DEFENDERS OF THE REICH

ROBERT FORSYTH

DEFENDERS OF THE REICH

THE LUFTWAFFE'S WAR AGAINST AMERICA'S BOMBERS

OSPREY PUBLISHING
Bloomsbury Publishing Plc
Kemp House, Chawley Park, Cumnor Hill, Oxford OX2 9PH, UK
Bloomsbury Publishing Ireland Limited,
29 Earlsfort Terrace, Dublin 2, D02 AY28, Ireland
1385 Broadway, 5th Floor, New York, NY 10018, USA
E-mail: info@ospreypublishing.com
www.ospreypublishing.com

OSPREY is a trademark of Osprey Publishing Ltd

First published in Great Britain in 2025

© Robert Forsyth, 2025

Robert Forsyth has asserted his right under the Copyright, Designs and Patents Act, 1988, to be identified as Author of this work.

For legal purposes the Acknowledgements on pp. 9–11 constitute an extension of this copyright page.

All rights reserved. No part of this publication may be: i) reproduced or transmitted in any form, electronic or mechanical, including photocopying, recording or by means of any information storage or retrieval system without prior permission in writing from the publishers; or ii) used or reproduced in any way for the training, development or operation of artificial intelligence (AI) technologies, including generative AI technologies. The rights holders expressly reserve this publication from the text and data mining exception as per Article 4(3) of the Digital Single Market Directive (EU) 2019/790.

A catalogue record for this book is available from the British Library.

ISBN: HB 9781472862860; PB 9781472862853; eBook 9781472862877; ePDF 9781472862891; XML 9781472862884

25 26 27 28 29   10 9 8 7 6 5 4 3 2 1

Maps by www.bounford.com
Index by Mark Swift

Typeset by Deanta Global Publishing Services, Chennai, India
Printed and bound in Great Britain by Clays Ltd, Elcograf S.p.A.

MIX
Paper | Supporting responsible forestry
FSC
www.fsc.org   FSC® C018072

Osprey Publishing supports the Woodland Trust, the UK's leading woodland conservation charity.

To find out more about our authors and books visit www.ospreypublishing.com. Here you will find extracts, author interviews, details of forthcoming events and the option to sign up for our newsletter.

For product safety related questions contact productsafety@bloomsbury.com

In memory of Christopher Shores and Jerry Scutts.
Gentlemen, both.

Contents

Introduction and Acknowledgements	9
List of Illustrations and Maps	12
Glossary	20
Table of Ranks	23

PART I. GUARDIANS AND GOLIATHS – 1939–42 — 25

1. 'Shoulder to Shoulder' — 27
2. 'An expensive mode of warfare' — 43
3. 'One swallow doesn't make a summer' — 58

PART II. HEAD-ON – 1942 — 65

4. West and South — 67
5. The Slender Sinews of Defence — 83
6. Imbalance of Power — 97

PART III. THE CORNERED WOLF – 1943 — 103

7. 'Once they have made contact with the bombers, the rest is easy' — 105
8. Defence in Depth — 133
9. Schweinfurt — 142
10. Bitter Harvest — 157
11. 'Defensive Victories' — 177
12. 'Without regard to losses' — 195
13. Battle Groups and Opera Houses — 209

PART IV. *STURM UND DRANG* – 1944	227
14 Pointblank and the Battle for Air Superiority	229
15 Big Gun – 'Big Week'	249
16 'Big B'	262
17 Bloody April	279
18 The Last Chance	305
19 Savage Skies	319
20 Imminent Danger West	336
21 All-Out Defence	350
22 Mass Against Mass	362
23 Darkening Skies	372
24 Blow after Blow	385
PART V. STORMBIRDS – 1944–45	403
25 Speed and Altitude – The New Weapons	405
26 Fire in the Sky	415
27 From 'Elbe' to the End	428
APPENDICES	441
Appendix 1 – Single-engined fighter aces with 20 or more Viermot victories	441
Appendix 2 – Zerstörer aces with ten or more Viermot victories	442
Sources and Selected Bibliography	443
Notes	448
Index	469

Introduction and Acknowledgements

My publisher has been generous in allowing the amount of content that forms this book, and so it would be unreasonable and impractical to include a lengthy introduction. I shall therefore do my best to keep it brief.

This volume is intended to offer a chronological portrayal of the Luftwaffe's efforts to defend against, and to counter, the Allied strategic daylight bomber offensive against the Third Reich and its occupied territories during World War II. I use the word 'strategic' in the way that Allied commanders used it to mean operations conducted by 'heavy' bombers, as opposed to the 'medium' or 'tactical' bomber forces which made an invaluable and equal contribution to ultimate Allied victory in the air over northwest Europe.

However, although the awesome might and efficiency of the United States Army Air Forces (USAAF) is often, and understandably, seen as the key plank of the ultimate Allied victory in the air in *daylight*, this book would not be complete without inclusion of the early attempts by the Royal Air Force (RAF) to mount daylight bombing raids on coastal targets in northern Germany in late 1939, during which the British trialled bombing formations with what were, at the time, modern bombers. But after receiving something of a 'bloody nose', the RAF would not make a significant return to daylight operations until much later in the war, preferring instead to deploy the squadrons of RAF Bomber Command against deeper penetration targets at night. Therefore, the bulk of this book naturally focuses on the Luftwaffe's war against the USAAF.

Sadly, but undisputedly, war focuses the mind, sharpens the intellect, develops initiative and accelerates invention – for good and bad. When one's homeland is under attack, these trends become essential. From mid-1942, as the United States inflicted the might of its air power against the Third Reich, the Luftwaffe – inherently an offensive force – was compelled to adapt quickly to a defensive stance and to adopt defensive measures.

Over the years, my interest in this subject has been drawn by the wide-ranging developments in the tactics, command organisation, aircraft, weapons, communications and technology devised by the Luftwaffe to respond to the bombers of the USAAF's Eighth and Fifteenth Air Forces and, increasingly, their fighter escorts. It was a battle between, quite literally, air *power* and ingenuity and sophistication, driven increasingly by desperation.

It has struck me that there were ironic similarities between the pilots of RAF Fighter Command defending southern England from German attack during the summer and autumn of 1940 and those of the Luftwaffe's home defence units from late 1943 onwards. The latter were, comparatively, a 'few' – trained increasingly under time pressure before being assigned to a small number of *Jagdgruppen*, *Zerstörergruppen* and *Sturmgruppen* comprised of limited numbers of aircraft. These airmen would spend much of their time waiting in primitive conditions for an *Alarmstart* order to intercept formations of enemy bombers sent to target their cities, airfields and factories, and these would usually be accompanied by squadrons of escort fighters. Invariably, the Luftwaffe pilots were outnumbered and outgunned, but at least they were operating over home territory,

I should stress that this is not a book about individual Luftwaffe fighter aces and their deeds. Indeed, while, inevitably, some of the *Experten* appear in the pages that follow, I have deliberately endeavoured to focus on the recollections and reports of lesser-known Luftwaffe pilots and of the commanders at *Korps* and *Division* levels who steered them into action.

I started gathering material for this book 40 years ago, and since then many people have contributed to it in one way or another. In no particular order, I would like to thank Hanfried Schliephake, Manfred Griehl, James H. Kitchens III, Erik Mombeeck, Eddie J. Creek, J. Richard Smith, Nick Beale, Martin Pegg, Steve Coates, Stephen Ransom, Roger A. Freeman, John M. Gray, Robert M. Foose, Keith Ferris, Dave Wadman, Martin Streetly, Don Caldwell, Eric Hammel, Donald Nijboer, Tim Harper, Dietmar Hermann, Neil Page, Gerd Kaschuba, Gary L. Moncur, Lt Col Harry D. Gobrecht, Hans-Heiri Stapfer, Tomáš Poruba, Chris Goss, Matti Salonen, G. J.(Rit) Staalman and Andy Thomas. I must also acknowledge Phil Reed and Stephen Walton, whose help over many years – and many years ago – at the archives of the Imperial War Museum has been greatly appreciated.

I was fortunate to be able to meet and correspond with several former Luftwaffe pilots, and my thanks go to Hans-Ekkehard Bob, Oscar Bösch, Fritz Buchholz, Hermann Buchner, Richard Franz, Adolf Galland, Horst Geyer, Walther Hagenah, Herbert Kaiser, Walter Loos, Gustav Rödel, Hans Schrangl, Franz Steiner, Franz Stigler, Willi Unger, Walter Windisch and Hermann Wolf.

INTRODUCTION AND ACKNOWLEDGEMENTS

Once again, it has been my good fortune to be able to work with Osprey Publishing, and I would like to thank Marcus Cowper, Tony Holmes, Bobby Kilshaw and the team at Oxford for their faith and support.

And my thanks, as always, to Sally, who remains my greatest motivation and source of encouragement.

Robert Forsyth
Sussex
March 2025

List of Illustrations and Maps

IMAGES

1. Wellington I bombers of the RAF's No. 9 Sqn in close formation on the eve of World War II. This unit would suffer heavy losses on the 18 December 1939 raid on Wilhelmshaven. (Robert Forsyth Collection)
2. This Wellington IA of No. 9 Sqn, flown by Canadian Flg Off Bill Macrae, was attacked by German Bf 110 fighters during the raid on Wilhelmshaven but, remarkably, made it home. (Robert Forsyth Collection)
3. American powerhouse – a B-17F Flying Fortress undergoes final manufacture in a vast, floodlit assembly shop at Boeing in Seattle in December 1942. (Farm Security Administration – Office of War Information photograph collection, Library of Congress)
4. In early 1942, Maj Gen Carl A. 'Tooey' Spaatz (right) was appointed commander of the new US Eighth Air Force in Britain, while Brig Gen Ira C. Eaker (left) was placed in command of its VIII Bomber Command. These two men became the architects of American air power in Europe. (Associated Press/Alamy Stock Photo)
5. The 'Mighty Eighth'. A formation of B-17 Flying Fortresses from the 381st BG based at Ridgewell, in Essex, on their way to bomb a target. The Eighth Air Force continually evolved the structures of its massed formations of 'combat boxes' to maximise self-defence against fighter attack. (Robert Forsyth Collection)
6. Reichsmarschall Hermann Göring inspects personnel from the Luftwaffe's two specialist anti-bomber units, *Sturmstaffel* 1 and E.Kdo 25, during an inspection at Achmer airfield

LIST OF ILLUSTRATIONS AND MAPS

on 17 November 1943. To Göring's right is Generalmajor Adolf Galland, while to his left is Hauptmann Horst Geyer, commander of E.Kdo 25. (Robert Forsyth Collection)

7 Generalmajor Adolf Galland (far left) peers down at an item of anti-bomber weaponry during a visit to the weapons evaluation unit E.Kdo 25 at Achmer in November 1943. Also seen (second left) is Major Hans-Günther von Kornatzki, driving force behind the '*Sturm*' tactic and units, and (fourth from left) Hauptmann Horst Geyer, commander of E.Kdo 25. (Robert Forsyth Collection)

8 Bf 109Gs of Major Walther Dahl's III./JG 3 undergo maintenance at Leipheim in March 1944. The aircraft are armed with two engine-mounted 13 mm MG 131 machine guns and a 20 mm MG 151 cannon as a centreline weapon firing through the propeller spinner. (EN Archive)

9 Mechanics take a break on the wing of an Fw 190A-7 of *Sturmstaffel* 1 at Salzwedel in April 1944, this aircraft being regularly flown by Unteroffizier Oskar Bösch. The aircraft has been fitted out as a '*Sturmjäger*', with 30 mm armoured glass panes attached to the canopy. (EN Archive)

10 In France in the summer of 1943, the *Kommodore* of JG 2, Major Egon Mayer, stands on the starboard wing of a B-17F that he has just shot down. In late 1942, it was Mayer who convinced Galland that a frontal pass against a B-17 offered the best chance of bringing it down. (EN Archive)

11 Two Bf 110G-2 *Pulkzerstörer* of 3./ZG 76 fitted with twin tubes for 21 cm W.Gr.21 mortars for breaking up bomber formations. Although able to fire such weapons at a distance from their targets, in reality, the slow Bf 110s were relatively easy prey for Allied fighter escorts. (EN Archive)

12 With the muzzle of its 5 cm Rheinmetall Bordkanone (BK) 5 covered, an Me 410A-1/U4 of 5./ZG 26 undergoes an engine test at Königsberg-Neumark. While the gun proved trouble-free and quick to mount and remove, it was less successful in action. (EN Archive)

13 Intrigued Me 410 crews of ZG 26 walk past B-17F *Miss Nonalee II* at Königsberg in 1944. The Flying Fortress, from the

385th BG, had force-landed in October 1943 and, having been salvaged, became a valuable war prize. It flew several 'instruction tours' around Luftwaffe bases so that fighter crews could familiarise themselves with the enemy bomber. (Hans-Heiri Stapfer Collection)

14 Initially, Generalmajor Josef Schmid was out of his depth when appointed to lead XII. *Fliegerkorps* (later I. *Jagdkorps*) from 15 September 1943, and thus put in command of all fighter units over the Western Front and the German homeland. But he adapted, making the best use of the forces at his disposal against an enemy with far greater resources. (EN Archive)

15 The purpose-built headquarters bunker of 3. *Jagddivision* from the autumn of 1943. It was from here that Luftwaffe fighter operations over northern Belgium, the Netherlands and areas of northwestern Germany were controlled and directed. (EN Archive)

16 Female Luftwaffe auxiliaries in a Luftwaffe control bunker with their light projectors, ready to project the positions of Luftwaffe fighters onto a large, illuminated, glass situation map. (EN Archive)

17 Controllers sit at their desks while the shadowy figures of female auxiliary plotters work on the other side of a large glass map of northwest Europe. Although photographed in the headquarters of 4. *Flakdivision*, the environment would have been very similar in a *Jagdkorps* bunker. (EN Archive)

18 Oberst Walter Grabmann (centre) served as the *Jafü Holland-Ruhrgebiet* and, later, commander of 3. *Jagddivision*. A competent tactical commander, he is seen here at Störmede in April 1944 talking with Major Heinz Bär (left), *Kommandeur* of II./JG 1, and Oberstleutnant Walter Oesau, *Kommodore* of JG 1. (EN Archive)

19 A veteran airman of World War I, Generalmajor Joachim-Friedrich Huth successively served from August 1942 as commander of 4., 5. and 7. *Jagddivisionen*. To the left is Oberst Max Ibel, commander of 2. *Jagddivision*. (Robert Forsyth Collection)

20 The purpose-built headquarters bunker of 2. *Jagddivision*, codenamed '*Sokrates*', was located at Stade, near Hamburg.

LIST OF ILLUSTRATIONS AND MAPS

From here, the *Division* deployed its fighter units against enemy incursions over northwest Germany. (Robert Forsyth Collection)

21 Grim expressions on the faces of three leading *Sturmgruppe* officers at Memmingen following Allied bombing attacks on the airfield there on 18 and 20 July 1944. From left to right are Hauptmann Heinz Lang of IV./JG 3, Major Walter Dahl, *Kommodore* of JG 300 and Major Wilhelm Moritz, *Kommandeur* of IV./JG 3. (EN Archive)

22 Using the time-honoured method adopted by fighter pilots, Oberst Hannes Trautloft, Galland's Inspector of Day Fighters, uses his hands to discuss air tactics with Major Hans-Ekkehard Bob. In April 1943 Bob collided with a B-17 during an attack and survived. Photo via Hans-Ekkehard Bob. (Robert Forsyth Collection)

23 German fighter pilots based in the West and the Reich were never allowed to forget their priority target. Here, the frontal view of a B-17 has been painted in scale on the doors of a hangar for range and gunnery purposes. (EN Archive)

24–26 Know your enemy. Luftwaffe tacticians, gunnery instructors and unit leaders used a variety of wooden and plastic models of bombers and fighters to teach newly assigned fighter pilots how to identify, approach and shoot down bombers. Especially important was awareness of the defensive fields of fire encountered from B-17s and B-24s. In photograph 25, an experienced pilot in the Mediterranean uses models to demonstrate to his young charges how to approach a Liberator using a diving frontal pass in a Bf 109. The Liberator has been fitted with wire cones to indicate the zones of fire from the bomber's various gun positions. Similar cones have been fitted to the B-17 model seen in photograph 26, and the location of its wing fuel tanks have also been highlighted. (EN Archive)

27 A B-17 is caught by the gun camera of a German fighter, having taken hits to its left inboard engine following an attack from the rear. Jagdwaffe pilots aimed for this area in the hope that the wing fuel tanks would ignite. (Robert Forsyth Collection)

28 Armourers of JG 26 load a 21 cm W.Gr.21 mortar shell into an underwing launch tube suspended from the port wing

of an Fw 190A-8/R6 at Lille-Vendeville in May 1944. Very inaccurate, the weapon was nevertheless successful in breaking up USAAF bomber formations. (EN Archive)

29 B-17F '*The Sack*' of the 379th BG made it back from the raid to Kassel and Oschersleben on 28 July 1943, despite having been hit by a 21 cm mortar fired by a German fighter. The B-17's oxygen cylinders exploded when hit by mortar fragments, blowing a hole in the fuselage. (Robert Forsyth Collection)

30 Unteroffizier Willi Unger of 12./JG 3 with his Fw 190A-8/R2 at Barth during trials with the 'Crab Device', a fuselage-mounted, rearward-firing, 21 cm mortar. The weight of the device adversely affected the Fw 190's speed and manoeuvrability and posed a risk to other Luftwaffe fighters following behind. It was abandoned. Photo via Willi Unger. (Robert Forsyth Collection)

31 A line-up of three Eighth Air Force P-51D Mustangs, four P-47D Thunderbolts and a P-38J Lightning – fighters which proved to be the nemeses of the Luftwaffe over the Reich. Photo via Jerry Scutts. (Robert Forsyth Collection)

32 For Oskar Bösch, photographed here when a Feldwebel, being caught in a bombing raid on a German city served as the impetus to volunteer for the *Sturmstaffel*. Bösch was credited with 18 victories, of which eight were USAAF four-engined bombers. Photo via Oskar Bösch. (Robert Forsyth Collection)

33 Five Fw 190A-8s of II.(*Sturm*)/JG 300 at readiness. Note, on the second aircraft from right, the armoured quarter panel fitted to the canopy to protect its pilot when flying close-range missions against bombers. (EN Archive)

34 The view from an Fw 190A-8 on 7 July 1944, captured by its gun camera, as Feldwebel Otto Erhardt of 10./JG 3 mounts a rear attack against a formation of Liberators. (Robert Forsyth Collection)

35 The steel wire tangled around the nose of a B-24D from the 44th BG was photographed upon the bomber's return to England following the raid to Emden on 11 December 1943. The wire, which was probably dropped from an aircraft

belonging to E.Kdo 25, wounded the Liberator's bombardier and navigator. (Robert Forsyth Collection)

36   The barrels of three 30 mm MK 103 cannon protrude obliquely from the fuselage of an Fw 190 of E.Kdo 25 in mid-1944. By means of a photo-electric cell, the weapons were triggered as the fighter passed beneath a bomber. (Robert Forsyth Collection)

37   A prototype Ruhrstahl X4 wire-guided air-to-air rocket suspended from beneath the wing of an Fw 190. Had the X-4 entered service against enemy bombers, it would have represented a significant advance over uncontrolled air-to-air mortars. (Robert Forsyth Collection)

38   A rocket-powered Me 163B is towed by a three-wheeled *Scheuch-Schlepper* (tug tractor) following its landing. When aloft, the *Komet*'s speed proved revelatory to USAAF bomber crews under attack from the Messerschmitt interceptor over Germany. (EN Archive)

39   The dawn of a new age. Use of W.Gr.21 mortars persisted through to the closing weeks of the war, and as seen here, they were fitted to a few Me 262A-1a jet interceptors of JG 7 in the spring of 1945. Their results were negligible. (EN Archive)

40   A standard battery of 12 R4M 55 mm air-to-air rockets in a wooden launch rack beneath the starboard wing, outboard of the turbojet nacelle of an Me 262 of JG 7. Used effectively, the R4M could be devastating against enemy bombers. (EN Archive)

41   The last, desperate attempt to counter Allied bombers was to be a manned, semi-expendable Bachem Ba 349 *Natter* (Adder) rocket-powered VTO interceptor. Seen here is the M22 prototype being readied for launch from a purpose-built tower. (EN Archive)

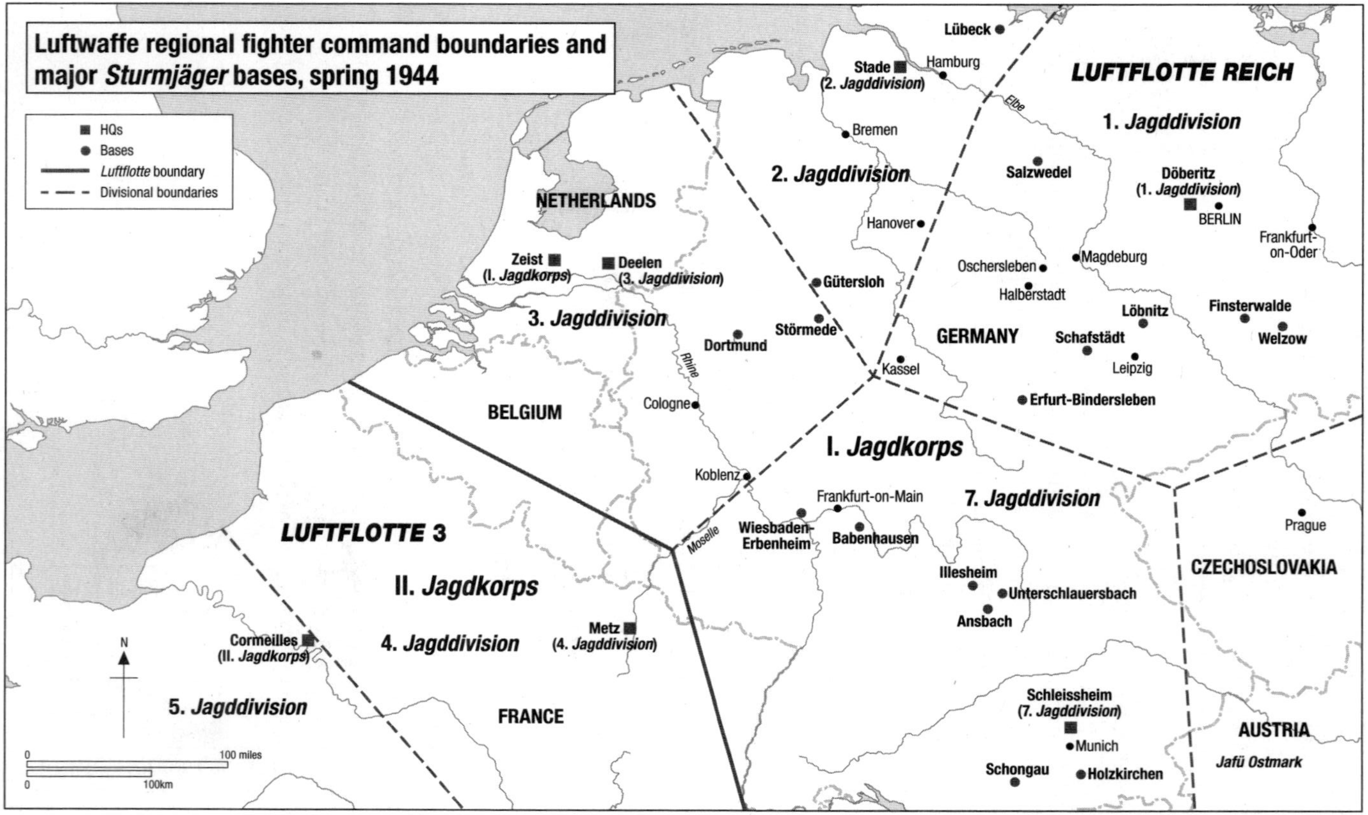
Luftwaffe regional fighter command boundaries and major *Sturmjäger* bases, spring 1944
HQs
Bases
Luftflotte boundary
Divisional boundaries
Lübeck
Stade (2. *Jagddivision*)
Hamburg
Elbe
LUFTFLOTTE REICH
1. *Jagddivision*
Bremen
2. *Jagddivision*
Salzwedel
Döberitz (1. *Jagddivision*)
BERLIN
NETHERLANDS
Hanover
Frankfurt-on-Oder
Zeist (I. *Jagdkorps*)
Deelen (3. *Jagddivision*)
Gütersloh
Oschersleben
Magdeburg
Halberstadt
3. *Jagddivision*
Störmede
Dortmund
Rhine
GERMANY
Löbnitz
Finsterwalde
Schafstädt
Welzow
Leipzig
Kassel
BELGIUM
Cologne
Erfurt-Bindersleben
I. *Jagdkorps*
Koblenz
Frankfurt-on-Main
7. *Jagddivision*
Wiesbaden-Erbenheim
Babenhausen
Moselle
Prague
LUFTFLOTTE 3
CZECHOSLOVAKIA
II. *Jagdkorps*
Illesheim
Unterschlauersbach
Ansbach
Metz (4. *Jagddivision*)
Cormeilles (II. *Jagdkorps*)
4. *Jagddivision*
N
5. *Jagddivision*
FRANCE
Schleissheim (7. *Jagddivision*)
AUSTRIA
Munich
Jafü Ostmark
Schongau
Holzkirchen
0
100 miles
0
100km

USAAF fighter escort ranges 1943–44

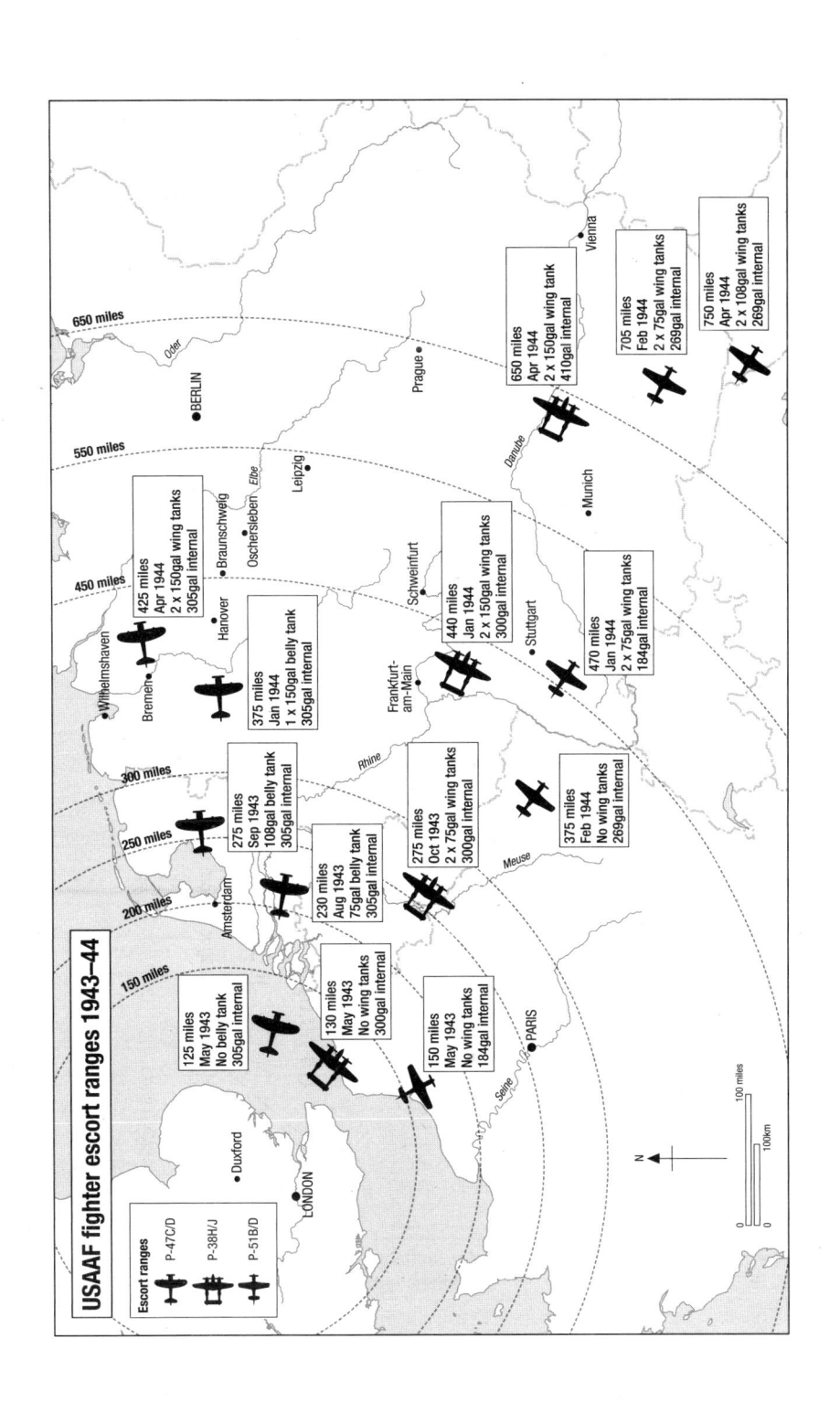

Escort ranges
- P-47C/D
- P-38H/J
- P-51B/D

125 miles
May 1943
No belly tank
305gal internal

130 miles
May 1943
No wing tanks
300gal internal

150 miles
May 1943
No wing tanks
184gal internal

275 miles
Sep 1943
108gal belly tank
305gal internal

230 miles
Aug 1943
75gal belly tank
305gal internal

275 miles
Oct 1943
2 x 75gal wing tanks
300gal internal

375 miles
Feb 1944
No wing tanks
269gal internal

375 miles
Jan 1944
1 x 150gal belly tank
305gal internal

425 miles
Apr 1944
2 x 150gal wing tanks
305gal internal

440 miles
Jan 1944
2 x 150gal wing tanks
300gal internal

470 miles
Jan 1944
2 x 75gal wing tanks
184gal internal

650 miles
Apr 1944
2 x 150gal wing tank
410gal internal

705 miles
Feb 1944
2 x 75gal wing tanks
269gal internal

750 miles
Apr 1944
2 x 108gal wing tanks
269gal internal

Glossary

Abschuss	Aerial victory
Abschusskommission	Commission for the validation of aerial claims
Alarmstart	Equivalent to RAF scramble
AOC	Air Officer Commanding
CBO	Combined Bomber Offensive
Dicke Autos	lit. 'Fat Vehicles' – Luftwaffe slang for Allied heavy bombers
DVL (*Deutsche Versuchsanstalt für Luftfahrt*)	German Research Institute for Aviation
Einsatzbereit	Operationally ready
Einsatzklar	Clear for operations
Ergänzungsjagdgruppe	Operational fighter training *Gruppe*
Erprobungsstelle	Test centre
Erprobungskommando	Test command
FluKo (*Flugwachkommando*)	Air Observation Unit and/or filter centre
Forschungsanstalt	Research institute
Fühlungshalter	Observation aircraft or 'shadower'
Funkhorchdienst	Radio listening service
Funkleit-Kompanie	Radio net control company
Gefechtsstand	Battle headquarters
Gefechtsverband	Battle group
General der Jagdflieger	General of Fighter Forces
Geschwader	Air unit equivalent to a wing, typically comprised of three *Gruppen* plus *Stab* flight
Geschwaderstab	Wing staff
Gruppe	Air unit equivalent to a group, typically comprised of three *Staffeln* plus *Stab* flight
Gruppenkommandeur	Officer commanding a *Gruppe*

GLOSSARY

Herausschuss	Term used for the validation of causing an enemy aircraft to leave its formation, resulting in its probable destruction
Höhenjagdgruppe	High-altitude fighter *Gruppe* (also high escort cover)
Industrieschutzstaffel	Industry (or factory) defence *Staffel* or unit
Industrieschwarm	Industry (or factory) defence *Staffel* or flight
Jagdabschnittsführer	Sector controller (Fighters)
Jagddivision	Fighter division
Jagdflieger	Fighter pilot
Jagdfliegerführer	(*Jafü*) Regional fighter controller
Jagdfliegerschule	(JFS) Fighter training school
Jagdgeschwader	(JG) Fighter unit equivalent to a wing, typically comprised of three *Gruppen* plus *Stab* flight
Jagdkorps	Fighter corps
Jagdstaffel	Fighter squadron
Jägerleitoffizier	Fighter control officer
Jägerschreck	'Fighter fear' (fear of enemy fighters)
Jägerstab	Fighter staff
Kampfraum	Battle (control) room
Kampfgeschwader	(KG) Bomber unit equivalent to a wing, typically comprised of three *Gruppen* plus *Stab* flight
Kampfstaffel	Bomber squadron
Kette	Formation of three aircraft
Kommando	Command/Detachment/Unit
Kommando der Erprobungsstellen	Commander of test centres
Leuchtpunktwerferinnen	(Usually) a female auxiliary operating a projector
Leuchtschirmkarte	Illuminated glass situation map
Luftlage	Air situation
Luftflotte	Air fleet
Luftnachrichten-Regiment	Air signals regiment
Luftwaffenbefehlshaber Mitte	Central air commander
Oberkommando der Luftwaffe (OKL)	Supreme Command of the Luftwaffe
Pulk	Luftwaffe slang for an enemy bomber formation
Reichsjägerwelle	Pan-Reich fighter commentary and control broadcast service
Reichsluftministerium	(RLM) Reich Air Ministry

Reichsluftverteidigung	Aerial Defence of the Reich
Reichswehr	Inter-war German armed forces
Rotte	Section of two aircraft
Schwarm	Flight of four aircraft
Sitzbereitschaft	Cockpit readiness
Stab	Staff
Staffel	Air unit equivalent to a squadron, usually comprised of nine or more aircraft
Staffelkapitän	Officer commanding a *Staffel*
Startbereitschaft	Take-off readiness
Sturm	'Assault' (in context, 'close-range attack')
Sturmjäger	'Assault fighter' (in context, 'close-range attack')
Sturmstaffel/-gruppe	'Assault' (in context, 'close-range attack') *Staffel/Gruppe*
Technisches Amt	RLM Technical Office
USSTAF	United States Strategic Air Forces
Viermot	'Four-engines/-ed' (Luftwaffe slang for four-engined bomber)
Viermotorschreck	Fear of four-engined bombers
Zerstörer	'Destroyer' (twin-engined 'heavy' fighter)

Table of Ranks

The table below lists the wartime Luftwaffe ranks, together with their equivalent in the RAF and the USAAF.

Luftwaffe	RAF	USAAF
Generalfeldmarschall	Marshal of the RAF	Five Star General
Generaloberst	Air Chief Marshal	Four Star General
General der Flieger	Air Marshal	Lieutenant General
Generalleutnant	Air Vice-Marshal	Major General
Generalmajor	Air Commodore	Brigadier General
Oberst	Group Captain	Colonel
Oberstleutnant	Wing Commander	Lieutenant Colonel
Major	Squadron Leader	Major
Hauptmann	Flight Lieutenant	Captain
Oberleutnant	Flying Officer	First Lieutenant
Leutnant	Pilot Officer	Lieutenant
Oberfähnrich	Acting Pilot Officer	Flight Cadet
Fähnrich	Officer Cadet	–
Stabsfeldwebel	Warrant Officer	Warrant Officer
Oberfeldwebel	Flight Sergeant	Master Sergeant
Feldwebel	Sergeant	Technical Sergeant
Unterfeldwebel	–	–
Unteroffizier	Corporal	Staff Sergeant
Hauptgefreiter	–	Sergeant
Obergefreiter	Leading Aircraftman	Corporal
Gefreiter	Aircraftman First Class	Private First Class
Flieger	Aircraftman	Private

PART I

Guardians and Goliaths – 1939–42

Clinging to the past will teach us nothing useful for the future, for that future will be radically different from anything that has gone before. The future must be approached from a new angle.

GIULIO DOUHET, AIR POWER THEORIST,
THE COMMAND OF THE AIR, 1921

The obvious lesson from the three raids is that we were lulled into thinking, as a result of the attack on December 3rd, that the German fighter pilot was rather a poor specimen somewhat indifferently mounted.

BRITISH AIR MINISTRY MEMORANDUM,
3 JANUARY 1940

1

'Shoulder to Shoulder'

Between 0900 and 0940 hrs on the cold morning of 18 December 1939, a formation of 24 twin-engined Vickers Wellington Mk IA bombers drawn from three squadrons in RAF Bomber Command's No. 3 Group took off from their bases in Suffolk and Norfolk and climbed into an overcast winter sky. Their crews, some 160 young men, had been tasked to 'destroy enemy warships' in or near the German port city of Wilhelmshaven in daylight or, as it was termed so innocuously in the higher-level jargon of RAF Bomber Command, they were being sent on 'coastal duties'.[1]

This mission was a diversion from the customary role of the Wellington units of No. 3 Group based at Mildenhall, the squadrons of which before the war had constituted a night bomber force. But with bombing of targets in the German hinterland expressly forbidden at this early stage of the European conflict, the War Cabinet in London set its priority on the sinking of a German capital ship instead.[2]

Methodically, the Wellington pilots assembled their aircraft into a great diamond-shaped formation over the rooftops of King's Lynn, a port town in some respects similar to Wilhelmshaven. There were four flights, each consisting of two 'vics' of three bombers, stepped up so as not to mask their defensive guns, with the aircraft of Nos. 9 and 149 Sqns, based at Honington and Mildenhall, respectively, in the leading vics, and those of No. 37 Sqn, based at Feltwell, intended to form the rearmost element. Leading the bombers in the air was Wg Cdr Richard Kellet, the commander of No. 149 Sqn. Kellet was a calm, quietly dashing man and an aviator of considerable experience who had once served in Iraq and as an engineering adviser to the Imperial Japanese Army Air Force.[3]

Unfortunately, things over Norfolk did not get off to a good start when the aircraft of No. 37 Sqn lagged behind at take-off, but Kellet, who had arrived at King's Lynn 90 seconds ahead of schedule, decided to press on regardless. No. 37 Sqn would just have to catch up with the main formation. The Wellingtons rumbled eastwards towards the shore of The Wash.

Aboard each bomber that morning was a crew of five or six. The minimum was a pilot, co-pilot, navigator (who could double as a bomb-aimer), wireless operator (who would double as a gunner) and tail gunner, although Kellet's crew was joined by a Fleet Air Arm officer who was to identify enemy ships and to direct the bombing accordingly.

As the aircraft climbed to 15,000 ft and freezing air sliced through the joins and gaps in the turret mountings, gusting into their unheated fuselages, each man did his best to huddle deeper into his bulky sheepskin flying clothing. Grp Capt Paul Harris recalled how the Mk IAs had been updated:

> Most Wellington Is were fitted with Vickers turrets which were useless. Sights did not follow the guns and ammunition belts stuck in the ducts. But soon Frazer-Nash turrets were fitted in the IAs, including the Frazer-Nash retractable under-turret 'dustbin' which rotated through 360 degrees and when firing aft could fire two degrees above the horizontal, which was very useful, backing up the rear gunner against stern attacks. All turrets, front, rear and mid-under, had two 0.303 Brownings firing 1,000 rounds per minute, and the 1,000-round belts, one to each gun, were fed in efficiently. Our gunners were volunteer groundcrew and not well trained. We had no gunnery leaders, and the only training they had was when they were able to come up with us when not working on the ground.[4]

And above everything was the constant, droning reverberation of each Wellington's pair of Bristol Pegasus XVIII air-cooled, nine-cylinder radial engines, rated at 1,050 hp at take-off and offering a top speed of 235 mph. The pulsation of the engines shuddered through the lattice-like shells of the fuselages, but those shells were what gave the 'Wimpys' their robust build, making them stronger than the Handley Page Hampden and Armstrong Whitworth Whitley bombers also operated by RAF Bomber Command at the time.[5] Indeed, these factors made the Wellington the RAF's most effective medium bomber type.

This had to be set against the reality that the RAF, like other European air forces, lacked 'heavy' bombers with which it could deliver significant blows against the enemy, and also bombers that were fast enough, despite carrying a crew, a bombload and armament, to evade high-speed enemy fighters.[6] This meant that, in effect, Kellet and his crews were undertaking a dangerous experiment, which had enjoyed nourishment following the results of an earlier raid to Heligoland on 3 December when he had led 24 Wellingtons to bomb German ships. The mission had fostered the belief among the leadership of RAF Bomber Command of the rationale of the 'self-defending' bomber formation. Ultimately, this would prove to be a mistaken judgement. Nevertheless, one 'Wimpy' pilot recalled that:

> From a combat point of view, they [the Wellingtons] were fantastic because you could shoot up to 50 per cent or more of the aeroplane away and it would still fly.[7]

Each aircraft could carry a bomb-load of up to 4,400 lbs for around 600 miles, but on this occasion they were each carrying three 500-lb Semi-Armour Piercing (SAP) bombs intended for dropping on any enemy warships they might sight.

The bombers' course was fixed for Germany, where their task, as set by the Air Officer Commanding (AOC) No. 3 Group, Air Vice-Marshal J. E. A. Baldwin, was 'to attack enemy warships in the Schillig Roads or Wilhelmshaven'. This target had come about, in essence, because there was a lack of suitable targets (due to the War Cabinet's aforementioned restrictions) and increasingly inclement weather overland in late 1939, and also because RAF Bomber Command was trying to grope its way towards a coherent bombing strategy – in fairness, not an easy thing to do at this point in time. So the Air Ministry had prepared 'Western Air Plan 7B', which selected attacks on the German fleet in and around its pre-war base at Wilhelmshaven fundamentally because attacking the port and the capital ships it harboured was just about the only way to strike Germany and eliminate the threat of attack on Britain's maritime supply routes.

Hanging over the young airmen in their draughty bombers that morning was the knowledge that the skies over the north German coast could be deadly. In the raid 15 days earlier, Kellet had commanded a force of 24 Wellingtons on an abortive attempt to bomb German cruisers off Heligoland. The Heligoland Bight was a vital passage of water, named after the island at its centre, across which plied a considerable amount of German naval and mercantile shipping. Somehow, on that occasion, all of Kellet's aircraft had returned home, but not without the Luftwaffe's fighters showing up and subjecting his crews to an alarming and punishing series of attacks. It was suspected that the Messerschmitt Bf 109s sent to intercept the Wellingtons had been alerted to the bombers' presence by a patrolling vessel.

But there was to be no escape for the unfortunate airmen who set off for the Schillig Roads in a following raid on the 14th amidst low cloud and poor visibility. That day, after the bombers had loitered in the target area for 30 minutes, five from a formation of 12 'Wimpys' failed to come back. Another crash-landed on British soil with the loss of three crew. On that occasion No. 3 Group had concluded that the high losses were down to the

German coastal Flak guns and not fighters, despite the fact that the RAF airmen had endured repeated attacks from Bf 109s.

But regardless of almost 50 per cent losses and German fighter attacks lasting 26 minutes, Air Commodore Norman Bottomley, the Senior Air Staff Officer (SASO) at RAF Bomber Command, opined that what he viewed as 'failure' on the part of the Germans was down to 'good formation flying' on the part of the Wellingtons:[8]

> The maintenance of a tight, unshaken formation in the face of the most powerful enemy action is the test of bomber force fighting efficiency and morale. In our service, it is the equivalent of the old 'Thin Red Line' or the 'Shoulder to Shoulder' of Cromwell's Ironsides.[9]

This, despite the fact that the surviving Wellingtons from that mission returned riddled with bullet holes which could only have been caused by the guns of enemy fighters, and not shrapnel from exploding shells fired by Flak batteries. Furthermore, Kellet, who had been in his post as commander of No. 149 Sqn for only a brief time, had not been given an opportunity to devise any firm tactical plans for conducting bombing missions at flight-, squadron- or group-levels. Nor had he been able to discuss tactics against enemy fighters with either senior or junior officers in RAF Bomber Command. This would prove to be a fatal shortcoming when commanding an inadequately prepared multi-squadron force.

When Kellet dutifully led his Wellington 'Ironsides' 'shoulder-to-shoulder' towards the North Sea that morning, senior officers in RAF Bomber Command believed there to be three principal means of sending bombers into hostile territory while simultaneously evading an enemy's fighter defence.

Firstly, to use an aeroplane that possessed such high-speed performance that neither fighters nor Flak would have a chance of inflicting loss or damage. But the development of a so-called 'speed bomber' was a long way off in December 1939. Secondly, the provision of a fighter escort, but as with the 'speed bomber', the RAF possessed no such fighter with sufficient endurance to cover the bombers all the way to their target. Thirdly (and this was really the only option), the bombers should fly in a tight, 'self-defending' formation which enabled mutual cover from the collective number of machine guns fielded by a large force of aircraft. However, in December 1939, this was still a largely untested means of defence, and it depended on *maintaining* formation come what may – regardless of Flak or attack by fighters – and having a *sustained* level of defensive firepower sufficient enough to ward off a fighter attack. Furthermore, the formation

'SHOULDER TO SHOULDER'

would need to hold firm even when manoeuvring over a target, buffeted by wind or, even more challenging, masked by cloud.[10]

And so the crews in the bombers flying over Norfolk that morning, heading for enemy territory, had no option other than to place their faith in the designers and workers of Vickers-Armstrongs (Aircraft) Ltd and the engines of the Bristol Aeroplane Company Ltd.

Reaching the coast, Kellet ordered all wireless communication to cease – future communication between the aircraft would be conducted only by Aldis signal lamps. The bombers headed out across a slate grey North Sea. It was about 50 minutes out from King's Lynn that the whole formation came together above the cloud and went up to 14,000 ft. The course set from The Wash was 040° True for 236 miles. But ahead, above the water, somewhat worryingly, the cloud had thinned, revealing areas of clear, sharp blue sky with visibility of around 50 miles. Whatever the RAF Bomber Command bigwigs thought, that meant ideal conditions for interception by German fighters. From this point, the young RAF airmen were on their own.[11]

Well out over the North Sea, some 250 miles from the British coast, the Wellingtons of No. 37 Sqn finally caught up with the main formation, but Kellet's lead aircraft was now two miles ahead of them. After the mission to Heligoland on the 3rd, one of Kellet's pilots had told him to, 'Go a little slower next time'.[12] Two hours into the flight, two aircraft turned back, and as a result the formation was down 12 defensive guns.

The remaining 22 'Wimpys' soldiered on, and at 1230 hrs, after some three hours in the now crystal-clear air, Kellet spotted the low, hazy strip of Sylt and the Danish and German coastlines. As instructed, he had followed a heading well north of the Frisian Islands so as to avoid German Flak, but he now swung his slightly depleted formation south, towards a point between Wilhelmshaven and Nordholz, near Bremerhaven.

1343 hrs, Central European Time. From the confines of a small building amidst the sand dunes on the East Frisian island of Wangerooge, Leutnant Hermann Diehl, a technical officer with a specialist Luftwaffe signals development unit, was demonstrating the vast, revolving antenna of an experimental radar installation known as *Freya* to a curious naval officer. This complex framework of metal sat directly above the men on the roof of the building, and was connected to a cathode ray tube inside the control room. Built by the GEMA company of Berlin, *Freya* was intended as the first in what would be a series of advanced early warning and search radars which would span the length of Germany on its western frontiers, detecting movement in the air to a depth of 120 km. That was the theory. At the start of the war, there were just eight such radar stations in operation along the coast of northern Germany.[13]

Around a month before Kellet led his bombers to Wilhelmshaven, Diehl and his little detachment had started to conduct experiments aimed at guiding fighters towards aerial targets in daylight. Initially, the system had proved unreliable because the azimuth measurements were not sufficiently precise and no data was available on the altitude of an incoming enemy force. Nevertheless, *Freya* was an impressive piece of technology, and although aware of German experiments in radar development, this was an aspect of the enemy defensive system that RAF Bomber Command's leadership had seriously underestimated to its peril.

At one point in Diehl's demonstration, he swung the antenna frame north, towards the waters of the Heligoland Bight and the sky above them. As he did so, he picked up an echo on his cathode ray tube at a range of 113 km. This was probably the point from which Kellet had first spotted the enemy coast, and although he did not know it at that precise moment, Diehl was about to enable direct control of airborne fighter aircraft on the basis of cathode ray tube readings for the first time.

If the *Freya* echo was correct, Diehl thought, then at such a range, there would be sufficient time to scramble the fighter units based around the northwest German coast to intercept. Indeed, as Kellet took his bombers in high towards the port, he knew that by taking an extended route, his formation had reduced the risk of attracting fire from the German Flak ships located around the Frisian Islands. But, in exchanging one risk for another, he had given the enemy's air defences maximum time to respond.

As luck would have it, another radar, operated by the Kriegsmarine on Heligoland, had also picked up the incoming Wellingtons. But where the German warning system failed was in its *relay* of the information gleaned by its radars to local Luftwaffe fighter units. Diehl immediately passed details of the enemy's location, height, course, estimated speed and strength to the naval signals exchange at Wilhelmshaven, which was meant to pass it on to the Luftwaffe's local fighter control centre in the town of Jever, some 15 km west of Wilhelmshaven and the Jade Bight – officially, this was the established route of communication.[14] Diehl watched the clock. The minutes ticked by without any acknowledgement from Wilhelmshaven – too many minutes. Taking matters into his own hands, he went to the telephone and called Jever directly.

But when the telephone jangled at Jever it was answered by a somewhat sceptical officer who apparently told the young leutnant from the Wangerooge radar station that his new-fangled device was either 'plotting seagulls' or that it was suffering from some kind of interference. He was then dismissed.

Undeterred, however, Diehl next attempted to call Major Harry von Bülow-Bothkamp, the *Gruppenkommandeur* of II./JG 77, the fighter unit based near the radar station on Wangerooge. Unfortunately, von Bülow-Bothkamp was in Jever, where he was meeting with Oberstleutnant Carl-August Schumacher, until recently commander of II./JG 77. On 30 November, Schumacher had been assigned the task of setting up and leading a composite group of fighter units based in northwest Germany whose mission it was to provide air defence of the coastal region stretching from the important ports of Emden, Wilhelmshaven, Bremerhaven, Cuxhaven and Hamburg to the western coast of Schleswig-Holstein and the Heligoland Bight.

Schumacher's new staff was named *Stab/Jagdgeschwader* (JG) 1, but it was also known as 'JG *Nord*' and 'JG *Schumacher*', and its prime mission was to direct fighter operations over the Bight in conjunction with the regional Naval and Luftwaffe Flak batteries. By mid-December, Schumacher had been assigned II./JG 77 under von Bülow with Bf 109Es at Jever and Wangerooge, ideally positioned for the defence of the Bight, with other units at Nordholz, Jever and Westerland.

Schumacher had worked hard to establish a beneficial liaison with the radar stations on Wangerooge, and he recognised the advantages that such technology could offer. For his part, von Bülow recalled:

When radar control called us up, no one could believe it. A substantial number of enemy aircraft were reported en route for our sector – we thought it must have been some kind of interference. However, a few minutes later, a naval *Freya* radar gave us identical information, which was also confirmed by eyewitness sightings. This time, there was no doubt.[15]

At least Schumacher viewed it to be 'splendid weather for fighters', although his adjutant remained convinced that the British were not foolish enough to come in such conditions. Perhaps they really were seagulls after all.[16]

Kellet pressed on, and with the Flak exploding around his long tail of bombers, he ordered bomb-bay doors open. Visible below them was a battleship and a cruiser moored in the Roads. But because of the vessels' proximity to shore, and thus the risk of further, land-based, casualties, in accordance with his orders, Kellet had no choice than to abandon the bomb-run. At around

1420 hrs Central European Time, over the Jade Bight, the doors were closed back up. The bombers turned north and back out to sea.

Seagulls or not, following Diehl's warning, Schumacher ordered the units of *Stab*/JG 1 to be placed on alert, and shortly after 1400 hrs, five Bf 109Ds from 10.(*Nacht*)/JG 26, ostensibly an experimental nightfighter unit led by Leutnant Johannes Steinhoff, were scrambled from Jever to intercept the enemy bombers over the Jade Bight. The *Staffel* was one of a small number that had been hurriedly formed by the Luftwaffe to provide nocturnal air defence, or 'Flak support' as it was deemed, a role which senior commanders had almost ignored and believed to be unnecessary. Notwithstanding this, Steinhoff's pilots had been well briefed on the Wellington and its armament.

After they left Wilhelmshaven, the RAF bombers split into two groups, one heading west, passing the Frisian Islands, the other going north, towards Heligoland. This was where the fighters intercepted them. The Messerschmitt pilots were amazed that the British were approaching in cloudless skies; they assumed that the raid mounted on 3 December had given the enemy confidence, but in doing so, it was astonishing that they made themselves such a target of opportunity. However, the fighters had to break off their initial approach as coastal and ship-mounted Flak continued to fire around Bremerhaven, Wilhelmshaven and the Schillig Roads. The Flak explosions forced the Wellingtons to loosen their formation and disperse, despite this being in contravention of the orders from No. 3 Group to retain close formation in order to provide mutual fire support. That was easier said than done.

First to reach the Wellingtons at 1430 hrs over the sea between Wangerooge and Heligoland was the grouping of four Bf 109Ds of 10.(N)/JG 26 and a *Rotte* from II./JG 77 up from Wangerooge, all led by the *Staffelkapitän* of the former unit, Leutnant Steinhoff.

Tall, intelligent, lean-jawed, blonde-haired and blue-eyed, his left cheek etched with a duelling scar in the time-honoured tradition from his time as a university student, 26-year-old Johannes Steinhoff fulfilled the Nazi ideal of a German fighter pilot. In the space of five minutes, he claimed the shooting down of two Wellingtons around 30 km south of Wangerooge. These claims represented his first aerial victories – or so he thought. And as with their leader, so the other pilots flying with Steinhoff that day each claimed a bomber downed.

This success may have been attributable to Steinhoff instructing his pilots to make only beam attacks, which required difficult deflection shooting and had to be driven to close range so that the Bf 109s' light 7.92 mm machine gun ammunition could count. In one case, Steinhoff had to make two beam attacks before flames engulfed the targeted Wellington and it went down inverted into the waters of the Bight. By the time he and his pilots returned to Jever they had expended all their ammunition.[17]

Following Steinhoff's formation came a second group of Messerschmitts, including a Bf 109E-1 piloted by Oberstleutnant Schumacher, which pursued the other group of bombers heading back to England just north of the Frisians. More Wellingtons appeared to fall to the guns of the Luftwaffe fighters. For the next 35 minutes, the German fighters harried the bombers some 120 km out to sea and as far west as Borkum.

As No. 3 Group later reported, the aircraft of No. 149 Sqn were subjected to several beam attacks:

Flying Officer Heathcote, second pilot to Sergeant Petts, in No. 1 Section of No.3 Flight, reports that this aircraft was left behind in a turning movement [presumably over Wilhelmshaven]. It was heavily attacked by fighters, the centre turret and wireless being put out of action, and both tail and front gunners being wounded. Flying Officer Heathcote replaced the wounded rear gunner until ammunition ran out and then replaced the wounded front gunner. Sergeant Petts dived to sea level to escape and was pursued down. The last they saw of their Leader was about 20 miles from the Schillig Roads when they got left behind. At about the same time they saw No. 2 Section suffer two casualties, one aircraft going down under control with the port engine on fire, and the other breaking up as a result of a direct hit.[18]

When Schumacher opened fire on his target, he shot both of its engines away. Elsewhere, another 'Wimpy' exploded in mid-air, while a third plunged towards the water with its port engine trailing flame. Schumacher recalled:

It was madness! The Tommies were chased in all directions by our fighters. I also attacked a British bomber. He defended himself well and hit my machine on three occasions. One of the bullets passed very close to my head. But then the bomber came into the centre of my sights. I fired at point-blank range and continued to follow my victim. There were no more than several metres between the two of us. I had to pull away quickly. I was preparing for another attack after a wide turn when I saw the aircraft fall into the sea like a stone. My wingman immediately confirmed my victory. The combat had already taken us more than

30 km to the west of Heligoland Island, and we were always on the tails of the British. We switched over during attacks and chased them out for some 150 km before returning.[19]

The wreck of the Wellington that Schumacher had shot down, a machine from No. 37 Sqn flown by Flg Off Lewis, remained protruding from the mud flats off the island of Spiekeroog for several days, like an abandoned monument to what had taken place. Only the body of the aircraft's tail gunner was recovered.[20]

A weakness of the Wellington was that its turrets were unable to traverse to a full right angle. On top of that, the air gunners had to battle with extreme cold. One young airman manning his twin 0.303-in. guns in the rear turret of a No. 37 Sqn Wellington on the Wilhelmshaven mission recalled watching the high-speed approach of an enemy fighter for the first time and thinking how small it appeared. But when the Messerschmitt was at 600 yards and the gunner attempted to fire, his guns froze after just one round. He then tried to traverse his turret, but that had frozen too.[21]

Logically, on 18 December, the German fighter leaders had instructed their pilots to mount beam attacks wherever possible, where there was no defence. Such an approach was also found to assist in breaking up the formations, but equally, where the formation maintained its rigidity, attacking also became easier. In only three instances did the Wellingtons adopt an evasive weaving pattern when under attack, and this proved difficult for the Bf 109s to counter.

Oberleutnant Berthold Jung, a pilot with II./JG 77, had had something of an initially luckless search for the bombers. Taking off in a new Bf 109E from Wangerooge, he had flown alone west over the Frisian Islands until he neared Borkum, where he saw Flak bursts and then a formation of Wellingtons, with two twin-engined Messerschmitt Bf 110s attacking them from the rear. Jung opened fire from the beam on the lead flight of bombers, but passed just above the Wellingtons, only narrowly avoiding a collision. Jung was later credited with his first kill.[22]

The Messerschmitts came in again and again, and although the rear gunners put up a stubborn defence, the more heavily armed Bf 110 fighters attacked from astern and the beam, firing, for the first time against RAF bombers, their 20 mm MG FF cannon from 500–800 m, which was beyond the effective range of the Wellingtons' 0.303-in. guns. This was frustrating for the air gunners, because although their Brownings had a high cyclic rate of fire, they could not match the range and calibre of the German cannon.

Some fighters pressed home at closer range, even as close as 45 m at one point. Indeed, one tactic adopted by more skilful Bf 109 pilots was to put a Wellington's rear turret out of action from further out than 365 m and then close in for a kill, aiming for the fuel tanks. Schumacher's wingman, Oberleutnant Johann Fuhrmann, had made three beam attacks on one Wellington, but all his attempts were in vain. Undeterred, and perhaps recklessly, he then made an approach from dead astern. In doing so, his Bf 109D attracted heavy crossfire from several rear gunners and it was hit. Although Fuhrmann successfully ditched into the water, he drowned before he could be rescued. The weight of cold, waterlogged flying clothing could be fatal.

Hauptmann Wolfgang Falck, the *Staffelkapitän* of *Zerstörergeschwader* (ZG) 76's 2. *Staffel*, also experienced just how effective the rear guns on a Wellington could be when repulsing a stern-mounted fighter attack. Falck and his parent *Gruppe* of Bf 110 'heavy' fighters had only transferred to Jever on 17 December, and the next day his unit took off in formations of four aircraft for its first familiarisation flight over the coast and the islands. As the Messerschmitt *Zerstörer* passed over the island of Borkum in a northwesterly direction, an alert was flashed over the radio warning of British bombers heading to Wilhelmshaven. The Bf 110s turned and headed for the northernmost part of the enemy force. As Falck recorded:

> We attacked at once and managed to shoot down a few British aircraft in spite of the intense fire from their tail guns. My aircraft was hit several times, the right engine stopped functioning, fuel was running out of numerous holes in the surfaces and the ammunition for the four machine guns contained in the fuselage was in flames. To make things worse, I had to open the cabin window because of the dense smoke inside the cabin. Shortly afterwards, the left engine also ceased working. Nevertheless, thanks to the altitude and loss of weight due to loss of fuel and the ammunition consumed, as well as a favourable wind, I was finally able to land smoothly with the accuracy of a glider on the aerodrome at Wangerooge.[23]

Falck was fortunate, however, and was credited with two Wellingtons shot down. He reported one as breaking up in mid-air and the other as crashing following damage to one of its engines.

The aircraft flown by Flg Off J. H. C. Speirs of No. 149 Sqn was shot down by a Bf 110 which carried out a beam attack on the squadron's first section at around 10,000 ft. The fuselage aft of the cabin and close to the wing root was seen to explode forward of its Astro dome. It dropped out of formation and dived vertically in flames from 10,000 ft towards the sea. There were no survivors.

During the attack, the German pilots observed how the Wellingtons burned very easily when hit, with tail units and wings being particularly inclined to burst into flames, suggesting that their fuel tanks had been struck. The failing here was that the Wellington lacked self-sealing fuel tanks. Thus, if a 'Wimpy's' fuel tank did take a hit, especially from an incendiary round in the port wing, despite any benefits from its geodetic construction, it could become, quite literally, a ball of fire. One pilot who flew the Wilhelmshaven operation remembered that Kellet's leadership in maintaining formation was 'immaculate', and that the only losses in his squadron 'were almost certainly due to having no self-sealing tanks'.[24]

Even if the tanks did not catch fire, any bullet holes would result in fuel being drained and the likelihood that a bomber would not make it back home.

According to the RAF crews, over some 40 minutes, 'probably 60–70' enemy aircraft, 'mostly Messerschmitt Me 109s and Me 110s', had attacked them. In his subsequent report Kellet wrote, in what could have been admiration, that 'The enemy pressed home their attacks in a splendid manner'.[25]

On 22 December, Headquarters, No. 3 Group summarised the enemy action as follows:

> Attacks by enemy fighters, which included Me 109s and Me 110s, were much more intensive and persistent than in previous operations. Attacks were continuous from a point a few miles South West of Heligoland on the way in, until our aircraft were some 70–80 miles from the coast on the way home, the only respite from fighter attacks being when the formation was being subjected to heavy AA in the Wilhelmshaven area.
>
> The total number of enemy attacks made has been estimated variously at 30 to 50. In most cases, attacks were made by a dive from the quarter developing into a stern attack. Attacks were also made from both quarters simultaneously. In about 50 per cent of the stern attacks, accurate concentrated fire at ranges of 400–600 yards from our aircraft caused the enemy to break away before reaching effective range.[26]

In its post-mission report, JG 1 commented sardonically:

> The British seem to regard a tightly closed formation as the best method of defence, but the greater speed of our Me 109s and Me 110s enabled

them to select their position of attack. Rigid retention of course and formation considerably facilitated the attack. It was criminal folly on the part of the enemy to fly at 4,000 to 5,000 m in a cloudless sky with perfect visibility. After such losses it is assumed that the enemy will not give the *Geschwader* any more opportunities of practice-shooting at Wellingtons.[27]

The Flak batteries also played their part, not just in aiming to hit bombers, but by damaging or breaking up their formation to a degree that the task facing the fighters was facilitated.

The crews of No. 149 Sqn claimed seven Luftwaffe aircraft shot down along with two 'probables'. In total, the RAF believed that 12 enemy fighters had been shot down and another 12 seriously damaged. These claims were wildly optimistic. The Germans lost four fighters and had nine damaged. The Luftwaffe fighter pilots believed they had shot down as many as 38(!) Wellingtons, although both Steinhoff and Falck were to be disappointed when their respective second claims were disallowed following review.[28] They were not alone. In accordance with the rigours of the claim verification process instigated by the *Reichsluftministerium* (RLM), at least ten other claims were not validated for lack of certainty.

Nevertheless, like the RAF, the Luftwaffe's claims were also wildly overstated. This can be attributed to the frantic, high-speed, lightning quick nature of aerial combat, where the approach to a bomber and the subsequent firing pass lasted no more than seconds. Furthermore, the action over the Heligoland Bight saw more than 30 German aircraft in the air, drawn from different units in either two-aircraft *Rotten* or four-aircraft *Schwärme*, with all of them making 'loose' beam or stern attacks, opening fire at varying ranges. In the case of the Bf 110 units, the observer/gunner in the rear seat, aware that his pilot was attacking an enemy aircraft, would *assume* that an enemy machine he witnessed going down would have been the work of his pilot.

For the RAF, 18 December 1939 had been a black day – 57 men had been lost, and of 22 aircraft that were engaged, only ten returned. For No. 37 Sqn, it had been a disaster. Of the six Wellingtons the unit had despatched to Wilhelmshaven, five failed to return, resulting in the loss of 26 aircrew. No. 9 Sqn had also suffered badly. Of its nine Wellingtons, seven failed to return and 23 men had been lost. However, almost as ominous were the damage reports covering the two aircraft which force-landed in Lincolnshire late that afternoon. Of one, it was noted:

> The starboard wing to the rear of the mid cell of wing tanks badly shot up and had been on fire, but the fire was localised. Armour plating kept fire from the tank. The armour plating was pierced, but the tank was not holed. Starboard side of the fuselage freely peppered.

Of the other . . .

> The armour plating to the rear of the starboard wing tank had been pierced and ragged edge had turned forward and holed tank. Rudder control rod pierced, and roller bracket shot away, causing partial jamming of the rudder control. Starboard tailplane and fuselage peppered.

Elsewhere, there were some lucky escapes for the survivors. On its way home, one aircraft of No. 149 Sqn had endeavoured to drop a dinghy to another Wellington which had force-landed in the sea, but the dinghy became snagged on its tail unit. With the dinghy thrashing about in the slipstream, the pilot managed to fly the aircraft with difficulty back to Coltishall. When it landed, the elevator was found to be riddled with bullet holes and there were more holes in the front turret and two of the geodetic members. Especially fortunate was one of the crew who took a bullet from a Luftwaffe fighter in his flying boot but, remarkably, escaped uninjured.[29]

Perversely, however, what made the day even blacker, was that the loss of life and aircraft had to be set against the stark fact that no bombs had been dropped since no 'legitimate warships' had been observed.

In his post-mission appraisal of the 18 December operation, the AOC of No. 3 Group, Air Vice-Marshal J. E. A. Baldwin, made it clear that he viewed the losses suffered that day as being attributable to 'poor leadership and consequent poor formation flying. I have not by any means given up hope of being able to drive home the lessons learnt'.[30] This view was echoed in a blunt review of RAF Bomber Command operations over the northwest coast of Germany by a senior RAF Operations officer at the Air Ministry to the Directorate of Operations on 3 January 1940:

> There is little more to be said. Poor formation flying (and in this I include poor sub-formation leadership) and the lack of self-sealing tanks.[31]

'SHOULDER TO SHOULDER'

Two days after the Wilhelmshaven raid, a concerned Air Chief Marshal Edgar Ludlow-Hewitt, Commander-in-Chief (C-in-C) of RAF Bomber Command, visited Mildenhall to discuss the operation with a dubious Kellet and his crews. Ludlow-Hewitt expressed his appreciation and condolences.

The same day, in the immediate aftermath of 'The Battle of Heligoland Bight', the Luftwaffe and the German press basked in the glory of the nation's *Jagdflieger* and their victory. Schumacher, Steinhoff, Falck and a small band of fellow pilots were summonsed to attend a lavish press conference in Berlin organised by the Otto Dietrich, Press Chief of the Reich. Flanked by Nazi dignitaries and officials from the Ministry of Propaganda and Public Enlightenment, Schumacher fielded questions from journalists as cameras flashed and popped.

For the RAF the evidence was clear that a 'self-defending' bomber formation was not, by any means, invulnerable to fighter attack. Three questions needed answering. Firstly, what would RAF Bomber Command be able to do about it? Secondly, how would future bombing policy adapt to the prevailing danger from fighter attack? Thirdly, would lessons be learned?

Ludlow-Hewitt did as much as to recognise the Luftwaffe's capability. He wrote on 27 December:

> The remarkable contrast between the resistance put up by the enemy Air Force on the 14th and 18th December as compared with the 3rd December suggests that in the interval there must have been a considerable reinforcement of the German fighter force in northwest Germany, probably by their best squadrons withdrawn from the Western Front. Up to the 14th December, our experience was that the morale and determination of the fighters in the northwest of Germany were appreciably inferior to that of their fighter units on the Western Front. Consequently, the vigour and determination of the fighter attacks, particularly on the 18th, came as a surprise to us.
>
> These engagements prove beyond any manner of doubt that bombers cannot maintain themselves in strength over enemy territory unless they are built to be as invulnerable as possible to enemy fire. Efficient self-sealing tanks and adequate armour to protect the crew and all vital parts is absolutely essential. The gun power of each bomber should be at least equal that of the enemy fighters. To stop fighter attacks, a bomber formation of manoeuvrable

size needs to be able to concentrate on each attacking fighter an intensity of fire at least double that of the attacking fighter.[32]

The next day, in a widely circulated memo, Kellet expressed his opinions of the Wilhelmshaven mission less charitably:

> It was a complete farce. We had no self-sealing tanks and silly First World War chaffer guns, hopeless against the heavy Flak we received. One good thing was that we got rid of Ludlow-Hewitt.[33]

Poignantly, the Operations Record Book (ORB) for No. 149 Sqn described the air battle as 'the biggest to date in the history of the Royal Air Force'. But greater – much greater – and ever more violent battles were to come in the skies over Europe.

2

'An expensive mode of warfare'

The RAF's attempted attack on German warships on 18 December 1939 had sent a clear signal to the more astute senior commanders within RAF Bomber Command that such raids could no longer be undertaken without considerable risk, especially against an alert and prepared enemy. The loss of 12 Wellingtons and their crews was way above acceptable limits for the still nascent RAF Bomber Command.

However, it seemed there were some within the higher echelons of RAF Bomber Command's leadership who retained faith in the self-defending formation, or they refused to acknowledge the true threat posed by the Luftwaffe's fighters and their detection and warning systems. No. 3 Group leaders believed that a 'very close' formation of six Wellingtons would be able to endure a sustained and heavy fighter attack and 'emerge with very few, if any, casualties'. In an operational instruction dated 23 December 1939, No. 3 Group told its crews that, 'If enemy aircraft are encountered, gunners will be able to practise shooting at real targets instead of drogues'. And even at the end of the year, RAF Bomber Command's SASO, Air Commodore Bottomley, continued openly to express his faith in the 'inviolability of a tight bomber formation'. Losses, he said, were down to 'straggling':[1]

> This operation has confirmed previous experience of this war that the Germans will always concentrate at once on stragglers, and that tight formation flying is absolutely essential for mutual protection and success in the face of enemy fighters. Vigorous action is necessary to ensure that all concerned are fully impressed with the necessity of maintaining tight formations in the face of fighter attack.
>
> It is also most necessary that attention should be directed towards the need for every crew to study thoroughly their fighting organisation in action, e.g. method of replenishing ammunition in turrets, fire direction and control, inter-aircraft communication and so forth.[2]

In the wake of the 18 December mission, the debate would rage. According to the official historians of RAF Bomber Command:

> If this was the kind of punishment which daylight formations of bombers might expect to receive in the future, then clearly the whole conception of the self-defending formation had been exploded. If, on the other hand, it could be shown that the action of 18th December had been a freak, then it was possible that a gain in experience, a revision of tactics and the improvement of certain equipment might restore the balance before Bomber Command was committed to larger scale actions against targets of deeper penetrations.[3]

The raid also gave the Luftwaffe a lesson. As early as the 1920s, planners in the inter-war Reichswehr were conscious of Germany being surrounded by countries with potentially hostile fleets of bombers, including Great Britain, France, Poland and the USSR. Doctrine stressed the need to at least limit the effects of enemy air bombardment against homeland targets.[4] By early 1940 the more insightful German air commanders believed it was a realistic, indeed, inevitable prospect that, in time, the RAF could and would attack targets within Germany, and that such attacks would be mounted from various directions and at various strength levels. Furthermore, developments in aeronautical technology, weaponry and aircrew training would not stand still, and so the enemy could be expected to become more aggressive and sophisticated in its endeavours.

It therefore became imperative that the Luftwaffe, in turn, 'sharpen its defensive blade' in order to respond in kind. This would have to occur at five levels: more intense and sophisticated fighter interception training; an improved tactical organisation and methods of deployment; fighter aircraft development; armament development; and the development of an efficient and quick-reaction warning system.

The Wilhelmshaven raid had highlighted a shortcoming in the latter. Albeit in a protracted way, the raid had demonstrated that fighters could be directed by radar and radio to a favourable point at which to intercept an enemy incursion and, as demonstrated on 18 December, achieve good results. Yet the advent of radar was a blind spot in Luftwaffe pre-war planning and it remained – mainly – a Kriegsmarine initiative.

After Wilhelmshaven, however, young, enterprising and technically minded Luftwaffe officers such as Hermann Diehl urged the establishment of a *Sofortauswertungen* (an immediate evaluation of a given air situation) to include direct landline links from radar stations to operational units. Although such proposals encountered strong opposition from senior officers who were concerned about security, the 'progressives' won the day. Eventually, from 1940, a series of *Meldeköpfe* (reporting centres) was set up to monitor and evaluate enemy direction finding (D/F) signals and to arrange speedy distribution of information to local tactical commands and day- and nightfighter units.[5] It was a first step towards organised, electronically controlled airborne defence.

Overshadowing all of this, however, was that fact that at the end of 1939 and into early 1940, the development and organisation of the Luftwaffe's fighter defences in the West were complex, riven to a great extent by competitive factors, and hamstrung by an offensive dogma. The latter issue, echoing the fears of the 1920s, had its foundation in the doctrinal guide *Luftwaffendienstvorschrift* (L.Dv)16 –'*Luftkriegsführung*' (Luftwaffe Regulation 16 – The Conduct of Aerial War) of 1935, in which it was stated:

> One's own armed forces and one's own land are constantly threatened by the enemy air force. This danger cannot be opposed merely by defensive measures in one's own territory. The danger of air attack against one's own land requires that the air force carry out offensive action against the enemy air force in his own territory.[6]

This offensive mindset dominated attitudes towards defence, although senior air commanders were also to oversee and coordinate the activities of the various defensive arms such as Flak, fighters and the reporting services, and that, 'The commander's command post requires a complete and effective communications net, uniting the air reporting system with subordinate units. Coverage of the whole area is desirable. This command post should be located near major targets'.[7]

From September 1939, the Luftwaffe's fighter *Geschwader* were assigned to, and controlled by, four *Luftflotten* (air fleets). Each *Luftflotte* – the highest level of operational command – comprised subordinate regional *Luftgaukommando* (Air District Commands) and *Fliegerdivisionen* (Flying Divisions), along with *Luftverteidigungskommando* (Air Defence Commands) – whose staffs had been formed during peacetime with a view, in time of war, to directing primarily *offensive* bomber, dive-bomber and reconnaissance operations. According to Generalmajor Walter Grabmann, of whom we shall read more from later, and who became a senior figure in the Luftwaffe's fighter defence infrastructure, these staffs 'had no practical experience in the commitment of fighter and twin-engined fighter forces in air defence missions'.[8]

Even within the Luftwaffe fighter command organisation, there was a lack of coherent and cohesive leadership. Many officers assigned to the tactical direction of regional fighter air defence were former army or anti-aircraft artillery officers, with little tactical air experience, and according to Grabmann:

> The coordination of fighter and anti-aircraft artillery operations was only possible at *Luftflotte*-level, and was therefore a complicated and time-consuming matter. The two *Luftflotte* headquarters committed in the West [*Luftflotte* 2, based at Braunschweig under General der Flieger Hellmuth Felmy, and *Luftflotte* 3, based in Munich under General der Flieger Hugo Sperrle] did not adopt uniform solutions to cope with this dilemma.[9]

With strategic ambitions focused on *offensive* operations, this unsatisfactory arrangement was allowed to continue because the apparent modest air activity of nations such as Britain and France gave German commanders a sense that air defence was not a priority. Grabmann noted:

> The reasons for the problem resided in the dual nature of the fighter arm as a weapon to be committed in support of strategic [in other words 'offensive'] air operations, and at the same time a weapon of air defence. It could be compared with a child who has two fathers and therefore no father at all.[10]

As such, emphasis remained on offensive operations, whether it be bombing of one kind or another, in the West or the East. But the RAF raids on Wilhelmshaven shook the tree, so to speak, and on 18 December Schumacher did his job well, as Grabmann concluded:

> The timely take-off of the interceptor fighter forces was due to the reliable advance warnings received through the naval radar instruments and the two *Freya* type radar stations of the Luftwaffe aircraft reporting services established on the island of Wangerooge.[11]

Long-term, the effect this had on RAF bombing policy was undeniable. Events over Wilhelmshaven had shown that German fighters had benefitted from radar-generated early warning. The Luftwaffe's fighters obviously enjoyed a greater speed advantage, and the twin-engined Bf 110 *Zerstörer* were able to fire cannon from beyond the range of the Wellingtons' defensive guns. This had nothing to do with what Air Chief Marshal Edgar Ludlow-Hewitt asserted in his memo to Air Vice-Marshal J. E. A. Baldwin of 24 December, alleging the Luftwaffe had deployed 'crack squadrons'.

In any case, Ludlow-Hewitt had identified a pressing problem closer to home – the poor quality of aerial gunnery amongst his crews. One report put this down to a lack of instructors and poor training methods and equipment, resulting in gunners unable to operate their turrets correctly.[12]

This must have preyed on Ludlow-Hewitt's mind when he sent his Wellingtons out in December. In early 1940, in the light of experiences over Heligoland and Wilhelmshaven, he knew that, if mounted, Bomber Command's pre-war 'Ruhr Plan', in which it was hoped to deliver a crippling blow to Germany's coal, coke, pig-iron, steel and chemical industries, would carry huge risk. The heavy losses of 18 December were a portent of what could be expected over the coming one to two years – losses as high as 50 per cent of an attacking force. RAF Bomber Command simply could not absorb such attrition and, in any case, at such a level of loss it would be unable to inflict the damage on the enemy with which it was tasked.[13]

The reality was that while the notion of daylight bombing had not been completely abandoned, as the authors of the official British history of the strategic air offensive against Germany succinctly put it, 'immediate confidence in the theory of the self-defending bomber formation, at least with existing types of bomber, had been seriously shaken'.[14]

Shaken enough for the Air Staff to peer into the dark night skies for an alternative to the dangers of mounting daylight raids. Indeed, RAF Bomber Command had been despatching the Whitley bombers of No. 4 Group on deep-penetration propaganda leaflet-dropping flights by night to targets in Germany since the outbreak of war and, from early 1940, to cities as distant as Prague, Vienna and Warsaw. These missions had encountered very little opposition.

The commander of No. 4 Group told Ludlow-Hewitt that the general absence of enemy fighters, along with ineffective Flak and searchlights, came as some surprise, and that the real 'enemy' was adverse weather (and the ensuing lack of moonlight), as well as the difficulties of locating and identifying targets in the dark. These latter factors could not be underestimated – the long, cold, lonely and tiring flights in darkness, deep into enemy territory, took a serious toll on aircrew morale.[15]

Nevertheless, in January 1940, the Wellington and Hampden squadrons had commenced some trial evening and then, gradually, night missions.[16] When Ludlow-Hewitt was replaced as C-in-C of RAF Bomber Command by Air Marshal Sir Charles Portal on 3 April, an Air Staff directive dropped onto the latter's desk in which it was stated 'the operations of our heavy bombers are to be confined mainly to night action'.[17] By May, and the German invasion of France and the Low Countries, RAF Bomber Command's Wellingtons, Hampdens and Whitleys were flying exclusively at night, attacking airfield and transport targets in the Netherlands as well as, on the night of 11–12 May, Mönchengladbach – the first German town to be targeted.

Ironically, however, those on the Air Staff and in RAF Bomber Command who still favoured daylight bombing were not helped in their views by the distinct lack of success achieved by the Luftwaffe's own bomber squadrons during their campaign in the summer of 1940 in what became known as the Battle of Britain.[18]

On 5 October, there was another change at the head of RAF Bomber Command when Portal was succeeded by Air Marshal Sir Richard Peirse. When he took over, Peirse could call upon 532 aircraft, comprised of Blenheims, Wellingtons, Hampdens, Whitleys and Battles – all twin-engined medium bombers, known by the Germans as '*Zweimots*' ('two-engines'), with the exception of the single-engined, and obsolete, Fairey Battle.

Night raids continued for the rest of the year, being conducted by small numbers of aircraft mainly against targets in Germany. It remained a common occurrence for bombers to turn back on account of the worsening autumn weather, and the level of operations gradually diminished until 1941.

On 27 September 1940, some nine months after RAF Bomber Command's first forays to Heligoland and Wilhelmshaven, a brief article appeared in the respected British aviation journal *The Aeroplane* entitled 'Boeings for Britain?', in which it was speculated that a new *four*-engined American bomber might soon be in service with the RAF. The article adopted a surprisingly derogatory tone about an aircraft that would go on to prove itself as one of the finest bomber types to fly in World War II – the Boeing B-17 Flying Fortress.

The origins of this aircraft lay in a US Army Air Corps (USAAC) tender of 8 August 1934 which called for a multi-engined, long-range bomber able to deliver a one-ton bomb load. The aircraft had to be capable of attaining a speed of 250 mph, have a range of 2,000 miles and an operating ceiling of 10,000 ft. The tender-winning company could expect to be rewarded with an order for 200 such aircraft. Boeing of Seattle, Washington, submitted its design to the USAAC as the Model X-299 (later amended to B-299).

The Model 299 showed promise over competing designs offered by the Martin and Douglas companies, and exceeded all USAAC requirements in terms of speed, climb, range and bomb load. In January 1936, the USAAC arranged to purchase 65 test machines under the designation 'YB-17', the 'Y' denoting an aircraft still at the experimental stage. Three years later, in January 1939, the 14th aircraft was fitted with turbo-supercharged engines and delivered to the USAAC. Following successful trials, an order for 39 further such aircraft was placed under the designation B-17B – the new 'Flying Fortress'.

The aircraft took the form of a low-wing, all-metal monoplane that, to some extent, drew on the aerodynamic features of Boeing's elegant twin-engined Model 247 airliner. Powered by four 1,200 hp nine-cylinder Wright R-1820-G205A engines, the B-17B was delivered to the USAAC from 1939, equipping two bomb groups that conducted high-altitude precision bombing trials in California with ostensibly encouraging results, albeit in near perfect conditions.

In Britain, however, the journalist from *The Aeroplane* remained caustically sceptical:

> The big Boeings, proudly dubbed 'Flying Fortresses' by the American press, are not new or formidable, except that they can carry a heavy load of bombs for a moderate range or a moderate load of bombs for a long range. By British standards, the B-17s are most poorly armed and, because of their size, should make easy targets in the air or on the ground. Their maximum speed of 268 mph is too slow to offset their poor defence, and they would be shot down easily by day.

Perhaps with the benefit of knowing how crucial tail armament had proved to be during RAF Bomber Command's daylight raids the previous year, the writer noted a valid point:

> These 'Flying Fortresses' have a defensive armament of five machine guns. The big single fin and rudder prevents the installation of a gun in the tail. Yet they are officially described as having 'exceptional defensive firepower'. They have no armour, nor are their tanks protected.[19]

The acid test came on 8 July 1941 when three of the initial batch of 20 B-17s made available to Britain following the passing of the Lend-Lease Bill, which had been signed by President Franklin D. Roosevelt on 11 March that year, carried out a 'high-altitude attack' from 30,000 ft on the same target that Wg Cdr Kellet's Wellingtons had journeyed to in September 1939 – Wilhelmshaven. Yet again it was a shallow penetration mission against a precision target – 'the submarine-building docks'.

The Boeing bombers had been assigned to the RAF's No. 90 Sqn based at Polebrook, in Northamptonshire, and were the new B-17C variant in which the removal of the bulbous gun blisters that had characterised the previous B-model resulted in the aircraft's four gunners enjoying workable positions with greater flexibility and field-of-fire. To the British, the B-17C was designated the Fortress I.

It had been arranged for the aircraft to be fitted with self-sealing fuel tanks and other British requirements prior to departing the USA, but to some extent the RAF proceeded under the strange and misguided assumption that the Flying Fortress had already been 'battle proven'.[20] And, aside from a fervent programme of cross-country flights and high-altitude aiming practice using the American-made Sperry bombsight, there had been little in the way of briefing or specialist training on the type provided by USAAC instructors.[21] One RAF crewman remembered how the aircraft's Browning machine guns proved unreliable and ill-fitting on their mounts, and that they had to be washed with petrol.[22]

Nevertheless, just as Wg Cdr Kellet had done in leading his (larger) force of Wellingtons, that afternoon, Wg Cdr Jeffrey 'Mad Mac' McDougall led the three Fortress Is to Wilhelmshaven in what would be the debut appearance of the Boeing bomber in the skies over Germany. Each aircraft carried a 'stick' of four 1,100-lb bombs. The Fortress Is climbed up to 32,000 ft above the North Sea in open formation in clearing weather, with unlimited visibility. Conditions were perfect, and as they approached the target each Fortress I descended to 27,000 ft. From then on, things did not go particularly well.

McDougall's aircraft was the second to fly over the docks, but as it did so, its on-board cameras suffered an electrical failure and prevented any photographs from being taken. The astrodome had also frozen up, making fire control impossible. Then, when the pilot tried to release his bombs, two of them remained stuck in the bomb-bay. McDougall made a second run, but still the bombs would not budge. Turning away from the target, a third and final attempt to release the bombs was made over the Frisian Islands, but that too failed, at which point McDougall gave up and returned home with half his bomb load still on board.

For the third aircraft, flown by Sqn Ldr MacLaren, the problems started as the aircraft had climbed away from Polebrook. At 20,000 ft oil began to leak from the breather valves on all four of the Wright engines. No. 90 Sqn's ORB how, 'At 27,000 ft oil was still spurting out and freezing on the tailplane, one inch thick. Gunners reported severe vibration and no more height could be reached. Oil pressure was falling off badly, and S/Ldr MacLaren decided to bomb targets on the Frisian Isles and return to base'.[23]

MacLaren and his crew attempted to bomb the island resort of Norderney, but they missed their target and the bombs exploded harmlessly on a beach. Then, as it turned for home, the Fortress I began to vibrate so severely that the wireless operator's key broke. As with McDougall's aircraft, the problem was leaking and freezing oil. Lateral flutter developed on the tailplane and the oil froze to a depth of about seven inches. The six-man crew had to endure a shaking airframe for 14 minutes and the aircraft fell to 12,000 ft. The pilot feathered all four propellers, but it had no effect. Eventually, at just 4,000 ft, the vibrations ceased, the tailplane became free of oil and the aircraft was able to return to base.

Some 40 miles off the island of Terschelling, a pair of Bf 109s had put in an appearance, climbing towards the bombers, approaching on the starboard beam and closing to within 600-800 yards, one of them attempting an attack over the target, but it turned away and was observed going into an involuntary spin. The other Messerschmitt followed it.

Despite the adversities, the bombing that there was had been accurate. Fourteen people were killed and 23 injured.

The RAF persevered. Between 8 July and 12 September, a total of 22 raids were mounted by the Fortress Is, involving 39 sorties, including attacks on German warships. During the course of these operations 18 aircraft aborted, two were shot down and two were badly damaged. There was doubt as to whether as much as half the bomb tonnage carried had been effective, and no enemy fighters had been shot down. Total combat and operational losses amounted to eight out of the 20 aircraft assigned.

In a measure of how determined the Luftwaffe response to such missions was becoming, on 16 August, during a raid intended to attack the capital ships *Scharnhorst* and *Gneisenau* in Brest harbour, a Fortress I of No. 90 Sqn was shot down. Operating as one of a pair, the bomber was bounced by a formation of Bf 109s immediately after it turned away from dropping its bombs. One of the Messerschmitts was flown by Stabsfeldwebel Erwin Kley, a Berliner of 1./JG 2, who claimed a Fortress at 10,000 m over the coast at Brignogan. It was his eighth victory.[24]

However, according to No. 90 Sqn's ORB, Kley's claim was optimistic:

The upper backward-firing gun was u/s, and soon after the e/a engaged our a/c, the two back gunners and wireless op. were wounded. Persistent attacks were made and the Fortress was considerably damaged. The pilot could not climb, and so began to lose height and take evasive action. Attacks continued down to 6,000ft, by which time the aircraft was nearing the English coast.

The pilot opted to force-land his aircraft near Plymouth, in Devon, but overshot and the Fortress I caught fire on coming to rest. Three crew were killed and one wounded.[25]

Despite this, one of the pilots on the Brest raid found himself speaking in a goodwill PR wireless broadcast to America:

> These Fortresses are wonderful aircraft – perfectly manoeuvrable, steady as a battleship, and incredibly efficient. We thank you in America for these bombers.

Yet in Britain, Peter Masefield, the bespectacled Technical Editor of *The Aeroplane* and air correspondent with the *Sunday Times*, described in an American report as 'Britain's most influential commentator on air power', opined that the B-17 was ill-prepared for air combat over Europe. He believed that American aircraft manufacturers should consider building the new British four-engined Avro Lancaster and use it in a switch to night bombing.

In some circles in Britain, the Flying Fortresses attracted the unreasonable moniker of 'Flying Targets', while in Germany, Joseph Goebbels, the club-footed Nazi minister for Public Enlightenment and Propaganda, afforded them the cruel sobriquet of 'Flying Coffins'.[26]

Just two days after the Brest raid, the conundrum facing RAF Bomber Command was accentuated by the arrival at its headquarters of the Butt Report, which had been compiled from photo-reconnaissance analysis of damage inflicted on 28 German targets during 100 night raids. The conclusion was that only around 20 per cent of crews were bombing within five miles of the target. For targets in the well-defended Ruhr area, evidence suggested that only seven out of 100 bombers managed to achieve this. The daylight versus night bombing debate was like an itch that could not be scratched.

Meanwhile, upon the conclusion of Fortress I operations by the RAF, a subsequent USAAC report commented, 'One long ton of bombs delivered at a cost of eight heavy bombers was an expensive mode of warfare'.[27] Indeed, there was exasperation on the part of the Americans, one USAAC officer recalling:

> I was in England when the planes arrived. We explained to the British our doctrine for the use of the planes. We told them that the crews had to be well trained, that a crew should drop 200 practice bombs before attacking a real target, that the planes were designed to fly in formation for protective purposes and that by using them as trainers, trained crews could be ready to operate the new, properly equipped Fortresses when we delivered them. For some reason, which only the British understand, they decided to use the planes offensively.[28]

'AN EXPENSIVE MODE OF WARFARE'

There was truth in this, but it could not overlook the fact that the B-17 had its weaknesses. On 28 July, one Fortress I suffered structural failure in its starboard wing as a result of turbulence during a test flight – it broke in two, resulting in the deaths of all seven on board, including an American officer.[29] However, it is fair to note that the B-17 had been designed to operate at 25,000 ft, whereas the RAF sent its Fortress Is over targets at altitudes in excess of 30,000 ft. In the aforementioned Brest raid of 16 August, the unfortunate aircraft attacked by Messerschmitts was flying at 32,000 ft. The bomber lacked the speed to escape swiftly, efficient defensive armament and unimpeded visibility.[30]

Valuable lessons had been learned by the British and the Americans. If Flying Fortresses were to be used in daylight raids, they needed to be flown in formations large enough to ensure a sufficient bomb pattern. The aircraft could not be overloaded – at least by USAAC standards. Bombing accuracy from high altitude would have to be improved, as would the functioning of defensive armament, and there would need to be the provision of better flight clothing, oxygen and heating systems, and windscreens and lubricants made resistant to frosting and freezing.

Also arriving in England in 1941 was another American four-engined bomber. The creation of the Consolidated B-24 Liberator had its origins in a 1938 request from the USAAC for Consolidated Aircraft of San Diego, California, to build the all-metal B-17 under licence. However, after visiting Boeing's plant in Seattle, Consolidated decided to advance its own design, intended to better that of the B-17, in the same time that it would have taken to prepare tooling for its mass production of the Boeing bomber.

Then, in January 1939, the USAAC officially invited the San Diego-based firm to produce a design for a bomber with greater range and superior performance to the B-17. Consolidated moved quickly and had finished a prototype – the XB-24 – by the end of the year. Early pre-flight orders from overseas were encouraging, with 120 aircraft destined for the French air force and 164 for the RAF. The German invasion of France in May 1940 resulted in the bulk of the initial production B-24s going to the RAF.

Designated the LB-30A, the aircraft was powered by 1,200-hp Pratt & Whitney R-1830-33 engines that produced a top speed of 280 mph. The aircraft had a service ceiling of 27,000 ft and – impressively – could carry 8,000 lbs of bombs. The LB-30A fielded six 0.50-in. machine guns, including a weapon mounted in the tail, and it took to the air for the first time on 17 January 1941. After receiving the first six machines, however, the RAF was disappointed by the lack of self-sealing fuel tanks and turbosuperchargers, and from March 1941 the aircraft were 'moved sideways' for transatlantic ferry service.

Consolidated had also produced a run of nine B-24As, similar in form to the LB-30A prototype, but finished in olive drab with a large Stars and Stripes painted on each side of the nose to signal a neutral American aircraft. Once more, however, the design was not considered sufficient as a bomber, and so the aircraft were passed on to the USAAC's recently formed Ferry Command. Another 20 such aircraft were purchased by the RAF and fulfilled from an order of 38 machines placed by the USAAC.

The RAF christened the aircraft the Liberator B I (effectively a B-24A), and because of its range and bomb load capacity, the Consolidated heavy bomber became the ideal aircraft for RAF Coastal Command in its operations against the growing U-boat threat. The Liberator II, which had a longer nose and powered turrets, followed in August 1941. Five months later, examples entered service with two squadrons of RAF Bomber Command – the first operational units to fly the type as a bomber. They were subsequently deployed to the Middle East and the China-Burma-India Theatre.[31]

In November 1941, the *Geschwaderkommodore* of JG 26, the innovative, raven-haired, cigar-chomping Oberst Adolf Galland, was appointed as the *General der Jagdflieger* following the untimely and unwelcome death of the previous incumbent, the highly respected fighter ace and tactician, Oberst Werner Mölders.

Galland had qualified for the position on account of his considerable frontline experience which went back to flying Heinkel He 51 biplanes with the *Legion Condor* in the Spanish Civil War. By early June 1940 he had been credited with 12 enemy aircraft destroyed, and took command of III./JG 26 in France. He led that *Gruppe* with distinction during the battles against the RAF over the English Channel that summer, being awarded the Knight's Cross with 17 victories to his credit on 29 July and, on 22 August, promotion to *Geschwaderkommodore* of JG 26.

As a tactician, Galland favoured his fighters making hit-and-run nuisance raids against targets in England, which gave advantage to the fast Bf 109. He experimented with a telescopic sight in his cockpit and he oversaw the complex air operation to cover the successful escape of the Kriegsmarine's heavy ships from their enforced confinement in Brest, through the Straits of Dover in daylight, to the sanctuary of the German coast in February 1942.

Galland successfully pushed for a revision of the Luftwaffe's prevailing bomber interception tactics and gained more freedom for his pilots to take on the Spitfires, which would pursue the Bf 109s as they broke away from their pass over the bombers they were escorting. Galland recalled the weight of fire from a Spitfire at this time as being 'very effective'. While he was with JG 26, his pilots had devised special tactics which saw them exploiting cloud cover to move slowly and carefully towards the RAF fighter escort without being noticed, before quickly assessing a vulnerable or 'convenient' part of the formation to attack. The German pilots would then climb slightly and dive quickly before the escort could have a chance to react.

Galland also experimented with the method of deploying some of his fighters to both the rear of and above an enemy bomber formation, thus diverting the attention of the escort, while he alone would climb slowly and gradually out of the clouds below the formation. Hopefully remaining unseen, he would close in on one of the lower elements, select a target, shoot it down, then make a quick dive into the clouds to get away.

Such tactics brought success on occasion, but they could also result in losses, such as on 13 October 1941 when, having attacked a formation of Blenheims from below and shot one down in flames, Galland veered away unscathed. His inexperienced wingman, however, was not so fortunate and drew fire from the turret gunner of the Blenheim he was targeting. Leutnant Peter Göring, a nephew of Reichsmarschall Hermann Göring, the Commander-in-Chief of the Luftwaffe, crashed to his death. These methods also depended to a great extent on weather and an ineffective or slow-to-react escort.

Somewhat more ominous had been the appearance, in July 1941, of a new British *four*-engined bomber – a '*Viermot*' (the German/Luftwaffe contraction of 'four-engines') – in the form of the Short Stirling, which carried a crew of six protected by no fewer than eight 0.303-in. machine guns housed in nose, dorsal and tail turrets. On 10 July, three escorted Stirlings bombed the Chocques power station in France.

Knight's Cross-holder Hauptmann Rolf Pingel, the *Gruppenkommandeur* of I./JG 26 and another veteran of the Spanish Civil War with 28 victories to his name, pursued one of the bombers alone from the Pas-de-Calais, across the English Channel, to England, where he managed to inflict damage on its tail section, before a burst of fire from the Stirling's upper gunner hit the engine of his Bf 109. Pingel descended to a lower altitude, whereupon he was attacked by a Spitfire and had to force-land, thus presenting the British with their first largely intact example of the new Bf 109F-2 fighter.

Six Stirlings were also used to attack the *Scharnhorst* at La Pallice on 23 July, one of them tellingly, but erroneously, claiming the destruction of two Bf 109s with its defensive armament during the raid. Likewise, in an indication of already heightened awareness of what probably lay ahead in the air war, pilots of JG 2 reported the Stirlings as being 'Boeing bombers'.

However, what really mattered to the Germans was that they accounted for the destruction of a Stirling when Leutnant Ulrich Adrian of 1./JG 2 shot down one of the six, thus becoming the first German pilot of his unit – and possibly the Luftwaffe – to account for a *Viermot* destroyed.

A freshly trained German pilot joining the Luftwaffe's western-based fighter units could expect to be engaged in combat against enemy fighters as well as, on occasion, RAF light and medium bombers which often lacked adequate defensive armament. Although Galland noted that at this time 'the strain on the men and material of JG 2 and JG 26 was much worse than during the Battle of Britain', providing a new German fighter pilot followed the instructions of his more senior and experienced fellow airmen, he would stand a fairer chance of life expectancy than his colleagues flying in the USSR or North Africa.

In Britain, the debate over deployment continued. In the autumn of 1941, a group of experienced RAF pilots was invited to the USA to give their opinions on the merits of the B-17 and B-24. They were not particularly favourable, and the Americans were left with the sense that there was a lack of interest in aircraft that were not British – especially aircraft which suffered from mechanical problems, lack of armament and losses. The British pilots opined that both the Flying Fortress and the Liberator should be used only as night bombers. Conversely, the Americans felt that the RAF had been negligent over maintenance and had demonstrated a lack of skill in handling the B-17.

Notwithstanding this, in October 1941, the USAAC carried out a study to determine whether the B-17 and the B-24 would be able to penetrate the expected German defences consistently enough to successfully undertake the bombing campaign against Nazi Germany set by the Air Staff's Air War Plans Division (AWPD).

The study pointed out that when operated by the RAF, the B-17 had shown great endurance under enemy fire, but inflicted little damage on enemy aircraft. Therefore, in order to avoid losses from Flak, bombing would have to be carried out from maximum altitude, where enemy defensive measures would be stretched. Furthermore, because of the lack of escort fighters, bombers would have to rely on their own defensive armament. The AWPD concluded that, like the British bombers, both the Flying Fortress and the Liberator should be armed with ten 0.50-in. machine guns, where possible mounted in turrets.[32]

In September 1941 Boeing introduced the B-17E. Six feet longer than the C-model and seven tons heavier than the original Model 299, it had a substantially redesigned airframe which featured an increase in the size of the horizontal and vertical tail sections in order to give the Flying Fortress the improved aerodynamic qualities necessary to turn the aircraft into a rugged and reliable bomber.

The B-17E's armament was formidable. The rear fuselage featured a tail gun turret (dubbed a 'stinger') for added defence against fighter attack from the rear, mounting twin 0.50-in. Browning M2 weapons hand-operated by a gunner in a sit-kneel position. Additionally, a 360-degree power-operated turret was installed into the upper fuselage immediately aft of the cockpit, while a remotely controlled turret, fitted with a periscope sight to be used by a gunner in a prone position, was built-in under the central fuselage aft of the bomb-bay. Both these turrets also fielded twin Brownings, meaning that the B-17E was truly a 'Fortress', armed with eight 0.50-in. guns in total and a single 0.30-in. gun in a framed Plexiglas nose cone which, together, protected its crew of ten.

Yet in England on 6 December 1941, Air Marshal Sir Richard Peirse drafted a letter to the Air Ministry expressing the view that neither the Fortress I nor II (B-17E) were suitable as daylight bombers. In his opinion, they would be better used for night operations with RAF Bomber Command.[33]

The day after Peirse sent his letter, on 7 December, the Japanese launched a pre-emptive air strike with more than 350 aircraft against Naval Station Pearl Harbor, home of the US Navy's Pacific Fleet in Hawaii, 3,400 miles from Japan. A number of American warships were sunk, including six battleships, three destroyers and three light cruisers. No fewer than 164 aircraft were destroyed and 128 damaged at nearby airfields. In total 2,403 service personnel and civilians were killed. The USA thus declared war on the Empire of Japan. In Nazi Germany, Adolf Hitler made his own declaration – 'The turning point!' he had exclaimed to Obergruppenführer Martin Bormann and other members of his inner circle.[34]

To many of those in the *Führer*'s court, it seemed America's entry into the war was driven by greed, self-confidence and pride. Such was his disdain that Hitler was heard to comment 'one Beethoven symphony contains more culture than America has produced in her whole history!'[35] From certain information he was receiving from his diplomats in Washington, D.C., Hitler had evidence that Roosevelt was reluctant to be drawn into a war. Yet hostilities between Japan and the USA would serve a purpose – to distract the Americans with war in the Pacific, at least for the coming year, thus allowing Germany to conclude its war in the USSR.[36] Four days later, on 11 December, Germany declared war on the USA.

3

'One swallow doesn't make a summer'

The USAAF's Eighth Air Force first arrived in Britain on 12 May 1942 – not by air, but by sea. The advance parties of the Eighth Air Force headquarters staff, VIII Bomber, Fighter and Base Commands and the 2nd Air Depot Group – constituting 1,850 officers and men – had sailed in convoy from Boston, Massachusetts, on board SS *Andes*, the ocean liner flagship of Royal Mail Lines, which had recently been converted into a troopship.[1] When these men docked at Liverpool, they formed the first element of what would grow to become a massive and formidable fleet of air power. By December of the following year, the Eighth Air Force would number 185,000 men, 4,000 aircraft and thousands of support vehicles spread across Britain in an extensive network of headquarters and communications centres, bomber, fighter and transport airfields, engineer depots and supply and ordnance bases.[2]

The establishment of what would become known as the 'Mighty Eighth' had been an ambitious, but militarily justified undertaking, and it had been neither hasty nor ill-conceived. Nearly a year before the attack on Pearl Harbor, in January 1941, when it became increasingly apparent that the USA would be drawn into the war in Europe, senior British and American staff officers commenced a series of conferences in Washington, D.C. which lasted just over two months. The objective was to agree on the methods by which the USA and Britain could defeat Nazi Germany and its allies, and to devise means of cooperation and military strategy. One key element of the strategy was to be 'a sustained air offensive against the German homeland and all territories under her control'.

Ensuing from this, a war plan was drafted in the USA – AWPD-1 – in which it was projected, with considerable accuracy, the number of men and aircraft needed to engage in an air war against Germany and its Luftwaffe.[3] The call was for the establishment of 54 air 'combat groups', with the aim of operating a 'substantial proportion of these forces from advanced bases in the British Isles in the event of US intervention in the war'. The objective was

'ONE SWALLOW DOESN'T MAKE A SUMMER'

to strike at three key German target types – the electric power network, the transportation system and oil and fuel refineries and their storage facilities.[4] This would weaken Germany's ability to wage war.

However, both Britain and America recognised that an air offensive of such magnitude would require deployment of air power that far exceeded prevailing capabilities of industrial production and military training. Both of these aspects would have to be accelerated.

For their part, the Americans believed that their bombers would have to fly deep penetration missions into Europe in daylight, using large numbers of aircraft with high speed, the necessary bomb lift and the requisite defensive armament. In addition, to provide protection against anticipated German fighter defences, work should proceed swiftly on a heavily armed and armoured escort fighter with speed in excess of, and range equal to that of the heavy bombers.

The Eighth Air Force was conceived as part of overall US war plans, but it had started life as the Fifth Air Force, intended to provide air support for American military operations in North-West Africa. When the European requirement manifested itself, however, on 2 January 1942, Maj Gen Henry H. 'Hap' Arnold, the commanding general of the USAAC, directed that the work and forces so far assigned to the Fifth Air Force should be diverted accordingly. To avoid confusion with a plan to activate a Fifth Air Force in the Far East, the proposed new command was renamed the Eighth Air Force, with headquarters and base commands to be established at Savannah, Georgia, by 28 January 1942, followed by Bomber and Interceptor Commands at, respectively, Langley Field, Virginia, and Selfridge Field, Michigan, by 1 February.[5]

Over dinner with senior USAAC officers in California, at which Air Chief Marshal Sir Charles Portal, Chief of the British Air Staff, and Air Vice-Marshal Arthur Harris, the new head of RAF Bomber Command, were also guests, Arnold laid out his aims for the Eighth. He stated that it would have no fewer than 3,500 aircraft and 200,000 men in England within 14 months, with the first cadre to arrive in March – just two months away.

These objectives were revised in February, with a target of 14 heavy bomber groups and two fighter groups to be in place before the end of 1942.[6] Time of initial movement was set for 15 May. The US Army would take care of supply, and the British would assist in organising air and ground protection, and arranging the necessary airfields.[7] Command of the Eighth Air Force was given to Maj Gen Carl 'Tooey' Spaatz, while the bomber element was to be led by newly promoted Brig Gen Ira Eaker.

While Spaatz remained in Washington, D.C. to oversee the shipping out of the first aircraft and crews, on 4 February Eaker departed for Britain, where, effectively and single-handedly, he became responsible for building the infrastructure of the entire Eighth Air Force.

On 1 June, Arnold, who had also arrived in Britain several days before, displayed an ebullient and confident mood when, having spent the previous night at Chequers, the Buckinghamshire country residence of Winston Churchill on the invitation of the British Prime Minister, he cabled Roosevelt. While at Chequers, Arnold had become aware of the effects of mass bombing following the RAF raid on Cologne the night before, when 890 aircraft had dropped more than 1,450 tons of bombs on the German city, killing 469 of its residents and injuring 5,027. More than 12,000 buildings were affected in some way by the raid, and water and electricity supplies, telephone communication and mail were inoperative or disrupted for two weeks.

Such results would have dovetailed with the aspirations of AWPD-42, a new war plan that saw assets for operations from Britain increase to 42 groups and 2,106 aircraft, with the target scope widened to embrace U-boat manufacturing yards, and aluminium and synthetic rubber plants.[8] 'England is the place [from which] to win the war', proclaimed Arnold to Roosevelt. 'Get planes and troops over as soon as possible'.[9] In his meetings with senior officers of the RAF, Arnold had stressed that every American-made aircraft would 'be manned and fought by our own crews'.[10]

As a result of negotiations between Arnold and Portal in London, on 21 June in Washington, D.C., the former signed off the commitment of 17 heavy bomber groups (595 aircraft) to operations against Germany and occupied Europe from Britain by 1 April 1943, along with ten groups of medium bombers (570), six light bomber groups (341), seven reconnaissance groups (399), 12 fighter groups (960) and eight transport groups (416).[11]

It would not be until 1 July that the first B-17E Flying Fortress bomber, with an American crew, from the 97th Bombardment Group (BG), touched down at Prestwick, in Scotland, after its gruelling 2,965-mile journey from the USA to Britain. For the bomber crews – despite being pitifully ill-trained on the aircraft, its radio equipment and armament, and destined to be quartered a long way from home – it was akin to the start of some great, adrenalin-charged adventure.

Aircraft transiting to British shores followed a main North Atlantic ferry route, staging firstly 569 miles from Presque Isle in northeast Maine to Goose Bay in Labrador, then 776 miles to a remote landing ground known as Bluie West One at Narsarssuak on the Tunulliarfik Fjord at the southern tip of Greenland, then a further 774 miles to a British base at Reykjavik

'ONE SWALLOW DOESN'T MAKE A SUMMER'

in Iceland, followed by a final 846-mile leg to Prestwick. Weather on the crossing was often atrocious, and for the first crews of the 97th BG, visibility on the approach to Bluie West One was so bad that several aircraft were forced to return to Goose Bay after 14 hours in the air.[12] Within six days, however, there were eight B-17s, seven Lockheed P-38 Lightning fighters and five Douglas C-47 Skytrains in Britain.[13] It was a slow start.

Each Flying Fortress carried a crew of ten men – pilot, co-pilot, bombardier, navigator, flight engineer/top turret gunner, radio operator, two waist gunners, belly turret gunner and a tail gunner. It was hardly surprising that as more bombers and their crews trickled in over the coming weeks into a new operating environment, there was much work to do in terms of training for formation flying, radio communication and, in particular, air gunnery. The Americans tackled all these areas with considerable endeavour, and by the end of August the Eighth Air Force's VIII Bomber Command had three operationally ready bomb groups to its name, representing a force of 119 B-17Es.

It was not all plain sailing, however. On 8 August, the headline in an article on the front page of the *New York Times* said it all – 'British–U.S. Rift on Planes Holding Up Air Offensive'. The article claimed this was down to 'British–American inability to agree on methods or objectives'. Apparently RAF officers did not believe that the American heavy bombers could 'do the job'. On the 11th, the *The Times* published Spaatz's response in which he stressed that any delay was because of the dispersal of so many personnel and aircraft, combined with bad weather and the need for training. There was no disagreement with the British over American aircraft or the USAAF's daylight bombing policy.[14] In any case, Eaker was quite clear as to how his bombers would target the enemy, as he noted in the summer of 1942:

> First the factories, sheds, docks and ports in which the enemy builds his submarines and from which he launches his submarine efforts. Next, his aircraft factories and other key munitions-manufacturing establishments. Third, his lines of communication. A subsidiary purpose of our early bombing operations will be to determine our capacity to destroy pinpoint targets by daylight precision bombing and our ability to beat off fighter opposition.

Irrespective of any bickering in the press, the nature of the air war over Europe changed indelibly when, in the late afternoon of 17 August, 12 Flying Fortresses of the 97th BG, escorted by four squadrons of Spitfire IXs from RAF Fighter Command, bombed the marshalling yards at Sotteville, near Rouen, in France, dropping 18 tons of bombs. 'Going along for the ride' as an observer in a B-17E (somewhat appropriately named *Yankee Doodle*) flying as lead bomber in the second flight of six aircraft was Brig Gen Eaker.

Focke-Wulf Fw 190 fighters of II./JG 26 (whose pilots, ironically, identified the bombers as RAF Stirlings) and JG 2, the Luftwaffe's only two fighter *Geschwader* based on the French coast at this time, launched an attack over Ypreville. Two B-17s were lightly damaged, but this was inflicted by Flak not fighters, and there were no casualties. According to the Eighth Air Force, there were 'a few brief exchanges of fire with enemy fighters; mission successful'. Just one American gunner 'got a shot at an FW'. An encouraging new dimension had opened in the air war over Europe, although Eaker was quick to comment to a note of congratulations from Air Marshal Sir Arthur Harris of RAF Bomber Command – 'One swallow doesn't make a summer'.

Following this inaugural operation, despite continuing sniping in the British press over the comparatively light bomb load of the B-17 against that of British bombers, as well as a perceived low speed and lack of armament, Spaatz was pleased with initial performance and results. He immediately wired Washington, D.C. enthusing that the Rouen raid had far exceeded the accuracy of any previous high-altitude bombing attack in Europe by either Allied or German aircraft. Spaatz felt the results entirely justified American belief in daylight bombing, and that for the task that lay ahead, the B-17 had proved itself in terms of speed, armament, armour and bomb load. He made it clear that he had no plans to substitute the Flying Fortress for any British bomber in production.[15]

Spaatz's commitment to the B-17 was given some justification by Generalleutnant Adolf Galland, who recounted to Allied interrogators shortly after the war that even in this opening phase of the battle against the *Viermots*, 'the defensive power of the bombers was regarded as extremely effective and actually instilled considerable apprehension into the minds of the fighter [pilots]. The actual effect of the weapons was more mental than material, but at first the German fighters simply would not attack'. The 'timidity of his men' served to irritate Galland.[16]

Throughout the rest of August, the USAAF launched more tentative raids on marshalling yards, shipyards and airfields in accordance with AWPD-42, but there was no contact of any significance between German fighters and the American bombers. Nevertheless, on the 20th, Unteroffizier Jan Schild of 2./JG 26 claimed a 'Stirling' shot down over the Channel, but the kill went unconfirmed and there is no reported corresponding loss of such an aircraft by the RAF. If anything, it is likely Schild damaged a B-17 from the small force that bombed the marshalling yards at Amiens that day.

'ONE SWALLOW DOESN'T MAKE A SUMMER'

All this changed in the fading light of the evening of 6 September, when Hauptmann Karl-Heinz Meyer, the *Kommandeur* of II./JG 26, became the first German fighter pilot to be credited with the destruction of an American-crewed Flying Fortress when he shot down a B-17F of the 97th BG near Amiens. It was Meyer's tenth aerial victory. The bomber had been one of a force of 51 aircraft sent by Eaker to bomb the Potez factory at Meaulte, used to repair and overhaul Bf 109s.

The raid had presented the Luftwaffe with the perfect opportunity to prove just how menacing it could be. Having failed to rendezvous with its Spitfire escort at the appointed time, the bomber formation flew on unprotected and was duly bounced by the Fw 190s of Meyer's *Gruppe*. When the Spitfires did catch up, they in turn were bounced by Fw 190s of JG 2. The accolade of the second B-17 to fall to German guns went to Oberfeldwebel Willi Roth of 4./JG 26, who was credited with the shooting down of a 92nd BG aircraft after a series of attacks by at least five Fw 190s. According to the Eighth Air Force's summary of operations, the German fighters had launched attacks from 'all directions' and 'out of the sun'.

From this point onwards, Luftwaffe fighters and VIII Bomber Command joined in a battle of steadily increasing attrition. The Allied fighter escort was always a problem for the Germans. One tactic that did prove effective was the 'sneak attack', whereby a single fighter targeted the bombers from below or from cloud cover while the bulk of the German fighters held the attention of the Allied fighter escorts. According to a post-war intelligence report, another rarely used tactic was to ease a group of fighters into the Allied fighter formation by simulating the latter. At the opportune moment, the German fighters would suddenly attack the bombers and dive away before the Allied pilots had realised what had taken place.[17]

From their early encounters with tail gun-armed B-17s, the Germans realised that in mounting attacks from the rear, they would, potentially, suffer damage and losses. To engage a Flying Fortress was a very different proposition to attacking twin-engined medium bombers of the kind that the British had deployed so far. Against 'mediums', Luftwaffe pilots encountered less intensive rear fire, but equally they could not be attacked head-on because of a greater closing speed than when attacking heavy bombers. Regardless, it was very apparent that both fighter aircraft armour and armament would need to be strengthened quickly.[18]

In reviewing German fighter tactics against B-17s to 15 September, a USAAF technical officer reported:

> A running commentary of enemy fighter activity is kept up between the fighter cover and the first pilots of the bomber formation. The co-pilots

and all other crew members of ships in the bombing formation are on the inter-phone system to give and receive information on enemy fighter attacks. Gunners are given sectors to search so that all fields of view are covered. At least three guns may be brought to bear on any point 400 yards from a B-17F. Mutual firepower from ships in formation greatly increases the number of guns that may be fired at enemy aircraft attacking the formation.

Enemy fighter attacks from all angles have been experienced. They started with astern attacks, then went to quarter, beam, below, bow and, on the last two missions, head-on attacks. The success of all these attacks has been about the same. The B-17s that have been shot down have been from the usual causes of straggling and gunners getting killed. Damage to airplanes returning has been slight, and there have only been two airplanes at any one time out of commission due to enemy gunfire.

Gunners have caused many fighters to decide not to attack by firing a burst just as the fighter begins the turn-in to attack. This has been done on some occasions when the fighter was 1,000 yards away or more.

The foregoing indicates the still random and arbitrary style with which German fighter pilots were conducting their attacks on heavy bombers at this time, although Eighth Air Force crews reported that from August to November 1942, 'tail attacks were the rule, and were the form of attack our bomber armament and armor plate was primarily designed to protect against'.[19]

That belief was about to be disrupted, very shortly, in a dramatic and lethal way, thanks to a man called Egon Mayer.

PART II

Head-On – 1942

The appearance of the bombers in mass was the turning point in the aerial warfare of World War II. The era of sportsmanlike, chivalrous hunting had ended. The airspace over Europe had turned into a battleground with fortresses and trenches – and it was our duty to storm these fortifications and break through.

GENERAL JOHANNES STEINHOFF, PROCEEDINGS
OF THE SECOND MILITARY HISTORY SYMPOSIUM,
USAF ACADEMY, 1968

4

West and South

In November 1942, most of the pilots, aircraft and groundcrews of JG 2 were deployed across airfields in France – from Beaumont-le-Roget in Normandy and Meucon in Brittany, to Marseilles on the coast of the Mediterranean. At one location or another, they had been in France since the German attack in the West in May 1940 (one *Gruppe*, II./JG 2, had, however, recently relocated to Tunisia, where it rendered support to Axis forces fighting in North Africa).

The *Geschwader* was, organically, one of the Luftwaffe's oldest fighter wings, its core having been formed from pre-war units at Döberitz in March 1939. Befitting its status, in one of its original guises during the 1930s, the wing had been granted the prestigious honour title '*Richthofen*' in commemoration of Germany's most renowned and revered fighter ace hero from World War I, Manfred *Freiherr* von Richthofen. He had been popularised as the 'Red Baron' on account of the blood-red Fokker Dr I he flew over the Western Front in 1918.

Until the summer of 1942, for its operations defending the airspace over France against incursions by fighters and medium bombers of the RAF, JG 2 had operated one of the latest types of the Luftwaffe's superlative standard, single-engined, daylight fighters – the Bf 109F. The sleek, neatly lined aircraft had entered service in September 1940 during the aerial campaign against Britain, and it represented a complete redesign of the earlier Bf 109E – the fighter with which the Luftwaffe had won its initial '*Blitzkrieg*' victories.

The Luftwaffe had instructed Messerschmitt to improve its tried and tested Bf 109 design in order to produce a fighter that could prevail over the RAF's Spitfire I/II in aerial combat. To achieve this, Messerschmitt reworked the entire airframe, from what emerged as a larger spinner to a refined horizontal stabiliser, based on thorough wind tunnel testing which would, it was hoped, result in both a more effective fighter and one that was better suited to time-saving mass manufacturing methods. This latter factor was no small consideration. Impressively, construction was reduced from 9,000 man-hours to 6,000.

The F-model – or 'ced to – saw the introduction of a new, longer cowling which faired in more aerodynamically with the propeller spinner, a new aerodynamically improved radiator housing and coolant tanks on both sides of the engine, a new hydraulics system, increased laminated Dural and steel armour protection for the pilot and fuel tanks (essential for dogfighting), a new wing layout with rounded tips to enhance handling in the air and a 100-litre increase in fuel capacity (later held in self-sealing tanks).

The earlier wing-mounted armament was also adjusted so that the guns were installed in the fuselage, with two 7.92 mm MG 17 machine guns fixed in the upper cowling to fire through the propeller arc and a 15 mm MG 151/15 (F-2) or 20 mm MG 151/20 (F-4) cannon through the propeller hub. Internally, in the narrow, tiny cockpit, the pilot's oxygen regulator was updated and a new remote compass and electrical turn-and-slip indicator were installed, together with adjustable rudder pedals.

JG 2 was equipped with the F-2 and F-4 main production sub-variants, powered by, respectively, the Daimler-Benz 1,159-hp DB 601N and 1,332-hp DB 601E inline engines. The former required 100 or 96 Octane C3 fuel, while the latter, despite improved performance, was able to run on lower-grade 87 Octane B4 fuel. The Bf 109F had a top speed of 635 km/h, some 65 km/h faster than the Bf 109E.[1]

In 1942, around 2,400 Bf 109Fs would be built, and several pilots in JG 2 had chalked up multiple aerial victories flying the Messerschmitt. Nevertheless, in the spring and summer of that year, the three *Gruppen* of JG 2 relinquished their Bf 109s for Germany's newest fighter, the radial-engined Focke-Wulf Fw 190.

If the Bf 109 was sleek in appearance, then, by comparison, the radial-engined Fw 190 with its wide-track undercarriage was a rugged-looking aeroplane, combining the benefit of manoeuvrability with stability as a formidable gun platform. Its existence was owed to an RLM requirement of 1937 for Bremen-based Focke-Wulf to design a fighter with a performance which would be superior to that of the then still new and largely untested Bf 109. Focke-Wulf's response was to think in terms of an aircraft built first and foremost for *interception*, which meant it would be able to absorb considerable punishment in action. The company's design was not specifically tailored towards offence or attack, like the Bf 109 had been. This philosophy did not prove popular with the RLM.

Dipl.-Ing. Kurt Tank, Focke-Wulf's Technical Director, and a resolute and exceptionally gifted designer, remained undaunted, and in some of the corridors of power, at least, he found support. This was primarily because the fighter's air-cooled radial engine was capable of withstanding considerable combat damage, and its production would not impinge upon the supply of the Bf 109's liquid-cooled DB 601. The RLM eventually relented, permitting the Focke-Wulf design to proceed.

The company took its time and made strenuous efforts to ensure that the build was second to none, and that the design would demand the minimum of maintenance in operational conditions. Company drawings of the first prototype, dating from the autumn of 1938, show proposals to install an armament of two 7.9 mm MG 17 and two MG 131 machine guns, all wing-mounted.

Powered by the BMW 801 engine, examples of the first production machine, the Fw 190A-1, were delivered to an operational unit, 6./JG 26, based in Belgium, in August 1941. Towards the end of the year, the A-2, fitted with an improved 1,600-hp BMW 801C-2 engine, reached the *Stab* and I./JG 26 in France. Deliveries of this variant were made to III./JG 2 in June 1942, and they came armed with an uprated weapons array which included two 20 mm Mauser MG 151/20 cannon built into the wing roots, with interrupter gear incorporated to allow synchronised fire through the propeller arc, as well as *Revi* C/12 D reflector gunsights.

Crucially, it was discovered that the Focke-Wulf enjoyed marginally heavier armament and a speed superior to that of the previously unassailable Spitfire V, but it was outclassed in the turn. If the balance had not turned in favour of the Germans, it was at least now equal. The production lines delivered 425 Fw 190A-2s between August 1941 and July 1942.

The ensuing Fw 190A-3 was delivered to III./JG 2 in June and July. This variant was fitted with the new 1,700-hp BMW 801D-2 engine, the uprated power achieved by increasing the compression ratio in the cylinders and refinements to the two-speed supercharger. Externally, the Fw 190A-3 was equipped with two MG 17s and, again, a pair of MG 151/20 cannon. III./JG 2 at Vannes-Meucon had around 30 Fw 190A-2s and A-3s on strength in November 1942, to be joined shortly by a similar number of the latest A-4s.

For the kind of operations against Allied heavy bombers which the Bf 109 and Fw 190 were destined to undertake, the MG 151/20 was an ideal weapon. Developed by Mauser of Berlin, the MG 151 was a recoil-operated, belt-fed aircraft cannon of high ballistic performance, blending a fast rate of fire with reliability, while its light weight favoured fitment into wings or fuselages. It had a muzzle velocity of 805 m per second, and a cyclic rate of 700 rounds per minute. The gun was electrically charged and fired, with 50 rounds stored for the fuselage-mounted cannon in the Bf 109, but a greater load for wing-mounted weapons in the Focke-Wulf. High-explosive, armour-piercing or incendiary rounds could be used.

Oberleutnant Walter Wolfrum flew the Bf 109 exclusively on the Eastern Front with JG 52 between 1943–45. Although he did not see action against the bombers of the Western Allies, he was a proficient fighter pilot, credited with 137 aerial victories claimed in 424 missions. Of the MG 151 he recalled:

> Originally designed as a 15 mm heavy machine gun in competition with the 13 mm Rheinmetall MG 131, it proved so promising that it was rechambered to fire 20 mm cannon shells. In its final configuration it weighed only 42 kg, and its rate of fire [700 rounds per minute] was better than most of the machine guns, and it had a velocity nine metres per second better than the MG 131. To give one an idea of how much firepower this cannon possessed, in one minute it could, theoretically, discharge nearly 90 kg of metal at the enemy, although no German aircraft cannon ever carried more than 200 rounds per gun – roughly enough for five seconds of non-stop firing.[2]

But by late 1942, if German armament was impressive, tactical deployment against enemy bombers needed tightening up – and the bombers were slowly, but surely, increasing in their numbers and their crews in experience. At their largest, German fighter interception formations were seldom greater than *Gruppe* strength, usually comprising 30 aircraft or fewer, depending on pilot availability and aircraft serviceability.

As previously mentioned, attacks were conducted from all directions often depending on the 'whim and skill' of individual pilots and/or units. Sometimes, however, attacks were made in twos or threes from several directions simultaneously. Skilful use was made of the sun and cloud cover at all times when executing surprise attacks. The condensation trails left by large formations of bombers were frequently exploited by the Luftwaffe. Straggling bombers were set upon by groups of fighters.[3]

On the American side, it seems the German fighters had made an impact, causing confusion – and wild overclaiming on the part of Eighth Air Force's gunners. During a raid to Lille and Abbeville-Drucat airfield by B-17s of the 1st Bomb Wing (BW) on 8 November, on some 20 occasions gunners claimed to have shot down attacking Luftwaffe fighters. For example, the crew of a Flying Fortress of the 306th BG reported how:

> E/A attacked from 7:30 o'clock low. Ball gunner fired, first hitting E/A at 600 yd. E/A 'wobbled', began smoking, but came in to 50 yd, then fell off apparently out of control.

Another:

> E/A came in at 5:30 o'clock below. Ball gunner fired: E/A hit first at 600 yd went down at 200 yd burning fiercely, after coming up in stall, exposing belly for perfect burst. Flames burst out evidently from tanks. Pilot not observed to bail out. No other US [aircraft] near enough to fire at same E/A.

And another:

> E/A came in at 3 o'clock level. Ball gunner fired, hitting lead E/A at 500–600 yds. At 300 yds, just as lead E/A started to peel off, it was hit by two bursts; cowling shattered and torn off. E/A dropped down in straight dive. Waist gunner couldn't fire as gun was jammed.[4]

In fact, JG 26, which attacked the B-17s that day, lost no aircraft or pilots in combat. The only consistent thing about these reports is that, with few exceptions, the *Geschwader*'s attacks were indeed made from the rear or rear quarters.

Since the beginning of November, III./JG 2 had been commanded by 25-year-old Oberleutnant Egon Mayer, a wiry farmer's son born close to the German border with Switzerland. As a young boy, like many of his contemporaries in 1930s Germany, Egon developed a keenness for flight and the sport of gliding. As a teenager, he would use the horses on his parents' farm to drag primitive gliders into the air at a local glider field not far from the town of Engen.[5] After Mayer completed school, in terms of a 'career path', it was a straight trajectory into the Luftwaffe, joining JG 2 as a leutnant in December 1939.

During operations in France in June 1940, Mayer shot down his first enemy aircraft, a French Morane-Saulnier MS.406 fighter. However, it was in the summer of 1941 and the spring of 1942 that Mayer (who had been awarded the Knight's Cross on 1 August 1941) would become something of a 'Spitfire killer', being credited with the destruction of no fewer than 47 over France and the English Channel by 19 August 1942. It was after an arid spell in terms of aerial success between August and November 1942 that Mayer would develop a new reputation as a 'slayer of Fortresses'.

By 22 November 1942, the Eighth Air Force had mounted 22 daylight bombing raids on targets in the Netherlands and western France – mainly airfields, industrial centres and U-boat pens.

Mayer may have been slight of stature, but aside from being a 52-victory fighter ace, he had a keen, analytical mind and an eye for tactics. For weeks, while serving in his post as *Staffelkapitän* of 7./JG 2, he had been studying as many of the combat reports lodged by pilots who had engaged American heavy bombers as he could. He compared their tactics, their gunnery techniques and their methods of formation flying. Mayer also took the occasional 'field trip', going out to inspect the wrecks of downed enemy bombers at their crash sites. From such visits, he realised that although some B-17s were equipped with a single 0.30-in. rifle calibre machine gun in the nose, this would be largely ineffective when contending with a high-speed fighter attack.

From such analysis, Mayer concluded that the most effective way to destroy or cripple a *Viermot* was to approach in a diving attack from the front. Due to the high combined closing speeds of the bomber and the fighter, this would place the latter in potential danger for the shortest possible time. At such an angle, a bomber's pilots became vulnerable in the lightly protected and lightly armoured cabin area. Additionally, a bomber's forward arc of defensive fire was its most restrictive and, therefore, weakest.[6] The attacking fighter would then proceed straight through an enemy formation, its pilot continuing to fire.

Mayer also believed that the high speed of a Bf 109 or Fw 190 meant that the enemy tail and waist gunners would not be able to track the fighter. In any case, the gunners would be reluctant to fire because of the risk of hitting their fellow aircraft in formation (although, sadly, this did happen on a number of occasions throughout the war).

The acid test came in the early afternoon of 23 November, when a force of 36 unescorted heavy bombers attacked the Saint-Nazaire U-boat pens. This time, a force of 28 B-17s was accompanied by eight of the recently arrived B-24 Liberators of the 93rd BG. Like the Flying Fortress, the Liberator bristled with defensive armament, incorporating ten or 11 0.50-in. Browning machine guns housed in nose, upper and tail turrets.

As the B-17s made their bomb run, Fw 190s from Oberleutnant Mayer's *Gruppe* swept in to meet them. The attack provided Mayer with the perfect opportunity to put his new tactic into practice. Forming into *Ketten* of three aircraft, initially the Focke-Wulfs went into attack from ahead and to the left, with Mayer leading one *Kette*. When in range, he opened fire with a no-deflection burst that gave him the impression that his cone of fire was reaching the area in front of the enemy aircraft. In pulling up to the left, Mayer observed hits in the starboard wing area of the B-17. The wing broke off and the Flying Fortress turned over and spun in, exploding as it went.

As Mayer's *Kette* made sharp pulls up to the left or right, initially there was no defensive fire. The bombers' gunners soon reacted, however, and both of the other pilots in his element received hits and one Focke-Wulf was shot down. The heavy defensive fire continued as the fighters moved over or beneath and behind the bombers using a climb or half-roll. Crucially, however, Mayer had experienced no defensive fire as he made his initial head-on approach.

After this initial pass, several more attacks were mounted from front low against other B-17s in the formation. On a final attack, strikes were seen in the fuselage areas and wing roots. When turning under one Flying Fortress, Mayer saw a 'light ball of fire' beneath the aircraft, moments after which the bomber 'spun in, twisting and turning and exploding after receiving more hits from the rear'.

Next, although his machine gun ammunition had been expended, Mayer aimed for the B-24s, attacking one from ahead and to one side with his cannon, keeping his speed as low as possible. As he opened fire on the Liberator, Mayer 'skidded' his Fw 190 in the direction of flight of the B-24 by applying simple rudder movement. Violent explosions were seen from the first shots, and the American bomber 'pulled up slightly and dived straight down without spinning. No one bailed out'.[7]

Mayer's attack certainly made an impact on the USAAF crews, causing shock, confusion and in at least one case, aboard B-17E *Banshee* of the 306th BG, wild over-claiming as it pulled away from Saint-Nazaire trailing behind its formation. The crew recounted being set upon by eight Fw 190s, which came in from all directions, but the top, ball and tail turret gunners all claimed to have fired at and hit the enemy machines, with, in one instance, the tail gunner observing his fire 'hitting the tail, and as the FW 190 turned, he got a spray of bullets in the nose. Heavy black smoke came out and the plane disintegrated. One wheel seen to fly through the air and the pilot to bail out'.[8]

The B-17 gunners aboard *Banshee* claimed seven Fw 190s shot down, but there was just a single loss on the German side, when one of Mayer's wingmen, Unteroffizier Theodore Angele of 7. *Staffel*, was killed over the Channel by return fire as he pulled his Fw 190 up behind the bombers after his attack. A second pilot sustained heavy damage to his aircraft at a similar moment.

It is easy to draw unreasonable conclusions regarding 'overclaiming' with the benefit of more than 80 years' comfortable hindsight, but the German attack must have been a terrifying ordeal of just a few minutes duration, which, to the men of the 306th BG, would have seemed like hours. Four bombers went down following the attack. Among the USAAF losses were two squadron commanders of the 91st BG, as well as that group's principal bombardier, navigator and gunnery officers.[9]

The HQ of the Eighth Air Force noted after the mission, 'A change of enemy fighter tactics was observed in this operation, nearly all attacks being frontal and apparently aimed at the right side of the nose.'[10] 'From that moment', one historian recorded, 'the B-17 was obsolete as a self-defending bomber'. Indeed, it seemed that Mayer had devised a way in which an initial head-on attack could be made with the aim of breaking up a formation *after* which other fighters operating in strength could concentrate on making attacks from the rear against a more dispersed enemy whose defensive firepower had been weakened.[11] Encouraged by Mayer's initial success, recently promoted Generalmajor Adolf Galland circulated a set of new Tactical Regulations to all his fighter units in which he listed five 'object lessons':

a. The attack from the rear against a four-engined bomber formation promises little success and almost always brings losses. If an attack from the rear must be carried through, it should be done from above or below and the fuel tanks and engines should be the aiming points.

b. The attack from the side can be effective, but it requires thorough training and good gunnery.

c. The attack from the front, front high or front low, all with low speed, is the most effective of all. Flying ability, good aiming and closing up to the shortest possible range are the prerequisites for success.

d. The exit can succeed only in a sharp, diving turn in the direction of the bomber formation or single bomber. The most important factor is the angle of curve in which the fighter leaves the bomber formation.

e. Basically, the strongest weapon is the massed and repeated attack by an entire fighter formation. In such cases, the defensive fire can be weakened and the bomber formation broken up.[12]

Mayer's tactics drew the interest and support of another young pilot who had only joined 7./JG 2 on 1 November – the day Mayer had been appointed *Kommandeur* of III. *Gruppe*. He was Leutnant Georg-Peter Eder, who, at just 21 years of age, was already an Eastern Front veteran, credited with ten kills. Despite being shot down and wounded in Russia, as well as having suffered a fractured skull following a collision on the ground with a Ju 52/3m, 'Schorsch' Eder would quickly prove his abilities in what would become a physically demanding and nerve-shredding new form of aerial warfare in the West.

Using Mayer's method of attack, Eder claimed his first B-17 on 30 December 1942 during a USAAF raid on the U-boat pens at Lorient.

Another followed four days later, these successes being the first in what would become an astonishing record of 'four-engined' kills.

In the final weeks of 1942, in the light of the new Tactical Regulations, Luftwaffe unit commanders issued instructions to their pilots to firstly determine a bomber formation's direction of flight, then to fly on a course parallel to and to one side of it until about 4,000–5,000 m ahead so that the formation could be seen over horizontal stabilisers. This was usually about five to seven minutes after overtaking the formation. The pilots were then to make a tight turn with engines throttled back, at which point they were to turn in by *Schwärme* and attack head-on. During this final approach to the target, the fighters were to fly level with the bombers for the last 1,400 m, open fire at 825 m and then get away by flying flat over the formation. The key aiming points were the cabin area of the target aircraft and the No. 3 engine.

When a pilot was executing a head-on attack, it was calculated that, on average, it required 20 hits with 20 mm shells from an MG 151/20 to bring down a heavy bomber. As the fighter closed in on its target, the combined approach speed would be approximately 805 km/h at 183 m per second, and this allowed only a half-second burst from the fighter before it would be forced to break away in order to avoid a collision with the bomber.

However, in reality, not many German pilots had the nerve to make their exit flat over the bombers, with most using a split-S to dive away many metres in front of the B-17s or B-24s, thus reducing firing time and shooting down fewer bombers.[13] After a successful head-on attack, they were to turn and complete the destruction of any bomber that had been knocked out of formation and isolated, or which was 'straggling'.

Despite this new doctrine, based on sound principles, German tactics against the bombers continued to sway between attacks from the rear and from head-on, although the Eighth Air Force admitted that 'from December 1942 through the end of January 1943, nose attacks predominated – in fact on some missions no other form of attack was reported. When nose attacks became a serious threat, the nose defense of our bombers was weak'.

In cases when rearward attacks were made, however, they were to be executed in a concentration of at least *Schwarm* (four aircraft) strength in rapid succession, from slightly high or low, with the fighters getting away flat over the formation. A diving exit behind the bombers was to be performed only if the fighter's speed was so low that a dive was necessary in order to evade defensive fire. Speed was essential, since the relative speed differential between the fighters and bombers was so low that the marksmanship of the bomber gunners was found to improve quite noticeably.

Those pilots persisting in rearward attacks found that the most vulnerable spot on a bomber was the wing area between the fuselage and the inboard engines. Again, the No. 3 engine on a B-17 was considered particularly important because it powered the hydraulics system.[14]

There is no doubt that Oberleutnant Egon Mayer's use of the head-on approach had both an effect against the enemy and an influence on German tactical thinking. However, it was not just over northwest Europe that Luftwaffe fighters had encountered the B-17, and nor was it in this theatre that head-on tactics had exclusively been devised and deployed.

The Luftwaffe's single-engined fighter presence covering the offensive by Generaloberst (from 22 June 1942, Generalfeldmarschall) Erwin Rommel's *Panzerarmee Afrika* against the Gazala Line in North Africa, the *Armee's* eventual capture of Tobruk and the subsequent push across the border into Egypt in mid-1942 primarily comprised the *Stab* and three *Gruppen* of JG 27, equipped with Bf 109Fs under Oberstleutnant Eduard Neumann. The Bf 109F force in-theatre had been bolstered in May with the arrival of III./JG 53 from Sicily.

In the early summer of 1942, these units, under the tactical control of the *Fliegerführer Afrika*, were hopping from one desert landing ground to another and had a strength of some 100 fighters, with serviceability averaging around 60 per cent.[15] Their tasks included providing escort for Junkers Ju 87 Stuka dive-bombers attacking both ground and maritime targets in the Mediterranean, endeavouring to achieve air superiority over the desert and engaging RAF Wellington 'mediums', as well as Blenheim, Maryland, Boston and Baltimore 'light' bombers which struck at Tripoli from Malta. Subsequently, such aircraft went on to be deployed against the Libyan supply ports of Benghazi and Tobruk when freshly taken by Rommel.

A number of the Africa-based Luftwaffe fighter pilots had made names for themselves over the desert, the most notable being Oberleutnant Hans-Joachim Marseille of I./JG 27, who became a darling of the German propaganda newsreels in which he was christened the '*Stern von Afrika*' ('Star of Africa') for his seemingly astonishing air combat record which stood famously at 101 claims by 17 June, including several multiple kills of Allied single-engined fighters in one day. Marseille became the first Luftwaffe pilot to shoot down 100 British aircraft.

When it came to tackling the bombers, up to 1942 it had not been necessary for the Luftwaffe to devise special tactics, as they posed no great threat. But from the spring of 1942, RAF Douglas Bostons operating from Bir el Baheira cooperated closely with their fighter escorts located just a few miles away at the main Allied fighter base at Gambut. The Bostons were faster than the Martin Marylands previously encountered by Bf 109 pilots in-theatre, and, mindful of the Luftwaffe's fighters, their methods of formation flying were improved. They avoided flying 'down sun', while radio communication was also established between the bombers and their escorts.[16]

When the bombers flew with fighter escorts, the tendency was for a small number of Messerschmitts to take on the Hurricanes or Kittyhawks so as to draw them away, while a larger group would then be deployed to go for the bombers. Initially, this worked well, but when the RAF increased its fighter strength, the number of Bf 109s available to the *Fliegerführer Afrika* was never enough to compete.

For the Allies, in April, the precarious situation on the vital island of Malta, which was under sustained bombardment by the Axis air forces, led to Mediterranean commanders calling for heavy bombers to attack enemy airfields on Sicily from where the Axis attacks were being mounted. By sheer good fortune, the following month, a detachment of USAAF B-24s staged through Egypt on their way to the Far East. The heavy bombers were held back in Egypt as, later, were RAF Liberator IIs bound for India, on the understanding that they would not be deployed on any 'local operations' or on any missions deemed 'unsuitable' to their type.[17]

Regardless, the Luftwaffe fighters in North Africa had a new type of enemy aircraft to deal with. What may have been the opening round in this new contest took place on 15 June when a B-24 was claimed shot down approximately 100 km south of Crete by Oberleutnant Hans-Joachim Heinecke, the *Staffelkapitän* of 9./JG 27 – his victim was actually an RAF Liberator II from No. 160 Sqn, which subsequently crash-landed in Egypt after being badly damaged. It was logged as Heinecke's 21st victory. The Liberators had been sent to bomb Italian warships.[18]

Things became much harder for the *Jagdflieger* from June 1942 with the arrival of the first Spitfire Vs in North Africa, although, in terms of manoeuvrability and armament, these were only just able to maintain a par with the Bf 109Fs. Nevertheless, they were a more formidable foe than the Hurricane IIs and Kittyhawk Is that had opposed German fighter units up until then.

The fighting in North Africa intensified in July as the exhausted forces of Rommel's *Panzerarmee* struggled to break the defensive line held by the British between the coast and the desert at El Alamein to the north and the salt marshes of the Qattara Depression to the south. Simultaneously, USAAF aircraft began to appear over the frontline, including B-24Es. The first such aircraft to drop bombs on North Africa, however, had been a lone

RAF Liberator II (examples of which had arrived in the Middle East in December 1941) on 11 January, when it had targeted Tripoli with 500-lb bombs in an 'experimental' daylight mission.[19]

It was on 9 July that the second B-24 was claimed shot down 100 km northwest of Bir-el-Astas by Feldwebel Günther Steinhausen of 1./JG 27, based at Turbiya, for his 34th victory. The bomber had been sent to attack an Axis convoy, and it plunged into the sea in flames. 1Lt Richard G. Miller was a pilot with the 376th BG operating from Fayid, east of Cairo on the shore of the Great Bitter Lake:

> On July 9 a bunch went out after some shipping and through an inexcusable lack of foresight, we lost a ship. The bunch went out in a 5-ship formation. First, the powers that handle our lives – so loosely – planned a route out that was 20 miles offshore from enemy territory; no excuse after our report of such a route being used the day before, only in shore. Anyway, from three to six M.E. 109s came out and got the trailing ship.
>
> The formation was foolish for it left one lad all alone. They hit so fast, he was in flames before he knew trouble was near. There was no confirmation that the plane absolutely went down. The last it was seen was when the rear was in flames and it dived for the water. I can't reconcile my thoughts to their loss; can't help but hope and believe they may still be alive – prisoners or something. The rear gunner certainly was out, for only one short burst came out of the rear turret, then the guns lurched down and were quiet.

USAAF B-24Es of the ad hoc Halverson Provisional Detachment (HALPRO) had been bombing Benghazi actively since 21 June, carrying out no fewer than 34 day and night raids through to month-end, including attacks on Tobruk, in which they were joined by RAF Liberator IIs.[20] In doing so they freed up the RAF's 'mediums', allowing them to strike at Rommel's supply lines. When elements of the *Panzerarmee Afrika* were on the coast road, 45 km west of Mersa Matruh, they reported being bombed hourly, and there were similar sustained attacks on Italian forces who were unable to bring fuel forwards as a result.[21]

In early July, the Liberators were joined by nine B-17s of the 7th BG arriving from India, HALPRO being redesignated as the 1st Provisional Bombardment Group, while another Heavy Bomb Group of 35 B-24s was due to arrive from the USA imminently.[22] The Flying Fortresses carried out their first strike on 2 July, when four bombed Tobruk. During July, the B-24s carried out 120 missions and the B-17s undertook 45 against Tobruk and

Benghazi, augmented by a small number of RAF Liberator IIs. Ports and convoys continued to be the target, and the bombers left large fires burning in the docks, exacerbating the *Panzerarmee*'s strained supply situation.[23]

On 23 July, the 1st Provisional Bombardment Group was reinforced by the B-24s of the 98th BG arriving from the USA with its four full-strength squadrons, thus tripling the number of USAAF bombers in the Middle East. Supported by a full-strength ground organisation, the 98th BG went into action, its 'Desert Pink' ('Titty Pink' to the crews) Liberators flying their first mission on 1 August. As a result, the port facilities at Tobruk were badly damaged, as were Axis supply ships. Tobruk's throughput fell from 2,000 tons per day to just 600 tons, and the figure would never again rise above 1,000 tons.[24]

The pressure was on the Luftwaffe fighter force, whose effectiveness, of course, was consequently compromised by fuel limitations. Eventually, like Oberleutnant Egon Mayer, the pilots of JG 27 worked out that one possibility would be to mount head-on attacks. While in Allied captivity in October 1945, Oberst Eduard Neumann, *Kommodore* of JG 27 between June 1942 and April 1943, explained to RAF interrogators:

> The head-on form of attack by massed fighters was tried, which was meant to scatter the RAF fighter screen, but this likewise demanded an aircraft and a degree of training on the part of the pilot, which was not available in Africa. Not until the Fw 190 arrived in the theatre did the plan work with any success at all. The Me 109 was quite inadequate for the purpose, since its manoeuvrability was not sufficient to allow the last-minute violent turns and dives which were an essential part of the tactics.
>
> In the head-on attack, at least six aircraft should be committed, approaching at high-speed in a shallow dive, opening fire at 650 m, closing to 180 m and aiming at the pilot's cockpit. In the rear attack, as many fighters as possible should approach from fine quarter, aiming at the wing roots. A variation of this method consisted of an approach at height, followed by a steep dive, the fighters coming up under the bomber's tail, shooting on the climb at the belly of the aircraft. All attacks were to be carried out at great speed to lessen the time within range of the bomber's defensive armament.[25]

Also responding to the war against the USAAF heavy bombers over the Mediterranean were the twin-engined Bf 110s of Hauptmann Georg Christl's III./ZG 26. The *Zerstörer* had been despatched to the Mediterranean in December 1940 to lend support in the bomber escort and ground-attack roles for the *Afrika Korps*' stop-start advance east.

Having been based in Crete since early August 1942, from where the *Gruppe* was carrying out convoy escort duties, it despatched a *Kette* of Bf 110s to cover a convoy of three merchant vessels southwest of Crete on the evening of the 21st. During their mission, Unteroffizier Fritz Lauff of 7./ZG 26 and Oberfeldwebel Walter Weiss of 9. *Staffel* each accounted for a B-24 of the 98th BG just off the coast of Gavdos. The Liberators were part of a formation of 11 sent to attack the convoy. One of the victims was a straggler, and the Messerschmitts duly took advantage.[26]

This action signalled the start of a spate of encounters over the coming weeks between the *Gruppe*'s Bf 110s and aircraft of the 1st Provisional Bombardment Group over the Mediterranean. On 3 September, while returning to Crete from a shuttle mission to Derna, Feldwebel Günther Wegmann of 8./ZG 26 spotted a formation of nine B-24Ds attacking a convoy. He went in to attack, and claimed one of the Liberators shot down, but during the engagement gunners aboard the bombers managed to get a bead on his Bf 110E-2 and hit it. Despite 50 per cent damage to the *Zerstörer* from the defensive fire, Wegmann nursed his Messerschmitt back to Crete, where he belly-landed near Kastelli. He and his gunner were unhurt, but no B-24s were lost.

There was to be almost a repeat of this incident four days later when Wegmann was scrambled in Christl's aircraft following another report of B-24Ds of the 98th BG to the south of Crete. Despite putting in another claim for a Liberator and damaging a further bomber, the hapless Wegmann returned to base riddled with 50 Browning machine gun holes in his *Kommandeur*'s aircraft. Wegmann's comrade in 8./ZG 26, Unteroffizier Heinz Sussemihl, also lodged a claim, but the American crews reported that the German attack was without effect, and again no Liberators are listed as lost.

Sussemihl struck again on the 16th, when B-17s and B-24s bombed Benghazi. The crew of one of the Liberators reported being attacked by a Bf 110, and two 20 mm cannon shells struck the bomber's right outer wing panel, but it survived. Another of the *Gruppe*'s NCO pilots, Oberfeldwebel Helmut Haugk, believed he had displayed prowess on 29 September while patrolling alone over the eastern Mediterranean. He spotted 11 B-24s and, after engaging them, he thought he had shot down two – but again that was not the case.

Haugk, who would be awarded the Knight's Cross for his service in the Mediterranean, and Wegmann would both go on to be credited with six four-engined kills by the end of the war. Their encounters with the B-24s in the second half of 1942 illustrate just how hard it was to bring down a four-engined bomber – with certainty – in aerial combat at this stage of the war.

As the American bombers persisted with their attacks on Benghazi into the autumn and early winter of 1942, so the clashes with German fighters continued. On 4 November B-24s bombed the 6,424-ton tanker *Portofino* in the port, resulting in Bf 109s from III./JG 27 being scrambled to intercept the Liberators from landing grounds around the city. Amongst those to take to the air was the *Staffelkapitän* of 8. *Staffel*, newly promoted Oberleutnant Werner Schroer. Pursuing the departing bombers towards Sollum, Schroer was able to shoot one down at 1215 hrs, as did his *Staffelkamerad*, Unteroffizier Alfred Stückler.

Twenty-four-year-old Schroer, a native of Mülheim in the Ruhr, was an ace who had been awarded the Knight's Cross three weeks earlier after reaching 49 aerial victories. His action that day between Benghazi and Sollum was significant, for it would mark his 60th kill and his first over a *Viermot*. By the time he left the Mediterranean in August 1943, Major Werner Schroer, as *Gruppenkommandeur* of II./JG 27, had claimed the destruction of 13 four-engined bombers. His remarkable rate of success against the bombers would continue to his final such victory, a B-17 shot down over Germany on 24 May 1944 while flying in the defence of the Reich. Schroer would end the war with no fewer than 26 confirmed four-engined kills, ranking him as the Luftwaffe's joint fifth highest-scorer against heavy bombers along with four other aces, including Oberstleutnant Egon Mayer.

However, the day that Schroer claimed his first 'four-engined' was the day that the Axis front at El Alamein broke. Lacking resources, Rommel could go no further and do nothing about it, so he began to retreat. By 12 November, the last Axis troops had left Egypt. That day, after pulling back to landing grounds in western Cyrenaica, where they were forced to abandon some of their Bf 109s, the *Stab*, I. and III. *Gruppen* of Oberstleutnant Neumann's JG 27 left North Africa.

Despite a worsening situation in the theatre in early 1943, the Luftwaffe continued to demonstrate innovation and resilience, occasionally in unconventional ways. According to Allied reports, at least one enterprising German fighter pilot serving in North Africa in February 1943 evolved a way of fixing four hinged containers to his Bf 109G-4, each one loaded with 34 standard infantry fragmentation hand grenades. Once packed into the container, the safety pins were removed and the detonator springs were held down only by the sides of the container and the tightness of the packing. One loaded container weighed just under 50 kg.

The aircraft would then be guided by a second fighter, which would report the height and speed of a targeted enemy bomber formation. The grenade-carrying Bf 109 then flew 1,000 m above the bombers and just so far ahead that vision of the leading bombers began to be observed off the wing, at which point the containers were dropped. The few flights that were made proved unsuccessful, primarily due to inaccuracy, but also due to the presence of escort fighters.[27]

The Luftwaffe would need every measure of innovation in its coming war against the enemy's daylight bombers over the Reich in the years ahead – and it would, in many respects, display considerable innovation. The direct combat experience gained by men like Schroer, Haugk and Wegmann over North Africa would provide invaluable tactical guidance for the younger generation of fighter pilots subsequently thrown into action in the great aerial battles over northwest Europe from 1943 through to war's end.

5

The Slender Sinews of Defence

As described by Oberstleutnant Eduard Neumann in the previous chapter, in 1942, the training required by Luftwaffe pilots to combat enemy bombers in North Africa was lacking. Furthermore, when it came to the early engagements with American four-engined bombers, there was also a tendency – not necessarily deliberate – for Luftwaffe fighter pilots to erroneously claim aerial victories. Knocking a *Viermot* out of the sky was hard, draining work that demanded an acute degree of flying ability, tactical awareness and gunnery skill. If this new air war was to be won, the necessary training was, therefore, an imperative.

It was for precisely these reasons that from late 1941, and with the prospect of a new 'air front' opening up above western Europe, every pupil in the advanced stages of daylight fighter pilot training was given two to three hours of airborne practice in bomber interception. However, this stage of training could only be reached after progressing through the Luftwaffe's established and well-proven, three-phase, day pilot training syllabus.

While, from 1943, the Luftwaffe would experience shortages of aircraft and fuel for training, for the first four years of the war, it never faced a shortage of eager young men hoping to become pilots. The 1930s had fostered a powerful sense of enthusiasm for aviation in a resurgent Germany. Thousands of young men – and many women – had been captivated by the glamour of flight. Boys grew up spellbound by the stories of Manfred von Richthofen and many other leading aces from World War I. This enthusiasm was fuelled further when Adolf Hitler rose to power in January 1933. He recognised the tremendous propaganda and potential military value in sports flying and formed, among other things, the *Nationalsozialistiches Fliegerkorps*, a branch of the Nazi Party that encouraged boys from the age of 12 to take up flying.

In line with this new 'air-minded' Nazi policy, in their free time, youth from all over the Reich flocked to embark on courses in fieldcraft, workshop duties, physical fitness and, ultimately, non-powered 'sports' glider flying at the myriad of 'sports' clubs and associations – some more para-military than others – that had sprung on up airfields across Germany. However enjoyable and 'educational' all this was for the youthful recipients was academic, for in reality, such 'sports' were intended by the Nazi overseers as semi-covert 'pre-military' flight training.

Invariably still in their teenage years, aspiring Luftwaffe aviators were required to demonstrate their proficiency by attaining three grades of the Civil Gliding Proficiency Badge (A, B and C), before being sent to a *Fliegerausbildungsregiment* (Flying Training Regiment) for a 12-month course involving physical fitness training and 'culture', military discipline, routine medical examinations, basic infantry training, lectures on radio and communications, map reading and orienteering, aircraft recognition and various sporting activities.[1]

Once they had met the required standards, they could be admitted for basic instruction at the Luftwaffe's various A/B-level *Flugzeugführerschulen* (pilot schools). To obtain the initial A1 certificate meant completing a loop in a light, powered single- or two-seat aircraft with an all-up weight of 500 kg, plus three landings without an error, an altitude flight to 2,000 m and a 300-km triangular flight course. The A1 certificate would mean that the student had undergone basic practical flying training in dual-control aircraft, with his instructors having taught him to take off and land, recover from a stall and be able to make basic solo flights in the vicinity of the airfield.

This would be followed by the A2, the B1 and the B2 courses and certificates. A2 certification was for aircraft with at least two seats and extended to 60–70 hours of familiarisation, mostly on trainers of around 90–120 hp. As most pilots in the Luftwaffe trained on dual-control machines, this was the usual starter qualification. The trainee was required to learn the theory of flight, including aerodynamics, meteorology, flying procedures and aviation law. The practical application of aeronautical engineering, elementary navigation and radio procedure was also studied.

In the air the student undertook solo cross-country flights, the duration of which was successively lengthened, and the flying of larger aircraft was practiced. An element of aerobatic flying was also incorporated into the course. These licences were normally gained over a six- to nine-month period. Initially, each instructor was assigned four pilots, but this had been increased to six by 1942.

Following on from this was the B1 certificate, for which pilots progressed onto high-performance and twin-engined aircraft of the 240 hp class, sometimes fitted with retractable undercarriages. To obtain this certificate, the student had to show that he had already achieved at least 3,000 km of flight experience, flown a 600 km triangular course in nine hours, completed an altitude flight to 4,500 m and made at least 50 flights in aircraft in the B1 category (single-engined and one- to three-seats, with a maximum weight of 2,500 kg).

On top of this, the pilot had to carry out three precision landings, two night landings and a night flight of at least 30 minutes. The course would total 20–30 hours of flying. The B2 certificate was progressively more difficult, requiring 6,000 km of flight experience involving 40–50 hours of flying time, including at least 3,000 km on B1 class and twin-engined aircraft. In addition, 50 further night flights were necessary, which had to include several difficult night landings.

Between 1939 and 1942, some 1,100 pupils per month passed through the A/B schools. They utilised a wide variety of powered biplane and monoplane training aircraft, including Arados, Bückers, Focke-Wulfs, Gothas, Heinkels, Klemms, Messerschmitts and Junkers. An initial instruction known as the '*Motor Auswahl*' (Powered Flight Selection) served to assess a pupil's performance, and to decide at an early stage whether he would be more suitable as a bomber or fighter pilot, or whether further training was futile.

Pilots deemed suitable for fighter training passed immediately from the elementary schools to a *Jagdfliegerschule* (JFS – Fighter School). During 1940–41, however, the A/B schools produced more potential fighter pilots than the, thus far, five *Jagdfliegerschulen* could process, and so long waiting lists developed. To counter any staleness and general loss of enthusiasm as a consequence of these waiting lists, in 1940–41, the Luftwaffe created an intermediate stage with the formation of three *Jagdfliegervorschulen* (Preliminary Fighter Schools). It was their job to absorb the surplus manpower and continue to provide some 20 hours of instruction on the same types of aircraft given at the *Jagdfliegerschulen*, as well as on ageing Ar 68 and He 51 biplanes, early Bf 109s and various captured foreign aircraft. By the autumn of 1942, however, the peak output from the A/B schools had passed, and the increased number of *Jagdfliegerschulen* (JFS 6 and 7 were established in late 1942) were once again able to handle the input.

Following the successful completion of training at a *Jagdfliegerschulen*, the pupil would be assigned to an *Ergänzungs-Jagdgruppe* (Erg.JGr. – Operational Training Group). The *Ergänzungs-Jagdgruppen* were intended as regional supply pools in France (*Süd*), Germany (*West*) and Poland (*Ost*), and operational units would have to draw their replacement airmen from them. The emphasis for the *Ergänzungs-Jagdgruppen* was the teaching of combat tactics against different types of aircraft, although according to a pupil at the *Ergänzungs-Jagdgruppe Süd* at Mannheim in May–June 1942, pilots were given no training with any gun of a heavier calibre than a 7.92 mm MG 17, and firing practice was air-to-ground against targets on gunnery ranges.

In addition to further flying, formation and altitude training using Bf 109s and Fw 190s, as well as instruction in air combat tactics and '*Kurvenkampf*' (dogfighting techniques), two hours were assigned to each pupil on bomber interception. For one exercise at least, in late 1942, 3./Erg.JGr. Süd at Nimes-Courbessac in the south of France called on the Ju 88s of IV.(*Erg*)/KG 77, which had just moved to Montpellier, to act as 'Allied bombers'.

On such exercises, an *Ergänzungs-Jagdstaffel* would wait 'at readiness' on the ground until an alert was given that an 'enemy bomber formation' was approaching at a given height and a given grid position. The fighters would then take off in *Schwärme*, with an instructor leading each flight. Once the aircraft were airborne and in formation, further operational instructions were given from the ground by R/T.

The object of the exercise was for the fighters to intercept the bombers, having gained an advantage in height of 900 m. When the bombers were sighted, the instructor would order one pair from each *Schwarm* to attack, whilst he and his No. 2 observed from above and provided theoretical cover against attack by enemy escort fighters. Three such interception flights were made, each lasting 30–40 minutes. The performance of each pupil was closely watched, and if his attack was not deemed satisfactory, he was made to go in again and again – and again, if necessary. Critical performance reports were then written up.

By October 1942 five fighter pilot training schools were functioning, and before the end of the year another five were established. These schools released a total of 1,666 pilots for assignment to frontline or replacement fighter units. During operations in 1942, 1,093 fighter pilots were lost, and after replacing them, the influx from the schools left a surplus of 573 pilots over and above existing units' authorised strengths. However, Luftwaffe fighter units regarded a large percentage of their assigned replacement pilots as not fully qualified for combat operations. Qualification was only confirmed after replacement personnel 'had given actual proof of their capabilities in a number of combat engagements'.[2]

By the end of the year, Germany was fighting on three massive battlefronts – in southern Russia, its armies were approaching the vortex of Stalingrad, and in North Africa the *Panzerarmee Afrika*'s grasp on Tunisia was slipping, while over occupied Europe, a new air war was intensifying. Fuel was at a premium, and priority was given to urgent operational needs in line with Hitler's war aims. Consequently, the training system fell to the back of an ever-lengthening queue. When the subject was raised with Generaloberst Hans Jeschonnek, the Chief of the Luftwaffe General Staff, he remarked insouciantly, 'First we've got to beat Russia, then we can start training'.

As German forces had advanced on various battlefronts in 1940 and early 1941, so the Luftwaffe's flying units moved forward into the freshly occupied territories. They were quickly joined by the administrative organisations essential to their support and maintenance. In due course these mid-level commands were followed by the *Luftflotten* and higher-level command staffs from their original headquarters in the Reich, which left only small skeleton staffs at their base headquarters. This left Germany with no organisation of *Luftflotte* status with the necessary staff for dealing with the activities and administration of flying units in the Reich. The net result was a somewhat fragmented arrangement, comprising a strong, semi-autonomous 'strategic' *offensive* air fleet in the West, with homeland air defence remaining as almost an afterthought – in other words, not much had changed in the Luftwaffe's mindset since the RAF had raided Wilhelmshaven in December 1939.

Between January 1941 and September 1943, the then Oberst Karl Koller was Chief of Staff at *Luftflotte* 3 in Paris. He recalled:

> It had already been seen in the West during 1941 that the British were doing what we did in 1940; that is to say they were carrying out daytime penetration raids with fighter cover – at all events, they tried to do so, albeit on a modest scale, using Blenheims, Bostons and four-engined Stirlings. This made us think seriously about what the future might hold.
>
> Numerical strength was a decisive factor for attacker and defender alike. There were only two poorly equipped fighter *Geschwader* in the West, however, and virtually no fighter defences in Germany itself. As things were, the British could have penetrated into the Reich even if they had been using older types of aircraft with poor defensive armament.[3]

In a move to roll up what was left in the homeland, on 24 March 1941 the *Luftwaffenbefehlshaber Mitte* was formed, with headquarters at Berlin-Dahlem under Generaloberst Hubert Weise.[4] The latter was a former artilleryman, in his late fifties, who had transferred to the Luftwaffe in 1935 and, because of his military background, he was appointed Chief of Staff to the Inspector of Flak, with further responsibility for the air protection of the Reich. Although awarded the Knight's Cross in June 1940 for his command of the I. *Flak-Korps* in France, he was not an airman, nor did he have experience in operational flying matters.

The *Luftwaffenbefehlshaber Mitte* took charge of all administrative, supply and defence requirements covering the airspace over the Reich. This included all Flak units, four regional *Luftgaukommandos* and XII. *Fliegerkorps* under Generalleutnant Hans Kammhuber, which had started life as a nightfighter division, but which had since been expanded to control the activities of both day- and nightfighter units.

The mission of the *Luftwaffenbefehlshaber Mitte* was the defence of Reich territory against air attack. During 1941, as a result of the ever increasing activity of RAF Bomber Command, Weise's operations staff was strengthened. However, during 1942, as German forces fought further and further from the Reich's borders, so Luftwaffe fighter and Flak units were regularly being called upon for operations at the various fronts. In terms of Flak, this meant that the home batteries became weaker in personnel and their mobility decreased, until finally they were forced to become static. In effect the Flak arm was denied one of its prime advantages – mobility as a basis for the rapid formation of strongpoints. Such a situation did not bode well for operational harmony, and counter-productive rivalries and spats developed between the Flak and flying arms of the *Luftwaffenbefehlshaber Mitte*, with one arm blaming the other for deficiencies.[5]

For the fighter units it was a similar situation. When *Luftflotte* 2, based in Brussels under Generalfeldmarschall Albert Kesselring and responsible for air operations in northwest and western Germany, northeast France and the Low Countries, was moved east in May 1941 in readiness for Operation *Barbarossa*, the *Jagd-* and *Nachtgruppen* in the Reich were reinforced, but their operational area was pushed further to the West and into the territory vacated by *Luftflotte* 2.

The first appearance of the USAAF's four-engined bombers represented another task for what was now an over-extended command, particularly since the 88 mm guns of the Flak arm were ineffective at altitudes above 8,000 m.

Day fighter operations within *Luftwaffenbefehlshaber Mitte* were coordinated by three regional *Jagdfliegerführer* (*Jafü* – Fighter Controllers). In military terms, a *Jagdfliegerführer* had the equivalent status of a division or brigade, and usually operated from the headquarters of a *Jagddivision*, coordinating, conducting and overseeing the operations of daylight fighter units assigned to its area of operations via a sophisticated monitoring and reporting system, as well as posting air situation maps within the divisional area during a given day.

In an attempt to expand fighter control infrastructure – at least on paper – on 1 May 1942, 1. *Jagddivision* (1st Fighter Division) was formed at

Deelen, in the central Netherlands, under Generalleutnant Kurt-Bertram von Döring, a former World War I aviator who, during the early 1930s, had represented German aeronautical interests in China.

2. *Jagddivision* was based at Stade under Generalleutnant Walter Schwabedissen, a burly, cigar-smoking man who, it seems, was deemed qualified to lead the unit on account of a varied service career going back to World War I as both an airman and artilleryman. After joining a Field Artillery Regiment as a Battery Officer in 1914, Schwabedissen had transferred to the Imperial Air Service the following year as an observer and artillery spotter over the Western Front. During the interwar years, under the shadow of the Versailles Treaty, he played a key part in the semi-covert development of training and flying operations in the Reichswehr, before transferring to the new Luftwaffe in 1933.

After making a name for himself as an adjutant of the Luftwaffe in no less an office than that of the *Führer* and Reichs Chancellor, Schwabedissen went on to lecture at the *Kriegsakademie* in Berlin, before being appointed Chief of Staff firstly to two *Luftgaue* and then to I. *Flak-Korps*. After service as Chief of Staff to the Commander of all German forces in the Netherlands, he was appointed to lead 2. *Jagddivision* from the summer of 1942.

3. and 4. *Jagddivisionen* at Metz and Döberitz, respectively, were formed at around the same time as 1. and 2. *Jagddivisionen*, but both of these commands controlled units equipped with nightfighters only.

These *Jagddivisionen* were nominally in charge of day- and nightfighter operations of larger geographical areas, including more than one *Jagdfliegerführer*, and, like the *Jafü*, they posted regional air situation maps on the basis of results obtained from all radio intercept and aircraft warning services. In reality, the *Jagddivisionen* were more administrative overseers, working with the *Luftgau*, and they had no authority over any ground staff or organisations.

Jafü Deutsche Bucht was based at Jever (covering the airspace over northwest Germany), *Jafü Holland-Ruhrgebiet* at Amsterdam-Schiphol (covering the Low Countries and western Germany) and *Jafü Berlin-Mitteldeutschland* at Döberitz (covering central Germany). The activities of these *Jafü* were consolidated under a coordinating *Jafü Mitte* (Centre) based at Stade.[6]

The headquarters and functioning of *Jafü Holland-Ruhrgebiet* in 1942 was typical of the *Jagdfliegerführer* during this period. It had been formed in September 1941 at Schiphol, in the Netherlands, with a subsidiary control at Zandvoort on the North Sea coast, both under the jurisdiction of Oberstleutnant Karl Vieck, former *Kommandeur* of I./JG 2 and *Kommodore* of JG 3 until August 1940.

The nerve centre at *Jafü Holland-Ruhrgebiet*, as with other such commands, was the control room, in which was housed a *Leuchtschirmkarte* – a 20 m-square, illuminated, semi-transparent, gridded glass map. At the base of this map sat a cohort of 80 female auxiliary *Leuchtpunktwerferinnen* (light projectors), each of whom monitored a geographic area or sector equivalent to one grid square on the *Leuchtschirmkarte*. This sector was reproduced on a map in front of each auxiliary onto which she would plot movements of hostile aircraft according to data received from *Würzburg* and *Freya* radar stations. The plots were 'drawn' using a special electric pencil, with each plot being reproduced automatically on the *Leuchtschirmkarte* as a red spot of light. Only one spot of light could appear at any one time in each grid square, irrespective of the number of aircraft covered, and a flashing display next to each spot would indicate the actual number of aircraft being reported.

From a balcony facing the *Leuchtschirmkarte*, another team of around 15 auxiliaries projected the positions of Luftwaffe fighters onto the map represented by white spots of light. The positions of the friendly fighters were based on plots received in the form of grid pinpoints from the 'Y' control stations. At Schiphol, and later at the *Jafü*'s subsequent headquarters near Deelen, there were three other transparent but smaller maps – one for reporting aircraft spotted by observer posts, another for tracking Luftwaffe bombers and transports passing through the zone, and a third for displaying shipping for which fighter cover was to be, or had already been, provided. On these maps, data was marked up in chalk on the reverse sides.

Facing the *Leuchtschirmkarte* were three tiers of seats, in the highest of which, at the back of the room, sat the *Jagdfliegerführer*, who held the equivalent authority of a divisional commander. The *Jafü* had direct communication with the operations rooms at the fighter airfields in his sector and could, if necessary, be connected directly to the airfield Tannoy system, although such an expediency was rarely used.

Seated to the right of the *Jafü* was an officer with a direct link to the 'Y' stations, and to his left sat the assistant *Jafü*, who handled telephone calls and messages which the *Jafü* was not in a position to take. Further to the left was an officer who liaised with the *Würzburg* and *Freya* radar stations, listening in to data received by the *Leuchtpunktwerferinnen* and checking their plotting. Immediately below the *Jafü* was a Flak liaison officer, along with around ten *Jägerleitoffiziere* who sat closest to the screen and whose task it was to control the movements of fighters in the air by means of their FuG 16ZY VHF transceiver sets. They were able to determine the bearing on which to instruct pilots to fly by flashing a compass rose over the appropriate spotlight plots on the *Leuchtschirmkarte*.

The tendency at this time was for a *Jafü* to control as large an area as possible, although on occasion fighter movements were handled by the 'Y' stations.[7] 'Y'-*Verfahren* was a means of fighter control used by the Luftwaffe, whereby the range and bearing of a friendly fighter were determined by radio/range measurement using a 'Y' *Bodenstelle* (ground site) consisting of five separate elements, each comprising a transmitter hut and mast (*Hans E-Mess Gerät*), a receiver pylon incorporating a direction finder (*Heinrich Peiler*) and a range-measuring unit. All five stations were connected to a plotting room also situated on the site, and each station required 27–30 men to operate it over a 24-hour period.

So as to extend control over a single fighter in the air to that of a larger daylight interception force, it was only necessary to include a single 'Y'-controlled aircraft amongst the fighters of the formation. The receivers of all aircraft in the formation would be tuned to a ground transmitter to receive R/T instructions from the plotting centre, as well as from the fighter formation leader. The Reich-based transmitters, known as *Berta I* or *Berta II*, had an output of 80–100 watts and a range of 400–500 km when controlling aircraft at altitudes of 5,000–7,000 m. Another transmitter was the S16B (*Sender 16 Boden*), a modification of the FuG 16 that had a maximum range of 250 km when used in conjunction with a *Rechlin* range-measuring unit, or a range of 250–350 km when used with the more accurate Siemens range-measuring unit.

In this manner, up to five separate interception formations could be controlled, each on a different frequency, from a single 'Y' site. If necessary, all five formations could be brought together to intercept one bomber formation, or alternatively, each of the five formations could be directed to engage the bombers or their escort at various points. The height of the aircraft under control was not measured by the 'Y' station, the pilot instead giving readings from the cockpit instruments over the R/T channel. Thus, all the data required for the plotting of a controlled aircraft, such as bearing, distance and height, were obtained.

In 1942, control was mainly effected by the '*Begleiter*' (escort) method, in which the lead aircraft in a formation – known as the *Führer* aircraft – also acted as the 'Y' aircraft, whilst the accompanying fighters in the formation were known as *Begleiter*. In the *Führer* aircraft, the receiver was linked with the transmitter and the receiver frequency was tuned to the ground transmitter frequency, whilst the aircraft transmitter was set to the frequency of the ground receiver. In all the other aircraft of the formation, the receiver was tuned to the transmitter frequency of the *Führer*, and in none of them was the receiver linked to the transmitter. The formation was thus plotted solely by the position of the *Führer* aircraft.

If the pilot of the 'Y' aircraft wanted to speak with his formation, he had to relay his message to the ground station and the plotting officer would repeat it on the *Gemeinschaftswelle* – a frequency of the ground transmitter to which the receivers of all the fighters in the formation were set.

During a combat operation, the fighter force was led by the 'Y' control officer only up to within sight of a bomber formation, at which point the R/T control ceased, allowing the formation leader to focus on directing the combat. It was only taken up again after combat when the fighters had re-formed for a second interception, and the 'Y' aircraft had made fresh contact with ground control. The ground station continued to plot the formation through the 'Y' aircraft.[8]

Ironically, and as a result of German military advances on three major fronts, despite the *Luftwaffenbefehlshaber Mitte*'s extensive command agencies and warning networks, in terms of fighter units, its cupboards were empty, with just one daylight *Jagdgeschwader*, JG 1, on its Order of Battle for defensive duties. In mid-1942, the war in Russia had consumed the bulk of the Luftwaffe's fighter force, with elements of six *Jagdgeschwader* based on the Eastern Front, while another seven *Gruppen* were in North Africa and the Mediterranean. The two '*Kanalgeschwader*' – JGs 2 and 26 – remained in France and the Low Countries, and there were other detachments in Scandinavia.

The four *Gruppen* of JG 1 covered a long stretch of the northern European coast from Norway to the southern Netherlands and were assigned to 1. and 2. *Jagddivisionen*. For the first half of 1942, JG 1's operations were generally not over-demanding, although there were regular claims made mainly against RAF fighter sweeps and medium bomber raids directed at the Low Countries, the northern German coast and shipping targets, with the most active *Gruppe* at this time being II./JG 1 from Haamstede, Stade and Katwijk. During the summer, this *Gruppe* had transitioned from the Bf 109F to the Fw 190A-2 and A-3. III./JG 1 operated in Scandinavia, continuing to patrol the coasts of southern Norway and Denmark, as well as undertaking convoy escort in the region. But as the summer of 1942 progressed, there was a growing sense within the ranks of the *Geschwader* that everything that had taken place thus far was merely a curtain-raiser for what was coming.

They were right. Directed by *Jafü Holland-Ruhrgebiet*, JG 1 clashed with B-17s for the first time on 21 August when nine Fw 190s led by Oberleutnant Robert Olejnik, *Staffelkapitän* of 4. *Staffel*, intercepted a formation of 12 B-17s from the 95th BG en route for the shipyards in Rotterdam. Although their fighter escort had turned for home, the bombers were well-grouped and repulsed the German attacks before they were recalled. Oberfeldwebel Detlef Lüth of 4./JG 1 was forced to make a belly-landing when his engine was hit by return fire from the Flying Fortresses.

A few days later, on 7 September, II. and IV./JG 1 were scrambled to intercept a formation of 29 bombers, escorted by Spitfires, on their way to attack Rotterdam once more, as well as Utrecht. II./JG 1 managed to put up seven Focke-Wulfs, but there was some apprehension on the part of the German pilots because, much to Generalmajor Adolf Galland's ire, stories about the apparent invincibility of the *Viermots* had begun to filter through. It took until December for II./JG 1 to bring down a B-17 when, on the 6th, a formation of 85 B-17s and B-24s of the 1st and 2nd BWs set out to attack Lille and Abbeville. Oberfeldwebel Hans Ehlers and Unteroffizier Eugen Wloschinski of 6./JG 1 each recorded a victory.

However, although JG 1 covered the coast, *Luftwaffenbefehlshaber Mitte* was bereft of single-engined interceptors within the Reich itself. Here, aerial defence had been left to a few combat-experienced instructor pilots in the fighter schools and to the small and newly formed 'factory defence flights'. These latter units had been created in direct response to the RAF bombing raids of 1939–40 when it was realised that aircraft factories in northern Germany were no longer safe from attack, and that the Luftwaffe was not available in sufficient strength to protect them.

The first such flight to be formed is believed to have been that of the Gerhard Fieseler Werke at Kassel on 16 October 1939. No less a figure than the owner of the company, the aircraft designer Gerhard Fieseler, led the flight, which was equipped with a small number of Bf 109Es that the company had licence-built, and which proudly bore the company logo on their cowlings.

Focke-Wulf had first formed a small factory defence unit, or *Industrieschutzstaffel* (ISS) *der Focke-Wulf GmbH, Bremen*, on 4 April 1940 to provide protection for its main works at Bremen – a city well within reach of the RAF's medium bombers. Equipped with three twin-engined Fw 187 fighters (just nine of which were built), the *Staffel* was headed by none other than the company's renowned director, Dipl.-Ing. Kurt Tank, and numbered six company test pilots, all of them civilians. The following month, Heinkel followed suit and set up a flight at its Rostock-Warnemünde plant using He 100 and He 112 aircraft, but the flight did not last long and was disbanded – the Focke-Wulf ISS was also disbanded in August 1940. Five months later, the RAF carried out its first raid on Bremen. More attacks followed, and on the night of 25–26 June 1942, 142 RAF bombers struck the city and a 4,000-lb bomb fell into one of the Focke-Wulf assembly shops and destroyed it.

Anticipating American daylight attacks, this must have acted as an incentive to re-establish the Bremen ISS, which the company did on 15 October 1942, assigning it the name *Industrieschwarm Focke-Wulf* and equipping the flight with six Fw 190A-4s. By this time, the company was able to muster 13 pilots, once more led by Tank, who held the honorary rank of Oberleutnant. The *Schwarm* was divided into two *Rotten*, with pilots interchanging between them. Focke-Wulf chief test pilot Flugkapitän Hans Sander recalled:

> Between test-flying aircraft, we Focke-Wulf test pilots had to fly service fighters in action when our factory was attacked by Allied bombers, and we knocked up quite a score in the process, although we lost several good test pilots in this way.[9]

Indeed, in the coming, large-scale air battles against the USAAF's bombers, both Focke-Wulf and Messerschmitt would deploy factory defence flights with some success.

Meanwhile, from mid-1942 at an operational level, in France and the Low Countries, the Luftwaffe's fighter command hierarchy continued to be overseen, ultimately, by *Luftflotte* 3 based in Paris under Generalfeldmarschall Hugo Sperrle, a brusque, bear-like figure who clamped a monocle in his right eye like a film caricature. But unlike Weise, Sperrle was at least a decorated aviator, having flown as an observer and a reconnaissance pilot during World War I. His air fleet had arrived in France during the German invasion of the West and it subsequently oversaw Luftwaffe operations against England.

Luftflotte 3 was, in essence, an 'air force' in its own right, responsible for offensive operations with its own bomber and fighter-bomber units, as well as defence with its two principle fighter *Geschwader*, JGs 2 and 26, based on the *Kanal* (English Channel) front. During 1941–42, the Bf 109s and Fw 190s of these two units had defended western airspace against coastal probes by the RAF's fighters and light bombers. Then, in 1942, they had played key roles in providing air cover for the Kriegsmarine's capital ships as they left Brest to return through the English Channel to German ports in the audacious 'Channel Dash'. They were also deployed in countering the Anglo-Canadian landings at Dieppe.

Operations by JGs 2 and 26 were coordinated by two regional *Jagdfliegerführer*, *Jafü* 2 at Le Touquet and *Jafü* 3 at Deauville. Towards the end of 1942, similar to the *Jafü Mitte*, the activities of the western *Jafü* were coordinated and monitored by a new *Höherer Jagdfliegerführer West* based at Chantilly, near Paris, and subordinated to *Luftflotte* 3. The *Jafü* was Oberst

Max Ibel, an extremely competent officer and a Knight's Cross-holder who had led JG 27 in the campaigns over France and England, before being appointed as leader of JFS 4 and then as *Jafü* 3 in France.

Men like Ibel would be needed. By late 1942, nowhere was safe. Even deep in southern Germany, at Schleissheim, near Munich, where relatively little had been felt of the Allied air forces so far, the staff of *Jafü Süddeutschland* under Oberst Harry von Bülow-Bothkamp, another World War I fighter pilot with six victories to his credit, prepared for the USAAF bombers. Von Bülow-Bothkamp understood fighter tactics – he wore the Knight's Cross and had served as *Kommandeur* of II./JG 77 and then as *Kommodore* of JG 2 in the West and over England.

By late December 1942, von Bülow-Bothkamp and his operations staff were left in little doubt that the enemy would soon be able to attack industrial targets linked to military production and oil refineries, and also carry out '*Terrorangriffe*' (terror attacks) against the civilian populations of cities and larger towns in southern Germany. In an appraisal of 28 December, *Jafü Süddeutschland* warned diligently, if not entirely accurately:

> The enemy approaches generally from the northwest and west, whereby a flightpath over Basel and Lake Constance in the direction of Augsburg–Munich is obviously favoured, as it offers the possibility of surprise and leads over areas with low air defence and, in places, even over neutral territory. The latest British and American four-engined bombers are used almost exclusively.
>
> The enemy's form of air warfare is very mobile, and despite long periods of rest, <u>surprises must always be expected – even during the day</u>.[10] [emphasis in original]

This review of defensive measures had probably been prompted by the 'surprise' Munich had received just a week earlier on the night of 21–22 December when 110 RAF bombers dropped their bombs wide of the city in the surrounding countryside. Munich had been fortunate on that occasion, but it was a wake-up call.

The *Jafü's* mistaken reference to the bombers routing 'over Basel and Lake Constance' was probably a reaction to recent RAF raids on the Italian cities of Turin, Milan and Genoa. In fact, the RAF followed a direct route across France and over Lake Annecy or the Alps. In any case, it was conceivable to the Germans that the USAAF could do the same in daylight.[11]

As *Jafü Süddeutschland*, the problem von Bülow-Bothkamp faced was a lack of day fighters with which to engage American bombers, and therefore his only course of action was to utilise the wholly inadequate forces at his disposal. These included instructor pilots flying the small number of Bf 109E and Bf 110 nightfighter trainers of *Nachtjagdschule* 1 at Schleissheim and Ingolstadt-Manching (later NJG 101), the worn and weary Bf 109E school machines of JFS 4 at Fürth-Herzogenaurach and Buchschwabach (later JG 104), elements of the Bf 110-equipped *Zerstörerschule* 2 at Memmingen (later ZG 101) and the Bf 109 civilian test and acceptance pilots of the '*Messerschmitt Industriestaffel*' (later the *Industrie Jagdeinheiten Messerschmitt Regensburg*). In case of operations, these units would be directed by the *Jafü's* area control rooms at Schleissheim, Echterdingen and Fürth.

Von Bülow-Bothkamp was not alone. The lack of daylight fighters just at the time that the USAAF was gearing up for increased operations in the coming year was also being felt in the crucial area of *Jafü Holland-Ruhrgebiet*. There too, in periods of 'extremely bad visibility' when, apparently, the Eighth Air Force was able to fly but the single-engined fighters of the '*Kanalgeschwader*' were not, the controllers resorted to sending up Bf 110 nightfighters in daylight, flown by pilots with blind-flying training, but controlled within their usual nightfighter 'box' zones.[12] It was a measure of expediency.

In a report of October 1944, the Luftwaffe's Historical Analysis Department reviewed and summarised the German fighter response to 'Anglo-American Air Operations against the Reich and Western Europe in 1942'. While honest, it did not make for cheerful reading – especially when it came to operations by JGs 2 and 26:

> Our operations against the enemy's numerous fighter sorties proved to be rather ineffective. Despite prompt location and recognition by means of radar, the situation remained unfavourable for our fighters. Due to the proximity of their airfields to the coast, the German fighters were flying at insufficient altitudes when contact with the enemy was established, and consequently had to fight from an inferior position.
>
> We suffered heavy losses, and it was therefore decided by the High Command not to oppose purely fighter sorties over wide areas. Our forces, limited in number, were from then onwards employed only in compact formations against enemy bombers. Even this type of operation resulted in great losses because of the enemy's strong fighter escort forming an air umbrella. Consequently, the forward airfields of our fighters had to be moved further inland; the distance between the new bases and the coast, however, made effective interception impossible.[13]

What was needed – and quickly – were more purpose-built interceptors over the West and the Reich with greater endurance, more fighter pilots and improved training.

6

Imbalance of Power

Sometime during the winter of 1942–43, Peter Masefield, the doubting Technical Editor of *The Aeroplane*, visited the 97th BG's base at Grafton Underwood, in Northamptonshire, for a USAAF press day. He was invited to board B-17E *Yankee Doodle*, actually an aircraft of the 92nd BG but assigned to the former group and the aircraft in which Brig Gen Eaker had flown in the mission to Sotteville in August. It appears Masefield had by then changed his mind about the B-17:

> Long, low, sleek, battle-scarred – a brown shape against the grey of the English Winter's afternoon. Inside, the rear fuselage looks like a scale model of a tube railway tunnel, long, cylindrical, massive. The interior of the Fortress is divided into seven compartments. Beginning at the rear, there is first of all the hand-operated tail gun position under the rudder. Next comes the compartment in which the retracted tail wheel is housed, and then the main rear cabin, with the two waist guns at the side and the top of the 'ball turret' in the floor, just behind the cabin's forward bulkhead. In front of the bulkhead is the radio compartment with a 0.50-in. machine gun in the roof, and then a narrow catwalk leads through the middle of the bomb-bay to the underneath of the top turret. Immediately in front of the turret is the pilot's cabin, with dual control and seats side by side. Between the two pilots, a little alleyway drops down and leads forward to the extreme nose with its accommodation for navigator, bomb aimer and front gunner.
>
> The crews of the Fortresses confirm that the 'Pursuit Effect' of the rearward-firing guns is very great indeed, and that a fighter hit when attacking from the rear breaks up almost invariably. In consequence, head-on attacks now appear to have been adopted by enemy fighters – an approach which reduces their time for aiming greatly. The German fighters have a healthy respect for the American formations in which crossfire from several bombers is used to deadly effect. The Germans

often stand off as far as possible and take pot shots at individual machines, hoping to cripple them by hitting a motor. Then if one bomber drops back from a formation, all the fighters pounce on it. This policy might be effective on long-range raids, but on the shorter hauls it has been proved of small account.

Apparently impressed, Masefield prophesised:

... no American-manned Fortress has flown over Germany, but when the time does come, the height and speed of the Fortress formations should enable them to show up against that opposition at least as well as any other aeroplane of their size now flying.[1]

There was, undoubtedly, truth in what the American crews told Masefield. Luftwaffe fighter pilots had indeed developed a 'healthy respect' for the B-17 and the B-24. But such respect on the part of the pilots was not shared by their portly Commander-in-Chief, Reichsmarschall Hermann Göring, who viewed USAAF aircraft with disdain. As far he was concerned, when it came to Americans, it was 'all bluff'. The Chief of Staff at *Luftflotte* 3, Oberst Karl Koller, recalled:

At this time, Göring was still the trusty paladin of the *Führer*, and he agreed unreservedly with Hitler's views on all important matters. The *Führer* and Göring both expressed themselves in a like manner, saying that the Americans might be very clever at manufacturing Fords, Chevrolets and refrigerators, but they were no good at turning out aircraft.[2]

Exasperated, senior Luftwaffe officers went as far as to bring in a hard-nosed engineering industry specialist, Wilhelm Werner, to convince the Reichsmarschall otherwise. Werner was a sensible choice. After working in the German engineering industry, he had spent several years in the USA in the employment of Chrysler in Detroit, with whom he studied American methods of mass production.

In 1941, General der Flieger Erhard Milch, the Secretary of State for Aviation, had appointed Werner to oversee and assess the production methods of German aero-engine manufacturers. He quickly spotted there was too much wastage in engine production in German factories, but when it came to enlightening Göring on the marvel of companies like Boeing and Consolidated Aircraft, it was hopeless. Werner had not been alone – industrialists such as Friedrich Siebel and Heinrich Koppenberg at Junkers, who had ambitions to create a mass-manufacturing concern following the principals of Henry Ford, had endeavoured to convince Göring of the long-term potential of American industry.[3]

This indicates denial on the part of Göring, who would have preferred the distraction of shopping trips to Paris and adding artefacts to his growing collection of plundered works of art, antiques, tapestries and statues. It is difficult to know what to make of his position, given that, at the time, details on the capacity, capabilities and expansion of the American aircraft industry appeared regularly in newspapers and international aviation journals. Copies of Peter Masefield's articles in *The Aeroplane* and elsewhere would have made their way to Germany, and photographs, drawings and specifications of new aircraft such as the B-17F and the North American Aviation Mustang I recently arriving from America to serve with the RAF were circulated widely.

Koller remembered:

> We had the details about the B-17 and B-24 aircraft, which were on their way over, and we studied them carefully. The General of Fighters [Galland] thought that enemy bomber operations without fighter escort would prove impracticable in the long run, but at the same time he pointed out the danger of the deep penetration powers which American escorts possessed. Any such allusions to the future were explained away, however, by calling the people who gave these warnings 'weak defeatists'.
>
> At the end of 1942, a ratio of four German fighters to every one Allied bomber was considered necessary in order to effectively prevent daytime penetration raids, and it was also considered that we must have the same ratio of fighters to cover the biggest escort force that the enemy might send over. At all events, this was the view held by the General of Fighters, and we people in the West thought the same. I know that the General of Fighters presented these estimates to the *Führer*.[4]

General Friedrich von Boetticher, the German military attaché in Washington, D.C., also delivered highly detailed reports on American developments in four-engined bomber design, and his reports were given support by experts like Wilhelm Werner. The writing really was on the wall, but when Generaloberst Hans Jeschonnek persuaded Boetticher to talk to the *Führer* in May 1942, it too proved a waste of time. Jeschonnek despaired and told the attaché:

> We are lost. We no longer have the air defence I requested and which is needed for our German soil. We now no longer have any time to

provide ourselves with the weapons to fight the dreadful threat which you have predicted and reported to us. We will be covered from the air with an enemy screen which will paralyse our power to resist. They will be able to play with us![5]

Yet just two months later, while on a visit to the Ukraine, Jeschonnek, accompanied by Oberst Josef Schmid, his Chief of Intelligence, attended a lecture in Kalinovka by Obersting. Dietrich Schwenke, head of the RLM Technical Office's *Auslandsluftrüstung* (Foreign Air Equipment Department), responsible for assessing enemy aviation equipment and development. As Schwenke expounded on the enormous military might of the Western Allies, and in particular the American four-engined bomber groups arriving in Britain, Jeschonnek interrupted him, exclaiming:

> Every four-engined bomber the Western Allies build makes me happy, for we will bring these four-engined bombers down just like we brought down the two-engined ones, and the destruction of a four-engined bomber constitutes a much greater loss for the enemy.[6]

This twisted logic overlooked the reality of German aircraft strength – or rather the lack of it – and the calculated requirement needed to counter USAAF power, as alluded to by Koller. Aircraft production had stagnated between 1939–41 as a result of the colossal demand for steel, machinery and armaments needed to satisfy Hitler's wider war aims.[7] Aircraft production in 1940 amounted to 10,826 completed airframes, while 1941 saw an increase to only 12,000.[8]

In July 1940, the RLM's *Lieferplan* (Delivery Plan) Nr.18 called for an increase in Bf 109 production from 5,070 machines to 6,116 by 31 March 1942.[9] In July 1941, Hitler ordered a new programme for aircraft production intended to quadruple the size of the Luftwaffe, but this ambition was thwarted to a great extent by the need for labour to achieve it. The economy required a further 2.9 million workers, but many skilled men had been drafted into the armed forces in order to fulfil Hitler's ambitions, leaving less skilled workers to build aircraft.[10] In 1940, 19.8 workers were needed, on average, to produce one airframe, but the following year that had risen to 21.[11] Yet, in 1942, German factories built 2,647 Bf 109s and 1,850 Fw 190s, as well as 853 twin-engined day- and nightfighters (Bf 110s, Me 210s and Ju 88s), and monthly production rose from 274 in January to 554 in December.[12]

Wear and tear took its toll as operational demands increased – the average service life of an Fw 190 in the West and South in 1941 was 12 months, offering 65 flying hours. The following year, it was four months and 25 hours.[13] Average monthly German fighter production (all types) in the first half of 1942 amounted to 373 aircraft, increasing to 435 for the second half. By comparison, in the US, on average 153 'four-engined aircraft' were being built per month over the first six months, the figure increasing significantly to 283 for the second six months. The American figures included a small number of civilian and military prototypes and the German figures have to take into account the fact that such production would have supplied Luftwaffe units on all fronts, including Russia.

But, the really intriguing statistic is that that year the production of military aircraft in the USA totalled 47,836, while in Germany the figure was 15,556.[14]

However ignorant Göring may have been when he repeated his charge that the US was only good for manufacturing 'fancy cars, razor blades and refrigerators', the irony was that in many respects he was, technically, accurate in his jibe. In 1940, American aircraft manufacturing methods using aluminium required intricate tooling and purpose-built jigs, most components were hand-fitted, and companies took advantage of the wide open landscape of states like California, where assembly could take place outside in warm air, under sunny skies. The prospect of mass-manufacturing warplanes on a scale similar to that of automobiles would have caused most US aircraft industry executives to pale. One reason, for example – a car had 15,000 parts, but a B-24 had a million.

In 1939, the USAAC had placed orders for just 435 aircraft from US factories. But in May 1940, President Roosevelt had set Congress an ambitious challenge: American plants would produce *50,000* aircraft per year – a figure which, according to one historian, Roosevelt had 'picked out of the air'.[15] As German forces sped into France and the Low Countries, despite contrary views from US isolationists, Roosevelt determined to create the world's largest military industrial powerhouse, and to supply France and Britain with bombers to take the war to the totalitarian Nazi regime.

Fifty thousand aircraft in a year. Maj Gen 'Hap' Arnold had wanted 100,000, but Roosevelt felt half that would be feasible, even if it was five times the number any nation had so far produced in a year.[16] If the automobile companies could do it, then so could the aircraft companies. The president even appointed the Chairman of General Motors, William Knudsen, to oversee production planning. Not surprisingly, Henry Ford moved in quickly, stating that he could build 1,000 aircraft per day, but the president of North American Aviation remained sceptical that car-builders could simply emulate the skills involved in aircraft construction – 'You cannot expect blacksmiths to learn how to make watches overnight.'[17]

Yet by the end of 1940, the car and aircraft manufacturers had gone a long way towards realising Roosevelt's ambition. Factory floorspace given over to airframes, engines, propellers and associated parts had doubled in 12 months, while the workforce tripled. In April 1941, Ford started work at its vast, 70-acre plant at Willow Run near Detroit, Michigan, dubbed 'the Grand Canyon of the mechanised world', and which featured a moving assembly line almost a mile long. The plan was to turn out a B-24 every hour (although this almost proved a bomber too far, even for Ford).[18]

One inherent drawback with mass production, however, is that in its very process, quality is compromised by the need for quantity. That meant that further development and/or enhancement of a type, beyond what was being built, could not take place, since such development might jeopardise the integrity of mass production schedules. However, the resourceful planners at companies like North American Aviation at Inglewood, Boeing at Seattle, Ford at Willow Run and Pratt & Whitney at East Hartford were not fazed by this and simply directed finished aircraft to purpose-assigned modification centres where work could be completed swiftly.

In 1941, the last year of peace which America would enjoy for four years, consumer confidence was at its highest since the 1920s, and it is intriguing to speculate what Göring would have thought of the nearly four million cars built in Detroit, plus the 26,000 aircraft produced by US factories, 6,000 more than those in Britain, the world's second largest manufacturer.[19] Building aircraft was one thing, however. How effective those aircraft would be operationally, a long way from home, in not so sunny skies, was another.

In conclusion, in Britain, in his assessment of the Flying Fortress, Peter Masefield wrote, 'The question remains – are the defences of industrial Germany such that daylight bombing in force in good weather will result in uneconomic casualties? We may soon know the answer'. That answer would come – with startling decisiveness – in the months ahead.

PART III

The Cornered Wolf – 1943

The cornered wolf fights the hardest.
GEN HENRY H. ARNOLD TO BRIG GEN IRA C. EAKER,
15 OCTOBER 1943

7

'Once they have made contact with the bombers, the rest is easy'

Perhaps justifiably, the strategic air offensive waged against Germany by the Allied air forces from 1942 to 1945 has been credited with bringing about the Third Reich's inability to continue the war. For nearly three years, almost day-by-day, night-by-night, the Allies systematically pulverised Germany's industrial cities and production centres, bombed its fuel plants, paralysed its transport system, attacked its airfields, terrorised and killed its civilians and eventually smashed its armies as they fought to defend their ever-contracting frontlines.

As the offensive ground on, the Luftwaffe, charged with defending the skies over the Reich, found it difficult to cope. This was a war of attrition; a battle to defend the homeland which tested both materiel and human resources to their limits. During this time, German aeronautical technology triumphed and failed; the reputations of the finest fighter pilots of the Luftwaffe were made when the fruits of victory were being enjoyed, but were denigrated when the Nazi leadership sought scapegoats for the suffering inflicted on the German people.

Some historians argue that until mid-1943, the air war in the West and over the Reich aroused only peripheral interest in the minds of Hitler and the German High Command. It was only alarming events, such as the RAF's 1,000-bomber night attack on the city of Cologne in May 1942 in which 469 civilians were killed, more than 5,000 injured and in excess of 45,000 made homeless, that galvanised Hitler and the leadership into response. But even then, the Luftwaffe mounted just three small-scale raids on the south of England in reprisal.

The fact was that Hitler and his generals had other, critical distractions. By the end of 1942, the Luftwaffe was still recovering from substantial losses incurred on the Eastern Front, where there was a growing crisis at Stalingrad. Difficulties in the USSR were compounded by the withdrawal of hundreds of aircraft to the Mediterranean, where there had been a high rate of aircraft and aircrew loss incurred during the race to build up Rommel's supplies in the four months prior to the battle of El Alamein. Only some 375 single-engined fighters were left to cover the entire Eastern Front. Thus military focus continued to be largely directed towards these theatres.

However, by 1943, the increasing damage inflicted by Allied strategic air power against the Reich forced focus away from the battlefronts. Between January and March, the heavy bombers of RAF Bomber Command struck at Berlin, Cologne, Dusseldorf, Essen and Hamburg during operations on 58 nights out of 78. In March, Air Vice-Marshal Arthur Harris opened his night offensive against industrial targets in the Ruhr, with Essen, Dusseldorf, Duisburg and Wuppertal being attacked. The damage was severe, with high-explosive bombs being dropped to blow off roofs, followed by incendiaries to cause fire. But by July, despite severe damage to the Ruhr's cities and a dire effect on civilian morale, the RAF had lost 1,000 aircraft and 7,000 aircrew in 22 major raids and had not completely secured its objectives of closing down the region as an industrial centre or significantly reducing its contribution to the German war effort.

That was the night war. It was different in daylight.

Since the opening of its operations in August 1942 to the end of that year, the Eighth Air Force had been 'blooded' in 30 missions, most of which had enjoyed RAF fighter escort. Eaker's VIII Bomber Command had been reinforced progressively and expanded throughout the second half of 1942 to a total of six bomb groups, four equipped with B-17s and two with B-24s, although two groups had left England in November for North Africa. VIII Fighter Command, under Brig Gen Frank O'D. Hunter, possessed four groups by late October, two with P-38 Lightnings and three with Spitfires. These routinely undertook fighter sweeps and patrols.

Confidence was perhaps unrealistically high amongst the crews of the B-17s, who, it was thought, had given a good account of themselves in their first skirmishes with the Luftwaffe in the autumn. For example, on 9 October, the Luftwaffe lost a single fighter from 7./JG 26 in aerial combat when B-17s bombed Lille, yet Eighth Air Force gunners claimed the destruction of 25 fighters and a further 38 'probables'. Such inflated claim levels gave rise to the belief that even if the accompanying Spitfire escorts had to turn for home at the limit of their range, a well formated group of bombers would be able to fight off German fighter attacks by bringing to bear its massed defensive armament.

The truth, however, was that general standards of nose and waist position air gunnery were poor, despite high claims made during initial clashes with the Luftwaffe, and incidents of damage from friendly fire were not uncommon. Understandably, the effective aiming and use of a heavy,

'THE REST IS EASY'

reverberating 0.50-in. machine gun in a 200-mph slipstream against a small, fast-moving target presented a challenge. Intensive gunnery training flights were conducted over British coastal ranges in an attempt to improve the situation. Furthermore, adverse weather conditions experienced in northwest Europe during the later months of 1942 proved difficult to deal with, hampered bombing accuracy and froze bomb-aiming equipment and guns.

Despite warnings to the contrary from their RAF counterparts, the Americans believed in the viability of undertaking longer, *unescorted* daylight missions to key targets within Germany. In January 1943 Churchill and Roosevelt met in Casablanca, accompanied by a galaxy of Chiefs of Staff and Joint Planners, to determine a plan for an ensured Allied victory.

It was here that the philosophy of daylight precision bombing of German targets was given the seal of approval by Allied leaders who were anxious to hone an air strategy that would swiftly and effectively destroy Germany's industry and its 'will to resist'. At Casablanca, the British again pushed for American involvement in night bombing, but Roosevelt and 'Hap' Arnold resisted this. Indeed, Arnold summoned Eaker from England to present the case for the continuation and expansion of daylight bombing.

On 20 January Eaker handed Churchill a single sheet memorandum on which were outlined his reasons for the pursuance of such attacks. With a keen and ambitious eye, the British Prime Minister picked out one particular sentence – 'By bombing the devils around the clock', Eaker wrote, 'We can prevent the German defences from getting any rest'. This was just what Churchill wanted to read, and the next day, during the Allied Leaders' conference, representatives of the USAAF and RAF were presented with a directive in which it was recorded:

> Given a force of 300 heavy bombers flown by trained crews, Gen Eaker believed he could attack any target in Germany by day with less than four per cent loss. Smaller numbers would naturally suffer more severely. Despite all problems and currently effective limitations, he stoutly maintained that 'daylight bombing of Germany with planes of the B-17 and B-24 types is feasible, practicable and economical'.

The final draft of the so-called 'Casablanca Directive' was quite clear in its instruction to the commanders of the proposed 'round-the-clock' Combined Bomber Offensive:

> Your primary object will be the progressive destruction and dislocation of the German military, industrial and economic system and the

undermining of the German people to a point where their capacity for armed resistance is fatally weakened.

Returning to England, Eaker, buoyant and confident, got on with the job. On 27 January 1943, a force of 91 B-17s and B-24s set out to bomb the U-boat yards at Wilhelmshaven in what was the first USAAF raid mounted against a German target. The result seemed to bear out what Eaker had proclaimed to Churchill – just three bombers failed to return. German opposition had come from the Bf 109s of Hauptmann Günther Beise's I./JG 1 which claimed five bombers shot down, but which lost five of its own aircraft and three pilots.

Shortly after the USAAF raid on Wilhelmshaven, Adolf Hitler asked to speak to Generalmajor Adolf Galland. He wanted to know what could be done about stopping the Americans. Galland travelled to the *Führer's* forested headquarters at Rastenburg in East Prussia – the so-called '*Wolfschanze*' ('Wolf's Lair'). Hitler still had much on his mind, not least of which was the recent military disaster at Stalingrad and the reversals in North Africa. But bombs falling on the Reich was of more immediate concern.

Galland was forthright. He told Hitler that the daylight fighter force would need considerable expansion. Hitler asked by how much. Galland replied, wisely, that he needed to discuss the matter further with his staff. Hitler accepted that, but wanted details as soon as possible. After speaking with his staff and the *Jagddivision* commanders, Galland concluded that three or four fighters would need to be airborne for each unescorted American bomber. But if American escort fighters were to penetrate Reich airspace, as was inevitable, then, in addition, one fighter would be needed for each enemy fighter. With such strength, and with no adverse changes to present training capabilities and fuel supply, Galland advised Hitler that losses of about 80 per cent could be inflicted on the bombers and the raids interdicted.[1]

The number of American bombing missions conducted in February was low – just three. This was a result of both adverse weather and the slow arrival of replacement crews and aircraft. On 4 February, 39 out of 65 B-17s despatched reached Germany, but freezing weather forced them to bomb targets of opportunity around Emden rather than the briefed target, the

'THE REST IS EASY'

marshalling yards at Hamm. The formation was strung out and vulnerable and the Luftwaffe struck, sending in fighters from II. and IV./JG 1. Pilots from 3., 4. and 12./JG 1 accounted for four B-17s, but no matter how hard they pressed home their attacks, the other *Staffeln* found it impossible to bring any of the bombers down.

Conversely, because of the general shortage of day fighters, 1. *Jagddivision* called upon the Bf 110 nightfighters of 11./NJG 1 based at Leeuwarden. The Luftwaffe controllers saw a desperate justification to deploying the nightfighters because of their comparatively longer range than the Bf 109s and Fw 190s, as well as the navigation skills of their crews and their ability to carry heavier armament, including mortars. But there was also a recklessness to sending up crews with no experience of intercepting American *Viermots* in daylight, along with the corresponding risk to highly trained specialist pilots and radio operators. Furthermore, such crews had little or no experience of flying formation attacks.

Eight Bf 110s of 11./NJG 1 were lead into action by Oberleutnant Hans-Joachim Jabs, a former *Zerstörer* ace. They made contact with the B-17s of the 1st BW over the North Sea as the bombers made their way back to England, with one of them falling to Jabs' guns and two others to his fellow crews. In making their attack, the Messerschmitts came under the full fire of the Flying Fortresses' defensive armament, and they all returned badly shot up. This meant that they could not be used against RAF Bomber Command raids over the coming nights.[2] It was also a stark warning – but would it be heeded?

American bomber gunner claims amounted to 25 German fighters shot down, with another eight probably destroyed and six damaged. This was not the case, for JG 1 had lost only two pilots. One crew of the 305th BG attacked by a Bf 110 of 11./NJG 1 reported:

> E/A came in from 6 o'clock level, was fired on by tail gunner at 700 yds, continued fire as E/A came up to within 10 yds. Hits shattered the entire nose of E/A, killing gunner and causing nose gun to fall out. E/A peeled off, trailing white smoke into clouds below.[3]

Clearly, in this case, aircraft recognition failed in the heat of combat and there was some degree of assumption on the part of the USAAF's crews.

On 26 February, VIII Bomb Command despatched 93 bombers in an attempt to attack Bremen, but they had to bomb the secondary target of Wilhelmshaven instead because of heavy overcast en route to the primary. Breaking out into clearing blue skies, JG 1 accounted for five B-17s and two B-24s shot down during a vicious engagement 50 km from the German coast. And once again Bf 110 nightfighters formed part of the Luftwaffe response, with 12 from IV./NJG 1 engaging. It is possible they may have shot down two Liberators into the North Sea.

By the time the USAAF force returned to England, 73 aircrew were missing and 14 wounded or injured. VIII Bomb Command commanders took heart, however, from the encouraging gunners' claims – 21 enemy fighters had apparently been shot down and a further nine damaged. But again, this was a travesty, for JG 1, the only *Jagdgeschwader* known to have engaged the bombers, reported no aircraft lost. For the nightfighters of NJG 1, the situation was much graver. Of the 12 Messerschmitts that went up, one failed to return – the aircraft flown by the *Staffelkapitän* of 12./NJG 1, Hauptmann Ludwig Becker, a 44-victory ace who, together with his long-time radio operator, had been flying his first daylight mission.[4] Becker had been instrumental in the introduction of *Lichtenstein* air intercept radar to the *Nachtjagd*. Would the Luftwaffe's High Command learn this time?

A similar pattern of operations continued through an unsettled spring. Inclement weather frustrated the Eighth's bombing capabilities throughout much of March, although on the 18th conditions cleared sufficiently to allow the most successful raid into Germany so far. A total of 97 B-17s and B-24s hit the U-boat yards at Vegesack. Once more, in what the Americans viewed as the toughest opposition to date, JG 1 fielded the main German defence. *Jafü Deutsche Bucht* did, however, call in other units, including Bf 110 nightfighters of 8./NJG 3, one of which, flown by the *Staffelkapitän*, Oberleutnant Walter Borchers, accounted for a Liberator over the mouth of the River Jade.[5] It was not just the Luftwaffe that responded.

Shortly after 1425 hrs at the Focke-Wulf plant in Bremen, the civilian works pilots of the ISS were placed at *Sitzbereitschaft* (cockpit readiness), and 35 minutes later *Jafü Deutsche Bucht* gave orders to take-off, course Wilhelmshaven, height 7,000–8,000 m. Focke-Wulf ensured that the pilots were assigned to their respective *Rotten* well in advance so as not to disrupt factory shifts and working practices. However, one of the Fw 190s suffered engine failure on take-off, which meant the ISS was down to five fighters led by Wolfgang Stein, the deputy *Schwarmführer*. Over Wilhelmshaven, Stein observed the bombers heading north in five large *Pulks* each of around 70–80 aircraft. He was the first to attack, head-on, targeting a B-17 flying in the outer right position of the second *Pulk* – 'Highly visible hits were observed. The inner right engine began to trail thick smoke'.

But as Stein made a wide turn back towards the bombers, he noticed that the Flying Fortress, its stricken engine now stopped, was attempting to manoeuvre into the middle of the formation for defence. He quickly levelled out and brought his Fw 190 in for an attack from the rear and opened fire, scoring more hits, as Stein later reported:

> The Fw 190 received several hits from the formation's strong defensive fire, as a result of which the elevator and the rear fuel tank were shot through, and another hit bounced off the armoured engine cowling. However, the Fw 190 was still capable of manoeuvring. The heavily damaged bomber now veered to the right, went into a glide and continued to be attacked by the Fw 190. At between 4,000–5,000 m one American crewman bailed out and the bomber showed no more attempt at defence. Nevertheless, it was attacked several times by two Me 109s at 4,000 m and, after four more crew members had bailed out, it was attacked again by an Me 110 at 1,000 m. The bomber then hit the eastern shore of the Jade Bay, 200 m from the shore, and sank in the water.

Company test pilot Hellmuth Bischof, holding the rank of an Unteroffizier in the Luftwaffe Reserve, pursued the first *Pulk* of B-17s as they flew north. He attempted a head-on attack near Cuxhaven, but he was unable to see the effects. He continued his pursuit of the bombers to the southeast, towards Stade, and attacked again but without effect. Undaunted, Bischof chased the B-17s as they turned west towards the River Weser and fired for a third time, and on this occasion small parts of one Boeing flew away. By this stage, Bischof had entered the Bremen Flak zone. Flying through the 'restricted area', with Flak bursts exploding at 500 m, he was beyond Oldenburg when he made a fourth attack against the now dispersed enemy formation.

In his post-mission report, Stein described what happened next:

> Two groups of six aircraft were flying ahead of him [Bischof]. Again, the aircraft on the right was attacked. After breaking away below the formation in a right turn in order to overtake, it was observed that this aircraft was already burning. Immediately afterwards it turned over and went down vertically to crash. At an altitude of approximately 3,000 m, it reared up once more and, after a large part of it fell away, it continued its vertical descent. The impact was not observed. The crash site must have been west of Oldenburg.

Still it was not over. The ever-determined Bischof remained with the enemy bombers and made an attack against the aircraft flying to the right in the same formation, but he was unable to see any effect. By that point his ammunition was expended and his fuel supply was running low. Bischof finally broke off the attack.

Elsewhere, two more Fw 190s, 'Black 5' and 'Black 3', had attacked the bombers near Cuxhaven, but without being able to observe the effects. However, during the approach, 'Black 3' was hit in its right wing and was forced to break off. 'Black 5' made a second attack, but again without any visible results. The bombers were now passing through the Bremen Flak zone, but near Vegesack, the pilot of 'Black 5' went in once again, despite the risk of being hit by friendly ground fire. As Stein later reported:

> 'Black 5' made a frontal attack against the third formation just beyond Vegesack and fired at the outermost machine on the left. This streamed white smoke from its right engines and veered slightly to the right. 'Black 5' approached again from below, and in an upward right turn fired on the damaged enemy aircraft from the rear left. First the right outboard and then the inboard engine started to burn, whereupon the aircraft turned over on its starboard wing and went into a spin and crashed. The crash took place from an altitude of around 6,000 m. The right wing came off at about 4,000 m. The aircraft then disintegrated almost completely after the engine fire went out.[6]

As determined as Bischof, the pilot of 'Black 5' attempted yet another attack, scoring hits on a second bomber as it headed towards the coast. Lack of fuel finally forced the pilot to break off and land at Jever with no ammunition remaining.

The efforts of Focke-Wulf's civilian ISS pilots were enough to generate a telex from no less a figure than the Secretary of State for Air, Generalfeldmarschall Milch, to Kurt Tank:

> I was delighted to hear about the valiant efforts of your *Industriestaffel* during the attack on Bremen. It fills me with particular satisfaction that your men were also successful. I would like to express my thanks and appreciation to all those involved, especially Gefreiter [sic] Stein.

According to Generalmajor Adolf Galland, the 'principal value' of the factory *Staffeln* 'was in raising factory morale'.[7]

JG 1 claimed ten bombers shot down during the enemy raid, but the reality was that only one B-17 was lost in combat as a result of the unit's attack, with a single B-24 also posted as missing. In another 'thumbs-up' for Eaker, 75 per cent of bombs dropped landed within 1,000 yards of the designated aiming point.

As Tank had believed, the Fw 190 was proving itself to be a rugged bomber interceptor. In the case of the Bf 109, in mid-1942 Messerschmitt had delivered the first examples of the new G-model, which were being utilised by many of the fighter *Gruppen* and which were fitted with the more powerful Daimler-Benz DB 605 engine. But Göring was not satisfied. The Bf 109G offered nothing new – it was simply a reworking of the F-model with a new engine, and the latest G-4, designed expressly as a fighter, had to have aerodynamically inefficient 'bumps' on the upper wing surfaces to allow new, larger mainwheels to fit into the wheel wells.

As the bombs fell on Bremen on 18 March, Göring chaired a production conference at Carinhall, his plush country residence in the Schorfheide Forest, northeast of Berlin. His view was that the aircraft and aero-engineering industries had failed the nation, and he was bitter about it. From the start, he harangued the assembled aircraft designers and engineers over their shortcomings:

> I can only express to you my absolute bitterness about the complete failure which has resulted in practically all fields of aeronautical engineering – bitterness too that I have been deceived in the past to an extent such as I had experienced only in variety shows at the hands of magicians and illusionists...

When it came to the crucial issue of day fighters:

> I by no means fail to recognise that, even today, the Me 109 is still an aircraft of very high performance. However, it has now reached the peak of its performance; no further improvement is possible. The aircraft cannot take a more powerful engine, whereas the British began to improve the Spitfire series very early with the result that this aircraft is now absolutely and unquestionably superior to the Me 109.[8]

Whatever German fighter design lacked in comparison with the enemy, there was no shortage of innovation at unit level in the war against the bombers. Throughout 1943, experiments with air-to-air bombing using both the Bf 109 and Fw 190 had been carried out by elements of JGs 1 and 11 and the test unit *Erprobungskommando* (E.Kdo) 25, using 250- and 500-kg bombs.

The first attempts had been reported by the Eighth Air Force in February when, during a raid to Saint-Nazaire on the 16th, it was claimed that enemy aircraft had dropped bombs on two crippled B-17s off the French coast. In early March elements of the Bf 109-equipped I./JG 1 based at Jever began experiments with dropping bombs onto bomber formations. The first batch of bombs arrived with the *Gruppe* on 8 March, and 'training' began immediately. This consisted of the somewhat unlikely method of a Messerschmitt attempting to drop bombs on sandbags which were towed endlessly across the sky by a Ju 88. It took ten days before the first practise hits were recorded.

On 22 March, I./JG 1 was ordered to intercept a formation of bombers heading for Berlin. As had happened on previous occasions, there was insufficient time for the mechanics to fix bombs under the fuselages of the unit's fighters. However, the *Staffelkapitän*, Leutnant Heinz Knoke, passed control of his 2. *Staffel* to Feldwebel Hans-Gerd Wennekers and waited until a bomb was attached to his Bf 109. Slowly, he rolled along the runway. Suddenly a tyre burst and the aircraft became unbalanced. Knoke quickly fired a red flare and some 20 mechanics came running to his aid. Under Knoke's direction, they changed the tyre in record time.

His aircraft finally took off, but it took Knoke 25 minutes to reach 9,000 m, the altitude necessary for an attack. Finally, he caught up with the enemy formation as it headed back to England after having set fire to the docks at Wilhelmshaven. Knoke placed himself above the leading bombers, but the defensive fire around him was intense. His left wing was hit and slightly torn, but the Messerschmitt still flew. At 1,000 m above the enemy aircraft, he released his bomb. It would take 15 seconds to detonate. Slowly, the bomb fell towards a group of three B-17s. Knoke counted the seconds until it exploded. The nearest bomber lost a wing and crashed into the sea, while the other two broke formation. Following his mission, Knoke's exploits became the subject of considerable interest. Göring even called to congratulate him on his initiative.

On 17 April, the air-to-air bombing method was tried once again. This time, Knoke's weapon passed harmlessly through a bomber *Pulk* without inflicting any damage. The Eighth Air Force noted:

> Inaccurate aerial bombing was reported. All in all, about 20 bombs were dropped; about half fell right through the formation. Believed to be 50-kg bombs, none of which burst closer than about 150 ft.[9]

By late August, however, Eighth Air Force Headquarters offered a realistic and balanced report on the Luftwaffe's air-to-air bombing enterprise:

> The difficulty of obtaining accuracy is obvious. A Fortress [formation] travelling at 250 mph at 25,000 ft is actually moving at the rate of 327 ft per second. If this were a constant speed it would take a nice calculation to hit. But the simple problem of speed is compounded both by the Fortresses' option to take evasive action and by differences in wind

velocity at different heights which have their own effect on the flight of bombs. For example, a [American] GP 500-lb AN-M43 fused for 1,500 yards would need an angle of drop of approximately 53° which, in its fall, would consume 17 seconds before even reaching the level of the Fortresses. It must be remembered that during this time, Fortresses can change direction at the rate of 327 ft per second.

The problem of assuring the burst, as well as the physical presence of the bomb, in such exact points of time and space is what has accounted for the relatively low effectiveness of air-to-air bombing to date. For the air-to-air bomb, unlike the one crashing into a fixed ground target, must explode at an exact second or be utterly wasted.

Over and against the difficulties involved, however, must be set the potential rewards of success with air-to-air bombing. These find their simplest explanation in a plain statement of the difference in the size of the lethal burst between the best Flak [shell] and a 500-lb bomb. The largest lethal burst for Flak is 50 ft. The lethal burst of a 500-lb bomb is 300 ft. When it is considered that this burst could encompass as many as four of our Flying Fortresses in tight formation, it can be seen why air-to-air bombing, for all its difficulties, holds out such dazzling attraction. It is the considerable possibility, rather than the likelihood of any high proportion of direct hits by air-to-air bombing, which must compel us to regard it as a serious and increasing threat.[10]

The 17 April raid also saw the Eighth unveil its new defensive formation. Up to this point, the Americans favoured an 18-aircraft combat 'box' comprised of three six-aircraft squadrons, with each squadron divided into two three-aircraft flights. Succeeding combat 'boxes' of a similar composition trailed in one-and-a-half-mile breaks behind the lead box. In a measure intended to maximise defensive firepower and increase protection, three 'boxes' were formated into a 'combat wing', with two boxes positioned respectively above and below the lead box. This resulted in an impressive sight – 54 four-engined bombers stretched across more than a mile of sky some half-a-mile deep.

In the first such deployment, two combat wings comprising 107 B-17s in six 'boxes' – the largest force thus far assembled – were despatched to bomb the Focke-Wulf plant at Bremen. This time, the bombers ran into even tougher defence.

Shortly after 1300 hrs, just as the Flying Fortresses commenced their bomb run, the Fw 190s of I. and II./JG 1 closed in at speed and mauled the 'heavies' for an hour. In determined, well-coordinated head-on attacks, JG 1 accounted for 15 aircraft destroyed, including an entire squadron –

the heaviest losses sustained to date in a single mission. Three of these fell to JG 1, including one claimed by Major Fritz Losigkeit, *Kommandeur* of I. *Gruppe* and a veteran of the air war over Spain. He observed how the Boeing tipped violently to the left, then went into a flat turn, before going down vertically. He recorded how the experience for the crew must have been 'terrible'. It was to be Losigkeit's sixth victory, and his first against a *Viermot*.

It was no mean achievement to shoot down a bomber with standard aircraft armament. At a range of 1,500 m, a B-17 would be seen in the centre of a Luftwaffe pilot's gunsight. At that distance, and at a combined closing speed of around 250 m per second, the target would fit into his graticule five times. Fire could be opened at 800 m, leaving a pilot with little more than two seconds from this point until opening fire effectively so as to shoot down a bomber. At a range of 900 m – half-a-second later – the pilot was to aim above the fuselage and then open fire. At 700 m – another half-second – the pilot opened fire, while moving the sight smoothly into the centre of the fuselage. At a range of 600 m, the pilot maintained fire. At a range of 300 m – just over one second to collision – the pilot was to make a hard turn away to avoid a collision, forcing the bomber's gunners to react to fast directional changes and presenting them with a large deflection target.

Also deployed that day were the Bf 109s of III./JG 54 based at Oldenburg, whose pilots were at *Sitzbereitschaft*. At 1229 hrs a red flare hissed into the sky above the airfield – it was the signal to scramble. Leading 9. *Staffel* was Hauptmann Hans-Ekkehard Bob, a 56-victory ace from Freiburg and veteran of the campaigns over France, England and Russia. He had been decorated with the Knight's Cross on 7 March 1941 for his service over the Channel Front, the award presented by Göring personally. Bob was responsible for his *Staffel*'s moniker of the *Teufelstaffel* ('Devil Squadron'), an image enhanced by the colourful unit emblem of a red devil's head on a yellow shield which graced the noses of his unit's Messerschmitts. Heraldry was forgotten, however, as he led his *Staffel* into the air to follow immediately behind the *Gruppenkommandeur*'s flight.

Even for a pilot of Bob's considerable combat experience, this would have been an anxious time. For the past two years, all of his aerial victories had been claimed in the Balkans or in Russia, amidst very different operational conditions to those prevailing in the West and over the Reich. Bob had scored his last kill on the Eastern Front just three months earlier, on 14 January 1943, when he shot down a Soviet LaGG-3 fighter southeast of Velikiye Luki. On 1 February, III./JG 54 was transferred from Smolensk to Lille, in France, where the *Gruppe*'s pilots chatted with their counterparts from JG 26.

'THE REST IS EASY'

The men of the *Kanalgeschwader* regaled their fellow airmen freshly arrived from the Eastern Front with unnerving stories about the mighty *Viermots* of the USAAF, and how difficult it was to shoot them down. For sure, the men of the *Teufelstaffel* had heard about *Viermotorschreck* – the fear of four-engines – which haunted many fighter pilots in the Reich.

After a brief and quiet spell in France, the *Gruppe* was transferred again, to Oldenburg in Germany, where at first things proved equally calm. This was to change for Bob on 17 April when he would encounter the *Viermots* for the first time. Even for a man of his calibre, it would be a daunting and almost fatal experience. Directed by the controllers at *Jafü Deutsche Bucht*, the Bf 109G-4s climbed at full power through cloudless skies, turning to the northwest and towards the waters of the Jade Bay. They had hardly reached combat altitude when the enemy was seen. As Bob later reported:

At around 2040 hrs we spotted in the region of 120–150 four-engined Boeing bombers flying at a height of between 7,000–8,000 m to the west of Wilhelmshaven. The enemy formation was flying a course south, southeast. We overtook the enemy formation on their port side in order to be able to attack them head-on. As we reached our estimated required distance to launch an attack, we observed that the enemy had made a turn to port, which placed us in a position to starboard of the formation. I corrected my flight course and lined up to attack head-on with my whole *Staffel*. In doing so, the enemy formation had continued to curve away, making it impossible for me to attain a suitable position for an attack.

While carrying out our manoeuvres, the enemy had bombed Bremen and was making its way south and then in a westerly direction. I immediately decided to make another attack, and was able to line up exactly with the leading enemy flight. I opened fire on the starboard aircraft of the lead flight from 500 m and continued on a ramming course, observing many direct hits in the cockpit area of the Boeing.

Just as I was about to break off the engagement by flying beneath the bomber, there was a loud explosion in my aircraft, which immediately caused it to spin out of control. I was able to jump out of the stricken fighter and take to my parachute, making a hard landing south of the village of Grossköhren, near Harpstedt. Besides receiving minor scratches and abrasions, as well as bruises to my head, I had no other injuries. I bailed out around 1245 hrs from a height of 6,000 m.[11]

Bob's victim was B-17F *"Hellsapoppin"* from the 91st BG based at Bassingbourn, in Cambridgeshire. As a result of his attack, the Flying

Fortress's nose Plexiglas was left with a one-and-a-half-foot hole. The bombardier was hit in the left leg by 20 mm cannon shells, the pilot was wounded in the head and the co-pilot was hit by shrapnel in the right eye, left arm, right hand and both legs. In the radio compartment, leaking oxygen from broken lines caught fire. The port wing was also burning, and three feet of the starboard wingtip had been torn off. The intercom had also been destroyed.

For his part, Bob had been unable to observe any further action against the enemy aircraft after he had abandoned his tailless Messerschmitt. Bailing out of a falling, spinning fighter after having just collided with a B-17 was a traumatic experience which many pilots flying in defence of the Reich had to endure. Bob recalled:

> I threw off the canopy and then unbuckled myself. I was thrown out of the aircraft in a flash and kept rolling over. When I was in a vertical position with my legs downwards, I pulled the parachute open. Immediately, there was a strong jolt, and I was hanging in the harness. I was now at an altitude of around 4,500–5,000 m. The parachute was swinging very sharply back and forth, and just before touching down it swung backwards, so that the impact with the ground was even harder. This meant I landed with the front of my body and head-first.
>
> The impact, which occurred in a relatively soft field just south of the village, was so strong that I lost consciousness for a moment. As a result, I was dragged several hundred metres along the ground. When I regained consciousness, I wanted to unbuckle the parachute immediately, but I was unable to do so as the predetermined breaking point was still being dragged by the straps to the inflatable dinghy. I only managed to free myself from the parachute by pulling it in.[12]

After coming down near Grossköhren, the dazed Bob was told by villagers, who initially mistook him for an American, that they had seen two enemy aircraft crash in the vicinity and several USAAF airmen taking to their parachutes. Bob was credited with the destruction of a Flying Fortress, but it had been a tough introduction to the defence of the homeland.

At 1243 hrs, 14 minutes after the Bf 109s of III./JG 54 had taken off, one *Rotte* of Fw 190s of the *Industrieschwarm Focke-Wulf Langenhagen* which had been formed the previous year and which comprised Oberfeldwebeln Heinz Finke and Hans Kampmeier, was roused with an *Alarmstart* and made course to Bremen. Some 15 minutes later, at 6,000 m over Verden, the two pilots observed the enemy formation flying on an easterly course over

'THE REST IS EASY'

Bremen. The *Rotte* climbed to 9,000 m and adopted a northerly course from Wesermünde to Sperre and then on to Leer.

At 1315 hrs, the Focke-Wulfs made contact with the enemy and attacked. Finke made a frontal pass on a B-17 and banked away, although he returned to make two further attacks along with some Bf 109s probably from II./JG 11 and Bf 110 nightfighters of either NJGs 1 or 3, which had also arrived. Some members of the bomber's crew bailed out and the aircraft went down. Finke then made two further attacks over the Norden–Westerede–Wittmundhafen area on a pair of straggling bombers that had been attacked earlier by the Bf 109s. Results were not observed. Low on fuel, Finke landed at Jever at 1332 hrs.

Kampmeier reported excellent strikes on one of the bombers during his first attack. On his third pass, he went after a machine turning away from the target and saw strikes on the fuselage, wings and rudder – the latter was seen to be jammed. Also short of fuel, Kampmeier made it back to Langenhagen.

The second *Rotte* from the ISS, comprising Unteroffizier Kurt Mehlhorn and Oberfeldwebel Bernhard Märschel, was scrambled at 1245 hrs, although Märschel's aircraft initially failed to start and he took off late. He failed to make contact with the enemy and returned to Langenhagen.

A native of Jena, 31-year-old Mehlhorn was the son of a machinist. He had studied at the *Technisches Hochschule* in Darmstadt and had learned to fly gliders as an engineering student. Following pilot training, Mehlhorn was assigned to the Luftwaffe's *Erprobungsstellen*, where he test flew various multi-engined aircraft to assess engine performance. Of his mission on the 17th, he reported:

> I took off in the reserve aircraft at 1245 hrs following the *Alarmstart*. In order to make contact with the other *Rotte*, I was ordered to fly in the direction of Oldenburg. In the hope of making contact, I took a direct course to Oldenburg. To the west of Verden at 6,500 m, Flak could be seen from the direction of Bremen. Being unable to find the *Rotte*, I received the warning 'Many "*Indianer*" in direction Oldenburg!' Before reaching Oldenburg, I saw enemy formations.
>
> Flying head-on, I quickly reached the highest formation and made a frontal attack to the right of the *Pulk* and opened fire. I observed hits and saw metal parts fall away. On breaking away to the right, I engaged another *Pulk* at around 7,000 m. I aimed for the outermost machine to the left of the formation. I observed hits again. On my second approach, this aircraft slipped back to the rear of the *Pulk*, and I made another attack from above left. Hits were observed, with burning pieces falling

away. By the next attack, the machine had lost height and was beginning to trail behind the *Pulk*. Upon my renewed attack, the Boeing tried to take evasive action, but I managed to attack again from the front and above and scored hits between the inboard engine and fuselage. More pieces were seen to fall off. Close to the rear of the aircraft, I saw a parachute fall away. The aircraft began to lose control and go down in a spiral. Together with another Fw 190, we observed the aircraft heading towards the ground. From around 1,000 to 1,500 m over Gründorf, white smoke and more pieces flew off into the air, some falling near the village.

To the north, not far from the crash, I could see a canal and could make out an airfield, which I decided to aim for due to lack of fuel. The other Fw 190 flew around the airfield. However, I observed that it would not be possible to land as there were many obstacles (concrete blocks and timber logs laid in triangular shapes on the runway). In any case, the airfield did not have a proper landing strip.

The other Fw 190 had lowered its landing gear, but after seeing the condition of the runway, it regained height and flew away in a northeasterly direction. After a short flight, I managed to land at Jever (1341 hrs). After landing at Jever, it was noticed that there was a bullet hole in my propeller and through the fuselage from the front to the rear. After changing the propeller, I left Jever for Langenhagen, landing there at 1841 hrs.

At around the time Mehlhorn landed at Jever, nightfighters of NJGs 1 and 3 went in to attack the bombers off the East Frisian Islands, sending three B-17s down into the sea.

During the mission on the 17th, the American gunners claimed 63 fighters shot down and another 15 probables. In fact, the figures were much lower – aside from Bob's Bf 109, just one aircraft, from JG 1, was lost in combat. The excessive levels of over-claiming by American gunners, even allowing for reasonable margins, amounted to more than nine times the known number of German fighters lost in the deeper penetration raids. VIII Bomb Command issued the following instructions:

> An enemy plane would be counted as destroyed when it had been seen descending completely enveloped in flames, but not if flames had been merely licking out from the engine. It would be counted as destroyed when seen to disintegrate in the air or when the complete wing or tail assembly had been shot away from the fuselage. Single-engined enemy planes would be counted as destroyed if the pilot had been seen to bail out.

'THE REST IS EASY'

The losses suffered by the USAAF on 17 April also gave warning that long-range fighter escort was now urgently needed. For example, it had been a tough day for the 91st BG, which lost six B-17s. Returning aircraft were damaged to the extent that the following day's mission was cancelled when it was found that sufficient machines could not be made ready in time.

The noise of the bombing, the bombers overhead and the sound of air combat must have brought a sense of purpose and urgency to a small cadre of Luftwaffe personnel that had been assigned to Wittmundhafen airfield, located 20 km to the west of Wilhelmshaven in the flat terrain of Lower Saxony. It was here, as, ironically, Bremen was attacked by USAAF bombers on 17 April, that the nucleus of a new, specialist unit known as E.Kdo 25 commenced work under the leadership of Major Heinz Nacke, a very experienced airman, veteran of the Spanish Civil War, holder of the Knight's Cross and previously the *Kommandeur* of III./NJG 3.

Nacke had been briefed to establish a new *Erprobungskommando* (Test Command) with the specific purpose of testing and evaluating new aerial weapons, with an emphasis on deployment against bombers in the defence of the Reich. It was a timely and necessary initiative. However, Nacke's command of E.Kdo 25 was to be brief, and he was replaced within a matter of weeks by another equally experienced *Zerstörer* pilot, Hauptmann Eduard Tratt, erstwhile *Staffelkapitän* of 1./ZG 1 in the East. Tratt was also a recipient of the Knight's Cross.

Once at Wittmundhafen, Tratt went about arranging the establishment of three *Staffeln*. Firstly, a *Jagdstaffel* (fighter squadron) was formed under Leutnant Wilhelm Sbresny and equipped with three Bf 109Gs and seven Fw 190s intended to conduct trials with numerous weapons and equipment – including rearward-firing armament, periscopes, acoustic fuses and wing-mounted rockets – for combatting heavy bombers.

Secondly, a *Zerstörerstaffel* was set up under Leutnant Vossel, equipped with around ten Bf 110s, a single Me 210 and a pair of the new Me 410s and intended to trial heavy calibre armament such as the 3.7 cm Flak 18 and Flak 43 and the 5 cm Flak 41 anti-aircraft cannon for use against bombers.

Finally, a *Kampfstaffel* (bomber squadron) was formed, equipped with two Do 217s, three Ju 88s, a solitary He 177 and four Bf 109Gs for escort purposes. This latter *Staffel* was intended to assess air-burst bombs, towed bombs, the radio-guided Henschel Hs 293 glide-bomb and underwing mortars and rockets, as well as conducting experiments in air-to-air bombing.

Like Nacke, Tratt would remain in command at Wittmundhafen for only a short time until his permanent replacement arrived in the form of Oberleutnant (soon to be promoted to Hauptmann) Horst Geyer. Geyer began his wartime flying career as a test pilot at the *Erprobungsstelle der Luftwaffe* at Rechlin. After service with a transport unit during the Polish campaign, he returned to Rechlin and became involved in developing a new automatic sight and bomb-release system for the Ju 88. His work caught the attention of the Director of Luftwaffe Supply and Procurement, the *Generalluftzeugmeister*, Ernst Udet, who snared Geyer for a desk job in the RLM.

Following repeated requests to Udet to allow him some frontline service, Geyer was appointed *Staffelkapitän* of 5./JG 51 in September 1941. At this time, JG 51 was the most successful *Jagdgeschwader* on the Eastern Front, being involved in supporting Army Group Centre during Operation *Taifun* – the drive on Moscow. However, when, on 17 November 1941, exhausted and depressed from working under Göring and Milch, the flamboyant Udet, one of Germany's greatest World War I flying aces, committed suicide, Geyer was transferred to the staff of the *General der Jagdflieger*, the renowned fighter ace Oberst Werner Mölders. Tragedy was to strike again when, while on its way to Berlin from the USSR on 22 November, the He 111 carrying Mölders to Udet's funeral crashed in bad weather near Breslau. Mölders and the aircraft's pilot were killed.

As a result, Geyer found himself on the staff of the new *General der Jagdflieger*, Oberst Adolf Galland, in Berlin. As Geyer remembered:

> It was a very busy time and we worked very hard. My role was that of *Technisches Offizier im Stab*, and amongst other things, I dealt with complaints from frontline fighter and *Zerstörer* units on matters of armament and technical equipment. Suddenly, one day in May 1943, Galland strode into my office and said, 'Geyer, I want you to go to Wittmundhafen tomorrow and take over E.Kdo 25'. That was that! I was to take over from Hauptmann Tratt, an officer I had not previously met, and who was returning to I./ZG 1. I think Galland viewed my new appointment as a kind of thank you for flying a desk for so long.

Geyer would rise quickly to the challenge of his new command, and would oversee the *Kommando*'s activities at the most active and urgent period of its existence, assessing and testing new weapons intended for the war against the American *Viermots*. He recounted:

> The *Kommando*'s main brief was to develop and test new and effective weapons with which to bring down heavy bombers. We tried many

things, but the ideas did not always originate from within. We received many letters and proposals from civilians, from companies and manufacturers, from other branches of the armed services and also from the Luftwaffe testing centre at Rechlin, suggesting 'Why don't you try this, or that', and so on. All suggestions were investigated, and if something looked hopeful, then we proceeded with trials. We were basically free to do what we liked, buy what we liked, design what we liked and test what we liked. But it fell to me to report everything to Oberst Galland and the *Erprobungsstelle* at Rechlin.

The unit undertook trials with heavy cannon, mortars, rockets, steel cable, cable bombs, chemicals and obliquely mounted automatic salvo weapons. These will be described later in this book. Suffice it to say that in the long term, nothing was considered too imaginative, bizarre or beyond consideration *if* it could bring down a bomber.

One of Geyer's initial tasks after taking command of E.Kdo 25 was to test the effectiveness of rockets and mortars. As a first trial, two Fw 190s were fitted with a pair of external, wing-mounted 'firing frames', each one built to carry four 65 mm spin-stabilised RZ (*Rauchzylinder* – 'smoke cylinder') 65 rockets.

First designed by E.Kdo Tarnewitz in January 1936 and then produced by Rheinmetall a year later under Luftwaffe direction, the RZ 65 were intended to be launched from tubes on an externally mounted rack or from a 'honeycomb' barrel of tubes. With a warhead of 840 g, the rocket had a velocity of 300–380 m per second. It was to be fired at a maximum range of 300 m from a target, and once launched, it had a maximum thrust of 200–220 kg. The flight path of the RZ 65 was erratic and followed a corkscrew trajectory, easily visible with the naked eye after launch.

The RZ 65 is believed to have first seen operational deployment with E.Kdo 25 when two Fw 190s took off as part of a four-aircraft *Schwarm* to intercept USAAF raids against Bremen and Kiel, targets close to the *Kommando*'s base at Wittmundhafen, on 13 June 1943. Geyer led one of the two-aircraft *Rotte*, each machine carrying RZ 65s. He recalled:

> This mission was to see my first *Abschuss* [aerial victory] as *Kommandoführer* of E.Kdo 25. Scattered bomber units were making their way home after their raid on the ports. There were no escort fighters in sight, so I attacked two B-17s that were flying close together. I fired all eight RZ 65s, and after the two bombers were forced to separate, I was able to wreak havoc on the machine flying lowest and to the right with several bursts from my 30 mm MK 108 cannon. From about 2,000 m,

I observed two parachutes fall out while the B-17 was evidently trying to go for an emergency landing somewhere. Meanwhile I had lost contact with my three comrades, but they all landed back at Wittmundhafen without damage. What was key here was that the rockets had weakened the bombers' defensive fire, shocked the crews and enabled me to get in close to make my shoot-down.

Despite this, further trials with the rocket on day fighters were dropped.

By May, the USAAF's bomber force was experiencing average losses of 1.6 per cent when under fighter escort, but this rose to seven per cent where escort was not present. And there was considerable pressure put upon men like Brig Gen Eaker at this time. At the Washington Conference of May 1943, the original plan, as agreed at Casablanca, for the 'progressive destruction and dislocation of the German military, industrial and economic system and the undermining of the German people' appeared less relevant because of a new commitment to embark upon an invasion of the European continent in May 1944. One fundamental prerequisite for this would be to clear the skies of the Luftwaffe. Eaker revisited priorities in the Central Bomber Offensive (CBO) Plan of 14 May 1943, and in doing so, he warned:

> The German fighter force is taking a toll of our forces both by day and night, not only in terms of combat losses, but more especially in terms of reduced tactical effectiveness. If the German fighters are materially increased in number it is quite conceivable that they could make our daylight bombing unprofitable, and perhaps our night bombing too.[13]

Despite these setbacks and pressures, Eaker considered that his bombers had proven their ability to penetrate the German air defences successfully, but that continued success depended on the quick expansion of his command. He asked for a further 944 B-17s and B-24s by July, 1,192 by October, 1,746 by January 1944 and 2,702 by April. In the short term, 13 May 1943 saw the arrival of six new bomb groups to strengthen his command, five of them fresh from the USA. Eaker recorded that it was 'a great day'.

In the meantime, there were many seasoned Luftwaffe pilots – those who were serving on the Eastern Front and in North Africa and the Mediterranean – who had still not encountered the *Viermots*. One such individual was Major Johannes Steinhoff, the veteran of the 1939 encounters with RAF Wellingtons over the North Sea, who, in the spring of 1943, had been appointed to command JG 77 based in Tunisia. As he recalled:

> It was in April 1943 that I first came into contact with the 'four-engine jobs' as we called the B-17s. At that time, the battle for North Africa was already lost, and we were defending, with little success, the beachhead of Cape Bon – that spit of land northeast of Tunis where the bulk of the *Afrika Korps* and the Italian Army were later taken prisoners by Allied forces.
>
> After a dogfight with Spitfires, we were prepared for landing when a glittering armada of bombers of a type we had never seen before, moved above us in the bright midday sun. It was too late to attack then, but I should soon have an opportunity to see these giant birds close-up.[14]

Over Germany on 3 May, a number of Fw 190s from I./JG 1 went into battle equipped with bombs, but their efforts were without success. Conversely, on the 14th, during an American raid against the Kiel shipyards, things improved when three *Viermots* were apparently destroyed by bombs. Brig Gen Frederick L. Anderson, commander of the 4th BW, reported:

> At 1313 hrs, I noted the first fighters in our vicinity – there were 23 airplanes off to our right front, and they appeared to be P-47s making a sweep. However, they suddenly turned out to be Fw 190s. They turned sharply to the right, the whole 23 attacking in a string. I noticed three of them drop bombs on this attack – other members of our crew reported as many as six bombs. They dropped these bombs in head-on attacks, apparently with very short time fuses, in an effort to break up our formation. Two of the bombs came very close to the lead plane and exploded behind us.[15]

VIII Bomber Command's Narrative of Operations stated:

> Three crews saw explosions within 50 yards of them, the shell or bomb disintegrating in a puff of black or green smoke from which streamers of black and green fluttered down, looking like strips of colored toilet paper. One a/c ran through these streamers and some hit the nose of the ship, but they did no damage. Two a/c reported aerial bombs with white parachutes; one a/c saw three and the other one. None seen to explode. Aerial bombs were observed by two other a/c, dropping down and exploding with blue, smoky bursts. No parachutes were attached. These bombs were seen bursting on the approximate position of the

preceding formation. One crew saw a shell or bomb disintegrating into a number of shell fragments, each of which in turn exploded with a pink, smokeless burst.[16]

Amidst such conditions, the American need for fighter escort was becoming ever more urgent. It was satisfied to some extent in the spring of 1943, when the Eighth Air Force was able to call upon three fighter groups, all of which were equipped with newly arrived P-47 Thunderbolts. However, how best the Republic fighter could provide escort would be a matter of experiment and debate for many months to come.

Deployed initially on shallow fighter sweeps over France and Belgium, the early reaction to the big, radial-engined Thunderbolt was mixed, with many pilots reporting engine and radio problems, but these were compensated by the aircraft's formidable firepower of eight 0.50-in. guns. For his part, Göring did not seem perturbed. He had told a production conference on 22 February that, in his view, 'the Americans haven't so far produced a fighter that is anything to write home about'.

On 4 May, 117 P-47s flew in the escort role for the first time when they accompanied 65 B-17s sent to bomb industrial complexes in Antwerp. However, the problem of providing escort all the way to German targets would remain until a workable drop tank design had been found, built, fitted and successfully used. Until such time as that happened, the tactical radius of the P-47 (200–250 miles) took it only into the Low Countries and just about as far as the Rhine, but not beyond. From thereon, bombers would be on their own, flying into the teeth of the increasingly hardening and capable German defence.

Throughout May, the reinforced VIII Bomb Command mounted further raids against German targets such as Kiel on the 14th, but the price was high. That day, the Fw 190s of Oberleutnant Knoke's recently formed 5./JG 11 claimed five B-17s shot down, three of them by air-to-air bombing – a method that had become something of a 'speciality' for this unit. The *Staffel* ended the day with its score of downed *Viermots* raised to 50. Elsewhere, while guided by 2. *Jagddivision*'s '*Johannisbeere*' radar station at Barkholt, nightfighter pilot Unteroffizier Hans Meissner of 6./NJG 3 shot down a B-17 into the sea 50 km northwest of Sylt for his second victory.

On 11 June, one of the largest raids so far was mounted against Bremen, but the target was cloud-covered, so the force altered course for Wilhelmshaven, the secondary target. As the 248 B-17s passed the port, the Luftwaffe launched a major response which lasted until 20 miles north of the Baltrum Islands. Elements of I. and II./JG 11, I. and III./JG 1, III./JG 26 and III./JG 54, together with nightfighters from IV./NJG 1 and

'THE REST IS EASY'

I./NJG 5 operating in a day fighter role, all pounced onto the bomber formation. VIII Bomb Command reported that:

> Attacks were persistent but seemed inexperienced, most coming from 11–1 o'clock level and from above. After initial attack, E/A would circle formation well out of range and then return to attack from head-on.

Eight B-17s fell from the sky, one of which was lost in a mid-air collision with an Fw 190. A further 62 were damaged and 80 American aircrew posted as missing in action.

Two days later, the 1st and 4th BWs journeyed to Bremen and Kiel. Although the main attack against Bremen met only light opposition, bombers from the 4th BW encountered fighters just after crossing the enemy coast – 22 B-17s were downed and 24 damaged. The 4th BW reported:

> Enemy fighter opposition was the strongest and most aggressive to date. Frontal attacks were predominant, but many angles were used taking advantage of sun and clouds. Attacks were made singly, in pairs and in threes. 'V' formations of three, six and eight in frontal attacks. Nose attacks in level and tandem made by series of three to five E/A. Several attacks of six and eight abreast were made against the rear.

Only six of the 16 aircraft from the 95th BG that crossed the coast returned to England. More than 250 crew were posted missing, including the CO of the 95th BG, Brig Gen Nathan B. Forrest, in the most devastating day of losses to date. The calls for a fighter escort grew ever more urgent.

Far to the south, in Sicily, things were not good at all for German forces. Tunisia had been evacuated and Sicily was being held in expectation of an Allied assault on the island. For the Allies, an invasion of Sicily made more sense than an invasion of Sardinia, to the north, because Sardinia was beyond the range of Allied land-based fighters, whereas the southern Sicilian beaches were within range of airfields on Malta.

The fighter pilots in the Mediterranean, drawn mainly from JGs 53 and 77, having retreated from North Africa, were not in the best of morale. They felt outperformed and outgunned by Allied fighter types and strength, but most of all, they had developed a *Viermotorschreck* largely from the fact that it was seemingly impossible to evade the fighter escort and get to within close enough range of a four-engined bomber to shoot it down. Göring held no truck with this, and his ire over the matter was sufficient for him to signal the staff of *Luftflotte* 2 in the Mediterranean:

> All fighter pilots stationed in Italy are to be informed that they are the most pitiful bunch of fliers I have ever commanded. If, by chance, they happen to encounter the enemy, they allow themselves to be shot down without obtaining any successes in return. Until further notice, I forbid any leave so that I do not have to be ashamed of these miserable personalities in the Homeland.[17]

Not surprisingly, this did little to improve the situation. Göring then despatched Galland to Sicily to sort things out. With the experience of fighting bombers over the Reich, Galland stressed to the Mediterranean-based fighter commanders that they should attack with large numbers of aircraft and at close range. But the pilots maintained they had little experience and no training in such operations. Furthermore, the Americans made life harder by being able to fly a 'dog-leg' route when attacking targets in the north, thus meaning the Luftwaffe fighters could only make contact at the limit of their range.

Caught between a rock and a hard place, Galland apparently had little alternative other than to pass on Göring's edict that the pilots should return with at least one victory after every mission or face court martial. The inevitable came on 25 June.

Major Johannes Steinhoff, the *Kommodore* of JG 77 (elements of which were based in Sicily), experienced a frustrating first encounter with the American heavy bombers. By this time, Steinhoff wore the Oak Leaves to the Knight's Cross and had been credited with 154 victories, making him one of the Luftwaffe's premier fighter aces. On the morning of the 25th he led a composite formation of 80 Bf 109s drawn from *Stab*, I. and II./JG 77 and II./JG 53 to attack what was the largest raid put up by the Northwest African Air Forces that month, with B-17s carrying 300 tons of bombs sent to attack Messina. Steinhoff recounted in 1968:

> Sicily had been softened up for an invasion by continuous bomber attacks. On 25 June 1943 our radar stations reported an enemy bomber formation approaching from the Mediterranean, about halfway between Sardinia and Sicily, heading for Naples.
>
> During the preceding days we had drilled in new tactics, and I had attempted to prepare the two operational wings, comprising about 120 aircraft, for their first encounter with the four-engined bombers. After

we had received take-off orders, it was determined that the bombers had not, as expected, attacked the Naples port installation, but had instead bombed the ferry traffic between Messina and the Italian mainland.

At this point the bomber formation was already flying in the direction of North Africa, returning to base, and it was almost impossible to make them out on the radar screens because they had gone down to low altitude. My formation was able to take off with about 100 aircraft and was directed to proceed to the area between Sardinia and Sicily. As we were approaching the area I was advised that the enemy had disappeared from the radar screens and was probably proceeding at almost surface altitude. Visibility was restricted due to strong haze, but just at the moment when I had decided to return to base because of fuel shortage, the armada appeared below me.

At this point, Steinhoff's formation was some 150 km northwest of Trapani. With fuel now low, options were limited, and only a small number of Bf 109s were able to launch a single attack:

The Fortresses were flying in a wide front, only a few yards above the sea, in a formation so huge you could hardly see from one end to the other. It seemed virtually impossible to launch a well coordinated attack – we had never practiced attacking bombers near the surface. The result was terrible. There was not a single kill, and the entire German formation went into panic because the majority of the pilots had to be directed to base by radar and were short of fuel. Altogether we lost six aircraft.[18]

Steinhoff may not be correct in this, for according to the German aviation historian Dr. Jochen Prien, Steinhoff did claim, and was credited with, a B-17 shot down that day. Yet, in contrast to his account above, in his book *Die Strasse von Messina* (*The Straits of Messina*) published a year later in 1969, Steinhoff *does* maintain that he shot a B-17 down into the sea and, indeed, that this was the only one destroyed that day. Again, this is suspect, for according to Dr. Prien, two other B-17s were listed as definitely shot down by II./JG 77, with eight more classified as 'w.b.' (for '*wirklich beschossen*' – shot up well enough to inflict severe damage and probably destruction) by pilots of I. and II./JG 77. Also, based on Dr. Prien's research, Steinhoff's claim that six German fighters were lost does not appear accurate – four Bf 109s were destroyed in combat during the day.[19]

Regardless, the net result was that for all the force assembled by JGs 53 and 77, just two B-17s were shot down. This was wholly unacceptable to Göring, who lost patience and promptly issued another edict, as Steinhoff recalled:

> The same evening, we received orders from Göring that were typical of the methods that the High Command used on us. They stated that one pilot from each fighter unit participating in the action against the bombers off Africa was to be court-martialled for cowardice in the face of the enemy. The unit commanders all volunteered for court-martial, and only through this decision could a completely ridiculous trial before a military court be avoided.

Steinhoff also concluded:

> The first taste of fighting four-engined bombers was completely sufficient for us. We started intensive training and were soon able to have opportunities to practice what we had learned.

Indeed, it seems lessons were being learned. The day after the episode over the Mediterranean, from his headquarters in Berlin, the Operations Officer at *Jafü Mitteldeutschland* signalled its units a message from Göring:

26.6.1943
Combatting enemy bombers
After approval by Herr Reichsmarschall, an urgent new revision is to be added to the instructions for combat by fighters and *Zerstörer* against bomber formations.

    With immediate effect, only bombers flying in formation are to be attacked, regardless of whether the formation is approaching or departing. Only when the entire bomber formation has been shot down or there is no prospect of striking it, may scattered and damaged individual bombers continue to be engaged until they are destroyed. The *Nebelwerfer* (mortar-carrying) aircraft have general authorisation to leave after successfully firing their shells. Extension of this exception is prohibited.

    Unit leaders and fighter pilots who violate this order are to be court-martialled for military disobedience in view of the serious consequences for the security of the Reich. This order is to be announced immediately to all unit leaders and fighter pilots.[20]

For his part, Göring continued to be rankled by what he viewed as a 'lack of backbone' in many of his fighter pilots when it came to combatting the

Viermots. Shortly after the war he told USAAF interrogators that 'the fear of firepower' from the tail guns of American bombers had lowered morale within the fighter *Gruppen* to such an extent that he 'found it necessary to visit all squadrons personally and give them pep-talks'.[21]

Moreover, despite drop tanks now being available universally to the fighter units in the West and the Reich, it was still taking the Messerschmitts and Focke-Wulfs too long to climb to combat altitude after an *Alarmstart*. One excuse was that the Bf 109's landing gear was too weak to permit carrying two drop tanks. Göring discounted that. He wanted flying time increased to ensure combat, and issued instructions that no fighter pilot was to release a drop tank unless it was actually hit by enemy fire. However, after a few weeks, the Reichsmarschall conceded that that was an absurdly impractical idea, but by then several pilots had been killed when their tanks exploded during combat.[22]

Disappointment in the fighter force – and a lack of understanding of military realities – was not limited to Göring however. It seemed that even the (slightly) more practical and objective head of Luftwaffe procurement, Generalfeldmarschall Erhard Milch, had also developed an acerbic attitude. Less than two weeks after Göring had issued his 'court martial' order, Milch chaired a crowded conference on aircraft development and production in Berlin. As he glanced around the room, he commented, 'Is Galland here? A pity, for I cannot tell him what I wanted to say to the fighter units – that once they have made contact with the bombers, the rest is easy'.[23]

As for the Combined Bomber Offensive proposed at Casablanca, there was little sign of it achieving its objective. Both Allied commanders and crews began to realise that the destruction of Germany was going to be a long haul. Plentiful numbers of longer-range escort fighters were badly needed, but until then the 'self-defending' bomber formation would just have to fight on.

The Eighth Air Force HQ's Operational Analysis Section carried out a study on the frequency and directions of Luftwaffe fighter attacks against bombers. It concluded, rightly or wrongly, that from August to November 1942, tail attacks were the most common, being the only tactic experienced by RAF 'medium' crews. At least USAAF crews were able to take satisfaction in the fact that that was what 'our bomber armament and armor plate were primarily designed to protect against'.

However, this had changed in December 1942 when nose attacks predominated following Oberleutnant Egon Mayer's tactical innovation and Galland's subsequent directive. On some missions no other form of attack was reported. When head-on attacks became a 'serious threat', nose armament in B-17s was at its weakest. Some Flying Fortresses had a 0.30-in.

hand-held gun firing through one of four eyelets just off-centre, while others had 0.50-cal side nose guns, but none had armament mounted in the dead centre of the nose. This left a blind spot to the front which neither the upper turret nor the ball turret could cover. B-24s were also equipped with 0.50-in. side nose guns and a single 0.50-in. central nose gun, but mounted to fire below the horizontal only. This also left a blind spot that the upper turret could not cover.

In consequence, the shift to concentrated attacks from the nose accelerated the development of improved armament for this area, and theatre modifications were rushed through which saw the fitting of single or twin 0.50-in. centre nose guns capable of offering defence from attacks mounted head-on. In February–March 1943, although the nose quadrant continued to receive about one-third of all attacks, beam attacks increased. Nearly half of the Luftwaffe's interceptions came from the 'two', 'three' and 'four o'clock' and 'eight', 'nine' and 'ten o'clock' directions. During April, May and June, tail attacks picked up, beam accounts decreased and nose attacks continued.[24]

July arrived. It was high summer.

8

Defence in Depth

The summer of 1943 found Germany's war effort floundering. On 10 July, in the USSR, five days after the launch of Operation *Zitadelle*, a major armoured offensive aimed at cutting off the Soviet-held salient at Kursk, Allied forces landed on Sicily. Forty-eight hours later, following an epic tank battle at Prokhorovka, the German thrust around the Kursk 'bulge' was halted and, by the 16th, the Panzers began to withdraw.

Ironically, despite the situation in Sicily, Generalmajor Galland used a lull in the American raids on northwestern Germany during the first three weeks of July as an opportunity to withdraw a number of day fighter units from the south to bolster the air defence of the Reich against the anticipated continuation of heavier daylight bombing. This went against the policy of Generaloberst Jeschonnek, who wished to maintain maximum commitment to the Eastern and Mediterranean Fronts, leaving daylight defence to the 250-plus fighters of JGs 2 and 26 in France and the Low Countries.

However, the general drain of deployment across three fronts throughout 1943 increased the need to terminate commitment somewhere, and in view of the threat posed by the Allied bomber offensive, there was little option but to defend the Reich and the West, where Galland had advocated the rapid reinforcement of fighter assets. He believed that it was necessary to inflict substantial losses on the USAAF now, at the outset of its strategic offensive, rather than waiting to attempt to engage it in strength later when crews would be more experienced and able to draw upon greater resources, including increased numbers of escort fighters.

Galland got his way, to an extent. From Sicily came Hauptmann Karl Rammelt's badly depleted II./JG 51, while the Bf 109s of II./JG 27 under Hauptmann Werner Schroer arrived at Wiesbaden-Erbenheim from Vibo-Valentia, in southern Italy. By the end of July, the previously fragmented elements of I./JG 27 had regrouped around Münster-Handorf under the command of its newly appointed *Kommandeur*, Knight's Cross-holder Hauptmann Ludwig Franzisket.

On 31 July 1943, some 11 day fighter *Gruppen* from JGs 1, 3, 11, 27 and 51, plus elements of JG 54, were based within the Reich, with half of the reinforcement being absorbed for the defence of northwest Germany. JG 2 and most of JG 26 remained in the Netherlands and France to protect the airspace in the West, while JGs 3 and 27 were to cover the Rhine and Main rivers.[1] In addition, JG 300 was about to form up at Bonn-Hangelaar for *Wilde Sau* night operations using day fighters under the command of former bomber pilot Major Hajo Herrmann.

This redistribution of fighter strength meant that the Luftwaffe was able to pursue a policy of 'defence in depth' in which, by expanding its defensive zones along the coast and also by holding the bulk of its fighter strength back in the Reich, its fighters would be beyond the range of USAAF fighters and, therefore, able to concentrate on the bombers with less risk.

Furthermore, single-engined fighter production had been increasing steadily throughout the first seven months of 1943 from about 480 to 800 aircraft per month, and by the time repaired fighters were added, some 1,000 were available monthly for replacement and expansion. In July, the actual total of Bf 109 and Fw 190 output was 1,050, against a target of 1,013 (an uplift of 3.7 per cent) representing an 8.9 per cent increase over June.[2]

By 1 July, there were approximately 800 single-engined fighters available for the daylight defence of the Reich and the West, but they were being steadily depleted in a growing battle of attrition against the Allied air forces at a rate that was difficult to sustain. That month, fighter aircraft losses (all fronts) stood at 31.2 per cent, while the loss in single-engined fighter pilots (all fronts and all causes) in July stood at 330, or 16 per cent – an increase of 84 pilots on the previous month and of 64 pilots when compared to May.

Particularly hard to bear was the accumulating loss of experienced fighter commanders. In June, the recently appointed *Kommandeur* of III./JG 26, Hauptmann Kurt Ruppert, had been killed when he had led a formation of 32 Bf 109Gs in a rear pass against the lead group of 72 B-17s attacking Kiel. His aircraft was hit by return fire from the bombers, and as he bailed out, Ruppert's parachute harness tore and he fell to his death. In July, during raids on Hamburg and Kiel, III./JG 1 suffered the loss of its *Kommandeur*, Major Karl-Heinz Leesmann, when, on the 25th, he crashed into the sea after attacking a group of B-17s. Although a search vessel was immediately despatched from Heligoland, there was no sign of Leesmann. His body was washed ashore on 16 August. In the meantime, Hauptmann Robert Olejnik took command of III. *Gruppe*.

An increase in non-combat losses reflected the pressures on fighter training. Reductions in the training programme meant that by the autumn of 1943, fighter pilots were reaching their operational units with an average of 148 hours on powered aircraft, compared to an average of 210 hours the previous year. In a measure of some expediency, the *Jagdfliegerschulen* were redesignated as *Jagdgeschwader* during the spring of 1943, placing them on what would be perceived as a semi-operational footing. JFS 1 at Werneuchen, for example, became JG 101, where the average duration of the fighter training course was three-and-a-half to four months, compared to an average of four to five months in 1942.

In June 1943, the four component *Staffeln* of *Ergänzungsjagdgruppe West* based in southwestern France supplied Bf 109- and Fw 190-ready pilots to the operational *Jagdgruppen*. Pupils were instructed by operationally experienced instructors over courses lasting normally a month, although demands from the operational units often shortened this period to 14 days. Courses consisted of circuits and bumps in the Bf 109F, followed by conversion to the Bf 109G, or in a Bf 108 Taifun prior to conversion to the Fw 190. Instruction in formation flying was similar to that received in a Fighter Training School, but in an *Ergänzungsjagdgruppe,* at least one flight was made in a formation of seven to nine aircraft led by an instructor. Heavy emphasis was placed in gunnery training and target practice, using both machine guns and cannon – something that would be needed in the war against the bombers.

Pressure began to mount on the German defence. On the night of 24–25 July, 741 aircraft from RAF Bomber Command undertook a major night raid against Hamburg. At midday on the 26th, 122 B-17s bombed the city again, disrupting rescue operations. The British returned on the night of 27–28 July with a force of 739 bombers that dropped more than 2,300 tons of bombs, setting 16,000 buildings ablaze in the infamous 'firestorm' raid. To paraphrase Brig Gen Eaker, 'the Devils were being bombed around the clock'.

As the daylight raids intensified still further, Galland reasoned that it would be prudent to limit the number of machines and operations flown by the home defence *Geschwader* against individual enemy raids so as to allow sufficient repair and re-grouping of aircraft that had landed on emergency fields. Only by carefully conserving strength and by efficient management of its most precious resources, namely its pilots, could the Luftwaffe hope to cause any damage to the bombers. Unimpressed, Göring brushed this theory aside and demanded that all available units be thrown against every raid wherever and whenever possible.

By July, in a turning point for USAAF fighter operations, P-47 Thunderbolts of the 4th Fighter Group (FG) appeared for the first time in German skies fitted with auxiliary fuel tanks that greatly extended their range. Initially, Galland failed to convince Göring that enemy fighter escorts had actually penetrated Reich airspace. According to Albert Speer, Reich Minister of Armaments and War Production, shortly after the first P-47 had been shot down over the German border in mid-1943, Göring had insinuated that the wreckage his fighter commander had seen near Aachen had been the product of 'fantasies'.[3]

During the summer of 1943, the residents of the Lower Saxony town of Stade in northern Germany, some 45 km west of Hamburg, close to the River Elbe, watched with a mixture of disquiet and wonderment as an enormous structure took form on a gentle rise of wooded ground to the west of the town.

The architecture was functional and brutal, a rectangular edifice some 60.5 m in length, 40.5 m wide and 16.6 m high, built of reinforced concrete and encased, during its construction, from top to bottom by wooden scaffolding. The walls and roof were 3.5 m thick, intended to be bomb-proof, and the thousands of tons of cement needed for its construction had to be brought from a storage depot on a specially built light railway. From the railway, the concrete travelled in a pressurised pipeline and was poured via a large chute into a fleet of on-site delivery vehicles. Other materials were moved up to the roof and upper levels of the building via a purpose-built lift, rigged up in the scaffolding. All day, every day, Stade endured the hammering and grinding of machinery, as well as clouds of dust.

This was the new purpose-built main battle headquarters bunker, or *Zentral Gefechtsstand*, for 2. *Jagddivision*, and it stood as a stark example of just how serious the Luftwaffe was taking its mission of Reich defence in mid-1943.

As much as the architecture was brutal, so was the construction process. Codenamed '*Sokrates*' (the 'S' denoted Stade), the bunker was built on fields that had been the subject of an Air Ministry acquisition order, and the small-holding farmers on whose land it now lay had had little choice in the matter. Neither did they receive compensation from the Air Ministry.

Hundreds of men had worked on the construction of the bunker as forced labour, including Russian and, later, Italian prisoners of war, supplied by the *Organisation Todt* (OT), the notorious Nazi body responsible for carrying out major engineering projects both in the Reich and the occupied territories. The treatment meted out to the Russians in particular was abysmal. They were subject to frequent beatings and were very poorly fed, to the extent that many of them resorted to stealing chicken feed from the barns of surrounding farms to stave off their hunger. Even on 'rest days', they toiled on drainage work in the nearby village of Haddorf.

Carpenters came from a joinery firm in Helmste, some ten kilometres away, to install the bunker's 98 windows, 230 doors, endless shelving and furniture. Since work commenced on *Sokrates* in early 1943, the cost was estimated at five million Reichsmarks.[4] Nothing about the bunker was small. And within its vast walls the workers laboured in a world of dim electric light, humming ventilators and kilometres of pipework and cabling.

By mid-July, the responsibility for all aspects of air defence in the Reich, Denmark, Bohemia-Moravia, Posen and areas of western Poland remained with Weise's *Luftwaffenbefehlshaber Mitte* at Berlin-Dahlem and Wannsee.

The fighter control structure was essentially as it had been in 1942, with overall control of daylight fighter operations in the Reich, the Netherlands, areas of Belgium, northeastern France and Denmark assigned to Kammhuber's XII. *Fliegerkorps* at Zeist. Reporting to XII. *Fliegerkorps* was 1. *Jagddivision* under von Döring covering northwestern Germany east of the Elbe, the Netherlands, and areas of Belgium, supported by *Jafü Holland-Ruhrgebiet* under Oberst Walter Grabmann, covering the same area.

Aside from the aforementioned 2. *Jagddivision* at Stade, 3. *Jagddivision* at Metz, under Generalmajor Werner Junck, coordinated activity in southern Belgium and northeastern France, while 4. *Jagddivision* at Döberitz under Generalmajor Joachim-Friedrich Huth handled northern Germany east of the Elbe, East Prussia, Silesia and central Germany, supported by *Jafü Mitteldeutschland* under Generalmajor Hermann Frommherz. 5. *Jagddivision* at Schleissheim covered southern Germany under Oberst Harry von Bülow, who also acted as *Jafü Süd*, while the semi-autonomous *Jafü Ostmark* based at the Schloss Cobenzl in Vienna, under Oberst Gotthard Handrick, covered Austria, Bohemia-Moravia and Hungary.

The Luftwaffe relied on this network of commands, control bunkers, observers and radars to detect the American raids as early as possible, and with the benefit of its long-range coastal *Freya* radars, hopefully as they assembled over England. Each *Freya* would constantly sweep the ether in its assigned zone of cover, which slightly overlapped that of its neighbour. Once the bombers were at sufficient height, sooner or later, they would fall within range of a *Freya*. From that moment, the operators of a particular radar would reduce its arc of sweep in order to focus on the incoming raid, leaving its neighbours to take over the sweeping of a wider area.

The *Freya* was able to read both range and bearing, so that it could provide information from which a continuous track could be plotted. In its earliest use, it took a *Freya* and its operators around two to two-and-a-half minutes to process and relay its information to a *Jafü* and or divisional *Gefechtsstand*, although as operators became more adapt, this could be reduced to one minute. It would take around ten seconds for a divisional plotter to 'throw' the plot onto the situation map. The senior fighter controller would take around a minute to assess and decide on what course of action to take, and if, and how, to deploy the units in his area, but usually he would wait for a second plot for confirmation. Depending on the position of the enemy bombers, the controller would then either bring fighters to readiness or order an *Alarmstart*. At this stage, the *Kampfraum* (Battle Room) would not have accurate data on enemy altitude.

As this was taking place, all available resources of the '*Auge-Ohr Flugmelde Dienst*' (Visual and Audible Air Reporting Service), regional *Flugwachkommando* (FluKo – Air Traffic Monitoring Unit) and *Funkhorchdienst* (Radio Listening Service) would swing into action, tracking and monitoring the enemy's progress. On the fighter airfields, pilots would be placed at either 30-minute *Bereitschaft* (readiness), five-minute *Bereitschaft* (pilots at dispersal with parachutes and life jackets worn loosely or close at hand), three-minute *Bereitschaft* (pilots at dispersal wearing parachutes and ready to climb into their aircraft) or *Sitzbereitschaft* (cockpit readiness, with mechanics waiting to start engines and runway clear).

At its best, the Luftwaffe was able to process and react to information in the following 'average' timeframe:

First detection by *Freya*:	65 seconds
First plot to first display in *Kampfraum*:	ten seconds
First display to second display:	60 seconds
From display to controller issuing first order:	60 seconds
Controller giving order to receipt of order by pilots:	15 seconds
From pilots receiving order to pilots in cockpits:	180 seconds
From pilots in cockpits to fighters airborne (one *Staffel*):	180 seconds
	(9.5 minutes in total)[5]

On 28 July, B-17 crews of the 4th BW were confronted by a new weapon in the skies over Germany. As previously mentioned, for the first time P-47s escorted the bombers right up to German airspace. However, on this occasion, the Luftwaffe waited until the escort had to turn back before launching a concentrated attack in bad weather on the then vulnerable bombers heading for the Fieseler works at Kassel-Batteshausen and the AGO works at Oschersleben. Ten *Jagdgruppen* were assembled by

DEFENCE IN DEPTH

2. *Jagddivision*, six from JGs 1 and 11, plus I. and III./JG 26, I./JG 3 and III./JG 54. These units were augmented by aircraft from E.Kdo 25 and the ISS from the Focke-Wulf plant in Bremen and the Fieseler factory in Kassel.

From head-on, spearheaded by the Fw 190s of JG 1 followed by the Bf 109Gs of Hauptmann Günther Specht's II./JG 11, the German fighters drove their way into the USAAF formation. The attack was described as 'intense and aggressive'.[6] Some 25 bombers went down.

In their first major deployment, aircraft from JGs 1 and 11, directed towards the Oschersleben force, carried newly fitted W.Gr.21 mortar tubes under their wings. Designed as an infantry weapon for use in ground warfare, the intention was to install the mortars under the wings of Fw 190s for use as an air-to-air weapon against formations of bombers. Fired from beyond the defensive range of the bombers' gunners, the mortar shells were intended to detonate within or even near to a formation, where the blast would be sufficient to scatter the *Viermots*, thus weakening their defensive firepower and rendering individual aircraft more vulnerable to attack.

In early June 1943, a consignment of 30 *Nebelwerfer* 42 mortar tubes and 200 mortar shells was delivered by the Wehrmacht to I./JG 1 at Schiphol, with a further 34 tubes and 200 shells going to II./JG 26 in France. Redesignated the *Wurfgranate* 42 and later as the *Werfergranate* (W.Gr.) 21, but less formally known as 'stovepipes' because of the shape of the tubes, the weapon was initially trialled by Hauptmann Tratt of E.Kdo 25. This unit had been seconded to I./JG 1 equipped with four Fw 190A-4s specifically to carry out the task.

At JG 26, Leutnant Otto Hummel of 5. *Staffel* was assigned to conduct similar experiments. Firing practice took place over the North Sea, and on 13 June, three B-17s were claimed by mortars over the German Bight, while on the 22nd, Oberfeldwebel Hans Laun and Oberfeldwebel Günter Fick of I./JG 1 claimed a further two *Viermots* shot down and two damaged. These initial results proved sufficiently satisfactory for trials to continue using Fw 190s of both JGs 1 and 26, as well as E.Kdo 25 at Achmer and the armaments *Erprobungsstelle* at Tarnewitz.

Hauptmann Horst Geyer of E.Kdo 25 recalled:

Unlike other missiles, the 21 cm '*Werfer*', which came to us from the Army, was not equipped with fins or stabilisers. Rather, this weapon was stabilised by its own spin, which, in turn, was created by the blast from initial ignition and the subsequent velocity. The 21 cm shell turned two or three times per second after leaving its launch tube, but speed increased rapidly thereafter.

We observed that the shell did not run straight to its intended target, but rather it spiralled and therefore often missed the target. To overcome this, the manufacturer built in a fuse intended to detonate the shell at a pre-set time. We usually fired the weapon from a range of 400 m, and from our experience with it, we were able to set the fuse correctly, compensating, of course, for the approach speed of the target. However, the closer to the target you were, so the greater the blast and the success of the weapon.[7]

One 1.3 m-long rifled mortar launching tube, 250 mm in diameter externally, was suspended from beneath each underside wing of an Fw 190 by means of four lugs and a central hook with a suspension bracket. The 112-kg shell with its 40-kg warhead was held in place by three retaining springs, located near the rear end of the tube. A screw bolt, also at the rear end of the tube, prevented the shell from sliding out. In an emergency, the launching tube could be jettisoned by activating an electrically primed explosive charge which severed the central hook. The mortars were controlled from a cockpit armament panel and aimed via a *Revi* 16B reflector sight. Two shells were fired simultaneously when the pilot depressed a button on his control column.

The mortar shells were fitted with their time fuses pre-set at 800 m prior to delivery to an operational unit and were not subsequently adjusted. The firing range was, therefore, invariable, and the weapon's low velocity meant that to be effective, it had to be aimed 60 m above its target and a shell had to detonate within 28 m of a bomber.

The rockets' psychological effect on the bomber crews during the mission of 28 July is evident from post-mission descriptions:

> Unidentified e/a were reported using rocket-propelled bombs with great accuracy. The rockets were propelled from a belly gun and looped over the top of our planes, where they exploded with great sheets of metal.[8]

Hauptmann Specht claimed one B-17 and the *Gruppenkommandeur* of I./JG 1, Hauptmann Emil-Rudolf Schnoor, claimed another for his ninth victory, while Unteroffizier 'Jonny' Fest of 5./JG 1 claimed three bombers destroyed, having dropped a bomb into the American formation. He was probably correct – one Flying Fortress from the 385th BG received a direct hit from a bomb over Oschersleben, and as the 4th BW reported, 'Air to air bombing is believed to have been responsible for the loss of at least three B-17s when one received a direct hit in its bomb-bay and crashed into two others'.[9]

Of the 25 bombers shot down, several were accounted for as a result of good guidance and cooperation with the respective *Jägerleitoffizier* at *Luftnachrichten-Regiment* (Air Signals Regiment) 201 at Nordhelle-Ebbe,

Luftnachrichten-Regiment 212 at the *Funkmess-Stellung* (radio warning and tracking station) '*Hummer*' on Heligoland and the '*Brombeere*' 'Y' station at Bredstedt in Schleswig.[10]

These encouraging results were tempered by the unexpected clash between P-47s of the 4th FG sent to cover the B-17s' withdrawal and a mixed formation of Focke-Wulfs and Messerschmitts of JG 1 and I./JG 26 which were in the process of launching an attack against the bombers near Emmerich. In a running engagement between Utrecht and Rotterdam, the American pilots claimed nine German fighters shot down. In its Narrative of Operations for 28 July, VIII Bomber Command reported, 'Heavy fighter opposition. Attacks were made predominantly from 12 o'clock high and 6 o'clock level, although scattered attacks were made from all directions'.[11]

Following research into escort protection throughout 1943, the Eighth Air Force's Headquarters' Operational Analysis Section concluded:

(1) Part-way escort offered little more protection than no escort; (2) in the summer of 1943, bombers with no escort suffered seven times the losses and two-and-a-half times the damage of bombers with full escort; (3) by the fall of 1943, growing enemy fighter power precluded bomber operations to targets deep in central or southern Germany until long-range fighters were able to provide full escort.[12]

And of the W.Gr.21 mortar, in a report prepared in late August 1943, the Headquarters of the Eighth Air Force warned, 'It would appear to be the most dangerous single obstacle in the path of our bomber offensive'.[13]

Encouraged by this early success, Galland instructed all units equipped with the Bf 110 *Zerstörer* and its successor, the new Messerschmitt Me 410, assigned to *Jafü Deutsche Bucht* to fit two W.Gr.21 tubes under each of their wings. From late 1942, the sleek, elegant Me 410 'heavy fighter' became the successor to the disastrous Me 210, which had been intended as a progressive development of the Bf 110, only for the aircraft to be plagued by delays, spiralling costs and appalling handling characteristics, and which, it was rumoured, had almost bankrupted Messerschmitt.

Meanwhile, by the end of July in the Mediterranean, no fewer than 600 Bf 109s and Fw 190s had been lost. The irrefutable fact was that heavy fighter losses incurred in and around Sicily had severely curtailed the Luftwaffe's ability to enhance its home defence operations, just as the USAAF was about to attempt a bold new step.

9

Schweinfurt

During the evening of 3 August 1943, after more than two years of operations on the Eastern Front, most of the Bf 109s of III./JG 3 arrived at Münster-Handorf, in northwest Germany, from Makejewka on the Mius Front, along with their support equipment and ground personnel carried in Ju 52/3m transports. The unit had been in action in the USSR as recently as the 1st, flying *Freie Jagd* and escort for bomber and Stuka units. That day, the *Gruppe* had lodged six claims against Soviet aircraft.

Now, III./JG 3 had been assigned defensive operations over the German homeland. The pilots and groundcrews would find this a very different form of warfare to that which they had experienced in the East. Furthermore, they had given up their single-cannon Messerschmitts to receive new aircraft in the form of Bf 109G-6s fitted with underwing, 'gondola'-mounted MG 151/20 cannon – weapons suitable for deployment against heavy bombers.

Leadership of the *Gruppe* had also undergone a change after the loss of its *Kommandeur*, Major Wolfgang Ewald, when his Bf 109 was hit by anti-aircraft fire near Belgorod on 14 July shortly after he had claimed his 65th victory – Ewald parachuted into captivity. The new *Gruppenkommandeur*, Major Walter Dahl, an exuberant but tenacious man imbued with self-confidence, greeted his new pilots with the terse welcome, 'Get ready for action as quickly as possible!'[1]

Dahl did not need to advertise his reputation. After being shot down in the early stages of Operation *Barbarossa*, he trekked for three days through enemy territory to return to his unit. Following service over the Mediterranean and the USSR, his victory tally rose to 50, for which he was awarded the German Cross in Gold. Appointed to lead III./JG 3 from 20 July, Dahl would earn himself a reputation as a leading exponent of tactics in the war against the *Viermots*.

III./JG 3 would be controlled tactically by *Jafü Holland/Ruhrgebiet* at Deelen, and within three days of its arrival in the Reich the *Gruppe* commenced tactical training in *Schwärme* for homeland defence, focusing on the use of the 20 mm cannon against bombers.

Overseeing similar training nearly 600 km to the south of Handorf, at Ansbach, was ZG 76, which had been re-formed and re-established under Oberstleutnant Theodor Rossiwall specifically for operations with Bf 110 *Zerstörer* armed with heavy calibre armament for combatting enemy bombers, its ranks drawn from various reconnaissance, nightfighter and flying school units. The nucleus of I. *Gruppe* came from former Bf 110-equipped reconnaissance units, while II./ZG 76, based at Wertheim under the leadership of Major Herbert Kaminski, was built up from elements of ZG 101 and some nightfighter units.

Some 70 km to the north of Handorf, at Plantlünne, was Hauptmann Fritz Schulze-Dickow, a Berliner and a Knight's Cross-holder who commanded the Bf 110-equipped III./ZG 26 *Horst Wessel* whose principal task, like ZG 76, was to combat the bombers. Schulze-Dickow had been with the *Gruppe* since 1940 and had flown many ground attack and escort missions in the West and the Mediterranean, but he was in no uncertainty as to what now lay ahead for his men.

On 12 August, he organised a day of instruction for all crews on day fighter tactics, high-altitude flying, communication and, in accordance with Galland's recent orders, the use of the W.Gr.21 mortar. To offer the *Zerstörer* crews a demonstration of the mortar, Hauptmann Geyer from E.Kdo 25 travelled to Plantlünne from Wittmundhafen, bringing his expertise. In a memo, Schulze-Dickow set out clearly the aim of the flying on the 12th:

> The focus of training is to maximise combat capability and to attain complete mastery of our respective aircraft types so as to ensure their ruthless deployment in combat against bomber formations.
>
> In accordance with this new task for the *Zerstörer*, great importance must be attached to fighter training, the approach to an enemy formation in *Gruppe* strength and mastery of new weapons.
>
> The deployment of the *Zerstörer* units in the Home Defence must be achieved in the *shortest possible time*. The aim of our training and deployment must be the complete destruction of incoming bomber units. Every *Zerstörer* must be able to get the most out of its weapon. With this attitude, our operations will always be successful.[2]

Schulze-Dickow and his adjutant, Oberleutnant Günther Wegmann, devised 'systematic' training plans for aircraft operating in *Rotte, Schwarm, Staffel* and *Gruppe*-sized formations, and directed them to 'attack' from different angles and approaches against an aircraft acting as a 'target'. The aircraft of

Schwarm- and *Staffelführer* would be fitted with 'robot' cameras to record what happened.

Each pilot was to fire at least two live mortars, as well as rounds from an MG 151 and later a 3.7 cm cannon, at a three-metre by three-metre disc on the ground from a range of 1,200 m. This would replicate the size of a four-engined bomber in the air. Gunnery practice would be followed by sessions in theoretical instruction on fighter control methods, radio usage, enemy aircraft types, new German types of armament such as large-calibre cannon, a lecture on the latest experiences gained in combat against four-engined bombers, the basics of formation and high-altitude flying and cooperation with single-engined fighters, pathfinder aircraft and Flak batteries.

In the initial stages of unit-sized *Zerstörer* deployment against heavy bombers in instances where no USAAF fighter escort was present, tactics were devised so that wherever possible *Gruppen* were based on airfields close to each other. Take-off in *Schwärme* followed receipt of the *Alarmstart* order from the *Jafü* or *Jagddivision* HQ. A *Gruppe* assembled by *Staffeln* in line astern over the airfield and continued to climb to the nominated *Geschwader* assembly area, which would lie over a prominent geographical point or, in bad weather, over a radio beacon.

At the assembly area, the *Gruppen* formed up into a column. Then, upon sighting the enemy, the formation deployed into line abreast, in which the *Gruppen* were stepped up – this was important if W.Gr.21 mortars were to be fired. The precise range for shooting down bombers in a *Pulk* was assessed either by using the *Revi* gunsight or with a ZFR 4 stereoscopic range-finding sight. Mortars were fired on radio orders from the *Zerstörer* leader. In frontal or beam attacks, it was common for pilots to overshoot, while in attacks from the rear, there was a tendency to undershoot. The most practical and ballistically effective method was dead astern. After discharging their mortars, which would take place at a range of 730–900 m, the *Zerstörer* closed up again and attacked using machine guns and cannon, following which the aircraft headed for home.[3]

Despite such admirable preparation, it would be some time before the Bf 110s of III./ZG 26 were deployed against the bombers.

It was a different story for III./JG 3 on the morning of 3 August. As Schulze-Dickow and Wegmann proceeded with their training programme, just 12 Bf 109s from Dahl's *Gruppe* took off for their first encounter with B-17s to the south and west of Cologne. These were part of a two-pronged attack by the Eighth Air Force, using 330 Flying Fortresses against targets in the Ruhr area and around Bonn.

Joining ten other *Jagdgruppen* committed to action that day, and guided by a Bf 109 of I./JG 27 fitted with 'Y'-*Führung*, the pilots of III./JG 3 sighted around 70–80 enemy bombers at 0910 hrs flying at an altitude of 8,000 m. Wasting no time, they launched an attack in *Schwärme* from head-on and forced two bombers out of formation to become stragglers. The Bf 109s passed over and around the bombers and turned back for a rear attack, coming in from above and below.

In the space of nine minutes, Leutnant Hans Schleef of 7. *Staffel* and Leutnants Erwin Stahlberg and Raimund Koch of 8./JG 3 each claimed a B-17 shot down. All of these pilots were Eastern Front veterans, but it seemed they had adapted quickly to taking on their new opponents. Schleef had been awarded the Knight's Cross on 9 May 1942 for his 41st victory credited over 200 missions. The B-17 represented his 95th kill. The Bf 109s of III./JG 3 attacked the bombers for 45 minutes, inflicting serious damage on three more of them. Finally, lacking fuel and ammunition, they landed either back at Handorf or scattered on airfields at Cologne-Ostheim and Mönchengladbach.[4]

In total that day, Luftwaffe claims amounted to 37 victories and *Herausschüsse*, while the Americans reported 25 B-17s lost.[5] The aircraft of the 1st BW bombing the Ruhr targets suffered 23 of these losses, and a further 103 Flying Fortresses were damaged, two of which crash-landed back in England and were written off. Five crewmen were killed, 232 posted missing and 49 returned wounded – by far the heaviest casualties inflicted on a USAAF bomber force so far. This was a significant achievement for the defenders, but there was a worrying portent in as much as that no fewer than 131 P-47s were able to undertake penetration and withdrawal escort using pressurised steel belly tanks.

Understandably, the presence of the Thunderbolt in Reich airspace, while not entirely a surprise, was still a nasty development for the defenders. Although Luftwaffe pilots were initially wary, they began to notice that the escort pilots tended not to attack, and so the Germans became more aggressive. Orders were thus issued to attack the bombers and to avoid the Thunderbolts unless they attacked. This measure quickly resulted in the USAAF pilots recognising the Luftwaffe tactics and counterattacking. But to a Luftwaffe pilot, orders were orders, and the *Jagdgruppen* stuck to targeting the bombers, seeing the presence of P-47s (and, later, P-51s) as 'an interruption of their appointed task of shooting down bombers'. Frequently, German formations were bounced by P-47s, and when under attack 'resorted to running away or detouring, rather than staying and fighting'.[6]

After the war, Galland described this time to Allied interrogators as 'the period of the Split-S and dive-away', as German pilots sought safety in diving towards friendly terrain, while invariably outnumbered and under pursuit by US fighters which could dive faster. The results were catastrophic for the Luftwaffe. This was the phenomenon Galland called '*Jägerschreck*' (fear of fighters), and it was usually only pilots from JGs 1 and 26 who would turn on the American fighters when bounced.[7]

On 15 August, at the third great conference held by Allied commanders that year in Washington D.C., and Quebec, the Chief of the British Air Staff, Air Chief Marshal Sir Charles Portal, presented a paper on Operation *Pointblank*, as the joint British–American Combined Bomber Offensive had been named, with which he intended to raise his concerns over what he perceived to be the growing strength of the Luftwaffe fighter force. Portal wrote:

> If we do not now strain every nerve to bring force to bear to win this battle during the next two or three months, but are content to see VIII Bomber Command hampered by lack of reinforcements just as success is within its grasp, we may well miss the opportunity to win a decisive victory against the German Air Force which will have incalculable effects on all future operations, and on the length of the war.[8]

The underlying 'future operation' to which Portal referred was the planned invasion of Continental Europe in mid-1944, codenamed Operation *Overlord* – without doubt the most important undertaking in Allied strategic plans.

Then came Schweinfurt. In the early morning of 17 August, the anniversary of VIII Bomber Command's first bombing raid on northern Europe, in the briefing room at Thorpe Abbotts airfield in Norfolk, the commander of the 100th BG, Col Neil Harding, spoke bluntly to his crews:

> Your primary is Regensburg. Your aiming point is the centre of the Messerschmitt 109G aircraft engine and assembly shops. This is the most vital target we've ever gone after. If you destroy it, you destroy 30 percent of the Luftwaffe's single-engined fighter production.

Another task force, Harding said, was to strike Schweinfurt, and as the 100th's Intelligence Officer subsequently explained, 'Their target produces most of the ball bearings in Germany. Three months after they get their target, there won't be an engine operating in the whole country'.[9]

The manufacture of ball bearings in Schweinfurt, an ancient Bavarian town on the River Main, stretched back to 1906. During Germany's economic recovery in the 1930s, this industry gave the place its affluence. In turn, it gave the Third Reich just under half the ball bearings it needed for its war effort, but *more* than half in terms of value.[10] Schweinfurt was therefore important. And that is how the Eighth Air Force mission planners saw it.

So it was that at 0645 hrs, the first B-17s took off from England for a mission which, in terms of size, surpassed anything that had gone before. The attack was carried out by two large formations. The first, comprising 146 B-17s from seven bomb groups belonging to the 4th BW, would attack the Messerschmitt works at Regensburg-Prüfening and continue across southern Europe to land at bases in North Africa. The second formation, consisting of 230 aircraft from nine bomb groups of the 1st BW, had as its objective the ball bearing complexes at Schweinfurt.

However, unsettled weather over the southeast of England hampered take-off. Just when it was thought that the missions would have to be scrubbed, the order to proceed was given. Precious time had been wasted and the raids had lost their synchronisation. It took more than an hour for the first-wave bombers to join up and assemble into formation. The fighter escort joined them over the North Sea at cruising speed to maximise fuel economy. Shortly after 0930 hrs, the complete formation crossed the Dutch coast south of the Scheldt estuary.

At the same time, the order for take-off reached III./JG 1. The unit's 32 serviceable Bf 109G-6s left Leeuwarden led by Hauptmann Robert Olejnik and headed for Deelen airfield, where they were to await further orders.

At 1048 hrs from a villa in Schaarsbergen, Oberst Walter Grabmann, *Jafü Holland-Ruhrgebiet*, ordered the Fw 190s of I./JG 26 under Hauptmann Karl Borris into the air from Woensdrecht, followed shortly by the Bf 109s of Hauptmann Klaus Mietusch's III. *Gruppe* from Schiphol. Once again the plotters at *Luftnachrichten-Regiment* 201 hunched over their maps and listened intently to their headphones, guiding the fighters towards their quarry. JG 26 established contact with the American armada over Antwerp. From this moment on, the Messerschmitts and Focke-Wulfs harried the bombers along their entire route over Europe.

From its position up-sun and slightly above the loosely dispersed enemy formation, I./JG 26 pounced in a classic head-on attack and inflicted fatal damage on several B-17s. The *Kapitän* of 1. *Staffel*, Oberleutnant Artur Beese, a veteran of the Channel Front, was one of the first to score, knocking down a Flying Fortress near Berendrecht at 1130 hrs for his 16th victory. It was his first *Viermot* kill, and he would soon score again, claiming another B-17 in the afternoon over Belgium.

A co-pilot aboard a bomber heading for Regensburg recorded:

> At 1017 hours, near Woensdrecht, I saw the first Flak blossom out in our vicinity, light and inaccurate. A few minutes later, two Fw 190s appeared at one o'clock level and whizzed through the formation ahead of us in a frontal attack, nicking two B-17s in the wings and breaking away beneath us in half-rolls. Smoke immediately trailed from both B-17s, but they held their stations.
>
> As the fighters passed us at a high rate of closure, the guns of our group went into action. The pungent smell of burnt powder filled our cockpit and the B-17 trembled to the recoil of nose and ball turret guns. I saw pieces fly off the wing of one of the fighters before they passed from view. The members of the crew sensed trouble. There was something desperate about the way those two fighters came in fast right out of their climb without any preliminaries.
>
> I watched two fighters explode not far beneath, disappearing in sheets of orange flame, B-17s dropping out in various states of distress, from engines on fire to control surfaces shot away, friendly and enemy parachutes floating down. The sight was fantastic; it surpassed fiction.

Seven confirmed bombers went down to the guns of III./JG 26 that day, including two accredited to Hauptmann Klaus Mietusch, the *Gruppenkommandeur*, and two to Oberfeldwebel Heinz Kemethmüller. Hauptmann Hermann Staiger, *Staffelkapitän* of 12./JG 26, claimed his sixth heavy bomber shot down within a month.

III./JG 1 took off again and intercepted just as the escorting fighters, at the limit of their range, turned back over the Belgian–German border. Hauptmann Olejnik recalled the interception:

> At a height of 7,500 m, about 50 to 60 km away, I sighted three formations of bombers. I changed course towards them. At this time we were over the Aachen region. The enemy was flying on a southeasterly course. After a chase of 35 minutes, I made contact over Saarbrücken. By this time my *Gruppe* had already been in violent combat for a quarter of an hour, the sound of which had reverberated in my earphones.
>
> I gained height to weigh up the position. They were Fortresses, with their very impressive defensive armament. These aircraft were better left

alone! Nevertheless, I attacked a bomber to the left of the formation from behind and slightly below. After my third attack, black smoke escaped from its right engine. Little by little, the enemy aircraft became detached from its group, but managed to correct itself 100 m behind, losing 80 m of height in the process — a very uncomfortable position for it, which meant it could no longer count on the protection of its colleagues. It released its bombs, which was the prudent thing to do.

During my fourth attack, the aircraft went out of control. Engulfed in flames, it made three large turns to the left. Seven crewmen bailed out. At 4,000 m, the turns became tighter. The right wing broke off, followed by the left wing. The fuselage continued to dive until it hit the ground in a wood near Darmstadt. Three men were probably still in the aircraft. It was high time for me to land.

Towards 1345 hours, I landed at Mannheim-Sandhofen, where my aircraft could be refuelled and rearmed. I found several of my pilots there, who had also chosen the base as a landing place. We were soon ready for further combat. In spite of that, we were ordered to take off late, and we were not able to attack the *Amis* on their return flight. We had four wounded, but claimed 12 victories.[11]

The reality, however, was that III./JG 1 was officially credited with just two victories on the 17th, one of which was Olejnik's.

Just before midday, Oberst Grabmann had called down the Bf 109s of III./JG 3 from Handorf. The Messerschmitts flew over Maastricht, then Aachen and Mainz, before finally landing at Woensdrecht without locating the bombers. After refuelling, they were airborne again at 1245 hrs to tackle a formation of enemy fighters. But on this occasion the *Jafü*'s guidance failed when the Bf 109s were directed towards a much larger formation of what was described as 'Spitfires' while the bombers were flying some 20 km away without any fighter escort.

In the dogfight that followed, Leutnant Hans Schleef of 7./JG 3 was forced to bail out, as was Unteroffizier Gerhard Pankalla, while Unteroffizier Norbert Geyer crash-landed. Two Bf 109G-6s were destroyed and the third damaged. Dahl fumed over the error committed by *Jafü Holland-Ruhrgebiet*. His mood was probably not helped by the fact that his own Bf 109 had suffered engine failure and he had been forced to land with a damage rating of 45 per cent.[12]

Other units, including elements of JG 2 and II./JG 27 from the south, took up the pursuit and attacked the bombers as far as Regensburg. By the time the B-17s reached the target at Prüfening, seven of their number had gone down. Paradoxically, over the target itself, only a loose formation of some

10–12 Bf 109s attempted to attack the bombers. These aircraft were from the ISS *Regensburg* commanded by Oberleutnant Gerhard Ladegast, a fighter pilot who was recovering from wounds suffered on the Channel Front.

Their lunch interrupted by the order to scramble, the pilots of the ISS *Regensburg* took off and launched a weak attack against the bombers. One of the pilots, Heinz Stemmler, who would score the only success over Regensburg when he fatally damaged a B-17 of the 390th BG, recalled that most of his unit dived away from the bombers without firing. He later commented:

> I think the idea of our little unit was a good one and the pilots were keen, but the difference between test-flying new fighters and operational flying was just too great for us to be effective.

At Wiesbaden-Erbenheim, a combined force of some 50 Bf 109s and Fw 190s drawn from JG 50 and aircraft flown by instructors from the fighter training units JGs 104 and 106 took off to intercept the vanguard of the American formation over western Germany.

JG 50 was commanded by Major Hermann Graf, the acclaimed fighter ace from the Eastern Front and holder of the Diamonds to the Knight's Cross. This small unit had originally been formed at Erbenheim in June 1943 as a high-altitude interceptor *Jagdgeschwader* equipped with just eight Bf 109G-6s. It was planned to equip JG 50 with the Bf 109G-5 fitted with a pressurised cockpit and GM-1/Nitro-oxide boost to enhance performance sufficiently to catch and deal with the threat posed by the RAF's fast, unarmed Mosquito reconnaissance aircraft and fighter-bombers. However, the delivery of this variant had been delayed and, in the meantime, a greater threat had been presented by the American 'heavies'. The high-altitude 'Mosquito-chasers' were, therefore, thrown into the battle. By mid-July, the unit had 12 Bf 109G-5s on strength, and by the end of the month Graf had claimed his first B-17 shot down.

On 17 August JG 50 was credited with 11 bombers shot down, but in the process it lost Unteroffizier Dietrich Barth, who was killed by defensive fire, and Feldwebel Horst Bilfinger after he was bounced by P-47s.

However, the bombers' ordeal was not over. As the B-17s turned south, making for their landing grounds in North Africa, they had to get through German fighter units based in southern Europe. More aircraft from II./JG 51 and I./JG 27 entered the fray from bases in Austria. Exhausted after a flight of 11 hours, the surviving bomber crews finally touched down in Tunisia at Bone, Telerma and Berteaux. They had left 240 airmen in Europe. Nevertheless, 126 bombers were able to unload their deadly cargo on the factories.

SCHWEINFURT

At 1120 hrs, the 230 four-engined bombers of the second wave had taken off. They would also suffer heavy losses. The Luftwaffe struck with more than 300 fighters. One hour after the bombers had left England, elements of I., II. and III./JG 1 and JG 11 intercepted a group of 100 B-17s. The result was carnage – 11 B-17s were claimed by JG 1 and 12 by JG 11, some of whose aircraft fired W.Gr.21 mortars into the bomber formations. II./JG 11's *Kommodore*, Hauptmann Günther Specht, accounted for two of the four B-17s credited to his *Gruppe*. Also downing two B-17s that day was Leutnant Hans Ehlers of 2./JG 1, as well as Berlin-born Knight's Cross-holder Hauptmann Erwin Clausen, *Kommandeur* of I./JG 11. He had shot down no fewer than eight Flying Fortresses the previous month, his record displaying a pattern of double claims for B-17s on three occasions – on 26, 28 and 29 July.

By the time the target had been reached, 21 bombers had been shot down, and a further three fell as the formation turned for home. Demonstrating his capabilities at this time was the colourful *Kommodore* of JG 26, Oberstleutnant Josef Priller. He already had two B-17s to his credit (both scored in June) when he downed his third late in the day as the surviving USAAF bombers from the second wave made their return flight from Schweinfurt. His *Stabsschwarm* and the Fw 190s of Major Wilhelm-Ferdinand Galland's II./JG 26 intercepted them over the German–Belgian border. Attacked head-on, Priller's B-17 erupted in flames and went down north of Liège.

Throughout the day, once again, nightfighters from five *Geschwader*, including instructor crews from NJG 101, were thrown – ill-advisedly – into the action. Fifteen Bf 110s from II./NJG 1 at Saint-Trond, in Belgium, were sent up at various times to pick off straggling bombers, but several of their claims were denied and credited to day fighter pilots operating in the same area at the same time, or they failed to get through the Luftwaffe's stringent verification process. Paradoxically, the crews from NJG 101, flying heavily armed but slow Dornier Do 217s and Bf 110s nearing the end of their operational lives, accounted for six of a total of ten B-17s shot down and credited to the nightfighters that day. For most crews, they represented their first kills.[13]

Even as the bombers crossed the English Channel, where they would enjoy some degree of protection from welcoming Allied escort fighters, aircraft of JG 2 kept the pressure up, chasing many B-17s out to sea, where two more were lost.

In total, 60 Flying Fortresses were shot down and 168 damaged. A good number of these had been claimed as a result of efficient direction from 1. *Jagddivision*'s *Luftnachrichten-Regiment* 201 based at Nordhelle-Ebbe, which was responsible for 27 of the 29 claims made against B-17s as a result of guidance. In each case such claims were logged officially as '*Abschuß einer Boeing in Zusammenarbeit mit 5./Ln.-Regiment* 201' ('Shooting down of a Boeing in cooperation with 5./*Ln.-Regiment* 201), with claims awarded to pilots from JGs I, 26 and 3.[14]

It seems fuel restrictions had impacted III./JG 3's ability to conduct effective operations at this time, for as the *Gruppe*'s war diary noted:

> An urgent solution to the fuel issue is obvious. The *General der Jagdflieger* has ordered 160-litre auxiliary tanks from industry, but they are not available at the moment. In future, therefore, aircraft will be flown with the 300-litre auxiliary tank, but only half-fuelled.[15]

In a mood of equal frustration, Oberstleutnant Priller was moved to register a complaint with Galland's staff about the combat effectiveness of III./JG 1, whose Bf 109s, led by Hauptmann Olejnik, had intercepted the bombers just as the escorting fighters, at the limit of their range, turned back over the Belgian–German border. Olejnik recalled the situation leading to 'interminable discussions'.[16] Priller had noted how JG 1 failed to make a concerted mass attack, preferring only to pick on lone 'stragglers' – they were 'easier' prey. Priller denounced such tactics as those of 'corpse looters'.

The unnerving experience of being a straggler over enemy territory is related here by the crew of 1Lt Helmuth F. Hansen of the 351st BG. Hansen's B-17 *Cherokee Girl* had been flying in the No. 3 position of the second element of the lead squadron heading for Schweinfurt – one of 21 Flying Fortresses from the 351st in action that day with the 2nd Air Task Force. It was *Cherokee Girl*'s 13th mission and, coming under fighter attack, it was to be her unluckiest. The B-17 was:

> ... hit in the No. 3 engine. The engine lost all oil pressure and could not be feathered. With the windmilling propeller, the plane could not maintain speed and was forced to leave the formation. As the bombs were salvoed to reduce weight, a fighter hit the plane with four bursts of 20 mm. The first came through the nose, taking the Plexiglas and nose gun completely away, and exploded under the cockpit among the oxygen bottles, starting a fire. The second burst hit the radio room, starting another fire. The third hit in the waist and the fourth struck the tail, taking away the tail guns and leaving the gunner staring into space.
>
> With the aircraft burning fiercely, Lt Hansen gave the order to bail out, before bailing out of the side window himself. He was on the wing of the plane, but found he could not get his right foot out. Looking

back, he saw that it was caught in his parachute which he had forgotten to take with him! Turning back, he grabbed the parachute, wrapped the harness around his hand and slipped off the wing. When the parachute opened he was left hanging by one foot and one hand. All the crew, except the top turret gunner, managed to get clear before the ship exploded, but all had severe burns.[17]

The Allies also lost three P-47s and three Spitfires. But even the destruction inflicted upon the factories did not compensate for the loss of more than 600 Allied airmen – especially so when the truth was that German production was interrupted for only a few weeks. This time, the German fighter force was able to celebrate a cautious victory, despite the fact that the losses for all participating *Geschwader* amounted to 17 killed and 14 wounded, with 42 aircraft lost. Amongst those killed was Major Wilhelm-Ferdinand 'Wutz' Galland, Adolf Galland's brother and *Kommandeur* of II./JG 26 – a respected formation leader who had 55 victories to his credit, including eight 'heavies'.

The Luftwaffe was not just affected by losses amongst its pilots. Hitler's reaction to Schweinfurt was to scold Göring for allowing such damage to be inflicted against two 'deep' targets. For his part, Göring blamed the lack of a centralised fighter control system and 'skulking' fighter pilots. The day after Schweinfurt, the Luftwaffe Chief of Staff, General der Flieger Hans Jeschonnek, shot himself.

A somewhat shy and sensitive man, Jeschonnek had long carried the burden of blame for the Luftwaffe's apparent lack of capability, particularly since the failure of the Stalingrad airlift. The raid on Schweinfurt (and the British raid on Peenemünde that evening) had been the final straw. Ethically reluctant to resign, and honour-bound not to advise the *Führer* of what he considered to be Göring's shortcomings, his bouts of depression had deepened when Hitler refused his request for a posting to command a *Luftflotte*. There was only one way out. Later, a piece of paper was found by Jeschonnek's body on which the former Chief of Staff had written, 'I can no longer work with the Reichsmarschall. Long live the *Führer!*'

The disturbing fact was that by the early autumn of 1943, Göring had begun to isolate himself from the reality facing 'his' Luftwaffe. Throughout that year, he became increasingly dependent on drugs, and more and more absorbed in expanding his art and jewellery collections. Cracks and strains in the relationship between the Reichsmarschall and his fighter commanders had begun to appear as early as the spring of 1943. So it was, that as the fighter force began to suffer unacceptable levels of attrition during the second half of the year, Göring could only assume that the lack of any decisive victory over the USAAF was down to a lack of fighting spirit on the part of his fighter pilots.

One week after the Schweinfurt raid, on 25 August 1943, the *Generalluftzeugmeister*, Generalfeldmarschall Erhard Milch, told subdued aircraft industry chiefs at a production conference:

> We are firmly convinced that our only chance of maintaining Germany's arms industry and labour lies in our hitting back at the enemy both by day and by night harder than before and above all harder than until a week ago. If we fail and the percentage of enemy aircraft shot down remains at the same level as up to the first half of July, we shall be crushed. I think it is idle to make up long-term plans for U-boats, tanks, aircraft and so on. Programmes of this nature can never be fulfilled; Germany would be brought to her knees.
>
> There is only one remedy. That is for our fighters to hit the enemy so hard, day and night, that he is forced to abandon the policy of destroying our arms production. The chance is there. In the daylight raids on Regensburg and Schweinfurt, our reports give 101 enemy aircraft brought down. We can show proof of these 101. As a maximum of some 400 machines were engaged on these operations, this is, in fact, a loss of 25 per cent. This is the first time since the bombing offensive began that enemy losses have been so high. Our losses are between 60 and 70 aircraft, 27 of them total losses. It is clear from this that the struggle will not be without cost, and that in order to be strong again quickly, we must first make a considerable outlay.
>
> I would further add that after the Regensburg raid, some 120 or more enemy bombers flew to Africa, and in the course of their flight many were probably damaged and forced down. But the enemy, who usually publishes his losses quite openly, was on this particular occasion, extremely reticent. This is proof that the blow went home. So is also the fact that these daylight raids were not continued on the following days. Yesterday, the bombers flew back to Britain, dropping their bombs on Bordeaux, where the weak defences cost them only one aircraft.
>
> Enemy bomber losses in May and June amounted to about 4.4 per cent of the total raiding force. In July there was a slight increase, the figure being 6.4 per cent. It is clear these losses are not enough to deter an enemy as resolute as ours. You know that the defence of our homeland is now in the forefront of our strategy. A large number of single-engined and twin-engined fighter *Gruppen* have been brought back to Germany. In my opinion, this is absurdly late in the day, but at least it has been done. Reichsmarschall Göring, too, is now bringing

pressure to bear in this matter. And as a result of the raid on two of our five largest repair centres, we shall be at least 150 fighters down on last month, even with no further raids being made. We are therefore about 220 fighters short of our actual programme. This is very serious.

Milch concluded chillingly. 'I would tell the front that Germany itself is the real frontline, and that the mass of fighters must go for home defence'.[18]

The Schweinfurt/Regensburg raid had also sent a clear signal to the OKL that the USAAF could reach just about anywhere in the Reich, and that the aircraft and aero engine plants in the south had to be secured. For this purpose, Dahl's III./JG 3 was ordered to relocate from Münster-Handorf to Neuburg an der Donau, from where the *Gruppe* was to provide air defence for the Messerschmitt factories and sub-plants in the Augsburg and Regensburg areas.

The problem was that Neuburg was already fully occupied by nightfighter and school units. Things then bordered on the farcical, with the unit's war diarist recording that in terms of operations and accommodation, conditions there would be 'impossible'. Dahl went to look at Gablingen and Leipheim as possible alternatives. 'Back and forth with the 5. *Jagddivision*', the diarist complained, '– no decision'.

Two days later, the *Gruppe*'s war diary bemoaned, 'No decision yet. The *Kommandeur* will explore [Bad] Wörishofen airfield'. This field was deemed more suitable, but the local military defence chief, who was apparently responsible for it, did not want to release it for occupancy. Only after intervention by the staff of JG 3 and the *General der Jagdflieger* was the field allocated to the *Gruppe* at around 2100 hrs. The *Gruppe* diarist remarked:

> As a result of this confusion over orders and the lack of interest shown by some departments in the welfare of the *Gruppe*, it becomes clear that we are approaching the fifth year of war. Why wasn't the issue of where the *Gruppe* was to be located resolved *before* it was moved?

Eventually, by the early evening of 26 August, the *Gruppe* had moved to Bad Wörishofen, with the airfield's previous occupant, a school unit, having been evicted.[19] One positive was that five 'Y' aircraft were assigned to the *Gruppe*, and the aircraft of 7. *Staffel* had been fitted with W.Gr.21 mortars.[20]

After Schweinfurt, both sides would now be given some breathing space, with the Eighth Air Force resting because it had to. In late August, following a tour of USAAF bases in England, Gen Arnold was left in no doubt that the Eighth lacked strength in B-17s to continue the offensive against Germany at the rate of operations so far.[21] In four missions conducted between

4–14 August, it had lost 148 heavy bombers.[22] The USAAF felt that the Combined Bomber Offensive had to be reassessed if there was to be an *increase* in offensive operations in the coming months. As an immediate step, in early September Arnold cabled the US Army Chief of Staff, Gen George C. Marshall, to request that 200 B-17s be sent to reinforce the Eighth in addition to the 217 already assigned.

For the Luftwaffe, the battering taken by the American bombers provided a much-needed respite. But that respite would be brief, and when it was over, the whirlwind that was coming would be more powerful and destructive than ever before.

10

Bitter Harvest

Schweinfurt provided the Luftwaffe with valuable lessons for future tactical deployment, and on 3 September 1943, Generalmajor Adolf Galland hurriedly issued revised directives to every fighter *Staffel* engaged in the defence of the Reich. Paramount in these new directives was the order for units to engage only *one* enemy wave of attack 'continuously' with 'the mass of all fighter units', and if possible to direct such an attack against the bomber incursion which appeared to be penetrating the deepest into German airspace.

But Galland recognised that there were shortcomings: even in mid- to late 1943, there was an insufficient number of fighter-ready airfields in the Reich, and he emphasised the need for early cooperation between neighbouring and rear *Jagddivsionen*. Often, a formation taking off from one divisional area was passed over to the control of another division only with some difficulty. Upon landing, a unit would find itself on an unfamiliar airfield, far from its home base, with no fighter fuel allocation, ammunition or repair facilities.

Galland worked with the *Luftwaffenbefehlshaber Mitte*, the *Luftgaue*, the *Jagddivisionen* and *Jafüs* to develop a network of airfields in western Germany, the Netherlands, Belgium and northern France where fighters could land, refuel and take off for second missions. These fields would be stocked with the correct types of fuel and ammunition, contain situation and weather rooms, refreshment and medical facilities and a direct telephone link to the home *Jagddivision*.[1]

A new fighter control commentary that spanned the entire German homeland was established known as the *Reichsjägerwelle* (Reichs Fighter Band) from which single- and twin-engined fighter formations not benefitting from 'Y'-*Verfahren* could be vectored. All day fighters, nightfighters operating in daylight and fighters from the *Industrie* units would have to remain continually tuned into the *Reichsjägerwelle* as an aid to understanding the wider *Luftlage* and for guidance. Twin-engined Bf 110 and Ju 88

Fühlungshalter (observation aircraft) were to shadow enemy formations and provide running commentaries on their strength, location, altitude and control.

'Upon landing on strange airfields', Galland wrote, 'the senior officer fighter pilot must immediately combine all fighter pilots present into one fighter formation, regardless of what units they belong to, and then attend to the quickest serviceability of the aircraft. Orders should be received from the area *Jagdführer*, who is to be kept informed as to unit strengths. If communication with the *Jagdführer* is not possible, the formation leader should act on his own authority. After take-off, he will use as a call sign the name of the airfield. The formation can only be dissolved on order of the *Jagdführer*, whereupon released pilots can then be turned over to their regular units'.

In the wake of Schweinfurt, Galland ordered JG 3 to southern Germany and JG 27 to the Vienna area, while ZG 26 was based in northern Germany and ZG 76 in the south.[2]

Acting on a request from the OKL, it was at this point that Galland also signalled a fundamental change in the tactical doctrine established the previous year. With immediate effect, all attacks mounted against heavy bombers were to be made from the rear, rather than by a frontal pass. This was chiefly because it was felt that a large percentage of the young, inexperienced pilots now filling the ranks of the *Jagdgeschwader* operating in the defence of the Reich and over the West encountered considerable difficulty in undertaking the latter type of attack. The high combined closing speed of the frontal pass demanded great skill in gunnery, range estimation and flying control. The slightest evasive action on the part of the bombers made this type of attack even more difficult. In contrast, evasive action taken against attacks from the rear was thought to be ineffective. Galland instructed that:

> Every fighter *Gruppe* and *Staffel* is to engage one and the same bomber formation. If the formation jettisons its bombs or is completely broken up, it is to be left alone and the next formation flying within visible range is to be attacked.
>
> All unit leaders from *Schwarmführer* up are to be identified in the air by white rudders. Single fighters and separated *Rotten* are to form up on these aircraft immediately, regardless of which formation they belong to. The leader of the *Schwarm* or larger unit thus formed must attack the bomber formation again without delay.
>
> The purpose of the first attack is to break up the enemy formation. The attack is to be executed in such a way that fighters go in close

together in *Schwärme*, with little interval between *Schwärme*, one after the other against the same formation. The exit, the direction of which is to be ordered before the attack, must allow for the quick reassembly of the entire fighter formation. Repeat attacks should be made using as many fighters as possible.

The head-on attack is, from now on, to be the exception, and is to be flown in only exceptionally favourable circumstances and by formations especially successful in it. As the standard method of attack, the attack from the rear with a small angle of approach is now ordered.

The closing up to effective range is to be supervised by all formation leaders; pilots who, without adequate reason, do not close up to the ordered minimum range are to be court-martialled for cowardice in the face of the enemy.

From now on, only bombers in formation are to be attacked (without regard of whether they are on the way to the target or on the way out). Only when the entire bomber formation has been broken up or when there is no further possibility of getting to the formation, are separated or damaged bombers flying alone to be destroyed. Aircraft carrying W.Gr.21 mortars are permitted after discharge of their mortars to destroy lone bombers separated from their formations. *Industrieschutzschwärme* and *Rotten*, nightfighters, as well as small operational elements from training units, may attack lone bombers separated from their formations as long as there is no possibility for them to join up into a larger formation either on the ground or in the air.

Formation leaders and fighter pilots who disobey these orders are to be court-martialled for military disobedience with serious consequences for the safety of the Reich.

Fire will be opened during frontal attacks at a maximum range of 730 m, and in all attacks at 365 m. The goal of every attack is one aircraft. Aiming at the centre of a bomber formation or spraying the whole formation with bullets never results in success. Attacks from an angle of approach greater than 30 degrees are ineffective. Combat will be continued even in the strongest Flak fire and in Flak zones.[3]

Galland's switch from head-on to rear-mounted attacks was timely. September 1943 saw the appearance of the new B-17G fitted with a Bendix twin-0.50-in. gun 'chin' turret which provided the Flying Fortress with the vital forward defensive armament it needed to counter frontally mounted attacks.

Just how effective rear attacks would be with W.Gr.21 mortars remained to be seen, but Hauptmann Georg Schröder, a former *Kommandeur* of

II./JG 2, told fellow Luftwaffe officers while in Allied captivity in 1945 that he recalled seeing a *Gruppe* of JG 27 making a mass rear attack on a *Viermot* formation:

> They fired from 1,200 m with rockets ('*Nebelwerfer*') [sic] – the whole *Gruppe*, but they used to fly in really close formation. Then the stream of fire came out, a few bombers went spinning down immediately, and in that way the formation was broken and then they could attack single aircraft perfectly calmly.[4]

During the summer, Galland had ordered mortars to be fitted to all Bf 110s and Me 410s assigned to *Jafü Deutsche Bucht*, and now twin-engined units based elsewhere had started to use the weapon. However, to deploy the *Zerstörer* effectively required a situation where they could operate beyond the range of American escort fighters and exclusively against the *Viermots*. If this could be achieved, then any lack of manoeuvrability would not be compromised by the addition of heavier armament.

E.Kdo 25 tested a modified *Revi* C/12 D reflex gunsight on an Fw 190 which was intended to offer greater accuracy when targeting the weapon. The sight incorporated an additional translucent mirror that provided a double image of the target, each of the images presented one above the other when the pilot took his aim. When both overlapped, the pilot was at the correct range and he could fire the mortars.[5]

One experimental installation of February 1944 comprised a large, revolving battery of six 21 cm mortar tubes in the manner of a Gatling gun or rotary cannon built into the lower nose of an Me 410. However, when fired, the aircraft sustained severe damage and the idea was abandoned. Nevertheless, with such weapons, a formation of bombers could be fired at and broken up from beyond its effective zone of defence. In conformity with Galland's directive, once a formation had been successfully broken up and scattered, individual bombers could be attacked and destroyed.

Kampfgeschwader (KG) 51's I. *Gruppe*, a bomber unit based at Illesheim, had somewhat optimistically converted to the Me 410 from the Ju 88. The *Gruppe* flew its first missions against bombers on 6 September when it sent up seven mortar-armed Me 410s to intercept a raid by 338 B-17s of the Eighth Air Force targeting aircraft component factories in Stuttgart. In heavy cloud, the bombers became separated and scattered, creating ideal circumstances in which the *Zerstörer* could operate. This may have been the case, but the crews of KG 51 still found their task daunting as they engaged the second wave of bombers at 5,000 m, firing their mortars in shallow, curved trajectories.

Despite the blast wave, the bombers flew on, and moments later the Me 410s were amongst them, drawing their defensive fire. The aircraft of Leutnant Eberhard Winkel of 1. *Staffel* had one of its engines shot out. He dived away from the enemy formation, emergency jettisoning the fuel from the reserve tank, followed by the remaining ammunition. By doing this Winkel retained altitude and managed to land back at Illesheim on one engine. Overall, I./KG 51's action had been a disaster, the *Gruppe*'s losses equalling the number of bombers shot down.

Another unit to engage the bombers that day was Hauptmann Walther Dahl's III./JG 3, which was scrambled from Neuburg at 1030 hrs and directed by *Jafü Holland-Ruhrgebiet* towards Mannheim with 25 Bf 109G-6s at 8,000 m. As the Messerschmitts, some of them probably carrying W.Gr.21 mortars, turned south towards Stuttgart, the bombers were sighted and the fighters went in to attack. Within 30 minutes, the *Gruppe* claimed, initially, four B-17s shot down, although after verification this figure was later revised to two, and eight *Herausschüsse*. Of the eight successful pilots, Dahl himself was awarded one in each category.

Following the mission, the unit recorded in its war diary, 'This successful attack was made from above and behind at very high speed!'[6] This was what Galland wanted to see.

Thick cloud had hampered the bombing operation from the start and many Flying Fortresses failed to bomb, 233 of them opting for targets of opportunity on their return leg. As a result of disorganisation and separation, 45 B-17s were lost, amounting to 16 per cent of the total force in one of the costliest missions so far. More than 300 crew were posted missing.

Verification of an aerial victory for a German pilot was not a foregone conclusion and could often be a protracted process, especially given the chaotic and super-fast nature of air combat, as well as the numbers of aircraft in the sky in a large air battle.

Oberfeldwebel Alfred Surau of 9./JG 3 was one of III. *Gruppe*'s 'old hares', and he enjoyed the reputation of being its highest scoring NCO pilot, his first victory being credited in southern Russia in February 1943. On 6 September he took off from Neuburg leading a *Schwarm* of Bf 109s:

> We met the enemy bomber formation of Boeing Fortress IIs at around 7,500 m altitude in the Stuttgart area and immediately attacked. Mounting my first attack from the front, I scored effective hits on the cockpit and the inner starboard engine. Following this attack, I had to

pull away under the enemy aircraft and, as a result, I received hits in the propeller and wing surfaces. As I pulled up, I saw how the Boeing I fired at was far behind the formation in a shallow dive, trailing a long white plume of smoke. Because of clouds, further observation was not possible.[7]

This, theoretically, represented Surau's 42nd victory. But soon after he returned to Neuburg to claim both this and another B-17 to add to his personal tally, the official verification process undertaken by the *Abschusskommission* (literally 'Shoot-down Commission') commenced. Surviving documentation presents a curious state of affairs. Admittedly, both Surau and another pilot of 9./JG 3 flying in his *Schwarm*, Leutnant Ekkehard Tichy, were unable to observe the B-17 to go down because of the cloud, but they both described the Flying Fortress as being damaged, losing height and trailing smoke. This was enough to award a *Herausschuss*. Surau's *Staffelkapitän*, Hauptmann Wilhelm Lemke, and Dahl, both supported his claim based on the combat and witness reports.

But for some reason a claim made by an Unteroffizier Busch, a nightfighter instructor with 9./NJG 101 based at Kitzingen, entered the picture for a claim over a B-17 shot down at Romanshorn, in Switzerland, on the shore of the Bodensee. It appears that a question mark then lay over the validity of Surau's claim. How Busch's claim could be interpreted as being connected to Surau's is not known, but from surviving records, as late as 14 November, Generalleutnant Schwabedissen at 7. *Jagddivision* was still attempting to get Surau's victory ratified.

However, by this time, Alfred Surau was dead. He had been shot down in aerial combat during the Eighth Air Force's second attack on Schweinfurt on 14 October when his Bf 109 was hit by return fire from a B-17. Surau managed to bail out, but died of his wounds later that same day, not knowing his final victory tally.

After Schweinfurt, Reichsmarschall Hermann Göring wanted a reorganisation of the Luftwaffe's fighter defence command structure. This was something that was overdue, and in early September Generalmajor Josef Schmid, a Bavarian known as 'Beppo', replaced General der Flieger Josef Kammhuber as commander of XII. *Fliegerkorps*. The reality was that although, nominally, XII. *Fliegerkorps* oversaw all fighter operations over the Reich and areas of northwest Europe, control of day fighters had been taken over by the *Korps'* five *Jagddivisionen* (1–5) and *Jagdführers*

(*Holland-Ruhrgebiet*, *Deutsche Bucht* and *Berlin-Mitteldeutschland*), while the *Korps* handled nightfighter operations.

Upon his brief appointment to XII. *Fliegerkorps*, and in accordance with Göring's wishes, the first thing Schmid did was to press for a new centralised command for the *Reichsluftverteidigung* (Aerial Defence of the Reich). His path was clear, and on 15 September a new I. *Jagdkorps* (Fighter Corps) was created, with Schmid as commander. The mission of the *Jagdkorps* was the 'direction of day- and nightfighter forces and activities in the northern area of Germany, Holland and northern Belgium'.[8] It set up its headquarters at the Villa de Breul, an elegant red brick manor house set amidst parkland with a moat and a lake between Zeist and Driebergen, to the east of Utrecht in the Netherlands, which had previously been used by Kammhuber and XII. *Fliegerkorps*.

In some ways Schmid was a curious choice, but not entirely surprising. Curious, because he was not an airman and lacked experience and understanding in the command of fighter aircraft, and was therefore arguably the wrong man to lead a fighter corps. Not surprising, because what he lacked in air warfare acumen he made up for in subservience and cronyism – especially to his master, Göring, to whom he was a confidant.

Schmid was born at Göggingen, near Augsburg, in 1901. His father owned a brickworks. By the time he was 18, young Josef's politics were clear, and he joined the right wing *Freikorps* movement initially in the Munich area, but later he was involved in tackling Communist unrest in the Ruhr, which meant taking part in street brawls and using whatever means were needed to suppress political opposition. An early member of the Nazi Party, he was involved in the infamous 'Beer Hall Putsch' of November 1923 and was awarded the Party's Blood Order for his troubles. Subsequently, he joined the Reichswehr and trained as an infantryman.

Schmid was commissioned as a Leutnant in December 1924 and thereafter his career progressed steadily, if unremarkably, culminating with a place at the *Kriegsakademie* in Berlin in October 1933. He transferred to the Luftwaffe in July 1935, assigned to the Operations Department of the Luftwaffe General Staff, and by April 1939, with the rank of Oberstleutnant and presumably on the basis of what he had studied at the Academy, Schmid was appointed head of 5. *Abteilung* of the Luftwaffe General Staff, and thus in charge of Luftwaffe Intelligence.

In this, Schmid proved to be out of his depth, underestimating the industrial capabilities and strengths of foreign powers such as Britain, Soviet Russia and the USA. This was a naïve and critical failing – particularly at the time of Luftwaffe operations against Britain in 1940 and then during Operation *Barbarossa* in the summer of the following year, when accurate intelligence was vital to German success.

As far as Generalfeldmarschall Erhard Milch was concerned, Schmid 'wasn't an airman and didn't understand the significance of the reports he received'. But he was protected by Göring, and he clung on in Intelligence until November 1942 when, finally, with a wholly undistinguished record, he was packed off to lead *Kampfgruppe Schmid,* a ground combat command assigned to the new *Division Hermann Göring* in Tunisia. Promoted to Generalmajor, Schmid commanded this Luftwaffe field division in North Africa until May 1943 when, with Göring's assistance, he was evacuated by air from Tunisia just ahead of the German collapse because he apparently knew secret information that would have been of value to the Allies.

After returning to Germany, he was promptly awarded the Knight's Cross. Oberst Hans-Joachim 'Hajo' Herrmann, an energetic and innovative Luftwaffe bomber ace who, in mid-1943, would become the driving force behind a new form of nightfighting tactics, met Schmid in 1942. He recalled:

> Some malicious tongues had said that we should have let the Americans have him because he would have told them as big a pack of lies as he had previously told his own leaders. The latter assertion I would have taken with a pinch of salt. I found him to be interested, ready to learn and of a practical turn of mind.[9]

After a few months in an 'advisory' staff capacity at the RLM, Schmid was posted to lead I. *Jagdkorps.* The only qualification he seems to have had for this appointment was that back in 1937 he had authored a paper on the employment of fighter aircraft.[10] In any case, this was the man that Göring entrusted with the fighter defence of the German homeland.

The establishment of I. *Jagdkorps* caused a simultaneous reorganisation and redesignations of the area fighter commands. As of 15 September, 4. *Jagddivision* in Berlin under Generalmajor Joachim-Friedrich Huth became 1. *Jagddivision.* The existing 1. *Jagddivision* at Deelen under von Döring became 3.*Jagddivision,* while 2. *Jagddivision* at Stade remained unchanged. In southern Germany, 5. *Jagddivision* under Schwabedissen became a new 7. *Jagddivision.* These divisional commanders were far more qualified for their tasks than was Schmid.

On 18 September 1943 Schmid called von Döring, Huth and Oberst Karl Hentschel, an experienced fighter staff officer who was destined to take command of 3. *Jagddivision,* for a meeting at the Villa de Breul. A range of fundamentals were discussed. Firstly, to avoid bomb damage, Schmid instructed that fighters parked on airfields should be dispersed more widely and, where possible, hangars should be moved and/or built further from core airfield areas. Secondly, aircraft tasked with 'shadowing' enemy bomber formations in one divisional area (which were often nightfighters or reconnaissance aircraft) should be grouped together under one *Staffelkapitän*, and, if possible, he should be an officer from the reconnaissance units. Thirdly, if possible, those *Gruppen* which had been deployed for longer periods of time on operations should be rotated with *Gruppen* based in 'rear' or 'less demanding' areas, for example, those in southern Germany.

Another issue was that the day fighter units employed on home defence were becoming critically short of ground personnel, and so it was agreed that the possibility of using personnel from the nightfighter units should be investigated. However, it was recognised that this should not be seen as a signal for a permanent reinforcement of the day fighter units, but rather a 'lending' from the *Nachtjagd*, whose personnel had specialist skills that were required by their own units.

Closer to home, Göring had expressed his dissatisfaction to Schmid over the fact that, as he saw it, *Jagdkorps* and *Jagddivision* staffs employed 'too many young people'. He wanted to see older personnel in the command centres so that younger personnel could be released for frontline service.[11]

Schmid also commented that attention should paid to stricter discipline among *Geschwader* officers. According to the minutes of the meeting, 'Criticism of organisational matters and matters that have nothing to do with flying and combat operations must be prevented. However, suggestions for improvements to attack tactics, technical matters etc. are accepted at all times'.[12] This last note in the minutes has resonance. Just four days after the meeting at the Villa de Breul, Galland circulated details of a proposal he had received from Major Hans-Günther von Kornatzki, an officer on the Staff of Oberst Max-Josef Ibel, the *Höherer Jagdfliegerführer West* based at Chantilly, to the north of Paris.

Von Kornatzki, the son of a general, was a fighter man who had completed his flying training in April 1934. He was also a widower, having married a secretary on Göring's personal staff who was killed during an air raid on Berlin. It may have been that the loss of his wife under such circumstances had hardened von Kornatzki's character and prompted him to devise more radical ways with which to fight back against the Allied 'terror bombers'. But von Kornatzki was also a seriously minded tactical innovator.

In the latter half of 1943, at Göring's personal request, von Kornatzki was seconded to E.Kdo 25 at Achmer, where he was able to discuss anti-*Viermot* tactics and weapons with Hauptmann Horst Geyer and other specialist officers. He was provided with a twin-engined 'hack' in which he toured fighter airfields in the I. *Jagdkorps* area, where he interviewed both fighter unit commanders and junior pilots about their experiences in combatting enemy bombers and listened to their suggestions regarding tactics. He also watched reels of gun camera films and studied pilots' combat reports in which they described their attacks on *Viermots*.

Resulting from his research, von Kornatzki concluded that during a rearward attack against an American bomber formation, a German fighter was potentially exposed to the defensive fire of more than 40 0.50-in. machine guns, resulting in only the slimmest chance of escaping damage during attack. Under such circumstances, it was even less likely that a lone fighter could bring down a bomber.

However, if a whole *Gruppe* of heavily armed and armoured fighters – some 30 aircraft – could position itself for an attack at close range, the bomber gunners would be forced to disperse and weaken their fire, allowing individual fighters greater opportunity to close in, avoid damage and thus increase the prospect of shooting a bomber down. The loss of speed and manoeuvrability incurred by the additional armament and armour carried by such '*Sturmjäger*' (assault fighters) would be countered by the presence of two regular fighter *Gruppen* which would keep any enemy escort at bay.

In September von Kornatzki met with Galland to propose adopting such tactics, but additionally he incorporated a radical new aspect – if necessary, and as a last-ditch resort, in instances where pilots were close enough and if their ammunition had been expended, a bomber could be *rammed* in order to bring it down. He further proposed that a smaller unit of *Staffel* size, rather than the proposed *Gruppe*, be established to train up volunteer pilots who would test and evaluate the new method under operational conditions.

Galland was in two minds. While he believed, rightly, that every fighter that actually 'rammed' a bomber could be assumed to be a complete loss, theoretically, it could still land or belly-land and its pilot survive to fight another day. On the other hand, it could not be guaranteed that every ramming would lead to the complete destruction of a bomber. However, it seems von Kornatzki was confident, and he assured the *General der Jagdflieger* that, 'Sufficient numbers of older fighter pilots will volunteer to form a full *Staffel*. Younger pilots, who are based in the west of the Reich and who have lost property and, in some cases, family members in bombing raids, will also volunteer'.

Galland knew that von Kornatzki had Göring's ear and that, ultimately, it would be futile not to comply. On 22 September he circulated a memo to the highest levels of Luftwaffe command:

A proposal has been made to the *General der Jagdflieger* to have enemy 4-engined bombers rammed by volunteer pilots who have not been significantly deployed in this war and who, due to their age, fitness or mobility, are unlikely to be used as full fighter pilots in the future. The spokesman for this proposal is Major von Kornatzki of the *Höherer Jagdfliegerführer West*.

The *General der Jagdflieger* is of the opinion that every enemy 4-engined bomber must fall if it is fired at from close range with a specially armoured aircraft and makes the following suggestion:

1. Establish a specialist *Staffel*, which will be called a *Sturmstaffel*.
2. Attack enemy 4-engined bombers with specially armoured fighters with heavy-calibre on-board weapons at very close range.
3. Ramming as a second option if fire from on-board weapons does not reach the target.

Galland intended that as a first step, two Fw 190s would be trial-fitted with armour plate at the former Arado factory airfield at Sagan-Küpper in Silesia in accordance with appropriate technical guidance issued by the *Kommando der Erprobungsstellen*. Each Focke-Wulf would have an armoured bulkhead installed in the front of the cockpit, armoured side panels screwed on to the existing panels beneath the cockpit and armoured glass panels fitted to the side panels of the glazed canopy. The Sagan-Küpper facility could cut and re-fit armour plate from the dismantling and disassembly plant there.

Providing this process went smoothly, a '*Sturmstaffel*' (assault squadron) of 16 such aircraft would be established, with the remaining aircraft fitted with armour and armament at the unit's airfield by a specialist *Kommando*.[13] For the time being, there the idea rested while Galland's staff set about scouring operational units and the training schools for suitable pilot candidates.

Away to the west, in France, Generalfeldmarschall Hugo Sperrle retained control over his *Luftflotte* 3, but, commencing 15 September, he was compelled to accept the formation of a new II. *Jagdkorps* which would operate along a similar operational brief to Schmid's I. *Jagdkorps* at Zeist. The new unit was founded from the Staff of Ibel's *Höherer Jagdfliegerführer West*, and as such it continued to be based at Chantilly in a purpose-built bunker codenamed *Komet* in the grounds of the Château des Fontaines. It was commanded by Generalmajor Werner Junck, a very experienced and competent civil and military aviator who, in 1941, had served briefly as the head of the Luftwaffe's ill-fated mission to Iraq.

Created in September 1943 as part of the Luftwaffe's defensive infrastructure in France and subordinate to II. *Jagdkorps* until June 1944 was *Jafü* 5 based at Bernay, to the east of Caen and Le Havre. The mission of the *Jafü* was to coordinate fighter defence against Allied bombers that might head across northern France for targets in southern Germany and western Austria. Work commenced on its bunker HQ, known as *Brutus*, in August 1943, and excavations went down to a depth of some ten metres to allow for a fully underground operations room.

Appointed as *Jäfu* 5 was Oberst Gordon Gollob, a former *Kommodore* of JG 77 and the third recipient of the Diamonds to the Knight's Cross, awarded on 30 August 1942 after his 150th aerial victory, all but six of which had been scored in Russia. Gollob was credited with multiple kills on one day on several occasions. By the end of that month, he was the leading Luftwaffe fighter ace, and it is believed he was withdrawn from combat operations by Hitler who wanted to protect such a talismanic propaganda figure. He was sent to France.

As a stern operational commander as well as an area fighter commander, Gollob oversaw a 'tight ship'. By January 1944, *Jafü* 5 received plotting information from 12 radar sites located along the Channel coast, in Normandy, on the Channel Islands and as far west as Saint-Malo.

In the '*Führungsraum*' (Command Room) at *Brutus*, which was the *Jafü*'s main nerve centre, Gollob and his staff overlooked three vertical maps on which, as with the map at *Sokrates*, 20 operators 'placed' illuminated plots denoting friendly and enemy aircraft on the reverse sides, using a large number of electric lamp sockets. To the left was a map displaying weather fronts and in the centre was the main operational map, measuring some four metres by three metres and covering an area from London to Le Mans and from Land's End to the Belgian frontier. The map to the right showed readiness levels of friendly aircraft and their locations.

During operations, Gollob sat at the *Führungstich* (Command Desk) together with his Operations Officer and a Feldwebel who manned a FuG 16 on the JG 2 frequency, conveying instructions to airborne fighters. On the desk were direct-line telephones to the fighter airfields and, according to a former member of his staff later captured by the Allies, an internal Tannoy through which 'Gollob could tear strips off any offending plotter'.

A team of 15 female auxiliaries, each with her own telephone, worked in an adjacent room, receiving messages from observation posts and other locations on movements of friendly aircraft, and this data was relayed to the *Führungsraum*. What the captured man described as the '*Jafü*'s Palace' was located at one end of the bunker. It was a small room where Gollob 'retired to his sanctum, put his feet up on the desk and let his hair down'.

However, by the end of January 1944, work had still to be completed on the bunker, and it effectively ceased at this point because the construction workers were needed elsewhere.[14] *Jafü* 5 was disbanded at the beginning of July 1944.

On 27 September, the Eighth despatched a force of 246 B-17s to attack port facilities at Emden. Despite cloud and poor visibility, for the first time the bombers were led by four Flying Fortresses equipped with the British H2S (US designation, H2X) blind-bombing radar which aided the observation of large geographic features through cloud. Their inward flight took them into a defensive zone covered by elements of JGs 1 and 11 and II./JG 3, and as such, 2. *Jagddivision* sent up just about everything it had.

The Fw 190s of I./JG 1 took off from Deelen at 1030 hrs and were the first fighters to engage the bombers, which offered a ferocious defence. Oberleutnant Georg Schott, *Staffelkapitän* of 1./JG 1 and a veteran of the Spanish Civil War with 16 victories, was hit by defensive fire. His body was found in a dinghy washed ashore on the island of Sylt three weeks later.

At 1040 hrs in the III./ZG 26 operations room at Plantlünne, the telephone link from *Sokrates* jangled. The operations officer at Stade gave the warning that American bombers were at 3,000 m over Lingen, and he told the *Gruppe* to get its aircraft into the air. The unit was to rendezvous with III./ZG 1, based at Vörden, which had not long returned to the Reich and was re-equipping with new Me 210s and Me 410s. Rendezvous of the two *Gruppen* was to take place over Lingen. If, together, they fired salvos of mortars into the American formation, they would break it up, thus assisting the single-engined fighters.

Five minutes later, 37 mortar-carrying Bf 110G-2 *Zerstörer* commenced their take-off to intercept led by Hauptmann Schulze-Dickow, but the process was delayed as a result of the twin-engined Messerschmitts' Daimler-Benz DB 605 engines failing to start properly. As a result, groundcrews had to rush out to the runway and hand crank them into life, for only four generator carts were available to the *Gruppe*. A frustrated Schulze-Dickow waited on the ground as his aircraft were re-started one by one. The minutes ticked by. The Bf 110s eventually took off, but assembly was complicated by low cloud, and this caused a further delay. A slow climb only exacerbated the situation.

III./ZG 1 would subsequently wait in vain for the enemy bombers. Confusing instructions and poor communication with 2. *Jagddivision* also plagued III./ZG 26's operation. At one point Stade informed the *Zerstörer* that there were '80 enemy fighters in the Emden area' and ordered the *Gruppe* to climb to 7,500 m. Once that altitude had been reached, Stade asked, 'Do you see enemy fighters?' From that point, communication with the fighter controller became difficult to comprehend and intercom communication aboard Schulze-Dickow's Bf 110 also failed, so he was unable to talk with his radio operator. The *Kommandeur* requested Stade for a home course for his aircraft, and the *Gruppe* followed him on the assumption that the mission was over. The *Gruppe* landed back at Plantlünne at 1215 hrs, having failed to engage the enemy.[15] It had not been an auspicious start to operations by III./ZG 26.

At 1050 hrs, the Bf 109s of Hauptmann Günther Specht's II./JG 11 were scrambled by *Jafü Deutsche Bucht* to intercept the bombers, and under guidance from 2. *Jagddivision*'s 5. *Funkleit-Kompanie* of *Luftnachrichten-Regiment* 202 based at the '*Johannisbeere*' radar station at Barkholt, assembled to the southwest of the approaching bomber stream. At the same time, the Fw 190s of II./JG 1 took off from Rheine. At around 1100 hrs, II./JG 11, approaching from Oldenburg, sighted the bombers. On its first attack, Oberleutnant Heinz Knoke's 5. *Staffel* fired W.Gr.21 mortars into the *Pulk* and two B-17s were seen to go down. However, the *Jagdflieger* were about to experience an unpleasant surprise.

Equipped for the first time with British-made 108-gallon 'paper' drop tanks that gave the P-47 an endurance of three hours, Thunderbolts from VIII Fighter Command's 4th, 56th, 78th and 353rd FGs were now able to escort the bombers all the way to Emden – for the first time a target inside the Reich. The American fighters surprised the Focke-Wulfs of II./JG 11, and a savage 15-minute aerial battle ensued, during which the *Gruppe* lost no fewer than 15 aircraft from across its three *Staffeln*.

Despite this setback, seven B-17s were claimed shot down in 12 minutes. This had been achieved through smooth cooperation with the operators of 5. *Funkleit-Kompanie*, who guided several pilots of I. and II./JG 11 towards their quarry.[16] Another Flying Fortress was claimed as a *Herausschuss*. The reality, however, was that because of the escort's presence, only three per cent of the bombers failed to return. There was some slight encouragement for the defenders when Oberleutnant Knoke claimed one of the Thunderbolts.

Just as the Fw 190s of I./JG 1 were taking off to engage the bombers, Generalmajor Schmid was in Döberitz visiting the *Gefechtsstand* of Generalmajor Huth's 4. *Jagddivision*, after which he flew to Stade with

Huth, to where he had summoned his divisional and day- and nightfighter *Geschwaderkommodoren* for a high-level meeting within the netting-draped, grey concrete walls of the *Sokrates* bunker.

It was an illustrious gathering. Joining Huth at command and control level was Generalleutnant Kurt-Bertram von Döring, Oberst Karl Hentschel and Oberst Walter Grabmann, while from France came Oberstleutnant Walter Oesau, an ace with a stellar reputation and a recipient of the Knight's Cross with Oak Leaves and Swords – only the third man to receive that decoration (for his 80th victory).

Oesau was probably present on account of the fact that he was one of the Luftwaffe's early anti-*Viermot* specialists, having claimed an RAF Lancaster in daylight over France on 17 April 1942 as his first four-engined victory – a relatively rare occurrence given RAF Bomber Command's nocturnal bombing policy. It had been achieved at a time when Oesau was, theoretically, 'banned' from flying because his exemplary record deemed him to be too valuable. He got around this by claiming that at the time he had happened to be on a routine 'test flight'. When he arrived for the meeting at Stade, Oesau had 114 victories to his credit.

Representing the day fighter arm alongside Oesau was Oberstleutnant Hans 'Fips' Philipp, *Kommodore* of JG 1, previously *Kommandeur* of I./JG 54 and a renowned Eastern Front *Experte* who had been only the second pilot to achieve 200 victories. He had been awarded the Swords on 12 March 1942 for his 82nd victory. Accompanying Philipp was Major Anton Mader, another Knight's Cross-holder and a former *Kommandeur* of II./JG 77 on the Eastern Front and in North Africa, who now led the Reich defence unit JG 11 based at Jever and Husum. Mader had 66 victories, including three B-17s. Also present was the *Kommodore* of JG 3, Knight's Cross-holder, Oberst Wolf-Dietrich Wilcke with 153 victories to his name. Four men with hundreds of aerial daylight kills between them.

Major Karl Boehm-Tettelbach, a former instructor pilot and staff officer who was overseeing the reforming of ZG 26 equipped with mortar-firing Bf 110s, also attended, while from the nightfighters came Major Werner Streib, *Kommodore* of NJG 1, Major Helmut Lent, *Kommodore* of NJG 3 and Major Günther Radusch, *Kommodore* of NJG 5 – all Knight's Cross holders and aces with, collectively, around 180 nocturnal kills to their names. In addition, the *Korps'* Operations Officer, Oberstleutnant i.G. Heinrich Wittmer, along with Major i.G. Hans Busold and Major i.G Schaller, the Operations Officers for 2. and 4. *Jagddivisionen*, respectively, were also present.

But if the attendees believed that this meeting was to achieve anything useful, they were probably disappointed. After a brief welcome, it appears as if Schmid 'lectured' the combat-experienced unit commanders on his methods of command and what he expected from his subordinates from his senior staff down to lower-ranking personnel. In his opinion, a staff was there to lead and to support operational personnel, but equally the operational personnel were there to fight, and there should be no criticism of the organisational leadership, and in this, presumably, Schmid was referring to the leadership of I. *Jagdkorps*. On a more practical level, he stressed the urgency of expanding airfields and, in particular, setting in place security measures against the risk of enemy parachutists.

Schmid then opened up the discussion. In terms of Reich air defence, the attendees spoke of a sense of military inferiority balanced with a sense of moral superiority arising from having to defend their own homeland. More aircraft were needed for the task, and those that they had suffered from technical shortcomings and weaknesses. There were also problems with armament.

Schmid responded that there would be improvement in all areas by the spring of 1944, but that debate over historical, technical and organisational deficiencies were pointless and should be gone over only after the war. When it came to daylight fighter operations, it seems that the suggestions of officers like von Kornatzki were gaining traction. Schmid advised those present that, as far as Göring was concerned, the emphasis was on destroying bomber formations by deploying mass formations of fighters in *Gruppe* and even *Geschwader* strength and with 'determination', if necessary to the point of '*Selbtsaufopferung*' – self-sacrifice.[17] Quite how this went down with the likes of Oesau, Phillip, Lent and Streib is not known.

Regardless, from surviving documentation it seems that by 29 September Schmid had co-opted Oesau onto the *Generalkommando* of I. *Jagdkorps*. He was present in that capacity at a further meeting chaired by Schmid at Zeist that day, along with Döring, Huth and Busold. Clearly, recent Allied air activity and the appearance of P-47s within the Reich had intensified the state of alarm within the Reich defence leadership. As the minutes from the meeting at Zeist noted:

> Assessment of the situation – the enemy has attempted to smash up our day fighter units in France and to force the withdrawal of day fighter units from the Reich and from Holland. Since no units have been withdrawn, it is assumed that, in the future, the enemy will attempt to destroy our fighters and ground organisation in Holland and northwest Germany.
>
> With reference to the range of the Thunderbolt. According to previous findings, its range takes it up to Aurich-Rheine and the

Ruhr area, including Cologne and Liège. Enemy fighters cannot be left unchallenged in this area. For this reason, three fighter *Gruppen* will be relocated and tasked with engaging in fighter-to-fighter combat wherever possible.[18]

On 4 October, 155 B-17s with strong P-47 escort were assigned the cities of Frankfurt and Wiesbaden as targets. German radar picked up the bombers at 0940 hrs 100 km northwest of the Scheldt. Towards 1100 hrs, II./JG 1, led by the *Kommandeur*, Hauptmann Walter Hoeckner, intercepted and attacked a group of about 100 Flying Fortresses at an altitude of 8,000 m over the Eifel/Wiesbaden area. The first attack was mounted from behind and at an angle, and was without success. Four Fw 190s were damaged by the bombers' defensive fire. While the *Gruppe* was reforming for a second pass, it was joined by several pilots from I. *Gruppe*.

Meanwhile, Hoeckner had spotted a lone Flying Fortress trailing the rest of its formation as a result of its left inboard engine being damaged during the earlier attack. He reported:

> Because only my MG 17s were functioning, I attacked this B-17 10–15 times with machine guns from all sides in short-duration attacks. After around eight such attacks, both left-side engines had failed. I attacked again and damaged the right side inner engine, whereupon the B-17 veered to the southwest. As I had only limited fuel, I made a decisive frontal attack at 600 m altitude from ten degrees to the upper left and fired at the B-17 until within ramming range. After this attack, the B-17 was finished and it hit the ground like an exploding bomb.[19]

This would be Hoeckner's 58th victory, and it was one of eight B-17s shot down during II./JG 1's second attack. Four more Fw 190s were hit in return.

Oberleutnant Rudolf Engleder, the *Staffelkapitän* of 1./JG 1, recalled of the raid:

> A tough encounter unfolded at an altitude of 9,000–10,000 m. Once again, the imposing American fighter escort engaged us in a cloudless sky. The bombardment no doubt hit the Hanau industries hard, because those responsible for its defence and the *Gauleiter* of Frankfurt visited Göring and protested strongly about his fighters: 'How is it possible that American bombers can fly over the city in almost parade ground fashion? And further, German fighters were seen at altitude, not attacking!' Göring went into one of his mad rages in which he knew

the answer to everything, and he despatched to all the fighter units responsible, the following orders:

1. There are no meteorological conditions which will prevent fighters from taking off and engaging in combat.
2. Every fighter pilot who lands in a machine not showing any sign of combat or without having recorded a victory will be prosecuted by a court-martial.
3. In a case where a pilot expends his ammunition, or if his weapons are unusable, he should ram the enemy bomber.

Some 304 tons of bombs had fallen on Frankfurt during the raid. The important Vereinigte Deutsche Metallwerke propeller factory in Heddernheim was hit, and that night, the RAF came with 406 Lancaster, Halifax, Stirling and Mosquito bombers. Frankfurt was turned into a 'sea of flame', with many of the buildings in the city centre destroyed. One source states that 529 residents were killed, including 90 child orphans and 14 nuns who were taking cover in a basement shelter.[20] When he heard the news that night, Hitler telephoned Göring, and one can only imagine the conversation.

Shortly after the raid Göring called Galland in a fury. The *General der Jagdflieger* attempted to balance the discussion by mentioning the heavy losses sustained by the fighter and *Zerstörer* units, but Göring cut across him. 'The German public doesn't care two hoots about your fighter losses. Go to Frankfurt and ask what impression your fighters that day left on them'. By this time, the Reichsmarschall's regard for his fighter units had reached an all-time low, and in his view, he was the only one who could remedy the situation. As he announced to Milch on 3 October, 'I believe that if I finished a tour in which I had spoken to every fighter group, we would soon see an undoubted victory'.[21]

Göring then headed south to his pseudo-rustic villa on the Obersalzberg in the Bavarian mountains, to where, over 7–8 October, he called Galland, Milch, Schmid, Weise and Kammhuber, as well as Generals Wolfgang Martini, the head of Luftwaffe signals, and Karl Koller, Chief of the Luftwaffe's Operations Staff, to an urgent conference. Also in attendance were several *Kommodoren* of the day- and nightfighter *Geschwadern*.

From the start of proceedings, Göring lashed out at what he saw as wholly inadequate fighter pilot training, failed technology, ineffective tactics, unreliable armament and low morale. In theatrical disgust, he threatened to remove his personal combat decorations gained in the last war and not wear them again until he was satisfied that the Jagdwaffe had restored its cutting edge. Milch endeavoured to reason with him, but Göring was not interested, claiming the fighter pilots were 'pussyfoots'. He scoffed at the notion of 'taking potshots at 1,800 m. They simply have to close to 400 m instead of 1,000 m; they simply have to shoot down 80 [bombers] rather than 20. Then their low morale will disappear, and I will tip my hat to them'.[22]

In something of a Machiavellian move, Galland placated Göring by assuring him that every unit commander would be assessed as to his fitness to command, and that gun cameras and altitude-measuring barographs would be installed in fighter aircraft in order to check just how close a pilot was to an enemy formation during an attack and at what height. But that was not enough for Göring. He argued that, quite simply, the *Jagdflieger* had to attack, attack and attack again.

'How long can you fire from every buttonhole?' he demanded of Galland. 'Seven minutes', Galland answered. Göring quickly calculated that each pilot could therefore make three sorties against the enemy during a four-hour deep penetration raid. Galland demurred, but Göring insisted that he was right.[23] Galland conceded, and agreed to ensure that in the case of deep penetration USAAF raids, daylight fighter pilots would attack, land, refuel, re-arm and go up again – at least once and, if possible, twice.[24]

To his generals, the *Reichsmarschall* confessed that the Luftwaffe was 'at the bottom of an abyss', that the fighter pilots were 'chicken', and that all they did was trail along behind the enemy bombers, leaving them to bomb German cities at will.[25]

Göring remained in the south for a few days. On 12 October he was in Munich, to where he summoned Walther Dahl and a number of pilots of III./JG 3. The *Reichsmarschall* lambasted them. According to the *Gruppe*'s diarist:

> The Jagdwaffe has lost its prestige, it has fought poorly. The *Führer* has lost confidence in his fighter pilots. The fighter pilots should once again become a 'Retaliation *Korps*'.
>
> Afterwards, the *Reichsmarschall* spoke with the *Kommandeur*. It transpires that our *Gruppe* has achieved two great successes – over Stuttgart on 6 September and over Switzerland on 1 October. The *Reichsmarschall* was satisfied with the *Gruppe* only, he said, because he was not addressing the individual fighter pilot or a *Gruppe*, but the entire Jagdwaffe. He took a very serious view about the fact that it did not seem possible to halt the enemy daylight attacks. General Galland and Oberst Lützow no longer wear any decorations.

The *Gruppe*'s pilots have recognised the seriousness of the situation, and will take steps to fight accordingly.[26]

Meanwhile, the Reich's factories were not producing enough Bf 109s and Fw 190s, with manufacturers failing to hit their production targets. For these two fighter types, actual production in August 1943 was 914 against a target figure of 1,024, representing a net fall of -10.7 per cent (a -13 per cent variance in output when compared to the previous month in percentage terms). For September, the figure was 853 against a target of 1,157, representing a net fall of -26.3 per cent (a -6.7 per cent variance).[27]

11

'Defensive Victories'

In October 1943, the daylight battle over the Reich reached its zenith, forcing the USAAF to accept that unescorted, deep penetration formations could not adequately protect themselves — just as the RAF had had to recognise the fact in 1939. Yet although the losses incurred reached unacceptable levels, such missions nevertheless forced the Luftwaffe into the air to fight, and in doing so inflicted attrition on a scale from which the Germans would find it difficult to recover.

USAAF operations commenced on the 8th with an attack on Bremen and Vegesack. At 1340 hrs, the *Funkhorchdienst* picked up radio traffic indicating a major bomber assembly to the northeast of London. Thus prepared, Generalmajor Josef Schmid was able to commit 441 aircraft from every day fighter unit within 1., 2. and 3. *Jagddivisionen* areas, as well as elements of 5. *Jagddivision*. Violent air combat ensued over Bremen and Oldenburg.

Thanks to the guiding hands of *Luftnachrichten-Regiment* 5./201 at Nordhelle-Ebbe-Geb (*Nelke*), 5./202 (*Johannisbeere*) and 5./211 and 5./212 at Bredstedt (*Brombeere*), 30 bombers were shot down and 26 damaged, with kills going to JGs 1, 3 and 11 and ZG 26. In addition, nightfighters from three *Staffeln* of NJG 3 were deployed, and they accounted for two B-24s and a B-17. Oberfeldwebel Mondry, flying an Fw 190 of Focke-Wulf's *Industrieschwarm Langenhagen*, also shot down a Flying Fortress. Airborne too were aircraft of the weapons testing unit E.Kdo 25. Hauptmann Geyer took off from Achmer leading a flight of three mortar-equipped Fw 190s:

> Together we attacked the 12 B-24s in the rearmost formation from the rear. From about 250 m range, I fired my mortars, but only one was functioning. I jettisoned both tubes, one still with its mortar shell, and then saw that the B-24 I had attacked was slipping away from its formation. I fired several long bursts from my 20 mm MG 151/20

cannon, following which I observed considerable damage to the fin assembly and heavy smoke coming from the inboard starboard engine. But right then several escort fighters suddenly rushed down on us and I gave the order to evade. One of my wingmen had also succeeded in shooting down a B-24 using his mortars.[1]

Indeed, Geyer was credited with destruction of a B-24, as was his comrade, Leutnant Wilhelm Sbresny, while Leutnant Paul Kaschuba and his radio operator, Feldwebel Krah, flying one of the new mortar-equipped Me 410s of E.Kdo 25, claimed a B-24.[2]

Mortars were also fired en masse by the *Zerstörer* of III./ZG 26, which scrambled 35 Bf 110s led by Hauptmann Schulze-Dickow from Wunstorf at 1430 hrs. Directed by 'Y'-*Gerät*, they sighted three *Pulks* comprising 'around 300' *Viermots* at 1520 hrs flying at an altitude of 7,000 m. The *Gruppe* fired its mortars, and also attacked with cannon. Nine bombers were confirmed as shot down, some as a result of mortar blasts, others by cannon, with a further two B-17s as probables. Evidently, the *Zerstörer* made an impact on the bomber crews, with the 1st Bomb Division (BD) later reporting that its crews saw 'twice as many twin-engined as single-engined fighters' and:

> Attacks were directed almost entirely on low groups and stragglers. Twin-engined E/A stayed 1,000–1,500 yards outside and fired rockets into formation as well as 20 mm cannon. Crews report rapid-firing rocket guns whose shells exploded with pink bursts the size of Flak.[3]

One Bf 110 of III./ZG 26 was lost and another landed shot-up at Hesepe. After the operation, Schulze-Dickow noted pointedly:

> It was repeatedly observed that our own fighters, contrary to orders, attacked enemy aircraft that had strayed from the formation.[4]

The Luftwaffe mourned the loss of the *Kommodore* of JG 1, Oberstleutnant Hans Phillip, who was shot down near Nordhorn by P-47s shortly after having claimed his first *Viermot*. Earlier that morning, Phillip had called together some of his senior officers and read out the recently arrived edict from Göring, instructing pilots to ram enemy bombers in instances where ammunition had been expended or weapons were not functioning. Apparently he was contemptuous of the Reichsmarschall's order and brushed it aside. Less than a fortnight earlier, Phillip had been one of the distinguished attendees at Schmid's high-level conference at Stade. Shortly

'DEFENSIVE VICTORIES'

before his death, he wrote a letter to his former comrade, fellow ace Oberst 'Hannes' Trautloft, about life and operations over the Reich:

> We are comfortably installed, the girls are numerous and we have all that we need. The bad point is that the aerial combat is very tough. Tough, not because the enemy are superior in numbers and the Boeings are better armed, but because to go over a group of 70 Flying Fortresses makes you see your whole life in front of you. And once you have made your mind up to go in, it is even more difficult to force each pilot of the *Staffel*, right down to the youngest 'green', to do the same.[5]

The next afternoon, the 9th, 53 B-17s and B-24s from the 2nd and 3rd BDs raided U-boat yards and port facilities at Danzig and Gdynia, while 202 B-17s from the 1st BD and other groups from the 3rd BD struck at aircraft industry targets at Anklam and Marienburg. After the war, Generalmajor Schmid summarised the response of I. *Jagdkorps*, and it is worth setting out his account at length, as he describes how the unit reacted tactically to such a scenario:

> The long detour of the enemy bomber units via the North Sea, Jutland and the Baltic Sea made the commitment of the daylight fighter units more difficult, since the bulk of them lay in Holland and northwestern Germany. Nevertheless, it was possible to bring all available fighters into contact with the bombers, and to inflict considerable losses on the USAAF. Since there were no daylight fighters stationed in eastern German territory, the enemy bomber groups could not be engaged over the target area. The commitment of the fighter units developed as follows;
>
> 1. *Jagddivision* took off from Holland and headed into the area over the North Sea. The fighter elements of this division could not make contact with the enemy due to the excessive range, and landed on fields in the Hamburg–Schleswig–Holstein area. After refuelling, the units of 1. *Jagddivision* successfully attacked the bombers on their return flights.
>
> The daylight fighter units of 2. *Jagddivision* engaged the enemy bombers during the approach and return flights. Single- and twin-engined fighters entered the fray over the German Bight and over Jutland.[6]

At around 0930 hrs 2. *Jagddivision* at Stade issued an *Alarmstart* order to III./ZG 26 at Wunstorf, but frustratingly, the *Gruppe*'s 26 mortar-carrying

Bf 110s became disoriented in cloud and 18 of them were forced to land at Leck and Schleswig, another five suffered technical problems and had to return to Wunstorf early and three turned back because they could not locate the rest of the unit amidst the adverse conditions.

Between 1155 and 1205 hrs, those aircraft at Leck and Schleswig took off for a second attempt to find the bombers and assembled over Kiel, but the 'Y' guidance failed. After hunting the skies for 30 minutes led by the redoubtable Hauptmann Schulze-Dickow, the Bf 110 crews eventually sighted three *Pulks* off the coast near Kiel at 4,500 m. The Bf 110s went into attack from the rear and launched their mortars, but nearly all the spin-stabilised shells exploded short of the bombers. Resorting to their MG 17 machine guns and two MG 151/20 cannon, the Messerschmitts accounted for eight B-17s shot down, with Feldwebel Scherkenbeck of 9./ZG 26 claiming two of them. The *Gruppe* suffered one loss.[7]

We return to Schmid's narrative of events:

> 3. *Jagddivision* successfully attacked the approaching bomber formations with weak fighter and industrial defence fighter units over the coastal area on the western edge of the Baltic Sea. For action against the bombers in the Bay of Danzig, only a few nightfighters based in Pommerania and East Prussia were available. The two fighter *Geschwader* of 5. *Jagddivision* from the Frankfurt basin were shifted in low-level flight to airfields in the German Bight, where they refuelled. These forces too were successfully committed against the American bombers on their return flight. All nightfighters that could be adapted to daylight operation [between 80 and 100] operated singly, and successfully attacked the enemy bombers during their approach and return flights in the area of the western Baltic Sea, over Jutland and in the North Sea area.

I. *Jagdkorps* launched 566 sorties against the bombers, including second take-offs and nightfighters. By the evening of the 9th, the *Korps* had suffered the loss of five Bf 109s, three Fw 190s and two Ju 88s (evidently III./ZG 26's sole loss had not been registered by that stage). Fourteen more aircraft were damaged, one pilot was lost, one wounded and ten missing. According to Schmid:

> Operations on 9 October were a considerable defensive victory for the units of I. *Jagdkorps*, achieved while suffering minor losses. The successes were achieved because of the superior armament of the German aircraft in their operations against the four-motor bombers. The successes were

made possible because the enemy chose to attack during cloudless autumn weather without fighter protection, and also because the deep penetration into German territory gave the defenders a great deal of time to attack the bomber formations.[8]

To what extent Schulze-Dickow would have agreed with Schmid's contention that 'the successes were achieved because of superior armament' is debateable.

Göring had issued 'explicit orders' to the headquarters of I. *Jagdkorps* to direct the efforts of those day fighter units under its command first and foremost against enemy four-engined bombers. The twin-engined *Zerstörergeschwader* were ordered to attack unescorted bombers, and at the same time instructions were issued that the equipping of certain units with W.Gr.21 underwing mortars was to be stepped up.

Evidence of the urgency surrounding the appetite for air-to-air mortars can be seen in the minute of a meeting held at Zeist during the afternoon of 27 October between Schmid and Haupt.Ing. Joseph Sedlmeyer, a specialist from the Luftwaffe main testing station at Rechlin. Sedlmeyer had been looking at the feasibility of fitting 21 cm mortars into a twin-engined Ju 88, an aircraft that was fast and had decent range. Unfortunately, efforts to install the tubes within the wing proved impossible and so, as a temporary solution, Sedlmeyer arranged for two launch tubes to be fitted in a 'makeshift' way beneath each wing in a similar fashion to such installations on the Bf 110 and Me 410. More permanent was the plan to install tubes in the aircraft's lower fuselage for automatic launching.

Sedlmeyer advised Schmid that modifications to the Ju 88 could be carried out very quickly, but that the difficulty was the procurement of the necessary components required for the work. Schmid told Sedlmeyer to draw up a list 'immediately', and to submit it to his Chief of Staff, Oberstleutnant Heinrich Wittmer, so that they could be requested directly from Generalfeldmarschall Milch.[9]

On 10 October, the USAAF struck the marshalling yards at Münster with 206 B-17s escorted by 216 P-47s. The *Funkhorchdienst* began intercepting American radio traffic at 1215 hrs, and it realised that a large assembly, accurately estimated as 'between 200–250 Fortresses' was taking place between the Thames Estuary and The Wash. The bombers crossed the Dutch coast at Goeree in cloudless skies and headed straight for the target, but around Bocholt and Wesel the numbers of P-47s had thinned, most of them forced to turn back on account of range. By then, the German fighter controllers were primed, and a force of 39 B-24s of the 2nd BD was quickly recognised as a diversionary ruse, allowing fighters of 2. *Jagddivision* to operate to the south. As Schmid described:

> All of the daylight fighter units gained combat with the enemy, operating in cloudless weather. The *Jagdgeschwader* of 1. *Jagddivision* [JG 25] engaged the enemy fighters over Dutch territory. Because of this, the daylight fighters of 2. and 3. *Jagddivisionen* were able to attack the unprotected swarms of enemy bombers repeatedly. In the Münster area, these units gained a defensive success in that they thwarted several bomber elements in aiming their bombs. Furthermore, 70 daylight fighters were committed by *Luftflotte* 3. None of these made contact with the enemy.

The Bf 109s of II./JG 3 reached the bombers first, and prepared to make an attack from the rear, only to be repelled by the heavy escort. In the skies above and around Münster, however, beyond the range of the P-47s, the USAAF bombers encountered vicious and determined aerial opposition, caught between waves of mortar-firing *Zerstörer* aiming to break up their formations, after which waves of Fw 190s came in from head-on.

This time, the Bf 110s of III./ZG 26 were able to reap chaos and destruction with their mortars in the way it was intended. Twenty-five Bf 110s had taken off from Wunstorf at 1419 hrs and flown under 'Y'-*Führung* at 6,500 m to the area north of Münster. The 'Y' had worked well, although the Allies did attempt to disrupt its function. At 1520 hrs, the *Gruppe* spotted the bombers some 20 km north of their target. The Bf 110s approached the rear of the B-17s and, at a range of around 1,000 m, they fired their mortars – anywhere between 50 and 100 of them. According to the *Gruppe*'s subsequent battle report:

> The mortar shells exploded in the enemy *Pulk*, which then fell apart. Two Fortresses were observed ramming into each other and crashing. In the following individual combats with aircraft armament, eight definite shoot-downs and one probable were achieved.[10]

Guided by the controllers of 2. *Jagddivision*'s 6. *Funkleit-Kompanie* at the '*Dattel*' ground station at Egestorf/Deister, southwest of Hanover, these included the *Gruppenkommandeur*, Major Boehm-Tettelbach, and his radio operator, Oberfeldwebel Martin Vipotnik, who accounted for the destruction of two B-17s. At least four other crews enjoyed success.[11]

'DEFENSIVE VICTORIES'

The way was cleared for the single-engined fighters. The 100th BG subsequently lost 12 of its 14 aircraft, with Eighth Air Force Intelligence reporting after the mission:

> E/A approached in groups, attacked on their own in formations of from 2–6 planes and flew level and straight at their targets. The attacks were pressed up to 50–75 yards, then E/A turned, took violent evasive action and kept coming back in for the attack. The attacking E/A showed definite tendencies to concentrate attacks on one group at a time, even to the point of flying through the lead group to attack the low (100th). After concentrating and disposing of the 100th Group, the attack was switched to the 390th, then to the 95th (especially the low squadron). The 100th Group received the first attack at 1453 hrs.
>
> Attacking aircraft would fly parallel to the formation, out of range in groups of 20–40, stacked in echelon down for frontal attacks. They would proceed on ahead of the formation and then peel in one or two at a time, attacking the lowest members. Many beam attacks from 4–5 o'clock were received by groups of 20–40 E/A at a time.[12]

As a result of losses sustained between June and October 1943, the 100th BG became known as 'The Bloody Hundredth'. Capt Frank Murphy was a navigator aboard the group's B-17F *Aw-R-Go* of the 350th BS flying to Münster. He recalled:

> The German aircraft came after the 100th in seemingly endless waves. As one element of fighters broke away, another was turning up for a head-on attack far ahead of us, and still others were forming up. Fighter after fighter flew directly into our formation, passing so close that we could distinctly see the German pilots in their cockpits. Although we were firing continuously, and could plainly see our own tracers as well as those from other B-17 aircraft seeming to be on target, they had no apparent effect. The fighters came on, at tremendous closing speed, with complete disregard for the curtain of defensive fire from our guns, the leading edges of their wings twinkling and glittering as they fired. Exploding cannon shells 'walked' through our formation.[13]

To the south, for the controllers at Generalleutnant Schwabedissen's 7. *Jagddivision*, it had been a frustrating day. Fifteen Bf 109G-6s of JG 50 were sent to the Münster area from their base at Wiesbaden-Erbenheim. However, the GM-1/Nitro-oxide-boosted high-altitude interceptors failed to engage. This lack of success was compounded by the fact the unit lost two of its Messerschmitts through crash-landings, with one pilot being killed. 7. *Jagddivision* also transferred 13 Me 410s from Hörsching to Illesheim and 22 Bf 109s from Neuburg to Wiesbaden-Erbenheim, but both formations returned to their bases the same day without achieving success.[14]

Further west, however, the *Jägerleitoffiziern* at the '*Nelke*' ground station at Nordhelle had a field day, directing several pilots from JGs 1, 3 and 26 towards victories. The ironically named Leutnant Leopold Münster of 4./JG 3, a Knight's Cross-holder, was credited with two Boeings for his 79th and 80th victories. He had shot down two B-17s a few days earlier. Other pilots who scored that day were Hauptmann Hermann Staiger of 12./JG 26, who already had seven B-17s to his credit (although some of these were unconfirmed at the time) and Oberfeldwebel Adolf Glunz of II./JG 26, who had been involved in the destruction or damaging of five Fortresses in August and September.

Thirty bombers were lost altogether on the Münster mission. VIII Bomber Command later reported that the passes made by JGs 1 and 26 on the 3rd BD were 'the most violent and concentrated attacks yet made on this Division by enemy aircraft. Attacks, from every clock position, appeared to have a definite method'.[15]

Based on the American accounts quoted here, it would seem that Göring's and Galland's tactical requirements were being executed. From his headquarters in Paris, the monocled Generalfeldmarschall Sperrle, commander of *Luftflotte* 3, signalled JG 26:

> *Jagdgeschwader* 26 displayed an outstanding spirit of attack in the defence against the terror attack on Münster by enemy 4-engined units on 10.10.43. During a fierce battle against the accompanying fighter escort and especially against the bomber units, 19 Boeing Fortresses were shot down and a further 19 bombers were shot out of formation.
>
> I would like to express my thanks and special appreciation to all the crews, especially the unit flight leaders, for this great success.[16]

In Münster, some 250 buildings were destroyed and a further 3,000 damaged, including the railway station and the cathedral. More than 300 inhabitants were killed and 602 injured.

It is most likely that Generalmajor Schmid was feeling Göring breathing down his neck. The former knew that the units of I. *Jagdkorps* had to

'DEFENSIVE VICTORIES'

demonstrate better results. Early in the morning of 11 October, he climbed aboard an aircraft at Soesterberg intending to fly to Stade and then on to Grove, in Denmark, for meetings with the staffs of 2. *Jagddivision* and the *Jagdabschnittsführer Dänemark*, but his plans were frustrated on account of the aircraft suffering engine failure. He decided, instead, to drive from his headquarters at Zeist to Deelen for an impromptu discussion with Oberst Grabmann at 3. *Jagddivision*.

Over coffee in an anteroom in the *Diogenes* bunker, Schmid and Grabmann were joined by Major i.G Erich Bode, 3. *Jagddivision*'s Operations Officer, and Hauptmann Emil-Rudolf Schnoor, the *Kommandeur* of I./JG 1 which was also based at Deelen, and which had taken part in the previous day's operations over Münster.

The conversation was frank. Schmid wanted to know how things were with 3. *Jagddivision*'s units. Schnoor commented that the *Kampfgeist* (fighting spirit) within his *Gruppe* was good, as had been demonstrated over Münster when I./JG 1's pilots had shot down three B-17s and claimed two *Herausschüsse*. For his part, Grabmann remarked that levels of operational readiness in his day fighter *Gruppen* had diminished considerably because of the intense number of sorties over the past few days. At that moment, 3. *Jagddivision* had only 40 *Einsatzklar* fighters.

The meeting turned to tactics against bombers. Schmid stressed Göring's request that *repeated* attacks must be made against bombers. Schnoor was an experienced fighter pilot who had first served in *Zerstörer* units prior to joining JG 1 in 1942. Having also flown against the recent enemy raid on Bremen, he told Schmid that in his opinion the best way to attack bombers was from the front, and that approaches from the side were not effective. Schnoor added that an Oberleutnant who had led I./JG 1's operations during the enemy raid on Münster managed to get the *Gruppe*'s fighters in close to the bombers, but that he had found it challenging to re-assemble after the initial attack because it took too much time.

With acidic humour, Schnoor also commented that the *Gruppe* had hit so many bombers over Münster and that so many American airmen had been seen bailing out of their Flying Fortresses that it looked like a whole parachute regiment was jumping out.

It seems Schmid raised the issue of the reported crash locations of enemy aircraft yielding no wreckage at purported claim sites when visited and inspected after the action had taken place. Grabmann and Schnoor responded that crashing aircraft often landed in soft or swampy terrain and could sink completely, and that aircraft could explode in the air, with their engines subsequently penetrating the ground by up to three to four metres on impact.

The meeting was joined by Major Streib, the *Kommodore* of NJG 1 whose Bf 110 nightfighters, based in Belgium and the Netherlands, acted as 'shadowers', tracking and reporting on the incoming routes taken by American bombers. Sensibly, Schmid instructed that shadowing operations should not just be conducted during the approach phase of a raid, but also immediately at the end of one so that all-clear information could be relayed to the firefighting and rescue teams in areas which had been subjected to attack.

Göring was under pressure. Allied bombs were falling all over the Reich, more and more Allied aircraft were flying ever deeper into Germany, and yet the Luftwaffe seemed unable to offer any credible response. The Reichsmarschall knew his prestige with those close to the *Führer* was waning rapidly. Both Albert Speer and Martin Bormann, Hitler's Machiavellian and loyal private secretary, used any opportunity to flag up the Luftwaffe's weaknesses. Bormann received reports from regional Gauleiter who made it their job to produce meticulous, but often inaccurate reports of Luftwaffe failings and the resultant damage inflicted on Germany's towns and cities and their vulnerable inhabitants after each major Allied raid. Invariably, these reports found their way to Hitler.

Generalfeldmarschall Erhard Milch, the ambitious and hard-nosed Secretary of State at the Air Ministry, had noticed that when it became apparent in mid-1943 that the numbers and range capability of American fighter escorts would only grow, it seemed 'Göring could just not grasp it'.[17] In a mixture of rage, megalomania and bewilderment, Göring blamed the nearest target – Galland and the fighter pilots. A few months earlier, Göring had convened a meeting of *Jagddivision* and *Luftgau* commanders at Schleissheim to thrash out the results of a major USAAF incursion into southern Germany. As Galland wrote in his post-war memoirs:

> Göring began to lay increasing blame on the Jagdwaffe, and as I felt I had earned the right to answer him back, we were soon at loggerheads. After some general remarks, he proceeded to comment on the *Jagdwaffe*'s lack of spirit. He may have been exasperated by my replies to his previous questions. At all events, he got into such a state that he hurled reproaches and accusations at us to the effect that we had been loaded with honours and decorations but had proved ourselves unworthy of them, that the Jagdwaffe had been a failure as early as the

'DEFENSIVE VICTORIES'

Battle of Britain, and that many pilots with the highest decorations had faked their reports to get Knight's Crosses over England.[18]

In a moment of fury, Galland, perhaps taking a swipe at Göring's own antics on the Obersalzberg a few days earlier, tore his own Knight's Cross away from his collar and, according to his testimony, 'slammed it down on the table'. Other *Ritterkreuz* wearers in the Fighter Arm offered to remove theirs too, but Galland did not permit it. For a year he himself did not wear the decoration. Göring apologised soon after, but Galland did not give in until a year later.[19]

According to Milch, this kind of atmosphere was not unusual:

> There was never a peaceful conference [with Göring]. I did not know of a single conference which was carried out from start to finish under quiet, reasonable terms, in which people kept to the point and which didn't immediately lead to furious attacks on someone or other. If one ventured to offer advice, one was shouted at – 'I don't want your advice! I know better myself!' If I ever wanted to bring something up, I had to try to say it to him privately, and then he accepted what I had to say. The only problem was that you could never get hold of him![20]

On 14 October, 229 of 291 B-17s despatched managed to reach Schweinfurt in a return to the aircraft industry targets which had proved so costly to the USAAF in August. It was planned that the bomber force would include 20 B-24 Liberators from the 2nd BD, but these, and their escort, were forced to abandon the mission due to bad weather and cloud. The P-47s of the 4th FG also had to turn back because of fog, leaving just the 56th and 353rd FGs to undertake escort for the B-17s.

However, over western Germany, the weather had cleared, and in cloudless skies I. *Jagdkorps* committed all of its daylight fighter units drawn from five fighter divisions – a total of 567 single-engined fighters, as well as twin-engined *Zerstörer* from ZGs 26 and 76 and some fighter training school aircraft and nightfighters. This was the kind of 'commitment' Göring was expecting, but against his orders, in the 3. *Jagddivision* area, Grabmann deployed the Bf 109s of III./JG 1 and I./JG 3 against the P-47 escorts between Woensdrecht and Antwerp. The escort stuck close to the bombers, however, and shot down seven Messerschmitts.

Just after 1330 hrs, and as the escorts began to turn back, the Fw 190s of I. and II./JG 1 dropped their auxiliary fuel tanks and turned to engage the American formation as it approached Eindhoven, attacking from '12 o'clock high', and almost immediately drawing in the fighter escort. A swirling, confused mêlée developed as the Germans took on both the US fighters and bombers. Oberfeldwebel Detlef Lüth claimed a B-17 for his 33rd victory:

> Around 1332 hrs we spotted between 250–300 Boeings flying in two large formations. As I was not able to jettison my auxiliary tank, I lost contact with the *Gruppe*. I joined up with three fighters that were flying some 1,500 m to the right of the Boeing *Pulk* which we were to attack. As I approached, I realised that they were three Thunderbolts. I positioned myself immediately behind these three Thunderbolts, but at exactly the same moment I was fired at by a fourth Thunderbolt and I dropped down to around 5,000 m away from the formation.
>
> I then attempted, at full power, to rejoin our own fighters. Since, after about 3–4 minutes' flying time, I did not succeed in doing this, I decided to make a lone attack. I climbed over a *Pulk* of around 15–20 Boeings, got in position on the right side, then went under the formation and made a sharp right turn upwards to around 150 m under the left, outer-flying Boeing. I gave a long burst of fire from 150 to 50 m. This dislodged large sections of the fuselage, tail and wing.
>
> Since the Boeing did not respond to the hammering from my cannon, I pulled back to fly at the same height and directly behind it, and fired for an extended time with my MGs until it fell to the left, away from the formation. Two members of the crew bailed out with parachutes. I saw that as the Boeing I had fired at went down on a westerly course, a Bf 109 fired at it from ahead and above and then it went down in a steep, gliding flight. Since I had not succeeded in releasing my drop tank, I attacked the Boeing once again from the side and below. Two more crew members bailed out with parachutes. The Boeing went over into a steep dive, lost its horizontal stabilisers and spun down from 3,000 m. I observed the impact with the ground 10 km southeast of Düren.[21]

Hauptmann Emil-Rudolf Schnoor, *Kommandeur* of I./JG 1, shot down a B-17 for his 13th victory and Oberleutnant Rudolf Engleder, *Staffelkapitän* of 1./JG 1, claimed another, plus a *Herausschuss*, taking his tally to seven *Viermots* shot down or damaged in just 15 days. JG 1's pilots would ultimately claim 21 B-17s destroyed on the 14th.

'DEFENSIVE VICTORIES'

By the time the 1st BD entered the target area, it had lost 36 bombers, with one group alone having just under half its strength shot down. The division's overall losses eventually reached 45 bombers, with one combat wing of 37 B-17s losing 21 aircraft.

2Lt Joel E. Punches was a navigator on board a Flying Fortress of the 385th BG in the 3rd BD:

> We had a P-47 escort for 20 miles inside Germany. When they left, the 109s started attacking, and continued for four hours. We were 'Tail End Charlie' today in 'Purple Heart Corner'. Carried incendiaries. It was clear over the target, and when we left it was a huge mass of flames. The whole town was burning, flames 500 ft high. Two B-17s burst into flames in the group ahead of us, on the bomb run. Ju 88s were sitting out, firing rockets at us. They had everything up today – Ju 88s, Me 109s, Me 210s.
>
> Thirty minutes later, a B-17 dropped down and two fighters went down after him. Twenty minutes later, he came out of cloud with his engines smoking. They all bailed out. Our No. 1 engine ignition system was shot out, and it sounded like a washing machine. I'm afraid things are going to be tough from now on. No 'milk runs'.[22]

To the west of Hanover, at Wunstorf, a force of 28 mortar-equipped Bf 110s of III./ZG 26 took off between 1249–1255 hrs and headed southwest under 'Y'-*Führung*. An hour later, near Remscheid, the crews spotted several *Pulks* of Flying Fortresses at 8,000 m. Two of them were over Mayen on a course to the southeast, while another three were on a similar course over München-Gladbach. The *Gruppe* positioned itself to the rear of the lead *Pulk* and, at a range of 1,000 m, fired its mortars. According to its later report:

> Explosions were well placed at long range, but despite being aimed an average of three degrees higher, they were too low. Bf 109s and Fw 190s were observed in the *Pulk*, which also fired their mortars too low. The enemy flew in a closed wedge formation and in echelons stepped up. The formation spread out after our mortars were fired and several aircraft veered off course. Very strong enemy defensive fire from machine guns.[23]

Leutnant Günther Wegmann was the only pilot to shoot down a B-17 by mortar, and he was also credited with the destruction of another Boeing bomber using his cannon, as were five other pilots in the *Gruppe*. Two crewmen were lightly wounded during the attack.

To the south, in the 7. *Jagddivision* area, Schwabedissen ordered the 25 serviceable Bf 109s of III./JG 3 – nine of them carrying mortars – to intercept the bombers. They took off from Bad Wörishofen at 1308 hrs and flew for 80 minutes before making contact with the bombers. By then fuel was low, and there was only time for two brief attacks. In total the *Gruppe* accounted for 11 Flying Fortresses shot down, five of them claimed using mortars, and a further seven *Herausschüsse*. One of the latter was credited to Feldwebel Herbert Zimmer of 8./JG 3, although on this day he was flying with his *Staffelkapitän*, Leutnant Erwin Stahlberg, who had taken temporary command of 7. *Staffel*. Zimmer, an Eastern Front veteran with 20 victories to his credit, took off in his Bf 109G-6 at 1310 hrs:

> We had reached the [enemy] formation in the Frankfurt/Main area. I had already twice made a frontal attack on the first *Pulk* of the formation, and then made a third attack from below and behind. I fired at the left wing of a Boeing Fortress II with a long burst, whereupon the enemy aircraft trailed two thick white streams, and at 1440 hrs, 20 km south of Schweinfurt, it fell away from the formation. After that, the wing caught fire, though for a short time it was extinguished. I then saw two Bf 110s attacking the Fortress.[24]

Moments later, Zimmer's Bf 109 was hit by machine gun fire from the bombers, and he was forced to bail out northwest of Seligenstadt.

Oberfeldwebel Alfred Surau of 9. *Staffel* claimed a B-17 for his 46th victory, but he too was hit by defensive fire from the bombers – a Browning machine gun round shattered the glass of his cockpit canopy. Badly wounded, he managed to bail out, only to later succumb to his wounds in hospital at Wertheim. Surau's loss was a hard one for III./JG 3 to bear, having been described as 'the *Gruppe*'s best Unteroffizier pilot'. He had shot down two B-17s on 6 September and two more on 1 October.[25]

Elsewhere, the confusion of battle had begun to tell. The War Diary of I. *Jagdkorps* makes mention of Unteroffizier Otto Monska of 6./JG 27 filing claims for the destruction of five enemy aircraft, but the reality was that he shot down just one B-17 for his sixth victory.

Only one escort fighter would be claimed that day, falling as a shared kill to the guns of the 'old hare' Oberfeldwebel Adolf Glunz of 5./JG 26 and his *Staffel* comrade Gefreiter Heinz Wyrich.

'DEFENSIVE VICTORIES'

Claims by *Geschwader* for the day were as follows:

I., II. and III./JG 1	17
I., II. and III./JG 2	12
Stab, I. and III./JG 3	21
II. and III./JG 11	4
I. and II./JG 26	10
II./JG 27	19
JG 50	6
II./JG 51	9
III./JG 54	2
JG 104	1
JG 106	1
Industrie Schwarm	1
E.Kdo 25	1
Zerstörer units	23
Nightfighters	11
Other	10
Total	148

Losses to the Luftwaffe from this mission were 31 aircraft shot down, 12 written off and 34 damaged – between 3.4–4 per cent of available fighter strength in the West.

After the raid, Göring turned up at JG 50's base at Wiesbaden-Erbenheim to inspect the unit. He was in a brooding mood. As he trudged down the parade of *Geschwader* officers, Major Graf presented the recently promoted Hauptmann Alfred Grislawski, one of the unit's best pilots, credited with 109 victories scored on the Eastern Front with JG 52 and a recipient of the Knight's Cross. He was 24 years old. Göring looked the young pilot in the eye and asked how many missions he had flown against American bombers. Grislawski answered, 'Four, sir'. Göring then asked, 'And how many have you shot down'. 'Also four, sir'. Göring scowled sceptically, 'I don't believe you!'[26] Clearly 'trust' of his fighter pilots had become an issue for the Reichsmarschall. He remained unconvinced about some of the claims being made by the aces, especially when the wreckage of an enemy bomber could not be found following an air battle.[27]

For the USAAF, the reality was that its Flying Fortress groups had taken a severe battering. The second Schweinfurt raid had cost VIII Bomber Command 60 B-17s and 600 aircrew. A further 17 bombers had been seriously damaged and 121 damaged but repairable.

Despite the catastrophe, a buoyant Brig Gen Ira Eaker wrote to Gen 'Hap' Arnold the next day with a sense of success, confident that 'there is not the slightest question but that we now have our teeth in the Hun Air Force's neck', and claiming that the Luftwaffe's response was 'pretty much as the last final struggles of a monster in his death throes'.[28] Arnold was unconvinced. He replied, 'The cornered wolf fights hardest'.[29]

Schmid recorded that 'the units of the German *Reichsverteidigung* achieved a great defensive success on 14 October 1943'.

Certainly, the losses from Schweinfurt forced a halt in the USAAF strategy of hitting deep penetration targets until such time that greater numbers of long-range escort fighters were available, and so missions were kept within range of the fighter escorts. Although it could not be said by any means that the Luftwaffe was 'winning' the battle for air superiority over Europe, it was nevertheless preventing the USAAF from doing so. Equally, however, on the German side, with 67 per cent of ball bearing production at Schweinfurt knocked out, the ball bearing industry was forced to disperse its manufacturing capacity, which, in turn, presented logistics problems.

In October, I. *Jagdkorps* reported 664 aircraft on strength. The month's operations had cost the Luftwaffe 284 fighters, eight more than in September. I. *Jagdkorps* recorded that 'the numerically inferior German daylight fighter units failed to prevent a single American large-scale raid during October 1943', but also that 'the enemy suffered noticeable losses, especially in bombers'.

Indeed, many of Galland's pilots were accumulating impressive results against the *Viermots*. Hauptmann Rolf Hermichen of JG 11 was typical of the new ilk of 'bomber-killers', ending the war with 26 B-17 and B-24 victories to his name. Pilots such as Hermann Graf, Walter Dahl, Anton Hackl and Kurt Bühligen were becoming household names. Another high scorer was Oberleutnant Herbert Rollwage of JG 53, whose 102 confirmed aerial victories included 14 four-engined bombers. From II./JG 11, Oberleutnant Heinz Knoke had been accredited with 15 four-engined kills, and his *Gruppekameraden* Hauptmann Günther Specht had 15 and Leutnant Hugo Frey 12.

Meanwhile, Göring was touring the Rhineland in his bullet-proof limousine, visiting Luftwaffe fighter airfields, Flak batteries and radar installations involved in the day and night battle against the bombers. He was bold enough to stop off in various towns and cities along the way.

'DEFENSIVE VICTORIES'

Pulling himself out of the luxurious leather confines of his car, he surveyed the ruins and the rubble left by Allied bombs. He saw the hollow, resigned expressions on the faces of the German people and their children, the burst water pipes and collapsed telephone wires, the queues for bread and the hastily prepared shelters in the basements of apartment buildings and shops. He expected insults, but all he got was a bewildered silence and some muted smiles, some of support and some of cynicism.

He called 'Beppo' Schmid to meet him at Bad Lippspringe airfield on 11 October, where the Bf 110s of I./ZG 26 were based, but other matters forced him to cancel. Schmid returned to Zeist, and at 2130 hrs that evening he convened a meeting of senior officers responsible for the control of day- and nightfighter operations in the I. *Jagdkorps* area. Those in attendance included Oberstleutnant Oesau, who had effectively become an adviser on daylight fighter matters at this time, and Major Heinrich Seeliger, a former *Kommandeur* of III./JG 77 and a graduate of the *Luftkriegsakademie* who had recently joined the *Korps* staff as Day Fighter Operations Officer, as well as key Flak, airfield support and intelligence officers.

Possibly for the first time, Schmid mentioned to the assembled officers about plans to relocate the *Korps Gefechtsstand* east, to Braunschweig, within the coming months. Work at the new location was already underway. This was perhaps recognition that even the bunker at Zeist could no longer be considered truly 'safe'. And in another indication of how the daylight war in the air was shaping up, a minute from the meeting noted, 'With immediate effect, *Sturmstaffel* 1 will be set up for a provisional period of six months'.[30] Von Kornatzki had got his way.

A week later, on 25 October, Schmid singled out Generalleutnant von Döring and 3. *Jagddivision* following rare praise from Göring. He noted in the *Korps* diary:

> On the occasion of an inspection of units of 3. *Jagddivision*, which lasted several days, the *Reichsmarschall* expressed his particular satisfaction with the attitude and the successes achieved in action by the units and staffs that he inspected.
>
> I would like to take this opportunity to express my thanks and appreciation to the commander of 3. *Jagddivision*, his staff and the units of this division for their unwavering commitment and the extreme dedication with which they have performed. I am convinced that the *Division* will continue to live up to the accolades it has won and the high expectations that our homeland has of its defence by bravely and effectively repelling all enemy air attacks.[31]

Meanwhile, following Feldwebel Herbert Zimmer's clash with USAAF bombers near Frankfurt on 14 October, during which he had claimed a *Herausschuss*, by 14 November, exactly a month later, the tough verification procedure was still ongoing. The issue was that there had been no witnesses to Zimmer's action. Both his *Staffelkapitän*, Hauptmann Emil Bitsch, and his *Gruppenkommandeur*, Hauptmann Dahl, supported his claim, as did Generalleutnant Schwabedissen. Despite Göring demanding more bombers shot down, confirmation of a pilot's kill could be an uphill process.

At a meeting at his Villa de Breul headquarters with the *Jagddivision* commanders on 4 November, Schmid referred to 'the well-known complaints regarding decisions made by the *Abschusskommission*'. He had recommended to Generaloberst Weise, the *Luftwaffenbefehlshaber Mitte*, that each *Jagddivision* should set up its own *Abschusskommission*, and that they should be comprised of personnel of a 'neutral' mind, as well as 'experts who understand the matter'. What he also wanted was a degree of permanence in these commissions so that understanding of aerial combat and decisions regarding claims of bombers shot down could be taken rationally, and thus avoid being adversely affected by the chopping and changing of personnel.[32]

Eventually, Zimmer was awarded the *Herausschuss*.[33]

12

'Without regard to losses'

As October gave way to November, the USAAF returned with a vengeance on the 2nd – from the south. Making its second raid over Europe, and the first against a CBO target, the newly operational Fifteenth Air Force, based in Tunis under the command of Maj Gen James H. Doolittle, sent 139 B-17s and B-24s to bomb the Messerschmitt plant at Wiener-Neustadt, in Austria, where Bf 109s were manufactured. The bombers were escorted by 72 P-38 Lightnings.

The Fifteenth Air Force was established from 11 combat groups that had been transferred to it by the Twelfth Air Force, including six heavy bomb groups of B-17s and B-24s and four fighter groups. Additionally, four more Flying Fortress groups arrived with the 5th BW.

This was a significant moment for Allied air power in Europe, and an inevitable, but catastrophic, development for the Luftwaffe. The mission of the Fifteenth was to assist, within the range of its aircraft, in the destruction of the Luftwaffe in the air and on the ground; to participate in the strategic destruction of German fighter production, ball bearing plants, oil refineries, synthetic rubber production, ammunition facilities and U-boat bases; to support Allied ground forces in the fighting on the Italian mainland; and to weaken the German position in the Balkans. The Allied command also banked on the Fifteenth's aircraft operating in better weather than in the north, especially in the winter months.

Nevertheless, for the Fifteenth Air Force's bombers, it was a 1,600-mile mission to Wiener-Neustadt. 'Greeted' by accurate Flak, they pressed on. In response, the Luftwaffe generated 147 sorties. Given that the bombers' incursion was mounted from the south, it was the overall responsibility of Generalleutnant Schwabedissen's 7. *Jagddivision*, headquartered at the *Minotaurus 1* bunker at Oberschleissheim, on the northern edge of Munich, to coordinate defensive operations.

However, in an instance of bad timing, on the morning of the 2 October Schwabedissen departed his HQ to visit 12. *Flugmelde-Leit Kompanie*, a part of Oberst Walter Dumcke's *Luftnachrichten-Regiment* 205, at Hofolding, southeast of Munich, where he inspected a training course being run for fighter guidance officers. This, apparently, left control of the region's fighters to the area's two *Jagdführer, Jafü Suddeutschland*, Oberst Harry von Bülow-Bothkamp, and *Jafü Ostmark*, Oberst Gotthardt Handrick.

As has been described earlier, von Bülow-Bothkamp was an experienced fighter pilot and an intelligent fighter leader. But it seems that on the 2nd he hesitated when he received the local FluKo reports about the approaching bombers and failed to bring his units – III./JG 3 and ZG 76 – to take-off readiness in good time. The result was that neither of these units engaged the *Viermots*.

The Luftwaffe claimed 17 bombers shot down, but only 11 failed to return to their Tunisian landing grounds. Ultimately, 11 crash wrecks of bombers were discovered by the German authorities. Pilots from I./JG 27, II./JG 51, II./JG 53 and the Wiener-Neustadt ISS claimed victories, but these came at a cost of two pilots killed, five wounded and the loss of eight Bf 109s in action.[1] Göring viewed this as abject failure.

As it happened, and to the detriment of 7. *Jagddivision*'s staff, he was back in the south of Germany, having visited the Messerschmitt plant at Regensburg on the 2nd, still wrecked from the American bombing of August. In the afternoon, he and his entourage travelled on to Lechfeld, where they witnessed a demonstration flight of the sixth prototype of the Me 262 jet-powered interceptor. However impressive this new aeronautical technology may have been, surviving photographs of this event show Göring appearing somewhat preoccupied and distracted. That may well have been because 'his' Luftwaffe's fighter defence had failed once again.

The bombers of the Fifteenth Air Force had dropped 327 tons of bombs on the Wiener-Neustädter Flugzeugwerke, with more than satisfactory results. One of the main assembly shops was destroyed and another damaged, and two hangars were also destroyed and one damaged. More damage was inflicted on ancillary buildings, and the Henschel and Steyr-Daimler-Puch works were also hit.[2] It is believed 115 partially assembled and five finished Bf 109s, along with 80 engines, were destroyed in the raid. Finally, a total of 102 people had been killed.

On the 3rd, Göring, in his powder-blue-uniformed magnificence, arrived at Salzburg-Maxglan airfield in Austria, and he came with copies of reports which offered a damning indictment of events of the day before. He asked to see Schwabedissen, Handrick, Dumcke and Oberstleutnant Hannes Trübenbach from the Staff of *Luftwaffenbefehlshaber Mitte*. Göring did not hold back. According to the war diary of 7. *Jagddivision*:

'WITHOUT REGARD TO LOSSES'

The Reichsmarschall reprimanded the leadership of the 7. *Jagddivision* in very harsh terms, describing this day as the *Jagddivision*'s darkest. In the course of the meeting, the Reichsmarschall used documents to identify the following leadership errors for the failure of individual units to approach the enemy in good time:

1. *Jafü Süddeutschland* ordered its units to *Startbereitschaft* too late due to an incorrect assessment of the FluKo reports, which inevitably led to a delayed take-off of III./JG 3 at Bad Wörishofen and ZG 76.
2. *Jafü Ostmark* ordered its units to be at *Sitzbereitschaft* in good time, but gave the take-off order too late, so that these units also reached the enemy too late or were unable to reach the required altitude in good time for a close-formation attack on the enemy bombers.

Göring did recognise the *Angriffsgeist* (spirit of attack) of the units that did engage, but he warned the assembled officers that this would be the last occasion on which he would address commanders without taking punitive action. After this dressing down, Schwabedissen spoke to Göring privately, stressing that he had not been at his *Gefechtsstand* at the time – Göring stated that he was aware of the fact. The next day, however, Schwabedissen was informed in a telephone call from Generalleutnant Walter Boenicke, a tough staff officer at *Luftwaffenbefehlshaber Mitte* who had seen some heavy ground fighting in Crete in 1941, 'that a change would be taking place in the leadership of the *Division*'.[3]

It seems Göring was trying to instil some order into what he perceived as a lax infrastructure within the Luftwaffe's fighter control. He urged Schmid to tackle the problem. During the afternoon of 4 November, Schmid gathered Huth, Ibel and von Döring from, respectively, 1., 2. and 3. *Jagddivisionen*, along with officers from his own staff, and asked that, following enemy raids, they contact him directly by telephone and relay 'their impressions of the enemy and their own activities'. Furthermore, he mentioned that he was aware 'that letters or orders are sent directly to the *Divisionen* from higher authorities. The *Korps* must be informed of such letters immediately'.

Göring's grip on fighter operations now began to filter through to operational policy. During the evening of 6 November at Berlin-Dahlem, the *Luftwaffenbefehlshaber Mitte*, Generaloberst Weise, chaired the opening of an important two-day conference attended by Schmid, Oberst Grabmann, at the time still the *Jafü Holland-Ruhrgebiet*, but very shortly to be appointed to command 3. *Jagddivision* at Deelen, and various officers on Weise's and Galland's staffs.

At the first session, attended by Weise, Schmid, Grabmann and Boenicke, Weise announced Göring's directive that in view of the higher altitudes and increased fighter escort adopted by the American bomber formations, there were to be two distinct areas in which German fighters should engage in combat. Firstly, in those areas within range of the fighter escort, and secondly, over territory free of escort.

Intriguingly, what followed at the meeting highlighted the differences in tactical thought at this time between key Reichs defence commanders such as Schmid and Grabmann, as well as the compromises, juggling of slender forces and enforced adjustments in aircraft armament that were having to be accepted in order to deal with the threat of the USAAF fighter escorts.

So as to allow *Zerstörer* units to carry out effective attacks, strong formations of faster and more manoeuvrable 'light' German single-engined fighters – Bf 109s without the aerodynamic encumbrances of W.Gr.21 mortar tubes or MG 151 underwing cannon gondolas – were to engage and 'divert' the escort. For this purpose, and in the first instance, the 'light' fighters would be concentrated against an enemy incursion.

The *Zerstörer* and 'heavy' units, equipped with the necessary armament to disperse the *Pulks* and blow up bombers, were then to be operated in areas beyond the range of the escort. They were to target only unescorted *Viermots*, with cover provided in daylight by the single-engined nightfighters of Oberstleutnant Hans-Joachim Hermann's *Wilde Sau* units of the new, specialist 30. *Jagddivision*, which, at night, conducted their principle tactic of freelance combat against RAF Bomber Command aircraft using searchlight guidance.

The problem was that I. *Jagdkorps* did not have enough fighters to cover all aspects of such a 'strategy', and so for it to work, it would be necessary to de-equip some of the 'heavy' fighter *Gruppen* into 'light' units. Grabmann recommended converting four existing 'heavy' *Gruppen* to light configuration, as, in his view, that would 'make it possible to effectively combat enemy fighter cover'.

Schmid was probably circumspect about this, and he waited until the next morning when the meeting reconvened at *Luftwaffenbefehlshaber Mitte*'s concrete command bunker, *Herold 1*, in Berlin's *Reichssportfeld* complex. For this second session, Weise had brought in another Divisional commander, Oberst Max Ibel from 2. *Jagddivision*, as well as Oberst Günther von Maltzahn, the *Jafü Oberitalien* (Upper Italy), who had travelled from his headquarters in Bologna, and Oberstleutnant Eduard Neumann, former *Kommodore* of JG 27, and at this time serving on Galland's staff. Also present was Flak officer Oberst i.G. Hans Schumann, Major i.G. Johann-Wolfgang Redlich, an experienced *Legion Condor* and North Africa fighter veteran posted to Weise's operations staff, and medical officer Major Dr. Ulrich Heynen.

Weise opened the meeting by explaining that because of the USAAF's recent methods of deployment with bombers flying at altitudes of around 8,000 m with stronger fighter escort, Göring had ordered that new basic directives should be issued to the commands of the daylight fighter units. In recent enemy incursions, the numbers of bombers and fighters deployed had remained broadly the same, but the Luftwaffe's heavy fighters had experienced difficulties in attaining the same high altitudes as the enemy and, therefore, had failed to engage in a timely and efficient manner. Göring wanted this fixed.

Suggestions were requested as to how Luftwaffe fighters should be deployed in future. The question posed by Weise was exactly how many *Jagdgruppen* should be converted to faster, 'light' *Gruppen*, and how fighters should best be deployed given that, on 3 November, the USAAF had ranged as far as Wilhelmshaven with strong fighter cover for the first time. This meant that, theoretically, the Eighth Air Force could now hit targets that fell within an arc running approximately from Bremen in the north, through Bielefeld and south to Koblenz.

Weise turned to the officers present. For his part, Ibel felt that *all* single-engined fighters should be converted to 'light' configuration. This can only be interpreted as an assumption that he believed 'light' fighters could undertake the whole defence mission on their own, or that more such fighters were needed at the expense of heavy fighters, or that the 'heavy' armament was not effective or necessary, or all of these things. Perhaps more realistically, Neumann proposed using as many fighters as possible, regardless of their configuration, leaving only 'thin' protection for the *Zerstörer*.

Grabmann believed that five light *Gruppen* would be sufficient for deployment against the present numbers of enemy fighter escorts. He also recommended that the two westernmost *Gruppen* – II./JG 3 with Bf 109s at Schiphol and I./JG 26 with Fw 190s at Grimbergen – should be located and deployed in such a way that they could reach any enemy incursion via 'the shortest possible route' in the manner of quick-response units. This, of course, relied on efficient and fast control by the *Jafüs* and *Jagddivision*, and Grabmann also advocated that those units equipped mainly with Fw 190s should be configured as heavy *Gruppen* and be deployed against bombers once their escort was tied down by light fighters.

Schmid recommended pulling II./JG 3 back if possible. 'It is currently very weakened and has always borne the brunt of the fighting recently', he explained. Indeed, just three days earlier, the *Gruppe* had lost its *Kommandeur*, 170-victory ace Major Kurt Brändle, who was posted missing over the North Sea after air combat against a formation of B-26 Marauders (his body was washed ashore on 17 January 1944). Eventually, it was decided to relocate the *Gruppe* some 40 km east to Hilversum, but this never happened and the unit remained at Schiphol until 14 December, when it moved to Volkel.

Also within the remit of 3. *Jagddivision*, it was proposed to convert Major Klaus Mietusch's III./JG 26 to light configuration, and move the unit to Grimbergen, while III./JG 1 under Hauptmann Friedrich Eberle would move from Leeuwarden and Eelde to Volkel. Furthermore, Hauptmann Emil-Rudolf Schnoor's depleted I./JG 1 would be relieved by exchanging it for a *Jagdgruppe* based in the southern Reich or with the Bf 109-equipped III./JG 54 at Schwerin. The Fw 190 heavy fighters of II./JG 1 under Hauptmann Walter Hoeckner would remain at Rheine.

No changes would take place with the units of 2. *Jagddivision*. Two *Gruppen* of ZG 26's Bf 110 *Zerstörer* would remain at Hanover, but the third would move to Grove for deployment against unescorted bombers passing over Jutland and the Baltic. The *Zerstörer* would receive protection from Oberst Herrmann's *Wilde Sau* nightfighters.

In accordance with Göring's orders, *Luftwaffenbefehlshaber Mitte* would draw up instructions for the *Jagddivisionen* to attack bomber formations 'with the strongest possible forces against the enemy fighter defence, so that, if possible, the *Zerstörer* can be brought up to engage unescorted bombers'. However, Schmid sagely voiced 'misgivings' about this plan, which would involve tackling bombers and their escorts simultaneously. He feared that the strength of the daylight fighter force was 'too limited' to deploy such tactics, but his was a lone voice.[4] Schmid was also concerned about the continued deployment of twin-engined nightfighters in daylight missions at this time. He told British intelligence officers after the war:

> Under orders, we sometimes sent up our nightfighters by day. This I considered lunacy. I was ordered to send them up as soon as the American bombers were beyond the reach of their escorting fighters — at that time the American fighters escorted them up to about a line from Emden to the Rhine. On 10th [sic] November 1943, early, at 0800 hrs, we suddenly heard to our surprise —'*Thunderbolts*'. That was the first time they went along as far as Wilhelmshaven. I then reported, 'This fact makes it impossible to use nightfighters anymore'. I was told

'WITHOUT REGARD TO LOSSES'

I was wrong in saying the American escort fighters accompanied the bombers as far as that. Then Galland took off himself and reported to Göring that he came into combat with American fighters near Hanover.[5]

Meanwhile, in the air over the Reich, despite Göring's admonishments and demands, there were still all too familiar failings. On 5 November, just two days after Göring's 'discussions' with Schwabedissen at Salzburg, the Bf 109Gs of III./JG 3 were ordered into the air from Bad Wörishofen to fly 750 km north to Oldenburg, from where it was intended they would tackle more than 300 B-17s of the 1st and 3rd BDs out to bomb an oil refinery and marshalling yards at Gelsenkirchen in the eastern Ruhr area. Eight bombers were lost, three damaged beyond repair and 216 damaged through Flak and fighters. But for Dahl's III./JG 3 it was to be a frustrating day, a lost opportunity and a waste of fuel, as the *Gruppe* diarist recorded:

> Unfortunately, the order to move the *Gruppe* to Oldenburg came too late. When the *Gruppe* landed at Oldenburg after almost two hours of flying time, the enemy units were already over the target. Despite good ground organisation, it was not possible for us to take off in time. In the air, we heard that all enemy aircraft were on course for home, having just reached the mouth of the Scheldt.[6]

When Schmid returned to his Villa de Breul from Berlin on the 8th, he chaired a meeting that evening with Grabmann, Oesau, Wittmer and Seeliger, as well as Oberst Günther Lützow, who was Galland's *Inspekteur der Tagjagd* as well as *Inspekteur der Jagdflieger West und Süd*. Schmid wanted to review the planned reorganisation of his *Gruppen* and Göring's strategy of combatting American fighters only with light fighters. He sought the assembled officers' opinions.

Lützow stated that Galland agreed with the conversion of individual *Gruppen* to light configuration, but was of the opinion that the forward coastal airfields should be vacated. II. *Jagdkorps* had also already proposed pulling back four *Gruppen* and leaving just two *Gruppen* at forward locations. Grabmann suggested moving back units to the rear if possible, locating the majority in the Deelen area. Schmid commented that an objection from the '*Reichskommissars*' and the Kriegsmarine was to be expected if the forward *Gruppen* were moved back. It was finally proposed that in weather conditions that did not favour large-scale USAAF raids, two *Gruppen* could be moved to the airfields of Bergen (in the Netherlands) and Grimbergen in order to counter lighter Allied operations over the coastal areas. The remaining *Gruppen* would be held further back to tackle major raids.

Herrmann's *Wilde Sau* fighters at Bonn-Hangelaar would be assigned to protect the *Zerstörer* units, but only after their training was completed and it had been established through exercises with ZG 26 that escort was operationally possible. Until then, protection of the *Zerstörer* would be handled by II./JG 1 at Rheine.

Lützow proposed that the battered II./JG 3 be pulled out and refreshed, while Oesau took the view that the *Gruppe*'s existing aircraft and crews should be distributed to other *Gruppen* in order to increase the combat capability of such units. Lützow was asked to put all this to Galland.[7]

That same day, Galland had been at work in Berlin carrying out Göring's wishes. He signalled his unit commanders:

> German fighters have been unable to obtain decisive successes in the defence against American four-engined formations. Even the introduction of new weaponry has not appreciably changed the situation. The main reason for this is the failure of formation leaders to lead up whole formations for attack at the closest possible range. Göring has therefore ordered the establishment of a *Sturmstaffel* whose task will be to break up Allied formations by means of an all-out attack with more heavily armed fighters in close formation and at the closest range. Such attacks that are undertaken are to be pressed home to the very heart of the Allied formation whatever happens and without regard to losses until the formation is annihilated.[8]

By this time, the *Sturmstaffel* had received its first complement of Fw 190A-6s that featured the introduction of a lighter wing capable of accommodating increased armament in the form of four MG 151/20 cannon located in the wing roots and the outer panels, thus phasing out the old, slow-firing MG FF cannon. Two fuselage-mounted 7.9 mm machine guns were also retained, and the aircraft featured additional protective armour around the cockpit.

These Focke-Wulfs constituted what was probably the first batch of aircraft to be armour-adapted specifically as *Sturm* (assault) fighters for close-range anti-bomber work. This also involved the fitting of 30 mm armoured glass panels – *Panzerscheiben* – around the standard glass cockpit side panels and a 50 mm plate of strengthened glass that would protect the pilot from fire from dead ahead. According to Focke-Wulf reports, some problems were experienced fitting the glass panels to the cockpit due to the angle of curvature of the cockpit's sliding hood, but these were eventually solved. The installation of external 5 mm steel plates to the fuselage panelling around the cockpit area and the nose-cockpit join offered further protection from defensive fire. Additionally, the pilot's seat was fortified by five-millimetre steel plates and a 12 mm head protection panel. All these additions, however, increased the aircraft's weight.

On 17 November 1943, Göring visited *Sturmstaffel* 1 at Achmer accompanied by Galland. In their presence, the first cadre of 20 or so pilots were reminded of the strict code they were required to follow during their operations, and were made to swear the following oath:

1. I volunteer for the *Sturmstaffel* of my own free will. I am aware of the basic objective of the *Staffel*.
 a. Without exception, the enemy will be approached in close formation.
 b. Losses during the approach will be immediately made up by closing up with the attack leader.
 c. The enemy will be shot down at the closest range. If that becomes impossible, ramming will be the only alternative.
 d. The *Sturm* pilot will remain with the damaged bomber until the aircraft impacts.

2. I voluntarily take the up an obligation to carry out these tactics and will not land until the enemy has crashed. If these fundamentals are violated, I will face a court martial or will be removed from the unit.

As testimony to the seriousness with which this oath was sworn, the volunteers were also required to draft a last will and testament. At least one pilot is known to have done so following this instruction, but another of the unit's pilots, Feldwebel Oskar Bösch, who joined the *Staffel* later, recalled, 'We were not forced to sign the declaration, but, in a way, we had worked ourselves up mentally to succeed at any cost. We simply recognised the need to defend our homeland'.

However, despite its state of readiness, the *Sturmstaffel* would not experience its baptism of fire until January 1944.

In southern Germany on 16 November, probably in the aftermath of the disappointing performance of his *Jagddivision* at the beginning of the month, Schwabedissen handed command of 7. *Jagddivision* to Generalmajor Joachim-Friedrich Huth. A native of Saxony-Anhalt, Huth, at 47 years of age, was an *'alte Adler'*, having flown as a fighter pilot during the latter months of World War I. Credited with shooting down an observation balloon over the Western Front in January 1918, he suffered wounds in combat two months later that resulted in him losing the lower part of his right leg.

Despite such a daunting impairment, Huth was appointed *Kommandeur* of the new Bf 110-equipped I./ZG 1 at Jüterbog-Damm in February 1939. Regarded as the 'Father' of the *Zerstörerwaffe*, Huth was awarded the Knight's Cross on 11 September 1940 and was appointed successively as *Jafü* 2, *Jafü Berlin-Mitteldeutschland* and *Jäfu* 4, and *Kommandeur* of 4. and 5. *Jagddivisionen*.[9]

To the north, at Stade, Knight's Cross-holder Oberst Hannes Trautloft, the former *Kommodore* of JG 54 (with whom he had flown more than 500 operational missions, most of them on the Eastern Front) and a *Legion Condor* veteran, arrived at the headquarters of 2. *Jagddivision*. He was there at Schmid's request and in his capacity as a senior officer on Galland's staff. I. *Jagdkorps* was a functionary body which directed operations, but it was the *General der Jagdflieger* that was responsible for supplying both the fighters and their pilots – and providing the training of the latter.

Schmid had some concerns, which he put to Trautloft as Galland's representative. Firstly, it was apparently the case that the Fw 190s of I./JG 11 based at Husum, a *Gruppe* which had only been formed in April from elements of III./JG 1, were unable to be deployed in strength against enemy formations because they had 'varying armament'. Schmid, understandably, wanted the *Gruppe* armed uniformly, otherwise it was, operationally, next to useless. Connected to this, and in accordance with Schmid's request, Trautloft stated that there were sufficient numbers of younger pilots now available.

Schmid signalled caution. He suggested that the *General der Jagdflieger* carry out a review of its *Staffelkapitäne*, 'as they are often too young to lead a *Staffel*'. Schmid further proposed that *Staffeln* could be merged to form stronger units as, in many cases, unit strength was very low. He also told Trautloft that 'the *General der Jagdflieger* should not hold too many courses at the same time, so that not too many crews are pulled out of operations, since the units are already so weak'.[10]

Indeed, manpower and morale were becoming increasingly strained in all of Germany's armed forces. In late 1943, memories of Stalingrad and defeat at the battle of Kursk in the summer were still fresh, and in ten days during November, no fewer than 6,473 German soldiers were killed on the Eastern Front.[11]

On the 20th Schmid called together his divisional commanders, along with some of his *Gruppenkommandeuren*. It was a stellar array of day- and nightfighter 'talent' that gathered around the conference table at Driebergen that evening, with the Knight's Cross decorating several necks. Aside from Grabmann, Ibel and Lützow, other Knight's Cross-holders present were the nightfighter aces Major Werner Streib, *Kommodore* of NJG 1, Major Günther Radusch, *Kommodore* of NJG 5, and Hauptmann Heinrich *Prinz zu Sayn-Wittgenstein*, *Kommandeur* of II./NJG 3, along with Major Karl Boehm-Tettelbach, *Kommodore* of ZG 26.

Schmid wasted little time in conveying what was, once again and without doubt, 'the gospel according to Göring'. It had been identified that within the units of I. *Jagdkorps* there was a negative attitude over the war situation. This could not be tolerated. Any officers or men found demonstrating such 'defeatist views, and thus effectively helping the enemy' were to be dealt with immediately. Furthermore, the *Korps' Divisionen* and *Geschwadern* were ordered to check that their component units did not contain men born from any time after and including 1901, who were not considered to be 'specialist' personnel, and as such fit for frontline service. If any such men were found, they were to be handed over for service in the field and replaced by female personnel.

When it came to the day fighter units, the message was that, 'It is to be expected that the supply of aircraft will continue to be low in the near future, so that units will remain inferior to the British and Americans. Unit commanders must therefore ensure that available aircraft are handled with care and that any loss is avoided'.

When an American bomber formation was identified as approaching, Schmid wanted 3. *Jagddivision* to send up dedicated shadowing aircraft as soon as possible so as to be able to report on the enemy's course and whether escort fighters were present. This way, operating nightfighters in daylight could be avoided. The intention was to assign a reconnaissance *Staffel* to each *Jagddivision* to act as shadowers in daylight operations and as reconnaissance for nightfighter units.

In addition, one aircraft in each daylight *Jagdgruppe* was to act as a 'pathfinder' to guide formations of fighters through bad weather and cloud. Nightfighters were instructed to use radio beacons in daylight operations, especially in bad weather. Only small fighter detachments – '*Jagdkommandos*' – were to remain at the more forward airfields, while the bulk of fighters were to be relocated to airfields further east.[12]

From surviving documents, there is no doubt that a degree of increasingly frantic inventiveness was seeping into the German mindset at this time, affecting even the likes of Galland – a rational man who liked to steer a steady ship. As an example, on 13 November he wrote to Milch's office proposing that the development of '*Rammflugzeuges*' (ramming aircraft) by the Blohm & Voss company, designed specifically for use against four-engined bombers, be allowed to continue.

The concept was that such an unmanned 'aircraft' be attached to a carrier aircraft. Galland was of the opinion that, 'If the loss in climb performance caused by its attachment to fighter and *Zerstörer* aircraft are kept within acceptable limits, the ramming aircraft could be used in conjunction with cutting devices to provide valuable support for homeland defence.'[13] He asked for further reports from Blohm & Voss.

At a marginally less radical, though equally experimental level, the Luftwaffe continued to explore the feasibility of deploying very heavy calibre Flak weapons fitted to aircraft against bombers – in essence to create 'airborne Flak'. To this end, in late August one of E.Kdo 25's Me 410s had been flown to Vechta, where the airfield workshop there set about installing a 3.7 cm Flak 43 light anti-aircraft gun in the Messerschmitt. This weapon promised a higher rate of fire (240 rounds per minute) than the same calibre Flak 18 (60 rounds per minute). By the end of November satisfactory experiments had still not been carried out, although there was a hope that a *Schwarm* of Me 410s could be so fitted and used operationally on a trial basis.

Much of this experimentation was driven by the expectancy that the USAAF would, at some point, deploy the larger B-29 Superfortress over Germany, and so it would be essential to prepare a fighter in good time that would have the power to reach altitudes of between 9,000–11,000 m and be able to engage the high-flying Boeing bomber in aerial combat.

In this regard, on 9 November 1943, Oberst Edgar Petersen of the *Kommando der Erprobungsstellen* wrote to the RLM advising that following discussions with Galland and personnel of E.Kdo 25, it was proposed to develop a 'prototype' Me 410 at Rechlin fitted with GM 1 power boost, a ZFR 4 telescopic gunsight and armament comprising 20 mm, 30 mm or 5 cm cannon arrangements or Flak 43 armament. Such weapons would have sufficient 'punch' to knock down a B-29, but the issue was weight, the ensuing loss of aircraft manoeuvrability and how close, realistically, an Me 410 could get to a formation of heavily armed Superfortresses.[14]

However, such was the awareness on the part of the Eighth Air Force of the continuing threat posed to its bombers by the Luftwaffe's daylight fighter force, and the depth of study of its attacks, that on 11 November intelligence officers on the staff of the 3rd BD issued a series of 13 detailed diagrams showing what were perceived to be the most common tactics used in attacks against Flying Fortresses. The diagrams were based on hundreds of reports from bomber crews on their returns from missions who had recounted more than 2,500 separate encounters with Luftwaffe fighters, and they were further verified by Allied fighter pilots who had flown as escort.

Graphically, each diagram was produced to a high standard, showing how Luftwaffe fighters were likely to approach and attack a squadron of six B-17s, as well as their exit routes. Each method of attack had a description of the tactic deployed, followed by a 'Tactics Lesson'. For example, during the Schweinfurt mission of 14 October, crews observed how six single-engined, mortar-equipped fighters would attack from the rear in line-abreast, astern and level, or slightly higher, at ranges of 1,200–2,000 yards. This attack was described as 'The Rocketeers' method. The outer four fighters would carry mortars, while those at the centre would be 'light' aircraft. The Tactics Lesson warned:

> It's a two-to-one bet that the e/a which will close in for attack is, or are, located in the center of the formation.
> THE STRAGGLER'S NUMBER IS UP. KEEP IN FORMATION AT ALL COST AFTER EXPLOSION OF ROCKET PROJECTILES.
> The tail gunner in Fortress No. 1 [lead ship in squadron] must be alert to this attack and warn formation leader when e/a are jockeying into position.
> DON'T BE LED AWAY FROM MAIN ATTACK BY E/A PEELING OFF.
> DON'T WASTE AMMUNITION ON LONG SHOTS.
> The best defense against rocket attacks from the rear is slight weaving of the formation. Due to high trajectory and low velocity of rockets, slight weaving will carry the formation out of the effective range of bursts [which is what frustrated the attack by III./ZG 26 during the Schweinfurt mission – see Chapter 11].

Each type of attack was given a satirical name – 'The Triple Threat', 'The Roller Coaster', 'The Sneak Attacks' (tail and head-on), 'The Sisters Act', 'The Swooper', 'The Scissors Movement', 'The Pepper Spray' and 'The Twin-Engine Tail-Pecker', plus its single-engined variation. Intended for distribution among the division's operations, intelligence and gunnery officers, the diagrams came with a perceptive warning:

> The Hun is an opportunist and is quick to change his approach if he can get a better shot. Tactics change from month to month. In their

desperation at losing the air war, the Germans will develop new aircraft and use old aircraft in new ways and with new weapons.

By 8 December the report had reached Eaker, who instructed that the diagrams should be enlarged to 'poster size for display on the walls of combat crew reading rooms' and that they should be made available for use by projectors and as a series, in handy, single sheets for use in post-mission crew debriefings. Intelligence officers were also to present 'chalk talks' based on the diagrams, and they were to be used in conjunction with aircraft recognition training.[15] Eaker knew just how important an understanding of German fighter tactics was to his bomber crews. The 'Cornered Wolf' was not going away any time soon.

13

Battle Groups and Opera Houses

Not surprisingly, on the other side of the North Sea, aside from Major Hans-Günther von Kornatzki's work, likewise the Luftwaffe had been similarly analysing the composition and methods employed by the Americans. Accurate drawings of how USAAF bomber formations assembled and then flew in formation, in wings, groups and squadrons, lead, low and high, were drawn up and circulated to fighter units. Others featured drawings of the B-17's and B-24's internal compartments, showing the positions of the various members of a crew as well as the gun locations.[1]

Scale models of four-engined bombers were made of wood and Bakelite, often with wire frames attached to represent the arcs of fire from a *Viermot*'s defensive guns. These models were used by veteran pilots and gunnery instructors who toured units to demonstrate to pilots how best to approach a *Pulk* and attack it. At many fighter airfields, life-size frontal views of B-17s were painted on hangar doors to assist in tactical awareness.

On 27 November, despite the snow showers and low cloud that covered southern Germany, 33 Bf 109s of III./JG 3 carried out mock training attacks on a pair of Heinkel He 177 bombers which stood in for American Flying Fortresses and Liberators. The *Jagdflieger* based in the West and in the Reich were never allowed to forget the number one enemy.

That enemy returned to Germany during the afternoon of 26 November in conditions that Schmid described as 'extraordinarily bad' for the defenders. The target was the city of Bremen and its port, which were to be bombed through cloud, and this time the weather and USAAF air power would give the Luftwaffe a double blow.

The German reporting services initially became aware of bombers assembling over Norwich and the London area at 0935 hrs, with the first attacking force approaching from Norfolk towards the German coast an hour later, followed by a second incursion at 1047 hrs. The Eighth Air Force had sent 505 B-17s and B-24s from all three of its bomb divisions, the aircraft flying along the Frisian coast before changing course in two thrusts at 60 km and 90 km, respectively, north of Norderney. The first thrust made directly for Bremen, while the second passed over 2. *Jagddivision*'s headquarters at Stade. Conditions were daunting for both sides, as I. *Jagdkorps* recorded:

> The approaching enemy bombers flew along a route leading through a zone of 5/10 to 9/10 shower clouds at the rear of a bad weather zone. Lower ceiling of the clouds around 500 m, upper ceiling from 5,000 to 6,000 m. In the coastal areas, scattered snow and sleet showers in thunderstorms. Cloudless above 6,000 m.
>
> Flying through clouds, the aircraft were exposed to icing above 1,000 m. In the area of Bremen at the time of the attack, 8/10 to 10/10 cumulus clouds reaching up into high altitudes, with snow and sleet showers extending over large areas. Upper cloud ceiling 6,000 m. The employment of our forces was hindered by showers extending over large districts in the area north of the general line Amsterdam-Rheine-Hanover-Rechlin. Single- and twin-engined fighter aircraft climbing through the clouds were exposed to strong icing.

To counter the Americans, Schmid deployed 294 day- and nightfighters and, once again, 24 Bf 110 *Zerstörer* of III./ZG 26, which took off from Wunstorf at 1100 hrs. After climbing through cloud, the Bf 110s assembled over the Dümmer See and rendezvoused with fighters from JG 11.

Things soon went wrong for the *Gruppe* when the equipment on both of its 'Y'-*Gerät*-equipped Messerschmitts failed, and the aircraft resorted to FuG 10 guidance to get them to the Wilhelmshaven area. Half-an-hour later, over that port, they caught sight of the *Viermots* flying southeast in seven *Pulks*, accompanied by a heavy screen of P-47s above and behind. The Bf 110s aimed for the rearmost B-17 grouping and fired off their W.Gr.21 mortars from the rear of the enemy at 700 m. Some of the shells exploded amongst the enemy bombers, while others detonated short of it. The Bf 110s then went in individually, with four pilots claiming to have downed Flying Fortresses. Three Messerschmitts were lost in return, with at least six others having crewmen either killed or wounded. According to the crews of the USAAF's 1st BD:

> Most of the attacks seemed to be against the leading groups. Attacks were from all directions. One cylindrical object dropped by an Fw 190 in a skip-bombing technique. An Me 109 attempted aerial bombing without results. One crew member saw an Me 109 with a rocket under one wing and wires swinging from under both wings come head-on through the formation.[2]

The last mentioned observation may have been the first time E.Kdo 25 had trialled a new form of weapon which will be described later, but if that was the case it would have been deployed from an Fw 190. Regardless, the *Kommando* lost four of its aircraft in this operation, accounting for half of 2. *Jagddivision*'s losses.

Schmid's units claimed the destruction of seven bombers, with 25 more as probables, as well as a sole Thunderbolt. The Eighth Air Force reported 440 of the 505 aircraft it despatched to Bremen as being effective, with 25 bombers and a solitary P-47 being lost. The USAAF claimed 16 Luftwaffe fighters shot down, three probables and a further ten damaged. Across its three *Divisionen*, I. *Jagdkorps* had 13 aircrew killed, 24 posted missing and five wounded. Eight aircraft were lost, 11 were listed as missing and 12 damaged.

American bombs fell in the port area of Bremen and on the main railway station, as well as on Delmenhorst airfield just to the west of the city.[3] In an indication that the air war was becoming increasingly savage, III./ZG 26 noted that one of its radio operators, having bailed out of his stricken Bf 110, was machine-gunned by a P-47 while hanging from his parachute at a height of around 5,000 m.[4]

On 29 November, the Eighth Air Force went back to Bremen. The bombers – 360 B-17s of the 1st and 3rd BDs, escorted by more than 300 P-47s and P-38s, less two combat wings which fell foul of icing and had to abort – were first detected in two thrusts, one at 140 km off the Dutch coast at Bergen at 1325 hrs, and another at the same time 100 km west of Texel. Around 15 minutes later, further groupings were picked up off Texel. Despite the inclement weather over northern Germany, Schmid committed all serviceable fighters from 1., 2. and 3. *Jagddivisionen* to the Bremen area. Of the 360 B-17s despatched, only 154 made it through high winds and cloud to reach the target area.

In conformity with Göring's wish to see greater forces deployed against the bombers, a composite '*Gefechtsverband*' (battle group) under the command of Major Karl Boehm-Tettelbach, *Kommodore* of ZG 26, formed of Bf 110s from II. and III./ZG 26, along with Bf 109s from III./JG 26 and Fw 190s from II./JG 11, headed north.

At 1436 hrs, III./ZG 26 sighted two *Pulks* of bombers flying east and went in to engage, mounting an attack with its W.Gr.21 mortars at 800 m from the right of the formation. As before, some of the mortars exploded amidst the bombers and others went off behind the formation. The *Zerstörer* then passed beneath the *Viermots* and climbed and turned back to make a second attack from the left with cannon. Three Flying Fortresses were seen to drop away to the left, falling out of their formation. As a result of this action, some of the bombers were forced to drop their bombs well away from Bremen. That evening Schmid signalled Boehm-Tettelbach. 'I send my special gratitude to the crews of the *Gefechtsverbände* of ZG 26 for their achievement in the large-scale combat today'.[5]

Also in the air that day were fighters from E.Kdo 25, trying out a new weapon. '*Gerät Liesel*' was a 500-kg fragmentation-parachute bomb developed by the *Forschungsanstalt Graf Zeppelin* based near Stuttgart. Suspended from a rack beneath an Fw 190, the bomb was designed to fall at 700 km/h, but upon triggering the parachute-braking device 100 m above the target, the speed would reduce to 500 km/h – a drop of 270 m could be achieved in 5.7 seconds. It was intended that a *Schwarm* of Fw 190s fitted with *Liesel* was to fly in the same direction and height as an enemy bomber formation, before overtaking it and then turning back towards it, approaching from the front and 100 m higher. In his fortnightly report for the second half of October 1943, Hauptmann Horst Geyer of E.Kdo 25 reported:

> It is intended that when attacking from the front with a slight elevation, the bomb should be released about 800 m from the enemy formation. Attempts on target drones have had good results. The devices are available immediately in acceptable numbers.

In his following report, however, Geyer noted:

> Since the '*Liesel*' devices must be carried out with at least one *Schwarm* each, and the *Erprobungskommando* has only six Fw 190s with crews available for this purpose, in view of the importance of this operational trial, four additional fighter crews are requested, as well as the assignment of four Fw 190A-6s.[6]

Evidently, the *Kommando* received them. After the mission on the 29th, one B-17 crew in the 45th Combat Wing (CW) 'reported seeing an object, thought to be an aerial bomb, dropping on low group', while crews in the 4th CW reported 'Fw 190s were observed to release parachute bombs. Me 110s were observed to drop aerial bombs from about 32,000 ft. Me 109 dropped a parachute bomb 100 ft over B-17 formation. This bomb made a very red explosion ten times larger than a Flak burst'.[7]

The main tactical problem facing the Luftwaffe was that its piston-engined fighters needed too much time to attain the required height for bomb-dropping. This meant that although well within sight of the enemy, the conventional fighters waiting to exploit the weakness in the bombers' defensive capability caused by the bomb-dropping were forced, for their own safety, to hold back their attack until the bomb-dropping had taken place. Nor were German aircraft equipped with a suitable bombsight for such operations, leaving bombs to be dropped according to the pilot's visual estimation.

By January 1944, the British had reached a measured conclusion when it came to air-to-air bombing:

> Very little success seems to have been achieved with air-to-air bombing. In recent reports of objects believed to be bombs falling through formations, the objects are frequently stated as having failed to explode. At the same time, there are many reports of Fw 190s and Me 109s being seen with belly tanks. In recent attacks some of the objects thought to have been bombs are recognised as jettisoned auxiliary fuel tanks. It is probable that this was the case with many earlier reports, and that air-to-air bombing has not in fact been used so frequently as was first thought. It has had little success.[8]

December 1943 saw, paradoxically, a weather-enforced lull in the activity of the Eighth Air Force, but also a focus on targets in the Ruhr. Operations opened on the 1st with a raid by 281 B-17s and B-24s of the 1st and 2nd BDs on the industrial towns of Solingen and Leverkusen in North-Rhine Westphalia, just to the east of Düsseldorf and Cologne. Despite early raids on German fighter airfields by B-26 Marauders of the Ninth Air Force, most aircraft of JGs 2 and 26 were moved in time to evade the 'mediums'' bombs.

The controllers at Junck's II. *Jagdkorps* had been ready, and they brought in units from *Jafüs* 3 and 4 to harry the heavy bombers when they crossed the Dutch coast. Gollob at his *Jäfu* 5 'palace' at Bernay was called to assist, and he sent up two *Gruppen* of JG 2 from Beaumont-le-Roger led by the redoubtable Major Egon Mayer, which it was planned would attack the bombers as they made their exit.

Just after 1130 hrs, 15 Bf 109s of II./JG 27 were scrambled from Wiesbaden-Erbenheim under the direction of 7. *Jagddivision* to intercept the Solingen-bound bombers. Flying a Bf 109G-6 'heavy' '*Kanonenvogel*' armed with underwing MG 151 gondolas in Leutnant Willy Kientsch's 6. *Staffel* was Unteroffizier Karl Schmitz. He reported:

> At an altitude of 6,000-7,000 m, an air battle developed with more waves of Boeing bombers which were flying west under English fighter escort. While making my second attack from behind and below on the Boeing

flying on the outer left position of the left low flight of the last *Pulk*, I caused hits in the fuselage and wings. After pulling up my machine, I observed how the bomber that I had attacked suddenly fell away to the left and below the formation. I attacked this Boeing again from below and behind, and fired the last of my ammunition with visible strikes.

As there was no defensive fire, I flew alongside this aircraft at a distance of about 500 m, and it was now falling away downwards. When the Boeing descended to 3,000 m, I was suddenly attacked from above and behind by three–four Thunderbolts. Because of the icing on my cockpit canopy, I saw them too late. I immediately banked away and headed into the cloud. Just above the cloud, at about 2,000 m altitude, I received hits in my engine and through the canopy. As I flew into the clouds my machine was on fire, and I managed to climb out just in time. Because I was attacked by the escort fighters I was no longer able to observe the Boeing at which I had fired.

Schmitz had closed in from 300 m to 50 m, firing 260 rounds from his 20 mm MG 151 cannon and 300 rounds from his 13 mm MG 131 machine guns. Despite visibility being masked by the cloud, Schmitz believed that the Flying Fortress had gone down around 20–30 km west-southwest of Aachen, in the area between Eupen and Malmedy. Wounded, he bailed out of his Bf 109 and came down near Eupen:

> A Canadian landed between five–seven kilometres from me at the same time. He had also been wounded and had been placed in the same ambulance as me, and together we were taken to hospital at Aachen. According to his statement, the crew of his shot-down Boeing was ordered to bail out just above the clouds. Since the time and place coincide exactly with my own shoot-down, I assume that the prisoner was a crewmember of my downed bomber.[9]

In the meantime, the B-17s of the 1st BD had bombed Solingen and other targets of opportunity through cloud, but their formation had become dispersed and, as such, so had their escort. The Luftwaffe's efforts resulted in the most successful engagement against the bombers in over a month, with I. and II. *Jagdkorps* mounting 283 effective sorties.[10] I. *Jagdkorps* noted:

> The units of 2. and 3. *Jagddivisionen* repeatedly attacked a number of American bomber units over the area east of Köln. They scored successes, sustaining moderate losses. The fighters of 1. *Jagddivision* engaged in combat over the area east of Gummersbach without success.

JG 26 claimed six confirmed B-17s, and the overall total that day was 27 bombers and 12 of their escorts shot down (the Eighth Air Force actually lost 24 bombers and seven fighters). The defenders in turn had 15 pilots killed and 16 wounded, with 27 aircraft destroyed.

Unteroffizier Schmitz of 6./JG 27 was eventually credited with shooting down his B-17, but 7. *Jagddivision* would not confirm it until 10 March 1944. It was Schmitz' second victory, the 133rd for 6. *Staffel* and the 701st for II./JG 27. His *Staffelkapitän*, Leutnant Willy Kientsch, was also credited with a B-17 that day for his 47th victory.

To the south, since its debut at the beginning of November, the USAAF's Fifteenth Air Force had continued its heavy bomber campaign, mounting 19 major raids against targets in Italy, Austria, Greece and Bulgaria, striking at Axis naval bases, airfields and rail yards. In mid-November, the Fifteenth's Flying Fortresses and Liberators had moved from their Tunisian bases to airfields in southern Italy.

By December 1943, in the wake of the Allied landing at Salerno followed by dogged fighting on the Volturno Line, Italy's disastrous and unexpected surrender, an ensuing Italian Armistice with the Allied powers and the forced abandonment of the key Foggia airfield complex at the end of September, the Luftwaffe's fighter presence in the Mediterranean was largely 'boxed in' on airfields in the north such as Udine and Villaorba.

Controlling the fighters in the region since early October was *Jafü Oberitalien* based at Bologna under Oberstleutnant Günther *Freiherr* von Maltzahn, the former *Kommodore* of JG 53. It is fair to say that von Maltzahn had had to grapple with a hectic and transitional situation as *Gruppen* arrived and left. IV./JG 3 and II./JG 53 returned to the Reich, while III./JG 77 departed for Rumania for 'rest' as I./JG 4 arrived from that country via Bad Wörishofen. Then II./JG 51 left Neubiberg in December for stationing in the Udine area.

In context, on 20 October, the Italy-based *Luftflotte* 2 reported 108 fighter aircraft in three *Gruppen* on strength, of which 43 were classified as *Einsatzbereit* (operationally ready). By 31 December those figures were 184 and 78, respectively.[11] These were slender resources with which to mount an effective defence against the combined Allied air forces ranged against Italy and southern Europe.

On 2 December, the Fifteenth Air Force launched a two-pronged attack, striking at the Bolzano marshalling yards with 35 B-24s, while a force of 118 Flying Fortresses went to the southern French port of Marseilles to bomb U-boat pens then under construction.

Scrambled to intercept the bombers by Oberst Friedrich Vollbracht, the *Jafü Süd* at Aix, was a *Schwarm* of Bf 109s of 2./*Jagdgruppe Süd*, an operational training and replacement unit based at Avignon-Pujaut, in France. Leading the four Messerschmitts was instructor pilot Feldwebel Werner Döring, and his charges were three of his junior student pilots.

To his dismay, as Döring, a North Africa veteran who had flown previously with 1./JG 27 and had claimed his first B-17 shot down in August, led the fighters into engage, all of his aircraft's weapons suffered a technical failure. Undaunted by the risk of defensive fire, he flew what were described by Vollbracht as 'several dashing attacks against the enemy formation' in an effort to demonstrate to his trainees how to close in on the bombers 'correctly and effectively'. Apparently Döring's action resulted in 'three successful attacks' and the shooting down of one Flying Fortress. 'I would like to express my special appreciation for his dashing and responsible behaviour', noted Vollbracht in the *Jafü*'s daily orders.[12]

The levels of attrition among experienced fighter pilots and formation leaders continued to bite during December. On the 4th, one month after replacing the loss of 180-victory Knight's Cross recipient Major Kurt Brändle as *Gruppenkommandeur* of II./JG 3, Hauptmann Wilhelm Lemke suffered a similar fate when he too fell to P-47s whilst on a patrol northwest of Nijmegen, in the Netherlands. Lemke had flown more than 600 missions, during which he had been credited with 131 victories, including 25 Il-2s in the East and three four-engined bombers in the West.

On 5 December, as the officers of I. *Jagdkorps* enjoyed a morning's hunting in the grounds of the Villa de Breul estate, they would have had no idea that an ominous event was taking place in the skies to the south. As if the P-47s were not enough, that day saw the feared debut of North American Aviation P-51B Mustangs of the 354th FG, temporarily assigned to the Eighth Air Force from the Ninth Air Force, escorting bombers to Amiens. This would herald a new and forbidding dimension to the air war. The appearance for the first time of the Mustang caused Luftwaffe fighter commanders considerable concern and forced a reappraisal of existing tactical methods. This high-powered fighter more than exceeded the speed and manoeuvrability of both the rugged, radial-engined Fw 190 and the re-worked Bf 109.

The next day another calamity took place when Generalmajor Schmid set off in a car from his headquarters at Zeist along the icy roads to Volkel, where he was due for a meeting with Hauptmann Friedrich Eberle, *Gruppenkommandeur* of III./JG 1, and his staff. At some point along the way, the car, driven by I. *Jagdkorps'* Day Fighter Operations Officer Major i.G. Heinrich Seeliger, collided with a Dutch cyclist. The unfortunate cyclist suffered a fractured skull as a result of the accident, while Schmid escaped with minor cuts to a hand.[13]

On 11 December, in an even more worrying development, 44 of the nimble new P-51s of the 354th FG, dubbed the 'Pioneer Mustang Group', shielded 523 bombers all the way to aircraft industry targets in the Lower Saxony port of Emden. A ferocious aerial battle ensued and, as will be described, it saw the introduction of another innovative if not radical aerial weapon on the part of the Luftwaffe.

The *Funkhorchdienstes* picked up the Eighth Air Force's bombers assembling over eastern England from 0808 hrs. At around 1035 hrs, the formation, comprising 437 B-17s of the 1st and 3rd BDs and 86 B-24s of the 2nd BD, commenced its northeasterly course across the North Sea. Reaching the East Frisian island of Norderney, the enormous armada of Flying Fortresses and Liberators stretching for several miles wheeled slowly south to head to Emden in three waves.

While II. *Jagdkorps* kept its units on the ground, I. *Jagdkorps* deployed 307 aircraft against the incursion, but those units of 1. *Jagddivision* which took off failed to engage because of bad weather over the Elbe. It was the 147 machines of 2. and 3. *Jagddivisionen* that made contact with the bombers during their approach to Emden and while they were over the city.

The first attacks against the lead group commenced off the island of Langeroog at 1212 hrs and continued against all four combat wings until 1250 hrs, when the fighter escort met the formation as it headed home via Leeuwarden. Attacks on the lead and low groups of the leading combat wing were 'pressed vigorously'. Mortars were fired simultaneously at the bombers, this time 'from high and at twelve o'clock' from around 400 yards, after which there was a massed attack, with fighters using both cannon and machine guns as they closed into around 200 yards. The fighters then dived against the low groups.

The mortar 'specialists' of I. and III./ZG 26 were active once more, these *Gruppen* sending up 23 and 17 Bf 110s, respectively, from Wunstorf at 1055 hrs. They assembled over the Dümmer See at 7,000 m, and at 1120 hrs hooked up with their fighter escort from III./JG 11. With I./ZG 26 leading, the formation made for Wilhelmshaven-Spiekeroog under 'Y'-*Führung*. The bombers were sighted at 1210 hrs heading for the mouth of the Weser river in '7 *Pulks*', with fighter escorts above and below them. The Bf 110s elected to mount a rear attack on the fourth *Pulk*, firing their mortars at a range of 1,000 m. The blasts had good effect, breaking up the bombers, but equally the *Zerstörer* were forced to scatter immediately after launching their mortars when they were attacked by the escort fighters.

The bombers flew directly over Oldenburg – the home of III./JG 11 – and were pursued by the Bf 110s of ZG 26, which made individual attacks.

Two B-17s were claimed shot down by Feldwebel Josef Scherkenbeck, but I./ZG 26 lost three aircraft and III. *Gruppe* one.[14]

The steadily increasing numbers of fighter escorts from late 1943 meant that a review of the tactics employed by the cannon- and mortar-carrying *Zerstörer* units became necessary. After being relocated to bases deeper in the Reich, the *Zerstörer* were assigned a standard fighter *Gruppe* to act as their escort. At this time, most of the *Zerstörer* units removed their underwing W.Gr.21 mortar tubes in order to remain manoeuvrable in the presence of USAAF fighters. Their own escort would fly with two *Staffeln*, in *Schwärme*, on either side and behind the *Zerstörer* some 450 m higher, while a third *Staffel* was positioned as top cover about 1,800 m higher.

The commanders of the *Zerstörer* and the escort had radio contact, but the escort fighters were forbidden from engaging the bombers until after the *Zerstörer* had carried out their attack, and only then if no American fighters were to be seen. If this was the case, the fighter leader would commence an attack, although the top cover *Staffel* was excluded from this.

At this time the *Zerstörer* usually attacked from head-on, approaching the lead *Pulk* in a column of *Schwärme* and passing once through the bombers, after which either the next *Pulk* back was attacked from head-on or the *Zerstörer* would curve back and attack it from the rear, continuously in *Schwärme*. Such tactical methods were used by I./ZG 26 working in cooperation with Major Günther Specht's I./JG 11, while II./ZG 76 worked with Oberstleutnant Walther Dahl's III./JG 3. According to senior Luftwaffe officers interrogated after the war, 'In this manner, losses remained within bearable limits and successes were good'.[15]

An immediate post-mission report on the Emden raid compiled by Eighth Air Force Headquarters provides a graphic synopsis of the combat:

> Attacks were repeated in same manner and appeared to be well coordinated. Three to four B-17s of the group hit were seen to go down from this attack. The usual concentrated attacks from all clock positions were reported against all stragglers. Parachute bombs were observed bursting 400–500 yards from the formation.
>
> E/A attacks were not vigorous against groups in the second combat wing. Fighters seemed to direct attacks against lead a/c of each squadron's low group, from high 12 o'clock. Fw 190s and Me 110s predominated. Attacking out of the sun, firing rockets from about 600 yards, attacking in formation and four to five abreast.
>
> Attacks against third combat wing were not pressed vigorously. Most attacks from rear – rockets being fired at approximately 900 yds, then fighters peeled off. Fourth combat wing reports as many as 100 E/A

seen. Attacks pressed home from mostly frontal and tail high. Fifty Me 109s and Fw 190s made continuous attacks from landfall to Dollard Bay on way out. E/A aircraft would line up in single file and come in at 12 o'clock high, returning to attack from six o'clock. Also attacks were made by four to six E/A abreast, some pressing attacks closer than others before peeling off left and right. Plane of the 385th Group was reported lost through air-to-air bombing.[16]

And it was on the Emden mission that E.Kdo 25 deployed another weapon for possibly only the second time.

Curiously, it was representatives from the German police and postal ministry who suggested to the RLM that steel cable could be used as a weapon by Luftwaffe aircraft. They foresaw cables being 'dragged' into enemy bomber formations to damage wings, control surfaces and engines.

Experiments with 'towed' bombs had first taken place at Rechlin in August 1943 when an He 111 trailed ten-kilogramme bombs through the air by means of 2.5-mm diameter steel cable some 60 m in length. Tests with high-tensile strength, carbon steel piano wire of one millimetre diameter, 100 m in length, trailing down to between 25.5–32.5 m, were also conducted. Piano wire was used for several subsequent experiments, with the aim of it being weighted and then released to wrap around the propellers of four-engined bombers, and with the hope of the wire being ingested by engines. Hauptmann Horst Geyer, commander of E.Kdo 25, recalled, 'Galland was very interested in the concept of using sharpened steel cable'.[17]

Problems were encountered when it was found that as the carrier aircraft changed course, the cables and wires flailed around uncontrollably. But at the end of August, despite the erratic and hazardous nature of these initial experiments, there was sufficient belief in towed or cable bombs to develop an automatic reeling and cutting device based on a cable drum for installation within the carrier aircraft.

Thus, in late September 1943, Rechlin delivered an experimental ten-kilogramme bomb attached to 'sharpened' 2.5-mm twisted-steel cable to E.Kdo 25 at Wittmundhafen for fitting to an Fw 190, with the objective of deploying such a weapon against the bombers. As well as the bomb itself, the developers at Rechlin were thoughtful enough to deliver a salvaged wing from a shot-down B-24.

E.Kdo 25's technical personnel then devised a means in which cable of 100–400 m in length could be stowed into a specially adapted cylindrical metal container, with the ten-kilogramme 'bomb' effectively used as just a weight to provide momentum, and left outside the casing. The whole apparatus, which was christened *'Schlinge'* ('sling') was then attached to a fuselage-mounted ETC 50 bomb rack. Geyer recalled:

> At first we carried out tests with a very small 'bomb' – about the size of a man's fist, with no charge or blast – attached to a length of 400 m, 2–3 mm twisted steel cable, which was extremely sharp. You could easily cut your hand on it.

It was planned to approach an enemy formation from the front and about 500 m above. The 'bomb' would be freed on impact with a bomber via means of a 'weak link' in the cable and the container jettisoned. The fighter would then exit flat over the bombers and subsequently be available to operate in a conventional role. One limitation was the fact that once the cable had been released, it could not be reeled in again, and so if a release was made in error, a danger existed if the cable had to be dropped straight down onto friendly territory.

Geyer undertook several test flights against the wing of the Liberator in order to assess the damage the cable would inflict, but results were disappointing, as he recalled:

> Some tests were made with a weight and others without, but approach and correction became very difficult. Rechlin then sent over the wing of an old B-24 Liberator, which was placed on a specially constructed wooden cradle. I flew several trials against this wing in an Fw 190 to assess the damage inflicted, but the cable just kept swinging about and didn't hit the target. The 400 m cable was carried in a cylindrical container beneath the Focke-Wulf's fuselage and was opened at a height of 500 m on the approach to the target. The bomb came free on impact with the target and the cable was released later whilst over open countryside. The device was made so that it could be fitted to virtually any aircraft.[18]

Undaunted by the results of the trials, E.Kdo 25 reported the weapon operationally ready in the first half of October. There, it seems, further work stopped until the raid on 11 December. As the B-24s of the 44th BG approached the target, an Fw 190 trailing a length of steel cable 'with a weighted object on the end' was seen to make a head-on approach towards the formation, followed by a shallow dive from slightly above. The German fighter was then seen to release the cable, which impacted with a B-24, entwining itself around the bomber's nose. The cable injured the bombardier and the navigator.

Shortly after this attack, the bomber's right-hand side bomb-bay door inexplicably blew in and was torn away in the slipstream. USAAF technical personnel later assumed this was as a result of the cable weight smacking against the aircraft. The Liberator was able to return to base, and the cable was removed and taken away for scientific analysis. This showed the cable to have been made of square section, seven-strand 7/48-in. steel that was capable of carrying a 550-lb bomb.[19] Chemical analysis tests showed the composition of the wire to include carbon, manganese, silicon, nickel, sulphur, chromium and phosphorus.

Two days after the raid on Emden, German radio broadcasts were heard proclaiming that this new weapon had been used against the American formations 'with devastating effect'. A more grounded assessment was given by Geyer in his report on the *Schlinge* for the second half of November:

> This device has been used twice so far on operations, firstly with two aircraft and on a second occasion with three aircraft. This showed that when attacking from the front, contact became difficult as a result of the enemy taking evasive manoeuvres. In one case the cable was apparently pulled over an engine, and the engine came to a stop shortly thereafter. In a second instance, a severe cut was seen across the centre of the wing of a Boeing. Further attacks and observations could not be made because of the commencement of combat with the accompanying enemy fighters. More accurate assessment can only be expected after further operations, which must be carried out at least in *Schwarm* strength.[20]

That time would not be long coming. The USAAF bomber crews had not seen the last of cable bombs.

Towards the end of December, work on *Sokrates*, 2. *Jagddivision*'s vast concrete control bunker at Stade, was complete and the wooden scaffolding brought down. The entire bunker was shrouded by a huge camouflage net intended to provide concealment from the air, anchored at its edges with concrete retaining blocks hammered into the ground with long spikes.

Under the command of Oberst Max Ibel, a staff of around 200 officers, Luftwaffe technicians and female auxiliaries moved into purpose-built rooms spread over three levels (later in the war, the number of personnel would increase dramatically). With no natural light, they worked under the glare of overhead lamps and with the perpetual sound of jangling telephones, urgent chatter, the echoes of steel doors slamming in long corridors, booted footsteps on metal steps in echoing stairwells and the latest in command, control, guidance and communications technology.

Because of the cavernous ambience of such buildings, they became known as '*Gefechtsopernhauses*' ('Battle Opera Houses'), and at their core was the largest room, the nerve centre, known as the *Kampfraum* (Battle Room). It would be from the *Kampfraum* at Stade that the staff of 2. *Jagddivision,* led by Oberst Ibel, would fight its day and night war against the bombers of the RAF and the USAAF.

The *Jagddivision*'s task was to defend the approaches to the Reich via the Heligoland Bight and the airspace over northwest Germany, including Hamburg and Bremen, as well as Hanover, Schleswig-Holstein and Denmark, directing tactical control of the fighter units assigned to the divisional area, in the process of which data was drawn from radar and observer stations and coordinated with other area and Flak commands. The *Jagddivision* was supported by *Jafü Deutsche Bucht* (shortly to be renamed as *Jafü* 2), with its quarters on the nearby Bremervörder Strasse. It was commanded by Knight's Cross-holder Oberst Johann Schalk, a former *Nachtjagdgeschwader Kommodore* who had recently taken over from Oberst Karl Hentschel.

In the *Sokrates* bunker, Ibel presided over a *Kampfraum* 32 m in length and 15 m wide, with a ceiling height of 13 m. Bathed in the low light from scores of overhead and desk lamps, the 'opera house' scale of the room was necessary to accommodate the 11 m x 11 m illuminated glass situation map that divided the space roughly two-thirds along its length.

Ibel sat centrally at floor-level, looking directly at the map, flanked to his left by three senior fighter control officers and to his right by his deputy Operations Officer and two Flak commanders. The map covered an area stretching from Paris in the west to the Oder in the east, and from southern Norway to the Donau. Within this area were shown all main rivers, radio, Flak and searchlight locations, nightfighting control 'boxes' and airfields within the divisional area.

The bases for the single-engined day fighters were at Jever, Oldenburg, Wittmundhafen, Nordholz, Heligoland-Düne and Husum, as well as Aalborg East and Frederikshavn/Knivholt, in Denmark, and Kristiansand (South) and Lista, in Norway. *Zerstörer Gruppen* could also be called upon from the airfields at Bad Lippspringe, Wunstorf, Achmer, Hesepe, Wittmundhafen and Hildesheim.[21]

Overlaying the situation map was a grid dividing it into large, lettered squares, with each square representing an airspace sector of 111 km x 70 km, and onto which would be portrayed the *Luftlage* – the prevailing air situation. The *Luftlage* was created and updated only after a long, complex and labour-intensive process involving many personnel at several locations who formed an *Auge-Ohr Flugmelde Dienst*. This service drew information from a network of regional FluKos in *Flugmeldebezirke* (Air Reporting Areas) which were based on former postal areas. Invariably, the 10–12-man FluKos were quartered in designated and suitable rooms of post offices and, to the autumn of 1943, relayed their information via telephone to a *Jafü* HQ, after which time reports went to the appropriate *Jagddivision*.[22]

In the *Kampfraum*, graduated floor levels or 'terraces' of work stations ran back from the situation map to the rear of the room. Immediately behind and slightly above Ibel and his senior staff, on the lowest 'terrace', were the desks for 22 fighter controllers responsible for controlling single or formations of aircraft and for monitoring activity in individual sectors. Above and behind them on the next level were the desks for the master 'Y'-*Führung* operator and the *Jagdgeschwader* operations officer, in contact with the operational fighter units, and his staff. To their right sat five keyboard operators assisting the fighter controllers.

On a fourth terrace were three *Klotsche Tische* (Klotsche tables) on which were indicated the locations and movement of Allied aircraft in large areas of airspace. Behind and above these were operators who projected light markers onto the situation map to indicate Allied air movement. Flanking them on either side were desks for personnel of the *Funkhorchdienstes* who listened for and evaluated enemy radio traffic. Across the room, seated in the 'gallery' behind the map, were more operators who projected different light markers to indicate the positions of Luftwaffe aircraft and formations. Elsewhere were desks for an electrical engineer and maintenance technicians, and also to one side, radio recorders.

The bunker was serviced by an extensive telephone network consisting of almost 1,000 lines connecting it with the *Luftwaffenbefehlshaber Mitte* in Berlin, *Jafü Deutsche Bucht*, which had relocated from Jever to 2. *Jagddivsion's* previous complex in Stade, and other divisional and *Jafü* command centres, airfields, radar stations, observation posts and Flak batteries.

Indeed, *Sokrates* was merely one component of an increasingly prodigious, sophisticated and expensive network of defence and interception control. Besides the bunker at Stade, other similar and equally large *Zentral Gefechtsstände* were under construction for 1. *Jagddivision* at Schaarsbergen, near Deelen in the Netherlands, codenamed Diogenes 2, and at Gedhus, near Grove in Denmark, for the *Jagdabschnittsführer Führer Dänemark* (Fighter Sector Commander Denmark), codenamed Gyges.

On the 29th, Schmid once again met with Galland and his divisional commanders. He stressed the importance of improving communication between day fighter units operating within individual divisional sectors, and to develop efficient methods of assembling *Geschwader* in the air.

In his opening remarks, Galland commented that use of 21 cm mortars had been more successful than previously assumed, but that when it came to tactics generally, he believed that the new plan of taking on the USAAF fighters had not brought any great success. In his view, this was down to recent inclement weather, the Luftwaffe's strength inferiority and the impossibility of assembling sufficient fighters in one area due to the constraints of time and space. It was also Galland's opinion that at least one entire enemy formation *had* to be *destroyed* in the air, otherwise the war against the bombers would never be won and attrition would continue to gnaw away at the Luftwaffe.

There was also further discussion about increasing use of the *frontal* attack method – further indication of the disagreements in tactical policy still prevailing. In a detailed review of Luftwaffe attacks, the Eighth Air Force's Operational Analysis Section noted:

> The period from July through December 1943 was marked by a high percentage of tail attacks and a decrease in the proportion of nose attacks. In five of the six months, attacks on the tail quadrant were 40% of the total or higher. Nose attacks did not rise above 29% in any month, and in December dropped to 20% of total attacks.

Also, a study carried out between July and November 1943 'indicated that B-17s were more efficient than the enemy when exchanging deflection shots on beam attacks'.[23]

Galland added too that although aircraft were fitted with drop tanks, pilots needed to learn to fly with more awareness of fuel consumption during assembly.[24]

Following the meeting, Schmid issued a directive to his *Jagddivision* commanders:

> In view of our numerical inferiority in operations against the American attacks, it will be necessary to concentrate our units for an attack relative to time and space. Fighter attacks should be conducted in such a manner that cohesive units of the strength of at least one fighter *Geschwader* attack the bomber stream at a specific spot. By applying this method it must be possible to destroy an American bomber unit completely.[25]

According to General der Flieger Karl Koller, who, in December 1943, was Chief of the Luftwaffe Operations Staff:

> At the end of 1943, Göring considered that the arming of the US Army Air Forces constituted merely a superficial show of strength. At this juncture he declared, in all seriousness, 'American reserves of manpower for aircrews are completely exhausted'. Göring frequently repeated this belief to General [Günther] Korten [Chief of the Luftwaffe General Staff] and to the General of Fighters, amongst others.[26]

Unfortunately for the Luftwaffe, the Reichsmarschall of the Greater German Reich was grossly misinformed. As at 31 May 1943, the Eighth Air Force numbered 45,569 personnel. In June 1943, heavy bomber crew personnel numbered 18,750 men, with the figures for September and December projected as rising to 25,000 and 38,000. At the end of May 1943, the USAAF had ten heavy bomber groups in the ETO. By December, that had increased to 21 groups. Total ETO combat aircraft strength for the same period rose from 1,260 to 4,242, with strategic bombardment being of primary importance.[27]

In the second half of 1943, the Luftwaffe had battled against an increasingly powerful enemy in the USAAF's heavy bomber forces, while having to weather attrition, reduced supplies of fighter aircraft, lowering standards of training and fuel limitations. It had made an impact in as much as that in four months (September to December) 516 bombers were lost, an increase of 147 over the previous four months. But these figures were based on all causes (fighters, Flak and weather), and as a percentage of the total of bombers lost from the numbers of those attacking, in the same periods the losses had fallen from 6.4 per cent to 4.4 per cent.[28]

On 8 August, the RLM had issued its Plan 233-II (the 'Reich Defence Plan'), in which production of fighters was to be accelerated dramatically to 4,150 single-engined types and 1,750 twin-engined types per month.[29] In the last quarter of 1943, production of Bf 109s and Fw 190s had been in steady decline:

	Target	Actual	Percentage drop
October	1,239	955	-22.9
November	1,370	775	-43.4
December	1,152	560	-51.4[30]

The Jagdwaffe did its best to employ the shifting tactics ordered by Göring. It devised the new *Sturm* concept that would be unleashed in the coming year. It had trialled new weapons such as air-to-air mortars and cable bombs, and more radical weapons were ready for operational evaluation. It had developed and expanded its sophisticated, but expensive command and control infrastructure with the building of giant concrete bunkers fitted out with the latest technology.

Yet the scale of the challenge the Luftwaffe faced would only increase in 1944, and its response would become only more desperate and radical the more limited resources became.

PART IV

Sturm und Drang – 1944

The outcome of a battle depends not upon numbers, but upon the united hearts of those who fight.

KUSUNOKI MASASHIGE (1294–1336),
ATTRIBUTED

The attention of all responsible commanders was focused on only one danger – the Flying Fortresses and their bomb loads.

GENERALMAJOR JOSEF SCHMID,
MAY 1944

14

Pointblank and the Battle for Air Superiority

On 27 December 1943, to welcome the coming New Year, Gen 'Hap' Arnold sent a straightforward message to the commanders of the Eighth and Fifteenth Air Forces:

Destroy the enemy air force wherever you find them – in the air, on the ground, and in the factories.

This objective he considered a '*MUST*', because without the Luftwaffe being eliminated it would be a 'conceded fact' that Operations *Overlord* and *Anvil* – respectively the planned invasions of northern and southern France – 'will not be possible'. Arnold also assured his commanders that American factories were turning out large quantities of aircraft, engines and support equipment, and air- and groundcrew training was proceeding apace.[1]

Behind the scenes, however, Arnold did not feel so bullish. On 20 December 1943, the Chief of the Air Staff, Maj Gen Barney Giles, had advised Maj Gen Carl Spaatz, commander of the United States Strategic Air Forces (USSTAF), that 'Arnold had not been satisfied with the efforts made to date'.[2]

Arnold also packed Brig Gen Eaker off to the Mediterranean as a result of his increasing dissatisfaction with his reluctance to mount deep penetration missions into the Reich, and replaced him with Maj Gen James H. Doolittle. He would soon 'loosen the reins' on his long-range fighters by allowing them the opportunity to strike at targets of choice – particularly airfields – once their escort duty had been completed. This would hopefully wreak mayhem on the Luftwaffe.

The fact was that along with cities such as Münster, Stuttgart, Schweinfurt, Regensburg and Wilhelmshaven, the Luftwaffe itself was now a target. In a poignant moment in January 1944, the newly appointed Doolittle walked into the office of Maj Gen William E. Kepner, commander of VIII Fighter

Command, at Bushey Hall, in Hertfordshire, and read a sign hanging on the wall:

Our mission is to bring the bombers back.

Doolittle considered this for a moment, and then told Kepner to remove the sign as it no longer applied. He duly told him, 'Your mission is to destroy the German Air Force'.[3]

Thus, despite atrocious weather conditions prevailing in Europe, January 1944 marked the beginning of an escalation in American offensive action. Furthermore, American production and the numbers of fighters and bombers reaching Europe were now beginning to swamp the Germans.

Generalmajor Schmid summarised that in addition to the poor weather:

> ... the technical deficiencies of German fighter aircraft and the low training standard of replacement fighter pilots precluded steadily successful and effective combat against American superiority at high-altitude. Thus, January 1944 was again characterised by the inability of German forces to provide an effective defence against American daylight attacks on the Reich, let alone prevent them. Only the utmost caution in employing aircraft in bad weather – especially when take-off and landing conditions were uncertain – was able to keep German losses within reasonable limits. Even so, approximately one-third of German aircraft losses was due to commitment under unfavourable weather conditions.[4]

January would see the Luftwaffe write off a staggering 30.3 per cent of its single-engined fighters and suffer a loss of 16.9 per cent of its fighter pilot strength. Furthermore, the beginning of the year showed a percentage decrease in the Luftwaffe's Order of Battle for Bf 109 and Fw 190 interceptors from 31 per cent in 1943 to 27 per cent at the beginning of 1944.

There was also a shake-up at the very top of the *Reichsluftverteigung*. Finally, the status of the central geographic command organisation, which to date had been founded on the *Luftwaffenbefehlshaber Mitte* under Generaloberst Weise, was retitled *Luftflotte Reich*, thereby giving it the same status as *Luftflotte* 3 and the *Luftflotten* in the eastern and southern theatres.

Furthermore, Weise was removed as commander of the air fleet. Appointed in his place was 55-year-old Generaloberst Hans-Jürgen Stumpff who, early in the war, had been chief of air defence at the RLM before commanding *Luftflotten* 1 (central and northern Germany and occupied Poland) and 5 (Norway). Grabmann felt that Stumpff was 'a commander versed in the direction of both air and anti-aircraft artillery operations and experienced in the execution of both offensive and defensive missions'.[5]

The 'new' *Luftflotte* would be headquartered in a hastily converted bunker previously occupied by the *Reichsluftschutzschule* at Berlin-Wannsee which became known as *Herold 2*.[6]

On the morning of 5 January, the German early warning system reported the assembly of large American formations over England. Just like the day before – which marked the first daylight attack against a German target in the New Year – the Baltic Sea port of Kiel was to be the target. Escorted by 70 P-38 Lightnings, 119 B-17s of the 1st BD and 96 B-24s of the 2nd BD set out to bomb the city's shipyards. The visual attack enabled a good concentration of bombs to hit their assigned target.

The way to Kiel had not been without adversity. At 1000 hrs, the first German fighters were scrambled to intercept, but the heavily armed and armoured Fw 190s of *Sturmstaffel* 1, together with the Fw 190s of I./JG 1 and Bf 109s of II./JG 27, were kept on the ground for another two hours. When these units did finally take-off, it was the more experienced pilots of I./JG 1 who met the first elements of the bomber formation over Belgium at 1245 hrs and subsequently scored one victory and four B-17 *Herausschüsse*. However, the *Gruppe* paid a heavy price, losing three of its pilots killed.

Immediately after the raid, across the three *Jagddivisionen* of I. *Jagdkorps*, one pilot was reported killed, six wounded and 15 posted as missing. Eleven fighters were missing, eight suffered more than 60 per cent damage and two others had lighter damage. The USAAF lost five B-17s, five B-24s and seven P-38s.

It was to prove an inauspicious start for *Sturmstaffel* 1, the unit failing to make contact with the enemy before returning to Dortmund. Oberleutnant Richard Franz, who had flown in North Africa and Italy with JGs 27 and 77, respectively, as well as serving as an instructor, recalled:

At that time we were the only unit which attacked the *Viermots* from the rear and all the other pilots who flew in the *Reichsverteidigung* thought we were a little bit crazy. They all preferred to attack head-on, with the advantages and disadvantages that came with it. The *Sturmstaffel* pilots, on the other hand, voluntarily bound themselves to bring down one bomber per engagement, either with their weapons or by ramming. I never had to ram, thank God.[7]

Despite the discussion at Zeist on 29 December, the War Diary of I. *Jagdkorps* commented: 'The technique of attack from the front, which has proved to be most generally successful, has not yet been mastered by all fighter units.'[8]

The pattern of American bombing throughout January was dictated to a great extent by the prevailing overcast weather over northwest Europe, which necessitated pathfinder-led missions against German ports and industrial areas. The only major visual operation occurred on 11 January when the weather was expected to be fine and Doolittle gave the go-ahead for a maximum-strength mission. However, conditions were to prove fickle, and the USAAF bomber force of 663 aircraft pushed on in deteriorating weather to hit several aviation and industrial targets in the heart of the Reich – Oschersleben, Halberstadt, Braunschweig and Osnabrück. This mission marked the commencement of Operation *Pointblank*, the strategic air offensive against Germany intended to bring about 'the progressive destruction and dislocation of the German military and economic system'.

Eighth Air Force Intelligence summarised the mission as:

The first deep penetration into the heart of the Reich under visual bombing conditions since the attack on Schweinfurt on 14 October 1943. It afforded to both the enemy and ourselves the first practical demonstration of the defence technique which the enemy had been developing and practicing during the three months' interval.[9]

The Luftwaffe committed maximum forces against the attack and put up the fiercest opposition since the last Schweinfurt raid. 1. *Jagddivision* would cover the area over Braunschweig, deploying aircraft from III./JG 54, III./JG 301, I. and II./JG 302, I. and II./ZG 26, nightfighters from NJGs 2 and 5 and the ISS *Erla* in 99 sorties. Fighters from 2. *Jagddivision*'s JG 11 (all *Gruppen*), III./ZG 76, E.Kdo 25 and nightfighters from NJG 3 operated over Hanover and Paderborn in 223 sorties, and 3. *Jagddivision*'s JG 1 (all *Gruppen*), I./JG 3, II./JG 27, I./JG 300, *Sturmstaffel* 1 and IV./NJG 1 generated 214 sorties, initially over Bremen and again over Münster as the bombers made their exit.

From the south, 7. *Jagddivision* deployed aircraft from I./NJG 6 and I./ZG 76, while to the west, II. *Jagdkorps* sent aircraft from the three *Gruppen* of JG 26 and 5. *Jagddivision* deployed III./JG 2, whose 10. *Staffel* had recently transferred from *Luftflotte* 3 to 3. *Jagddivision* specifically so that it could train up in the use of 21 cm mortars.

Quite accurately, Eighth Air Force Intelligence described the Luftwaffe effecting a three-stage form of defence, with the first stage operating between the Dutch coast to just east of the Dümmer See. In this zone, around 50–60 single-engined fighters were deployed to attack the bombers and their escort on the way in, while a few nightfighters were brought down from the north. It was noted that:

> As distinguished from previous occasions, there was no apparent effort to engage our fighters, and thus to force their early return to base. Attacks were principally against the leading bomber formations, but the enemy exploited through his highly developed reconnaissance and control system any lapses in escort which facilitated his attacks at any point along the column.[10]

In readiness, *Sturmstaffel* 1 and I./JG 1 had transferred from Dortmund to Rheine and waited for the order to take-off. It came at 1030 hrs. Thirty minutes later, I./JG 1 executed a frontal attack against the USAAF formation and shot down three bombers in as many minutes between 1108–1110 hrs. The *Sturmstaffel* separated from I./JG 1 and, in conformity with its intended tactics, attacked an American combat box from the rear. Approaching at close range, Oberleutnant Othmar Zehart opened fire simultaneously with the other pilots of the *Staffel* and scored the first kill – a B-17 – for his unit.

Fifteen Fw 190s of II./JG 1 led by the *Staffelführer* of 5. *Staffel*, 23-year-old Austrian five-victory ace Leutnant Rüdiger von Kirchmayr, also scrambled from Rheine at 1030 hrs, their pilots having been waiting at cockpit readiness. Guided by 'Y'-*Verfahren*, they made contact with three *Pulks*, numbering 50–60 Flying Fortresses, at 1126 hrs at 6,300 m in the Göttingen area heading southeast without an escort – the best conditions the German fighter pilots could hope for. Von Kirchmayr duly led the Focke-Wulfs in for the first of three close-formation frontal attacks, taking aim with his Fw 190A-7's four MG 151s and two MG 131s. He recounted:

> After a close-formation frontal attack by the *Gruppe*, I started a second closed attack on the first *Pulk* of about 20 B-17s in Plan-Qu. KU. Coming out of the sun, I fired at the Boeing flying on the outside right from 600 m, closing in from the same height. The cockpit and individual parts of the fuselage and wings flew away, whereupon the Boeing extended its undercarriage and spiralled off to the right.
>
> After two further closed attacks by the *Gruppe*, I commenced a third frontal attack. Due to the Boeing formation making a slight change of course, I had to start the attack at an angle of 15–20 degrees from the front right and from the same height. Coming out of the sun, I fired at the Boeing flying in the first group of about 20 B-17s to the upper right, and was able to observe hits in the left inboard engine, which trailed dense black smoke. The ball turret and individual parts of the

cockpit, fuselage and wings flew away. The Boeing lagged far behind its formation and slowly lost altitude. Impact took place at 1130 hrs in *Plan-Qu*. KA2 – four kilometres southwest of Osterode/Harz.[11]

Von Kirchmayr had despatched the bomber with 90 rounds of MG 131 and 60 rounds of MG 151 ammunition.

After these attacks, a number of Fw 190s turned back for a rear attack, apparently of a kind devised by the *Gruppenkommandeur*, Hauptmann Walter Hoeckner, and known as the '*Schlangenbiss-Angriff*' ('Snakebite Attack') in which the Focke-Wulfs would approach from behind and below in waves – not a method mentioned in the Eighth Air Force's November 1943 graphical guide to Luftwaffe fighter tactics. Regardless, in the space of minutes, II./JG 1 claimed 11 B-17s shot down and one *Herausschuss*.[12]

The Bf 109Gs of the *Wilde Sau* nightfighter *Gruppe* I./JG 302 based at Jüterbog-Waldlager also accounted for a B-17 shot down. Twin-engined nightfighters were deployed in some strength and with some success, claiming 12 B-17s downed – Oberleutnant Rolf Bokemeyer, *Staffelkapitän* of 3./NJG 5, was credited with three *Viermots* shot down in his Bf 110 between 1240 and 1312 hrs and three *Herausschüsse* between Quakenbrück and Hoya. However, these successes were negated by the loss of nine nightfighters.[13]

In what the Eighth Air Force described as the 'Second Defensive Stage':

> At 1030 hrs twin-engined day fighters were assembling over Wunstorf awaiting the arrival of single-engined fighters which were being sent there from other points, including bases in southwest Germany [single-engined fighters were instructed to assemble over Wunstorf at 26,000 ft]. The rendezvous was not completed. The single-engined fighters, however, under the guidance of a 'shadower aircraft', engaged the bombers just south of Wunstorf, the twin-engined fighters following shortly afterwards. This concentration of 150–200 E/A continued to harass the bombers of the 1st Task Force from that point to and around the targets at Oschersleben and Halberstadt, while a lesser force engaged the trailing 3rd Division formations which were attacking Brunswick [Braunschweig].

The 'Third Defensive Stage' saw more nightfighters brought down from the north:

> Well-timed interceptions along the withdrawal routes were effected, and since no withdrawal escort was available to the bombers, the results were very profitable to the enemy – full exploitation of nightfighters against stragglers.[14]

As the bombers withdrew, 4. *Jagddivision* directed several *Gruppen* against the bombers, including the 30 or so Fw 190s of I./JG 26 based at Florennes, in Belgium. This was what Eighth Air Force Intelligence described as the 'Withdrawal Offensive Stage'. Led by Hauptmann Karl Borris, the Focke-Wulfs headed north with drop tanks and intercepted 19 B-17s of the 306th BG near Nordhorn. With a *Staffel* of Fw 190s providing top cover, Borris flew past the Flying Fortresses, then turned and lined his fighters up for a classic head-on attack. Eight B-17s were shot down, with five crashing around the Zuider Zee and the remaining three making it back to England, where they crash-landed, never to fly again.[15]

A small number of aircraft from E.Kdo 25 were also in action, once more attempting to take down bombers of the Oschersleben force with cable bombs. These unconventional weapons seem to have generated some degree of 'cable fever' among the USAAF crews, who reported seeing 'Ju 88s, Me 110s, Fw 190s and Me 109s' carrying such bombs. Indeed, following a conversation with officers of the Eighth Air Force after the mission, Air Commodore S. O. Bufton, Director of Bomber Operations at RAF Bomber Command, was so alarmed that he sent a 'Most Secret' memo to the Air Staff on the subject. According to Bufton, the tactics employed by E.Kdo 25 were:

> ...head-on, with the object of either severing the wing or bringing the bomb into contact with some part of the aircraft's structure. The observed results achieved were that one aircraft was hit by a bomb, exploded and went down; one aircraft had the end of the wing sawn off by the cable but returned safely; one aircraft was struck on the nose of the fuselage by the cable and the bomb hit the underside of the fuselage. It failed to explode and fell away; 15 ft of cable remained with the aircraft.[16]

Those B-17s of the 1st BD going to Oschersleben reported opposition as being:

> ...heavy and sustained. Most groups report up to 200 E/A encountered, with approximately 50 percent twin-engined. Enemy fighters first encountered in the vicinity of the Dummer Lake and around the target area. Attacks were from all angles and levels, both singly and in fairly large groups. Rockets [sic] were used extensively with unknown results. Ju 88s were once again reported swinging bombs on the end of cables, and one report was received of unsuccessful air-to-air bombing. It seems that the heaviest and most concentrated attacks came in the

target area and all the way back to the coast. Some groups report they had no withdrawal support from fighter escort and other groups report no escort at all.[17]

It seems that the Flying Fortress crews had paid attention to the posters pinned on their briefing room walls. The B-17 crews of the 3rd BD striking Braunschweig described Luftwaffe fighters as adopting the 'Tail Pecker', 'Sister Attack', 'Rocketeers' and 'Tail Gunner's Headache' methods of attack, with mortars being used extensively. The B-24 crews of the 2nd BD, also bombing Braunschweig, experienced the weakest attacks, deemed to be generally 'unaggressive', around Lingen. Here, Luftwaffe fighters attacked in pairs and in *Ketten* from 'six o'clock', not closing any nearer than 400 yards, and with Fw 190s firing mortars inaccurately.[18]

Schmid recorded how:

> All three *Jagddivisionen* succeeded in assembling their units in close combat formation. Excellent high-altitude visibility enabled these to attack the American *Viermots* repeatedly and from the front. Our high-altitude fighters were able to keep the numerically inferior American escort fighters so occupied that our twin-engined fighters were free to attack the unprotected bomber aircraft.[19]

By the end of the mission, the USAAF had lost 62 bombers – almost 11 per cent of the total force, with one formation losing 19 per cent of its strength to enemy action. I. *Jagdkorps* reported 21 aircraft lost and a further 19 rated at more than 60 per cent damaged. Schmid enthused that German defensive operations were:

> ... crowned with success, while our own losses were within reasonable bounds. Despite their numerical inferiority, the German single- and twin-engined fighter units demonstrated on 11 January that the employed tactics and striking power of the fighters were capable of inflicting such high losses on the Americans, under favourable weather conditions at any rate, that they would soon exceed the limit of expendable loss.[20]

Publicly at least, Göring was pleased. His concept of '*Klotzen Nicht Kleckern*' ('Hit them heavy and hard, don't just stroke them') had paid off. He signalled the *Jagdkorps*:

> On 11 January, units of North American *Terrorflieger* [terror-flyers] experienced the full effectiveness and force of a massed German air

defence during a large-scale attempt to attack central German territory. The attack was largely dispersed.

I would like to express my full appreciation and thanks to all those who contributed to this success through their energetic and effective leadership, sacrifice and courageous commitment.

However, both leadership and servicemen must continue to be on their guard, as this success must not remain a one-off.[21]

The Germans should have been concerned about one development. By 11 January VIII Fighter Command had sufficient fighter groups available for escort to allow the 56th FG to undertake freelance missions in which the P-47s would fly ahead of the bombers, freely hunting Luftwaffe fighters in order to harass them as they attempted to form up for massed deployment against the following B-17s and B-24s.[22]

As a measure of the intensity of operations at this time, on the 16th, JG 2 claimed its 2,000th aircraft destroyed (a total that included no fewer than 350 *Viermots*), but the *Geschwader* also suffered the loss of three *Staffelkapitäne* and the *Geschwader-Adjutant*, Hauptmann Fritz Edelmann, that day.

In the south, Flying Fortresses and Liberators of the Fifteenth Air Force continued their assault on airfields and marshalling yards around Rome and in northern Italy, as well as targets in Yugoslavia, Bulgaria and Greece. Often, the raids were unescorted, but some came with an escort of P-38s, as was the case on 24 January when B-24s and B-17s, screened by a strong Lightning escort, attacked marshalling yards in Sofia, while more B-17s bombed the rail yards at Vratsa, just over 100 km to the north of the Bulgarian capital.

IV./JG 27, under Hauptmann Otto Meyer, had been in the Balkans since May 1943, operating from bases in Greece and Bulgaria. It had always struggled with serviceability, and at the end of 1943 the *Gruppe* had just 12 serviceable Bf 109Gs. On the morning of the 24th, IV./JG 27 scrambled its Messerschmitts from Skoplje, led by Meyer, to intercept the B-24s. Twenty-five minutes after take-off, at 1220 hrs, the Liberators were spotted flying towards Sofia, some 30 km northwest of the city, and the Bf 109s made a head-on attack at an altitude of 6,500 m. Meyer targeted a Liberator and closed in from 500 m to 150 m. He later wrote:

I fired at the flight leader of the centre flight and scored strikes to the cockpit and the wing surfaces. The Liberator immediately started to trail extraordinarily thick white smoke and sheared away beneath the formation. I was no longer able to track the whereabouts of this aircraft as I attacked the formation again and became involved in combat with fighters. The Liberator crashed at 1225 hrs in Schar, 30 km west of Skoplje.[23]

Meyer was able to verify the crash location because a railway official at Schar had spoken with an officer on the *Gruppe Stab* of IV./JG 27 to inform him that a Liberator had come down a short distance from the station. Four of the crew were found dead, but the remainder had escaped. Meyer had observed six parachutes at the time of the combat. It was his 11th victory, and the 17th for the *Gruppe Stab*. Of note is that claims for two other B-24s shot down during the engagement were not credited to individual pilots, but rather as '*Staffel*' and '*Gruppe*' victories respectively, in a reflection of the speed and wild nature of the action.[24]

At around the same time, Major Erich Hohagen's I./JG 2 relocated to Aix-en-Provence, in southern France, before eventually moving to Italy, thus depleting the strength in the north of a valuable and experienced fighter *Gruppe*.

When things go wrong, they can go very wrong. In a classic example of this, calamity bordering on embarrassing farce befell the commanders of both the Eighth Air Force and the air defence of the Reich on 24 January.

Early that morning, reports from both the *Funkhorchdienstes* and coastal radar stations arrived at Schmid's headquarters to the effect that a force of approximately 700 bombers and 300 fighters was assembling over eastern England. At 0957 hrs, a large enemy formation was reported crossing the coast between the Scheldt and Dunkirk. The weather was bad.

At 1020 hrs, the *Funkhorchdienstes* picked up an American radio signal cancelling the operation. The German tracking had been accurate, reflecting the difficulty the USAAF experienced in forming up the intended, colossal armada of 857 B-17s from the 1st and 3rd BDs, along with 678 fighters, amidst the wintry gloom that shrouded northern Europe. Only 563 bombers headed out across the North Sea, the Liberators of the 2nd BD having already been called back while still over England.

Of the force despatched, many bombers, having received the recall signal, lumbered around and made course back to their mist-covered bases. However, the Flying Fortresses of the lead wing of the 3rd BD pressed on, and by 1020 hrs they had almost reached the German frontier.

Notwithstanding that, I. *Jagdkorps* assumed that the bombers crossing the coast and heading to the southeast would be aiming for targets along the Rhine and Main rivers. The *Korps* ordered units of 1. and 2. *Jagddivisionen* to cover the Koblenz area and 3. *Jagddivision* to cover Brussels – a total of 410 aircraft. However, only a small number of fighters made contact with the bombers over Düren and Koblenz, including some *Zerstörer* that also engaged enemy escort fighters over the latter city.

Meanwhile, at its headquarters at Berlin-Wannsee, the nascent *Luftflotte Reich*, through reports generated by the *Funkhorchdienstes*, aircraft observation stations, various Luftwaffe regional commands and Flak units, had understood that American bombers had flown east as far as the 'Koblenz, Frankfurt and Mannheim areas. Here, they separated into two groups, one of which would continue to Berlin, the other to Nuremberg and Pilsen'.

But once the controllers at the Villa de Breul at Zeist realised that the bulk of the bombers had been recalled, they ordered all aircraft to land. Yet, according to Schmid:

> On the basis of the situation picture available at the Headquarters of *Luftflotte Reich*, the Commander-in-Chief of the Luftwaffe [Göring] assumed that a large-scale attack on Berlin was forthcoming, and took a personal hand in operations. So as to ensure adequate defence against the anticipated attack on Berlin and, later, Pilsen, he ordered headquarters *Luftflotte Reich* to send up all available fighter aircraft, including day- and nightfighter units belonging to the *Jagddivisionen* and the fighter pilot schools. The headquarters of *Luftflotte* 3 in Paris also received orders to attack the American units when they flew back from Berlin.[25]

This resulted in 411 single- and twin-engined fighters and nightfighters from 7. *Jagddivision* and *Jafü Ostmark*, as well as several training units, being committed pointlessly, with the only noteworthy aspect being the needless consumption of a significant quantity of fuel. Göring, however, seemed impervious to any sense of wrong-doing on his part and was not about to cry *mea culpa*. On the 25th a signal arrived at Zeist:

> To Generaloberst Stumpff and Generalmajor Schmid:
>
> Yesterday's little manoeuvre may be considered a success, except for the fact that April Fool's Day is still two months away. I should like to express my appreciation, both to myself and to all participating commanders, for our excellent work in warding off the attack on the fortress of Köpenik.
>
> Göring[26]

In his post-war summary of activity, Schmid was seemingly aghast at Göring's actions, and the 'resultant senseless mass commitment of aircraft and personnel of the day fighter units'. In the hours after the 24 January debacle, he drafted a memo intended for the RLM which he sent via the new office of *Luftflotte Reich*. What he wanted was to avoid repetitions of what had happened earlier that day, and thus to secure the authority of his I. *Jagdkorps*, if not to expand its influence:

> In order to assure successful air defence measures within the territory of the Reich, the following conditions must be met:
> 1. One central agency should be given the responsibility of preparing the situation picture
> 2. All the reporting agencies engaged in home air defence activity (radio reconnaissance, radar and visual observation/listening reporting stations) should report to a single central agency, and should be made subordinate to this agency
> 3. A central command should be set up to direct the commitment of day- and nightfighter units in home air defence activity.[27]

It remained to be seen whether this would happen, and if it would have an effect.

Meanwhile, the bad weather temporarily halted further Eighth Air Force raids over German territory. This frustrated Spaatz, who wrote to the US Assistant Secretary of War for Air in Washington, D.C., 'Nothing is more exasperating than trying to run an Air Force continuously hampered or grounded by weather'.[28]

The weather cleared on 29 January. That day, the Eighth despatched 863 B-17s and B-24s to targets in the Frankfurt area. Escorted by 632 fighters, a record 806 bombers dropped more than 1,895 tons of bombs over the primary target and the escorts allegedly shot down 44 Luftwaffe fighters between 1100–1305 hrs along the route over France, Belgium and Germany. However, despite dense cloud cover, 21 aircraft from Major Klaus Quaet-Faslem's I./JG 3 and others from 10./JG 2 took off from Rheine and clashed with USAAF fighters over Frankfurt and Aix la Chapelle (Aachen), but suffered no losses.

At Bad Wörishofen, after waiting at cockpit readiness, 28 Bf 109G-6s of III./JG 3 under Major Walther Dahl took off at 1008 hrs and were guided by 'Y'-*Führung* to Mannheim, where the formation sighted nearly 60 B-17s at 1052 hrs over the Mannheim-Ludwigshafen area. Shortly thereafter, after climbing 1,500 m through heavy cloud, the *Gruppe* formed up into position and made a frontal attack.

As the Messerschmitts passed through the bombers, the defensive fire was intense. Nevertheless, the pilots claimed 12 *Abschüsse* and three *Herausschüsse*, with Dahl and Oberfeldwebel Kurt Graf of 7./JG 3 each claiming two and raising their individual scores to 58 and 14, respectively. Leutnant Ekkehard Tichy, who hailed from the Sudetenland and was the *Staffelkapitän* of 9./JG 3, was credited with a *Herausschuss*, the event having been witnessed by his wingman, Feldwebel Paul Wielebinski, a pilot of 7. *Staffel*:

> As the bombers had dropped their bombs and were on a westerly course, we made a sweeping turn and attacked from the front. During the attack I saw how a Boeing fired at by Leutnant Tichy took hits in the cockpit and the left engines trailed thick black smoke. During the exit I observed how the Boeing sheared out of the protective fire of the formation away to the lower left, losing a lot of altitude. As I attacked another Boeing in the further course of the combat, I was unable to observe the Boeing shot down by Tichy any further.[29]

Unteroffizier Kurt Clemens of 8. *Staffel* shot down his first Flying Fortress at 6,000 m. His *Staffel* was being led by Leutnant Raimund Koch, and Clemens was flying in a *Rotte* with Feldwebel Heinz Gosemann. Clemens reported:

> We sighted the enemy formation at 1055 hrs, flying approximately 2,000 m above us. There were about 60 Boeing Fortress IIs, the first bombs had been dropped and they were flying on a westerly course. We carried out the first attack at 1107 hrs from head-on and at the same height. For me, this attack was without success.
>
> In the second attack, which was made from above and behind, I was not successful either. I made a third attack at 1119, frontal from the left. I fired at a Boeing from about 300m, which flew as the second-to-last aircraft in the formation to the right. After exiting, I observed how the aircraft I was firing at flipped over several times, went into alternating spins, and then fell into the clouds at 1119 hrs. The Fortress did not trail any smoke. I was not able to observe the crash because of the cloud layer.[30]

By 12 May, Clemens had claimed five B-17s shot down.

The *Gruppe* suffered two losses, including Leutnant Bruno Bolowski of 8. *Staffel* who went down near Konken, around 100 km west of Mannheim, after destroying a B-17.[31] Navigator 2Lt Joel E. Punches was aboard a B-17 of the 385th BG that day, flying as No. 2 ship in the lead squadron, high group. He described the carnage in the air:

> We were attacked by at least 100 German fighters from target onward, for about one hour. No escort showed up. An Me 109 hit head-on

with a Fortress over the target. The fighter blew up and the Fort went down. Five minutes later [1Lt Robert L.] Bostick went down. Five chutes opened. Ten minutes later a Fort broke apart. A few minutes later in the group next to us, one Fort came up under another and cut its tail completely off. We saw two bodies fly out. It spun down and one chute finally got out. The other plane tore its wing off and went down. Didn't see any chutes. P-47s finally arrived. German fighters sure looked new and all painted up red and black. They came straight through the groups.[32]

In France and Belgium, II. *Jagdkorps* committed most of the *Staffeln* of JG 26 against the bombers not long after they had crossed the French coast, and the fighters harried the *Viermots* well into the afternoon. Several of the *Geschwader*'s long-serving veterans gave a good account of themselves.

Feldwebel Heinz Gomann of 6./JG 26 claimed the destruction of a B-17 near Le Cateau shortly before 1300 hrs, and just under an hour later he claimed a B-24 shot down in the English Channel, west of Calais, for his 20th victory. Leutnant Wilhelm Hofmann of 8. *Staffel*, who had also been with JG 26 since 1942, shot down a B-17 north of Lutrebois. It was his eighth claim, and third *Viermot* kill that month. Hofmann would later become distinctive for the eye patch he wore, the result of an injury suffered when the bolt of a machine gun suddenly slammed closed, injuring his eye. He refused to stop flying combat missions. By the end of the day, JG 26 had claimed 11 B-17s shot down or cut out of formation and five B-24s suffered similar fates.[33]

In total, the USAAF lost 24 B-17s (11 from the 3rd BD, which lacked a fighter escort) and five B-24s, equating to 299 aircrew missing and 22 killed.

For all that was happening in the skies above the Reich's cities and factories, Generalmajor Josef Schmid continued to feel the pressure. Certain organs within the Reich defence infrastructure were not pulling their weight, and in some quarters there was evidence of a pervading sense of inferiority. This had to be stamped out. During the afternoon of 25 January he hauled in Galland, the commanders of 1., 2. and 3. *Jagddivisionen* and other senior staff officers for a meeting at the Villa de Breul. He opened proceedings with a tongue-lashing, scolding the highly decorated officers around the table because there were still too few enemy bombers being shot down – both during daylight and at night. He attributed this lack of success to inadequate preparations ahead of operations, and in this regard, in his view, the divisional staffs were just as responsible as individual *Gruppen* and *Staffeln*.

Schmid was also aware that complaints had been made about the inferiority of Luftwaffe high-frequency technology. In his view that was utter rubbish. The reality was that there had been a lack of technical training, organisation and suitable preparation. He wanted his divisional commanders to be 'much tougher' with the *Gruppenkommandeuren* in their respective zones, and also with their divisional signals officers. It was the latter that were responsible for high-frequency technology and the associated training, not unit technical officers.[34] Schmid also informed the attendees:

> The numerical strength of the American air forces in Great Britain has increased. We must face the fact that American offensive activity against the Reich will probably become greater during the coming weeks and months, and that American fighter escort will become much stronger than at present. The estimated flight range of the Thunderbolt as far as Braunschweig has not yet been confirmed.
>
> On the other hand, we know that Lightnings, equipped with auxiliary fuel tanks are able to provide a protective screen for the bombers as far as central Germany. It is extremely important that our high-altitude fighter units provoke the Lightnings to engage in combat so that they will be forced to dump their auxiliary tanks. If they can be forced to do so, they will have no alternative but to break off combat and return to base before running out of fuel. It does not seem likely that American fighters will be able to penetrate as far as Berlin at present.
>
> As regard the commitment of our day fighter units, we must try to follow the technique of assembling light, heavy and twin-engined fighters at combat altitude, and of bringing them to bear against the incoming bombers in closed combat formation. In this way, we should be able to maintain numerical superiority at a given time in a given place.
>
> The practice of moving fighter units early in the morning will be discontinued. Experience has shown that these units have not regained the required state of operational readiness by the time the Americans appear. If weather conditions or the military situation should render the transfer of fighter units necessary, they should be transferred on the evening before an attack is expected.
>
> In order to assure the smooth transfer of fighter units in the air from one divisional area of control to another, all fighter divisions will announce their control frequencies every evening. Each divisional command will inform its neighbouring commands of the transfer of any of its units. Before fighter units are ordered up for a second time against the same formation of bombers, they must be given all available information regarding the position of the enemy aircraft, especially when the fighter units are not in their own divisional command or have landed at fields other than those specifically assigned to fighter aircraft.[35]

Oberleutnant Richard Franz of *Sturmstaffel* 1 recalled:

> Although the Allies had gained air superiority in 1943, I think that the morale of our fighter pilots was not bad, especially when it is realised that the young pilots we had in the frontline units had very little experience, and a life expectation of something like ten missions. It was a hard time for both the young pilots and their leaders.
>
> Normally, we were informed at about 0700 hrs of a '*grosse Versammlung*' (a large enemy assembly) over the Great Yarmouth area. After breakfast, we were driven to the *Staffel*'s dispersal and then had 30 minutes readiness. About 45 minutes before the expected take-off, and after determination of the probable target area, cockpit readiness was ordered until, finally, the scramble order was given.
>
> After being scrambled, all units were ordered to meet at a certain point and then form up into a battle formation (sometimes numbering up to 100 aircraft), before being directed to a pre-assigned attack position from where we would separate from the main formation for our rearward attack. The main formation would always try to overtake the bomber stream in order to get into position for a head-on attack.[36]

Over the coming days, Generalmajor Schmid maintained a busy pace of meetings with his staff and technical officers, drumming home the need for improved communication and greater operational efficiency. During the afternoon of 1 February he chaired a meeting on the welcome allocation of new aircraft for units of I. *Jagdkorps*, and then talked with Grabmann and Oesau about day fighter operations. On the 4th, he flew with Wittmer to Berlin for discussions with Stumpff at *Luftflotte Reich*, most probably in the wake of his memo of 24 January on the need for a central fighter command. The following evening, Schmid and his Daylight Fighter Operations Officer, Oberstleutnant Heinrich Seeliger, drove from Zeist to Deelen for dinner with Grabmann, where they discussed aircraft allocation for 3. *Jagddivision* and matters concerning fighter tactics.

There was a real urgency now, as the effects of the Allied bombing were becoming debilitating. Despite thick cloud, the Eighth Air Force had targeted Wilhelmshaven again on the 3rd, inflicting considerable damage on both industrial and residential areas. Fires were raging in the southern districts of the city, and there was bomb damage as far afield as Westerstede, 25 km northwest of Oldenburg, and at Farge on the Weser River, 20 km from Bremen, beyond Vegesack. A Flak battery was also hit.

On 9 February Schmid set off on a four-day inspection tour of a selection of day and nightfighter units under I. *Jagdkorps* command, as well as visiting two divisional *Gefechtsstände*. In terms of day fighters, departing Soesterberg, he went firstly to Venlo, where he met with Major Franz Beyer and officers of IV./JG 3, who that day reported 45 Bf 109G-6s on strength. His next stop, as snow showers fell, was München-Gladbach, where he inspected the men and machines of I./JG 3 under Hauptmann Josef Haiböck, then on to I./JG 1 and *Sturmstaffel* 1 at Dortmund. Schmid was cautiously encouraged by what he experienced during these visits:

> The morale and military attitude of the flying crews is excellent. In those units commanded by exemplary officers, it is better than excellent. The young crews of the daylight fighter units are ready and eager for battle. The recent heavy losses, however, are ample indication of the fact that they are lacking in flying and tactical experience. I propose that even after they have been assigned to their units, their training be continued until they are actually needed for operations. Intensive training on Fw 190s, in conditions that closely simulate air combat, is needed urgently from the point of view of personnel economy, and the additional time required would more than pay for itself in the form of more experienced crews with improved tactical ability and increasing effectiveness with fewer losses.
>
> The *Staffelkapitäne*, as deputies of their *Kommandeuren*, should be give continuous training in the exercise of command, even to the extent of granting them greater initiative during operational missions. There must be extremely careful personnel management so as to select only the best-qualified men to fill these positions as they become vacant. Bureaucratic practices, which prioitise length of service when making such appointments, while ignoring tactical ability and training, can only lead to a serious decrease in the effectiveness of our command.[37]

In this regard, Schmid then makes the pointed remark '*Bedeutung der Versetzung aus dem Osten nach dem Westen*' ('Transfer from East to West is significant') – a reference to his view that combat experience gained in Russia would count for nothing in combat against the USAAF daylight raids. Simply bringing in pilots from the East to replace those lost in the *Reichsverteidigung* was not necessarily a solution. The air warfare and tactics in each of these theatres was very different. While no one doubted the tactical skills and awareness needed to fight the Il-2s and Yak fighters of the Red Air Force, or to engage small formations of Tu-2 or Pe-2 bombers in the open skies in the East, it was impossible to compare it to flying against massed formations of USAAF four-engined bombers with their strong defensive firepower and formidable escort fighters that were bombing the homeland's cities and their people.

Schmid continued his tour with a visit to the new *Sokrates* bunker of 2. *Jagddivision* at Stade, before heading southeast to III./JG 54 at Ludwigslust. Finally, he stopped at Döberitz to meet with Oberst Günther Lützow, commander of 1. *Jagddivision*, at the division's bunker, codenamed *Dädalus*. Following his conversations with Ibel and Lützow he noted that:

> Last-minute transfers from one airfield to another, which are often necessitated by tactical considerations or by weather, are having a detrimental effect on the smooth functioning of the command organisation. In future, every effort should be made to allow each unit to take off from its own airfield and then to assemble all the units at an airfield which is most favourably located for the purposes of a specific operation. In carrying out such assembly procedures, care should be exercised to ensure that all *Staffeln* belonging to a *Gruppe* be assembled at the same airfield. Provided the airfield in question is large enough, it is desirable to assemble two entire *Gruppen* there at once.
>
> The enemy fighter escorts are increasing in numbers and power. Some way must be found to meet the escorts effectively, otherwise our fighters will be unable to get at the *Viermots*. A concentrated blow against the enemy fighter escort forces would represent a success both tactically and in terms of morale.[38]

On 10 February, Schmid deployed 303 single- and twin-engined fighters from all three of his divisions when 143 B-17s of the 3rd BD, protected by 466 P-38, P-47 and P-51 fighters, were despatched to bomb the aircraft plants around Braunschweig. Again, the weather was awful, but the day would see some of the hardest-fought aerial combat ever to take place over northwest Europe.

Units from 1. *Jagddivision* covered Braunschweig amidst ten-tenths cloud, beginning at 300 m and extending to 5,000 m, with intermittent snowfalls. Fighters of 2. *Jagddivision* were sent to the Soltau and Hanover areas and aircraft from 3. *Jagddivision* went to Diepholz and Bremen, the weather in both zones seeing scattered snow flurries, although visibility at high altitude was good. According to Schmid:

> Despite the wintry weather, all the *Jagddivisionen* were able to carry out their assemblies according to plan, and the close combat formations were able to stage repeated attacks on the American bomber formation.

The air combat with American fighters over Bremen, Braunschweig and Osnabrück was violent and resulted in heavy losses for our units.[39]

At 1030 hrs *Sturmstaffel* 1 and I./JG 1 took off and, together with II./JG 1, were directed to attack the B-17s heading for the aircraft plants around Braunschweig. Under the overall leadership of the *Staffelkapitän* of 6./JG 1, veteran ace and Knight's Cross-holder Major Heinz Bär, the German fighters hit the bombers north of Osnabrück.

Behind the presence of Heinz Bär in this action lies a somewhat tortuous story which highlights the Machiavellian environment of the Luftwaffe fighter force. Bär was one of Germany's most experienced and accomplished fighter pilots. His service career stretched back to 1939, the year he scored his first victory in the west. Concluding the campaign over England in 1940 with 17 confirmed victories, Bär subsequently flew in the East with JG 51, and within two months had accumulated 60 kills.

The award of the Knight's Cross came in July 1941, followed by the Oak Leaves in August, a month which saw him down six Soviet aircraft in one day. Leaving Russia in 1942, Bär was given command of I./JG 77, with whom he flew over the Mediterranean, claiming another 45 victories and gaining the Swords to the Knight's Cross, despite contracting a bout of malaria and being stricken by gastric ulcers. Some sources also state that his fighting spirit took a dent at this time.

In the summer of 1943, after an apparently difficult relationship with Major Johannes Steinhoff, the *Geschwaderkommodore* of JG 77, Bär was transferred to France for 'cowardice before the enemy', where he took over command of the operational training unit *Jagdgruppe Süd*. One Luftwaffe airman commented of him, 'Actually, from what one has heard about Bär, he was a "tough" who was avoided as much as possible by the officer corps. There must have been some fellows who behaved arrogantly – young airmen – and he must have given them hell'.

Ill and exhausted by endless combat, Bär returned to Germany for a period of convalescence, before embarking on a long, hard stint as one of the foremost operational commanders in the defence of the Reich. However, once home, his plain speaking on tactical policies did not enamour him to Göring, who saw fit to 'demote' him. Thus, Bär's first posting was as a *Staffelführer* for 11./JG 1 at Volkel, but he soon became *Kapitän* of 6. *Staffel* in II. *Gruppe* at Rheine. However, when he arrived at his new *Geschwader*, Oberst Walter Oesau found himself in the uncomfortable position of having to remind his new officer that he had given Göring an assurance that Bär would not be given any senior command positions.

On 10 February, 13 B-17s were claimed as brought down by JG 1, as well as one *Herausschuss* and four P-47 Thunderbolts destroyed, for the loss of two pilots. Bär accounted for two bombers – his 180th and 181st victories – as did Oberfeldwebel Karl-Emil Demuth of 2./JG 1. Successes for the *Sturmstaffel* were still proving to be hard-won, and the unit claimed only one victory when a B-17 was shot down by Oberfahnrich Heinz Steffen near Rheine. There were no losses.

Six Fortresses were claimed destroyed by the pilots of II./JG 3 and five by those of I./JG 11, while the *Zerstörer* of I./ZG 26 were credited with six bombers downed. Schmid summarised the day's operations as follows. 'Due to poor bombing visibility and the successful attacks by our fighter units on the bomber stream, the American attack on Braunschweig was robbed of full effectiveness.' The losses incurred by the Eighth Air Force during the Braunschweig mission were considered 'unsustainable'. In all, 295 crewmen and 29 bombers were listed as missing, or 20 per cent of the force.

A young USAAF radio operator flying on board a B-17 of the 388th BG thought that the raid on 19 February 1944 was 'the roughest so far'. Despite flying 19 missions prior to attacking Braunschweig, he admitted freely to being scared, and had 'never prayed harder to come through'.[40]

15

Big Gun – 'Big Week'

It was just a short train journey from the '*Wolfschanze*' to Insterburg airfield, which lay 80 km east of Königsberg. It was 26 November 1943. Reichsmarschall Göring had invited the *Führer* to Insterburg in an attempt to restore his declining prestige, setting up a display of some of the Luftwaffe's latest aircraft and weaponry, including the advanced Messerschmitt and Arado jet- and rocket-powered prototypes. As he climbed down from his train and took the car to the grass airfield, Hitler seemed generally indifferent to the flying display. At this stage in the war, he had many things that were of concern to him, and he was keen to know what immediate steps were being taken to retaliate against Allied bombing raids on the Reich.

But one item of hardware did catch Hitler's eye when a sleek, twin-engined Me 410A-1 fighter flew past at low level, its underside brandishing the long barrel of a 5 cm cannon. It certainly *looked* formidable. Hitler suddenly turned to Göring and enthused that such an aircraft/weapon combination could form 'the backbone of the home air defence', demanding that two *Gruppen* or a *Geschwader* immediately be equipped with such machines. Göring had to pluck up courage and advise the *Führer* that only two or three aircraft could be equipped with the cannon since, although there were limited stocks, no further examples were available at that time. Despite the fact that Hitler's attention had already been snared by the next display, the die was cast.

In December 1942 the Luftwaffe *Technisches Amt* issued a requirement for a gun with a muzzle velocity of at least 600 metres per second and with a rate of fire of 300 rounds per minute, the concept being to have a weapon capable of causing the almost certain destruction of an enemy bomber with just one shell, without the attacking aircraft coming within range of the enemy machine's defensive fire. But the dichotomy was that while there was a requirement for accuracy and extremely low dispersion due to the heavy-calibre ammunition required, it would be impossible to achieve a high rate of fire. Every shot would have to count. Two aircraft selected to trial such a weapon were the Ju 88 and the still embryonic Me 410.

By early 1943, design of the intended weapon had proceeded quickly and construction commenced. The inspiration was the 5 cm KwK 39 L/60 tank gun as used in the *Panzerkampfwagen* III medium tank. This gun incorporated the latest armament developments and was available in sufficient quantities. The small number of alterations required to fit the weapon into an aircraft was considered to be worthwhile as it was not necessary to design and develop an entirely new gun. A magazine feed mechanism would make it fully automatic, and the gun, its mounting and its feed were to be combined so that the complete weapon was an interchangeable whole. This was impressive in its own right – the gun measured almost 4.5 m in length and weighed 540 kg. Because of its weight, the weapon had to be hoisted into an Me 410 by means of a hydraulic jack.

Using the *Revi* C/12 D or ZFR 4 telescopic gunsight, a hit with one 5 cm round was thought to be enough to bring down a bomber. However, successful employment of the ZFR 4 required considerable gunnery and flying skill, or much practice, as well as the ability to stay in a firing position for an extended period of time. The gun had a rate of fire of 50 rounds per minute and a muzzle velocity with a high-explosive shell of 965 metres per second. The 1.52 kg shells were loaded electro-pneumatically and were fired electrically. The recoil of nearly three kilogrammes was absorbed by two hydro-pneumatic cylinders mounted above the gun cradle.[1]

The idea of using such a large weapon, which became known as the BK 5 cm, in the Me 410 in combat had also been proposed by officers on Generalmajor Galland's staff to E.Kdo 25 in July 1943.[2] This was somewhat ironic, as, apparently, it was over this gun that the relationship between Göring and Galland sank to a low.

Galland recalled being ordered to Burg Veldenstein, Göring's hilltop castle in Bavaria, where he found himself once again being berated for the 'cowardly' attitude of the fighter units. Galland ignored the tirade and countered by demanding 'increased production and better fighters'. Göring was enraged at Galland's implied criticism, and retorted that German aircraft were the best in the world. He then told Galland that the BK 5 would be built into the Me 410. Galland was appalled, and told the Reichsmarschall that the Me 410 could not be used against bombers because of its vulnerability to enemy fighters.

So inflamed was Galland by what he considered was a ludicrous decision that he 'flatly refused to carry out the order' and asked to be relieved as *General der Jagdflieger*. Göring agreed and Galland left, but when Galland arrived at the local airfield to fly back to Berlin, the Reichsmarschall's adjutant telephoned him and told him he was to remain in office until a replacement was found. Two weeks later, Göring apologised and reinstated Galland.[3]

In conformity with Hitler's decree, however, on 12 January 1944 Göring instructed Milch to set about equipping two *Gruppen*, each with a strength of 45 cannon-fitted aircraft. Milch wrote to Göring in response two days later:

> The first experimental aircraft have been equipped with a 50 mm gun. The first delivery of ten guns was to be made in December. This was not possible since the magazine feeding device suffered stoppages due to broken belt links whereby the cartridge was hitched on the belt conveyer table. These defects have now been eliminated. There have been difficulties experienced with the high-explosive shells on account of casting defects in the casings and also in respect to the dispersion because of the rotating bands. Alterations are being carried out in the plants. The results have still to be tested.

From early February 1944, after just over three months of further testing, the weapon was fitted to the Me 410s of II./ZG 26 at Hildesheim. By the 8th, 5./ZG 26 had 12 cannon-armed aircraft, and trial operations commenced over southern Germany and Austria. This, despite the fact that there were prevailing electrics problems, small switches were found to break easily and ammunition belts continued to break. Also, the BK 5's recoil and feed mechanisms were unable to cope with the g-forces of aerial combat, and it was rare for more than one shell to be fired without the weapon jamming. At most, the BK 5 could expend just ten rounds.[4]

II./ZG 26, under the command of Hauptmann Eduard Tratt, was the sole *Gruppe* in the *Reichsverteidigung* equipped with the Me 410. Prior to the advent of the BK 5, the aircraft was usually armed with four 20 mm cannon and four underwing mortars. For a newly qualified pilot, assignment to II./ZG 26 was tantamount to 'buying a one-way ticket'. One such pilot was Feldwebel Fritz Buchholz, who joined 6./ZG 26 on 3 February 1944. He recalled:

> The Me 410 was a mixed bag. It had good, stable flying characteristics, but it wasn't good in the turn – here, the Bf 110 was better. Other than that, in flying the aircraft, generally there were few problems. In air combat, however, it was a different story. For a start, it was easy prey for enemy fighters, and in formation it was unwieldy, while it made a nice, big target for the bomber gunners.

Generally, we were ineffective. The *Zerstörer* units were too slow and unmanageable. Our *Gruppe* was frequently the target for enemy fighters, and so we only ever got a short time to deal with the bomber *Pulks*. There was rarely a chance to make a second formation attack because after our first attack, the enemy formation was usually broken up. Also, the way the Americans staggered their formations was very effective, and it made it very difficult for us to attack.

The increasing numbers of escort fighters made a hard job harder, and whenever they appeared, we were usually forced to break off because of the risk of being shot down because of our lack of adequate defensive armament. Our ground controllers always tried to get us to the bombers when there were no fighters in the vicinity. Most of our crews just focused on safety and survival – there were few daredevils.

After breakfast at around 0800 hrs, there was an operational briefing at battle HQ. There would be a large, black table with small yellow markers with the names of the crews and their formation positions in the air. Then a meteorologist would brief us on the expected weather situation over the enemy airfields in England and over the likely operational areas in Germany.

As soon as word came through that the bombers had taken off in England, we were placed on 60 minutes readiness. When they had assembled and were en route, we were ordered by loudspeaker to go to 30 minutes readiness. At that point we went to our aircraft. At ten minutes readiness, we pulled on our lifejackets and flare cartridge belts and gathered our maps and other items. We were also advised on the course and progress of the bombers. Once at cockpit readiness, we waited for the yellow star flare to be fired and then started our take-off procedure.

Up until March 1944, our Me 410s were fitted with four 21 cm mortars and four 2 cm cannon, but from April to August 1944, they carried the BK 5 cm cannon. With the BK 5, it was best to attack at an angle of ten degrees to the upper part of the rear of the enemy formation. But because of the rear defensive guns, and our lengthy approach, this was not popular. Because of the trajectory [80 cm to about 1,000 m], we often fired too early, and we were hampered by so many stoppages.[5]

The employment of such large-calibre guns, forced onto the units by Göring and the high command, proved a fallacy. It would have been better to have employed air-to-air rockets then under development. Generalmajor Schmid remained distinctly unimpressed about the deployment of the Me 410. He recalled:

It was sheer suicide. The *Führer's* crazy orders were carried out and the 5 cm cannon was to be put in the Me 410. I said, 'If you really intend throwing in a twin-engined fighter with its own fighter protection, then use one with as many cannon as possible. You use a shotgun for hunting game, not a rifle'. You want to be able to fire a lot of ammunition in a little time, and a 5 cm cannon, which fires very slowly, is no use at all – you can't fire at aircraft in that way. In the summer of 1944 I only used these units to attack damaged aircraft or such as had engine trouble and were taking evasive action towards Sweden, or else those which had been hit in the southern area and were trying to escape to the east.[6]

Prompted by Gen Arnold's directive the previous Christmas, in late February 1944 the Eighth Air Force launched Operation *Argument* – dubbed 'Big Week' by the crews charged with carrying out the offensive. This was a concerted and intense bombing campaign against German aircraft production centres commencing on the 20th, specifically the principal airframe, final assembly and component plants responsible for the output of single- and twin-engined fighter aircraft such as those at Leipzig-Mockau, Halberstadt and Regensburg.

'Big Week' was intended to do two things – destroy German aircraft on the ground and the means of replacing them, and force the Luftwaffe into the air to defend against the attacks. In all, 16 combat wings of heavy bombers, totalling 1,000 aircraft, were committed to the operation, together with fighter protection from all available fighter groups in both the Eighth and Ninth Air Forces. It was to be the largest force ever assembled in the history of American strategic air power.

On 17 February, Maj Gen Doolittle wrote to VIII Fighter Command and all the bomb divisions. He was clear:

This Air Force is now approaching the most critical phase of the war with Germany. During the next few months it is mandatory that we secure complete air superiority over the German Air Force in this Theater. In order to accomplish this end in the time allotted, we must adopt every expedient to improve the effectiveness of the Air Force, and to keep it at a high level of operational efficiency.[7]

Doolittle's mention of 'the time allotted' was perhaps deliberately somewhat cryptic and also serious, for overshadowing all Allied grand strategy since mid-1943 was a ticking clock – and it was counting down to *Overlord*, the planned invasion of Continental Europe.

In Germany, between them, I. and II. *Jagdkorps* could muster approximately 750 serviceable aircraft.

The scale of the first 'Big Week' raids came as a shock, and they were mounted against objectives in the Braunschweig and Leipzig areas. They saw an 'unaggressive' and 'remarkably weak' reaction from the Luftwaffe, mainly because of adverse weather and uncertainty as to where the bombers were heading.

On the 20th bombers penetrated as far east as Tutow airfield and Poznan, in Poland. Schmid was able to send up only limited forces on account of the weather, which 'precluded the assembling of our aircraft into large, closed combat formations'. Despite 362 fighters being employed, only 155 engaged. Nevertheless, I. *Jagdkorps* lost 28 machines, with a further 21 being seriously damaged. Ten aircrew were killed, 19 wounded and 34 posted as missing. The USAAF lost only four aircraft and four pilots.

Crucially, on this day, VIII Fighter Command aircraft used 150-gallon drop tanks for the first time, giving pilots 'the legs' to get as far as Leipzig. It was also the first time that the escorts had undertaken two missions in a single day.[8]

Things ramped up on 22 February, when the Eighth and Fifteenth Air Forces mounted their first successful coordinated attack. Despite the weather forcing a recall or abandoning of the mission by 544 of the Eighth's B-17s and B-24s, 81 aircraft of the 1st BD managed to bomb factories at Aschsersleben and Bernburg, while to the south, the Fifteenth struck the Messerschmitt plants at Regensburg, Obertraubling and Prufening. A force of 118 B-24s targeted Obertraubling, while 65 B-17s were assigned to Prufening, although they bombed another location in error. The Fifteenth's bombers came with an escort of 122 P-38s, but they had only sufficient range to reach the Alps before being forced to turn back.

From his bunker, *Minotaurus*, at Schleissheim, the commander of 7. *Jagddivision*, Oberst Huth, mustered his forces, deploying aircraft from I./JG 5 (which was re-equipping with Bf 109G-6/R6 '*Kanonenboote*' ('cannon ships') at Obertraubling at the time, having recently arrived from Sofia), II./JG 53, 2./JG 104, I./JG 301 and II./ZG 1 to attack the bombers. Seventeen bombers and two fighters went down. Leutnant Heinrich *Freiherr* von Podewils was a pilot with I./JG 5. He and a small number of fellow airmen just managed to take off in their new Bf 109G-6/R6s before the bombs fell on the factory airfield. He remembered:

> We had no vectoring from the ground, and had to look for the bombers. We made three attacks on them – from behind, and then

to the left and right. One can hardly imagine today what it meant to attack such a heavily armed bomber formation. We were met with such a concentrated barrage of fire that our hearts sank into our trousers. It called for a competent degree of self-control to dive into that defensive fire and approach the bombers to firing distance.

Von Podewils did shoot one of the Liberators down, but when he landed back at the Messerschmitt airfield he found hangars, assembly buildings, workshops, storage facilities and other factory buildings destroyed, with flames raging through them. The small accommodation area assigned to the *Gruppe* had also been hit. Some 27 Messerschmitt workers had been killed and 48 injured. Furthermore, 120 new Bf 109s had been destroyed and many more badly damaged.[9]

Also operational were ten Me 410A-1/U4s that took off from Oberpfaffenhofen under the command of the *Staffelkapitän* of 5./ZG 26, Oberleutnant Fritz Stehle, and which were directed towards Regensburg. This would be the first operation on which the 5 cm BK 5 cannon would be used, but it was still classified as a 'practice flight'. Shortly before 1300 hrs, Feldwebel Baunicke opened fire with his cannon and shot down the weapon's first bomber. Around ten minutes later, Stehle claimed another south of Dachau. What this 'practice flight' did tell the crews was that they would need to get within 400 m of the bombers to score a hit, rather that than the 800–900 m as claimed by the armament handbook.

This day also brought a serious loss when Hauptmann Eduard Tratt and his gunner, Oberfeldwebel Gillert, were shot down and killed over Nordhausen. Tratt's 30th (on 29 November 1943) and 38th (on 20 February 1944) victories were B-17s. This total brought him to the top in the *Zerstörer* pilot rankings when it came to aerial kills. He was promoted to Major posthumously.

The next morning, Schmid flew to Berlin and journeyed on to meet with Göring at the Reichsmarschall's country estate at Carinhall. Even as they talked about the spectre of a possible Allied invasion in the West, more American bombs were falling on the Reich's aircraft factories. Almost certainly as a result of their meeting, Schmid hastily convened another for the following afternoon, this time at Ibel's headquarters in the *Sokrates* bunker at Stade.

In attendance were Galland and Trautloft (now the Inspector of Day Fighters), both of whom had been touring fighter units and airfields in northern Germany, along with Ibel, Grabmann (commander of 3. *Jagddivision)*, Oberst Otto von Lachemaier from the RLM planning staff, Oesau (*Kommodore* of JG 1) and Graf (*Kommodore* of JG 11).

Although lessons had been learned from the successes and failures during operations over the past few weeks, one can imagine that it must have been a sombre atmosphere as Schmid spoke. He commenced with a finger-pointing admonishment:

> The enemy obviously plans to assure air supremacy as a prelude to a large-scale invasion. The air situation in the Reich is tense and serious. The damage the enemy has inflicted on our air armaments industry is not inconsiderable. In order to meet the inherent threat from the enemy daylight attacks, all available units must be prepared for all-out commitment. We must find a way to turn back the enemy before he can enter the Reich, otherwise we may soon be faced by attacks from the British by day. The tactical mistakes made during the last few days are not the fault of the operational units, but of the *Jagddivision* HQs. Chief among these was the failure to recognize in time the American diversionary manoeuvres for what they were.

Schmid informed Galland that his suggestion to form a specialist high-altitude *Gruppe* assigned to each *Jagddivision* specifically to combat enemy fighter escorts had been approved by Göring. These *Gruppen* would be equipped with Bf 109s and eventually with one *Staffel* of aircraft benefitting from GM-1 nitrous-oxide-based injection power-boost. They would operate in small formations of *Rotten* (two) and *Ketten* (three) aircraft.

Galland replied that the American bomber streams also enjoyed high-altitude protection, and that further:

> ... the *Jägerschreck* [fear of fighters], which hides in all the *Jagdgruppen*, must be overcome by deploying skilful tactics. You have to reorganise, equip and train forces for fighter combat, and especially for combat against the escorts. The Bf 109G-6 and G-5 with GM-1 are suitable for this. These *Gruppen* must reach altitude in good time. They will have an easy fight from this elevated position. The aircraft must be well prepared technically in order to maximise their performance. In addition to training the crews, it is important to equip these aircraft with additional tanks. The issue of jettisonable auxiliary tanks will need to be resolved in the shortest possible time.

Galland stressed that the fighter escort should be engaged further to the east, commencing at the Rhine, and wherever possible attacked from as high an altitude as possible so that an element of surprise could be ensured. Schmid added that with immediate effect the 'special task' *Gruppen* were

1. Wellington I bombers of the RAF's No. 9 Sqn in close formation on the eve of World War II. (Robert Forsyth Collection)

2. This Wellington IA of No. 9 Sqn, flown by Canadian Flg Off Bill Macrae, was attacked by Bf 110 fighters during the raid on Wilhelmshaven but, remarkably, made it home. (Robert Forsyth Collection)

3. A B-17F Flying Fortress undergoes final manufacture in a vast, floodlit assembly shop at Boeing in Seattle in December 1942. (Farm Security Administration – Office of War Information photograph collection, Library of Congress)

4. In early 1942, Maj Gen Carl A. 'Tooey' Spaatz (right) was appointed commander of the new US Eighth Air Force in Britain, while Brig Gen Ira C. Eaker (left) was placed in command of its VIII Bomber Command. (Associated Press/Alamy Stock Photo)

5. The 'Mighty Eighth'. A formation of B-17 Flying Fortresses from the 381st BG based at Ridgewell, in Essex, on their way to bomb a target. (Robert Forsyth Collection)

6. Reichsmarschall Hermann Göring inspects personnel from the Luftwaffe's two specialist anti-bomber units, *Sturmstaffel* 1 and E.Kdo 25, during an inspection at Achmer airfield on 17 November 1943. (Robert Forsyth Collection)

7. Generalmajor Adolf Galland (far left) peers down at an item of anti-bomber weaponry during a visit to the weapons evaluation unit E.Kdo 25 at Achmer in November 1943. Also seen (second left) is Major Hans-Günther von Kornatzki. (Robert Forsyth Collection)

8. Bf 109Gs of Major Walther Dahl's III./JG 3 undergo maintenance at Leipheim in March 1944. (EN Archive)

9. Mechanics take a break on the wing of an Fw 190A-7 of *Sturmstaffel* 1 at Salzwedel in April 1944, this aircraft being regularly flown by Unteroffizier Oskar Bösch. (EN Archive)

10. In France in the summer of 1943, the *Kommodore* of JG 2, Major Egon Mayer, stands on the starboard wing of a B-17F that he has just shot down. (EN Archive)

11. Two Bf 110G-2 *Pulkzerstörer* of 3./ZG 76 fitted with twin tubes for 21 cm W.Gr.21 mortars for breaking up bomber formations. (EN Archive)

12. An Me 410A-1/U4 of 5./ZG 26 undergoes an engine test at Königsberg-Neumark. (EN Archive)

13. Intrigued Me 410 crews of ZG 26 walk past B-17F *Miss Nonalee II* at Königsberg in 1944. (Hans-Heiri Stapfer Collection)

14. Initially, Generalmajor Josef Schmid was out of his depth when appointed to lead XII. *Fliegerkorps* (later I. *Jagdkorps*) from 15 September 1943. (EN Archive)

15. The purpose-built headquarters bunker of 3. *Jagddivision* from the autumn of 1943. (EN Archive)

16. Female Luftwaffe auxiliaries in a Luftwaffe control bunker with their light projectors. (EN Archive)

17. Controllers sit at their desks while the shadowy figures of female auxiliary plotters work on the other side of a large glass map of northwest Europe. (EN Archive)

18. Oberst Walter Grabmann (centre), commander of 3. *Jagddivision*, in conversation with Major Heinz Bär (left), *Kommandeur* of II./JG 1, and Oberstleutnant Walter Oesau, *Kommodore* of JG 1. (EN Archive)

19. Generalmajor Joachim-Friedrich Huth successively served from August 1942 as commander of 4., 5. and 7. *Jagddivisionen*. To the left is Oberst Max Ibel, commander of 2. *Jagddivision*. (Robert Forsyth Collection)

20. The purpose-built headquarters bunker of 2. *Jagddivision*, codenamed '*Sokrates*', was located at Stade, near Hamburg. (Robert Forsyth Collection)

21. Grim-faced Hauptmann Heinz Lang (officer on the staff of IV./JG 3), Major Walter Dahl (*Kommodore* of JG 300) and Major Wilhelm Moritz (*Kommandeur* of IV./JG 3) at Memmingen following raids on the airfield on 18 and 20 July 1944. (EN Archive)

22. Oberst Hannes Trautloft, Galland's Inspector of Day Fighters, uses his hands to discuss air tactics with Major Hans-Ekkehard Bob. Photo via Hans-Ekkehard Bob. (Robert Forsyth Collection)

23. The frontal view of a B-17 painted in scale on the doors of a hangar for range and gunnery purposes. (EN Archive)

This page (24., 25. and 26.). Luftwaffe tacticians, gunnery instructors and unit leaders used a variety of wooden and plastic models of bombers and fighters to teach newly assigned fighter pilots how to identify, approach and shoot down bombers. (EN Archive)

27. A B-17 is caught by the gun camera of a German fighter, having taken hits to its left inboard engine following an attack from the rear. (Robert Forsyth Collection)

Above 28. Armourers of JG 26 load a 21 cm W.Gr.21 mortar shell into an underwing launch tube suspended from the port wing of an Fw 190A-8/R6 at Lille-Vendeville, May 1944. (EN Archive)

Right 29. B-17F '*The Sack*' of the 379th BG made it back from the raid to Kassel and Oschersleben on 28 July 1943, despite having been hit by a 21 cm mortar fired by a German fighter. (Robert Forsyth Collection)

30. Unteroffizier Willi Unger of 12./JG 3 with his Fw 190A-8/R2 at Barth during trials with the 'Crab Device', a fuselage-mounted, rearward-firing, 21 cm mortar. Photo via Willi Unger. (Robert Forsyth Collection)

31. A line-up of three Eighth Air Force P-51D Mustangs, four P-47D Thunderbolts and a P-38J Lightning – fighters which proved to be the nemeses of the Luftwaffe over the Reich. Photo via Jerry Scutts. (Robert Forsyth Collection)

32. For Oskar Bösch, photographed here when a Feldwebel, being caught in a bombing raid on a German city served as the impetus to volunteer for the *Sturmstaffel*. Photo via Oskar Bösch. (Robert Forsyth Collection)

33. Five Fw 190A-8s of II.(*Sturm*)/JG 300 at readiness. (EN Archive)

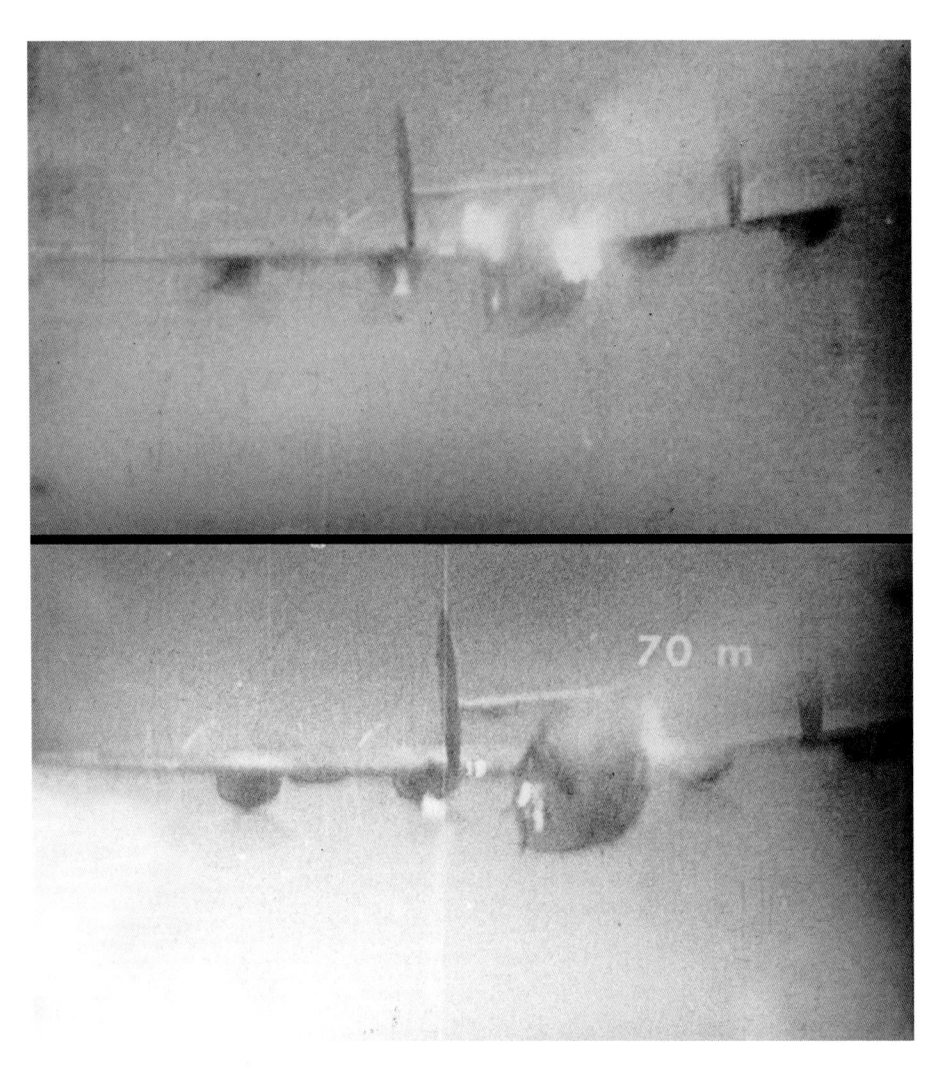

Above 34. The view from an Fw 190A-8 on 7 July 1944, captured by the Focke-Wulf's gun camera. (Robert Forsyth Collection)

Right 35. The steel wire tangled around the nose of a B-24D of the 44th BG was photographed upon the bomber's return to England following the raid to Emden on 11 December 1943. (Robert Forsyth Collection)

Above 36. The barrels of three 30 mm MK 103 cannon protrude obliquely from the fuselage of an Fw 190 of E.Kdo 25 in mid-1944. (Robert Forsyth Collection)

Right 37. A prototype Ruhrstahl X4 wire-guided air-to-air rocket suspended from beneath the wing of an Fw 190. (Robert Forsyth Collection)

38. A rocket-powered Me 163B is towed by a three-wheeled Scheuch-Schlepper (tug tractor) following its landing. (EN Archive)

Top 39. Use of W.Gr.21 mortars persisted through to the closing weeks of the war. They were fitted to a few Me 262A-1a jet interceptors of JG 7 in the spring of 1945. (EN Archive)

Above 40. A standard battery of 12 R4M 55 mm air-to-air rockets in a wooden launch rack beneath the starboard wing, outboard of the turbojet nacelle of an Me 262 of JG 7. (EN Archive)

Right 41. The last, desperate attempt to counter Allied bombers was a manned, semi-expendable Bachem Ba 349 *Natter* (Adder) rocket-powered VTO interceptor. (EN Archive)

to be known as '*Höhenjagdgruppen*' ('High-altitude Fighter Groups'), and that their aircraft were also to be used for combatting RAF Mosquitos at night. The *Höhenjagdgruppe* for 1. *Jagddivision* was still to be determined, but 2. *Jagddivision* was assigned II./JG 11 and 3. *Jagddivision* III./JG 1 as high-altitude units.

Following his meeting at Carinhall, Schmid advised the attendees at Stade that Göring wanted the *Korps'* units grouped more closely on the ground to aid rapid assembly in strength in the air at the time of an enemy incursion. Ibel emphasised the need to choose an easily identifiable point, such as the Steinhuder Meer, to assist with assembly. In this regard, 1. *Jagddivision* was to decide immediately which assembly points were possible, either using points in the terrain or recognisable navigational points such as radar stations or communications masts. Directional firing by an entire Flak zone could also be considered as an aid. *Luftflotte Reich* was to advise whether it was feasible for Flak batteries to fire when there was no alarm.

Schmid commented that Göring did not believe guidance of fighters from the ground was possible. The *Jagdkorps* commander conceded that there was still much work to be done to improve guidance procedures. An essential prerequisite was that *Geschwader* command posts had efficient telephone links to operational airfields, and that it should be possible to talk with the *Gruppenkommandeuren* before understanding enemy intentions. Furthermore, every *Geschwaderkommodore* should able to talk to his *Gruppen* in the air.

Implementation of voice communication, distribution of the 'Y'-lines, coordination with the *Reichsjägerwelle* and the setting up of necessary transmitters were to be organised immediately by the signals officers of the *Jagdkorps* and the *Divisionen*. The *Höhenjagdgruppen* were to have their own net so as not to 'bleed over' or interrupt other *Gruppen*.

At the time enemy bombers made their return route to England, it was vital that as many Luftwaffe fighters as possible should be deployed against them in second missions, but in reality, by that stage, many had landed on unfamiliar airfields. Small groups of aircraft were not informed when and to where they should take off again. Thus, new, designated '*Jägereinsatzplätze*' ('operational fighter fields') were to be established, supplied with ammunition, oxygen, oil and fuel. If a fighter landed at a field that was not a *Jägereinsatzplatz*, it was to refuel quickly and depart immediately for a designated field where fuel would be topped up and from where it would be deployed to the west to pursue the enemy. It would be the responsibility of local airfield commanders to ensure that emergency stocks of fuel were always on hand for such a purpose.[10]

At the same time Schmid's conference was taking place at Stade, at the RLM in Berlin, Generalfeldmarschall Milch addressed another conference on aircraft production attended by senior officials from the ministry and aircraft manufacturers. As the first 'Big Week' bombs rained down, Milch had undertaken a timely fact-finding tour of the fighter manufacturing plants. Returning to Berlin on 23 February, he was in a grimly honest mood, telling the meeting that the situation at the plants was 'very strained to say the least'. He lamented:

> The effect on our day fighter production has been very severe and we are faced with great difficulties. If you go into a fighter plant – I have seen Erla-Leipzig and Oschersleben – there is nothing to be seen but bent wires, like a bombed block of flats here in Berlin. Outside, there are bomb craters eight to nine metres deep and 14–16 metres across. But the struggle is not hopeless. It can be managed.
>
> [However] we must face the fact that our fighter production has encountered difficulties since last July. For the first time our monthly output then exceeded 1,000 single-engined fighters and 150 to 200 twin-engined fighters, including nightfighters. We were making considerable progress and we were going to reach 2,000 single-engined fighters and 250 twin-engined fighters in November. We did not succeed.
>
> Instead, our output was constantly reduced by the heavy attacks which were directed first of all against Me 109 production. There were several attacks on Regensburg and Wiener Neustadt – both of these plants were producing 400 aircraft and would soon have increased this output. Then came a series of attacks on the Fw 190 factories. These plants were hit again recently. We inspected a number of these damaged factories. The only plant which has not yet been heavily hit, although it has been attacked once, is the Erla works at Leipzig, which is scheduled to produce about 450 fighters this month. It withstood the Saturday night attack quite well, but then this industry has been hit very hard.
>
> We should have reached a monthly output of 2,000 fighters by February. However, there is no prospect of this programme being carried through. Considering the present situation, we can be very content if we produce 1,000–1,200 fighters. At most factories we have already dispersed plant in all directions. The Erla works was perhaps still too close to the Leipzig area, but the other factories were much more widely dispersed. However, even dispersed installations have been hit.

Milch had been told that the BBC had broadcast that the destruction of the fighter factories was the primary Allied objective:

Once the fighter plants were destroyed, they would have the upper hand and Germany would be at their mercy. The other types of production would then be dealt with similarly, and it would be a simple matter to carry out carpet-bombing in the American style at any given target and from any height desired as there would no longer be any defence.[11]

But Milch – the pragmatist, the hard-nosed businessman, the shrewd optimist – was not to be cowed. Within hours he formed the *Jägerstab* (Fighter Staff), a select committee comprised of industrialists and representatives of the RLM tasked with regenerating the flagging and now bomb-stricken fighter production industry.

Yet none of these challenges – a lack of aircraft, restrictions on fuel, inadequate training – prevented the Luftwaffe from showing its teeth intermittently during 'Big Week'.

Following its mission to Gotha on 24 February, the 2nd BD reported its B-24s as 'being attacked for almost the entire period over Germany'. It seemed that the German fighters had gained a new confidence, the Fw 190s of JGs 1 and 26 'pressing home vicious nose attacks', whilst elsewhere, 'some groups were forced far off course, and these formations and especially stragglers were attacked unceasingly'.

At Wunstorf, following an *Alarmstart* order, III./ZG 26 was able to get only four Bf 110s into the air just after midday. Under guidance from the controllers at *Sokrates*, they joined up with ten Bf 110s from I./ZG 26 and Bf 109s from Hauptmann Günther Specht's II./JG 11 as escort over Braunschweig. At 1315 hrs, the Luftwaffe formation spotted eight *Pulks*, each of 15 B-24s, at between 4,000–7,000 m heading southeast in what Schulze-Dickow described as an 'unstable' formation. Upon sighting the German group, the bombers turned to the south and then to the southwest. III./ZG 26 launched its attack at 1330 hrs in the Holzminden area from left and above. One Liberator was claimed by Oberleutnant Werner Meltz of 8./ZG 26 and a *Herausschuss* by Major Johann Kogler, the acting *Kommandeur*. Schulze-Dickow noticed how:

> The enemy flew with Thunderbolts as fighter escort. I realised that the lead *Pulk*, which I wanted to attack, always turned to the right just as I had positioned myself in front for an attack. It is possible that this pushed them away from the target.[12]

That day, the 2nd BD lost 33 Liberators.

The Fifteenth Air Force 'twisted the knife' into the German defence when it launched a simultaneous raid on aircraft components factories at Steyr, in Austria. Mortar-equipped fighters from JGs 3 and 27 and ZG 1 attacked B-17s of the 2nd BG, shooting down a 'box' of ten bombers. III./JG 3 based at Leipheim did well, claiming six *Abschüsse* and three *Herausschüsse* in the Linz area.

In their BK 5 cannon-equipped Me 410, the crew of Oberfeldwebel Willi Frös and Unteroffizier Gerhard Brandl of 5./ZG 26 shot down a B-17 of the Fifteenth Air Force at 6,000 m over Steyr. Frös would eventually be accredited with three *Viermots* shot down. More missions with the BK 5 would be flown throughout the spring and summer of 1944, but they brought virtually no success. Furthermore, the operational losses suffered by aircraft fitted with such armament were disproportionately high in the relatively few missions flown. Their envisaged capability had been nullified by loss of aircraft speed and the defensive fire of enemy bombers.

'Big Week' in some ways caused unexpected reactions. In summarising operations in his sector during February, Schmid wrote:

> In the interest of the overall conduct of the war, the Luftwaffe must face the fact that its most important mission is the prevention of American daytime attacks on the Reich. The most vital prerequisite to the successful accomplishment of this mission is the regaining of air supremacy over the territory of the Reich. It is doubtful if this goal can be attained with the fighter aircraft types presently available, especially in view of the fact that Germany is not in a position to rival the United States in the production of fighter aircraft.[13]

Under Göring's directive of February 1944, aptly entitled 'Imminent Danger West', Generalfeldmarschall Sperrle's *Luftflotte* 3, which maintained overall tactical control throughout northwest France and the Low Countries, was haltingly reinforced. It was, of course, realised that the drain of the defensive campaigns in the East as well as the continual need for an effective fighter umbrella over the Reich, would prevent any satisfactory level of reinforcement in the event of an Allied invasion in the West, although it was hoped that the relatively short distances involved would assist in the rapid transfer of the required fighter units to the invasion zone when needed.

Sperrle's *Luftflotte* was, in reality, ill-suited for the task demanded of it. A total of 815 combat aircraft were based in northern France and Belgium. The single- and twin-engined day fighter strength, consisting of the 220 aircraft of JGs 2 and 26, along with two *Zerstörergruppen*, continued to be marshalled under the command of II. *Jagdkorps*.

But it was to the north east, in the area of *Luftflotte Reich* and I. *Jagdkorps*, and where the need for air defence was greatest, that Galland had assembled the bulk of the fighter force. Yet the odds were depressing. The air fleet calculated that the prevailing numerical ratios were as follows:

Total USAAF strength (bombers and fighters) – 3.6
German single- and twin-engined fighter strength (I. *Jagdkorps*) – 1

USAAF fighter strength – 1.6
German single- and twin-engined fighter strength (I. *Jagdkorps*) – 1

I. *Jagdkorps* undertook 2,861 sorties in February, and losses in the area by the end of that month stood at 299 aircraft, or 10.3 per cent of the total number of aircraft committed.

The death toll for February had been devastating, and it included several valued *Experten* and Knight's Cross-holders. Others would follow. And yet, that month the Luftwaffe's propaganda war reporters were filing ever more colourful, even lurid, reports of the apparent deeds of the heroic fighter pilots. The war diary of the I. *Jagdkorps* for early 1944 is peppered with accounts with titles such as '*Stolze Leistungen unserer Jäger*' ('The Proud achievements of our fighter pilots'), '*vernichtet im Rammstoss*' ('Destroyed in a ramming attack'), '*Ohne Waffen gegen eine Boeing*' ('Without weapons against a Boeing'), '*Im Pulk der USA Bomber*' ('In an American bomber formation') and '*Beim ersten Feindflug, zwei Abschüsse*' ('First mission against the enemy, two victories').

16

'Big B'

On 2 March 1944, Hauptmann Egon Mayer, *Kommodore* of JG 2, the first pilot to accumulate 100 victories solely on the Channel Front and the tactical mastermind behind the Luftwaffe's classic frontal attack against the bombers in late 1942, led a *Schwarm* of Fw 190s of *Stab./*JG 2 against a formation of around 200 B-17s heading for Frankfurt am Main. The *Stab* flight had failed to link up with the Focke-Wulfs of II. and III./JG 2, and recent research suggests Mayer later lost contact with his own *Schwarm*.[1]

As he made a lone diving pass through the bombers, Mayer fell prey to P-47s that he had failed to spot above him. He came down near Montmédy in France. Mayer's loss was especially hard to bear, for at that time he was the highest scorer against the bombers with 24 *Viermots* to his credit. The commander of II. *Jagdkorps*, Generalmajor Werner Junck, offered the following typically overcoloured tribute:

> Together with his victorious *Geschwader*, the entire II. *Jagdkorps* remembers him in mourning for his heroic death, but also with pride because he was one of our own. He lives on in our hearts as a dear comrade, as a model of the unwavering will to win, and brave heroism. The fighter pilots in the West will continue to fly and fight in his spirit, which was equal to that of von Richthofen.[2]

Two days later, Mayer became the 51st recipient of the Swords to the Knight's Cross with Oak Leaves, awarded posthumously.

In the main, the flying and combat skills of many younger Luftwaffe fighter pilots flying in defence of the Reich were questionable. As Schmid had described in his post-inspection tour report in February, 'intensive training' was needed urgently because of the lack of 'flying and tactical experience' of the replacement pilots being sent to the units of I. *Jagdkorps*.

'BIG B'

Paradoxically, whereas in the six months to June 1943 fewer pupils were leaving the A/B schools (1,100–1,300 per month) and the fighter schools (350–400 per month), between July 1943 and June 1944 there was an increase to 2,250–2,550 per month from the A/B schools and 850–1,000 per month from the fighter schools. But quantity does not necessarily equate to quality. Up to the end of 1943, a German fighter pilot could expect to fly approximately 20 operational training hours before becoming engaged in aerial combat, but in 1944, generally, a newly qualified pilot reaching an operational unit was thrown into action on his first, second or third flight. Nor were such pilots given instruction on blind-flying.

From October 1942 to June 1944 there was a marked reduction in the total elementary and operational training instruction time. In the periods October 1942 to June 1943 and July 1943 to June 1944, total training hours fell from 185–225 to 165–175, and there were corresponding falls in the time allocated to operational types of aircraft. Gunnery training also suffered. In an effort to overcome this, in 1943 Galland set up six mobile gunnery training staffs equipped with the latest armament, sights and training aids to tour fighter airfields.

Senior officers in the Luftwaffe training establishment had little say or influence in the effectiveness of the tuition being given, since the amount of fuel available for it was determined by the RLM and OKL, who also decided upon the numbers of pilots to be trained.[3]

Swimming against this tide, Galland proposed the opening of new schools with sufficiently qualified instructors and facilities for blind- and bad-weather flying – skills that were now needed in order to equal the capability of the Allied opposition. He was even prepared to take the surplus pilots of other branches of the Luftwaffe as a means of reducing overall training hours and fuel usage. In March 1944, Galland took the drastic initiative of signalling all the major flying branches of the Luftwaffe:

> The strained manpower situation in the units operating in defence of the Reich urgently demands the mustering of experienced flying personnel from other arms of the service, and in particular, so as to maintain the fighting strength of the Luftwaffe, tried and tested pilots from ground-attack and bomber units, especially officers suitable as formation leaders. The basis for all this is still to be voluntary. Every officer and official from the Staffs is to be called upon to give his very last ounce in the performance of his duty, as is demanded by the manpower difficulties in this fifth year of war. *Luftflotte Reich* and *Luftflotte* 3 need officers who will give their utmost as fighter and formation leaders in defence of the Reich.

However, such proposals when submitted to OKL were quietly brushed under the carpet.

February saw production of Bf 109s and Fw 190s slide yet again from a target figure of 1,651 to 1,016 machines – a shortfall of 38.5 per cent.[4] To a great extent this could be attributed to the American 'Big Week' bombing raids on the production centres. It remained to be seen what the new *Jägerstab* would or *could* do about it.

In March, following the attacks on the enemy aircraft manufacturing centres, the Americans felt sufficiently confident to concentrate their efforts on Berlin. With a population of just over 4,300,000 in 1939, the German capital was the greatest commercial and industrial centre on the continent of Europe. Berlin was also the hub of Germany's war effort, housing the administrative and ministerial headquarters of all three armed services, and it was a major rail centre with 12 main lines meeting there.

After a delayed start, the first strike was mounted on 4 March when a force of 500 B-17s and B-24s escorted by 770 fighters headed for the capital. The concept behind the 'Big B' missions was not solely to bomb the important industrial targets in the city, nor even to dent civilian morale, but rather it was an attempt to coax the Jagdwaffe into the air in order to inflict further hopefully unsustainable losses. In this, the Eighth Air Force's trump card was the P-51B Mustang. Equipped with twin 108-US gallon underwing drop tanks, the North American Aviation fighters were now able to escort the bombers as far as Berlin.

Surprisingly though, despite this new, but not altogether unexpected menace, the German response to this first, crucial raid was light, with I. and II. *Jagdkorps* deploying just 149 aircraft in response. USAAF losses that day were incurred more as a result of poor operating conditions rather than the sporadic reaction of the German fighters. Luckily for the city, adverse weather prevented all bar 30 aircraft from one combat wing of the 3rd BD from reaching its primary target and unloading 68 tons of bombs. Little damage was inflicted. Of this force, five aircraft were shot down. Two days later, however, the story was different.

On 6 March, the USAAF despatched a force of 730 bombers, with a formidable escort of 796 fighters drawn from 19 fighter groups of the Eighth and Fifteenth Air Forces, to target the capital. Bitter fighting waged from the moment the bomber streams crossed the Dutch coast, and it lasted all the way to Berlin and back.

The Luftwaffe had been expecting the raid, and had prepared itself by practising the assembly of large formations of fighters drawn from more than one unit – so-called *Gefechtsverbände* (battle groups). This was broadly in accordance with Göring's wishes as expressed to Schmid the previous month at Carinhall, and it would see greater numbers of fighters brought together into smaller geographical areas so that they could be deployed against the bombers more quickly and at reduced intervals.

The basic tactic employed by *Gefechtsverbände* saw mortar-equipped 'heavy' fighters and/or *Zerstörer* being used to break up and disperse enemy *Pulks*, with standard cannon-armed fighters following in their wake. All of these would be covered by *Höhenjagdgruppen*, which would exclusively engage the escort.

Each *Gefechtsverband* covered an assigned area of operations and comprised a commanding *Jagdgeschwader*, which controlled the battle formation in the air and to which other units were assigned for a specific mission. The leading *Geschwader* was directed from the ground by its overseeing headquarters. Thus, JG 1 covered the Netherlands and was controlled by 3. *Jagddivision*. JG 3 (also 3. *Jagddivision*) and JG 11 (2. *Jagddivision*) covered the Rhine and Westphalia regions, respectively. JG 27 covered Linz, Passau and Vienna, and was controlled by the *Jafü Ostmark*. Additionally, a staff body, the *Jagdgeschwader zur besondere Verwendung* (Fighter Wing for Special Deployment), would be formed in April to cover the Rhine and Main basins, and to which could be assigned independent units on an ad hoc basis.[5]

In readiness for a USAAF attack on Berlin, several days earlier the Luftwaffe had been practising the assembly of large numbers of fighters over the Steinhuder Meer, northwest of Hanover, in an attempt to meet mass with mass. So it was that on 6 March no fewer than 19 *Jagdgruppen*, three *Zerstörergruppen* and four *Nachtjagdgruppen*, together with a handful of miscellaneous units, were available to take on the *Viermots*.

At 0850 hrs, the first USAAF aircraft took off. From that moment, the German radar and listening services were continually tuned into the Eighth Air Force's 250th bombing mission. More than an hour before the first American aircraft crossed the Channel, preparatory orders had been issued to the German fighter units. For this attack, the units of 2. and 3. *Jagddivision* would work closely together under the tactical directorship of the *Gruppenkommandeur* of I./JG 11, Hauptmann Rolf Hermichen, a former *Zerstörer* pilot who had shot down two B-24s in one day on 1 December 1943, followed by four more Liberators on 20 February 1944.

The first B-17s reached the coast of the Netherlands at 1052 hrs. With engines running at cruising speed to conserve fuel, the escort fighters slowly made up the distance between themselves and their charges.

At last, the interminable *Sitzbereitschaft* came to an end on the majority of Luftwaffe fighter bases across western Europe. At Twente, Major Schnoor's I./JG 1 took off at 1055 hrs, setting course for the Steinhuder Meer. I. *Gruppe* was joined over Rheine by the 21 Fw 190s of II./JG 1, led by Major Bär. The two *Gruppen* were the last to arrive over the lake, meeting up with 50 Bf 109s and Fw 190s from JG 11 and 20 Bf 109s of III./JG 54. JG 1's arrival meant that more than 100 fighters would go into action simultaneously – a force which far exceeded the usual German strike capability. For the first time in a long while, the young Jagdwaffe pilots experienced a feeling of invulnerability. However, their numbers could still not compare with those put into the fray by the USAAF.

Shortly after 1130 hrs, seven Fw 190s from *Sturmstaffel* 1 joined the Bf 109s of IV./JG 3 as they took off from Salzwedel and headed towards Magdeburg. Once there, they were due to form up into a *Gefechtsverband* comprised of units drawn from 1. and 7. *Jagddivision* under the command of Major Johann 'Hans' Kogler, *Kommandeur* of III./ZG 26. Rendezvous was made at 8,000 m near Magdeburg.

Once assembled, this large *Gefechtsverband* comprised a lead element of 41 Bf 110 and Me 410 *Zerstörer* from II. and III./ZG 26 and I. and II./ZG 76, many equipped with underwing batteries of four W.Gr.21 mortars. Behind the *Zerstörer* came no fewer than 72 Bf 109s and Fw 190s from I., II. and IV./JG 3, *Sturmstaffel* 1, JG 302 and the Erla works defence flight.

At around 1230 hrs the enemy bombers were sighted – 112 B-17 Flying Fortresses of the 1st and 94th CWs of the 1st BD. The twin-engined heavy fighters went in first, firing their mortars. As they did so, P-51s of Lt Col Don Blakeslee's 4th FG dived out of the sun to intercept them. Their intervention forced the *Zerstörer* pilots to break off their attacks early, resulting in many of the mortars exploding way off target.

Following behind the Bf 110s and Me 410s, the Bf 109s of IV./JG 3 attacked the bombers head-on and from out of the sun. By the time the action was over, the *Gruppe* would claim 12 of the bombers either shot down or struck out of formation, as well as one P-51 destroyed.

For *Sturmstaffel* 1, it was to be the most successful day since the unit's formation. Moving in to attack from the rear, the unit closed in on B-17s of the 91st BG. Unteroffizier Kurt Röhrich scored his third victory at 1235 hrs, together with Unteroffizier Willi Maximowitz, who claimed a *Herausschuss*, and Leutnant Gerhard Dost, who scored his first victory. Three minutes later, Feldwebel Hermann Wahlfeld, who had shot down two bombers just two days before, added to his personal score and recorded his third victory.

Oberleutnant Othmar Zehart followed at 1255 hrs when he scored his second victory. Oberleutnant Richard Franz remembered:

> The close 'V' formation gave us a very strong attacking force with extreme firepower so that when we engaged the bombers we were pretty well always successful. The problem was to bring our heavy birds into position before we were caught by the escort fighters, which sometimes happened, bringing us severe losses – especially when the P-51s arrived. I also recall the defence of their bomber formations was very effective, because while attacking a formation you couldn't find one angle that did not have defensive fire.[6]

These early combat experiences, combined with the highly hazardous nature of their missions, may have served as the motivation behind some *Sturmstaffel* pilots experimenting with the wearing of steel infantry helmets as a form of additional armour protection during the initial period of operations. Feldwebel Oskar Bösch remembered what his fellow pilots told him. 'It, not surprisingly, proved impractical. Wearing a steel helmet in the cockpit resulted in the complete inability of the pilot to move his head when in combat!' The idea was soon abandoned.

Just north of Magdeburg, one Fw 190 of *Sturmstaffel* 1 collided with '*My Darling Also*', a B-17G of the 91st BG. The Focke-Wulf descended slightly as it approached and took hits, but then climbed 'relentlessly' towards '*My Darling Also*', which was already badly damaged by fire from the German fighter. The Fw 190 struck the Boeing, knocking off the entire right stabiliser and then cartwheeling away through the sky, streaking flames.

As the bomber lurched in the air and began to fall out of control, Sgt Dana E. Morse, the left waist gunner, was thrown away from his gun. He glanced over to his fellow waist gunner, Sgt Sydney A. Barratt, but he had been wounded badly and was clutching his stomach. Morse then peered out of the right waist hatch and saw flames rushing past as the Flying Fortress began sinking away to the right, its engines howling. Smoke filled the fuselage and the intercom had been knocked out, so there was no way that he could communicate with the cockpit of the aircraft. Morse groped his way forward to try to reach the ball turret gunner, SSgt Harold J. Rhode, but he was either unconscious or dead.

By that time Barratt had collapsed to the floor, and Morse could see no life in the tail gunner's position either. With the g-forces growing stronger as the Flying Fortress lost more height, Morse kicked out the rear escape door and jumped.[7] Shortly afterwards, '*My Darling Also*' crashed to Earth near the village of Letzlingen, 12 km southeast of Gardelegen. Eight crew were killed and the two who managed to bail out, including Morse, were taken prisoner.

In all, by the time the *Gefechtsverband* broke off its attack, having expended both fuel and ammunition, eight B-17s had been shot down and three more destroyed in collisions. Four P-51s also went down in the Berlin area. However, for the Germans, the price of this 'success' was high. Of the seven Bf 110s of III./ZG 26 thrown into action, five were destroyed and the remaining two damaged. Eleven further *Zerstörer* were destroyed and at least two more damaged. For the single-engined fighters, losses were five Bf 109s and two Fw 190s.

JG 1's score for the day was a gratifying total of 26 claims – 23 B-17s shot down and one *Herausschuss*, plus a P-51 and a P-47 destroyed. Heinz Bär downed two B-17s during a first mission and a third during a following sortie. Unteroffizier Helmut Stiegler of 4./JG 1 who flew with Bär, opened his tally with two B-17s, one on each mission. Hauptmann Segatz shot down two B-17s in two minutes, the *Kommodore*, Oberst Walter Oesau, claimed a P-47 and another B-17 15 minutes later, Oberleutnant Rüdiger Kirchmayr was credited with a B-17 and a P-51 and Feldwebel Walter Köhne claimed two B-17s.

In total, the Luftwaffe suffered 87 single- or twin-engined fighters lost or damaged on 6 March, resulting in the deaths of 36 pilots, with a further 27 wounded. Among those lost were Knight's Cross-holder Oberleutnant Gerhard Loos of III./JG 54, who had 85 victories to his credit. Having attacked the bombers, Loos was bounced by P-51s. He bailed out over Oldenburg, but drifted towards high-tension wires and was forced to release the harness to his parachute. He fell to his death. Schmid issued a *Korpstagesbefehl* on 10 March regarding Loos which typifies the solemn grandiloquence used by the armed forces of the Third Reich customary on such occasions:

> Inspired by the genuine hunter's spirit which always seeks victory, Loos achieved proud and heroic successes in action in various theatres of war, and was an inspiring example to his crews in battle. His memory will not be forgotten in the German fatherland.
>
> For all of us, his fulfilment of duty, to his heroic death, is a reminder to show the same serious devotion to the *Führer* and the Reich![8]

Leutnant Hugo Frey, *Staffelkapitän* of 7./JG 11, claimed four bombers destroyed that day before being shot down and killed near Sleen, in the Netherlands. He had 32 victories, including 26 four-engined kills, to his name, and would be awarded the Knight's Cross posthumously.

On the American side, 53 B-17s and 16 B-24s failed to return, 293 B-17s and 54 B-24s were damaged and five B-17s and one B-24 written off. Seventeen crew were killed, 31 wounded and 686 listed as missing. It was the highest loss rate for a mission to date.

Both sides withdrew to lick their wounds and assess losses, devastated by the savagery of the combat. The USAAF questioned whether attacking such targets was worth the cost, while the Luftwaffe contemplated how it could possibly continue defending cities like Berlin in the face of such harrowing losses to its pilots. But of even greater psychological impact on the Germans was the fact that Berlin could no longer be considered immune from attack, no longer out of range. The pressure on the pilots of the outnumbered fighter units operating in the defence of the Reich could only now grow.

And yet, there was to be no let-up. On 8 March, 320 B-17s and 150 B-24s attacked the VKF ball bearing plant at Erkner. More bombers hit targets of opportunity in the German capital. As an indication of the dramatic odds at which the Luftwaffe defence now fought, a record 891 USAAF fighters provided escort and support. Eighteen of these were lost and a further 16 written off as a result of the raid.

At Salzwedel, IV./JG 3 was scrambled to intercept at 1348 hrs, and it is more than likely that the unit took off accompanied by the six operational Fw 190s of *Sturmstaffel* 1. At 7,500 m over Magdeburg, the fighters formed up into a *Gefechtsverband* with a small number of Bf 110 *Zerstörer* from ZG 26 and other elements of JG 3. Following a course to the northwest, the *Gefechtsverband* sighted the American bombers at 1325 hrs flying east-southeast at 6,000 m with strong fighter escort.

Once again, the *Zerstörer* went in first, followed by JG 3, which mounted a frontal attack – the *Gruppe* demonstrated its tenacity by claiming seven B-17s shot down or cut out of formation.[9] One of the claimants was the *Kommandeur*, Major Karl-Friedrich 'Tutti' Müller, a veteran of the *Kanalkampf* and a holder of the Oak Leaves to the Knight's Cross. He had shot down his first B-17 on 31 January 1943 while serving in North Africa, but owing to exhaustion, he was given extended leave. Then, on 26 February 1944, Müller was appointed to command IV./JG 3. During the early afternoon of 8 March, he shot down a Flying Fortress for his fifth *Viermot*, and 120th victory overall.

Flying as *Rottenflieger* to the *Geschwaderkommodore*, Oberst Wolf-Dietrich '*Fürst*' Wilcke, Müller was scrambled at 1516 hrs for the second mission of the day to pursue the retiring bombers, the pair of Bf 109G-6s climbing south out of Salzwedel, heading for Gardelegen. They made contact with a formation of 20–25 B-24s north of Gardelegen just after 1530 hrs at 5,000 m.

Going in head-on, Müller fired at a Liberator, shooting it down, and then dived through the bombers, turning to come back from below and behind, opening fire again with his MG 151s at another bomber. Two of its engines started to burn, and as he closed, Müller observed further strikes to the tail and fuselage. The bomber immediately went into a steep glide away from the formation. Müller was awarded a *Herausschuss* for his 122nd victory. He landed back at Salzwedel six minutes later.[10]

As Müller and the pilots of IV./JG 3 battled with the *Viermots* above Gardelegen, the same day, 200 km to the west in the spa town of Bad Eilsen, Dipl.-Ing. Hans Multhopp, a softly spoken aerodynamicist who led the Focke-Wulf *Entwurfsabteilung* (Design Department), and his assistant, Dr. Wendland, signed off a somewhat radical proposal. The *Entwurfsabteilung* was a branch office of the main Focke-Wulf works in bomb-battered Bremen, one of several departments that had been dispersed to less urban areas for reasons of safety since the heavy bombing raids in the north had begun.

Multhopp and his team were involved in highly important projects, including developmental work on the Fw 190 and new jet engine technology. They had inventive minds. But with Bad Eilsen lying directly under the route taken by the bombers of the USAAF as they flew to attack targets in Hanover, Braunschweig and Berlin, Multhopp and Wendland would have seen the USAAF formations flying in and out, seen the smoke from fires on the horizon, and witnessed the aerial battles between the *Viermots* and the Luftwaffe's fighters above them in the skies over Lower Saxony.

Like many loyal German civilians, and in a departure from their day-to-day aircraft design work, Multhopp and Wendland made their own contribution to the Reich's defence against the Allied *Terrorflieger* – albeit one that could be viewed as radical, fantastical, innovative, impractical or ingenious. They proposed to destroy enemy bomber formations by artificially generated gusts, or squalls, of air. The gusts were to be created by the 'combustion of fuels in the atmosphere'.

They envisaged replicating the levels of natural energy which were contained in the 'storm clouds of nature' – around 6.5 kilocalories to a kilogramme of air – which created updrafts with speeds of more than 25 m per second. If, however, combustion could occur without excess air, enormous levels of energy – up to 680 kilocalories to a kilogramme of air – could be produced. Multhopp and Wendland proposed producing such energy by blasting volatile explosive fuels directly into the atmosphere from specially designed tanks, two of which could be carried externally beneath the wings of an Fw 190 fighter-bomber.

The upper half of each tank would contain fuel and the lower half the necessary ignition material. The mixture would be released using a valve, of which a type had been used for flame-throwing experiments on a Ju 88. This valve would allow a quantity of approximately 35–40 kg of mixture to be jetted out at an altitude of 6,000 m. As a 'simple and quick solution', it was suggested adapting the existing 295-litre external drop tanks used by Ju 87 dive-bombers.

The mixture in the tanks would be released and an uplift would result, into which the bombers would fly and then collide or even physically break up. According to the proposal, 'the ignition of such fuels in the atmosphere would produce updrafts of tremendous strength. Aircraft which have less resistance to gusts, for example bombers, would suffer extreme flows of wind on their wings of sufficient strength to the cause rupture of their airframes'.

When using the tanks operationally, the two technicians allowed for the fact that USAAF bomber formations were organised in such a way that saw them fly at a considerable depth and staggered back upwards or downwards. The discharging Fw 190 would fly below and ahead of the bomber formation at right angles or diagonally to the formation's direction of flight. As Multhopp and Wendland commented:

> [The discharging aircraft] is therefore exposed only minimally to targeted defensive fire. Our fighters also no longer need to expose themselves to the massive defensive fire of the enemy bomber formations; their primary task is to protect the fuel-discharging aircraft from attacks by enemy escort fighters and to attack bombers that have been blown off course.

Two discharging aircraft could be used, approaching diagonally from the rear of the enemy formation and opening the valves to their tanks as they curved past it.[11]

However imaginative Multhopp's and Wendland's proposal may have been, it did not progress beyond the report stage.

On 15 March, the enemy was the weather. Spring was nowhere to be seen. Flying via instruments, the crews of 185 B-17s of the 3rd BD and 145 B-24s of the 2nd BD bombed aircraft industry targets in Braunschweig. In Europe heavy fog blanketed the airfields in the area of 1. *Jagddivision* at all altitudes, while varying cover of nimbus clouds hung over the 2. and 3. *Jagddivisionen* zones at between 200–5,000 m. There were also snow flurries and the danger of icing in the clouds, and over Braunschweig the cloud cover was six-tenths to ten-tenths, although high-altitude visibility was good. Such conditions meant that it was incredibly difficult – and dangerous – to attempt to assemble individual units of fighters, let alone *Gefechtsverbände*.

But on such occasions, those at unit level were often unwilling or unable to see the bigger picture. For example, that morning at Wunstorf,

III./ZG 26's airfield just east of the Steinhuder Meer, despite the poor conditions, Major Johannes Kogler fumed as his Bf 110 'destroyers' were ordered by I. *Jagddivision* to remain on the ground, despite the fact that their airfield lay almost directly on the bombers' incoming flightpath.

There had been confusion in orders and timings emanating from *Division* headquarters at Döberitz. At 0923 hrs, when the bombers were reported as being 200 km from Wunstorf, Kogler's crews had been placed at 15 minutes readiness. Then, at 1000 hrs, when the Americans were 50 km closer, they were ordered to go back to 30 minutes readiness and told to disperse their Messerschmitt *Zerstörer* around the airfield. That, despite the fact that the single-engined fighter units of 2. *Jagddivision* also based at Wunstorf had been given the *Alarmstart*. Twelve minutes later, Kogler asked Döberitz for clearance to take-off. The *Jagddivision* responded two minutes later, bringing III./ZG 26 to cockpit readiness. The *Viermots* were now 100 km from Wunstorf.

Kogler advised that he would 'have to decline responsibility for a take-off' because, based on three recent enemy low-level attacks on the airfield, a further attack could be expected. He was right — 60 seconds later, American fighters streaked across the airfield. Four minutes after the attack, at 1019 hrs, the order to take-off finally came when the bombers were just 15 km from Wunstorf, but on this occasion, the *Gruppe* was ordered to head for a new assembly area — the seventh — over Cottbus, 400 km to the east, and just over 300 km away from the target at Braunschweig.

Miraculously, during take-off there were no accidents or losses, but once the Bf 110s were in the air, they flew straight into a snow shower and their formation broke up. One aircraft and crew were lost.[12] The operation proved futile and simply consumed fuel.

I. *Jagdkorps* managed to scramble 161 aircraft in total, of which 115 engaged the enemy and claimed eight bombers shot down, but at a cost of 12 of its own aircraft lost and a further five categorised as more than 60 per cent damaged. Two airmen were dead, three wounded and 12 posted missing. The USAAF lost just three bombers, but also five fighters. The 745 tons of bombs dropped on the city of Braunschweig and the surrounding areas caused widespread damage to both factories and residential areas.[13]

The attrition continued over Berlin throughout the month, forcing the Eighth Air Force to write off 349 bombers over a period of 23 operationally active days, 13 of which involved all-out effort.

For the Luftwaffe, the months of February and March 1944 marked a grim chapter in its history. Pilot losses had been crippling and were no longer confined to the younger and less experienced, hurriedly trained replacements. Galland's dilemma was the continuing and increasing losses of experienced and irreplaceable unit leaders such as the 108-victory Knight's Cross-holder, Hauptmann Emil Bitsch, *Staffelkapitän* of 8./JG 3, who was a victim of British fighters over Volkel on the 15th.

At unit-level, such losses were real blows to morale. In a communiqué of the 16th, Schmid implored – again with solemn grandiloquence – his fighter pilots to keep the faith and fight on:

> We are fighting under the eyes of our homeland. This means the greatest obligation for each of us. At a time when German cities are being destroyed, when an inhuman enemy is killing our women and children, I demand of you, comrades, the greatest dedication to duty and the greatest soldierly spirit.
>
> I am happy to be able to lead the best German pilots in my *Jagdkorps* against the enemy and to inflict the greatest losses on them. But we have not yet hit the British and Americans sufficiently at their core, in their substance. We must double and multiply our blows and increase them so much that they forget to come back. Our defence must reach a high point from which we can finally leap forward and go onto the offensive.[14]

As an example of the attrition being suffered, in the four days from 15–18 March 1944, III./JG 3 flew four combat operations stretching from the Netherlands to Augsburg and lost five pilots, with a further six wounded and seven forced to either make emergency landings or bail out.

The same day that Schmid issued his plea, 465 B-17s from the Eighth Air Force set out to bomb targets at Augsburg and Ulm. Throughout the day the Eighth also despatched 868 fighters, swamping the defenders. If Schmid thought that his *Korps* was in a position to 'double and multiply' its blows, he was mistaken. The fickle spring weather over Germany was bad, enabling I. *Jagdkorps* to deploy only 111 fighters. The 'impenetrable' cloud rendered take-off, assembly and approach manoeuvres very difficult, and ground visibility was so poor that the units of 1. *Jagddivision* and those based in the northern part of 2. *Jagddivision*'s zone were unable to take-off at all. One entire *Gefechtsverband* was forced to return to its bases, abandoning the mission because of poor visibility and icing in the cloud layers, while from 3. *Jagddivision*, which was assigned to cover the Koblenz area, only 37 fighters made contact with the enemy.

At 1054 hrs Leutnant Ekkehard Tichy, *Staffelkapitän* of 9./JG 3 at Bad Wörishofen, led nine Bf 109s of III./JG 3 along with some Bf 110s from II./ZG 76 to Augsburg to engage the bombers. They were joined by 24 Bf 109s from I./JG 5 and formed a *Gefechtsverband*.

Pilots from III./JG 3 accounted for one bomber shot down and four classified as *Herausschüsse*. Leutnant Raimund Koch of 8. *Staffel* was one of the successful pilots, claiming a *Herausschuss*. That day, he had taken command of the *Staffel*, replacing Hauptmann Emil Bitsch who, as mentioned, had been lost the day before. Koch was airborne in a *Schwarm* of Messerschmitts three minutes behind Tichy. At 1140 hrs, the Bf 109s sighted a widely spaced formation of B-17s in the area between Stuttgart, Augsburg and Ulm, with a strong fighter escort flying around 1,000 m higher and off to the right of the bombers. The Messerschmitt pilots moved quickly to try to beat the Mustangs. As Koch reported:

> I approached the formation from a slightly elevated position and pulled back for a frontal attack. For my first attack I approached a Boeing Fortress II from the front and a little below which was flying to the right of the formation leader in the second flight, and I fired some good shots. I observed some good strikes to the cockpit and around the inboard engine. As I made a left turn behind the formation in order to make another frontal attack, I saw that the Fortress at which I had fired was slowly falling away and steadily losing height.
>
> On my second attack, I fired from ahead and below at the lead flight, but was not able to observe if I was successful. As I exited, I once again attacked the first Fortress, which was already flying very much behind the formation and which no longer had covering defensive fire from the main formation. I turned to the left again, and made a new attack from the front and saw that two of the Boeing's engines had stopped. Then I was attacked by fighters and could no longer observe the aircraft.

It was Koch's 12th victory, and the 2,047th in the war for his *Gruppe*. Koch's *Staffelkamerad*, Feldwebel Georg Ströbele, who was flying in a *Rotte* with Leutnant Herbert Zimmer, also claimed a *Herausschuss*. Ströbele targeted a B-17 flying out on the right side of the formation, expending 90 rounds from his three 20 mm cannon and 200 rounds from his two MG 131s. As he passed through the formation, he saw white smoke streaming from the B-17's two starboard engines and it immediately started to trail behind the other bombers. Seconds later, before he could finish the Flying Fortress off, Ströbele was attacked by escorting Mustangs.

III./JG 3 duly had one pilot killed by the USAAF fighters, while Leutnant Erwin Stahlberg, the *Staffelkapitän* of 7./JG 3 who claimed a *Herausschuss* for his eighth victory, was wounded in the action and crash-landed near Kirchheim. Unteroffizier Franz Neujahr of 8. *Staffel* managed to shoot down a P-51 before he too was hit and forced to bail out wounded, while

Ströbele's *Rottenflieger*, Leutnant Herbert Zimmer, crashed near Ulm after falling victim to a Mustang. Pulled from the wreckage of his fighter alive, he subsequently died of his wounds.[15]

By the end of the day, the Eighth Air Force had lost 24 bombers and 12 fighters and claimed 184 enemy aircraft shot down. The Luftwaffe claimed 36 victories, of which 23 were four-engined, but this was negated by the loss of 30 pilots, with a further 25 wounded.

On 18 March, the target for the Eighth Air Force was the aviation industry in southern Germany, while the Fifteenth Air Force was active over northern Italy and southern Austria. III./JG 3 sent up 19 Bf 109s to intercept the latter, but they failed to locate the bombers. A second mission took place at 1315 hrs when 17 Messerschmitts – 11 from III./JG 3 and six from I./JG 5 – were assembled and ordered to Mannheim to meet up with units of 3. *Jagddivision*. Pilots from III./JG 3 claimed three B-17s and Leutnant Tichy a P-51, but in the course of shooting down the Mustang, he too was hit and had to take to his parachute with a badly wounded eye. One pilot was killed and two others bailed out wounded.[16]

The following day, the Fifteenth Air Force launched the first of four attempts to bomb the Steyr-Daimler-Puch industrial complex at Steyr. A total of 234 B-17s and B-24s left their bases in Italy in bad weather but were unable to reach the target, so they opted to bomb targets further south. Most bombers struck Klagenfurt airfield, where 589 tons of bombs were dropped, while 76 Liberators expended 183 tons of ordnance on Graz airfield.

Three days earlier, the Bf 109G-6s of Hauptmann Otto Meyer's IV./JG 27 had departed their base at the former Royal Yugoslav Air Force airfield of Nisch, 200 km southeast of Belgrade, to transfer to Graz-Thalerhof, a busy pre-war airport and training base in southern Austria. Thalerhof had already been targeted by the Fifteenth, suffering some light damage as a consequence. Meyer's *Gruppe* was still in the process of settling in when the Liberators struck on the 19th.

In the wake of the bombing, the Messerschmitts took off in the early afternoon and, under direction of 7. *Jagddivision*, pursued the bombers south over Yugoslavia. Five B-24s were claimed, two of them credited to the *Staffelkapitän* of 12./JG 27, Leutnant Franz Stigler, who downed one over Marburg an der Drau and another 28 minutes later northwest of Cirkle for his 23rd and 24th victories.[17]

Stigler was one of JG 27's true combat veterans, having flown hundreds of missions over North Africa, Sicily and Italy. He had scored 17 of his kills over the desert, and had been shot down on no fewer than 17 occasions, bailing out six times. But Stigler found attacking bombers easily the most demanding form of aerial combat.[18]

Elsewhere on the 19th, IV./JG 27 lost five pilots from 10. *Staffel* in combat over Budapest.[19]

As bombs continued to fall on Berlin, 45-year-old aeronautical scientist Dr.-Ing. Ulrich Schmieschek was impelled to investigate how the American *Viermots* could best be dealt with. Schmieschek, a Silesian, was not, naturally, a hostile man – he was married and an academic, although he did experience World War I as a soldier and had languished for two years in French captivity.[20] After that, his life was spent in the pursuit of scientific research, specialising in photochemistry.

By March 1944, Schmieschek was working in the sprawling, futuristic complex of the *Deutsche Versuchsanstalt für Luftfahrt* (DVL – German Research Institute for Aviation) in Adlershof, on the southeastern edge of Berlin, as head of the Institute for Education. The DVL was where Germany's aeronautical engineers, aerodynamicists and scientists worked amidst vast, strangely shaped buildings that housed wind tunnels, engine testing platforms, cooling towers and sound-proofed chambers.

It was here that Schmieschek came up with a variation on a theme – extended length cable bombs, and this time bombs which would be ignited electrically from a carrier aircraft. He proposed that the cable was to be made of steel, to which was secured an insulated copper cable, and both were connected to the bomb's detonator. The carrying aircraft, foreseen as a Bf 109, would be escorted by other fighters at a height of around 1,000 m on its flight from its airfield towards a bomber formation. The option would be available to use just the steel cable if copper was not available and/or the bomb was to be detonated without control.

The pilot of the carrying fighter would view both an enemy bomber and the bomb through the means of a stereoscopic sight. Using the latter, the pilot was to manoeuvre his aircraft as close as possible to the bomber. At the moment of the closest possible range (the coincidence point), the bomb would be electrically triggered and the bomber damaged or destroyed by the ensuing blast.

When suspended from a 1,000-m cable, the bomb would behave like a pendulum, but the oscillations could be negated or compensated for by the movement of the carrying fighter.

Schmieschek outlined the tactical method to be deployed using a 50-kg bomb as follows:

> The fighter flies with the cable retracted until he sees an enemy bomber or formation of bombers. After spotting the enemy bomber(s), the fighter flies as far behind as possible on the same course and at an elevated

altitude. As soon as he is at the right altitude, he releases the cable, which is wound around the cable drum, as well as the 50-kg bomb until it is suspended at approximately the same altitude as the enemy aircraft.

Because lowering the bomb takes a certain amount of time, the fighter pilot reduces speed at this moment so that he is flying only slightly faster than the speed of the enemy bomber.

Deviations in azimuth and elevation were to be corrected by means of a stereoscopic sight. At the moment the enemy aircraft and the bomb were at the closest range, the bomb would be detonated electrically in order to destroy the targeted bomber. According to Schmieschek:

> Assuming that a 50-kg high-explosive bomb has a radial range of 40 m, the bomb must be brought to within 40 m of the bomber. This should be possible with a stereoscopic view and the corresponding correction of the bomb's position by the movement of the fighter. Since the aircraft and bomb have practically the same speed, the stereoscopic measurement ultimately amounts to measuring a fixed target from a fixed position, which is known to be a major advantage for stereoscopic measurement accuracy. The fact that the bomb and the enemy aircraft are moving at practically the same speed means that the most favorable moment to release the bomb can be selected optimally over a longer tracking period, which makes it much easier to release it at the right moment.[21]

Schmieschek calculated that the optimum rear-mounted approach height was 1,000–1,500 m to minimise effect from defensive fire. Once the fighter was above the enemy aircraft or formation, the pilot would then descend gradually to about 360 m before releasing the cable.

It is not believed that Schmieschek's idea advanced beyond a proposal.

In early 1944, the German fighter force was outnumbered, outgunned and undertrained. In March, the Luftwaffe lost, for one reason or another, 56.4 per cent of the single-engined fighters available to it at the beginning of the month, while losses in fighter pilots amounted to 22 per cent of the strength available at the end of February. Within that number were several formation leaders.

March saw output of Bf 109s and Fw 190s miss the monthly production target by 541 aircraft – the target was 1,918 aircraft, but output was 1,377 machines, a decline of 28.2 per cent. Meanwhile, in the same month at Ford's 65-acre Willow Run plant near Detroit, 14 B-24 Liberators were being built per day, each comprising 1.25 million parts. Ford had achieved this impressive figure by redesigning the bomber and dividing it into 73 sub-assemblies so that its construction became easier. Pilots and crews slept on cots while awaiting new aircraft to roll off the assembly line.[22]

At the end of March Schmid noted that:

> Despite the growing numerical superiority of the American forces, there had been no change in the organisation or operation of the Reich air defence forces. There could be no increase in the strength of our daytime fighter units since the production of fighter aircraft had fallen far behind schedule as a result of the successful enemy attacks on our aircraft factories. For the same reason, no new units could be activated. There seemed to be no chance of withdrawing fighters from other fronts. The command organisation of the *Reichsverteidigung* had not been altered in any way, and thus no effective concentration of fighter strength was possible.[23]

Nevertheless, the 'cornered wolf' continued to fight back. The Eighth Air Force lost 349 bombers in March 1944. Schmid believed that:

> The striking power of the few remaining daylight fighter units assigned to the *Reichsverteidigung* remained unbroken. Whenever weather conditions permitted the concentrated employment in close combat formation in a single area, noteworthy success was achieved in bringing down enemy aircraft and in keeping our own losses down to a reasonable limit.
>
> The success of our defensive operations over Berlin on 6 and 8 March gave ample evidence of the fighting morale of our fighter pilots, and of their ability to execute effective combat despite the technical inferiority of their aircraft. If the *Reichsverteidigung* had had 1,000–1,200 fighters available, it would doubtless have been in a position to alter the air situation, at least by day, in Germany's favour within a very short period of time, assuming of course that there was no appreciable increase in American fighters.[24]

On 23 March, Oberstleutnant Wolf-Dietrich *'Fürst'* Wilcke, *Kommodore* of JG 3 and holder of the Knight's Cross with Swords and Oak Leaves, was lost to Mustangs over Schoppenstedt, east of Braunschweig. Wilcke was a veteran of the Channel Front and North Africa and had commanded fighter operations over Stalingrad. He was an extremely respected figure within the Jagdwaffe, and upon his death was accredited with 162 victories scored in more than 730 missions.

17

Bloody April

April 1944 brought little respite, but Schmid had managed to win one battle – on the last day of March Göring finally agreed that, with immediate effect, Huth's 7. *Jagddivision* in southern Germany, including *Jafü Ostmark*, was to be assigned to I. *Jagdkorps*. Thus, at this point, although subordinate to *Luftflotte Reich*, Schmid's *Korps* was in control of all fighter units and their operations within the Reich, from north to south. This meant, in theory, that one overseeing command could react to activity by both the Eighth and Fifteenth Air Forces without conflicting and competing priorities.

Junck's II. *Jagdkorps* in Paris would be employed for the defence of the occupied western territories, and in particular the important supply and transportation centres, as well as key German construction projects such as the vast concrete bunkers and storage sites being built in France for the planned new 'revenge weapons' to be targeted against England. Göring instructed that, 'These forces will be committed in the *Reichsverteidigung* only against such enemy forces intruding or leaving the Reich via southwest Belgium and France. Transfers of these units over longer distances into the Reich's territory will be avoided in future'.

Göring also stressed that close cooperation between *Luftflotte Reich* and *Luftflotte* 3, and between I. and II. *Jagdkorps*, was imperative and was to be achieved through 'prompt communication of situation information and operational objectives. Special directives will be issued regarding signal communications and improvements in radar and fighter control systems, as well as the possible transfer of the I. *Jagdkorps* command post'.[1]

The USAAF bomber offensive ground on, targeting the aircraft production centres in central and southern Germany. On the 2nd, the Fifteenth Air Force returned to Steyr with 450 of its B-17s and B-24s to bomb the ball bearing and Daimler aircraft components plants there. The bombs were to be released through cloud, and the bombers were again escorted by P-38s and P-47s.

In response, I. *Jagdkorps* deployed 226 fighters of 3. *Jagddivision* from the Frankfurt area towards Wels and, with its new remit of control, units of 7. *Jagddivision* based in Bavaria towards Passau and Salzburg and from Vienna towards the Graz area. These were considerable distances, but the *Jagdkorps* had been under pressure from the Luftwaffe *Führungsstab* to fly longer range interception flights (for example, from Vienna to Frankfurt). However, such flights simply strained the endurance of both men and machines, usually accomplished little, and resulted in logistical confusion after a raid. Also, after covering such distances to intercept, fighters had barely enough fuel to make one brief attack before forced to break off.[2]

Once again, IV./JG 27 based at Graz-Thalerhof under Hauptmann Meyer was ordered to intercept the American formation as it approached from the direction of Linz. The *Gruppe* made contact with the bombers shortly after 1030 hrs in the area between Graz and Klagenfurt. At a height of 7,000 m, the *Gruppe* manoeuvred for a rear attack, and in a short, intense aerial battle, the Bf 109s swept in from behind and below, opening fire with their MG 151/20 cannon from 200 m.

In a series of attacks lasting 15 minutes, the *Gruppe* claimed four *Abschüsse* and three *Herausschüsse*. Meyer was credited with two of the *Herausschüsse* for his 13th and 14th victories, while at 1047 hrs, Feldwebel Werner Döring of 12./JG 27 (the former instructor pilot who once flew into a formation of bombers with his guns jammed to instruct his pupils – see Chapter 13) was leading a *Schwarm* of Bf 109s and targeted the rearmost flight of Liberators of the last box.

Döring selected one bomber and scored hits on the fuselage and left wing. The B-24 fell away from its formation and the German pilots watched as it passed below them trailing thick smoke. Döring saw one crewmember take to his parachute as the Liberator went down. The bomber hit the ground about 25 km northwest of Thalerhof. Later that day, Hauptmann Meyer and Leutnant Stigler, *Staffelkapitän* of 12./JG 27, approved Döring's claim for a *Herausschuss*. It was his 12th victory, the 20th for 12. *Staffel* and the *Gruppe's* 86th since its formation in Greece in May 1943.[3]

Leutnant Franz Stigler recalled that attacking bombers was a draining, dangerous process:

> B-24s suffered from fuel fumes in the fuselage, and that was their weak point. We found that they were easier to shoot down because they burned. The B-17s took a lot more punishment. It was terrifying. I saw them in some cases with their tail fins torn in half, elevators missing, tail gun sections literally shot to pieces or ripped away, but they still flew.

We found them a lot harder to bring down than the Liberators. The Liberators sometimes went up in flames right in front of you.

Attacking bombers became a very mechanical, impersonal kind of warfare, one machine against another. That's why I always tried to count the parachutes. If you saw eight, nine or ten 'chutes come out safely, then you knew it was okay, you felt better about it. But when you flew through a formation, the B-17s couldn't miss you. If they did, something was wrong. I never came back from attacking bombers without a hole somewhere in my aircraft.[4]

Also in action against the Steyr attack on 2 April was III./JG 3, which put 17 Bf 109s into the air at 0956 hrs led by Leutnant Jürgen Hörschelmann. Assembling with aircraft of I./JG 5 over Passau at 7,000 m, the Messerschmitts headed for Steyr and soon sighted B-17s of the 5th BW. As the *Gruppe* made its attack, USAAF escort fighters intercepted, resulting in the unit immediately suffering two losses when one pilot was forced to bail out and the aircraft of Unteroffizier Alfred Damaschko was hit and seen to plunge into cloud. Damaschko crashed to his death 40 km southeast of Steyr.

However, breaking through the escort, the remaining fighters attacked the bombers and claimed five *Abschüsse*, including single kills for Leutnant Hörschelmann and Leutnant Raimund Koch, each of whose claims represented their 14th victories. Nevertheless, the unit returned to Bad Wörishofen missing three further aircraft which had crash-landed.

Increasingly, the Luftwaffe was using composite *Gefechtsverbände* as a means with which to tackle mass with mass. In this regard, the *Gruppen* of JG 3 often flew into action alongside the heavily armed and armoured Fw 190A-6s and A-7s of *Sturmstaffel* 1. For example, on 8 April, fog prevented a large part of the 1st BD from taking off to attack its assigned airfield target at Oldenburg. The 3rd BD despatched 255 B-17s to airfields across northwest Germany and the B-24s of the 2nd BD headed for aircraft production plants at Braunschweig, as well as the Focke-Wulf airfield at Langenhagen and other targets. The whole force was protected by 780 fighters.

In response, a *Gefechtsverband* comprising *Sturmstaffel* 1 and *Stab*, I., II. and IV./JG 3 was sent up to intercept the bombers northwest of Braunschweig. Launching a massed frontal attack over Fallersleben, a great aerial battle commenced, the sky swirling with P-51s, P-38s, Bf 109s and Fw 190s as the B-17s and B-24s lumbered on into their bomb run. The *Sturmstaffel* attacked a box of Liberators, and within a matter of minutes had shot down four of them, with Unteroffizier Kurt Röhrich claiming his fifth victory, Leutnant Siegfried Müller his third, Unteroffizier Heinz Steffen a

Herausschuss, representing his third victory, and Leutnant Richard Franz his third. The latter pilot recalled:

> After this mission, I had the opportunity to meet a crew member of the bomber I had shot down. I landed at Magdeburg airfield and met him there in the operations room. He was a lieutenant, his name was Andy, and he was the only member of the crew who had survived the attack. We had a good talk, and he presented me with his flying jacket – half leather and half silk, with 24 previous missions written in ink on the silk part of the jacket, including the date and target. He told me that this was their last mission, and that had they returned, they would have been posted back to the States. But he also felt lucky to be alive. I had that jacket until the end of the war, when I was shot down for the last time on 25 April 1945 by a Russian fighter over Berlin.[5]

That same day, two more experienced unit leaders were lost. Just after 1345 hrs, Oberleutnant Josef Zwernemann, *Staffelkapitän* of 1./JG 11, attacked and shot down one of the 190 B-24s of the 2nd BD attacking Braunschweig. One minute later, east of Salzwedel, he claimed a P-51 escort fighter. A short while after that, however, his Fw 190A-7 was hit during an aerial battle with Mustangs near Gardelegen. Bailing out, he was reported to have been machine-gunned by an American fighter as he hung from his parachute. Zwernemann was one of three pilots lost from 1./JG 11 that day. He held the Oak Leaves to the Knight's Cross and had flown 600 missions, from which he had been credited with 126 aerial victories (including five *Viermots*).

At 1545 hrs, Oberleutnant Karl Willius, *Staffelkapitän* of 2./JG 26 and another veteran of the *Kanalfront* and the battles over England, was shot down by P-47s of the 361st FG following a head-on attack against the same stream of B-24s. Willius' Fw 190A-8 was seen to spin into the ground and explode. His Knight's Cross was awarded posthumously for his 48 victories, of which 11 were against the *Viermots*.

On 9 April the USAAF targeted aircraft plants and airfields in northeast Germany. More than 400 *Viermots* were effective over the range of targets, escorted by 719 fighters, most of them P-47s. Eleven fighter *Gruppen* were sent to intercept, with II./JG 1 in operation as part of a *Gefechtsverband* during the morning in which Oberleutnant Georg-Peter Eder claimed a B-24 for his 35th victory, followed by a P-47.

Another *Gefechtsverband* comprising *Sturmstaffel* 1 and IV./JG 3, under the command of the Major Friedrich-Karl Müller, was assembled over the Baltic coast near Rügen, where an aerial battle broke out shortly before midday between the German fighters, B-24s and their P-51 escorts. IV./JG 3 accounted for seven *Viermots*, with Oberleutnant Otto Wessling (who would be killed in action ten days later) scoring his 77th victory and Leutnant Hans Iffland knocking down two for his sixth and seventh. *Sturmstaffel* 1 also claimed a bomber.

Following the action of the morning, Oberfeldwebel Leo Schuhmacher of *Stab* II./JG 1 and Feldwebel Kurt Niedereichholz of 5. *Staffel* both landed at Rothenburg, along with aircraft of I./JG 11, where their Fw 190s were rearmed and fitted with drop tanks. At 1450 hrs, these two pilots, with Schuhmacher leading the JG 1 *Rotte* in his Fw 190A-7, took off on an *Alarmstart* with six aircraft from I./JG 11 on a course north for Schleswig-Holstein, where they were vectored to intercept returning bombers of the 1st and 3rd BDs. Spotting '50–60 B-17Fs' north of Schleswig, the JG 1 pilots lined up to attack the Flying Fortresses to the right of the formation head-on, following in the wake of JG 11. Niedereichholz, also flying an A-7, closed into within 500 m, but he had problems:

> As my radio was not working, I could not hear who was directing our unit towards the enemy. At 1530 hrs we got sight of 50–60 B-17s in Plan-Qu.SU3-6. The enemy formation flew on a west-northwest course. After JG 11 had made their pass, with my *Rotte* I attacked the Boeing to the right outer position from level and ahead, and scored hits in the cockpit. Pieces of the cockpit flew away and the Boeing went down in a sharp spiral to the left. At around 3,500 m altitude, the tail and rudder broke away, whereupon three men from the crew bailed out with parachutes.

Schuhmacher had targeted the flights to the right of the bomber formation, approaching dead level from the front, but without success. Then, as he made his pass though the B-17s, he flew close to Niedereichholz and also experienced problems:

> After my exit, I wanted to drop my auxiliary tank because we were being attacked by Thunderbolts. The tank remained stuck on one side and I had to head down. As I did so, I saw a Boeing spiralling downwards. I also saw parts of the tail end come away and three crew members parachute out.[6]

Five minutes after the JG 1 pilots had spotted the American formation, the B-17 hit the ground north of Schleswig and exploded in flames. It was

Niedereichholz's 16th victory, and one of 21 bombers claimed shot down or cut out of formation by the JG 1/11 grouping that day.

On the 11th, the USAAF launched an all-out assault against centres of aircraft production in eastern Germany. A record-breaking force of 917 B-17s and B-24s was assembled to strike at the Focke-Wulf plants at Poznan and Sorau, the Junkers plants at Bernburg and Halberstadt, the Pommerische Motorenbau works at Stettin and Cottbus and various assembly plants at Oschersleben. This enormous armada was protected by more than 800 aircraft drawn from 13 fighter groups from the Eighth Air Force and four from the Ninth Air Force's Third Division. However, with bomber resources stretched over such a wide range of deep penetration targets, even this escort was barely adequate, and weather conditions had improved only marginally over those prevailing on 9 April.

In response, I. *Jagdkorps* sent up a total of 432 single- and twin-engined fighters drawn from 1., 2. and 3. *Jagddivisionen*. JG 1 gave a good account of itself once again. Twenty-four Fw 190s of II. *Gruppe* had been waiting at *Sitzbereitschaft* for eight minutes at Störmede when, at 0958 hrs, *Alarmstart* was ordered. The *Gruppe* flew over Lippspringe to assemble with I. and III./JG 1 at Paderborn, after which the *Geschwader* was supposed to link up with elements of JG 27, but this did not take place.

Led by Major Heinz Bär in his Fw 190A-7, the *Gruppe* then passed from 3. to 2. *Jagddivision* control and was directed towards a stream of some 200 B-17s and B-24s heading on a northeasterly course. Upon visual contact with the enemy formation north of Braunschweig, II./JG 1 swung to the left and formed up to make a mass head-on attack against a *Pulk* of approximately 15–18 Flying Fortresses. At 1059 hrs, approaching Fallersleben, and at an altitude of 6,000 m, Bär selected the lowest squadron to the left of the *Pulk* and closed in:

> I attacked the B-17 flying lowest in the left, smaller *Pulk* from front and below, and scored hits in the fuselage and cabin, whereupon the B-17 immediately trailed light coloured smoke. After the pass, I watched the Boeing spin vertically over on its left wing and crash.

Flying with Bär as his wingman, Oberfeldwebel Leo Schuhmacher aimed at the same part of the formation, and one minute later opened fire at the same range with 160 rounds of incendiary and armour-piercing ammunition. This time he would enjoy more success than he had done on the 9th over Schleswig:

> I attacked the B-17 flying lowest in the second smaller *Pulk* from the left, from the front and from below. I was able to score hits in both right

engines and the cockpit, whereupon the underside of the right wing immediately caught fire, trailing a broad white plume of smoke. After descending, I saw a jet of flame come out of the right wing and the Boeing crash after this wing came off.

The pilots of 5./JG 1 proved equally deadly. At 1100 hrs, Oberfeldwebel Otto Bach fired at a B-17 at close range. The left wing came away, followed quickly shortly thereafter by pieces of the cockpit canopy. Bach saw three men bail out, but the aircraft then plunged into the earth north of Fallersleben. The Boeing was Bach's 13th victory.

At precisely the same moment at 6,000 m, the *Staffelkapitän* of 6./JG 1, Oberleutnant Georg-Peter Eder, had closed in to 100 m in his Fw 190A-7, raking a B-17 with cannon fire from slightly below, sending strikes into its starboard wing as well as along the fuselage. While the bomber was seen falling towards the earth by four of Eder's fellow pilots, Eder himself was attacked by the escorts as he came out of the *Pulk*, and he had to veer away quickly in an evasive manoeuvre. The bomber came down 10–15 km north of Fallersleben for Eder's 37th victory.

After the *Gruppe*'s pass through the bombers, due to the strength of the fighter escort, it was not possible to reassemble for a second attack, and the subsequent combat broke down into individual engagements fought at *Rotte* and *Schwarm*-strength. By the time II./JG 1 returned to Störmede, it had shot down seven bombers in 60 seconds, including another unconfirmed kill. Four pilots were lost to the escort fighters. In total, JG 1 claimed 16 *Viermots* downed, while I. and III./JG 11 claimed 19.

At 1005 hrs, *Sturmstaffel* 1 and IV./JG 3 received the *Alarmstart* order and took off from Salzwedel to form up into a *Gefechtsverband* with elements of various units drawn from 1. and 3. *Jagddivisionen*. The USAAF aircraft were sighted some 40 minutes later between Braunschweig and Halberstadt. *Sturmstaffel* 1 separated from IV./JG 3, with the latter unit directing its attack against a combat box of B-17s, whilst the *Sturmstaffel* closed in on a formation of some 50 B-24s from the 2nd BD in the Hildesheim area.

The engagement that ensued wrought carnage on the American bombers, with the *Sturmstaffel* enjoying the most successful action in its short-lived history. Five B-24s were either shot down or cut away from their formation in just 60 seconds. IV./JG 3 claimed a staggering 23 B-17s shot down or severely damaged, including three by the redoubtable Oberleutnant Otto Wessling, who raised his score to 80 victories.

In its Narrative of Operations, the Eighth Air Force reported as follows on the combined attack:

The leading group on Oschersleben was not attacked until it reached the IP near Hildesheim, where about 50 Fw 190s and Me 109s were seen. A number of enemy aircraft passed through the formation in ones and twos from 10 o'clock, making unpressed attacks. The last combat wing on Oschersleben encountered about 25 Fw 190s and Me 109s, which attacked aggressively just after the target. Enemy aircraft would come in three or four abreast or in a V formation from ahead or high and level.

1Lt Raymond E. Smith was flying a P-47 as a Flight Leader with the 84th FS/78th FG based at Duxford, in Cambridgeshire. His group had been assigned to provide support for the bombers as they went in. His combat report reveals that flying escort on a big mission, even with superior numbers, was not necessarily an easy job. At 1140 hrs he was heading east, south of Bremen, in clear skies with scattered cloud below:

> My flight was six to eight miles southwest of the tail box of B-24s and about 6,000 ft below them, near the Dummer Lake, when we saw about 50 single-engined Jerries come through them from about ten o'clock. We were with the first box of B-17s at the time. I saw hundreds of flashes from the Jerries' cannons, and they came through like a swarm of bees. One Liberator went down like a torch and one Jerry fell in a flat spin. I didn't see anything else because at that moment we were bounced by eight P-38s. We waggled our wings violently and they didn't fire. Meanwhile, we had dropped our belly tanks and were climbing towards the Libs with full throttle, but when we got to them, all was quiet again. The Jerries had all disappeared.[7]

Thirty-one minutes after the IV./JG 3 *Gefechtsverband* had taken off, 13 Bf 110s of III./ZG 26 led by Major Kogler were airborne from Königsberg, under orders to fly a course to Stettin. But just as the Messerschmitts reached the port city at the mouth of the Oder, their 'Y'-guidance failed and the fighters continued to fly on using the *Geschwader* frequency.

From there they headed some 70 km to the area north of Cammin. The fog and dense cloud were atrocious, with visibility down to between five and 15 kilometres, but eventually, slipping through the gloom, the crews spotted two *Pulks* of Flying Fortresses heading east at 4,400 m. These were some of the 274 B-17s from the 3rd BD that had made it into Germany to bomb the aero engine plant at Arninswalde, shipyards at Stettin and targets in Rostock and Pölitz. This time the Americans appeared to be using a new formation, with the combat wings flying in a broad front beside each other, rather than being stepped vertically.

Under considerable difficulty, Kogler immediately led his *Zerstörer* in for a frontal attack, but the pass had to be abandoned for fear of collision amidst the cloud. For more than an hour, from Stettin to as far as Rostock, III./ZG 26 attempted three more level frontal attacks and finally a fifth attack, diving from an acute angle. Several bombers were hit by mortars and exploded or broke apart. In all, nine claims were made by Kogler and six of his pilots, although two Bf 110s were hit by defensive fire from the bombers and exploded in the air. Only one crewman was able to bail out, suffering burns to his face and legs.[8]

Controlled by 1. *Jagddivision*, the Me 410s of II./ZG 26 under the command of former nightfighter pilot Hauptmann Günther Weyl took off on their first mission from Königsberg-Neumark, from where, following closely behind III./ZG 26, they also engaged the B-17s of the 3rd BD over the Baltic, northwest of Kolberg. The Me 410A-1/U4s claimed between eight and ten Flying Fortresses shot down, but these successes again came at a heavy price, with the *Gruppe* losing no fewer than eight aircraft, from which just four of 16 crew survived.

After their first attack, a few *Sturmstaffel* aircraft, together with elements of IV./JG 3, joined up and flew in formation back to Salzwedel. Once landed, they quickly refuelled and rearmed for a second mission directed against the withdrawing bombers. They took off at 1240 hrs. Heading to the northwest, it took them only 15 minutes to seek their prey. Thirty minutes later, having assembled into attack position, they closed in on a formation of B-17s most probably from the 3rd BD returning from bombing Rostock and Stettin. *Sturmstaffel* 1 shot down one bomber, whilst pilots of IV./JG 3 claimed nine more.

The Eighth Air Force recorded what happened to the 3rd BD:

> The enemy contrived one of his most severe and well coordinated defenses marked by the skilful handling of a considerable number of twin-engined day fighters in the Stettin area and single-engined fighters in the Hanover–Oschersleben area. Immediately after the bombing assault, 30 to 35 Fw 190s and Me 109s began aggressive and vicious frontal attacks, with enemy aircraft coming in abreast and flying through formations. At least 15 aircraft were lost in the combination of these attacks.[9]

The Eighth Air Force reported 12 B-24s and 33 B-17s lost, including one which landed in neutral Sweden as a result of battle damage, whilst

I. *Jagdkorps* reported the loss of 36 aircraft. Thirteen German pilots were reported killed, 17 wounded and 24 missing. Nevertheless, Schmid noted that, 'Flying against American forces three times superior, the day fighter units of the *Reichsverteidigung* shot down a considerable number of enemy aircraft. However, they did not succeed in preventing the air attacks on the German air armament plants which were of utmost consequence'.[10]

Aircraft manufacturing facilities were again the targets for the Eighth Air Force on 13 April, as the USAAF offensive switched to southern Germany. This time it was to be the turn of the ball bearing factories at Schweinfurt, the Messerschmitt production plant at Augsburg, the Dornier plant at Oberpfaffenhofen and Lechfeld airfield. Some 566 of the 626 bombers despatched were effective over their assigned targets, the B-17s and B-24s being escorted by nearly 900 fighters.

Sturmstaffel 1 and IV./JG 3 took off following an *Alarmstart* at 1245 hrs, forming up into a *Geschwader*-based *Gefechtsverband* with the *Stab*, I. and II./JG 3. Towards 1400 hrs, enemy condensation trails were sighted east of Giessen at 6,500 m, but the formation was flying with an immensely strong escort of Mustangs. At 1400 hrs over Aschaffenburg, the German fighters launched a frontal attack against the third wave of bombers. Ignoring the Mustangs and powering through a formation of some 150 B-17s, the Fw 190s of *Sturmstaffel* 1 shot down five *Viermots* in a matter of seconds. The Eighth Air Force recorded:

> Of the three Bombardment Divisions, 1st met the heaviest air opposition. Around 14.00, another series of attacks was launched ten minutes before Schweinfurt, and continued for about half an hour. The lead Combat Wing, which sustained the heaviest losses, was first attacked at about 13.50 near Klingenberg. Eight B-17s of the high group were shot down in about three minutes.[11]

II./JG 1, already on *Sitzbereitschaft* at Störmede, was given an *Alarmstart* at 1247 hrs and assembled with the rest of the *Geschwader* at 1,000 m over Paderborn, heading on a southerly course to intercept the incoming bombers. At 1350 hrs visual contact was made with an enemy formation (elements of the 1st BD), with a strong P-47 escort, at 6,500 m in the Frankfurt area. Five minutes later, I. and II./JG 1 launched a massed frontal attack on a *Pulk* of approximately 50 B-17s. Once again, Oberleutnant Georg-Peter Eder was in the fray, and at 1357 hrs he 'attacked a Boeing on the right wing of the *Pulk* from the front and below from a range of 600–100 m. The Boeing took hits in the fuselage and in the cabin, veered off course, went straight down 100 m and then blew apart in the air'.

Leading a *Rotte* from 5. *Staffel* was Unteroffizier Hubert Swoboda. At the same moment Eder shot down his B-17, Swoboda, flying an Fw 190A-7, opened fire from 300 m, closing in on a bomber flying in the second to right position to the right of the *Pulk*. Swoboda recorded that 'the cabin and part of one of the right-hand engines flew away and the Boeing burned, going steeply down'. It was Swoboda's sixth victory. Both Eder's and Swoboda's targets had crashed in an area 20 km southwest of Aschaffenburg. In this attack, II./JG 1 knocked down three *Viermots*. There were no losses.

Following this operation, fighters returned to various airfields around Frankfurt and Darmstadt. At Wiesbaden-Erbenheim, aircraft from I. and II./JG 1, having been rearmed, were formed into a *Gefechtsverband* and sent up on a second *Alarmstart* at 1505 hrs to engage returning bombers. Contact was made around 1530 hrs south of Heidelberg, but the bombers, heading on a northwesterly course, were protected by a strong escort, and only one success was possible when, for the second time that day, Swoboda managed to break through at an altitude of 6,500 m:

> I positioned myself for an attack from the rear and below and fired at the outer right-hand Boeing in the rearmost *Pulk* at a range of 200 m to almost ramming range, at which point sections of the left wing and tail assembly flew away. I then saw three of the crew bail out with parachutes. The Boeing went steeply over onto its right wing and down, and exploded in flames on the ground. During my exit I received hits and I was wounded, forcing me to bail out.[12]

Swoboda's victim crashed near the village of Ittlingen, northeast of Eppingen. Swoboda landed about a kilometre northwest of Eppingen and was taken to hospital in the town by a Luftwaffe officer, where he was treated for a head wound. His aircraft had crashed 200 m from the headquarters of a Luftwaffe ground unit.

Meanwhile, simultaneous to the Eighth's attack on 13 April, the Fifteenth Air Force launched its largest mission to date. It involved 535 bombers, from which a force of 324 B-24s was sent to bomb the Dunai Repülőgépgyár Bf 109 airframe factory in the Hungarian capital, Budapest. The air defence of the Reich was caught in an ever-strengthening USAAF vice.

Intended to cover the south, the day before, Major Walther Dahl, *Kommandeur* of III./JG 3, and his *Gruppe*'s Bf 109s and pilots had returned to their usual base at Bad Wörishofen from Leipheim. No sooner had they arrived than they were in action over the Vienna area alongside aircraft from I./JG 5. They shot down two Liberators. Then, on the morning of the 13th, the *Gruppe* received more transfer orders, this time to Vienna-Markersdorf, from where they attempted to intercept aircraft from the Eighth Air Force, but failed to make contact.

At that point, the eight serviceable Bf 109s of the *Gruppenstab* and 7. *Staffel* were ordered to land at Tulln, from where, at 1355 hrs, they were scrambled to intercept B-17s heading towards Augsburg. Exactly an hour later, Dahl spotted several *Pulks* of B-17s with fighter escort west of the Ammersee. Instinctively, he gave the order for his small formation of Bf 109s to go in for an attack from the rear of the bombers.

Northeast of Augsburg, Leutnant Jürgen Hörschelmann, leading 7./JG 3, approached level with the formation of bombers and aimed at one of the rearmost Flying Fortresses. Opening fire with his two MG 131 machine guns from a range of 100 m, he closed in to 60 m, firing all the way. His shells struck the bomber's starboard wing and inboard engine, causing the propellers to immediately stop turning. But by then Hörschelmann's Bf 109 had been hammered by 0.50-in. rounds from the B-17s' guns, so he dipped away, and as he did so, he observed the bomber also fall away to the north and enter cloud.

Dahl went in five minutes later:

> I attacked the forward *Pulk* immediately with all our aircraft, and in doing so shot one down. I subsequently flew with my wingman, whose guns had jammed, for a second attack against the same *Pulk* and definitely hit two Fortresses, but without seeing either of them crash. During a third attack, I came in from behind and above the B-17 flying in the outer left rear position, and at a range of about 200 m, got into firing position and fired all my remaining ammunition at this aircraft in one long burst. After exiting, I saw the B-17 descend steeply with a long black plume of smoke, leaving the firing range of the formation and disappear into the cumulus clouds that were at about 3,000 m with six- to eight-tenths coverage.

In addition to his determined attitude in combat, Dahl was also mindful of his higher responsibilities as a formation leader:

> I could not descend with the B-17 and determine its whereabouts, because as *Gruppenkommandeur*, I had to report to the *Division* on the bomber formations that were following, and the air situation. I stayed above the target and the bomber formations for about ten minutes and continuously reported the air situation. I then had to land due to a lack of fuel.[13]

By the end of the mission, Hörschelmann was credited with two *Herausschüsse* and Dahl one B-17 kill and a *Herausschuss*.

That day, Major Dahl had been flying a Bf 109G-6/U4, a variant of the Messerschmitt fighter produced by the Wiener Neustädter Flugzeugwerke in which the standard engine-mounted 20 mm MG 151/20 was replaced by a 30 mm MK 108 *Maschinenkanone* (machine cannon). Dahl had fired 20 rounds from his MK 108.

The advantage of the MK 108 lay in its simplicity and economic process of manufacture, the greater part of its components consisting of pressed sheet metal stampings. By mid-1943, the Luftwaffe had need of a long-range, heavy calibre gun with which a fighter pilot could target individual bombers, expend the least amount of ammunition, score a kill in the shortest possible time and yet stay beyond the range of the defensive guns. It was a virtually impossible requirement, and yet the MK 108 almost achieved this.

First designed in 1940 by Rheinmetall-Borsig, the MK 108 was a blow-back operated, rear-seared, belt-fed cannon, using electric ignition, being charged and triggered by compressed air, although once installed into any aircraft, there was no method of adjustment for harmonisation. One of the most unusual features of the gun was its extremely short barrel, earning it the name *Kurzgerät* (lit. 'short device'), which gave the weapon its low muzzle velocity of between 500–540 m per second, with a maximum rate of fire of 650 rounds per minute. A total of 60 rounds was fed by means of a disintegrating belt from an ammunition canister mounted above the gun.

As will be seen, the MK 108 would quickly gain a fearsome reputation amongst both German pilots, particularly the pilots of the *Sturmgruppen* who would use it to devastating effect, and Allied bomber crews on the receiving end, the latter dubbing the MK 108 the 'pneumatic hammer' on account of its rate of fire and impact.

As ammunition, the cannon could be loaded with the *Minen Geschoß* ('Mine Shell'), which had been developed by the Luftwaffe's armaments engineers at the Rechlin test centre and ballistics specialists at Rheinmetall-Borsig's main testing ground at Unterlüss. They calculated that maximum destruction to an enemy aircraft could be created by causing the largest possible explosive effect in its interior, but that this in turn was dictated by the size of the enemy aircraft and by the quantity of explosive that could physically be placed into a projectile. The thicker the shell wall, the more energy was needed for the destruction of the shell itself, and thus less energy remained for the destruction of the target by the ensuing explosion.

This theory led to the development of the *Minen Geschoß*, which combined a minimum thickness in shell casing with a maximum load of explosive to produce the greatest possible blast effect. This rendered it extremely destructive to the stressed skin of a bomber aircraft. Using such ammunition, the entire enemy aircraft could be regarded as the target area, it making no difference where the hit was actually made. As such, with Mine Shells a fighter pilot had an inherently greater chance of scoring a kill. Following tests carried out at Rechlin it was discovered that five hits from a 30 mm Mine Shell carrying 85 g of explosive were needed for the destruction of either a B-17 or a B-24.

Incendiary shells were also an extremely potent form of ammunition, but they were only effective when targeted at fuel tanks. The vulnerability of an enemy aircraft could therefore be measured by the area and/or size of its tanks. However, a certain degree of force was still needed in order to penetrate the airframe or any protective armour carried by the target without breaking up and igniting prior to actually striking the fuel. To achieve this, the 30 mm incendiary shell was fitted with a hydrodynamic fuse which activated only when making contact with a fluid.

When attacked by a fighter directly from behind, the area of a B-17 taken up by its fuel tanks was approximately one-fifth of the total surface area, and it was assumed that by the time an attack was made the tanks would be half-empty. Thus, in combat conditions, this area was reduced to one-tenth of the surface area. It was calculated that between five and ten 30 mm incendiary shells were needed to cause inextinguishable burning. However, in the case of the B-24, an effective attack using incendiaries was slightly more difficult since the bomber's main fuel tanks were located in the fuselage, with only reserve tanks located in the wings behind the engines.

On 15 April, Generalmajor Galland visited Salzwedel to brief officers of the *Geschwaderstab* JG 3 and *Stab* IV./JG 3. Accompanying him was Hauptmann Wilhelm Moritz, whom Galland introduced as the new *Gruppenkommandeur* of IV. *Gruppe*, replacing Hauptmann Heinz Lang, who had stepped briefly into the role following Major Friedrich-Karl Müller's appointment as *Geschwaderkommodore*. Dark haired, square jawed, with blue eyes gazing from a stern face, Moritz was an experienced fighter pilot who had joined JG 3 from 11./JG 51 in October 1943.

During the meeting, Galland spoke of his plans for the tactical reorganisation of IV./JG 3. In the 'Big Week' raids of early 1944, pilots such as Leutnante Hans Weik, Willi Unger and Hans Iffland had achieved impressive personal victories against the *Viermots*. Indeed, as a result of the whole *Gruppe*'s encouragingly consistent successes against the bombers, Galland intended to convert the unit into a fully fledged *Sturmgruppe* which would apply the tactics of the original *Sturmstaffel*, but in *Gruppe* strength.

Galland also announced that every *Geschwader* operating in the defence of the Reich would eventually include its own '*Sturmgruppe*'. Reaction to this proposal on the part of IV./JG 3's pilots, however, appears to have been mixed, and led to considerable debate. Although Galland's reasoning was appreciated, many officers felt that it was unnecessary to sign oaths and documents of obligation in the same way as the *Sturmstaffel*, let alone volunteer for tactics which would involve ramming or court-martial, when those already employed were achieving results. Indeed, many years after the war, Galland reiterated that *he* had been of the same opinion, stressing how, in early 1944, he had deterred von Kornatzki from the idea of ramming units:

> At that time I was able to convince him that ramming was unnecessary because fighters that were able to approach very near the bombers were absolutely certain to shoot them down, and then had a chance for their own survival. Subsequently, the very successful '*Sturmjäger*' tactics and techniques evolved from this original ramming idea.[14]

Moritz recalled:

> When I took over the leadership of the *Sturmstaffel* at Salzwedel, the two ranking officers of the unit, von Kornatzki and Bacsila, were not fit for action – one was ill, the other wounded. I have to admit that my relationship with these two officers was not the best because I had the impression that they allowed their *Staffel* to go into action without their leadership. This was not acceptable practice for responsible officers. In their absence, Leutnant Werner Gerth led the *Staffel* on operations.
>
> For my part, I never accepted the fighting tactic favoured by von Kornatzki and never bound a pilot to ram a bomber. My IV./JG 3 scored many victories attacking bombers with traditional tactics, and the successes came from the sense of duty felt by my men and the tactics they employed, namely attacking in closed formation and opening fire at close quarters.[15]

Perhaps the most immediate change for the *Gruppe*, however, was Galland's announced planned replacement of its Bf 109G-6s with the more heavily armed and armoured Fw 190A-8 – an aircraft considered to be better suited for work as a close-range '*Sturmjäger*'.

The Fw 190A-8/R2, many of which would equip the *Sturmgruppen*, featured two 20 mm MG 151 cannon installed in the wing roots and two 30 mm MK 108 cannon in the wings. The cowl-mounted MG 131 machine guns fitted to the standard A-8 were removed to reduce weight and the empty gun troughs and slots left by their deletion covered with armoured plate. Additionally, a panel of six-millimetre armoured glass was mounted on each side of the cockpit canopy, and a sheet of six-millimetre armour plate, extending from the lower edge of the cockpit canopy to the wing root, was mounted externally on each side of the fuselage to protect the pilot from lateral fire. Another armoured panel on the underside of the aircraft protected the pilot's seat to a point sufficiently forward to cover the feet and legs.

In mid-April, one of the Luftwaffe's top Eastern Front aces, Major Günther Rall, arrived at Wunstorf from Russia, where he had commanded III./JG 52 and accumulated 273 victories, ranking him at the end of the war as the Luftwaffe's third most successful fighter pilot. At Wunstorf, Rall's new assignment was as *Gruppenkommandeur* of the Bf 109-equipped *Höhenjagdgruppe*, II./JG 11. The other two *Gruppen* of JG 11 operated Fw 190s, and as Rall recorded in his memoirs the Focke-Wulf was:

> . . . ideally suited to attacking the carefully staggered, heavily armed bomber boxes. But with a critical height of around the 5,000 m mark, the Focke-Wulf's BMW 801 twin-row radial engine is of little use against the enemy's fighter escort. Fighter combats over the Reich are now often being fought at altitudes of between 8,000 to 11,000 m, where the air is too thin for the BMW powerplant to deliver sufficient output.[16]

Feldwebel Willi Unger of the new 11.(*Sturm*)/JG 3 summarised the Fw 190A-8 thus:

> Advantages – wide undercarriage, large twin-row radial engine which protected the pilot from fire from the front, electric starter motor and electric trim system. Disadvantages – there was a danger of turning over when braking hard on soft or sandy ground. In combat against enemy fighters, more awkward because of the heavy armour plating. Strong at low altitudes, inferior to the Me 109 at higher altitudes. In my opinion, the Fw 190 – in this version – was the best aircraft used in formation attacks against the *Viermots*.[17]

Oberleutnant Richard Franz, who flew with *Sturmstaffel* 1 and then JG 11, opined:

> The Fw 190A-8/R8 was a very good aircraft in its '*Sturmbock*' ['Stormbird'] version due to its armament of two 13 mm machine guns, two 20 mm MG 151s and two 30 mm MK 108s, and its additional armour plating. Also, the radial engine gave some protection. Due to its weight, however, the aircraft showed a great disadvantage when we had to engage enemy fighters. In the normal configuration, the Focke-Wulf had some advantage in comparison with the Bf 109 up to 4,500 m, whereas the Bf 109 was better at higher altitudes. But the Spitfire was top in a dogfight.[18]

The onslaught against the German aircraft industry continued with the Eighth Air Force mounting attacks on a range of targets around Berlin on 18 April.

The tactical partnership of *Sturmstaffel* 1 and IV./JG 3 was ordered into the air at 1330 hrs, but bad weather prevented assembly with other units. This meant that only these two units, together with Bf 109s of the *Wilde Sau Gruppe* II./JG 302 from Ludwigslust, carried out a close-formation attack, targeting 350 B-17s escorted by 100 fighters.

Sixty kilometres west of Berlin, *Sturmstaffel* 1 attacked first, with Gefreiter Wolfgang Kosse claiming one of the Flying Fortresses as his 21st victory and Unteroffizier Kurt Röhrich another a minute later as his eighth. From 6./JG 302, Oberfeldwebel Eberhard Kroker claimed a *Herausschuss* over a B-17 for his second victory in two days, although the *Gruppe* would suffer the loss of the *Staffelkapitän* of its 4./JG 302, Oberleutnant Willi Klein, when he was shot down over Alberode near Eschwege.

Closely following the *Sturmstaffel*, IV./JG 3 showed its mettle once again by claiming no fewer than 19 B-17s destroyed, although the actual American losses for the entire mission were 19 Flying Fortresses, including one aircraft which was interned in Sweden. Only one pilot was lost from IV./JG 3. This not insignificant accomplishment was deemed sufficient enough to gain Major Friedrich-Karl Müller a mention in the official Wehrmacht bulletin of the day.[19]

From JG 3, Oberleutnant Otto Wessling, *Staffelkapitän* of 11. *Staffel*, was killed on 19 April when he made an emergency landing in his burning Bf 109G-6 near Eschwege following operations against heavily escorted bombers in the Göttingen/Kassel area. Wessling had been presented with the Knight's Cross in September 1942, and the Oak Leaves were awarded posthumously. He had accounted for 12 bombers in his total of 83 victories.

Five days later, 1./JG 3 lost its commanding officer when Leutnant Franz Schwaiger was forced to make an emergency belly-landing in his Bf 109G-5, having engaged large numbers of B-17s and their P-51 escorts north of Augsburg. He had exited his downed aircraft but was shot at and killed on the ground by P-51s. Schwaiger had been awarded the Knight's Cross on 29 October 1942 and had been accredited with 67 victories, 56 of them on the Russian Front and four *Viermots*.

The events of 24 April 1944 bear testimony to the destructive power of the MK 108 cannon. That day, Hauptmann Hermann Staiger, *Staffelkapitän* of 12./JG 26 claimed his sixth *Viermot* shot down. Staiger had formerly led 7./JG 51 in Russia, where he proved his skill in anti-bomber work when he accounted for the destruction of three SB bombers in one day on 22 June 1941, with a further four in one day on the 30th of that month, for which he was awarded the Knight's Cross.

In the early afternoon of 24 April 1944 Staiger led a *Gefechtsverband* from III./JG 26 based at Neubiberg and Walther Dahl's III./JG 3 at Bad Wörishofen to attack a formation of 84 B-17s out to bomb the Dornier factory airfield at Oberpfaffenhofen. The two *Gruppen* rendezvoused over Ulm at 7,000 m and were directed by 7. *Jagddivision* until, a short while later, three large *Pulks* of B-17s were sighted flying east in the direction of Munich and Augsburg. Shepherding the bombers either side and above was a strong escort of P-51s.

Flying a Bf 109 fitted with an MK 108 cannon in the nose, Staiger shot down two B-17s in one minute over Donauwörth. Twenty-five minutes later, he claimed a *Herausschuss* for two more B-17s, before destroying another south of Munich – again all within one minute. Staiger would survive the war having shot down 26 four-engined bombers, making him one of the Luftwaffe's leading specialists in their destruction.

The pilots of III./JG 3 also enjoyed significant success, although many of them were still relatively new to the experience of air combat. Regardless, Dahl led his men against the centre *Pulk* of around 80–100 bombers. Leading one of the two *Rotten* in Dahl's *Schwarm* was Feldwebel Paul Wielebinski of 7. *Staffel*.

During the first pass against the Boeings he failed to score any strikes, but as he followed Dahl, climbing and turning back to make a second attack from behind and above, he opened fire with both machine guns and his MG 151/20 on the Flying Fortress flying in the furthest position to the right of the *Pulk*. The metal skin of the bomber's starboard wing and right outboard engine flashed little flames as the German fighter's shells hit home and then pieces of the wing shot through the air towards Wielebinski's Bf 109.

As Wielebinski raced through the bombers, he saw how his victim started to lose speed and fall behind the formation, flames streaking from its underside. But as the Bf 109s turned for the second time to make a frontal attack, Wielebinski felt the thump of 0.50-in. rounds punching into his wings and engines as a Mustang latched itself onto his tail. The German pilot dived away and was forced to make an emergency landing near Dachau. The B-17 had been just his second kill.

Like Wielebinski, Unteroffizier Gerhard Pankalla also of 7./JG 3 failed to make any impact in his first, rearward pass against the bombers. But together with his *Rottenflieger*, Unteroffizier Georg Spittler, he would perform no fewer than five attacks on the enemy formation. As he returned for a second, frontal attack on the same *Pulk*, Pankalla:

> ... fired at the second aircraft from the left and observed effective strikes to the cockpit and outer left engine. The engine immediately caught fire and pieces flew away from the cockpit. The enemy aircraft tipped over onto the left wing and crashed 10 km southwest of Dachau, where it exploded in flames and was destroyed.
>
> I then continued to engage the same enemy formation, and during my third frontal attack I set fire to the two left engines of the B-17 flying at the left. The enemy aircraft then veered to the left of the formation and began to lag far behind. After another attack, I had to abort because my weapons were no longer firing.

Pankalla was credited with the destruction of a B-17 and a *Herausschuss* for his fourth and fifth victories, while Spittler also accounted for a bomber cut out of formation, having opened fire at a range of just 50 m – it was his first victory. Oberfähnrich Heinrich Seel of 7./JG 3 claimed a *Herausschuss* for his third victory, but sustained damage from a P-51 to his Bf 109's radiator and tail. Having been wounded, he too had to make an emergency landing.

Six B-17s were confirmed shot down and there were five *Herausschüsse*. At least four of III./JG 3's pilots were killed in the engagement and two were wounded. Four more Bf 109s were either written off or badly damaged. It was a grim balance sheet.[20]

At Salzwedel, the *Sturmstaffel* continued to draw in a small number of volunteers. Twenty-year-old Feldwebel Oskar Bösch from Höchst, in Austria, was already a proficient glider pilot by the time he joined the Luftwaffe fighter arm in 1943. He recalled:

> I was lucky enough to have completed full training as a glider pilot before being accepted into the Luftwaffe for pilot training in August

1942. To be able to qualify for entry into the fighter arm, I had to undergo intensive training. I was first in the *Flugzeugführerschule* A/B 118 at Stettin, then I was transferred to JG 101 in Nancy, France, in July 1943 for advanced training on the Bf 109F and G-6. I must have done what was needed correctly because my transfer to a unit in the defence of the Reich came as early as February 1944, while I was with the *Ergänzungs Jagdgruppe Süd* at Avignon. On 22 April 1944, while I was heading to my first operational posting in JG 3, something happened that really influenced my commitments.

That day, the Eighth Air Force, flushed with its success against the German aero industry, despatched 779 B-17s and B-24s, escorted by 859 fighters, to 'lower priority' targets, most of them to the marshalling yards at Hamm. Bösch remembered:

> Stopping over in Hamm, the taste of heavy bombardment gave me a real shock. I was there with three other pilots from my training unit, and we had driven up from Avignon, in the south of France. It was good to be back in Germany.
>
> The bombs came down close to the main station. I had to rush down into a basement along with terrorised women and children. When the first bombs landed, the lights in the cellar went out. They lit candles for light. Children cried. I had never been so frightened in my life. There was total panic. I spent a few hours there, in the dark and dust, listening to the bombs falling above our heads. When we got out, the town was nothing but fire and ruins, a place like Hell. The following night, and the night after, the bombs fell again. I made up my mind. I would volunteer for the *Sturmstaffel* then stationed at Salzwedel.[21]

On the 27th, during a month which had seen the loss of 489 pilots and the arrival of only 396 replacements, Galland addressed the *Jägerstab* in Berlin. He told Karl-Otto Saur, the *Jägerstab*'s Chief Executive:

> I need not say too much about the situation regarding the Luftwaffe. Unfortunately, you too are living with it every day. The problem which the Americans have set the Jagdwaffe is quite simply the problem of air superiority. The situation is already beginning to be characterised by enemy mastery of the air. The numerical ratio in daylight operations is approximately 1:6 to 1:8. The enemy's standard of training is astonishingly high. The technical capabilities of his aircraft are so manifest that we are obliged to say that something must be done immediately.[22]

On 29 April, the Eighth Air Force struck Berlin, committing 368 B-17s and 210 B-24s for the attack on the German capital, whilst 38 B-17s were to bomb various targets of opportunity in the Berlin and Magdeburg areas. Escort was to be provided by 814 fighters. To meet the American aircraft, I. *Jagdkorps* was ready to deploy 275 single- and twin-engined fighters. After the raid, a German press reporter somewhat sensationally described the Luftwaffe's tactical preparations as follows:

> When at noon on Saturday the sirens wailed over Berlin and, a little later, single groups of US gangster aircraft appeared over the capital to drop their terror bombs aimlessly on a widespread residential area of the city, the operation rooms of the German air defences had been working at a high pitch for a long time.[23]

Schmid directed that units of 1. *Jagddivision* were to assemble over Magdeburg for deployment in the Braunschweig area, although the *Zerstörer* of ZG 26 were kept in readiness over Küstrin for commitment against any bombers that attempted to exit via the north. The fighters of 2. and 3. *Jagddivisionen* were to assemble, respectively, over Hamburg for deployment to Hanover and over Kassel for deployment to Braunschweig.[24]

It would be on this day that the newly trained Feldwebel Oskar Bösch received his baptism of fire with *Sturmstaffel* 1:

> Towards the end of April 1944, I arrived early one morning at Salzwedel airfield. I didn't have time to admire the scenery. Instead, I was introduced to my Fw 190A-7, a 'pure-bred' and massive machine, of which a fellow pilot explained all the refinements before letting me off on a flight, as I'd never flown one before! Everything went fine. I made four flights before taking the aircraft back to the hangar. My initial contact with the aircraft had lasted 60 minutes. My fifth flight took place the following morning, 29 April. It was serious this time; the aircraft was armed and I was sent off against the '*Dicke Autos*'. I didn't have time to be afraid. The *Sturmstaffel* went through the raging defensive fire to get really close from behind to get optimal efficiency for the attack.
>
> In the beginning, attacking the bombers was almost easy. It was exciting. Your adrenalin really pumped. Everybody had their own tactics, their own tricks, but generally we attacked from behind and high for additional speed, offset by five or ten degrees and about 500 m above

the formation, opening fire upon the order by radio at 400 m. The air was pretty thin at 7,200 m, and often there was a lot of turbulence behind the bomber formation. This sometimes made our approach very difficult. Positioning was also made difficult because of the escort fighters. [Oberleutnant Othmar] Zehart, for example, had guts. He flew right into the *Pulk* and we just followed him in.

When the escort fighters were late to react, we had time to line up – like being on parade – before diving to attack. The bomber gunners usually started to fire and waste their ammunition while we were still out of range at 2,000 m from them. It was obvious they were just as scared as we were. Shaken by the slipstream of the B-17s and blinded by condensation trails, we were subjected to machine gun fire for minutes or seconds that seemed endless before being able to see the results of our attack. Despite the armour plating of our cockpits, we had good reason to dread the defensive fire of the bombers.[25]

At 0940 hrs, 27 Fw 190s of II./JG 1 were given the *Alarmstart* and, led by Major Bär, assembled with the other *Gruppen* of the *Geschwader* over Paderborn. The formation firstly made for Kassel, but was then directed towards Braunschweig to intercept an incoming formation of 150–200 *Viermots* heading east, past Hanover, with a fighter escort. At 1055 hrs JG 1 intercepted the enemy at 7,500 m in the Braunchsweig area. Because of the strength of the escort, the *Geschwader* was forced to break up, and combat ensued in *Rotten* and *Schwärme*, although II. *Gruppe* was initially able to make a *Gruppe*-strength frontal attack on a *Pulk* of about 60 B-17s and B-24s.

At 1058 hrs, Oberleutnant Eder, leading 6./JG 1, targeted a B-17 to the right of the formation and opened fire from 600 m. He observed hits on the left wing, then the bomber entered into a spin and the left wing broke away. The aircraft crashed into the city of Braunschweig. Within the space of eight minutes, I. and II./JG 1 shot down or 'cut out' eight B-17s and one B-24. II. *Gruppe* lost two pilots in return, including Eder's wingman, Obergefreiter Werner Triebel. Low on fuel and ammunition, the unit's aircraft landed at various airfields between Braunschweig and Berlin either singly or in *Rotten*.

Following the morning mission, Hauptmann Rüdiger Kirchmayr, the 23-year-old Austrian leader of 5./JG 1 with 13 victories to his credit, found himself at Salzwedel in his Fw 190A-7. As he recorded:

Following air combat I took off at 1245 hrs with a *Schwarm* from Salzwedel towards outward-flying bomber units flying on a west-northwest course. In Grid GB I had sight of the enemy of around 200 Boeing B-17Fs and Liberators. I attacked the furthest left Liberator of a *Pulk* of 30-40, coming behind from out of the sun and opened fire at the aircraft from close range. The left outer engine began to burn immediately, pieces flew away from the fuselage and left wing and two crewmembers bailed out. Then the Liberator went down into a steep spiral to the right, during which fire spread over the whole left wing and another three crewmembers bailed out. The impact of the Liberator followed, close to a small village east of Fallersleben north of the canal at 1310 hrs.

Two minutes later, Kirchmayr flew over a *Pulk* of B-17s at 5,500 m, with the sun still behind him. He opened fire on a bomber to the left of the formation:

Following the first burst, the left inboard engine remained in place, a crewmember bailed out with a parachute and the Boeing veered down steeply to the left and out of formation. Shortly after, two more crewmembers jumped out with parachutes and the left wing of the Boeing began to burn fiercely. The aircraft fell steeply and disappeared into clouds.[26]

It is believed the bomber crashed around Fallersleben, but the kill was witnessed by Feldwebel Arnold Jansen of 5. *Staffel*, and Kirchmayr was awarded his 14th and 15th victories, adding two more to II./JG 1's tally of eight *Viermots* that day.

At 1010 hrs, *Sturmstaffel* 1 and IV./JG 3 took off together from Salzwedel led by former instructor pilot Leutnant Hans Weik, *Staffelkapitän* of 10./JG 3. Once assembled with other *Gruppen* over Magdeburg, the *Gefechtsverband* headed towards Braunschweig at 1045 hrs. Shortly before 1100 hrs, the German formation sighted the USAAF bombers, and Weik turned his aircraft 180 degrees to launch a frontal attack. Simultaneously, the *Sturmstaffel* formed up for a rearward attack on another part of the formation, trusting in its armour-plated cockpits to afford the pilots protection whilst closing in to killing range.

By the time the *Gefechtsverband* had finished its work, nine B-17s had gone down under the guns of IV./JG 3, including two claims from Weik and one each from Unteroffizier Walter Loos and Unteroffizier Willi Unger, both of 11./JG 3. The *Sturmstaffel* had accounted for a further 13 Flying Fortresses, including one shot down by Feldwebel Oskar Bösch for his first victory on his first mission, and he may well also have caused a *Herausschuss*. The Eighth Air Force reported:

The 4A Combat Wing experienced difficulty with PFF [Path Finder Force] equipment and lost visual contact with other bombers and fighter escort. Reaching the Magdeburg area, the Wing was attacked by packs estimated as totalling 100 enemy aircraft, which attacked in waves from nose to tail. Attacks were pressed home vigorously and closely, and lasted for about 20 minutes. The Wing lost a total of 18 B-17s.[27]

But the day was not done for the Liberators of the 2nd BD, nor for the pilots of IV./JG 3. At Salzwedel, just 45 minutes after IV./JG 3's Bf 109s had returned from their first mission, the *Alarmstart* was sounded for another take-off at 1235 hrs, this time to engage the B-24s as they made their way home. Leading ten Messerschmitts, the *Kommandeur*, Hauptmann Moritz, headed south to intercept, and 23 minutes later in the area northwest of Gardelegen, the German group spotted a formation of '400–500 Liberators' – this cannot have been the case, for only 212 B-24s were rated as effective bombers that day by the Eighth Air Force.

At 1313 hrs, Moritz formed up his fighters for a frontal attack and then returned for a second pass, again from the front. At 1320 hrs he targeted a B-24, opening fire at a range of 300 m and closing in to 100 m, dispensing with 40 rounds of mixed tracer, armour-piercing and incendiary ammunition from his MG 151/20 cannon and 80 rounds from his MG 131 machine guns. The Liberator sustained hits in the cockpit area and right wing, with thick white smoke pluming back from its inner starboard engine. Immediately, the bomber lost altitude and fell behind the formation.

Flying as *Rottenflieger* to Moritz, Oberfähnrich Erhard Nolting of the *Gruppe Stab* flight had a similar experience to his commander, but he kept firing until he was within 50 m of his target. Nolting noticed how the Liberator 'tilted forwards and started trailing black smoke' as it descended into cloud. For Nolting, it was his fifth kill, and for Moritz, his 35th. By the time the Messerschmitts returned from the second mission, they had accounted for five B-24s cut out of formation.

There were other notable successes that day, such as that of Oberleutnant Hans-Heinrich 'King' Koenig, *Staffelkapitän* of 3./JG 11 based at Rothenburg. The 23-year-old from Halle was a former nightfighter pilot who had lost an eye during a nocturnal combat with an RAF bomber over the Baltic in June 1942. Evidently, this did not preclude his daylight marksmanship, and on 29 April he claimed no fewer than four B-24s shot down in two sorties.

When it was over, the war diary of I. *Jagdkorps* recorded:

In spite of good visibility and high numerical strength, the large-scale attack on Berlin was, for the American Air Force, no success of great importance in respect to the overall war effort. Industry in Berlin sustained only slight damage. Damage to buildings and the losses of personnel were heavy. The strafing attacks on airfields showed no results.

By assembling combat units beyond the approach routes of the American bombers, German fighter units could be launched in a concentrated attack against the bomber units. During these operations the day fighter units of I. *Jagdkorps* scored a considerable defensive success by destroying ten per cent of the American bombers committed.[28]

As a percentage, this was a remarkably accurate figure. Altogether, the Berlin raid cost the USAAF 38 B-17s and 25 B-24s from a total of 618 'effective' bombers, with 18 crewmen killed and 606 missing.[29]

The German press was quick to exploit what had been perceived as a failure for the Eighth Air Force and a victory for the Luftwaffe. '*One of the biggest air battles ever fought!*' proclaimed one headline, and '*US fighters inferior to Messerschmitts and Focke-Wulfs!*' announced another. German reporters did not restrain the sense of melodrama:

> The battle was turned when the German fighter formations broke through the US fighter screen from several sides, making direct attacks on the four-engined bombers. The Boeings and Liberators attempted to put up a wall of fire around them by their many hundreds of guns, but were unable to stop the furious onslaught of the German fighters. A great many US four-engined bombers perished in one of the biggest air battles ever to be fought over central Germany.
>
> Several combat box formations lost so many aircraft in this battle over the Elbe that the survivors had to draw closer together to form a new formation capable of offering resistance.[30]

The flip side of the coin was that 765 tons of high-explosive bombs had fallen on Berlin, along with 733 tons of incendiaries. The Germans stated that 'during the period from 1041–1130 hrs about 1,000 demolition bombs were dropped on Berlin.' The centre of the city was hit, as were the southwestern districts of Steglitz and Zehlendorf. A total of 294 buildings were destroyed and another 1,808 damaged, while 375 people were killed, 470 injured and 13,700 left homeless.

Meanwhile, as the Luftwaffe marked a great 'defensive victory', an order was received from OKL officially redesignating IV./JG 3, under the command of Hauptmann Moritz, to IV.(*Sturm*)/JG 3 in line with Galland's intentions. *Sturmstaffel* 1 was dissolved and its pilots and groundcrews formed the nucleus of 11.(*Sturm*)/JG 3 under the command of Leutnant Werner Gerth.

In summarising operations for April 1944, Schmid stated that the emphasis for those units of the Jagdwaffe engaged in the *Reichsverteidigung* was to combat bombers and to not tackle fighters and win air superiority:

The daylight air warfare over the Reich with the increased American offensive action had brought about a psychological effect on all Luftwaffe command staffs and dominated them. Nowhere, at no command headquarters, neither at OKH, nor at OKL, nor on the staff of the *General der Jagdflieger*, nor at *Luftflotte Reich*, nor at the headquarters of I. *Jagdkorps* was an adequate plan under consideration for operations to gain air supremacy by a victorious fighter battle. The attention of all responsible commanders was focused on only one danger – the Flying Fortresses and their bomb loads. The persistent demand for destroying American bombers by an incessant commitment of fighters originated with the *Führer*.

The intensity of the air fighting in April 1944 saw a host of 'bomber-killers' rise to the fore. Alongside the aforementioned trio from IV./JG 3 was Feldwebel Hans Schäfer of 10./JG 3, who 'cut out' three *Viermots* from their formation and shot down two more in that month. Of his final score of 18 victories, 12 would be four-engined. His *Staffelkamerad*, Feldwebel Walter Hagenah, shot down a B-17 and claimed a *Herausschuss* on the 18th over the Nauen area for his ninth and tenth victories, while Oberfeldwebel Helmut Rüffler of 4. *Staffel* downed a pair of Flying Fortresses on the 19th for his 57th and 58th victories.

The loss sheet for April included Hauptmann Hans Remmer, commander of 1./JG 27. He had attacked B-24s of the Fifteenth Air Force over Graz on the 2nd and shot one down over Jüdenburg, but his Bf 109G-6 was hit by defensive fire and, upon bailing out, his parachute failed to deploy and he fell to his death. Remmer, who had achieved 16 victories over North Africa, had taken his tally to 27 (nine of which were four-engined bombers) by the time he was killed. He was awarded the Knight's Cross posthumously.

I. *Jagdkorps* estimated the following force ratios for March and April 1944:

Total USAAF strength (bombers and fighters) March 1944 – 7.5
I. *Jagdkorps* total single- and twin-engined fighter strength – 1

Total USAAF strength (bombers and fighters) April 1944 – 4.5
I. *Jagdkorps* total single- and twin-engined fighter strength – 1

USAAF fighter strength March 1944 – 3.6
I. *Jagdkorps* single- and twin-engined fighter strength – 1

USAAF fighter strength April 1944 – 2.2
I. *Jagdkorps* single- and twin-engined fighter strength – 1

18

The Last Chance

Sometime in the spring of 1944, during one of the big Eighth Air Force raids on northern Germany, Generalmajor Adolf Galland decided to experience at first-hand what it was like to fight the bombers. He took Oberst Hannes Trautloft, his Inspector of Day Fighters based at his headquarters at Hottengrund, southwest of Berlin, with him. The two aces took off from nearby Staaken airfield on the western fringe of the city in a pair of Fw 190s and climbed to the west to 7,600 m. Crossing the Elbe north of Magdeburg, they found the bomber formation. After observing from a distance for a short while, Galland spotted a straggler – a B-17 flying sluggishly and endeavouring to join the protection of another part of the American formation. Telling Trautloft of his decision, he decided to go in. As he related in his memoirs:

> There was nothing heroic in the decision. We had to act very quickly before he joined the next formation. I was 100 m behind on his tail. The B-17 fired and took desperate avoiding action. The only thing that existed in the whole world was this American bomber, fighting for its life, and myself. As my cannons blazed away, pieces of metal flew off, smoke poured from the engines and they jettisoned the entire bomb-load. One tank in the wings had caught fire. The crew was bailing out.

Suddenly, Trautloft's voice was yelling in Galland's headset. His friend warned of Mustangs, and that his own guns had jammed. Moments later, the gunfire from four P-51s flew all around Galland. 'I sobered up. There was no mistake about the B-17; she was finished, but I was not. I simply fled'. At full throttle, Galland dived away, back towards Berlin, his Fw 190 peppered with bullet holes. With the Mustangs hot on his tail, the veteran ace resorted to a ruse which had twice saved his life during the campaign over England back in 1940:

I fired everything I had simply into the blue in front of me. It had the desired effect on my pursuers, who suddenly saw the smoke which the shells had left behind coming towards them. They probably thought they had met the first fighter to fire backwards or that a second attacking German fighter was behind them. My trick succeeded, for they did a right-hand climbing turn and disappeared.[1]

On 27 April 1944, Galland was at a fighter production conference. The chairman, Karl-Otto Saur, concluded his opening remarks by stating what should have been obvious:

> The character of air combat is being transformed to an ever-increasing extent from encounters between bombers and fighters to encounters between opposing fighters. We can win this struggle only if we have aircraft of superior quality.

But this was much easier said than done. The point was the Allies had inflicted an increasingly unsolvable problem upon the Luftwaffe and its ability to fight. Quite simply, the more the production factories were bombed, the fewer fighters could be made available for air defence, and thus the Allied bombers could carry out their work with impunity and against a broadening range of targets. When Galland rose to his feet to address the meeting, he did not pull any punches:

> It is very unfortunate that the Fighter Staff's efforts to increase aircraft production must be carried out under the pressure of bombing and very heavy losses. I am convinced that the Fighter Staff will meet with success if its present efforts are maintained. It must succeed. It is the only chance; I might even say that it is the last chance. The concentrated effort which has been applied to the technical side of the matter is not evident in our planning and training and in the exploitation of possibilities. Gentlemen, I have also noticed this on our staff. I must tilt at windmills in this matter.
>
> In the last four months well over 1,200 day fighter pilots have been lost, including, of course, many of the best unit commanders. We are having great difficulty in closing this gap – not in a numerical sense, but with experienced leaders.

And that very day, as Galland was in Berlin, almost 1,000 km away in France, his words were being proved true.

THE LAST CHANCE

JG 2, one of the two *Jagdgeschwader* operating in France under 4. *Jagddivision* control, suffered particularly badly at this time when it lost its recently appointed *Kommodore*, Major Kurt Ubben. He had taken over command of the '*Richthofen Geschwader*' following the loss of Oberstleutnant Egon Mayer to American fighters in March – a month during which JG 2 had lost three *Staffelkapitäne*, all of them to P-47s. On 27 April, Ubben was also attacked by Thunderbolts west of Reims during his third mission of the day. Although the veteran of the Eastern Front and North Africa, and 110-victory *Experte* who held the Oak Leaves to the Knight's Cross, managed to bail out of his Fw 190A-8, his parachute failed to open. The *Geschwader* lost another *Staffelkapitän* in combat with Allied fighters in April as well.

In Berlin, as Galland continued, he must have felt a sense of weariness:

> However, this will be managed. My only request is that if this Staff can give me help by way of the *Reichsmarschall*, it should be given now.
>
> I have often spoken of the last chance and the danger of the Luftwaffe collapsing. The enemy's numerical superiority has reached such proportions that we must realise that operations are beginning to become extremely unproductive for us – i.e. we can hardly manage defensive operations, let alone carry out offensive activity.

Galland implored the *Jägerstab* to produce a guaranteed number of fighters with which the Luftwaffe could allow basic training and the strengthening of its operational units. He cited the fact that following a recent decision that 'training would come first at all costs', even at the expense of operations, 'decisive progress' had been achieved for the first time that month. But he warned:

> In each of the last ten daylight attacks we have lost, on average, over 50 aircraft and 40 pilots – i.e. 500 aircraft and 400 pilots in ten major operations. In view of the present state of training and the rate of these losses, units cannot be kept supplied with fresh pilots. This is simply not possible. Replacements can be found in a purely numerical sense, but this will not give us organised units.[2]

Indeed, the continual and increasing low-level Allied attacks on German airfields, the constant alerts and general feeling of insecurity had badly disrupted training. Yet there was a paradox, for in the spring of 1944 the channels of the fighter training system were almost full to capacity. One contributory factor was that, as Galland had hoped, the schools were being sent qualified pilots from disbanded bomber, transport and second-line units with the intention of providing them with short conversion courses to fighters.

It was also true that the training schools had no shortage of aircraft, whether they be ageing German trainer types, worn out and often repaired fighters cast off by operational units or captured foreign machines pressed into service. The problems they faced were a shortage of fuel and components, the decline in the numbers of proficient fighter instructors, many of whom had already been sent off to the fill the depleted ranks of the *Jagdgruppen* in light of the operational losses described by Galland, and the pressure to continue to replace pilot losses quickly.

In April 1944, General der Flieger Werner Kreipe, the commanding general of the flying schools, agreed to make 80–100 flying instructors available to the Jagdwaffe, but when it came to fuel, Generalmajor Hans-Joachim Rath, who commanded 1. *Flieger-Schul-Division*, described allocation for training in July 1944 as being 'hand to mouth' across the training infrastructure.[3]

The net effect of these factors was a reduction in total training hours per pilot, unlike the USAAF, which was able to provide full, specialist, uninterrupted training in clear, peaceful skies. According to a report by the US Strategic Bombing Survey, in the early part of the war, newly trained British and American fighter pilots had 95–100 more hours in operational type aircraft than German fighter pilots, and from 1943 the margin was even greater.[4]

Because of the continuing losses in combat of pilots, in early 1943 the *Jagdfliegerschulen* (JFS – day fighter schools) were necessarily placed on a semi-operational footing to become *Jagdgeschwader*. For example, JFS 2 based at Zerbst was redesignated as *Stab* and I./JG 102 on 25 February 1943, with its 3. *Staffel* at Magdeburg-Ost. This *Vorschule* (Preliminary School) *Staffel*, which, in 1943, was equipped with the high-wing Focke-Wulf Fw 56 Stösser, two-seat Bücker Bü 131 biplanes and even old pre-war Heinkel He 51 biplanes, as well as, by spring 1944, some advanced, closed cockpit Arado Ar 96 trainers and a handful of Bf 108 monoplanes, supplied pilots to the main school at Zerbst.

By May 1944, however, Zerbst was overcrowded, with many pilots who had completed their preliminary training being held up. An attempt to alleviate this situation across the Luftwaffe fighter schools was the introduction of the '*Windhund*' (Greyhound) programme, a fighter conversion course intended for experienced multi-engined pilots hurriedly brought in from bomber and transport units, which lasted just eight days.

Windhund had its origins in mid-1943, when the Inspector of Fighter and *Zerstörer* schools, Generalmajor Gerd-Albrecht von Massow, instituted the programme in response to the need to increase the output of pilots by reducing the standard 50–60 hours of training down to 15–20 hours. To oversee *Windhund*, a quota of instructors was drawn from the elementary A/B schools, which meant that twice as many instructors could be trained on the same amount of fuel required for instructing ordinary students. After a brief, experimental period, *Windhund* courses became established, with a complete switchover to the course taking effect in late 1943. In mid-1944, *Windhund* courses were extended to include the conversion of former bomber, reconnaissance and transport pilots for fighters.[5]

At 1./JG 102, this brief course comprised 'circuits and bumps' in the Ar 96 and formation flying in the two-seat, dual-control Bf 109G-12. The *Staffel* also had a small number of Bf 109G-6s which, in line with the semi-operational status of the fighter schools by mid-1944, were always flown armed and with drop tanks attached.

Similarly, in southern Germany, JFS 4 at Fürth and Herzogenaurach was redesignated JG 104 in March 1943, with 1. *Staffel* at Herzogenaurach acting as the *Vorschule* for the other two *Staffeln*, which together formed the *Endschule* (Advanced School) at Fürth. 2. *Staffel* was known to have been formed of three instructional groups of 30–40 pilots, with some of the former bomber and transport pilots benefiting from a longer, three-week conversion course. JG 104 numbered Bü 131s, Ar 96s, Bf 108s and two-seat Gotha Go 145 preliminary biplane trainers, as well as a range of Bf 109D, E, F and G fighters and G-12 trainers.

Unteroffizier Willi Unger, for example, a future *Sturmgruppe* pilot, was posted to 1./JG 104 under Oberleutnant Josef Unterberger. Here, he received training at the *Vorschule*-level, carrying out 'circuits and bumps', spot landings, turns, aerobatics, long-distance flying, navigation, diving, formation flying and some minimal awareness of battle formations and blind-flying – altogether expected to last approximately 25 hours, and conducted on the same type of aircraft as used by the A/B schools.

The task of the ensuing *Endschule* was to prepare and convert the pupil onto either the Bf 109 or Fw 190 in a series of 'circuits and bumps' in dual-control aircraft, followed by ten solo flights. Students would then be taught formation flying in pairs and fours, followed by a high-altitude flight with oxygen, a practise flight concentrating on weak points and, finally, two firing training flights, each comprising three approaches to a ground target. This covered another 16–18 hours.

Once those pilots with JG 102 at Zerbst had completed their training, they were transferred to *Jagdgruppe Ost*, an operational training unit based, from February 1944, at Liegnitz. This unit, established originally as the *Ergänzungs-Jagdgruppe Ost* in February 1942, was intended to supply pilots with basic operational qualifications to fighter units on the Eastern Front, but by 1944 it was supplying personnel additionally to units in Norway and, increasingly, the defence of the Reich. In the case of 1. and 3./JGr Ost, they prepared pilots for service with JG 54 on the Fw 190 and Bf 109, respectively, with the instructors all being former pilots from the *Geschwader*.

Posted to 1./JGr Ost in late April 1944 was 21-year-old Silesian Leutnant Norbert Hannig, who had previously flown Fw 190s with 5./JG 54 in Russia. Exactly what qualified him as an instructor is not clear as, by his own admission, 'There was no formal training involved in becoming an instructor. It was just something you got on with and did'. Hannig joined a small team of instructors, all '*alte Hasen*' (old hares) – combat veterans like himself who wore Iron Crosses and Combat Clasps in Gold. Each instructor took charge of three trainees, which, as a group of four, allowed flight training to be conducted in the Luftwaffe standard two-aircraft *Rotte* and four-aircraft *Schwarm* formations.[6]

On 20 May 1944, 1./JGr Ost had a strength of 43 pupils and 48 Fw 190s, including A-6s, A-7s and a small number of A-8s. One former member of the unit recalled that an average of ten aircraft were damaged in training each day.[7] Some of this 'accidental' damage would have been attributable to the general feeling of risk and vulnerability felt by trainees because of the increasing numbers of Allied fighters hawking through the skies over the Reich. Indeed, as American bombers penetrated ever more deeply into German airspace it became necessary to set up an efficient air warning system at each school in order to get airborne students back down on the ground before a raid passed into, or through, the general area of the school.[8]

Hannig's first cadre were all former instructors themselves, of officer rank. In his memoirs, he describes the shortcomings in fighter training at this time:

> They were complete novices when it came to operational flying and combat tactics. It was my task to impart to them the knowledge I had gained at the front. But even at this late, indeed final, stage of a fighter pilot's training, there was still one glaring deficiency. I was unable to provide them with any sort of gunnery practice against either air or ground targets.

Jagdgruppe Ost lacked gunnery ranges, aerial drogues and instruction manuals, and it was down to the *Gruppe*'s instructors to work out how to teach their charges. Furthermore, the unit had no two-seat Fw 190 trainers, and so, in essence, a pupil's first flight would be his first solo, but because the trainees were experienced pilots already, after some 'circuits and bumps', they had grasped the basics of the Fw 190A-4 and A-5 fighter variants. Then, with that done, formation take-offs and flights would follow which involved turns, stall turns and dives, slip turns, flick half-rolls and basic combat manoeuvres, with such flights lasting around 60-75 minutes.[9]

When a pilot was deemed ready for fighter operations, his training was considered finished, providing he had qualified for the single-engined blind-flying certificate – something that was mandatory for all pilots destined for units operating in the defence of the Reich. This was carried out variously at the school or with *Jagdgruppe Ost*, and at Fürth, for example, JG 104 had two Go 145s for this purpose.[10]

Despite all the adversities faced and the restrictions on pilot training, output from the fighter schools between July 1943 and June 1944 numbered between 850 and 1,000 students per month – an increase of 500–600 per month compared to the first six months of 1943. This was partly due to the introduction of the aforementioned *Windhund* measures. But, as Galland had told the *Jägerstab*, just producing replacements did not necessarily result in combat-effective units – particularly those expected to fight a well organised, well trained, confident and numerically superior enemy.[11]

From Norbert Hannig's perspective, when it came to his pupils, 'I pushed them and myself hard in the belief that a drop of sweat now might save a lot of blood later'.[12]

Throughout the spring of 1944 Luftwaffe fighter tactics against USAAF bombers remained fundamentally unchanged, although from May, wherever strength and time permitted, efforts were made to form mixed *Gefechtsverbände* of Me 410s with single-engined fighters as escort. Such *Gefechtsverbände* were led by the *Kommodore* of a *Jagdgeschwader* along with his *Stab Schwarm*, and it became a question of skilful vectoring and formation leadership or simply being lucky enough to meet a bomber formation whose fighter escort was not to hand at a given moment.

On the few occasions circumstances worked in the favour of the German defence, as has been recounted, carnage could be inflicted on a USAAF bomber formation. In this regard, the partnership between the Me 410s of II./ZG 26 and the Bf 109Gs of Major Walther Dahl's III./JG 3 was especially successful.

On 8 May, the targets were once again Berlin and Braunschweig. Nearly 750 B-17s and B-24s escorted by 729 fighters reached Germany, with the Liberators of the 2nd BD leading the formation in a straight line to Berlin, passing over the Zuider Zee and onwards, north of Hanover. East of Uelzen, the 2nd BD, together with the 45th CW from the 3rd BD, which had become separated from the Berlin force, turned south to bomb Braunschweig.

Despite dense, multi-layered cloud blanketing central Germany, at 0842 hrs a *Gefechtsverband* formed of *Stab*/JG 3, IV(*Sturm*)./JG 3 and *Sturmstaffel* 1, and led by Major Friedrich-Karl Müller, *Kommodore* of JG 3, scrambled from Salzwedel to intercept. Initially, the formation was directed towards the Hamburg area, where the cloud had begun to clear, allowing the *Gefechtsverband* to initially rendezvous with II./JG 3 from Gardelegen. However, contact with the *Gruppe* was soon lost, and the Salzwedel aircraft were duly led to the south.

At 1000 hrs, despite worsening weather, unescorted B-24s were intercepted northwest of Braunschweig. Flying an Fw 190 with *Sturmstaffel* 1, Feldwebel Oskar Bösch recalled many years later:

> I particularly remember the 8 May 1944 mission, the details of which are engraved in my memory and which went wrong from the beginning. We were flying at 3,000 m beside a box of B-24s at a slightly lower altitude when our own Flak mistook us for a target! A shell exploded near my aircraft and riddled it with shrapnel. Almost immediately, a trail of oil appeared on my windshield and hood. An oil pipe had been hit. I called on the radio to my comrades that I had to leave the flight. This I did without losing a minute, getting closer and closer to the B-24s.
>
> As I flew my aircraft down through the bomber formation, I found that I had to fire at the last B-24, which burst into fragments. I continued to fire as I flew through the formation, but I had no time to observe the results because, in a brief matter of time, I had passed through some 60+ bombers.
>
> I was in a relatively secure position – in between the bombers, where I could not be fired at without the gunners risking hitting one of their own bombers. Out of ammunition and over-excited, I decided to ram one! I moved into an oblique attack on a B-24. I could feel the eddies from the slipstream. My aircraft was thrown off balance and I missed my intended victim by only a few metres. Then the sky became clear in front of me.
>
> Looking around, I could see no bombers, only some kind of hell of fire. My aircraft vibrated as shots hit home, and I am sure that the lateral armour plating saved my life. Pushing my stick forward, regardless of the terrific negative G forces, I was now in a straight dive at 1,000 km/h, engulfed in bullets and hits. Without wasting time, I undid my harness and ejected the canopy – a freezing wind snatched me from my seat.

I felt terrified during my free-fall of 6,000 m, waiting to pass through the clouds before opening my parachute. I landed at Goslar in the Harz. I was lucky to have been only lightly wounded in the head by some shrapnel and slightly burned on the face from my fall in the freezing air, as my parachute had been pierced many times by bullets![13]

Bösch was credited with a B-24 *Herausschuss* following this operation, while the *Gruppenkommandeur* of IV.(*Sturm*)/JG 3, Hauptmann Moritz, claimed two. The JG 3 machines approached for their frontal attack, and Moritz, flying a Bf 109G-6 armed with an MK 108, closed from 1,000 m to 200 m before opening fire at 1007 hrs on a Liberator at the right of the nearest *Pulk* of around 40 bombers. He saw his burst striking home on the B-24's starboard wing between the two Pratt & Whitney radials. 'Large pieces came away', Moritz reported, 'and the machine tilted over on its right wing'.

Seven minutes later, after the *Gruppe* had flown through the bombers and made a wide left turn to come around for a second pass, Moritz approached again in exactly the way he had done for his first run, targeting another Liberator. This time he saw strikes hit the starboard wing root. On this occasion, 'At first the machine flickered with bright flames, then stopped and finally spun downwards with a plume of black smoke'.[14]

USAAF Intelligence later reported:

The B-24s attacking Brunswick were strongly attacked in the target area. Some mass attacks were made, but the majority of passes were made by groups of four to eight, head-on, level, and slightly high out of the sun. The formation was subjected to fierce fighter opposition in the Nienburg area, when nearing Brunswick, without escort. About 75 enemy aircraft, mostly Fw 190s, attacked in a square block formation, massing and assaulting from the nose. These pilots were experienced and viciously aggressive, pressing so closely that in one instance a bomber was destroyed by collision with an enemy fighter.[15]

Moritz was credited with two *Herausschüsse* for his 36th and 37th kills. Although IV.(*Sturm*)/JG 3's total claims amounted to 11 *Abschüsse* and *Herausschüsse*, with *Sturmstaffel* 1 registering another eight within the space of seven minutes, only 11 B-24s were lost in total and a further seven written off.[16]

Perhaps the greatest blow to hit the Jagdwaffe so far occurred on 11 May when the Eighth Air Force attacked marshalling yards in northeastern France, Belgium and Luxembourg. Nearly 550 bombers took part, and escort fighters mounted more than 1,000 sorties. At Paderborn, the Bf 109Gs of *Stab* and III./JG 1 took off in the afternoon, with the *Geschwaderkommodore*, Oberst Walter Oesau (by this time a 123-victory '*Experte*' who wore the Knight's Cross with Oak Leaves and Swords), leading three aircraft of the *Stabsschwarm*. They were followed by the Bf 109G-6s of III./JG 1, led by Major Hartmann Grasser.

The *Stabsschwarm* was diving towards the bombers when it was bounced by American fighters. Oesau was forced into a circling combat against five enemy aircraft. His wingmen, themselves fully occupied by the encounter, could do nothing to help. Attempting to escape his opponents, Oesau progressively lost height. Oberfeldwebel Leo Schuhmacher of II./JG 1 recalled:

> Several times I had said to Oesau that the Fw 190 was better than the Bf 109, but being an old 109 pilot, he preferred it. On 11 May, [Heinz] Bär [*Gruppenkommandeur* of II./JG 1] remained on the ground because of technical problems, and Oesau led the formation totalling 30 aircraft. At high altitude we spotted the enemy fighters, and Oesau ordered me over the radio to take II. *Gruppe* with me.
>
> As I was later told by his wingman, a young Oberfähnrich, Oesau was attacked by P-51s, which forced him into a turning dogfight. Each turn became tighter, and the Bf 109 slowed down, more so than his adversaries. Oesau was probably shot down near the ground. I saw Oesau's body – the whole left side of him appeared to have been hit by a burst. Thus wounded, he no doubt tried to carry out a makeshift landing.[17]

The remains of Oesau's Messerschmitt were found several kilometres from Saint Vith in Belgium. His body, having been thrown clear on impact, lay not far away. Several years after the war, Major Hartmann Grasser commented on Oesau's loss:

> At that time, Oesau was physically and mentally exhausted. The German fighter pilots had to fight right through the war, without respite. I consider it a grave error on the part of our High Command. I personally took part in the combat when Oesau was lost. Alone, chased by Lightnings and Mustangs, he had no chance of escaping. Neither did we. It was in this way that we lost the majority of the best among us.[18]

In a sad twist of fate, several hours after Oesau's disappearance, a letter signed by Galland arrived at the unit. It was an order posting Oesau to

Galland's headquarters staff, but by then it was too late. All that could be done was to honour the fallen hero. From henceforth, the premier fighter unit would be known as *Jagdgeschwader* 1 '*Oesau*'.

Since March 1944, Maj Gen Spaatz, commander of USSTAF, had been closely monitoring Germany's oil storage and production capacity. The bombing policy directive issued by Air Chief Marshal Sir Arthur Tedder on 17 April 1944 to Air Chief Marshal Sir Arthur 'Bomber' Harris and Spaatz stipulated that:

> . . . the overall mission of the strategical Air Forces remains the progressive destruction and dislocation of the German military, industrial and economic system, and the destruction of vital elements of lines of communications. In the execution of this overall mission, the immediate objective is first the destruction of German combat strength by the successful prosecution of the combined bomber offensive.[19]

Despite the omission of oil as a specific target, two days after the directive, Gen Dwight D. Eisenhower, Supreme Allied Commander of the Allied Expeditionary Force, provided Spaatz with verbal authority to proceed with a 'limited offensive' against German oil targets. Encouraged, Spaatz ordered the Eighth Air Force's commander, Maj Gen Doolittle, to begin attacking as many oil targets as possible in central Germany.

The weather gave the Germans a badly needed respite, and it was not until 12 May that the first massed bomber formations, drawn from 15 combat wings, and with an escort provided by both the USAAF and the RAF, headed out on a carefully plotted course to bomb the synthetic production plants at Zwickau, Merseburg-Leuna, Brüx and Lützkendorf. Once again, however, the skilful German fighter controllers had been watching developments and, in a refreshingly successful operation, sent up a total force of 470 single- and twin-engined fighters to intercept.

These units harassed the bombers from Frankfurt to the targets in well-coordinated attacks, and the USAAF reported confronting the largest numbers of *Zerstörer* for several weeks. Some even reported ramming, and the sheer aggression of the attacks caused at least one combat wing to become completely disorganised, resulting in contact being lost with half of its bombers.

The *Stab* and the three *Gruppen* of JG 3 were particularly successful once again, collectively claiming 24 B-17s shot down and 17 cut out of formation, along with three P-51 escorts. Among the multiple scorers were Leutnant Hans Weik, leader of 10./JG 3, who continued to demonstrate a formidable aptitude for anti-bomber work when he shot down two B-17s in seven minutes for his 32nd and 33rd victories, while Leutnant Rudolf Metz of 11./JG 3 excelled himself, claiming three *Herausschüsse* in nine minutes for his third, fourth and fifth kills.

From the *Stab* of IV.(*Sturm*)/JG 3, Oberfähnrich Erhard Nolting claimed a first *Herausschuss* at 1230 hrs northeast of Frankfurt, observing hits to the B-17's cockpit, wing root and engines, and watching the bomber shear away from its formation, falling earthwards to crash into the ground at a sharp angle. Seven minutes later, coming in for a second pass, Nolting selected a Flying Fortress on the outer right of the formation, opened fire and, as before, scored hits to the cabin area and right wing. He was credited with two *Herausschüsse*, taking his personal tally to seven.[20]

Thirty Me 410A-1/U4s of II./ZG 26 took off in the early afternoon led by Hauptmann Günther Weyl. This time amongst them was at least one machine, formerly of E.Kdo 25, fitted experimentally with the 3.7 cm Flak 43 that featured a wide muzzle brake and longer barrel than the BK 5. The aircraft was crewed by pilot Leutnant Paul Kaschuba and his radio operator, Feldwebel Karl Bredemeier, both having been recently seconded to II./ZG 26 from the *Erprobungskommando*. This was to be another draining, savage mission, as Gefreiter Richard Wilde recalled:

> The *Kommandeur*, Hauptmann Günther Weyl, set up the attack by bringing us in behind the B-17s on a wide, curving, right-hand turn with a slight height advantage, allowing for accurate firing. Following a corresponding order, he broke off his own attack very early, while the rest of the group continued the attack to the closest range. During our closing approach my right neighbour caught fire. Dark red flames generating deep black smoke appeared in the front under the hull. The flames billowed out about one or two fuselage lengths behind the tailplane. Almost certainly the cannon rounds were burning, which also happened to me shortly thereafter. As I recall, the aircraft peeled away to the right with a half-roll.
>
> I managed seven or eight firing rounds with the heavy cannon on the approach with no problems. Not a single jam. Even the smaller cannon worked well that day. I could see the impacts of my firing on the right inboard engine of the B-17, and now fired the cannon hoping for a direct hit in the fuselage. As I was attacking, I took numerous hits as we closed in. I could hear the impacts and see their effects on the port wing. There were streaks of oil around the port engine.[21]

THE LAST CHANCE

Elsewhere, Kaschuba and Bredemeier also attacked with their Flak 43-equipped Me 410, but as they did so, defensive fire from a B-17 hit the underside of the *Zerstörer* as it passed close by. The aircraft's right engine had been damaged and was on fire as Kaschuba attempted an emergency landing. But 200 m above the ground, the engine fell away and the Me 410 crashed, probably in the immediate vicinity of Schleiz, some 30 km west of Plauen. On impact, Kaschuba was thrown out of the aircraft and died from a skull fracture. Bredemeier perished in the burning aircraft.

II./ZG 26 lost four aircraft and two crews during the encounter, and claimed three victories in return. Eight of the A-1/U4s suffered stoppages with their BK 5s after firing just a few rounds.[22]

Yet at a meeting between Göring, Galland and Schmid on 15 May, the Reichsmarschall 'allowed' II./ZG 26 to remain as the only BK 5-equipped *Zerstörergruppe*, despite the gun being a politically favoured weapon that was failing to live up to expectations and indirectly, if not directly, causing losses.[23] Indeed, just two days earlier, five Me 410A-1/U4s had fallen prey to Mustangs before they had even managed to reach bombers out to strike at the Focke-Wulf plant at Tutow. One of the Messerschmitts was flown by Oberfeldwebel Wolfgang Martin of 4./ZG 26, who had been awarded the Knight's Cross on 30 December 1942 while flying with KG 3. He had joined ZG 26 just ten days before his death. Lost alongside Martin was his radio operator, Feldwebel Johann Ahlgrim.

Returning to the action on 12 May, the USAAF strike force lost 46 bombers that day. For the Luftwaffe, however, the cost had again been high, with losses in the I. *Jagdkorps* sector amounting to 34 aircraft, with a further 31 machines recording damage in excess of 60 per cent.

In February 1944, following a suggestion made by *Stabsingenieur* Reyle of the RLM's Technical Office, Hauptmann Horst Geyer oversaw another development of the W.Gr.21 mortar – a rearward-firing version. Geyer noted that initial ground tests with such a weapon had brought 'positive results', although further, presumably airborne, tests still had to be carried out. He reported:

> This installation is ready to go, and it is expected that with little effort, the W.Gr.21 used this way will be much more advantageous compared to the previous attack methods used.[24]

The intention was that a pilot would fire the mortar, known as the '*Krebsgerät*' (Crab Device), after he had made a firing pass using forward armament against a bomber formation and was in the process of passing through the enemy *Pulk*. The fuse would be set to detonate at 1.5–2 seconds after the weapon was fired, giving sufficient time for the carrying fighter to fly ahead and clear. There was a plan to make the tube jettisonable after firing, but it is not thought that this was ever followed through. It was hoped that a rearward-firing mortar would achieve surprise in the manner of a 'Parthian shot'.

In May 1944, Galland ordered that 20 Fw 190A-8s were to be fitted with the *Krebsgerät*, while Oberst Trautloft, Inspector of Day Fighters, required one Me 410 to be installed with the rearward-firing mortar for trials with the *Zerstörerstaffel* of E.Kdo 25. On the one occasion the weapon was fired, the Me 410 suffered from a strong blowback, thick smoke filled its cockpit and the aircraft's hydraulic system was very badly damaged.

Despite this, by 15 July it was planned to have 60 *Krebsgeräte* ready for installation into Fw 190s, with 16 fighters of E.Kdo 25 fully fitted out by 15 August. A new automatic, optically controlled firing mechanism, known as the '*Wurzen*', was also being worked on by the Hugo Schneider AG (HASAG) company in Leipzig. By the end of August, however, Geyer recorded that only one Fw 190 had been fitted with the automatic device.[25]

In the meantime, in May 1944, pilots of the Fw 190-equipped 12./JG 3, while based briefly at Barth, had attempted trials with a single rearward-firing 21 cm mortar tube. Four of the *Staffel*'s aircraft were installed with a form of the *Krebsgeräte* fitted beneath their centre sections, and they proved unreliable mechanically. The additional armour already added to the unit's Fw 190A-8 *Sturmjäger* affected performance, and Unteroffizier Willi Unger, who tested the weapon in combat, reported that the *Krebsgerät* caused a further deterioration in the fighter's speed and manoeuvrability.[26] By late September, trials with both E.Kdo 25 and other operational units seem to have petered out.

19

Savage Skies

On the morning of 14 October 1943, while over the North Sea en route to bomb the Focke-Wulf plant at Marienburg, in East Prussia, B-17F *Miss Nonalee II* of the 385th BG, piloted by 21-year-old 1Lt Glyndon D. Bell, suffered pitch control problems on its No. 2 engine, resulting in the powerplant becoming locked on a take-off setting.

Miss Nonalee II had rolled off the Boeing production line at Seattle the previous year, and like many B-17s, had received various armament and technical enhancements at United Airlines' Cheyenne Modification Center in Wyoming before leaving the US. It had arrived at the 385th BG's base at Great Ashfield, in Suffolk, in June 1943, after which it was assigned to the 548th BS. Since then, the bomber had flown several missions – and survived. On 14 October it was one of 23 Flying Fortresses despatched by the 385th BG as part of the 3rd BD mission to Marienburg. In addition to its usual crew, the aircraft carried an aerial photographer who was to take shots of the bombing for Group command.

As *Miss Nonalee II* approached the Danish coast at an altitude of 11,600 ft, Bell feathered the propeller blades on the malfunctioning engine. With the resulting loss of speed, the bomber began to lag behind the rest of the 385th formation. It was now vulnerable, but continued on course to the east. After some eight minutes, Bell decided to turn around and head back to England. As he did so, *Miss Nonalee II* succumbed to further engine problems. In such a condition, Bell knew that to attempt to make it back to England would be impossible. His navigator then called out that he believed they had just crossed into neutral Sweden. He was wrong.

Nevertheless, on that assumption, Bell gave his ten-man crew the option to either remain with the still bombed-up aircraft or to bail out, starting with the tail gunner and working forward to the front of the ship. The crew chose the latter. The radio operator had accidentally opened his chute inside the aircraft, however, so Bell gave the man his own. For Bell's crew as they parachuted down unwittingly into German-occupied Denmark, the war was over.

Alone now, without a parachute, and carefully nursing the limping bomber slowly towards the ground, Bell successfully landed *Miss Nonalee II* in a meadow near the Danish town of Varde, 25 km from the coast. Clambering out of the B-17, and in accordance with Eighth Air Force instructions, he hurriedly attempted to set fire to the aircraft, but was unable to. Bell was fortunate enough to be discovered by friendly Danish farmers, who passed him to the Resistance. He eventually made it to Sweden later that month, but in failing to ignite *Miss Nonalee II*, he had gifted the Luftwaffe a very welcome 'war prize'.

The Luftwaffe moved quickly. On 15 October, an ungainly Arado Ar 232 transport carrying a team of salvage specialists from the test centre at Rechlin, together with their necessary equipment, landed close to the B-17, which was lying on soft ground in a tree-lined clearing. The Arado, known as the *Tausendfüßler* ('Millipede') on account of the row of 22 closely set, independently sprung, 'millipede' wheels beneath its box-like fuselage, in addition to its main tricycle undercarriage, was perfect for operating in such rough conditions.

Accompanying the salvage team was a highly experienced test pilot from Rechlin, Flieger-Haupting. Hans-Werner Lerche. Importantly, Lerche had flown a captured B-17 before. Assessing the site, he was of the opinion that if the aircraft could be stripped of every item of non-essential equipment such as armour plating and armament, and its tanks drained to leave just enough fuel to reach the airfield of Esbjerg 16 km away, then he could fly it out.

The next morning, Lerche sat in the cockpit where, a few days earlier, 1Lt Bell had flown the bomber from England. His expert eye surveyed the well laid out instruments – the small, ladder-shaped throttles on their mount ahead of and between the pilots' seats, below which was the auto flight control panel, and immediately ahead of the throttles, the altimeter, airspeed, turn and bank and rate-of-climb indicators. Above the panel was the expansive windscreen, offering good vision forwards. Behind Lerche, the Rechlin engineers worked hard to remove the last of the Boeing's surplus equipment and stow it into the Arado.

After the necessary repairs and a trial take-off run, once all was ready and with engines running, Lerche applied the brakes, gave full power and then slowly released the brakes, allowing the lightened B-17 to roll and bump along the clearing, hauling it up just above the tall trees and into the grey October sky. *Miss Nonalee II* turned slowly over the Danish countryside and nosed its way towards Esbjerg, followed by the curious, lumbering *Tausendfüßler*.

Some days later, at its new home base at Rechlin, *Miss Nonalee II*'s USAAF white national recognition stars, tail serial number and unit markings were painted over. They were replaced with German black crosses, and a small Swastika was applied to the tail. It was now a Luftwaffe aircraft. The one concession was that the bomber's name was retained in its place on the forward fuselage just behind the Plexiglas nose cone.

Miss Nonalee II provided the Luftwaffe with two valuable services. Firstly, it provided an insight into the latest American aero engine technology, especially the superchargers, which were activated by exhaust-driven turbines, and which helped the B-17 to perform well at higher altitudes. As such, German engine experts were keen to examine the aircraft, and Hans-Werner Lerche recalled how 'the most varied measuring instruments were installed for this purpose, so that the fuselage behind the bomb-bay was like a laboratory with engineers in attendance'.

But the test flight that followed became hair-raising when, at 2,750 m, an engine fire broke out in the starboard outer engine, with flames licking back some 4.5 m in length. Lerche managed to land the Flying Fortress on three engines at Jüterbog-Damm, taxiing to a standstill just in front of the workshop hangars.

Secondly, from May 1944, *Miss Nonalee II* was used as a touring demonstration and instructional aircraft for the Luftwaffe's fighter units, who were also understandably keen to have the opportunity to look over one of their arch opponents at close quarters. On a pre-arranged basis, Lerche would fly the B-17 low over fighter airfields in northern and central Germany, making several passes, so that the fighter pilots were able to study the bomber at all angles from the ground. Upon departure from one airfield to fly to another, Messerschmitts and Focke-Wulfs would accompany *Miss Nonalee II* in the air to allow the fighters to carry out mock attacks.

Taking off from Rechlin early on the morning of 14 May 1944 in order 'to avoid being molested by enemy aircraft', Lerche commenced the first stage of a tour of the fighter units based in the southern Reich, which would see the B-17 fly via Munich, Vienna and Prague. In his memoirs, he recalled an aerial training session at Munich:

That afternoon we made the first flight that brought us into contact with Luftwaffe fighters. At that time, attacking the B-17 from ahead was considered a particularly effective tactic. However, during preliminary discussions, I had already pointed out that the B-17 had a rather tall fin – a point that had to be kept in mind when sweeping in towards the bomber. Be that as it may, I must say that the fighters dealt pretty hard with the 'enemy' afterwards, and sometimes my fingers itched to make a timely evasive manoeuvre. To be sure, the fact that I was flying a 'friendly' B-17 must have had something to do with their wild attacks. However, the training session passed without incident, and finally I was relieved to land with an undamaged tail unit after all.

While at Munich-Riem, *Miss Nonalee II* generated much interest amongst personnel of the Luftwaffe, Wehrmacht and Party. 'So much so in fact', noted Lerche, 'that even generals were queueing up to have a look!'

Lerche made several more instructional flights in the B-17, high above the clouds which hung over the Lower Alps, before heading to Vienna. Such was the value that the *Jagdgeschwader* took from Lerche's demonstrations that he would be in the air for as long as four hours at a time:

> One can imagine that it must have been an exalting feeling for the fighter pilots to fly so close to a Flying Fortress without being shot at 'out of all buttonholes'.

In Austria, Lerche carried out a low-level demonstration flight for the benefit of Oberst Gotthardt Handrick, the *Jafü Ostmark*, although as Lerche admitted, 'There was always the danger that the spectators would get the impression they were watching an easily manoeuvrable plane – which was certainly not true of the B-17!'

In the end, Lerche clocked up 35 hours on B-17s. He remembered:

> I really enjoyed flying the 'Fort', as it made a most reliable impression, and the engines always performed perfectly. Perhaps there were other aircraft that were more pleasant to fly than the B-17, because it did have its drawbacks. For example, the forces acting on the ailerons were relatively high, and the rudder felt as if were set in concrete. But it was much more important that the aircraft was easy to fly and land. When one had become accustomed to the higher all-up weight and the strange instruments, it could be compared with our He 111 in the degree of effort needed to fly it.

Miss Nonalee II continued to be operated by the Luftwaffe until the end of 1944. It is believed the aircraft was written off in April 1945.[1]

Schmid and Galland travelled south to the Obersalzberg for a two-day conference with Göring over 15–16 May. The atmosphere was tense.

Galland, who was having to scrape the barrel for manpower for daylight defence, had become more ruthless and even a little desperate in his demands. He wanted 'qualified nightfighter pilots' transferred over to daylight operations and two *Jagdgruppen* withdrawn from the East for employment in defence of the Reich. Göring agreed, and issued orders for II./JG 5 and IV./JG 54 to be relocated accordingly.

Galland then recommended that the Fw 190-equipped ground-attack *Gruppe* II./SG 2, which was fighting in the Crimea, be converted over to fighter operations. His rationale was that the *Gruppe* numbered 11 pilots, each credited with between five and 90 aerial victories. Their capabilities would be valued by the *Jagdgruppen*. Göring refused, but Galland continued to press. If that was not possible, then he suggested the *Schlachtflieger* should release all pilots with more than five victories. Göring demurred and decreed that ground-attack pilots could only transfer voluntarily.

Next, Galland asked that *Luftflotte* 3 release its fighter units assigned to II. *Jagdkorps* for employment in the *Reichsverteidigung*, and that any *Gruppenkommandeur* absent from his post for more than 14 days owing to sickness or wounds should be replaced. Surprisingly, this was more than Göring could stomach, and again he refused. The Reichsmarschall did agree with one of the *General der Jagdflieger's* requests – that to improve training there should be a rolling withdrawal of one fighter *Gruppe* from each *Jagddivision* for a period of eight days to four weeks, but as long as the removal of II./JG 5 and IV./JG 54 from the East took place. However, as Oberst Martin Mettig, the former Chief of Staff of II. *Jagdkorps*, wrote in November 1944 on Galland's proposals for withdrawing *Luftflotte* 3's fighter assets to the Reich:

> The fighter forces available were utterly insufficient – up to the beginning of the Invasion, they comprised two *Geschwader* with a total operational strength of 60–80 aircraft. It was decided to send one *Gruppe* at a time from each *Geschwader* back to the Metz-Nancy area for training under more peaceful conditions. The suggestion that these units might more profitably be transferred to Bohemia or Silesia for training was turned down by the *Luftwaffenführungsstab* with the comments that a) no airfields were available, and b) that the danger would exist of both *Geschwader* being incorporated into *Luftgau Reich*, and therefore being lost to II. *Jagdkorps*.

With an eye on a worrying future, Schmid proposed that all fighter *Gruppen* deployed in the defence of the Reich should remain in the Reich 'even if the Allies should invade'. In response, and according to the minutes of the conference:

... the Reichsmarschall decides that only the third *Gruppe* of fighter *Geschwader* will stay in the Reich on surrender of their serviceable aircraft and pilots who are fit for flying, in accordance with orders already issued.

This was astonishing. Under such terms, quite how the airspace of Germany was to be defended in the aftermath of an Allied invasion was not clear.

Towards the end of the conference, Göring advised that he had proposed to Hitler 'that American and British aircrews who fire indiscriminately on towns, civilian trains or men descending by parachute should be executed on the spot'.[2]

The increasingly fast, furious and large-scale aerial battles taking place in the skies over Europe put pressure on some of the most combat-seasoned fighter aces, leading them, occasionally, to take uncharacteristic risks and to make mistakes.

Twenty-eight-year-old Thuringian Hauptmann Ernst Börngen had joined the Luftwaffe as an officer cadet in 1937, and in June 1940 he was posted to 4./JG 27 in France, from where, on 18 August 1940, he shot down a Spitfire over the south coast of England. He demonstrated an aptitude for engineering, and within 18 months Börngen had been appointed Technical Officer in his *Staffel*. By late 1941, after service in the Balkans and Russia, he was in North Africa with five victories to his name. Over the next year-and-a-half, Börngen would fly regular combat missions in a Bf 109 against the Allied air forces over Libya, Egypt, Tunisia, Sicily and Italy, adding five more Spitfires to his tally.

As Technical Officer of II./JG 27, he was responsible for the smooth mechanical functioning of his *Gruppe*, and by July 1943 he was *Staffelkapitän* of 5. *Staffel*. On the 16th of that month, Börngen's unit, operating from San Vito des Normanni in Apulia, was vectored to engage B-24s of the Fifteenth Air Force near Bari. He shot one down, for his 28th victory, but was hit in his cockpit by defensive fire. Badly wounded, Börngen had to force-land back at San Vito des Normanni, during which he was further injured and had to be removed from the wreckage. While recovering, he spent a few months as a fighter instructor with *Jagdgruppe Süd* in southern France.

By the spring of 1944, Börngen was back on active duty as *Staffelkapitän* of 2./JG 27, which by then was operating in the defence of the Reich at Fels am Wagram, northwest of Vienna. The *Staffel*'s parent *Gruppe*,

I./JG 27, had sustained heavy casualties protecting the airspace over southern Germany, Austria and northern Italy. Amongst those wounded was its *Gruppenkommandeur*, veteran Knight's Cross-holder Major Ludwig Franzisket, whose Messerschmitt was hit by defensive fire from a B-17 on 12 May. Börngen was announced as his replacement the following day. By then, he had been credited with 36 victories, including eight B-17s and four B-24s.

At 1143 hrs on 19 May, the *Geschwaderstab* and I./JG 27 were scrambled from Fels am Wagram and rendezvoused with III. and IV./JG 27 to form a *Geschwader Gefechtsverband*.[3] They were directed north by *Jafü Ostmark* and 7. *Jagddivision* to the Magdeburg area, where they would reinforce units of 1. *Jagddivision* and engage a force of 272 B-24s of the Eighth Air Force's 2nd BD routing via the Zuider Zee, the Dümmer See and Hanover to attack aircraft industry targets in Braunschweig.

But the Luftwaffe fighter force found itself stretched to the limit, dealing with an Eighth Air Force double thrust aimed at targets in Braunschweig while two bomb divisions of B-17s approached Berlin via the north German coast. I. *Jagdkorps* reacted quickly to the first attack by the 2nd BD over the Dümmer See, bringing in fighters controlled by Gollob's *Jafü* 5 in France. The USAAF noted:

> Perhaps as many as 150 singles and 10 twin-engined fighters were in this attack, the first to take place so far to the west since 15 March. This first attack was followed up by a second one, which paid the only real dividends of the day. Once the fighter escort of the 2nd Division was saturated, the enemy followed up with the old 'one-two' technique. In the Celle area 100 more single-engined fighters launched an attack against the hard-pressed escort, and the lone fighter group, now already well occupied, was insufficient to cope with this added weight of attack.[4]

Among these 'singles' were the aircraft of I./JG 27, which engaged the Liberators northwest of Magdeburg shortly after 1300 hrs, while those of III. and IV./JG 27 'saturated' the escort. At 1315 hrs, Hauptmann Börngen attacked a Liberator and shot it down six kilometres east of Helmstedt, then turned back to attack the main formation for a second time. Five minutes later, he was over the bombers. As he recalled:

> I had shot down a four-engined bomber, but my unit had been broken up in non-stop dogfights. A whole squadron of American Mustangs hung behind my aircraft, firing wildly. I no longer had the slightest

chance. It was over, and I was terrified! Out of sheer fear, I rushed at the bomber formation flying below me. All I could do was ram. If I hadn't rammed, the Americans would have shot me down.

I could clearly see a huge bomber in front of me. Another 20 seconds and the game would be up. I caught the B-24 on the tail and sliced off the whole tail fin. The wreckage of my aircraft detached itself from the crashing bomber. But there was no longer any control.

At an altitude of 7,000 m, I threw off the Plexiglas canopy and jumped. There was a terrible blow. I had been thrown directly into the tail unit of my own aircraft. Despite the shock, I kept my nerve. I let myself descend from 7,000 m and only opened the canopy at an altitude of around 1,500 m. My whole right side was covered in blood. My right arm was hanging lifelessly in the shreds of my flying suit. I pulled with my left hand and suddenly had my arm in my hand. I dropped it, and tied the stump of my arm with scraps of my shirt. The Americans were still after me. They fired at me in cold blood. My parachute was shot through in several places, but it still carried me.

Börngen came down in a field of corn. He staggered to his feet, fighting back the feeling that he was going to pass out, and stumbled forward to look for help. At one point he came upon a small group of Russian prisoners of war, but they simply stared at the horrific image before them and made off. Shortly afterwards, some German civilians arrived and dragged Börngen to the house of an elderly man who had once worked as a medic at the coal mine near Helmstedt. 'The old man skilfully stitched up the stump of my arm. If it hadn't been for him, I would have bled to death in the middle of Germany'.[5]

Börngen was credited with the destruction of a second bomber north of Helmstedt. The remains of his right arm were amputated at a Luftwaffe hospital.

With more than 150 victories to his credit, Major Anton Hackl, *Gruppenkommandeur* of III./JG 11, was a highly regarded unit commander and a leading 'bomber killer'. He had been decorated with the Oak Leaves to the Knight's Cross. On 20 May 1944, Hackl sent a paper to Galland in which he offered his suggestions – bluntly – on what was required to deal with the *Viermots*:

The aim of all fighter formations in operations against bombers when the target of the bomber stream is known should be:

a) To attack as late as possible, causing bombers to jettison, even though a late approach excludes the possibility of a second operation, or –

b) To attack as early as possible, thus allowing *Gruppe* after *Gruppe* to attack at one-minute intervals. Allied fighter relief would then be forced to deal with the main body of attacking elements, one after the other, necessitating a splitting of forces, and would not be in a position to hamper individual *Gruppen* making repeated frontal attacks, even where there was Allied high-altitude fighter cover. Secondly, on the second sortie, auxiliary tanks should be retained as far as possible in order to challenge Allied formations as deep as possible inside the Reich. Fighter protection is less bold and weaker here, and relief does not always arrive as scheduled. Thirdly, it is certainly possible to break up Allied formations through these tactics; rear attacks are then possible so that even bad gunners would have to get a victory or be suspected of cowardice. Experience of frontal attacks show that only older (experienced) pilots get victories and, for the most part, they get hit. Younger pilots do not approach correctly, nor go in near enough. Fourthly, my *Gruppe* proposes therefore 1) to continually bring young pilots over from the Russian Front with few victories so that the East would become a kind of battle school for the West, and 2) every pilot, even when his ammunition has been expended, must attack in formation as long as the *Kommandeur* does, in order to split up defence and prevent our own from refusing combat.[6]

The same day that Hackl drafted his paper, Galland summoned Major Walter Dahl, the commander of III./JG 3 (one of the most successful units serving in the *Reichsverteidigung*), to a meeting at Wiesbaden-Erbenheim. Galland advised Dahl that he had been monitoring the operations of his *Gruppe* for the past few months and congratulated him on his considerable achievements.

Since the first daylight raid on Berlin in March 1944, there had been pressure on the command of the Jagdwaffe to improve the control and coordination of its fragmented *Gruppen* based across the Reich so as to launch quick, concentrated responses to the American bomber threat.

Galland had put forward proposals for the formation of a special *Gefechtsverband* of only *Geschwaderstab* strength to be known as the *Jagdgeschwader zur besonderen Verwendung* (JGzbV – Fighter Wing for Special Deployment), which would oversee a number of *Jagdgruppen* based in southern Germany under 7. *Jagddivision*. The JGzbV would operate as a cohesive force, with the prime role of attacking bombers from both the

Eighth and Fifteenth Air Forces. In effect, with Schmid having pulled 7.*Jagddivision* into the fold of I.*Jagdkorps*, Galland was fine-tuning Schmid's restructuring, and it was hoped lessons would be learned and experience gained.

On 23 April 1944, Knight's Cross-holder Major Gerhard Michalski, *Kommandeur* of II./JG 53 and a veteran of the Mediterranean Front, was appointed to set up the *Stab* JGzbV at Kassel. On 1 May however, just days after his appointment, Michalski was wounded in action and was temporarily assigned as a unit leader instructor. Galland subsequently asked Dahl if he would lead the JGzbV. Dahl agreed enthusiastically, and after further discussions with Major Gerd Müller-Trimbusch, Galland's Chief-of-Staff, he climbed into his Bf 109 and flew back to his unit the same day to put things into immediate effect, firstly overseeing the transfer of the *Gruppe* from Bad Wörishofen to Ansbach. The next day, 21 May, Dahl – still at Bad Wörishofen – officially handed over command of III./JG 3 to Hauptmann Karl-Heinz Langer, the current *Staffelkapitän* of 7./JG 3. He then left for Ansbach, where he established the headquarters of the new JGzbV.

In the meantime, Müller-Trimbusch had assigned five *Jagdgruppen* to Dahl – III./JG 3 under Langer at Ansbach; I./JG 5 under Major Horst Carganico at Herzogenaurach (planned as a *Höhenjagdgruppe* with the high-altitude Bf 109G-6/AS); II./JG 53 under Hauptmann Julius Meimburg at Frankfurt-Eschborn; III./JG 54 under Hauptmann Werner Schroer at Lüneberg; and II./JG 27 under Hauptmann Ludwig Franzisket at Unterschlauersbach. As previously mentioned, Franzisket was wounded and replaced by Börngen, who was also wounded and replaced by Major Karl-Wolfgang Redlich. The latter was killed attacking B-24s on 29 May, his place then being taken by Hauptmann Walter Blume. Like Redlich, Blume had been with the Fighter Unit Leader School immediately prior to joining II./JG 27.

On 24 May, the JGzbV flew its first major operation against the enemy in which a successful engagement took place, fighters intercepting some of the 517 B-17s that had set out to bomb Berlin under the cover of nearly 400 escorts. I. *Jagdkorps* threw 255 single-engined fighters at the raid, drawn from 1., 2., 3. and 7. *Jagddivisionen*. Bounced by P-51s over Rangsdorf, the German force, believed to have comprised elements of II./JG 27, II./JG 53 and III./JG 54, engaged in a massive, violent fighter-versus-fighter air battle, although a few aircraft did manage to break through to the bombers – the Fw 190s of III./JG 54 accounted for ten B-17s (including three *Herausschüsse*). Thirty-three B-17s were lost in total and a further 256 damaged. Dahl sent an ebullient report of events to Galland.

However, the Jagdwaffe suffered a blow in the north of Germany that day when Oberleutnant Hans-Heinrich Koenig, the one-eyed, provisional commander of I./JG 11 and the man who had been credited with the destruction of four B-24s on 29 April, was lost over Kaltenkirchen. He had just led his *Gruppe* into an attack in a wide 'arrowhead' formation against two or three *Pulks* of B-17s. As he closed in, he failed to pull away in time and his Fw 190 collided with his target. The B-17 exploded and one of the wings was torn off the Focke-Wulf. The fighter spun and spiralled helplessly towards the earth. No parachute was seen. It was Koenig's 28th victory. He was awarded the Knight's Cross posthumously on 2 September and promoted to Hauptmann.

Meanwhile, to the south, the Fifteenth Air Force despatched some of its B-24s to drop 265 tons of bombs on the marshalling yards at Toulon, one of 14 such targets in southern France. The bombers were picked up while still over the Mediterranean by 8. *Abteilung* of *Luftnachrichten-Regiment* 51 at the '*Rüsselkäfer*' ('Weevil') post at Saint-Raphaël on the French Riviera. '*Rüsselkäfer*' duly reported the enemy incursion to Oberst Friedrich Vollbracht's *Jafü Südfrankreich*, which had not long moved from Aix to a building in the idyllic grounds and vineyards of the Chateau La Nerthe, between Orange and Avignon.

The *Jafü* scrambled a small number of Bf 109s flown by the fighter instructor pilots of the *Einsatzkommando/Jagdgruppe Süd*, the operational training unit based at Orange-Caritat. Guided by the operators at '*Rüsselkäfer*', three Liberators were shot down and a B-17 was also claimed by a pilot of 3./*Jagdgruppe Süd*.[7]

Two days later, on 27 May, the Eighth Air Force's 3rd BD despatched 102 B-17s to bomb aircraft industry targets and a marshalling yard at Strasbourg, in France, and a further 98 Flying Fortresses to strike a railway yard in Karlsruhe. As the bombers crossed the French coast at Dieppe in two waves, the JGzbV ordered I./JG 5 airborne at 1100 hrs to intercept the bombers heading for Strasbourg. The *Gruppe* clashed with enemy fighters over the Alsace, losing seven pilots including Major Horst Carganico, the *Gruppenkommandeur*.

At 1126 hrs III./JG 3 took off with 21 Bf 109s, heading for Karlsruhe under 'Y'-guidance. Oberfeldwebel Georg Ströbele claimed a B-17 destroyed and Hauptmann Langer, the newly appointed *Gruppenkommandeur* who was also leading the *Gefechtsverband* in the air in his Bf 109G-6, a *Herausschuss*.

At 1217 hrs Langer led his *Gruppe* in for a frontal attack against the first wave of some 50–60 bombers, selecting the Flying Fortress in the outer right position in the right flight of the centre squadron. He fired two bursts, expending 55 rounds of 20 mm and 60 rounds of 13 mm ammunition, and saw strikes registering in the B-17's cabin area and on the starboard inboard engine and wing root. Thick white smoke plumed back as the bomber dropped away from its formation, and at the same time the defensive fire from the other Flying Fortresses stopped. The stricken B-17 plunged into the ground 70 km southwest of Strasbourg. It was Langer's 17th victory, and the 51st for the JGzbV.[8]

Operating together, II./JG 27 and II./JG 53 engaged B-17s in the vicinity of Nancy at 1215 hrs. The former *Gruppe* managed to destroy two Mustangs and a B-17, while II./JG 53's Oberfeldwebel Herbert Rollwage claimed one of the unit's score of three B-17s, as well as a P-51. But II./JG 27 lost three pilots and six Bf 109s to enemy action, including Feldwebel Rudolf Philipp of 6. *Staffel*, one of the unit's most accomplished aviators.

The fact was that throughout May, I. *Jagdkorps* still found it increasingly difficult to concentrate its forces against large-scale American raids, as its units were scattered across the Reich, had to fly great distances to reach the bombers and required long periods to assemble into *Gefechtsverbände*. Consequently, German fighters were often late in intercepting the *Viermots* or were forced to land early as a result of fuel shortage. Feldwebel Willi Unger of 11.(*Sturm*)/JG 3 recalled:

> The operational bases of our fighter units in the *Reichsverteidigung* were spread all over Germany. Attempts to maintain strength at critical times and in critical areas were made by the rapid redeployment of fighters to northern or southern Germany. Several *Gruppen* would combine together in the air from various airfields and were then led together from the ground to attack the approaching bombers. This did not always work.
>
> The bombers often 'cheated', flew towards one town, then changed their course and bombed a completely different target. As the flying endurance of our fighters with an auxiliary drop tank was maximum 2.5 hours, we were often forced to break off. There is no question of German fighters having the advantage – only disadvantages, since the numbers of American escort fighters were far superior to us, and they also operated at higher altitude, to our disadvantage.[9]

On the 28th, a record 1,341 heavies were despatched against six oil and rail targets in Germany, but nearly 500 were forced to abort due to weather. Against the balance of this force, I. *Jagdkorps* deployed 333 single- and twin-engined fighters, of which 266 engaged in combat. The bombers caused serious damage to a tank depot at Magdeburg, a sugar refinery at Dessau and three hydrogenation plants.

Amongst units sent to intercept the bombers aiming for Magdeburg was Hauptmann Ernst Düllberg's III./JG 27, whose Bf 109G-6s took off from Götzendorf/Leitha at 1247 hrs to intercept. Over the Wittenberg area of central Germany, however, the *Gruppe* sighted a small formation of B-17s on its way to bomb the Junkers works at Dessau, and engaged the *Viermots* at 7,000 m over the town of Zerbst to the east of Magdeburg.

Flying as a *Kettenführer* with 8./JG 27 was Unteroffizier Hans-Joachim Burkel, who selected a B-17 and made his approach from behind, below and to the right of the bomber, opening fire with his MG 151/20 cannon at a range of 350 m. Closing to 200 m, he saw hits in both starboard engines, after which the Flying Fortress started to burn and trail dense smoke. Burkel saw crew members bail out, but was not able to see the bomber go down since a pair of P-51 escort fighters appeared and unsuccessfully attempted to attack him. Burkel was able to escape and land safely at Bürnburg, following which he was awarded a *Herausschuss* (his second), along with four other pilots from the *Gruppe*. III./JG 27 claimed eight B-17s shot down for the loss of Unteroffizier Günther Weth of 7./JG 27 and three other aircraft, the pilots of which survived.

I. *Jagdkorps* recorded 39 aircraft destroyed in total, five missing and 34 badly damaged. The USAAF lost 26 B-17s and six B-24s, as well as 14 escort fighters.

On 29 May, the USSTAF launched a dual attack against oil and aircraft industry targets. In Austria, the Fifteenth Air Force's B-24s targeted the Messerschmitt assembly works at Wiener-Neustadt and a components factory at Atzgersdorf, while B-17s and B-24s bombed the airfield at Wollersdorf. Over all three targets, factory buildings and hangars were wrecked and the airfield peppered with craters, with its workshops and other buildings destroyed or badly damaged. To the north, the Eighth Air Force endeavoured to stretch the defence once again by bombing air industry targets in eastern Germany with its B-17s and sending its B-24s to attack oil and aircraft manufacturing plants along the Baltic coast.

B-17G *Ol' Dog* was one of 251 bombers from the 3rd BD which was assigned to attack aircraft plants at Leipzig. An aircraft of the 334th BS/95th BG based at Horham, in Suffolk, *Ol' Dog*, embarking on its 41st mission, had 2Lt Norman A. Ulrich at the controls. As the 95th crossed the English Channel that morning, navigator 2Lt Ralph W. Smithberger recalled:

> During this time, I checked my maps and charts. While over the Channel, I test-fired my two guns and our bombardier, 2Lt Don Payne, did the same with the chin turret guns. You could hear the clatter of 'fifties throughout the plane as all of our gunners followed suit. The crew was really tired because we had flown a maximum effort mission to Dessau the day before, and today was another big mission. On these deep penetration missions, we didn't get much sleep the night before.

As the B-17s of the 3rd BD neared their target, the low groups of the 2nd and 4th CW were attacked by '40 to 60' German fighters making frontal and rear attacks whilst the escort was not present. For the crew of *Ol' Dog*, a nightmare was about to begin, as Ulrich recalled:

> Flying formation is total monotony. We'd see fighters far off in the distance and wonder if they were ours or theirs. Suddenly, over the intercom, I heard, 'Fighters at ten o'clock' – and when I looked out the window, I could see the fighters in front of us. They were coming at us, and fast! Within seconds of this sighting, the world exploded and total monotony became total terror.

1Lt Peter P. Pinas was at the controls of B-17 *Able Mable* of the 334th BS in the Lead Flight of a Composite Group flying with the 100th BG. His crew later reported that the German fighters 'came in from dead ahead, straight and level, and passed between low and lead squadrons. Saw 3 B-17s at IP down from low squadron. 5 chutes out of one ship. Did not see others. All three under control. Two FWs came back and attacked stragglers, but ships stayed up'.[10]

According to 2Lt Ulrich:

> I remember two Fw 190s coming at us, but one in particular seemed to have us in his sights with his cannon blazing away. I could feel the impact of his shells hitting our plane, but at the same time I saw the Fw 190 getting hits and a large piece of it falling off. Suddenly, he began to smoke, and I watched him fly by the cockpit, going down.
>
> This attack happened in a matter of seconds. In the meantime, the Fw 190 had done a good job on us. I remember seeing the Plexiglas nose explode. Cannon shells had made a shambles of our cockpit instruments. Our number two engine was hit and windmilling. The radio compartment and bomb-bay had been destroyed. Our left gun position had been knocked out, with Sgt [Eugene H.] Buhler being wounded. Cannon shells tore off a large chunk of our left rear stabiliser. Air streaming through our nose and the windmilling number two engine caused a severe drag on the plane, which seemed to stop in mid-air.

Ol' Dog peeled away to the left, remarkably still under control and with no fire or smoke trailing from it. The crew pulled on their parachutes and prepared to bail out, but then from the cockpit Ulrich asked his men to wait as the Flying Fortress was still flyable. However, due to the general battle damage, *Ol' Dog* had fallen behind its formation and was alone – a straggler, damaged and vulnerable, but still flying. Ulrich dropped from 29,000 ft to fly as low as possible to avoid Flak and fighters. The decision was then taken to turn north towards neutral Sweden, the closest friendly territory. All surplus weight was jettisoned – guns, ammunition, Flak suits, radio equipment and parachutes. Even the ball turret was released. Eventually, the B-17 was flying just 50 ft above the ground.

At around this time, two Fw 190s of IV.(*Sturm*)/JG 3 were returning to Salzwedel from their mission against the bombers. One of these was flown by Unteroffizier Karl-Heinz Schmidt, who had joined *Sturmstaffel* 1 several weeks earlier. As of 8 May, Schmidt had been credited with three victories. Approaching Salzwedel, he spotted the stricken B-17 and manoeuvred to intercept. Ulrich recalled:

> The first Fw 190 came at us head-on, firing away. I thought he was going to come right through the pilot's window. Andy [SSgt Leon E. Anderson] opened up on the approaching fighter from his turret. In a split second, cannon shells hit the turret, knocking Andy from it, and he fell on us, wounded and bleeding. The Fw 190 flew to the right of our cabin and over the wing. You could see him circling to come around for a second attack.
>
> I realised it was over at this point, with our only turret knocked out and with wounded aboard. I knew we were about to be shot down in flames, so I immediately ordered George [co-pilot 2Lt George D. Reiff] to lower the landing gear as a sign of surrender. While all this was happening, the second Fw 190 was coming in for a side attack. At the last second, he recognised that we were surrendering and waggled his wings, but not before buzzing our cockpit and veering off. He flew so close to our cabin that I thought I could touch him. As we flew on, the two Fw 190s circled us, and you could see them waving in their cockpits and we waved back.

This moment is borne out by one of Unteroffizier Karl-Heinz Schmidt's former *Sturmstaffel* comrades, Feldwebel Oskar Bösch, who remembered:

> As he [Schmidt] told the story, the B-17 was in bad shape flying at 50 m above ground level when he intercepted it on the flight back to Salzwedel. He flew formation and signalled it to land. After some hesitation, it finally belly-landed into a farmer's field. After landing at Salzwedel, Schmidt drove out to the B-17 to extend 'welcome' greetings. It was still a gentleman's war.[11]

Ol' Dog came down close to the town of Packebusch, around 30 km southeast of Salzwedel, with 'gasoline pouring out of the fuel lines where

[the] number two [engine] had been'. Briefly, the Boeing stood up on its nose and then crashed back down. It was one of 34 bombers lost by the Eighth that day.

In a further blow to the Luftwaffe, Major Friedrich-Karl Müller, the *Kommodore* of JG 3, collided with another machine and he was killed when he attempted to crash-land at Salzwedel. Having flown some 600 missions, Müller's death added to the growing list of valued formation leaders who had lost their lives defending the German homeland.

29 May also saw Me 410s of I. and II./ZG 26 scrambled from Königsberg. According to a later-captured, unnamed *Staffelkapitän*, one *Staffel* received information that B-17s were attacking Schneidemühl airfield unescorted, and the plan was for four Me 410s to attack the top, rear squadron of Flying Fortresses head-on in a dive. When the bombers were encountered, however, and the Messerschmitts began their turn to attack from 900 m and above, they were unexpectedly bounced by P-51s, and three of the four *Zerstörer* were shot down. The *Staffelkapitän* was able to escape and crash-land, although his radio operator was killed.

Schmid summarised the month of May 1944 thus:

> American fighters, the strength of which had increased considerably, were in a position to demonstrate their air superiority in various respects. Especially impressive was the perfect and accurate cover they provided for the bombers as they made their incursions, and also as they returned to their bases. The fighter escort, flying up to an hour ahead of the bombers, made the commitment of German air defence against the bombers extremely difficult, and sometimes even impossible. Whenever German fighter units succeeded in attacking an American bomber stream, it was surprising in what short period of time American fighters were concentrated in the area in which the bombers were under attack.[12]

I. *Jagdkorps* calculated that the ratio of total American air superiority (bombers and fighters) stood at 7.7 to 1 over German strength, whilst in fighters alone, American strength stood at 3.8 to 1.

Meanwhile, the OKL had been encouraged by the performance of both the *Sturmstaffel* and IV.(*Sturm*)/JG 3. It was decided to increase the strength of the *Sturmgruppe* in late May by assigning to it 2./JG 51, an Fw 190-equipped *Staffel* that had returned from the Eastern Front under the command of the very experienced Oberleutnant Horst Haase. Haase's *Staffel* would eventually be fully integrated into IV.(*Sturm*)/JG 3 as

16. *Staffel* in August. Furthermore, OKL ordered the establishment of two new *Sturmgruppen*, II.(*Sturm*)/JG 4 and II.(*Sturm*)/JG 300.

Despite all the adversities faced by the Luftwaffe's fighter pilots over the Reich, according to the Eighth Air Force the numbers of bombers being lost 'increased steadily up to April 1944' as a result of the expansion of bombing operations. This, in itself, showed that the Luftwaffe's deployment of *Gefechtsverbände*, its attacks at carefully chosen times and places, such as at the limit of escort protection, and determined, mass operations by close-range *Sturm* fighters continued to take their toll. No fewer than 361 bombers were lost in April, and the figure fluctuated thereafter at around 200–300 per month.[13]

In mid-May 1944, Oberstleutnant von Kornatzki was ordered to set up II.(*Sturm*)/JG 4 at Salzwedel and Welzow. As the new *Gruppe*'s personnel had previously served with a Ju 88 long-range fighter *Staffel* employed against Allied convoys over the Atlantic, von Kornatzki decided that to assist with conversion and combat training he would gather together a solid core of pilots from *Sturmstaffel* 1 who understood what was required and possessed the necessary combat experience. Consequently, a number of former *Sturmstaffel* 1 pilots joined the *Gruppe*, and the former Ju 88 pilots were hastily converted to the Fw 190 at Hohensalza.[14]

However, II.(*Sturm*)/JG 4 had to wait until late July to receive its first Fw 190A-8/R2, and for most of the summer its personnel were occupied undertaking type conversion, as well as technical and tactical training.

20

Imminent Danger West

In the late autumn of 1943, despite his priorities being directed towards the aerial defence of the Reich, Generalmajor Josef Schmid, along with most senior German military commanders, was not blind to the strong likelihood that the Allies would launch an invasion of Europe at some point in 1944 – indeed, it was inevitable.

During the summer, Göring had devised a system of codewords intended to trigger such defensive measures as organised by the Luftwaffe in the event of an invasion. Transmission of the codewords 'Imminent Danger North' signalled an invasion of Norway or Denmark, 'Imminent Danger West' signalled a landing in the coastal areas of the Netherlands, Belgium or western France, and 'Imminent Danger South' signalled an invasion in southern France.

Schmid understood that a successful aerial interception of any invasion would be of 'decisive significance' to the course of the war, and in December 1943 he ordered the establishment of a small but dedicated 'Transfer Staff' within I. *Jagdkorps* and tasked it with preparing and arranging the transfer of fighter units from the *Reichsverteidigung* into any possible invasion zone. Formed on 8 December 1943 under Oberst Otto von Lachemaier, the Transfer Staff was based within I. *Jagdkorps'* headquarters and comprised, aside from von Lachemaier, three officers of Hauptmann rank and a limited number of junior personnel, all of whom reported directly to Schmid.

Provisional schedules were drawn up taking into account all possible eventualities, with lines of communication established between the Transfer Staff and the staffs of the respective *Jagddivisionen* and *Luftgau* in the areas of potential risk. Attempts were also made to train the home defence fighter units in bombing and strafing of ground and water-borne targets. Finally, studies were made into tidal and meteorological conditions along the French coast. By the spring of 1944, more than 1,000 fighters were on standby in the Reich.

Schmid also arranged conferences at which he explained to the commanders of the home defence units the measures being taken. This included briefing von Lachemaier and his staff, whose job it was to ensure the availability of equipment, ammunition and motor vehicles, as well as personally reconnoitring the proposed forward airfields and preparing them in cooperation with their staffs. They also drew up the air and land transfer routes, and were to ensure adequate supplies for the units during their transfers and immediately upon their arrival at receiving airfields. Von Lachemaier and his staff found their job tough, as he later wrote:

> In itself, preparation for the transfer of flying units from the Reich to France and for the conversion of these units' role and equipment to another type of employment was nothing unusual. But it was the conditions existing during the period of preparation that were unusual.
>
> The Reich defence fighter units were almost daily engaged in fierce combat against Allied air attacks. They sustained heavy losses and their operations absorbed commanders and their pilots to such an extent that anything not regarded as essentially necessary for the task in hand was liable to be classed of secondary importance.
>
> The great number of written orders, supplements and amendments issued by OKL as a result of the constantly changing overall situation in the *Reichsverteidigung* not only impaired the transfer operation, but caused much confusion in the staff and units of the heavily strained home air defence.
>
> An officer responsible for preparation of the transfer operation was appointed in each *Jagddivision*, *Jagdgeschwader*, *Jagdgruppe* and *Staffel*. One officer from the Transfer Staff remained at I. *Jagdkorps* headquarters to receive orders, to receive and forward reports and to receive and answer inquiries related to the 'Imminent Danger' policy. However, the head of the staff and two of its officers were constantly on the move in aircraft or by car, offering assistance to the units and clarifying problems. This activity showed its results especially in respect to the speeding up of additional supplies of ammunition and other materiel and vehicles effected in close association with the supply agencies of *Luftflotte Reich* and I. *Jagdkorps* headquarters.

At the end of March 1944, von Lachemaier reported to Schmid that preparations for an 'Imminent Danger' codeword had been completed, and that the time required from the moment the codeword was issued by I. *Jagdkorps* headquarters to the time the *Jagdgruppen* were ready for transfer would be approximately two hours. In a summary of his mission, von Lachemaier concluded:

> Upon orders of the I. *Jagdkorps*, I inspected all fighter units in the area of the *Reichsverteidigung* during the months preceding D-Day. Combat morale and bearing of the men in the *Reichsverteidigung* were admirable. This did not only apply to the flight crews, but was also true of the technical ground personnel.
>
> There were only two sources from which the fighter units could gather strength to keep up their unique attitude. These were, firstly, their recognition of the necessity of their fight for their bleeding homeland and their commitment in combat which was beyond any reproach; and secondly, the confidence in their commanders up to their commanding general, who demanded total commitment in combat, but who also appreciated their accomplishments and protected their honour as soldiers.
>
> At that time there was not much to inspire the heart of a young soldier with enthusiasm. The fighting became more unequal from day to day, the numerical superiority of the attackers became overwhelming, the homeland more and more damaged, the successes obtained necessarily more and more limited, confidence decreased steadily, and finally, the disgraceful reproaches by the German High Command became the worst enemy of all.[1]

In light of recent operations against naval vessels supporting the Allied seaborne invasion of Italy, OKL envisaged the need for both Fw 190s and Bf 109s to make close-formation diving attacks in *Gruppe* and *Staffel* strength with bombs against ships in the landing area, followed, where possible, by strafing attacks against ships and troops, again in *Staffel* strength.

Schmid later described the condition of the Jagdwaffe a few days before the Allied invasion of France:

> Heavy losses, as well as the great physical and psychological strain imposed on German fighter pilots, reduced the combat value of our units in April and May 1944. The young replacements showed deficiencies in flying and radio usage. They lacked combat experience, particularly in respect to high-altitude operations. Time and opportunities for training in the operational units was lacking to an increasing extent. The shortage of qualified formation leaders increased. The excessive strain caused by almost uninterrupted commitment resulted in combat fatigue. Experienced fighter pilots

reached the limit of their efficiency. They were worn out by the many missions they had flown and needed a rest. All these factors resulted in a number of failed missions.

For the first time, branches of the Wehrmacht, Luftwaffe, Government and Party unjustifiably reproached the fighter units of the home air defence for cowardice. In view of these accusations, it should be noted that the inferior German day fighter forces fought bravely and were subjected – especially in May – to the heaviest strain, which admittedly reduced the substance of their personnel and materiel, yet did not seriously obstruct the overall structure of these forces. The limited American offensive activities against the Reich's territory in the first week of June offered the day fighter forces of the home air defence a brief respite for regeneration. Thus, it was possible that the day fighter *Geschwader* were reasonably intact and ready for defensive operations against the invasion in France.

In February 1944, on the suggestion of senior Luftwaffe officers, E.Kdo 25 explored the feasibility of spraying fouling chemicals onto the engines and windscreens of enemy bombers. The proposals became the subject of much debate and investigation, and resulted in a salvaged engine from a downed USAAF bomber being sent to the chemical firm of IG Farben, which was instructed to conduct experiments with prospective chemicals. Hauptmann Horst Geyer recalled:

> One member of the unit had contacts with the IG Farben company, and he worked with them on trials designed to foul and clog up an aircraft engine using certain chemicals. They found that the quantity of chemical needed even to 'kill' one engine was too great, so to have brought down a four-engined bomber would have been impossible.

Indeed, by June 1944, Geyer noted that all efforts in this direction had thus far proved without success. The *Kommando* also consulted Dr. von Harz of the research laboratories at the chemical and weapons company Dynamit Nobel A.G. in Troisdorf. Von Harz advised the officers of E.Kdo 25 that the agents available did not possess sufficient energy to destroy an engine.

It had also been suggested that the use of ozone could damage the engines of enemy aircraft, but Geyer conceded that procuring it was extremely difficult, and, in any event, there were no devices available to carry and spray the required quantities of the substance, other than at the

DVL at Berlin-Adlershof. He recommended that no further testing should be carried out. Geyer also recalled that:

> Tests were carried out at Rechlin with chemicals designed to spray over cockpit and gun turret Plexiglas to adhere to it and to mask it, but not, necessarily, to destroy it. Civilian laboratory researchers analysed fragments of windshields from downed B-17s and B-24s in an effort to determine the manufactured composition of the Plexiglas. They subsequently developed certain types of chemicals in liquid and powdered form which could be dispersed over the glass. Rechlin then asked us to conduct trials using an Fw 190, and we found that, depending on which kind of chemicals were being used, it was not necessary to use large quantities.

Geyer remembered a group of chemists visiting the *Kommando*'s airfield at Parchim one day in the summer of 1944 to deliver a sample of one such 'white liquid', which was duly sprayed over a large piece of Plexiglas:

> As soon as the liquid hit the glass, you went blind – you couldn't see anything in front of you. But I wasn't sure about it, and I sent a report to Galland, warning him that, if necessary, American bomber crews would attempt to break their windshields if they were sprayed, thus nullifying the effect. Galland understood what I was saying. But Göring also grew worried about the idea and instructed Galland not to pursue it, since he was concerned that the enemy would employ the same methods against us.[2]

Geyer did remember one Fw 190 being fitted with underwing tanks with valves designed to eject a chemical spray. The valves were of an open-or-shut, one-use only, jettisonable type, and they were intended to be used following a head-on attack against an enemy bomber formation. The Fw 190 would make a standard approach, using cannon, pass over the formation and then the pilot was to open the valves to the tanks to spray the American aircraft. No such operations were ever carried out, however.

On 6 June, the Allies landed, pouring 155,000 men and hundreds of vehicles onto the beaches of Normandy. Operation *Overlord*, better known as D-Day, remains the greatest amphibious invasion in history. The planning was unprecedented, the risks colossal. Allied air cover was immense, with sufficient capability to fly more than 14,500 sorties within the first 24 hours. Only two Luftwaffe fighter sorties were flown that morning, when the *Geschwaderkommodore* of JG 26, Oberstleutnant Josef Priller, and his wingman swooped in at 15 m over the British landing area at 'Sword' beach, their Fw 190s raking disembarking troops and armour with cannon and machine gun fire.

In the early hours of the 6th, teleprinters at the OKL had chattered out a string of warnings and situation reports from the *Jagddivision* headquarters, but the vital instruction to proceed with the transfer of the home defence units to the invasion zone never materialised. OKL dithered in indecision. The threat of bad weather over the central German mountain range risked jeopardising the whole transfer, but late that morning, despite misgivings voiced by Galland, I. *Jagdkorps* acted unilaterally and ordered the transfer to proceed.

By early afternoon the first units began to move, although poor weather conditions prevented many from transferring until evening. Nevertheless, by the morning of the 7th, 400 fighters had arrived in France. On 6 June, II. *Jagdkorps* had just 121 operable aircraft. When contacted, Göring was bewildered at OKL's lack of reaction.

The day the Allies landed in Normandy, Galland was apparently making a visit to E.Kdo 25 at Parchim to inspect new, experimental fighter weapons in the war against the bombers. Whilst the technology on display was admirable for the time, by definition, their experimental status meant the weapons could be dangerous to the operator.

That day, Galland watched as Unteroffizier Günter Lüdke took off in an Fw 190A-8 fitted with a 'shotgun' device known as '*Laternenpfahl*' (Lamp Post). The latter consisted of two 128 mm cannon installed in the fuselage immediately aft of the cockpit with the barrels protruding downwards that were intended to fire 88 mm shrapnel grenades. The grenades were loaded with 300 fragmentation shards, and they were designed to be fired into a bomber's fuel tanks from above.

Sensibly wearing a steel helmet and goggles, Lüdke attempted a trial firing, but was badly wounded in the process, sustaining head injuries as a result of the ignition and blast. The aircraft was written off and further work on the '*Laternenpfahl*' abandoned.[3]

As von Lachemaier had promised, within days of the invasion just under 1,000 fighters had arrived in France from Germany drawn from JGs 1, 3, 11, 27, 77 and 301. These aircraft moved into a 100 km-long belt of airfields running parallel to the Channel coast constructed by *Luftflotte* 3. But then the debacle began. Von Lachemaier recorded, 'The transfer operation was, as everything was at that time, only a drop in the bucket. This drop was unable to bring about any change in the overall situation'.

The Chief-of-Staff of II. *Jagdkorps* reported:

> Our own day fighter forces were at first employed exclusively on low-level attacks on landing craft and landing points and as fighter cover for the fighter-bomber formations of II. *Fliegerkorps*, which were attacking the same objectives. Often, the enemy's superior fighter defence intercepted our own formations before they could reach the invasion front, and after the latter had run out of ammunition and fuel, they were forced to return without having carried out their actual mission.[4]

Operating from barely prepared emergency strips, most of them without sufficient buildings, ammunition or fuel, and completely lacking dispersal points, blast shelters, teleprinters and radio installations, the German fighters struggled throughout June and July to make even a dent against the Allied air forces. As early as mid-June, *Luftflotte* 3 had lost 75 per cent of the strength it possessed immediately prior to the landings, and the units were plagued by technical problems and accidents.

The emergency movement of a German home defence unit to the Invasion Front in June 1944 is typified by Hauptmann Karl-Heinz Langer's III./JG 3 at Ansbach – the *Gruppe* Galland had identified as the Luftwaffe's premier Reich defence unit under Dahl. It first became aware of what was happening on the Normandy coast at 0830 hrs on the morning of 6 June when Langer received the 'Imminent Danger West' code. Advance detachments and transport were placed on standby. At 0916 hrs, the unit's war diary records 'Reich defence is now out of the question for the *Gruppe*. Transfer in two hours is to be ensured'.

Just over an hour later, 49 Bf 109s and eight Ju 52/3m transports loaded with groundcrew and essential equipment were ready for the move to Normandy. The unit was to transfer 'as a fighter *Gruppe*, not as a fighter-bomber *Gruppe*. The ETCs [bomb racks] will follow overland'. At 1215 hrs, the *Gruppe* was advised that it was to head for Saint-André-de-l'Eure, a poorly equipped airfield with two concrete runways, south of Évreux, 800 km from its German base. The rest of the *Gruppe*'s personnel and equipment would follow by road.

However, if the unit's staff felt good reason to complain about operational shortcomings in the Reich, they had a shock when they arrived at Saint-André-de-l'Eure. The airfield had been subjected to Allied air attack on several occasions, leaving just one useable runway. The field lacked sufficient telephone lines, and this meant that operational orders would usually only arrive at time of take-off. The aircraft dispersals were so far away from the runways that it was impossible to effect a mass take-off. Engine coolant heated up in the aircraft before they reached the runways, and they had to be guided carefully past bomb dumps when taxiing.

Langer immediately requested an alternative field that could adequately meet the requirements of a *Jagdgruppe* and one that was not so vulnerable to attack from the air.

Notwithstanding, the unit went straight into action the following day (7 June), when 28 of its Messerschmitts attacked shipping and landing craft at the mouth of the Orne. Later in the day, the *Gruppe* sent up 18 Bf 109s to escort fighter-bombers attacking enemy armour. Six pilots were shot down or lost to shipborne Flak and 75 per cent of the aircraft which saw operations were reported damaged to some degree. Over the next three days, III./JG 3 bombed shipping targets with 250-kg bombs, engaged P-47s and P-51s and acted as escort for fighter-bombers and bombers over the Orne.

On the 9th, the RAF bombed Saint-André-de-l'Eure and the *Gruppe* was forced to transfer to Marcilly, a poorly equipped airfield five kilometres to the south. This inconvenience was countered to some extent on 10 June when the unit claimed three Mustangs shot down.[5]

Following a day when the unit flew three fighter-bomber missions against landing craft, on the 13th another transfer ensued when III./JG 3 moved to Francheville, from where it operated under Oberst Karl Hentschel's 5. *Jagddivision* based in Paris. Over the next two weeks, working with II./JG 3 and elements of JG 11, II./JG 53, JGs 1, 26 and 27 and III./JG 54, the *Gruppe* conducted several 'Freie Jagd' patrols and fighter-bomber, ground-attack and tactical reconnaissance missions. It also engaged heavy bombers.

The following week, the unit conducted further ground-attack sorties, during which four more pilots were lost and five posted missing. The *Staffelführer* of 9./JG 3, Leutnant Dieter Zink, told a fellow prisoner after he was shot down by enemy anti-aircraft fire in his Bf 109G-6 near Bretteville-sur-Odon on 11 July 1944:

> Allied numerical superiority is quite colossal. You could say that their superiority in numbers is in the ratio of 20-to-1, and then their materiel is better, and also their personnel. All our pilots are inexperienced, while theirs are all fairly experienced. Better aircraft too – but there's nothing

we can do about that. We had to stand on our airfield looking up at the sky, watching them fly over. We had six aircraft on the ground ready for operations, and they used to circle about up there with between 80 and 100 aircraft. To take off is suicidal.[6]

The Allies constantly strafed and bombed the airfields, and a new pilot, lacking in training and flying time, was lucky to survive more than three sorties. Major Hans-Ekkehard Bob, who commanded II./JG 3 operating out of Dreux, recalled:

We were often attacked taking off, causing one aircraft taking off to be blocked by another. Our position was extremely unpleasant. We reckoned in operating strength we were outnumbered ten-to-one. In fact, operations were really more an exercise in self-preservation.[7]

Self-preservation must have been uppermost in the minds of the men of II./JG 1 in the days immediately following the invasion when the unit was based at Le Mans under the temporary command of Oberleutnant Rüdiger Kirchmayr. On the night of 9–10 June, 109 RAF Lancaster and Halifax bombers, led by Pathfinder Mosquitos, targeted the airfield. Many of the *Gruppe*'s Fw 190s and vehicles were destroyed or damaged and the unit was subsequently grounded while the 300 bomb craters which scarred the airfield's surface were filled in and numerous unexploded bombs dealt with.

Finally, after days of frustrating inactivity, the unit moved to Essay, which was also bombed three days later, forcing another transfer to Semalle, a rough landing strip some six kilometres northeast of Alençon. By late July, although II./JG 1 was able to report a relatively full complement of pilots, most of these were fresh arrivals from the training schools. None of the *Gruppe*'s component *Staffeln* possessed an experienced *Staffelkapitän*, but rather temporary, field-appointed *Staffelführer*, two of whom were experienced NCOs.

Oberfeldwebel Herbert Kaiser, a veteran airman who flew with 7./JG 1, was rushed to Normandy in June 1944. He had joined the *Geschwader* at the beginning of that year from JG 77, with whom he had seen earlier action in North Africa, the Mediterranean and Russia, and had been awarded the Knight's Cross in March 1943 when his victory tally stood at 45. Despite being a combat veteran, Kaiser remembered the air fighting on the invasion front as some of the toughest. He recalled the Luftwaffe being, as he put it, 'ground into the earth':

At the end of June 1944, I was with 7./JG 1 on an airfield just outside Paris and experienced an excellent example of the almost complete air superiority enjoyed by the Allies. We were detailed to intercept a formation of incoming Allied bombers in the Normandy area. We had to take off in the smallest of flights (usually two to four aircraft) due to the Allied fighters, which almost always waited above our airfields for our fighters to emerge from cloud cover. We would be forced to sneak towards the target area by hedge-hopping over the terrain to take advantage of as much natural camouflage as possible. Flying just a few metres above the ground kept us off the radar screens, but sometimes put us into the side of a hill. We would only climb to altitude once we reached the point of attack.

My flight of four aircraft sighted a formation of escorting Spitfires, and we positioned ourselves to engage them. But right at that moment, we were jumped by another formation of Allied fighters and, in the process, I lost all three of my fellow pilots. Escape for me seemed impossible, and it was only because of my experience as a flier that I was able to get myself into some nearby cloud and save my skin.

At this time the odds were against us, and you could count on the fingers of one hand the days you expected to live. Frankly, I am amazed Luftwaffe fighter pilots had any nerve left at all, let alone the ability to attempt to fight under such conditions.[8]

On 9 August, Kaiser's *Staffel* was assigned to intercept a formation of some 300 Allied aircraft. Preparing to attack a group of RAF Lancasters, he was bounced from out of the sun by Spitfires near Paris and his Bf 109G received severe damage. Badly wounded, Kaiser opened the canopy of his burning fighter and bailed out, but his right leg became entangled in his parachute lines. He landed behind German lines with multiple fractures to his right thigh and was hospitalised until February 1945.

Galland, too, spent several days with the units in the West, after which he wrote:

My impressions were shattering. In addition to the appalling conditions, there was a far-reaching decline in morale. This feeling of irrevocable inferiority, the heavy losses, the hopelessness of the fighting, which had never before been so clearly demonstrated to us, the reproaches from above, the disrepute into which the Luftwaffe had fallen among the other arms of the forces from no fault of the individual, together with all the other burdens that the war at this stage had brought to every German, were the most severe test ever experienced by the Luftwaffe.[9]

4. and 5. *Jagddivisionen* had concentrated the four *Jagdgeschwader* under their command in the Paris–Lille area, but it quickly became evident that even

Lille was too exposed to danger. German fighters were forced to take off as soon as plots of enemy aircraft were received, if they were not to run the risk of being pinned to the ground by prowling Allied fighters. Even with drop tanks, this often resulted in German fighters being short of fuel by the time they were expected to engage US bombers. Consequently, II. *Jagdkorps* suggested the withdrawal of these fighters into the Reims–Romilly–Creil area, but as a result of poor preparation and the risk of overcrowding on these more easterly airfields, which were already being used by Luftwaffe bomber and nightfighter units, this did not take place.

Perhaps the most drastic transfer was the movement of some 50+ Fw 190A-8s of IV./JG 3 to the invasion zone, thus, briefly, depriving the defence of the Reich of its first, dedicated *Sturm* unit. The *Sturmjäger* arrived at Dreux from Salzwedel on the afternoon of 8 June, with the first ground equipment and crews arriving in six Ju 52/3ms shortly thereafter. Subsequent attempts at operations were continually disrupted by air raids and the threat from Allied fighters.

It has been argued that the transfer of such heavily armed and armoured fighters for work over Normandy was inappropriate. Equally, the Fw 190A-8/R2s of 10. and 11./JG 3 perhaps offered greater protection to their pilots whilst deployed with SC 250 bombs as fighter-bombers against enemy shipping and landing craft and on battlefield support north of Caen than did the Bf 109s and Fw 190s of other units. No casualties or aircraft losses were suffered by the unit while it was in Normandy, but on 10 June Dreux was bombed by B-24s and, with the unit having achieved only marginal results, it was decided to send IV./JG 3 back to the Reich. By 15 June the *Gruppe* was based at Eisenstadt, an airfield 45 km southeast of Vienna.

The rush to Normandy brought a realisation among many younger, lower-ranking fighter pilots of just how great the odds were stacked against them wherever they served and how strained resources were. But there was a great difference between being shot down over Normandy and over Germany. Feldwebel Hans Knabben of 6./JG 1 bailed out of his Fw 190A-8 near Isigny, in France, on 22 June 1944, while Unteroffizier Heinz Römer of 9./JG 3 was shot down in his Bf 109G-6 and bailed out over the Orne 13 days earlier. Both pilots were captured. While being held by the British, the two men struck up a conversation with a curious German paratrooper who had been captured in the fighting near Carentan.

'They had intended having 1,000 aircraft for the Defence of the Reich', Römer told the paratrooper, 'but actually they only have 400'. 'How is it that they only have 400 aircraft?' the paratrooper enquired, adding that he had seen plenty of Luftwaffe units in the Homeland. 'Just look at those

"*Geschwader*", Römer retorted. 'How many pilots fit for flying are there among them? So many crashed and most of them are in hospitals'.

For his part, Knabben did concede, albeit with some disingenuity, that there was a 'benefit' to bailing out over the Reich. 'Whenever a pilot bails out over Germany, they can get into the nearest aircraft and take off again'. 'The good thing about being in the Reich Defence', added Römer, 'was that when you bailed out, you could make a service call and return by Second Class [train], and you could claim a sleeping compartment if the train had any. You had a pass enabling you to apply for assistance to all the authorities so that you should be able to get back to your unit in the quickest possible way'.[10]

But bailing out was always hazardous. Oberleutnant Johannes 'Focke' Naumann, the *Kommandeur* of II./JG 26 and a veteran fighter pilot, was hit by British anti-aircraft fire southwest of Caen in his Fw 190 and had to leave his aircraft at a height of 200 m. As he did so, his legs struck the rear of the Focke-Wulf and he suffered severe injuries.[11]

In committing virtually its entire defence force into the wasting cauldron of Normandy, the Luftwaffe made it easier for the Allies to resume their strategic bombing campaign against the Reich and, in particular, against oil targets. In June, during the course of 17 major raids, 20,000 tons of bombs rained down on key oil installations throughout Germany, Hungary, Romania and Bulgaria. Aviation fuel output had fallen from 214,000 tons in March to 120,000 tons in May and to 74,000 tons in June. At the beginning of June, Luftwaffe fuel stocks stood at 540,000 tons. By 1 July, this was down to 218,400 tons.

On the 17th, Generaloberst Hans-Jürgen Stumpff ordered the units under his command at *Luftflotte Reich* to actively conserve fuel:

> The fuel situation and the present rate of consumption at the front necessitate the imposition of immediate measures to save fuel. Only by making utmost reductions, above all in general air activity and also in operations, will it be possible to overcome the present situation. Unnecessary use of fuel is equivalent to sabotaging the war effort.[12]

Luftflotte Reich also evaluated operations in June in a report to OKL. It made for sombre reading:

> As a result of the invasion, the main effort of fighter commitment was, to a considerable extent, shifted to the area of *Luftflotte* 3. The relief of Reich territory from enemy air attack which had been expected as a result of the invasion was realised to only a very small extent.

On the contrary, the enemy directed the main effort of his offensive action against those war production plants most important at the time, against fighter production and, above all, against oil supply. Further effective support on all defensive fronts, especially the West, can be insured only if there is an undisturbed production of aircraft and the required fuel. Only then can an acceptable balance of power in the air be maintained.

It is therefore of decisive importance for the outcome of the war that primarily gasoline supply does not suffer any further interruption. The systematic and continued attacks against oil production constitute, at present, the most acute danger.

As a result of the transfer of fighter units to France, the defence of the Reich was left seriously depleted. Immediately after the invasion, only a scratch force was available to intercept USAAF daylight raids comprised of the single-engined *Wilde Sau* nightfighter *Gruppen*, four twin-engined *Zerstörer Gruppen*, three operational training *Gruppen* in Silesia and East Prussia, some fighter school units, a Bf 109-equipped Hungarian fighter unit and a test unit equipped with a small number of the new rocket-powered Me 163 interceptors.

On 20 June 1944, Oberst Ulrich Diesing, a former *Zerstörer* pilot attached to the RLM, addressed a gathering of *Gauleiter* and Party officials as the representative of Generalfeldmarschall Milch:

In regard to day fighters, our defences have already shown an improvement. But operations are still shouting for more and more aircraft, and with justification, for we have to combat not only enemy fighters but also hordes of four-engined bombers, which constitute a formidable adversary, particularly during the day.

We must, therefore, far exceed our present production. The opportunity is there. All our fighters are capable of being used offensively and of carrying bombs. That was done because in addition to the grave threat of the four-engined bomber to our homeland, the danger of invasion was obvious. We are all aware that the fate of the war rests with the Invasion. The Invasion has now been with us for 14 days. Now the enemy has a foothold on the Continent. But there is no cause for alarm. We must master the situation, and from what we hear it can be mastered, provided that we rapidly build up a frontline air force on a par with the enemy.

Yesterday, I spoke with General Galland, who had come back from the front. Galland stated quite clearly that as far as performance goes, our fighters are adequate and indeed, in most cases, superior at the altitudes at which the Invasion fighting is taking place, but that unfortunately, they were by no means sufficient in numbers. The morale of our fighter pilots, however, was high, as high as in the days of the great offensives on the Western and Eastern Fronts.

A considerable number of enemy aircraft have been shot down. To name but one example, in the initial stages, Oberstleutnant [Josef] Priller [*Kommodore* of JG 26] had five successive kills.

The problem now is to provide the necessary numbers. If we can keep up a supply of these aircraft to the front during the next few months, I believe that we shall be able to force a decision in the air war. I believe that a decision must come this summer. Our aircrews have the spirit to fly these fighters and they have the faith that they can turn the tide of battle against our enemies in the West, however bitter the struggle.

21

All-Out Defence

While the bulk of the German daylight fighter force from the Reich was fighting its battles over France, there was still the need to provide an adequate and effective air defence over the Homeland. Obviously, and in accordance with the Allies' strategic plan, the scale of damage inflicted as a result of the bombing offensive was having a serious effect on German production capability. In reporting to the *Jägerstab* on 30 June 1944, the senior engineer at the RLM, Generalstabs.-Ing. Roluf Lucht, described what he had seen during a recent post-raid tour of aircraft production plants in the Leipzig and Magdeburg areas:

> From above, Oschersleben looked devastated. All the sticks of bombs missed the target, but incendiaries fell right on the works. There were major fires. They will probably be able to carry on production except for small parts, where it is too early to tell. They have lost ten to twelve aircraft. Four Mustangs were shot down and destroyed when they hit the ground. The factory gun detachment did its best to defend; the works representative was firing too. They brought down one of the raiders but that was all. At Bernburg – little damage. Two aircraft hit, one hangar wrecked. There was nothing in it – just a small fighter hangar. A second assembly shop received four direct hits, but it will be fully working again today. For the present they are working under the open sky.[1]

Elsewhere, the 5 cm BK 5 cannon that had been fitted into the Me 410 continued to prove troublesome. Galland had had enough, and spoke to Göring's adjutant, Oberst i.G. von Brauchitsch. During the evening of 6 July, Brauchitsch informed General der Flieger Karl Koller, Chief of the *Luftwaffenführungsstab*, that Göring wanted II./ZG 26's operations with the weapon stopped because they were achieving 'no practical results', and that the unit should be moved to the East for deployment in the anti-tank role.

While Koller thought this 'not a bad suggestion in itself', the fact was there were no aircraft and crews available to replace the *Gruppe* in the defence of the Reich.[2]

The next day (7 July), the aircraft and synthetic oil plants were targeted again by the Eighth Air Force when it sent 939 B-17s and B-24s, escorted by more than 650 fighters, to attack a range of targets in central Germany, but this time the defenders were ready and they were to inflict a devastating blow on the USAAF.

As the Liberators of the 492nd BG approached Oschersleben from the west, a *Gefechtsverband* led by the recently appointed *Kommodore* of JG 300, Major Walther Dahl, comprising the 44 Fw 190A-8s of Hauptmann Wilhelm Moritz's IV.(*Sturm*)/JG 3 from Illesheim, along with Fw 190s from the recently attached 2./JG 51, escorted by Bf 109G-10s from I., II. and III./JG 300, evaded the fighter escort and closed in on the bomb group's Low Squadron. It had been planned initially to make a frontal attack against the bombers, but this was changed to a rear attack, undertaken at 0940 hrs, 5,600 m over Oschersleben.

Despite the massed defensive fire from the bombers, the Fw 190s spread across the skyline abreast in a formidable broad front and closed to 100 m before opening fire. It took the '*Sturmjäger*' about a minute to shoot down 11 Liberators – an entire squadron. When the B-24s of the 2nd AD returned home, 28 of their number had been lost, most of them to the *Sturmgruppe*, which had had nine of its own aircraft downed during the attack. Altogether, the Eighth Air Force lost 37 heavy bombers, with a further 390 damaged, during the day's raid.

Moritz claimed a *Herausschuss* for his 40th victory, while Leutnant Hans Weik, *Staffelkapitän* of 10.(*Sturm*)/JG 3, who would receive the Knight's Cross on 20 July, was credited with a B-24 for his 35th. Also successful – and one of the first to score at 0940 hrs – was Leutnant Oskar Romm, a 23-year-old Sudetenland German assigned to 2./JG 51. For Romm, who had been decorated with the Knight's Cross in February when his score stood at 76 victories, all of which had been achieved over the Eastern Front since December 1942, it was also to be his first aerial victory over the Reich:

On 7 July I flew my first sortie with this unit and the heavier Fw 190A-8 against a tight formation of B-24 Liberators. I searched out a bomber, and from very close range I poured short bursts into the fuselage and starboard engines. The impact of our new, improved 20 mm shells was devastating. The crippled B-24 immediately lost altitude and sheet metal as it began to burn, the aircraft exploding as

I completed my overflight. I watched as the wing split away from the fuselage, the powerplants spinning off the wing like Olympic torches. I had also received some hits from the bomber during the attack, both in my engine and fuselage, but the heavily armoured Fw 190 just kept flying.[3]

Other notable claims were lodged by pilots who had become masters in the art of 'bomber-killing'. Two minutes after Romm shot down a Liberator, Feldwebel Hans Schäfer of 10.(*Sturm*)/JG 3 got another, and then a second five minutes later for his 16th and 17th victories. Leutnant Werner Gerth of 11.(*Sturm*)/JG 3 was credited with his 13th and 14th claims within one minute, and Feldwebel Willi Unger of 12.(*Sturm*)/JG 3, who was flying as *Schwarmführer* in an Fw 190A-8, his tenth and eleventh also within one minute at an altitude of 5,600 m over Oschersleben. Unger was not one to be over-concerned about ammunition expenditure. When he fired, he intended it as a deadly assault – nothing less. He reported:

> At 0942 hrs the *Gruppe* launched an attack from behind on a *Pulk* of Liberators numbering about 25–30 enemy aircraft. I opened fire from 600 m on a Liberator flying in the centre, and after my first burst of fire, the right wing and both right engines were burning. With further continuous fire up to a distance of 350 m, the enemy machine reared up to the right. A real fireball enveloped the fuselage and the right wing, the aircraft tilted to the right, and immediately afterwards it broke apart, burning.

Unger had fired 160 rounds from his two 20 mm MG 151s and 40 rounds from his pair of 30 mm MK 108s. Seconds later, he targeted a second B-24:

> Immediately after my first attack, I shot down a second Liberator that was flying in the right half of the *Pulk*. By levelling off, I was able to attack this second Liberator. At about 300 m I opened continuous fire up to 100 m. The hits were in the centre of the fuselage and tail unit. The tail gunner was hit immediately and then parts of the tail unit came off. The Liberator immediately spiralled downwards to the right. On my descent, I passed close to the enemy aircraft, behind which two to four parachutes had opened.

For this second kill, Unger had used 220 rounds from the MG 151s and 55 rounds from the MK 108s.[4]

Marring the *Gruppe*'s sense of success, however, was the loss of Leutnant Hans Rachner, the *Staffelkapitän* of 12.(*Sturm*)/JG 3, who was killed by

Mustangs as he searched for a landing ground near Stassfurt.[5] He would be replaced by Leutnant Oskar Romm before the day was out.

In one of their earliest missions as day fighters, the pilots of JG 300 also lodged claims for nearly 30 aircraft downed or shot out of formation. Later that day, Schmid signalled the unit commanders in Dahl's *Gefechtsverband*:

> Under the excellent leadership of Major Dahl, the *Gefechtsverband* achieved great successes today. The *Sturmgruppe* played an outstanding part in this. These achievements mean more than a serious defeat for the enemy at the present time. In such tough battles against superior enemy forces, our day fighters have once again demonstrated the effectiveness of the German Jagdwaffe under the most difficult circumstances, especially in the important area of Reich defence.
>
> I would like to congratulate you, comrades, on this success. May traditional fighting spirit and determined leadership continue to lead you to the same, and greater, successes.[6]

Somewhat belatedly, from Carinhall, Göring ordered his gushing praise to be circulated to the home defence units concerned:

> The outstanding success of the *Sturmgruppe* in combatting the North American terror airmen has filled me with the greatest pride. I wish to express my deep recognition to the brave crews who, scorning death and with a furious spirit of attack, destroyed a close formation of bombers. The *Sturmgruppe*, by its complete and decisive will to fight, has shown the enemy the valour of the German soldier to high perfection. This operation in defence of the Homeland, carried out regardless of danger, embodies an attitude worthy of admiration. The *Sturmgruppe*, with this pitiless battle, has started a new page of glory in the high tradition of the German fighter force and expresses the fanatical will to win of my fighter pilots, the boldest of whom have placed themselves in the ranks of the *Sturmstaffeln*.[7]

Such decisive success was attributable to the determined mass-against-mass tactics employed by the *Gefechtsverbände* and *Sturmgruppen* during the summer and autumn of 1944. According to Dahl, from mid-1944, operations hinged on three 'ifs': if the prevailing clear weather allowed the possibility of an incoming daylight raid; if conditions permitted the Luftwaffe to undertake large-scale defensive operations; and if German radar and listening services had detected enemy formations preparing for assembly.

If all of these conditions applied, then the standard tactical drill for a *Gefechtsverband* or *Geschwader*-strength mission, including a *Sturmgruppe*, against a heavy bomber incursion over the Reich would typically commence with a telephone call from the *Jagddivision* commander to the *Geschwaderkommodore* or *Gefechtsverbandführer* at around 0530 hrs. In this conversation, the Divisional commander would advise on weather conditions, outline the battle plans issued by *Luftflotte Reich* and/or I. *Jagdkorps*, give the unit commander his specific mission orders and tell him to prepare all his *Gruppen* for 15 minutes readiness.

The *Kommodore* and his Staff, who would have been working since dawn, would then relay this information to the *Gruppenkommandeure*, who, in turn, would hold a pre-briefing with their pilots. The *Geschwader* HQ would assign a FuG 16ZY-equipped 'Y'-aircraft for fighter control purposes, as well as issue call signs and advise the chain of command.

Once confirmation of an incoming raid had been received from the *Division* – usually at the point when enemy bombers were either assembling or crossing the English coast – the *Geschwader* would go onto three minutes readiness. As more information arrived, the pilots would be moved forward to *Sitzbereitschaft*, or cockpit readiness, and appraised of further developments via loudspeaker at the dispersal point.

At the order to scramble (*Alarmstart*), all three *Gruppen* would then take off and assemble over their own airfields at 900–1,800 m within six to ten minutes, before flying to the *Gefechtsverband* assembly point, where, under strict radio discipline and control, the *Gefechtsverbandführer* formed up the whole battle formation. As Dahl explained to his Allied captors in September 1945:

> Behind him lies the *Sturmgruppe*, and the close and top escort hang on to them. The assembly altitude has been ordered beforehand and fixed at 3,000 m, under the ceiling. The assembly and forming up of the *Gefechtsverband* can take no more than 20 minutes, calculated from the time of take-off of the *Gruppen*. After this space of time, the *Gefechtsverband* must be ready to set course and start for its objective. The *Geschwaderkommodore* announces by radio to the *Division* the completed assembly and the readiness of the formation to set course.[8]

The formation would then climb to a combat altitude of 7,500–8,000 m.

In the case of IV.(*Sturm*)/JG 3, following assembly, the *Gruppe*'s Fw 190s flew in two stacked-down 'Vee' or '*Sturmkeil*' formations, each comprised of eight to ten aircraft from the *Stab* and three *Staffeln* (depending on serviceability), the second formation flying 140–180 m behind and about 45 m below the lead formation.

Meanwhile, the Bf 109 *Begleitgruppen* (escorts) would split to either side of the *Sturmgruppe*, stacked up from front to rear. Another, smaller escort – usually formed from the aircraft of 2./JG 51 (to be redesignated 16./JG 3) – would fly high cover at about 900 m above the rearmost aircraft of the second Vee of the *Sturmgruppe*. The Bf 109s would fly in a sufficiently loose formation to avoid slipstreaming and allow aircraft to weave without the risk of collision.

Within sight of the enemy bomber formation and some 90-150 m above and 900–1,520 m behind it, the *Sturmgruppe* would drop its external tanks, then reformate from its Vee formation into its line abreast *Angriffsformation* (attack formation) or *Breitkeil*. This was carried out by climbing where necessary and fanning out into a slightly swept-back line abreast formation of usually more than 20 fighters, either level with or slightly above the enemy, with the commander of the *Gruppe* and his deputy flying at its apex. As Dahl described it:

> Upon sighting the enemy bomber formation, the formation leader gives the signal to attack by rocking his wings, or by radio. The wings of the Vics now pull up until the aircraft are in line abreast, with the formation leader throttling back a bit so the others can catch up. The approach is made from behind and the fighters attack in a line, the formation leader dividing up the target according to the formation of bombers, for example – 'Bomber formation on a broad front with little depth (from top to bottom)'. The CO will attack the centre, and the forces to right and left will go [after the bombers] to right and left respectively.

In cases where the interval between the bomber formation selected for attack and the succeeding bomber group within the stream was reasonably large, the *Sturmjäger* found little difficulty in manoeuvring into a good attacking position, but when bomber groups flew more closely together, a very tight turn was necessary, which demanded total concentration as a formation.

Once the Focke-Wulfs were in position, and upon clearance being received from the *Jagddivision*, the formation leader gave the order to attack over his FuG 16Z radio, together with instructions for reassembly afterwards. Each pilot selected one bomber as his target, closed in to about 360 m and, aiming at the tail gunner, opened fire with his two 20 mm MG 151 wing root cannon. As the *Angriffskeil* closed into 180 m, each pilot opened fire with his 30 mm MK 108 cannon, aiming at either of the inboard engines. Should the selected bomber have been damaged or set on fire by a fellow pilot, a *Sturmjäger* would move through the formation and pick another target.

Having made their attacks, some pilots broke away 45 m from the bomber and sideslipped in the direction of the reassembly area on the basis that this was the quickest and safest means to get clear of defensive fire and debris. Others either broke away after passing their target bombers or flew further into the formation before slipping out. Dahl maintained that exit from a *Pulk* should be made:

> ... to the side and down, and reassemble at the same altitude with the bombers about 2,750 m to the side and 900 m below. The basic principle to be observed in reassembling is that the assembly is to be made on the same side from which the entry into the bomber stream was made. The advantage thus gained is that the escort *Gruppen* are on the right side after the attack to protect the reassembly of the *Sturmgruppe* without having to change sides. If little or no further opposition is encountered, a second attack can be carried out by the *Sturmgruppe*.[9]

Variations to the basic tactics did occur. For example, the pre-attack flight formation of II.(*Sturm*)/JG 4 usually consisted of three stacked down Vees, unlike IV.(*Sturm*)/JG 3's two-formation method. Furthermore, pilots of II.(*Sturm*)/JG 4 are reputed to have favoured diving *below* the level of the bomber formation prior to making an attack, nosing up immediately before opening fire.

On 18 July, more than 500 B-17s and B-24s of the Fifteenth Air Force operating from Italian bases attempted to strike at the aircraft production facility at Manzell and Memmingen airfield in southern Germany, to which IV.(*Sturm*)/JG 3 had recently moved (although it was the presence of 70 Bf 110 and Me 410 *Zerstörer* trainers there which had caught the attention of a USAAF reconnaissance aircraft).

A force of around 45 Fw 190s of IV.(*Sturm*)/JG 3 was scrambled to intercept the raid. Assembling over Holzkirchen, the *Gruppe* headed south towards the *Viermots*, which were reported to be approaching from Innsbruck and Garmsich. For the second time in less than two weeks, the *Gruppe* hacked down an impressive number of bombers – this time B-17s from the 5th BW, heavily escorted by P-51s and P-38s.

Adverse weather prevented the greater part of the Memmingen force from hitting the target, with two groups and their escort turning back and another bombing an alternative target. However, the Flying Fortresses of the 483rd BG became separated, failed to receive the recall message and pressed on alone without their P-38 escort. As the 483rd doggedly neared the Starnberger See at around 1050 hrs, the *Sturmgruppe* struck, and 14 of the bomb group's Flying Fortresses went down. In total, the pilots of IV.(*Sturm*)/JG 3 and their comrades in 2./JG 51 who operated alongside them, claimed 34 B-17s shot down and 13 *Herausschüsse*. Two P-51s were also destroyed.

Leutnant Oskar Romm, *Staffelkapitän* of 12.(*Sturm*)/JG 3, claimed two B-17s and a P-51 for his 78th–80th victories, scored within five minutes. Oberleutnant Horst Haase, *Staffelkapitän* of 2./JG 51, accounted for his 49th victory. The *Gruppenkommandeur*, Hauptmann Wilhelm Moritz, claimed his 41st. For his unit's accomplishments on 18 July, he was awarded the Knight's Cross.

Several former *Sturmstaffel* 1 pilots also proved their mettle. Leutnant Werner Gerth, Unteroffizier Oskar Bösch and Feldwebeln Willi Maximowitz and Gerhard Vivroux, all of 11.(*Sturm*)/JG 3, and Feldwebel Kurt Röhrich of 12.(*Sturm*)/JG 3 claimed a total of seven victories.

Bösch graphically recalled what it was like to go in against the bombers, and the methods employed by the *Sturm* units:

> We always went in line abreast. That was our normal tactic. If you went in singly, all the bombers shot at you with their massive defensive firepower, and as you went through them, you drew fire from the waist gunners. But as a tactic, the psychological effect of a mass attack formation on the bomber gunners was much greater.
>
> First of all, you tried to knock out the tail gunner. Then you went for the intersection between wing and fuselage, and you just kept at it, watching your hits flare and flare again. It all happened so quickly. You gave it all you had. Sometimes, after the first attack, all your energy seemed to go. Your nerves were burned out. But we had this kind of theory that when you were in the middle of a bomber formation – flying through it – you were, in a way, 'protected'. The bombers wouldn't open fire because they didn't want to shoot at their own aircraft.
>
> We would break off the attack just before we were about to collide with our target. The devastating effect of our 30 mm guns was such that we would often fly through a rain of fragments, some being complete sections of aircraft.[10]

One negative of the 18 July operation was that having broken away from the main JG 3 attack formation, the Fw 190A-8/R2 of Oberleutnant Hans Weik, *Staffelkapitän* of 10.(*Sturm*)/JG 3 since February 1944, was hit by defensive fire from a B-17 which Weik had attacked alone and shot down for his 36th victory. However, he was himself shot down and badly wounded in the shoulder and arm.

The loss of Weik's contribution to the *Sturmgruppe*'s operations was a difficult one to bear. Regarded as a fearless pilot, he was an inspiration to others in the *Gruppe*. Weik had joined I./JG 3 in February 1943 and scored ten victories before being transferred as an instructor to *Jagdgruppe Ost*. Returning to III. and then IV./JG 3 in the autumn of 1943, he subsequently shot down no fewer than 21 four-engined bombers in just 85 operational missions. Weik, who mostly flew the Bf 109, had survived being shot down on several occasions in early 1944.

Despite heavy losses, IV.(*Sturm*)/JG 3 continued to battle against the bombers for the rest of July, and at the end of the month moved to Schongau, near the Austrian border, to operate against the Fifteenth Air Force. On 3 August, the Fifteenth sent its B-17s and B-24s to bomb aircraft and steel factories at Friedrichshafen and the chemical plants and marshalling yards at Immenstadt. By this time the entire *Gruppe* had only 16 aircraft and could put up only four *Schwärme*. When the *Gruppe* took off to intercept the bombers that had targeted Friedrichshafen, they were on their way back to Italy. The *Schwarm* from 12.(*Sturm*)/JG 3 was led by Feldwebel Willi Unger, who later recalled:

> On 3 August 1944, I led 12. *Staffel*, which was the strength of a *Schwarm* – just four aircraft to sortie; myself and three *Unteroffizieren*: Hermann Christ, Hans-Joachim Scholz and Heinz Zimkeit. In fact, the entire IV. *Gruppe* consisted only of four *Schwärme* – 16 aircraft. Our attack was directed at a bomber unit which had bombed Friedrichshafen and was flying over the Alps to Italy. The attack took place at 1130 hrs at an altitude of 6,500 m over the Lechtaler Alps.
>
> We shot down six Liberators, but during our attack the American escorts rushed at us from behind. As a result we lost eight Fw 190s to escort fighters and defensive fire from the bombers. Six German pilots met their deaths, two were able to bail out and landed high up in the Alps. Of my flight – four aircraft – only one machine made it back home. Two comrades were killed [Scholz and Zimkeit].
>
> I myself was hit in the engine by fire from a tail gun. My windshield went black with oil and I couldn't see a thing. I was saved by my parachute and landed with a thump some 2,000 m up in the mountains. Fragments of my machine still lie scattered today at another spot in the mountains. Of the six dead fighter pilots, two are still recorded as missing. Sixty-seven people were killed by bombs in Friedrichshafen,

among them 22 Flak gun helpers aged 17. I took part in greater air battles over Germany, but for me, this was the most dramatic.[11]

During the attack, Unger shot down one Liberator for his 15th victory. Christ and Scholz also each shot down a bomber. In total, IV.(*Sturm*)/JG 3 accounted for 19 B-24s either shot down or classified as *Herausschuss*, but suffered the loss of five pilots and one wounded. Unger walked 16 km to the nearest village, where he found a car and arrived back at Schongau at midnight.

In the summer of 1944, as part of its continuing efforts to devise weapons with which to shoot down Allied bombers, E.Kdo 25 worked with several leading technical institutions, RLM test centres and armament manufacturers on a range of inventive and technologically advanced forms of air-to-air weaponry. At its base at Parchim, the *Kommando* carried out tests with the SG 116 '*Zellendusche*' (*Sonder Gerät* – 'Special Apparatus'/*Zellendusche* – 'Cell Shower'), a recoilless, single-shot 30 mm weapon based around the barrel of an MK 103 cannon fitted to a breech block which was intended to be fired upwards as a fighter passed below a bomber.

In attacking a heavy bomber 'conventionally' from the rear, a Luftwaffe fighter risked drawing the combined defensive firepower of several 0.50-in. machine guns mounted in the bombers' top turrets, lower 'ball' turrets, tail and waist gun positions as it passed through a formation to make its exit. In attacking from the front, although the intensity of the defensive guns was not so strong (even allowing for the twin-gun Bendix chin turrets on the later B-17G), the combined closing speed of the fighter and the bombers, as well as the narrower and much more challenging target profile, meant that the chances of shooting down a bomber, as Major Anton Hackl, *Gruppenkommandeur* of III./JG 11, had stressed to Galland in May, were frequently beyond the capability of all but the most skilful '*Experten*'.

The tactical rationale behind the SG 116 was that by approaching from the front of a target, the fighter could avoid the collective mass of a formation's defensive firepower by flying beneath it, while a bomber's underside presented a much larger, and closer, target to hit. Furthermore, the technology incorporated into the weapon meant that aiming depended more on the sighting apparatus rather than the human eye and the skill of deflection shooting needed with conventional guns.[12] Hauptmann Horst Geyer recalled:

> The intention with the SG 116 was to make a frontal approach, fly under an American bomber and release the shot which was fired by

means of an explosive charge built into the base of the tube designed to be mounted into the side of an Fw 190 fuselage. The intention was good, and the aiming technology impressive. We believed that with such a weapon we could inflict fatal hits in the B-17's and B-24's wing fuel tanks.

Devised by the Hermann Göring Luftfahrtforschungsanstalt (Aeronautical Research Institute) near Völkenrode, the weapon was built by Rheinmetall-Borsig. It was developed in a very short time using stocks of MK 103 cannon barrels.

The SG 116 comprised a rifled MK 103 barrel without a finished chamber, and the breech block with the ignition system. The complete round consisted of the 3 cm shell, a cardboard container and the propelling charge, and the counterweight with the firing mechanism. Three barrels were to be fitted on the left fuselage of an Fw 190, the forward barrel being just aft of the point where the rear of the cockpit joined the fuselage when closed. The distance between each barrel was about 15 cm. The barrels pointed aft, but were slightly displaced from the parallel, projecting about 50 cm above and 25 cm below the fuselage.

The weapon was to be activated and fired automatically using a photoelectric cell, or *Magisches Auge* ('Magic Eye') developed by the *Institut für Waffenforschung* (Institute for Weapons Research) and manufactured by AEG. The device was built into the fuselage of the Fw 190 immediately forward of the barrels and comprised four reduction lenses placed one below the other, with a photoelectric cell fitted to the lowest lens. This was connected to a solenoid on which a contact arm functioned. When the photoelectric cell was activated by an image in the lens, the solenoid was energised and the circuit to the barrel firing gear completed. The diameter of the external part of the 'Magic Eye' was 8 cm. The maximum range from the target aircraft at which the 'Magic Eye' was sufficiently sensitive to operate the firing gear was around 55 m.

E.Kdo 25 commenced trials with the SG 116 fitted into an Fw 190F-8 at Parchim on 1 July 1944. As Hauptmann Geyer recorded:

> An optical automatic release system had also been developed. On one occasion, on 1 July 1944, Galland and some of his staff made an inspection trip to Parchim, and we demonstrated the weapon using an Fw 190 fitted with three such tubes mounted immediately behind the cockpit, and each loaded with a 3 cm mine shell. We put an NCO pilot into the specially rigged fighter and arranged for an Fw 58 *Weihe* to fly simultaneously overhead, about 200 m above the Fw 190.

The *Weihe* was to tow a target drogue. The Fw 190 flew in very low, at about 100 m, so that we on the ground could observe the weapon being used to its full effect.

In the interests of safety, and because the Fw 190 was not a large aircraft, we developed a firing system designed to allow the pilot to fire only one tube at a time, thus minimising and avoiding the risk of any blast damage from all the tubes firing at once. Unfortunately, however, the NCO made a mistake and fired all the tubes simultaneously. There was a loud explosion in the air, with a huge cloud of smoke. Then, emerging from the smoke came the *Weihe*, flying gracefully on, undamaged. However the Fw 190 was destroyed in the process. Fortunately, the pilot somehow got out, but like the *Weihe*, the drogue was also untouched. The pilot of the Fw 190 landed by parachute and limped up to Galland and I. He pulled off his flying helmet, and his first words were 'Permission to have a cognac, *Herr General!*'[13]

By late August 1944, photoelectric cells had been fitted into 19 Fw 190s, but the following month the decision was taken not to use the SG 116 operationally until greater accuracy could be assured.

22

Mass Against Mass

In May 1944, a third *Sturmgruppe* had begun forming up when 4. and 5. *Staffeln* of the single-seat *Wilde Sau* nightfighter *Gruppe* II./JG 300, under the command of former reconnaissance pilot Major Kurd Peters, commenced conversion to the day fighter role together with I. and III./JG 300, commanded respectively by former bomber pilots, Knight's Cross-holder Hauptmann Gerhard Stamp and Major Iro Ilk.* Based successively at Dortmund, Merzhausen, Frankfurt/Main and Unterschlauersbach, II./JG 300 took delivery of Fieseler-built Fw 190A-8/R2s, while I. and III. *Gruppen* retained their Bf 109s for the escort role. In late June 1944, Major Walther Dahl relinquished command of the JGzbV and was appointed *Kommodore* of JG 300.

Within II./JG 300, Dahl was able to draw on a number of battle-hardened pilots such as Leutnant Klaus Bretschneider, one of the most successful *Wilde Sau* aces who had been credited with 14 victories in only 20 night missions during the first four months of 1944. Bretschneider was made *Staffelkapitän* of 5./JG 300 on 19 July. In addition, with IV.(*Sturm*)/JG 3's departure to France in June, a number of officers from Oberleutnant Horst Haase's 2./JG 51, which had been seconded to the original *Sturmgruppe*, were temporarily detached to II./JG 300 to assist with training on the Fw 190.

The new *Sturmgruppe* was officially designated II.(*Sturm*)/JG 300 in July 1944, and by 4 August, Major Peters reported to Dahl that the conversion and training of the unit as a *Sturmgruppe* was complete. Ten days later, on the 15th, II.(*Sturm*)/JG 300 received its baptism of fire as a *Sturmgruppe*.

The day dawned as a perfect summer's morning, with cloudless blue sky and almost limitless visibility. The Eighth Air Force used the conditions to despatch a force of nearly 900 B-17s and B-24s to bomb a range of airfield

---

*6./JG 300 was detached from JG 300 to remain on nightfighter operations as 8./NJG 11.

targets across Germany. Amongst the aircraft despatched were 219 B-17s of the 1st BD, which would target airfields around Wiesbaden, Frankfurt and Cologne. Of the 426 fighters sent to escort the strike force, 112 were assigned to the 1st BD.

The German *Funkhorchdienstes* first reported the build-up of enemy bombers at around 0745 hrs, with isolated plots continuing for the next two hours, and it relayed regular updates to the various *Jagddivisionen*. At Bad Wörishofen, Major Dahl placed his 100 or so available fighters on readiness and drew up plans for a *Gefechtsverband* comprising the *Geschwaderstabsschwarm* and I./JG 300 at Bad Wörishofen, II.(*Sturm*)/JG 300 at Holzkirchen and IV.(*Sturm*)/JG 3 at Schongau.

Within two hours, Dahl was airborne in his Fw 190A-8, accompanied by the 30 Bf 109G-10s and G-14s of Hauptmann Stamp's *Höhenbegleitgruppe*. The formation headed south to Augsburg, where it made a textbook rendezvous with the Fw 190s of the two *Sturmgruppen* just after 1000 hrs. Meanwhile, the Flying Fortresses of the 1st BD had departed the Suffolk coast over Orford Ness at 0837 hrs, and they were not picked up by the German monitors until 0929 hrs.[1]

Under radio silence at 7,000 m, and with Dahl at the head of a great wedge-shaped battle formation, the German fighters turned towards Frankfurt, some 260 km away, in accordance with directions received from 7. *Jagddivision*. Thirty minutes later, the *Division* ordered a change in course to Trier, on the Mosel, 150 km further west, and passed control of the formation to Oberstleutnant Fritz Trübenbach, the *Jafü Mittelrhein* at Darmstadt.

After one hour of flying, and in slowly deteriorating weather, the *Gefechtsverband* finally sighted three *Pulks* of 60–80 Flying Fortresses of the 1st BD just west of the Mosel river, and Dahl reported the observation to the *Jafü*, whose Operations Officer gave clearance to attack. Just before 1145 hrs, Dahl manoeuvred his *Angriffskeil* for a classic attack from the rear, with Moritz's IV.(*Sturm*)/JG 3 assigned to the *Pulk* flying to his left and Leutnant Bretschneider's II.(*Sturm*)/JG 300 to the right (Major Peters had broken a leg bailing out of his aircraft a few days earlier). Dahl and the *Stabsschwarm* would tackle the centre *Pulk*.

Dahl lined up on a Flying Fortress flying to the left of his selected group and commenced firing at 300 m, continuing to fire as he closed in, with hits striking home in the fuselage and both wings and debris flying away. A few seconds later, the B-17 veered to the left, with flames and smoke from the left wing trailing over the fuselage. Three crewmen bailed out. As Dahl passed through the formation, the bomber's wing broke away and the aircraft nosed downwards.

The 303rd BG had 39 B-17s committed to the strike on Wiesbaden airfield that day as part of the 1st BD's 41st 'B' CW. The bomb group was returning from having attacked the airfield, its fighter escort having left the bombers when some 25 Fw 190s from Dahl's *Gefechtsverband* attacked the Low Group B-17s from the 358th and 427th BSs. Nine out of 13 aircraft were shot down. 2Lt R. W. Davis was piloting B-17 *Flying Bison* of the 427th BS in the No. 4 position of the squadron's high element. He recalled (in third person narrative) the *Sturmgruppen's* devastating attack:

> Immediately after being warned by Tail Gunner Sgt. W. F. Foley, Lt. Davis began violent evasive action. Two Fw 190s engaged them, making one pass before disappearing. *Flying Bison* sustained numerous hits, causing Lt. Davis to lose altitude from 22,000 ft to 17,500 ft, and become separated from the rest of the formation.
>
> Fighting to get the aircraft back on an even keel, Lt. Davis began to take stock of his aircraft and crew. The Engineer, Sgt. R. D. Hughes, had been instantly killed by a 20 mm cannon shell while flying in the waist gunner position. Radio Operator Sgt. E. R. Gorman was wounded in his right ankle and Tail Gunner Sgt. Foley in the leg and foot. The Navigator, Lt. G. L. Lange, and the Bombardier, F/O. F. W. Bryan, were sent back to administer First Aid.
>
> Aircraft damage was very severe. The amplifiers and turbos were shot out, rudder controls were useless, the fuselage looked like a sieve, and the No. 4 engine was not functioning properly. The No. 4 propeller then ran away and was feathered. Fortunately, cockpit instruments still worked. The engine was restarted and began spurting oil and dropping pressure. It was again feathered for the remainder of the mission. To maintain the 17,500 ft altitude, airspeed was dropped to 140 mph. The wounded were made as comfortable as possible. Friendly fighters were attracted by firing flares, and provided escort for the return journey, but the aircraft was damaged to such an extent that no attempt was made at repairs.[2]

Meanwhile, Dahl ordered his formation to reform and make a second attack. Selecting a second *Viermot*, Dahl once again closed in from 200 m to 80 m, firing with machine guns and cannon. The port inboard engine started to burn and the Flying Fortress began to drop away sharply from formation. Dahl hurriedly counted five parachutes just as the USAAF P-51 fighter escort arrived, at which point, with fuel low, the *Sturmjäger* disengaged and turned for freshly bombed Wiesbaden-Erbenheim and Mainz-Finthen (the nearest airfields cleared for their arrival), leaving Stamp's Bf 109s to take on the Mustangs.

The USAAF reported that the attack on the 303rd BG was 'from 6 o'clock low, with no definite pattern in the attack – 81 men are missing from these aircraft'. The bomb group also reported expending 50,050 rounds of 0.50-in. ammunition against German fighters during the mission.[3]

When Dahl landed at Mainz-Finthen, his Focke-Wulf was rated as 35 per cent damaged as a result of defensive fire from the bombers, but 17 heavy bombers had been lost by the Eighth Air Force. Among the scorers from IV.(*Sturm*)/JG 3 were Oberleutnant Horst Haase from 16. *Staffel* (formerly 2./JG 51), who claimed one B-17 for his 51st victory, Leutnant Werner Gerth of 14.(*Sturm*)/JG 3, whose B-17 destroyed was his 23rd victory, and Unteroffizier Klaus Neumann and Feldwebel Kurt Gren, both of 16.(*Sturm*)/JG 3, who each claimed a Flying Fortress for their 19th victories. One pilot was shot down and wounded as he bailed out and Unteroffizier Hermann Christ of 15.(*Sturm*)/JG 3 was killed in action.

Once he had received reports from each of his *Kommandeure*, Dahl telephoned the *Jafü*, Oberstleutnant Trübenbach, and delivered a full report on the battle.[4]

The Eighth Air Force lost 12 B-17s and five B-24s.[5]

Another idea assessed by E.Kdo 25 during the summer of 1944 was the possibility of dropping *Nitropentaschnur* (15 m-long strips of detonating cord) in clusters on enemy formations. *Nitropentaschnur*, more widely known as PETN cord, was made from pentaerythritol tetranitrate. This form of explosive compound, which is similar to nitroglycerin, was first manufactured in 1894 by the Rheinisch-Westfälische Sprengstoff A.G. of Köln, with production commencing in 1912. It was used by German forces during World War I, and in World War II it formed a component in ammunition used in the Luftwaffe's MG FF/M series of cannon, as well as in the *Minengeschoß* high-explosive shell.

The rear fuselages of a small number of the *Kommando*'s Fw 190s were fitted with specially designed containers manufactured by the Max Baermann engineering firm at Cologne-Dollbrück. These containers could carry 20 lengths of 15 m-long cord.

The plan was that a frontal approach would be made against a bomber *Pulk*, and as the fighter passed through the enemy formation, the container would be released and the cords dropped down onto the bombers, the flight of each piece of cord being controlled by two small parachutes. They would either become wrapped around propellers or strike the metal of the enemy machines to hook and embed themselves into their panels with the aid of small, sharp-clawed 'anchors'. The fuses were set to detonate seven seconds after impact. Such contact with an enemy aircraft would result in detonation.

Initial test flights against static targets on the ground demonstrated flawless opening of the containers and discharge of the *Nitropentaschnur* cord, but it was also found that the fuse delay was too short, and it was recommended that the period be extended to 20 seconds. Furthermore, it was believed that a load of 20 cords would be insufficient, having little effect as they scattered harmlessly through an enemy formation. In cases where the anchors managed to embed themselves in the metal of the static test targets, it was observed that while the outer metal skin was punctured, the cord had failed to entwine itself around any parts, and thus would fail to detonate.

In July 1944, Geyer departed E.Kdo 25, his position as *Kommandoführer* being taken by Major Georg Christl, a Knight's Cross-holder who had previously commanded III./ZG 26. By the beginning of August, the *Kommando* had been redesignated *Jagdgruppe* 10 (J.Gr.10). In September, Christl noted that:

> ... further experiments with *Nitropentaschnur* has revealed new factors. Dropping tests with 60 m-long detonating cords are inconclusive due to technical deficiencies with the parachute system. When the length of the cords are extended from 15 m to 60 m, the number of cords carried in the container has to be reduced from 20 to seven, thus meaning that the additional cords would have to be transferred to suspended external holders in a further development. Since the fundamental problem of looping the cord around aircraft components has still not been resolved, it does not seem promising to continue with further tests based on the [negligible] measure of success so far achieved.

In their war against the bombers, an often overlooked but key element for the Luftwaffe's day fighter pilots was their use of an advanced gyro gunsight manufactured by the Askania firm in Berlin. At the outbreak of war, the Luftwaffe relied on more rudimentary, fixed reflector sights which, at the time, were adequate for firing lower calibre fixed guns from fighter aircraft.

However, in 1935, the RLM's Technical Office commenced development work on gyro sights, with Askania eventually producing a small number of

EZ 40 combined single AC gyro and head sights between 1935 and 1942. Such a sight, it was hoped, would aid aerial gunnery and marksmanship. Certainly, when tested in a Bf 109F, strike probability increased by 50–100 per cent over a standard Revi C/12 D reflector sight. An EZ 41 gunsight was developed by Zeiss, but it was found to have too many faults.

In mid-August 1944, a small *Kommando* from the *Schießschule der Luftwaffe* (Luftwaffe Gunnery School) at Værløse, in Denmark, led by Oberleutnant Karl Maier, a gunnery specialist, spent time with II.(*Sturm*)/JG 300 at Holzkirchen and Erfurt-Bindersleben. Maier had received training himself on the sight at the *Erprobungsstelle* Tarnewitz, the main Luftwaffe armaments testing centre on the Baltic coast, 40 km northeast of Lübeck.

During periods of bad weather, which meant no flying, five Fw 190A-8s of II.(*Sturm*)/JG 300 were fitted with EZ 40 sights. The task of Maier's *Kommando* was to train the pilots in their use, to instruct the *Gruppe*'s own technical personnel and to use operational experiences with the sight to add to the training of combat units. Maier used a model sight (a model aircraft within a target circle) as part of his 'classroom' instruction to explain the construction of the EZ 40, as well as a training film aimed at coaching pilots in assessing distances to a target. According to Maier, the film was greatly appreciated by the pilots.

A Bücker Bü 181 twin-seat monoplane trainer was also made available in which it was intended to offer pilots a 20-minute practice flight accompanied either by Maier or II. *Gruppe*'s *Staffelkapitäne*. This was easier said than done since due to operational requirements, the *Gruppe* was 'continuously being called up [into the air]', which interrupted and disrupted training sessions, leaving only short time periods available. Nevertheless, the whole *Gruppe* was trained, remarkably, within ten days, and as Maier later reported:

> The average number of aircraft shot down by the *Gruppe* is very satisfactory. The training of pilots in fixed gunnery varies. The pilots always received the *Kommando* well, and they took great interest in the training, especially the fighter pilots. The instructors and the pilots had close contact, and so any questions arising and any doubts were dealt with on the spot. An improvement in flying and gunnery technique was clearly evident.

No special selection was made as to which pilots should fly the EZ 40-equipped aircraft in action, although the deliberate exception was Leutnant Klaus Bretschneider, the *Staffelkapitän* of 5.(*Sturm*)/JG 300. He had brought down more enemy aircraft than any other pilot in the *Gruppe*. According to Maier, Bretschneider was 'greatly interested in improvements to methods of attack and sighting'. He was given the first instruction on the EZ 40, including flights in the Bü 181.

While Maier's *Kommando* was with II.(*Sturm*)/JG 300, five operational sorties against four-engined bombers were flown. On the morning of 22 August, over Hungary, a large *Gefechtsverband* formed of 'light' Bf 109s from I./JG 300 and I./JG 302, as well as some Hungarian-flown Messerschmitts, along with the 'heavy' Fw 190s of II.(*Sturm*)/JG 300 and IV.(*Sturm*)/JG 3, intercepted B-24s of the Fifteenth Air Force heading for targets in Germany and Austria. Bretschneider was flying an Fw 190 fitted with an EZ 40 gyroscopic sight, and Maier noted afterwards what Bretschneider had told him (emphasis in original):

> Attack on two Boeings flying close together over Lake Balaton. Height 6,000 m. Attack commenced from the left side at an angle of 30 degrees because of the appearance of enemy fighters. Pursuit curve. Commenced firing from a range of 300 m. Pilot fired at both enemy machines. First shots already scored hits in the wings and fuselage of the first machine. Fire developed. The second machine also showed direct hits after the first few shots on one of the left-side engines. A strong fire developed. <u>Hits were obtained exactly</u> where the *Zielstachel* [aiming needle] was directed. The fighter escort diverted us off our course. One enemy aircraft shot down [Bretschneider] – the only aircraft shot down during this sortie [on this occasion, Bretschneider's victim was a B-24, which went down at Celldömölk-Sümeg/Herend from a height of 7,300 m].[6]

Two days later, in an afternoon sortie against Fifteenth Air Force bombers over Czechoslovakia, Bretschneider struck again, leading nine Fw 190s of II.(*Sturm*)/JG 300 with aircraft from four other *Gruppen*:

> Attack against one Boeing by whole unit, height 8,000 m. Attack commenced from rear, left side, above, flight angle at 20 degrees. Opened fire from a range of 400 m. Pilot reported to have stated verbally: '*Zielstachel* aimed at left inner engine: a hit there. *Zielstachel* aimed at *Turmstand* [centre section of aircraft]: hit secured there. It was like regular target shooting!' Significant outbreak of fire on account of fact that aircraft did not fall away. Aircraft hit from side. Attack was filmed. Copy of film will be sent to *Schießschule der Luftwaffe*. The description given by the pilot was very matter-of-fact and trustworthy. One aircraft shot down – only downing of an aircraft by unit [5. *Staffel*] that day.

During sorties against *Viermots* using the EZ 40, the pilots of II.(*Sturm*)/JG 300 found that after measuring range and deciding on a target, the first shots they fired hit home. The younger, less experienced pilots were very impressed by this degree of automated accuracy – something that was important in the short firing opportunities available when escort fighters were present. The pilots also commented that this increase in success had occurred as a result of the new training methods, whereas when flying with the standard *Revi* sights, very little, if any, formal gunnery training had been given.

While Maier's *Kommando* was with the *Gruppe*, five sorties were flown with the EZ 40 in which three bombers were shot down, two were classified as *Herausschüsse* and three were hit in such a way that their engines burned for an extended period.[7]

In late 1942, as speed, firepower and calibre improved on enemy aircraft, Askania introduced the new EZ 42 gyroscopic sight, comprising a separate gyro assembly with two AC gyros, single-stage amplifier and sight head.[8] With the EZ 42, a pilot could fire at a moving target regardless of fixed guns built into the longitudinal axis of the carrying aircraft.

When approaching a target, a pilot had to ensure that he continuously twisted the range-finding button on the aircraft's control column so that the growing target was permanently encapsulated in the dial, as well as making sure that the cross-wire was contained within the target circle. The precise angle of deflection was obtained within two seconds. Accuracy could be guaranteed to within 15 per cent of the angle of deflection in the longitudinal direction of the enemy and ten per cent perpendicularly.

On 11 September 1944, Oberstleutnant von Kornatzki's II.(*Sturm*)/JG 4 flew one of its most successful operations against the bombers since its formation in the summer. That day, the Eighth Air Force launched 1,016 heavy bombers from all three of its bomb divisions, escorted by 411 fighters, against eight synthetic oil plants and marshalling yards and an ordnance depot in central Germany. I. *Jagdkorps* challenged this huge armada by fielding fighters from 15 units, including the point defence Me 163 rocket interceptors of I./JG 400.

At 1030 hrs, II.(*Sturm*)/JG 4, with III./JG 4 providing its escort, received the *Startbefehl*. More than 60 Fw 190s and Bf 109s took off from Welzow and Alteno to form part of a *Gefechtsverband* which would fall under the tactical control of Major Günther Specht and the *Geschwaderstab* of JG 11. With accurate guidance from the ground, the two *Gruppen* of JG 4 were vectored towards Chemnitz, and at 1210 hrs the unit had its first sighting of the bombers, although by this time aircraft from IV.(*Sturm*)/JG 3, I./JG 76 and II.(*Sturm*) and III./JG 300 were already engaging the 1st BD and its escort.

JG 4 would take on elements of the 3rd BD southwest of Chemnitz, with *Stab*/JG 11 and III./JG 4 deploying against the Spitfire and Mustang escort. Major Specht shot down one of the P-51 escorts for his 31st victory, while III./JG 4's Bf 109s accounted for the destruction of two P-51s and two Spitfires.

Minutes later, at about 1210 hrs, and at an altitude of 8,000–9,000 m, with the Allied fighter escort occupied, II.(*Sturm*)/JG 4 went to work on the bombers to such effect that 15 pilots, including Hauptmann Manfred Köpcke, *Staffelkapitän* of 6.(*Sturm*)/JG 4, and Hauptmann Erich Jugel, *Staffelkapitän* of 5.(*Sturm*)/JG 4, each later claimed a B-17 either shot down or a *Herausschuss* within three minutes. But the attack had not been without cost, for 5. *Staffel* lost three pilots, 6. *Staffel* five pilots and 7.(*Sturm*)/JG 4 three pilots, all some 20 km south of Chemnitz.

At 1219 hrs, the Fw 190s of 8.(*Sturm*)/JG 4, which had formed a high rear escort element for the *Sturmgruppe* in case the *Begleitjäger* of III./JG 4 were not able to offer sufficient protection, also waded in from the rear of the *Pulk* at around 8,000 m. However, due to intervention by American fighters, their formation was not as tight as it should have been. Nevertheless, eight claims were made by eight pilots, including the *Staffelkapitän*, Hauptmann Gerhard Schroeder. Leutnant Alfred Rausch rammed a B-17 with his Fw 190A-8/R2 over Reitzenhain/Komotau and was killed in the process. Apart from Feldwebel Josef Tüssner, who was wounded, Rausch represented 8.(*Sturm*)/JG 4's only casualty.

By the end of the action, II.(*Sturm*)/JG 4 had claimed 16 Flying Fortresses shot down, with another seven classified as *Herausschüsse*, while III./JG 4 claimed nine B-17s destroyed with three *Herausschüsse*, plus the four escort fighters. However, these victories came at a heavy price, with II. *Gruppe* reporting 12 pilots lost, together with nine from III. *Gruppe*. The cost in aircraft was high too, with JG 4 estimating that as a result of this operation, between a third and a half of its machines needed repair. Twenty-three Fw 190s were classified as 60–100 per cent damaged, with 27 Bf 109s reported at the same level.

For the USAAF, the cost was equally high, with 40 heavy bombers and 17 fighters lost during the raid.

But the next day (12 September), JG 4 was to receive a further blow when Oberstleutnant Hans-Günther von Kornatzki, the popular tactician and 'father' of the *Sturm* concept, was killed after an engagement with

USAAF bombers. During the late morning, he had shot down a B-17 at 8,000 m some 30 km west of Magdeburg during another American attack on the oil plants, but his aircraft was damaged by the bombers' defensive fire. Pursued by a USAAF escort fighter, von Kornatzki attempted to make an emergency landing, only for his Fw 190A-8 to crash after hitting power lines at Zilly, near Halberstadt. Major Gerhard Schroeder, *Staffelkapitän* of 8.(*Sturm*)/JG 4 and a former bomber pilot, assumed command of II.(*Sturm*)/JG 4 following von Kornatzki's death.

The notion of using bombs dragged through the air at the end of cables against four-engined bombers would not go away. In September 1944, Dr.-Ing. Walter Wundes of the Gothaer Waggonfabrik of Gotha, a prolific designer of radical anti-bomber proposals such as one-time-use ramming aircraft, put forward a proposal for a method to destroy an enemy bomber by means of:

> . . . a bomb towed on the end of a wire cable towards the path of an oncoming enemy aircraft. Upon the impact of the enemy bomber with the cable, the explosive charge would be forced by its momentum towards the bomber and explode. The wire cable would be released from the tow aircraft at the moment the enemy aircraft makes contact with the cable.

Nothing came of it.

23

Darkening Skies

After the loss of Normandy and the Wehrmacht's retreat to the Seine, one by one, the battered fighter *Geschwader* were pulled back into the Reich for badly needed rest and refitting. Occasionally, the German Ministry of Public Enlightenment and Propaganda was able to make good press from those *Experten* who had survived the summer. For example, in July, Major Josef Priller, *Kommodore* of JG 26 was awarded the Swords to his Knight's Cross for his 100th victory and Hauptmann Anton Hackl received the decoration for his 162nd. In August, Major Kurt Bühligen, *Kommodore* of JG 2 received the Swords for reaching 104 victories. Their faces were splashed across the pages of the Party magazines.

But by the autumn of 1944, however, periodic individual accomplishments, no matter how meritorious, did little to salvage the Luftwaffe's deteriorating prestige in the eyes of the German leadership. In August, unable to contain his anger any further at the Jagdwaffe's perceived abject failure as a fighting force and its evident inability to defend the homeland against the bombers, Adolf Hitler dragged in its Commander-in-Chief for a confrontation. For Göring, it was a humiliating experience. In the presence of Generaloberst Alfred Jodl and Generaloberst Heinz Guderian, Hitler chided, 'The Luftwaffe's doing nothing! It's no longer worthy to be an independent service – and that's your fault!' As the two Wehrmacht generals diplomatically left the room, tears trickled down the Reichsmarschall's cheeks.

On 10 September, an advance party from the staff of Generalmajor Grabmann's 3. *Jagddivision* based at the *Diogenes* bunker at Deelen, in the Netherlands, was despatched to prepare for a relocation eastwards to a new *Ausweichgefechtsstand* (alternative battle headquarters) at Duisburg, more than 100 km to the southeast, within the building used by the FluKo there. The target date for the move of the entire operational staff was set for 17 September, although a signals *Vorkommando* (advance detachment) under Oberleutnant Dr. Wilhelm

Behlen, the divisional Adjutant, flagged up that facilities at Duisburg might not be sufficient for the functioning of a full divisional battle HQ. Behlen was able to locate suitable accommodation for the divisional *Führungsstab* but not for its administrative, signals and support personnel. They would have to take quarters in a Flak barracks in Dortmund.

Compared to the facilities at Deelen, this was far from ideal, but clearly the risk from the advancing Allied armies and air forces was now forcing Schmid's and Grabmann's hands. Better a proactive relocation now than a reactive one under pressure later. Over the next four days, crates containing 3. *Jagddivision*'s transportable light equipment, files and documents were moved by train from *Diogenes* to Duisburg. Any remaining material would be moved by road at the time of the final stage of relocation.

On 16 September, a column of lorries was ready to move the entire divisional staff, and departure was set for 1000 hrs the next morning. However, that evening at the regular Divisional conference, as a result of a conversation between Grabmann and Schmid, it was decided to place the planned movement on hold. At this point, 3. *Jagddivision* at Deelen was left with the minimum necessary *Führungsstab* with which it could function.

The next morning pandemonium broke out.

On Sunday, 17 September, the Allies launched Operation *Market Garden*. In an unusually headstrong move, Field Marshal Bernard Montgomery had successfully persuaded Eisenhower that under his control, the British Second Army, led by Gen Miles Dempsey, could mount a 'rapid and violent' air–ground thrust across the Rhine and the Maas to form the spearhead of an advance into the German plain. The US Army's 82nd and 101st Airborne Divisions would seize the Nijmegen and Eindhoven bridges, respectively, whilst the British 1st Airborne Division would take the bridge at Arnhem. Ultimately, bridgeheads would be established east of the Ijssel while working with the US First Army to eventually isolate and surround the Ruhr. It was also hoped that the operation would affect the German ability to launch V2 rockets against London.

As a first move, in the early hours of the morning, a force of 200 Lancasters and 23 Mosquitos of RAF Bomber Command struck at Luftwaffe airfields near the Dutch–German border. At 1130 hrs, a few poorly aimed bombs fell on Deelen airfield and around 3. *Jagddivision*'s staff accommodation area not far from the *Diogenes* bunker. It was here that Grabmann had to shelter as the bombs exploded. He, wrongly, assumed that *Diogenes* was also being attacked, and had no means of communicating with the bunker.

Meanwhile, in the bunker itself, the Divisional Operations Officer and his small team took matters into their own hands and declared a full alert. He ordered troops to tackle the fire in the accommodation area and for two companies of soldiers to form a defensive line south of the bunker. He also instructed his team to destroy all secret files and documents.

At one point, the Operations Officer was alarmed to notice a glider land about a kilometre from the bunker. Indeed, by late afternoon, hundreds of Allied gliders had landed in the Netherlands, depositing more than 20,000 troops, 500 support vehicles, 330 artillery pieces and hundreds of tons of equipment. Simultaneously, as part of *Market Garden*, British tanks and vehicles had started to advance north from Eindhoven.

Grabmann appeared at the bunker at 1530 hrs and, following consultation with Schmid, at 1600 hrs ordered the Divisional personnel, with the exception of a minimal *Führungsstab*, to evacuate along the predetermined lines to Duisburg.

Using two 1,000 kg and eight 500 kg bombs which had been acquired earlier and placed in the *Führungsraum* specifically, Grabmann's Operations Officer instructed the officer in charge of the soldiers to ignite the bomb at first sight of any British paratroopers. At 1815 hrs he left for Duisburg. Forty-five minutes later, *Diogenes*, the Battle Headquarters of 3. *Jagddivision* responsible for Luftwaffe fighter control over the Western Front and northwestern areas of the Reich, was blown up.[1]

Hardly had Grabmann and 3. *Jagddivision* arrived at *Diogenes III*, their new headquarters at Duisburg-Kaiserberg, than I. *Jagdkorps* signalled the *Division* during the evening of the 17th to instruct that in cooperation with II. *Jagdkorps*, its new task was to combat 'enemy transport and bomber units' in the Allied landing area around Arnhem, with fighters 'provided by I. *Jagdkorps*'. The priority was to destroy enemy gliders and their transports and to fire on landed paratroops, who would probably be dropped at dawn and dusk. To this end, Schmid would be sending Grabmann the Fw 190s of IV./JG 54 and III./JG 11, which were to operate as a *Gefechtsverband* under Major Wolfgang Späte.[2]

But on 18 September, a day when the Jagdwaffe – unlike the USAAF's fighters – had flown few sorties due to bad weather, Hitler told Generalleutnant Werner Kreipe, the Luftwaffe Chief-of-Staff, that he thought the Luftwaffe 'incompetent, cowardly and letting him down. I have no desire to speak to you again'.[3]

The problem was that, by degree, the Luftwaffe's fighter units based in the Reich were having to shoot down ever larger numbers of bombers while tackling ever larger numbers of escorting fighters, defend their own airfields from attack, deal with increasing losses of both experienced and freshly arrived pilots, endure shortages of fuel and parts – the latter affecting serviceability – and respond to new threats, such as the *Market Garden* landings.

For example, on the 19th, from his hastily readied *Führungsraum* at *Diogenes III*, Grabmann ordered that two *Gefechtsverbände* (one consisting of IV./JG 54 and III./JG 11, and one comprising II./JG 27, III./JG 4 and I./JG 76) were to be deployed in the Arnhem and Nijmegen areas, respectively, to strike at Allied ground forces, while another (comprising elements of JG 4 with I./JG 3, III./JG 300 and III./JG 53) would operate around Eindhoven. Clearly, undertaking such missions would pull these units away from air defence.[4]

Despite such a worsening predicament, the OKL still saw the Jagdwaffe's prime mission in September 1944 as one of air defence and ensuring 'domination of the air over friendly territory and the destruction of enemy aircraft by day and night', as well as 'the shooting down of as great a number of bombers as possible before they reach their target'. Accordingly, the OKL Operations Staff issued a new pamphlet for distribution among all freshly trained pilots reaching units flying in defence of the Reich in which this philosophy was emphasised. It also detailed how such a crucial task was to be organised and achieved.

The pamphlet explained how ultimate control of all forces engaged in the air defence of the Reich continued to lie with *Luftflotte Reich* in accordance with directives from the OKL. It also noted that the production of area-based air situation pictures, the ensuing fast and 'unfailing' relaying of information derived from such pictures to all commands in the *Reichsverteidigung*, the day-to-day overseeing of daylight fighter operations and the control of air raid warning services was managed by the *Jagdkorps*, which reported to the *Luftflotte*:

> The *Jagdkorps* is responsible for the marshalling of fighter forces according to time and place, and for determining the points of defence according to the given situation. The *Jagdkorps* appoints the *Jagddivision* which leads the mission and ensures timely transfer of control to a neighbouring *Divisional* area.

At this time, the *Jagddivisionen* or the *Jafüs* directly controlled the fighter units assigned to them in combat. They were responsible for all measures taken before and after a combat operation to ensure the correct tactical and technical conduct of the units, as well as efficient cooperation with other arms of the *Reichsverteidigung*, such as with *Flakeinsatzleiters* (Flak operations directors). For the duration of the battle over its own area, a *Jagddivision* also controlled all units sent into its zone from other *Divisional* or *Jafü* areas.

The included *Jagdgeschwadern* were responsible for the operations, supplies and replacements for their component *Gruppen*. The *Geschwaderkommodore* was responsible for the correct tactical execution of a mission. Each *Gruppe*, as a tactical command, was equipped with personnel, machines and signals to enable it to operate independently in combat operations. The *Gruppenkommandeur* directed his *Gruppe* depending on the briefing and mission assigned to him in the air.

The OKL recognised that the size and strong defence of enemy bomber formations by September 1944, and their fighter escorts, meant that only deployment of 'strong, concentrated fighter formations promises success'. As usual, the assemblies of larger *Gefechtsverbände* were to take place beyond the approach routes of enemy escort fighters. In cases where second missions against bomber formations were possible, greater *Gruppe*- or *Gefechtsverband*-strength fighter formations were always preferable to 'small, split-up forces'.

The prevailing, and tried and tested, tactical doctrine was very much geared towards deployment of fighters in '*Division* strength'. In instances where the enemy deployed several bomber formations, the German fighters were to engage just one formation, rather than diluting striking strength by attacking several formations. The *Höhenjagdgruppen* would be used primarily against the enemy escort, preferably 'destroying' them or leading them away from the bombers before other Luftwaffe fighters engaged. The use of *Zerstörer* units was only beneficial against unescorted bombers or when the escort was engaged with the *Zerstörers'* own escorts. Depending on the composition, strength and exit route of a bomber formation, second attack missions against retiring bombers were always favoured.

In terms of attack tactics:

> The first attack by the fighters has the goal of breaking up the enemy formation. In further attacks, the simultaneous attack by several fighter or *Zerstörer* units is always to be aimed for. If, however, an enemy formation breaks through to the target, at least the dropping of its bombs should be hindered with all available strength and means.
>
> The target of the attack for each fighter is one aircraft. Aiming at the centre or spraying of bullets over the bomber formation does not lead to success. From a flying point of view, the easiest method is the attack from the rear with a slight stepping down of the attack formation. Attacks from head-on and from the side require a high measure of flying ability and exceptionally good gunnery.[5]

But in reality, before OKL's aforementioned wished-for 'domination of the air over friendly territory' could be achieved, a more immediate goal was 'equality', and even on that count, the Jagdwaffe was significantly outgunned by Allied strength. On 20 September Grabmann's 3. *Jagddivision* reported 223 Bf 109s and 84 Fw 190s on strength for a total of 307 machines. Of these, 168 Messerschmitts and 45 Focke-Wulfs were *Einsatzbereit*. Over the next ten days, this strength increased to 178 Bf 109s (122 serviceable) and 71 Fw 190s (40 serviceable).[6]

The Fw 190s of the *Sturmgruppen* were active again on the morning of 27 September. In what was one of the most formidable missions of its kind, three waves of *Sturmgruppen* numbering some 120 aircraft, escorted by the Bf 109s of I./JG 300, attacked the B-24s of the 2nd BD whilst on a mission to Kassel. The first wave comprised IV.(*Sturm*)/JG 3 led by Hauptmann Moritz, the second comprised II.(*Sturm*)/JG 4 led by Oberleutnant Othmar Zehart and the third, II.(*Sturm*)/JG 300 led by Leutnant Klaus Bretschneider. II.(*Sturm*)/JG 4 shot down 26 Liberators of the 445th BG in three minutes – the largest loss suffered by any single USAAF group in one mission in the entire war. Oberleutnant Hans-Martin Markhoff, *Staffelkapitän* of 8.(*Sturm*)/JG 4, recalled that:

> The 30 mm Mk 108 cannon proved remarkably effective. Those fortunate enough not to be peppered by the bombers' fire during the closing approach were almost always assured of a victory. Moments later, the sky was scattered with chunks of debris and aircraft parts – pieces of wing, rudder, occasionally even complete engines – whistling around your ears. The debris momentarily appeared to be flying in formation with the bombers before tumbling away.[7]

German pilot losses from this action amounted to 18 (including Zehart who was listed as missing in action), with a further eight wounded. Thirty-two aircraft were damage-rated at 60 per cent or more.

The next day (28 September), the Eighth Air Force came back to bomb an oil target at Magdeburg, but in bad weather only 23 of 417 bombers despatched found the main target and the rest bombed the city. Of the Flying Fortresses that made it to Magdeburg, 27 were from the 303rd BG. They had completed their bomb run and had turned for home when their combat box was attacked from the rear in a *Breitkeil* formation at 1250 hrs by the Fw 190s of IV.(*Sturm*)/JG 3, which, together with II.(*Sturm*)/JG 4 and II.(*Sturm*)/JG 300, formed a *Gefechtsverband*.

Leutnant Oskar Romm of 15.(*Sturm*)/JG 3 claimed two B-17s for his 84th and 85th victories, while Feldwebel Willi Maximowitz, also of

15. *Staffel*, scored his 13th victory. Unteroffizier Hubert Chlond of 5.(*Sturm*)/JG 4 was flying an Fw 190 that day:

> I eased my target into the Revi and let him have the first bursts at a range of 150 to 200 m. As on previous sorties, my fire chewed into the rudder and tail fin, wiping out the tail gunner's position which posed us the greatest threat. The gunner's compartment detached from the body of the aircraft and went spinning down. I couldn't see whether or not its occupant had managed to bail out. By modifying the angle of fire slightly, I was able to rake the length of the fuselage right up to the cockpit – a huge sheet of flame erupted from this section almost immediately. This was one B-17 that was done for.

Chlond passed over the Flying Fortress and momentarily found himself in empty sky. He turned east and spotted another B-17, but seconds later he was attacked by a USAAF fighter and was forced to bail out of his burning Focke-Wulf. Chlond came down in a tree, trapped by his parachute. He had suffered facial burns and remained in hospital for five months.[8]

A similar fate befell Major Alfred Lindenberger, a 47-year-old reserve airman from Stuttgart who had flown fighters with the Imperial Fliegertruppe during World War I. After flying as observer on the Western Front in 1917, as a fighter pilot he had shot down his first kill – a Breguet XIV over Villers-Cotterêts – on 30 May 1918 while at the controls of a Fokker Dr. I triplane from *Jasta Boelcke*.[9] He ended the war credited with 12 aerial victories. Now, ostensibly as *Kommandeur*, Lindenberger had determinedly clawed himself back into one of the most dangerous and demanding forms of aerial combat at the controls of an armoured Fw 190A-8 assigned to *Stab* II.(*Sturm*)/JG 300.

Flying as wingman to an NCO pilot, Lindenberger closed on a B-17 to within 50 m, firing four lengthy bursts and attracting no return fire. The bomber fell away – it was Lindenberger's 13th victory. Remarkably, 14 minutes later, he shot down a P-51, but two other Mustangs latched onto his tail and, despite evasive manoeuvring, forced him to bail out over a farm in the Halberstadt area. Lindenberger subsequently ended up in hospital with sprains and bruises.[10]

Particularly badly hit by the *Sturmgruppen* attacks was the Low Squadron of the 303rd BG, which was flying as the 41st CW's 'B' group. In less than a minute, 11 of the squadron's bombers were shot down. According to the 303rd's records, 'Attacks were chiefly from five to seven o'clock, from low to level. The tactics utilised by the enemy pilots demonstrated that they were determined, efficient and experienced'.

Once again, the lethality of the MK 108 and its mine shells was demonstrated. Two of the latter exploded in the waist position of the B-17 of 1Lt V. L. Howard and the left wing started to streak fire. The Boeing went down in a spin from 20,000 ft. Four parachutes were seen prior to the bomber hitting the ground near Ohrum. Another Fw 190 shot a large hole in the right wing of 1Lt James T. Hahn's Flying Fortress. What then happened was awful, as the 303rd's history records:

> The gas tank behind the No. 4 engine was hit and was on fire, then fire enveloped the entire right wing. The aircraft was forced out of formation and then started down. 1Lt Hahn ordered his crew to bail out and his Fortress blew up while in a spin. He died at his controls. The aircraft crashed near Ohrum, south of Wolfenbüttel. S/Sergeant Hans Howald (Tail Gunner) died in the aircraft. T/Sgt John R. Conkling (Radio Operator) and S/Sgt Robert D. Proctor (Waist Gunner) bailed out, but their chutes had been damaged by 20 mm shells and failed to open properly. They died on impact with the ground. 1/Lieutenant Jack H. Benford died in his aircraft.

2Lt Lorin W. Hamman was the bombardier on board *Minnie the Moocher*, a B-17 flying in the 'tail-end Charlie' position in the Low Low Flight – it was a dangerous place to be. Hamman recalled:

> I heard Sergeant [Charles R.] Coughlin, the Tail Gunner, call and report 'Here come the fighters'. The pilot told him to keep cool and try to get a few of the Focke-Wulfs. I heard Coughlin's gun firing while his interphone button was still down. Then he said 'Jesus'. That was the last I heard from him. The plane went into a tight spin and I bailed out at 18,000 ft.

Six cannon shells punched through *Minnie the Moocher*'s fuselage, killing the pilot, co-pilot, flight engineer and the ball turret and tail gunners.

Feldwebel Klaus Neumann of 16.(*Sturm*)/JG 3 shot down his 29th victim, and Oberleutnant Horst Haase, also of 16. *Staffel*, was to enjoy success too. 360th BS B-17 *Miss Umbragio*, flown by 1Lt Willam F. Miller in the Low Low Flight alongside *Minnie the Moocher*, suffered hits to two engines. Burning gasoline also streamed out of the bomber's ruptured fuel tanks. The bomb group's history recounts how:

> The first Fw 190 burst badly injured S/Sergeant Calvin G. Tarkington, the Tail Gunner. He crawled out of the tail compartment, asked the Waist Gunner, Sergeant Tony Zelnio, to help him and died.

Tarkington's body was found in the wreckage of the aircraft when it crashed southeast of Wolfenbüttel. The radio operator was blown out of the aircraft, but the rest of the crew managed to bail out.[11] *Miss Umbragio* was Haase's 56th victim.

The Eighth Air Force recorded the relentless tactics of the Luftwaffe fighters as follows:

> The enemy aircraft attacked in waves of 15 to 20 at a time, coming in from 6 o'clock high, in a line abreast. They broke away in all directions, then returned to come in from below as the next wave attacked from above.[12]

In total, the USAAF lost 34 heavy bombers in the raid, with IV.(*Sturm*)/JG 3 accounting for ten of them. An 11th bomber also failed to make it home. By the end of a month of intensive operations, IV.(*Sturm*)/JG 3 was able to field only 30 aircraft.

As noted in the previous chapter, during the late summer E.Kdo 25 was redesignated J.Gr.10 and placed under the command of Major Georg Christl, a Knight's Cross-holder who had previously commanded III./ZG 26.

Under Christl, J.Gr.10 pressed on with E.Kdo 25's trials with the SG 116 *Zellendusche* automatic weapon. By 22 August 1944, the unit had commenced fitting the photoelectric cell, which by that time was under manufacture as the '*Wurzen*' at the Hugo Schneider Aktiengesellschaft Metallwarenfabrik in Leipzig, into 19 of its Fw 190s at Tarnewitz. However, further development was dropped, forcing the various parties involved in the weapon's manufacture back to the drawing board. By 18 September the decision was taken not to use the SG 116 operationally until greater accuracy could be assured, although fitment of the optical devices was nearing completion.

In late September, one of the RLM's senior armaments officers calculated that in a pass below a bomber at 50 m, a fighter equipped with five upward-firing SG 116 barrels triggered by a photo-electric cell could look to achieve three hits on the target aircraft.

In his fortnightly work reports, Christl admitted that the automatic triggering device in the *Zellendusche* was not proving reliable. However, in ground tests, it was found that when fired at a wing salvaged from a crashed B-17 from a range of 60 m, the equipment and detonator functioned correctly, with the shell achieving a velocity of 845 m per second.

In the air, tests using the SG 116 were conducted against an Fw 58 and a He 177, both of which had been rigged with specially constructed automatic steering devices. After a pre-determined period of time, the pilots of both aircraft bailed out and they flew on unmanned, at which point the Fw 190s made their attacks at altitudes of 1,000 m against the Focke-Wulf and at 6,000 m against the Heinkel. It was noted that problems arose at heights in excess of 6,000 m when the automatic triggering device became too sensitive, with premature and random firings being a problem. The Fw 58 was hit and damaged, but the Heinkel flew on undamaged and is believed to have eventually crashed into the Baltic as planned.[13] Whatever the case, the results of these aerial tests failed to tally with the optimistic theoretical results calculated by the *Technisches Amt*.

During September, the Eighth Air Force lost 248 B-17s and B-24s or 1.6 per cent of the total number of heavy bombers that attacked Nazi-occupied territory. That was a reduction of 216 over July and August – an encouraging sign for the USAAF. And yet as the Operational Analysis Section at the Eighth's Headquarters warned starkly:

> It would be a mistake, however, to conclude that the enemy fighter problem has been licked, when the average number of bombers lost per month in the first eight months of 1944 was more than twice that for the last eight months of 1943. Furthermore, in September 1944, the Luftwaffe staged a comeback after a three-month lull, and on two successive days destroyed more bombers with fewer fighters in a shorter time than on any previous occasion. Losses in four days in September totalled 144 bombers, more than half of which were attributed to enemy fighters.[14]

For the Luftwaffe, September did see record deliveries of more than 3,000 new or repaired single-engined fighters, largely the results of the *Jägerstab*'s efforts. By October, new, improved fighter types were reaching the units. III./JG 27, under Hauptmann Dr. Peter Werfft at Cologne-Wahn, took delivery of the first 75 enhanced and aerodynamically refined Bf 109K-4s, whilst III./JG 54, under Hauptmann Robert Weiss at Oldenburg, received the first of the vaunted, 'long-nosed' Fw 190D-9 *Doras* in late September. The latter machine, powered by the Jumo 213A engine, would later prove to be an outstandingly manoeuvrable and fast fighter when pitted against Allied types.

The immediate problem facing the Jagdwaffe was a lack of sufficiently trained pilots able to defend the skies over the Reich or the Western Front.

This was exacerbated by the ease with which the USAAF was able to overcome damage inflicted on its heavy bombers by German fighters. Between 21 January and 30 April 1944, for example, in the 33,065 heavy bomber sorties conducted by the Eighth Air Force, 8,859 aircraft suffered battle damage. But the Eighth's infrastructure of repair depots and mobile repair units fixed 83.44 per cent of the damaged bombers within five days and almost 50 per cent within 24 hours. As one USAAF officer remarked, when it came to repair support, there were 'almost more than enough men, equipment and accumulated experience'.[15]

For the Germans, the Western Front had so deteriorated by this stage that neither Generalfeldmarschall Walter Model, the *Oberbefehlshaber West*, nor his replacement, Generalfeldmarschall Gerd von Rundstedt, were able to stem the rapid pace of the Allied advance. Virtually unopposed, the troop-laden armour of the British Second Army broke out of France and swept on into Belgium, taking Brussels and the key seaport of Antwerp with its vital harbour installations still intact in early September. By late October, Montgomery's troops had reached the southern banks of the Scheldt, where their task was to flush the estuary of resistance so as to open Antwerp to Allied shipping.

Worse still, in mid-September and further to the east, the first US troops had crossed the Sauer north of Trier and penetrated the frontier of the Reich itself. Two weeks later, elements of the American First Army breached what was thought to be the impenetrable Siegfried Line north of Aachen. The front was collapsing, with the Allies now engaging German troops within the borders of the Reich.

But from what seemed disaster, Galland was attempting a recovery and ultimately a reprisal:

> Our fighter units arrived at the Rhine in a chaotic condition. The *Gruppen, Geschwadern* and even *Staffeln* had got into a complete mix-up, and except for a few, had shrunk to a fifth of their normal strength. It took a long time for the decimated groundcrews to find their units. They had sustained great material losses. The existing ground organisations on both sides of the Rhine were in no position to cope with all these new units. Each *Luftgau* now had additional airstrips under its care. To re-establish order within the Jagdwaffe, we introduced a complete regrouping. My main desire was to create a new reserve.

Other *Gruppen*, only slightly less scathed, returned from the Balkans and the East. Elements of JG 302 came from Rumania and IV./JG 54 and III./JG 11 arrived from Poland.

Galland continued:

Oddly enough, my proposal to give priority to the replenishing and formation of reserves instead of sending forces to the front was accepted without demur by the Supreme Command. As on my two previous attempts in this direction, I maintained that this was the only possible way to deliver the necessary *Grosse Schlag* – 'Great Blow' – in the defence of the Reich. This phrase was taken up in the highest quarters.

With his *Grosse Schlag* policy sanctioned by both Hitler and Göring, and the short luxury of a halt in the extended Allied advance, Galland began working to create a 'new' reserve of such strength that the Jagdwaffe would be in a position to send up at least 2,000 fighters against a major American raid, with the intention of making an impact on the escort fighters as well as harrying the bombers at any point between Sweden and Switzerland if necessary. Galland was prepared to sacrifice 400 aircraft and 150 pilots if 400–500 *Viermots* could be brought down in one massive operation.

He began by stripping the southern front and Austria of fighters. Such moves meant, for example, that the four *Gruppen* of JG 27 previously scattered across France, Germany and Austria could be reunited within the Reich. The nominal strength of each home defence *Gruppe* was increased, as was the amount of specialist training given to pilots serving in the *Reichsverteidigung*. Practice manoeuvres were run through again and again, taking into account all possible variations of approach flight the bombers might take and using the lessons gained in the sector of I. *Jagdkorps* over the past seven months. Sufficient fuel was scraped together and stockpiled to cover 2,500 sorties, and command infrastructure was revised.

Nor did the challenging regeneration of the Jagdwaffe distract it entirely from its ability to wage defensive warfare. On 15 October, Maj Gen Doolittle told the RAF that he considered 'the German day fighter force was becoming a more and more serious threat'. There had been noticeable increases in the numbers of enemy fighters deployed, as well as improvements in tactics and armament.

These were limited initiatives, however, and were not enough to satisfy Hitler. By the end of October, he was again losing patience with what seemed yet more inertia on the part of the Luftwaffe fighter arm, only this time it was dressed up as 'strategic regeneration'. He had had enough. He wanted bombers brought down, but still the fighter pilots made excuses. What mattered was that the bombers were still getting through, inflicting continual damage to his oil supplies.

In this respect, the *Führer* had observed a dangerous new cycle beginning to emerge. Despite record aircraft availability, fuel supply was low, which meant that the production plants and refineries were not being protected and, despite Galland's efforts, many of those pilots who were flying had been insufficiently trained due to the lack of fuel!

Göring was prompted to gather a number of his key home defence commanders at the headquarters of *Luftflotte Reich* at Berlin-Wannsee on 26 October to address the problem. Galland recalled of this meeting:

> All formation leaders down to and including *Gruppenkommandeure* were present and a *Staffelkapitän* from each *Gruppe*. Apart from that, this glorious speech was also recorded and sent out to the units. It lasted for about three hours. He just kept chewing the same old stuff over and over again; the operations against England and how the fighter escort had not worked properly, and then came reproach after reproach – Africa, Sicily, escort missions to Malta, what had the Jagdwaffe achieved in the East? etc. In the end, there was doubt cast upon the fighting spirit of the fighters. There were a few who contradicted, and they had a very bad time of it. Afterwards, it was so bad that he could no longer bear to look at my face without getting worked up.

Then Göring announced:

> I want 500 B-17s brought down next time or I'll have you transferred to the infantry! The Allies know how to put up a good show at fighter protection – use them as an example!

By the end of the first week of October, 18 of J.Gr.10's *Wurzen*-fitted Fw 190s had returned to the *Gruppe*'s base at Parchim from the *Erprobungsstelle* at Tarnewitz, where the circuitry work was completed. One machine remained at Tarnewitz, along with one of the *Erprobungsstselle*'s Focke-Wulfs, and both aircraft were to take part in further firing trials against another He 177. These resulted in only one Fw 190, equipped with five barrels, firing two shots and achieving two hits, but with three barrels suffering misfires. The other Focke-Wulf failed to get off the ground due to technical faults.

Tests continued through until the end of December 1944, and saw a series of revisions and enhancements to the weapon and its firing system. It was planned to mount the SG 116 *Zellendusche* in three different ways in the Fw 190 for operations: firstly, four barrels in a rhomboid mounting in the fuselage; secondly, six barrels in two triangular blocks; and thirdly, three barrels in a line, with a 'fan' spread that saw each barrel angled at two degrees. However, nothing more materialised in terms of operationally ready equipment.[16]

24

Blow after Blow

At dawn on 2 November 1944, there were nearly 30 operational day fighter *Gruppen* at readiness in Germany, with a further 16 refitting or training, totalling 695 aircraft. That day, these units were once again to be tested to their limits. The targets were the refineries at Gelsenkirchen and Castrop-Rauxel and the Leuna hydrogenation plant southeast of Merseburg. Furthermore, Allied commanders were taking no chances on a repeat of the savage punishment their bomber crews had received over the preceding weeks and had arranged a fighter screen of approximately 600 P-51s.

Some 500 German fighters were scrambled to intercept in conditions of nine-tenths cloud and extremely poor visibility. Nevertheless, it was to be an all-out effort. At midday, a *Gefechtsverband* formed around Hauptmann Moritz's IV.(*Sturm*)/JG 3 hit the B-17s of the 91st BG in a head-on formation, clawing 13 of the bombers out of the sky. Knight's Cross-holder Leutnant Werner Gerth was one of 11 pilots from IV.(*Sturm*)/JG 3 killed that day when he rammed a bomber over Bitterfeld and his parachute failed to open. Gerth had accumulated 25 four-engined kills and was a veteran of *Sturmstaffel* 1.

Major Gerhard Michalski led the Fw 190s of II.(*Sturm*)/JG 4 up from Welzow and met the Americans over Köthen. Whilst the Bf 109s of JG 4's escort *Gruppen* took care of the Mustangs, the heavily armoured *Sturmjäger* went for the Flying Fortresses of the 457th BG, sending down nine of them.

The battle raged all afternoon, spreading across Saxony and Thuringia, yet in a moment of supreme irony, at the headquarters of *Luftflotte Reich*, Generaloberst Hans-Jurgen Stumpff was penning a new order to his regional airfield command:

The fuel situation makes further restriction of flying operations essential. I therefore issue the following orders:

1. A sortie is justifiable only if weather reports and the available tactical information promise success. Those responsible for operations must bear this in mind when issuing operational orders.
2. Training flights within units are prohibited until further notice unless specific quotas are issued for the purpose. My approval is required for exceptions to this rule.
3. No flights may be undertaken except for operational transfer, test and transport purposes.

Meanwhile, Oberst Gustav Rödel's JG 27, its four *Gruppen* of Bf 109s operating together for the first time since being brought back into the Reich, tried in vain to get to the bombers but clashed with Mustangs around Leipzig instead. It was to be the blackest day in the *Geschwader*'s history. Fighter after fighter plunged towards the earth, and by the time the battle ended JG 27 had had no fewer than 38 pilots killed or wounded. Rödel remembered:

> I flew and survived more than 1,000 missions, but attacking four-engined bombers flying in formation still remains a nightmare in my memory. Each attack had a different pattern. There were too many odds and unknown factors during an approach, such as weather, the counter-action of the fighter escort and the difficulty in manoeuvring in a large formation. The sole aim of the flight leader was to get his formation into a position which allowed a virtual collision course attack. Thereafter, it was every pilot for himself – he could hardly even keep an eye out for his wingman.

Figures still differ as to the exact casualties that both sides incurred during the battle, but sources place the Eighth Air Force losses at between 40 and 50 bombers – almost four per cent of the total force – and 16 out of 873 fighters. Galland had lost 120 aircraft and 70 of his pilots, with another 28 wounded.

The battle had been so severe that Doolittle thought it perfectly reasonable to assume the Germans capable of bringing down up to 100 bombers on any future deep-penetration raid. In a letter to Spaatz after the mission, he warned that as a result of improved, heavier calibre armament, the enemy fighters might soon be in a position to open fire on the bomber boxes beyond the range of their defensive weapons, and he complained about a shortage of available fighters in his air force.

As Galland told an American interrogator in May 1945:

> If the weather from the middle of November and during December had been decent, you might have been attacked by 2,500 to 3,000

fighters. With those numbers, our Fighter Arm would have been in a better position to cope.

The *Grosse Schlag*, however, had become little more than a pipe dream.

On 5 November, the Chief of the Luftwaffe General Staff's Military Science Branch, 8. *Abteilung*, produced a stark study in which it was admitted, among other things, that 'German fuel production is now almost at a standstill'. The same report also estimated that only one to three per cent of enemy bombers were being destroyed in daylight attacks.

Given the prevailing attitudes of the Nazi high command at the time, 8. *Abteilung* was brave to put things into such candid perspective, and in doing so, it confronted the bleak reality facing the fighter force employed in the defence of the Reich:

> Our day fighters are facing the best aircraft of the Allied air forces. Our one standard day fighter aircraft, the Fw 190, can equal the performance of the Spitfire, Thunderbolt and Mustang at altitudes up to approximately 4,000 m, but at greater heights is undoubtedly inferior to these latter aircraft. Recent modifications have made the performance of the Me 109 equal to that of the enemy fighters at all altitudes. Similar modifications will have to be undertaken to improve the performance of the Fw 190.
>
> Such measures are, however, of an emergency nature, dictated by the necessity of attempting to counter our marked numerical inferiority by an increase in performance. Should the enemy decide on similar modifications, any temporary advantage that we may have gained will once more be lost.
>
> The inferiority of our personnel is also an important consideration. We are obliged to train our crews in about half the time allowed by the enemy for the purpose. In comparison with the enemy figure of 400 hours on training flying, our men can only be given 200 hours of instruction before being sent on operations. Total operational flying training time in the Luftwaffe at present is only 60–80 hours, as compared with the Anglo-American figure of 225 hours. Our pilots must attempt to counter-balance this obvious disadvantage by greater enthusiasm and courage.[1]

Five days after 8. *Abteilung* published its study, on 10 November, the concerns of Major Gerhard Stamp, the *Kommandeur* of the light fighter *Gruppe*

I./JG 300, highlighting the rise of Allied fighter strength operating over Germany, and the Luftwaffe's means to counter it, were also published in a report. The 24-year-old Stamp was a former bomber pilot from Bamberg who had flown Ju 88s with distinction in the Mediterranean, specialising in anti-shipping missions, and had been decorated with the Knight's Cross in March 1943 in recognition of one of the highest mission tallies for a bomber pilot in the Mediterranean theatre.

In the summer of 1943, he requested a transfer to the *Wilde Sau* nightfighters, joining newly formed 8./JG 300 as its *Staffelkapitän* in August. In May 1944 he was appointed commander of I./JG 300, and thus became increasingly involved in daylight operations over the Reich, and especially in combatting American escort fighters. Less than a month earlier he had shot down a P-51 west of Leipzig. Then, on 2 November 1944, Stamp's *Gruppe* had become embroiled in a controversy when Mustangs had strafed the unit's base at Borkheide, having followed some Bf 109s of JG 3 there, which, with their fuel levels low after combat, were seeking a place to land.

In a moment of opportunity, the USAAF fighters had destroyed 19 of I./JG 300's precious Bf 109s and damaged another 13 during a series of strafing passes. The *Jagddivision* had viewed this as incompetence, and Stamp was told to make a report for Schmid, who visited the *Gruppe* to personally investigate the disaster a few days later.[2] Stamp took the situation as his opportunity to enlighten the Luftwaffe's senior leaders about the realities of trying to attack bombers:

> The enemy's fighter defence of bomber formations is divided into two groups: one operating freelance around the whole bomber formation, and the other giving close protection to the bombers. This system of fighter protection is very effective owing to its manoeuvrability, and this, coupled with the loose-flying formation of the bombers, makes it unlikely that the present rate of [bomber] losses will increase.
>
> The problem of the air defence of the Reich is at present not so much a question of how to concentrate our fighter strength, but of how to attack effectively the enemy's fighter cover, and thus be able to strike at the bombers; and of how our own fighter losses can at the same time be reduced.
>
> Having regard to the performance of the Me 109 and Fw 190 against enemy types, it is apparent that to achieve any decisive rise in successes, the ratio of [Luftwaffe] escorting fighters to assault aircraft [*Sturmflugzeug*] would have to be increased to at least four-to-one to combat the enemy fighter cover alone. At present, not only are too few enemy aircraft being shot down, but losses inflicted by escorting enemy

fighters are so high that the units are being drained of their resources. The position will be worsened by the fact that Tempests and Spitfires can now operate over the centre of the Reich.

The solution to the problem of successful defence lies, therefore, in counter action against the enemy fighters which are superior both in numbers and performance. At present, our aim is to secure numerical superiority over the opposing fighter escort in the centre of the combat area. By putting a large number of fighters into operation, we should undoubtedly succeed in shooting down a considerable number of enemy aircraft in the first operations, and our own losses should be within reasonable limits. As countermeasures, the enemy might then either change the tactics of his fighter escort or avoid making attacks in weather conditions which would favour the operation of strong German fighter formations.

It is possible that the enemy, recognising the limits of large-scale operations by German fighters, would, by constant attacks, attempt a war of attrition. The German fighter force could not keep pace with such conditions for very long as the number of serviceable aircraft would be so reduced that the use of the term 'large-scale operation' would no longer be justified. The enemy could also change the tactics of his fighter escort, and by concentrating his forces, soon establish equality or superiority. The above considerations lead me to the conclusion that a change in the air situation over the Reich is not possible with the forces at present available.[3]

Stamp's prescient warning about the prospect of a worsening situation given that RAF and Commonwealth Spitfire and Tempest V squadrons were able to operate over Germany – adding to the threat already posed by the USAAF's fighters – would not have been welcome news to Göring, in particular.

Throughout 1944, aside from the already described *Zellendusche*, several other air-to-air weapons using photoelectric cell firing technology were proposed by German armaments manufacturers, ballistics engineers and Luftwaffe personnel for combat against enemy bomber formations.

One such weapon was the 2 cm SG '*Bürste*' (Brush), a rigid, vertically-mounted, spin-stabilised, volley-shot design for firing upwards, believed to have been the brainchild of Luftwaffe officer Oberleutnant Herbert Schlitter. The name *Bürste* reflected the weapon's 189 barrels, each just

200 mm in length, giving the appearance of the dense hairs of a brush. The *Bürste* was intended to fire 15 mm incendiary shells to achieve the equivalent rate of fire, in three volleys, of 20,000 rounds from an MG 151 at a velocity of 200 m per second. However, after ballistic calculations, the proposed weapon was considered ineffective and led to cancellation of the project.

Conceived by the HASAG concern in Leipzig, another design based on a 25 mm barrel with 2 cm MG 151 ammunition was the SG '*Harfe*' (Harp) which comprised one or two rows (one row either side) of 20 smooth tubes mounted to the fuselage side of an Fw 190, perpendicular to the direction of flight, giving the appearance of a harp. The forward tube of each line was placed just aft of the rearmost point of the Focke-Wulf's closed canopy glazing. The spacing between each tube was about one centimetre. The tubes were recoilless and electrically ignited, with powder gas being burned and discharged from an outlet in the base of each tube. They were set at an angle of 74 degrees to the horizontal axis of the aircraft. After firing, the tubes were jettisoned so as to avoid any aerodynamic interference to the fighter.

E.Kdo 25 first trialled the weapon in August 1944 when it fired 30 rounds of 2 cm incendiary shells simultaneously without any problems. An aerodynamically improved projectile was introduced which featured three flexible steel fins which folded up when loaded into the upper end of the tube and sprang into position when fired. Trials showed a satisfactory hit pattern and sufficient stability. However, as with the *Bürste*, the effect of the 2 cm Mine shells was deemed insufficient, so development of the *Harfe* was stopped in favour of larger calibre armament.[4]

Oberleutnant Schlitter also proposed a 2 cm system known as the '*Schlitter-Projekt*'. In this design, an obliquely mounted, multi-barrel weapon fired projectiles upwards or downwards following an optically operated triggering. After due consideration and some revision to the design, initial construction was taken over by the Reichswerke Hermann Göring at Salzgitter.

The weapon emerged as the '*Handfeger*' (hand brush) and took the form of no fewer than 60 2 cm tubes loaded with standard 20 mm MG 151 shells. It was intended as a single-shot weapon that had to be primed before take-off of the carrier aircraft and it could not be re-loaded during flight. The projectiles were fired at the equivalent rate of 20,000 rounds per minute, with a velocity of 180 m per second. Recoil was kept within a limit of five to six tons, but ultimately the weapon was not released for production for the same reasons as the *Harfe*.

In the meantime, as a progression of the *Handfeger*, 60 3 cm tubes were assembled on a spring-loaded platform mounted behind the pilot, based on a recoilless system and discharging balancing gas downwards, to become a basic prototype of the SG '*Bombersäge*' ('Bomber Saw'). The adverse course of the war prevented any further practical development of the weapon, however.

On 30 December 1944 the *Erprobungsstelle* Tarnewitz drew up a table which compared the number of hits expected on a B-17 by a fighter equipped with each weapon during a pass below at a distance of 50 m. This indicated that while the *Bürste*, *Harfe* and *Schlitter* weapons were heavier, greater impact could be expected when compared to the earlier mentioned SG 116 *Zellendusche*.[5]

Weapon	Calibre	Barrels	V⁰ m/sec	Operational Weight	Anticipated Hits to:			
					Fuselage	Inner Wing	Engine	Outer Wing
Bürste	15 mm	189	200	382 kg	40	16.6	20.3	12.2
Harfe	20 mm	15–20	325	37.8 kg	26.2	16.6	20.3	12.2
Schlitter	20 mm	60	385	107.2 kg	23.6	16.6	20.3	12.2
SG 116	30 mm	3	845	102.2 kg	4.9	4.5	4.9	3.5

On 30 November 1944, Göring visited the *Stab* of JG 300 at Jüterbog, and almost immediately embarked upon an angry confrontation with the *Kommodore*, Oberstleutnant Dahl. That morning, nearly 900 Eighth Air Force bombers were making for German oil refineries and transport targets, but the skies over Jüterbog airfield had been heavy with fog.

As the Reichsmarschall's cavalcade drew to a stop outside the hangars, Göring hauled his overcoated bulk from his Mercedes saloon under parting clouds through which the weak beams of a winter sun filtered. He stomped across the tarmac clutching his diamond-encrusted baton and demanded to know from Dahl why his *Geschwader* was not airborne to intercept the American 'terror-bombers'. Dahl replied that the adverse weather conditions had prevented a safe take-off and assembly of his formation. Göring exploded:

> You cowards! Now I know why your *Geschwader* holds the record for parachute jumps – you jump so as not to fight! Why have you not obeyed my orders? I shall order my Flak to have you shot from the skies. You and your rotten fighter pilots are going to feel my hand. Before the sun sets tonight, I shall have you shot!

In November 1944, the various organs of the Reich defence infrastructure continued to be overseen by *Luftflotte Reich* under Generaloberst Stumpff at Berlin-Wannsee. Fighter control over the central Reich was maintained by I. *Jagdkorps* under Schmid, his command having moved to new headquarters known as *Meteor 4* in a former hospital at Treuenbrietzen in April 1944. Schmid would be replaced by Generalleutnant Joachim-Friedrich Huth on 30 November.

The *Korps* remained responsible for 1. *Jagddivision* under Generalleutnant Kurt Kleinrath at Döberitz, covering northern Germany east of the Elbe, and 2. *Jagddivision* under Generalmajor Ibel at Stade, which continued to protect the Heligoland Bight, Hamburg, Bremen, Schleswig Holstein and Hanover. 3. *Jagddivision* under Generalmajor Grabmann was at Duisburg, with the *Jagdabschnittsführer Mittelrhein* under Oberstleutnant Hans Trübenbach at Darmstadt. The latter covered parts of northwest Germany, the north of the Netherlands, east towards Wiedenbrück, in North Rhine-Westphalia, south to Aachen and Mannheim and parts of Belgium.

Southern Germany, including the Frankfurt Plain and western Austria, remained the jurisdiction of 7. *Jagddivision* recently installed at Pfaffenhofen, while directly to the east, 8. *Jagddivision* was at Cobenzl under Oberst Gotthardt Handrick and covered eastern Austria, Bohemia-Moravia and parts of Hungary.

From 21 September 1944, *Luftflotte* 3 was redesignated *Luftwaffenkommando West* under Generalleutnant Alexander Holle at Limburg an der Lahn, and it oversaw the fighter operations of II. *Jagdkorps*. The latter had moved east to Flammersfeld under Generalmajor Dietrich Peltz, with Generalmajor Karl Hentschel's 5. *Jagddivision* at Durlach, both units covering the Western Front. In the east was *Jafü Ostpreussen* at Insterburg and *Jafü Schlesien* at Cosel.[6]

From October through to the end of November, *Luftwaffenkommando West* reported the following strength figures for day fighters:

	Actual Strength	Effective Strength
2/10/44	343	214
18/10/44	353	191
1/11/44	345	223
28/11/44	494	249

It is intriguing to observe that the more adversity the Nazi war machine faced, the more inventive, extraordinary and technically brilliant some of its designs were. One such example was the X4, a highly advanced, remotely-controlled, wire-guided, rocket-propelled, fin-stabilised air-to-air missile intended for launching by fighters against formations of heavy bombers. It was originally conceived in June 1943 by Dr. Max Kramer, a scientist and aerodynamicist employed by the Ruhrstahl AG Presswerke at Brackwede.

The X4 had a 20 kg warhead carrying a dinitroglycol-based explosive. It was cigar-shaped, with the warhead section made of steel. This was attached to the central section of the missile by wooden screws together with an adaptor for the fuse attached to the nose in the same way. It was designed to be launched from beneath the wing of an Fw 190.

Once fired, ideally from a range of 1.5–2.5 km, the X4 was guided by the pilot using visual observation and a control stick in conjunction with signalled corrections applied to a Telefunken transmitter and receiver from a small control unit in the aircraft. Shortly after release, the X4 would reach a speed of some 250 m per second. This was the kind of weapon which Maj Gen Doolittle feared, and about which he had warned his RAF counterparts in October.

Propulsion came from a bi-fuel BMW 548 rocket motor which functioned from the reaction between a nitric acid oxidant formed of 96 per cent nitric acid HNO_3 and four per cent ferric chloride $FeCl_2$, and Tonka 250 rocket fuel comprised of 57 per cent crude oxide monoxylidene and 43 per cent triethylamine.

Ballistics research showed that as the X4 flew past a B-17 at speed from behind, it was vital that the warhead detonated within what had been determined as the area of 'lethality for explosions'. In launching a missile at the tail of a bomber with a miss distance of seven metres from the aircraft's centreline, overtaking at a speed of between 120–150 m per second, the missile would fly through the lethality zone for a 20 kg warhead in less than a tenth of a second. The X4 was therefore to incorporate a proximity fuse which would detect the bomber as its target and trigger the warhead within the lethality zone.

The first air-launched tests of prototype X4 missiles were conducted in August 1944 at Peenemünde-West using an Fw 190, an He 111 and, later, a Ju 88 as a carrier aircraft. They were considered partially successful, although weapons specialists always remained somewhat hesitant over the missile's deployment in numbers because of the volatility of its fuel system. Furthermore, it was thought that vulnerability of the parent aircraft to fighter attack would restrict the effective use of the missile in a combat situation, or at least restrict operations to missions against unescorted bomber formations.

Guided firing trials ensued using a command-link transmitter in January 1945, by which time around 130 flight trials had been carried out. However, development is believed to have been officially terminated on 6 February 1945. Some 100–200 missiles are estimated to have been completed, but many of the intended BMW 548 rocket motors were destroyed in air attacks on the company's works at Stargard.[7]

In April 1944, Air Marshal Sir Norman Bottomley, the Deputy Chief of the Air Staff, wrote to Air Chief Marshal Sir Arthur Harris in an attempt to persuade the reluctant head of RAF Bomber Command that he should reconsider his resistance to RAF heavy bombers mounting daylight raids on German targets. For its part, the Air Staff had concluded that such was the situation in the air war over Nazi Germany that deployment of Lancaster and Halifax heavy bombers in daylight would be 'both practicable and profitable'. The Air Staff believed that 'under cover of an adequate fighter escort', RAF Bomber Command's aircraft would be able to reach targets in western Germany, provided conditions were favourable and routes carefully planned. It was felt that losses 'should not be unduly heavy'.[8]

By June, however, Harris' viewpoint had changed remarkably, not least because he saw the significant impact Allied fighter escorts were making on Luftwaffe daylight fighter operations. Limited daylight bombing operations thus commenced on 27 August when RAF Bomber Command carried out its first major daylight raid to Germany for three years. A force of 216 Halifaxes, 14 Mosquitos and 13 Lancasters attacked the Rheinpreussen synthetic oil refinery at Homberg/Meerbeck.

Then, throughout the autumn of 1944, the pace of RAF daylight heavy bomber raids picked up, with oil remaining a key target when it came to mission planning, although, for example, in December 1944, the focus was on transport, with RAF Bomber Command conducting 17 daylight raids in that month alone.[9]

On 12 December, the target was the Ruhrstahl steelworks at Witten, a part of the same concern that manufactured the previously described X4 air-to-air missile. A force of 140 Lancasters set out in the morning in poor weather conditions from No. 3 Group's bases in East Anglia to head across the North Sea to Blankenberge.

Just under 180 km northwest of the target at Achmer airfield were the 50 or so Bf 109G-14s and G-10s of IV./JG 27 under Hauptmann Hanns-Heinz Dudeck, who had been a fighter pilot since the beginning of the war, but who had experienced several forced landings and being shot down, as well as bailing out at least once.

At 1230 hrs the *Gruppe* received an *Alarmstart* from 3. *Jagddivision* to intercept enemy *Viermots*, which, by then, were over the Brussels area. The bombers had just picked up their escort of 90 Mustangs from No. 11 Group, RAF Fighter Command, and were heading towards the Ruhr, flying through multi-layered cloud. After Dudeck had hurriedly briefed some of his pilots, and despite the bad weather, 20 Bf 109s took off and assembled in *Schwärme* over the airfield. With Dudeck as his *Rottenflieger* was Fähnrich Oswald Pejas of the *Gruppenstab*.

From under the dense cloud the Messerschmitts climbed to find patchy, clearer conditions at 5,800 m, after which they headed southwest towards the incoming Lancasters. According to Dudeck, it had been intended that the formation would be guided by 'Y' control, but his FuG 16Z became unserviceable, as did his R/T, and so he flew by dead reckoning. The Messerschmitts flew in five loose *Schwärme*, forming a Vic, stepped up from front to rear.

Then, as they were over the Ruhr, the German formation came upon a large break in the clouds and Dudeck led his pilots upwards. Pejas looked back over his shoulder to see a long row of Bf 109s climbing in a tight spiral. Once above the clouds and still well north of the Ruhr, they spotted the bombers and their escort in a stream some 30 km long and three to eight kilometres wide, dispersed and with no contrails. From the nature of the formation, Dudeck knew the bombers were RAF and not USAAF.

Initially, Dudeck zigzagged to allow time to assess the enemy formation, and then led his own formation across the course of the bombers, before turning back to the northwest. As he did so, he confirmed that the bombers were Lancasters. Dudeck then indicated to his Bf 109s to make a 180-degree right-hand turn so as to attack the tip of the bomber formation as it turned south to commence its bombing run on Witten.

Because of the failure of his R/T, Dudeck was unable to issue last minute instructions to his pilots, but they automatically adopted the tactics they used against USAAF formations. Dudeck entered the stream from the left and led his *Schwarm* under or between the boxes of Lancasters to attack the lead and lowest box, which he assumed would be carrying radar devices and marker bombs. Simultaneously, a second *Schwarm* flew in under the bombers, circling about 300 m beneath them so as to pounce on any which might lose height after being attacked. The third *Schwarm* climbed above the bomber stream and attacked in a steep dive, during which one Lancaster was shot down. The remaining two *Schwärme* entered the stream from the left and attacked boxes further back.

As the lead *Schwarm* reached the head of the formation, Dudeck targeted a bomber from the rear on the left side of the first box. He fired from 400 m in an effort to silence the tail gunner, and then aimed short bursts into the wing roots, closing in to about 20 m before breaking away. The Lancaster fell away in flames and crashed north of Wuppertal. Fähnrich Pejas opened fire at the same moment and his aircraft was pelted by spinning debris and twisted fragments of the Lancaster he had selected, which also crashed near Wuppertal.

In the space of seven minutes, IV./JG 27 claimed six Lancasters shot down. One was observed to drop its bombs when attacked and another apparently fired green flares, which Dudeck assumed was to call in the Mustangs. But by the time the escorts arrived, it was too late. Dudeck still had ammunition left, and so despite the Mustangs, he led his *Schwarm* around in a tight left-hand turn, which brought him back into the bomber stream at a point several hundred metres back from where he carried out a similar attack on another box. Most of the other *Schwärme* followed in the turn, and they delivered a well-coordinated attack.

By this stage the Lancasters were even more dispersed on account of the violent evasive action that they had been forced to take. The Bf 109s then broke away to the northwest in a shallow dive, entering the cloud about ten minutes' flying time away from the bombers.

The German pilots put in claims for eight Lancasters shot down, including three *Herausschüsse*, which match RAF losses. The wrecks of the bombers lay scattered around Wuppertal, Bochum and Dortmund. At 5.7 per cent of the attacking force, this was a high loss rate. The actions of IV./JG 27 prevented the bombers from making a successful attack on the Ruhrstahl works, with bombs falling widely over the Witten area. However, this caused the destruction of 126 houses and five industrial premises, killing 334 people. A further 64 were listed as missing and 345 injured. IV./JG 27 suffered no losses.

After the mission, Fähnrich Pejas had to land at Gütersloh, where he stayed the night. The next morning, as he prepared to head home, the local groundcrew handed him a package containing pieces of the Lancaster he had shot down that had become embedded in his Messerschmitt.[10]

The last great German offensive in the West began at 0530 hrs on 16 December 1944. It was a plan so audacious that no senior Allied commander expected it. Codenamed *'Wacht am Rhein'* ('Watch on the Rhine') and under the overall command of the C-in-C West, Generalfeldmarschall Gerd von Rundstedt, the offensive was devised by Hitler, who wanted to drive an armoured wedge between the Allies by thrusting through the forests and hill country of the Ardennes to retake Antwerp. He also hoped that he could trap the US First and Ninth Armies around Aachen, thus eliminating the threat posed to the Ruhr.

In mid-November, Göring had issued orders to II. *Jagdkorps* that its main tasks in the offensive were 'to attack enemy fighter-bombers at airfields near the frontline' and, even more importantly, 'to fly fighter cover for the Army to give it freedom of movement'. In command of II. *Jagdkorps* at Flammersfeld, Generalmajor Dietrich Peltz, a highly regarded former Stuka pilot and bomber commander, became increasingly concerned as reports reached him of German fighter pilots breaking off engagements with enemy fighters without good reason and jettisoning drop tanks to race back to the relative safety of Reich airspace.

But as SS-Oberstgruppenführer Josef 'Sepp' Dietrich's 6. *Panzerarmee* drove west, encircling Bastogne and trapping several thousand American troops, the Allied air forces remained largely grounded by bad weather. This in turn allowed the Jagdwaffe to fly ground-attack missions for the offensive. Such sorties proved to be extremely hazardous for the pilots involved due to withering Allied anti-aircraft fire.

The first half of December had seen only 136 pilots lost in home defence operations, but in the week 23–31 December, as weather conditions slowly improved, German fighter losses on the Western Front were 316 pilots killed or missing. Over Christmas, in the area of *Luftwaffenkommando West*, the units assigned to the Ardennes offensive reported in excess of 260 casualties. It was a level of attrition which could not be sustained.

Finally, on 23 December, the fog lifted and Allied air superiority was quickly re-established. The rail system upon which the German commanders were so dependent for their supplies was subjected to attack by RAF and Eighth Air Force bombers. Hardly a train got through from the railway yards in Germany without being attacked, and Dietrich's tanks were slowly starved of fuel. Simultaneously, P-38 and P-47 fighter-bombers of the Ninth Air Force began a systematic ground-attack campaign in support of recovering Allied ground forces.

Hampered by Allied air power, improving weather and boggy terrain, starved of fuel and now meeting firm opposition, the German mechanised assault, having penetrated 112 km at its deepest point, but still far short of Antwerp, faltered and stopped. By 30 December, the last German attempt to close the Bastogne corridor failed. With the initiative now lost, General der Panzertruppe Hasso von Manteuffel's 5. *Panzerarmee* abandoned any hope of further offensive action.

Meanwhile, Peltz, supported by an increasingly despondent Göring, had decided that, logically, the best way in which to offer support to the armoured thrust in the Ardennes was to neutralise Allied tactical air power where it was at its most vulnerable – on the ground. By using the element of surprise, Peltz had concluded that as an alternative to the costly dogfights against numerically superior and skilled enemy fighter pilots over the front, such an attack would incur minimum casualties and consume less fuel. Originally intended to coincide with the launch of the ground offensive, the weather frustrated the plan and the operation, known as '*Bodenplatte*', was deferred, despite the commencement of *Wacht am Rhein*.

However, on 14 December, Peltz briefed the assembled regional *Jafü* and stunned fighter *Kommodoren* at Altenkirchen. At first light, under complete radio silence on a day when meteorological conditions were favourable, and guided by Ju 88 nightfighter 'pathfinders', virtually the entire strength of the Luftwaffe's single-engined daylight fighter force on the Western Front would be deployed in a low-level, hit-and-run style operation mounted against 11 key Allied fighter airfields in Belgium, the Netherlands and northeastern France.

The component *Geschwader* of 3. *Jagddivision* would attack bases of the RAF's 2nd Tactical Air Force in the north at Antwerp, Brussels, Sint-Denijs-Westrem, Maldegem, Ursel, Eindhoven and Volkel. Units of *Jafü Mittelrhein* were to strike at USAAF fields at Sint-Truiden (St Trond), Le Culot and Asch, while to the south, JG 53, under control of 5. *Jagddivision*, would attack Metz.

At the first suitable break in the weather – dawn on 1 January 1945 – German fighters from 33 *Gruppen* left their forward bases and roared in tight formation towards the Allied lines.

The experiences of Major Karl-Heinz Langer's III./JG 3 are representative of the operation. Despite earning a good reputation – and Göring's rare praise – while on home defence operations in late 1943 and early 1944, the *Gruppe* had been so badly mauled in Normandy that it had to be withdrawn to Esperstedt to rest and refit. The *Gruppe* then transferred to Bad Lippspringe with 45 Bf 109s, but in return for shooting down 13 USAAF aircraft over the Ardennes, a further 25 of its Bf 109s were destroyed and 13 damaged. Fifteen pilots had been killed and six wounded.

On 31 December, in the company of the *Kommodore*, Major Bär, Major Langer briefed his pilots and advised them of the forthcoming operation against Eindhoven airfield, planned for the next morning. The pilots were then confined to their quarters at 2000 hrs and were forbidden to drink alcohol to welcome in the New Year. After a good night's sleep, they were awoken very early the next morning and given a final briefing by Langer, during which the target, course and attack plan were outlined. Pilots were given specially prepared maps and instructed to make repeated low-level attacks in *Schwärme*.

The *Gruppe's* Bf 109s took off from Lippspringe at 0825 hrs and were joined by the Fw 190A-9s of the *Geschwader Stabsschwarm*. The *Gruppe* then assembled with the rest of JG 3 over Lippstadt and set course for Eindhoven. At 0915 hrs, disaster struck when one of III./JG 3's aircraft flown by Leutnant Hans-Ulrich Jung, *Kapitän* of 7./JG 3, collided with a power line and his fighter exploded when it hit the ground. Shock gripped the formation.

Soon, however, the *Gruppe* reached the target and, in formation, went in to strafe the field which was home to a number of Typhoon, Spitfire and Mustang squadrons, as well as some Boston medium bombers. As the Messerschmitts swept in, their cannon fire striking fuel and ammunition dumps, fires broke out all over the airfield, personnel ran for cover and, amidst it all, some Typhoons attempted to take off. Leutnant Oskar Zimmermann, *Kapitän* of 9./JG 3, shot down a Typhoon over the airfield for his 30th victory.

Another *Staffelkapitän* was lost when Oberleutnant Eberhard Fischler *Graf* von Treuberg, commander of 12./JG 3 and a former member of JG 52 on the Eastern Front with some 20 victories to his credit, was shot down either on the approach to Eindhoven or during the early stages of the attack.

At the end of the mission, around ten Bf 109s of III./JG 3 returned to Lippspringe. The unit War Diary recorded:

> Our *Gruppe* started with 15 aircraft within the formation of our *Geschwader* and was ordered to 'clear' Eindhoven airfield. It would be the last big victory of the Luftwaffe in which *Jagdgeschwader* 3, destroying 116 aircraft on [the ground at] Eindhoven, had a major part.

Although complete surprise was achieved and moderate success gained at Eindhoven, where two Canadian Typhoon squadrons were virtually destroyed, as well as at Brussels and Sint-Denijs-Westrem, the attacks on Antwerp, Le Culot and Volkel were nothing short of catastrophic. JG 1 lost 25 pilots (from 70 that had sortied) for the destruction of 60+ aircraft. Aside from the fighters lost, a further 29 were damaged. Over the Malmedy–Aachen battle zone, JG 2 lost half of its aircraft.

In many cases, the German formations failed to even find their allocated targets, or they fell as victims of their own Flak or became lost or collided. JG 53 lost 30 Bf 109s out of 80 attacking aircraft, or 48 per cent of its strength. It is believed that nearly 300 Allied aircraft were destroyed as a result of the raid, of which some 145 were single-engined fighters. A further 180 Allied aircraft were damaged and 185 personnel killed or wounded.

Bodenplatte was, without doubt, an unexpected blow for the Allies, but the effect on long-term Allied tactical operations would be negligible. For the increasingly beleaguered Jagdwaffe, however, the cost was much higher. In total, 143 pilots were killed or reported missing, including three *Geschwaderkommodoren,* five *Gruppenkommandeure* and 14 *Staffelkapitäne,* with a further 21 pilots wounded and 70 taken prisoner.

On 23 January 1945, Göring officially announced Galland's dismissal, ostensibly on the grounds of his 'health', and his successor. In reality, Galland had become a scapegoat, the loser in a personality clash with Göring in which the latter could not cope with resistance:

> In place of Generalleutnant Galland, I have appointed Oberst Gollob to safeguard the duties of the *General der Jagdflieger.* I expect that the Jagdwaffe will support Oberst Gollob. It should be remembered that it is neither the organisation nor the man that is important, but only the goal that is common to us all – the regaining of air supremacy over German territory.

On 2 November 1944, a special test unit designated E.Kdo 152 was established at Rechlin for developing, to operational readiness, what many have perceived to have been the ultimate piston-engined fighter of World War II, Kurt Tank's superlative Ta 152. The unit was led by the 35-victory Knight's Cross-holder and former *Kommandeur* of III./JG 2 and I./JG 11, Hauptmann Bruno Stolle, and was equipped with a small number of Ta 152H-0 pre-production aircraft all fitted with GM-1 power boost.

During early tests, the pilots of the *Kommando* found that the aircraft possessed superb performance, especially at altitude, making it more manoeuvrable than both the P-51 Mustang and P-47 Thunderbolt. During one flight, Stolle reached an altitude of 12,000 m, and was only prevented from climbing higher by lack of oxygen. This was the perfect aircraft with which to counter the anticipated deployment of the USAAF's B-29 Superfortress over northwest Europe.

A plan was then issued on 9 January 1945 to expand the *Kommando* to *Gruppe* strength. However, this was abandoned almost immediately, and operational testing was placed in the hands of III./JG 301 under the command of Hauptmann Wilhelm Fulda. Formed in October 1943, JG 301 had been one of the original *Wilde Sau* nightfighter units before adapting to all-weather day fighter duties. III./JG 301 operated in Austria, Rumania, Bulgaria and Hungary, where its primary mission was the defence of the oilfields and where it suffered heavy losses. The unit returned to the Reich in August 1944 for refitting with the Fw 190A-8. By January 1945, the *Gruppe* had moved to Alteno, near Berlin, and exchanged its previous equipment for the Fw 190D-9. One of the unit's pilots at this time was Feldwebel Rudi Driebe of 10./JG 301, who remembered:

> In January 1945 we received about 24 to 26 Ta 152s. Quite a number of these were lost during conversion training due to crash landings and other causes. The remaining Ta 152s were then taken over by the *Stabsstaffel* of the *Geschwader*. To my knowledge, only one operation was flown by the Ta 152 at that time. It was during an air raid on Berlin. The Geschwader suffered heavy losses on that day and only the Ta 152s returned safely. If the Ta 152 had seen action a year earlier, things would have looked bad for the P-51.

In combat it was found that the Ta 152 was inferior in the initial turn to the P-51, but it then tightened, enabling the Focke-Wulf to position itself behind the Mustang and bring its guns to bear. The aircraft was more sensitive on the controls than the Fw 190D-9, but possessed a much improved performance, especially at altitude. Furthermore, the Ta 152 was much easier to take off and land than the Fw 190D-9.

Feldwebel Willi Reschke of III. and *Stab*/JG 301 recalled:

> From 27 January 1945, I only flew the Ta 152 as escort protection for our standard *Reichsverteidigung* units, and I have to say that the later development of the Ta 152 was much superior to all propeller aircraft of the Second World War, but we only had so very few machines in operation. The Ta 152 enjoyed very high climbing ability, very high speed (750 km/h) and a very small turning radius thanks to its larger wing.

As pilots gained experience with the Ta 152, they became more and more impressed with its capabilities. Leutnant Hagedorn of 9./JG 301 reported:

> We reached the remarkable altitude of 13,200 m. Our ground speed, which we later worked out with a Focke-Wulf test pilot, was somewhere

between 820–830 km/h. I'd never had such a fast aeroplane under me in my life. Take off was incredible when you shoved the throttle fully forward. The runway at Alteno, where I flew it, was 600 m long. The aircraft took off, and I mean really took off, in 300–400 m! I had never previously seen such a thing, and also its performance was above anything I had experienced in any other aircraft, as was its incredible manoeuvrability.

It was known that even an Fw 190 would buffet very easily on the verge of spinning out in a dogfight if you pulled too hard, but we noticed in the Ta 152 that you could practically twist it around its tail. The thing really went round. Others experienced aileron snatching, but I managed this seemingly impossible turning radius without any problem at all in the ailerons. We often said among ourselves, 'Why didn't we get the Ta 152 earlier?'

PART V

Stormbirds – 1944–45

It will be the fastest aircraft any of us have seen.
2LT DONALD M. WALTZ, 305TH BG, RECALLING
WORDS OF 305TH BG INTELLIGENCE OFFICER
REGARDING THE MESSERSCHMITT Me 163

25

Speed and Altitude – The New Weapons

To those Luftwaffe personnel, civilian aeronautical designers, engineers and ballistics specialists tasked with defending the skies over the German homeland, in early 1945 the air war took on daunting new dimensions. As hard as the Luftwaffe's fighter units had fought against the USAAF's bombers, as battered and starved of resources – human, mechanical and industrial – as they had become, there was no hiding the fact that the stakes would only rise.

The main threat came in the form of the USAAF's new four-engined bomber, the Boeing B-29 Superfortress. With its smooth, metallic, tubular fuselage, the B-29 was twice the aircraft that the B-17 was in terms of weight, range, bomb load (20,000 lb), engine performance, maximum range (4,200 miles) and cost, at an eye-watering $600,000 per aircraft. But it was the 'tool for the job', streamlined and deadly, with none of the aerodynamically unrefined bumps, bulges and turrets of the Flying Fortress.

The Superfortress incorporated four 2,200 hp engines able to deliver a top speed of around 360 mph, a pressurised cabin, freeing the crew from the need for oxygen masks during high-altitude bombing missions and remotely controlled, low-profile gun turrets carrying an armament of 10–12 0.50-in. machine guns and 20 mm cannon.

The USAAF had intended to use the B-29 on raids against targets in Germany mounted from bases in North Africa when bad weather prevented operations from England, but perhaps fortunately for the Luftwaffe, the first squadrons were deployed to the Far East instead.[1]

The Germans had not been blind to the threat. As far back as early 1943, the Luftwaffe's commanders had known that it would be essential to prepare a fighter in good time that would have the power to reach altitudes of between 9,000–11,000 m quickly, and be able to engage in aerial combat. Much design work and experimentation ensued in the race to be ready.

For example, as with Boeing, Junkers had undertaken considerable work in the field of cockpit pressurisation for high-altitude fighter, bomber and reconnaissance types. In another initiative, the RLM held a competition amongst all the leading aircraft manufacturers calling for a new-generation, jet-powered 'emergency' interceptor which would be capable of taking on predicted Allied jet fighters, as well as being able to deal with the B-29.

In October 1944, a first series batch of 50 cheap, wooden Ba 349 rocket-powered 'point interceptors' – known as the *Natter* (Adder) – was ordered from the small Bachem company for delivery up to January 1945, and thereafter, once that batch had been delivered, it was planned to order 200 more. It was hoped that these would offer a stop-gap defence against the B-29.

In November 1944, Heinkel assessed the best armament to fit into its prospective cheap-to-build He 162 *Volksjäger* ('Peoples' Fighter') single-engined jet fighter in readiness for combat with the Superfortress.

In a memo that same month, Rheinmetall-Borsig, whose 30 mm MK 108 cannon would be fitted into a number of the He 162 prototypes, advised Heinkel that with the weapon installed, the *Volksjäger* would be ready to attack formations of new generation Allied heavy bombers. In mounting such attacks, it was foreseen that the He 162 would approach from 1,000–1,500 m above and behind the enemy aircraft, then dive below the formation and pull up at an 80-degree angle, closing to between 600–800 m before opening fire. Fire was to cease when a 60-degree angle had been reached and the engagement broken off. 'We need to know the speed in such an attack', Dipl.-Ing. Carl Francke, Heinkel's Technical Director, noted, 'and duration of effective firing times when attacking B-17s and B-29s'.[2]

As an example of the alarm caused by the prospect of the Superfortress, at the daily OKL situation conference on 31 March 1945, a Luftwaffe intelligence officer reported that:

> ...in the last attack on Berlin, ten American four-engined B-29s were seen for the first time, flying at an altitude of 9,500 m. The appearance of this American high-altitude and long-range bomber in Europe would mean that the present four-engined types are already going out of production and are being replaced only by the B-29. Intelligence is assigned the duty of further investigating the matter with the means of reconnaissance at its disposal.[3]

The reality, of course, was that there were no operational B-29s in Europe. Nevertheless, to the Germans, the development of Allied jet fighters and B-29s posed a clear and imminent danger.

But all was not lost. Germany was, historically, a nation of accomplished designers and engineers. Since the 1920s, German inventors had been

SPEED AND ALTITUDE – THE NEW WEAPONS

attracted to new and alternative means of propulsion, such as rocketry, and from the 1930s, the turbojet engine. In 1935, former marine engineer Hellmuth Walter established his own company to produce engines powered by hydrogen peroxide, an oxygen-rich fuel capable of developing power by combustion without the need for atmospheric air. The chemical breakdown of hydrogen peroxide produced oxygen, heat and a large increase in volume, creating a mass flow of gas with sufficient power for an engine.

Walter's early work centred on using hydrogen peroxide for submarine turbines and torpedoes, but in 1936 he began developing liquid-propellant rockets for rocket-assisted take-off for aircraft, as well as aircraft engines, using C-*Stoff* (known as 'cold' start, using a mixture of hydrazine hydrate, methanol and water) and C-*Stoff*/T-*Stoff* (known as 'hot' start, T-*Stoff* being an aqueous solution of concentrated hydrogen peroxide).

Then, in mid-1939, Heinkel became the first company to get an aircraft powered by jet engines into the air. The diminutive He 178 flew for the first time on 27 August powered by a single 500 kp-thrust Heinkel HeS 3b engine. Further development resulted in the He 280, a design intended as a fighter powered in prototype form by twin HeS 8 engines which produced 700 kg of thrust.

Work on such technology continued before and after the outbreak of World War II, and the aircraft and aero-engine design industries benefited considerably from Nazi support. Companies such as Walter, Heinkel, Junkers, BMW, Messerschmitt and Junkers were all engaged, one way or another, in rocket and jet aircraft and engine projects.

In January 1944, a specialist Luftwaffe test unit, E.Kdo 16 based at Bad Zwischenahn, took delivery of its first Messerschmitt Me 163Bs – small, bat-like interceptors with stubby, swept-back wings, each powered by a Walter HWK RII 211 rocket motor providing around 1,700 kg of thrust. Known as the *Komet*, the aircraft's maximum speed was a remarkable 830 km/h at sea level and 955 km/h between 3,000–9,000 m. Its climbing time to 9,000 m was 2.6 minutes.

Although few in number, the tactical advantage of the *Komet* was its ability to be scrambled quickly and to climb fast and high from airfields close to the bombers' targets, and to attack a bomber formation at speed with impunity. The rocket interceptors would use their extraordinary speed (increasing from 320km/h to around 850km/h) and rate of climb to ascend as high as 12,000 m in three minutes. With the Me 163's fuel quickly being consumed, the pilot would dive at a formation of bombers at an angle of 45 degrees to make his attack, firing his cannon in a single pass through a *Pulk* before descending to the ground in an unpowered glide.

Such missions were not for the faint-hearted. The extreme stresses placed on both the pilot and the aircraft, combined with the latter's highly volatile fuel, demanded aviators of a certain stamina, skill and courage.

From early July 1944, a new fighter *Staffel*, 1./JG 400, initially under the command of Oberleutnant Rudolf Opitz, but recently taken over by Hauptmann Robert Olejnik, began relocating from Wittmundhafen to Brandis. The latter airfield, on low-lying land just a few kilometres east of Leipzig, was ideally located for covering the defence of the synthetic oil plants which had been the subject of Allied bombing.

By 31 July, 1./JG 400 reported 16 Me 163s available, only four of which were serviceable. Sixteen days later, on 16 August, 1,090 bombers set out to strike a range of oil, aircraft industry and airfield targets. Eighty-eight B-17s of the 1st BD struck at Braunkohle-Benzin AG's plant at Böhlen, while 101 Flying Fortresses of the 3rd BD bombed the same organisation's facility at Zeitz and another 105 B-17s from the same bomb division went to Deutsche Petroleum AG's refinery at Rositz. Additionally, a force of 87 B-24s from the 2nd BD attacked Braunkohle-Benzin AG at Magdeburg-Rothensee.

2Lt Donald M. Waltz, the pilot of B-17 *Towering Titan* of the 305th BG recalled the mission:

> Our Bomb Group had been briefed for the previous ten days on the possibility of attack by a new German 'jet' [*sic*] fighter plane – the Me 163. At our early morning briefing on 16 August, our Group Intelligence Officer again described the Me 163. He said the airplane was in early production – not too many in operation, so we were 'unlikely to see the Me 163 on this Leipzig mission.' He further indicated that if we did encounter the Me 163, we would have no problem with aircraft recognition: 'it will be the fastest aircraft any of us have seen.' I recall that mission being long and rough.

The bombers came with more than 600 escort fighters, almost swamping the defence. Nevertheless, 77 piston-engined fighters attacked the bomber streams.

At Brandis, the fighter controllers once again waited until the bombers were virtually over the airfield before issuing the *Start* order. Just five Me 163s of 1./JG 400 were operationally ready, and they took off in quick succession, climbing sharply and fast. In the late morning, as the 1st BD neared Böhlen, the rocket interceptors headed down towards the lead element of B-17s from the 365th BS, sweeping through the formation.

The first to go in was the Me 163 flown by Feldwebel Herbert Straznicky, who dived 600 m from 'six o'clock high' towards 2Lt Waltz's *Towering Titan*.

SPEED AND ALTITUDE – THE NEW WEAPONS

Manning the tail gun position was Sgt Howard J. Kaysen, known as 'Red' to his fellow crew. He opened fire on the Messerschmitt at 1,000 yards, but Straznicky levelled out and closed in to just 50 yards. *Towering Titan*'s navigator was 2Lt Paul Davidson, who later recalled:

> 'Red' was our best gunner. The Me 163 came within 50 yards and then peeled off as 'Red' plastered him. The Me 163 went into a dive trailing black smoke.

As Straznicky's Me 163 fell earthward, he was able to bail out and land safely not far from Brandis airfield, although his aircraft exploded on impact with the ground. Metal splinters had embedded themselves in his left arm and thigh, but Straznicky soon recovered and returned to operations.

A second *Komet* closed in from 'six o'clock high' on the B-17 flown by 1Lt Warren E. Jenks, who was leading the 365th BS that day. Through the Plexiglas dome of the top turret, gunner TSgt H. K. Tubbs opened fire at 800 yards, watching the enemy interceptor speeding in to 200 yards before it broke away below the Flying Fortress. Other than being subjected to this fruitless attack, Jenks' bomber remained unscathed.

It would be a different story for two other B-17s attacked by 28-year-old Leutnant Hartmut 'Bubi' Ryll. A combat-seasoned fighter pilot who had joined 1./JG 400 from 2./JG 77, Ryll had initially been assigned for 'jet fighter' training back in October 1943. Flying Bf 109Gs over Italy, he had been credited with six victories. Ryll's tactic was to attack a bomber in a vertical dive, even when he risked being pursued by an escort fighter. He recounted:

> If you go into a vertical dive, the aircraft following you will fire his munitions over you! The guns in a fighter aircraft are harmonised for horizontal flight. The guns are adjusted up so that the trajectory of the shells will follow a ballistic curve to compensate for the pull of gravity. Therefore, the enemy has too much lead since there is no longer any deflection of the trajectory caused by the gravitational pull of the earth.
>
> Naturally, you have to keep your nerve, keep the aeroplane in a vertical dive, and then, with your chin tucked in for support, pull hard to level out. And by the time the airspeed dissipates to back out of the 900 km/h area, you're already back in the local area and under the protection of our own Flak.

Ryll fell upon the B-17 flown by 2Lt Charles Laverdiere, closing in with such speed that the startled tail gunner bailed out. Ryll was very aggressive and accurate in his attack, the fire from his two 30 mm cannon killing one of the gunners, striking both of the B-17's inboard engines, shooting up the flaps and damaging the tail. But that was not enough for Ryll, who climbed and turned in again from 'two o'clock' for a second pass, during which he hit the ball turret, its gunner being literally shot out into the sky.

Somehow, Laverdiere managed to fly the damaged B-17 back to base. He later told intelligence officers how his aircraft had been shot up by a heavily armed 'bat-shaped' aircraft which was so fast that his gunners were unable to track it.

After damaging Laverdiere's B-17, Ryll went for another as he passed through the enemy formation. This time he made for a 'straggler' from the lead squadron of the 91st BG based at Bassingbourn, in Cambridgeshire, and one of the component groups of the 1st CW of the 1st BD. This Flying Fortress had endured a particularly heavy earlier attack by Bf 109s and an Fw 190 while on its inward route. The German fighters had knocked out the superchargers in the bomber's Nos. 3 and 4 engines, and also damaged the No. 2 engine. This meant the power output of the engines had been roughly halved. The tail gunner had been left badly wounded in his right leg and the top turret gunner had received a head wound, albeit more superficial.

The pilot, 1Lt Reese Walker Mullins, ordered his bombardier to jettison the bombs to lighten the aircraft, but he determined to fly on with just one-and-a-half engines, alone, below and some way north of the main 91st BG formation.

At 1045 hrs, Ryll climbed back up to around 18,000 m, his Me 163 trailing white vapour, before banking over and coming in from 'six o'clock', gliding, as his fuel was expended, and firing his cannon all the way. 'Here he comes', called in gunner Sgt Robert D. Loomis from the waist hatch. Mullins immediately started to rock the B-17 up and down, before, according to co-pilot 2Lt Franklin P. Drewery from Franklin, Virginia, 'skidding back and forth' in an attempt at evasive action. In a subsequent newspaper interview, Mullins recounted how:

> The 'Jettie' looked like a bat. Its fuselage was a minor part, for it was practically all wings. When it made a vertical climb at high speed it left a vapour trail. After gaining altitude above us, the pilot seemed to shut off the power, for no vapour trail was seen.

For all his aggression, Ryll did not succeed in hitting the damaged bomber. According to the crew's statements, after his firing pass, Ryll banked to the right and glided on a parallel course to the B-17, but just out of range of its guns. The ball turret gunner, SSgt Kenneth J. Blackburn, asked Mullins to dip the left wing so that he could attempt a burst from his twin Brownings,

SPEED AND ALTITUDE – THE NEW WEAPONS

but just at that moment Flt Off O. V. Chaney, the bombardier, who was standing in for the wounded top turret gunner, told him to hold fire as he had spotted a P-51 diving on the Me 163.

Pursued by a pair of Mustangs and taking strikes from the American fighters, Ryll met his end when his Me 163 crashed vertically into the ground west of Brandis at 1052 hrs, a tall column of smoke emitting from the wreckage.

The small number of Me 163s of 1./JG 400 had been in action for 15 minutes. In that time, Ryll had been lost and Straznicky wounded. On the plus side, it is believed that Feldwebel Friedrich Schubert accounted for a B-17 shot down with just three brief bursts of fire from his MK 108s. A subsequent USAAF report noted of the action on 16 August:

> The gunners of the bomber formation stated that the enemy aircraft were so fast that it was impossible to track them with turrets or free guns. Speed was in excess of that of an escort fighter diving at 400 ASI (595 TAS) at 25,000 feet, although at one time the speed of the enemy aircraft when flying straight and level was estimated to be as low as 150 mph.

For the next eight months, JG 400's 40 or so pilots maintained an intermittent level of operations to defend the oil plants in the central Reich, engaging the bombers when weather and fuel supply permitted. The latter commodity was the Me 163's nemesis, with a shortage of C-*Stoff* in the autumn of 1944 affecting training. Even if all available fuel had been diverted to the Me 163 training programme, only ten pilots per month could have been taught to fly the demanding rocket fighter, but that would have meant that there would have been insufficient fuel for JG 400 to conduct missions.

In Focke-Wulf's 'long-nosed' Fw 190D-9 *Dora* and Kurt Tank's Ta 152, Germany had produced two superlative fighters. In terms of performance, they were aircraft to rival the P-51D, Spitfire XIV and Tempest V, representing almost the pinnacle of piston-engined fighter design. Almost.

For despite the advances in rocket and jet propulsion, deep in southern Germany, on the shores of the Bodensee, work had been underway at Dornier since early 1943 on an aircraft that promised to give the piston engine its last hurrah. This was in accordance with a specification requirement issued by the RLM for a high-speed fighter-bomber powered by twin, back-to-back engines that was able to carry 500 kg of bombs at 750 km/h over a range of 2,000 km. Dornier won the tender and, ultimately, on 26 October 1943, the first prototype of the Do 335 took to the air.

It was a big, brutal-looking and yet innovative aeroplane. Resting on a tricycle undercarriage, the Do 335 was intended as an all-weather *Zerstörer* powered by a 'push-pull' arrangement comprising two Daimler-Benz DB 603 engines, one located in the nose and the other at the rear of the aircraft, immediately behind the tail fin. The DB 603 was a 12-cylinder, liquid-cooled, inverted vee inline engine giving 1,750 hp at 2,700 rpm. Despite the aircraft weighing more than 10,000 kg, theoretically, it could achieve a maximum speed of 750 km/h at 6,400 m, which would make it the fastest piston-engined aircraft produced by Germany so far.

In November–December 1943, the prototype made 23 test flights. The aircraft reached 600 km/h at sea level during climb and speed tests, and even with its rear engine stopped, the Do 335 could still attain a speed of 560 km/h.

Armament comprised two 20 mm MG 151/20 cannon mounted above the engine, synchronised to fire through the propeller arc. There was capacity for each cannon to have 200 rounds. A single, long-barrelled Rheinmetall 30 mm MK 103 cannon, a weapon that had a greater muzzle velocity than the 30 mm MK 108 cannon, was mounted between the engine cylinder banks and fired through the spinner. This was truly a *Zerstörer*.

Later prototypes were delivered to the Luftwaffe's test centre at Rechlin in the summer of 1944. The fifth such aircraft was handed over to the armaments testing ground at Tarnewitz towards the end of September, where firing trials took place. However, the MK 103 cannon proved problematic and was prone to jamming in flight, and although some 1,400 rounds had been test-fired by the end of November, it was still not fully satisfactory. By comparison, the twin MG 151s worked well.

Further tests conducted at Rechlin between late 1944 and early 1945 showed that while speeds of around 730 km/h were achievable at 8,000 m, the Do 335 was plagued by undercarriage and hydraulics problems. Nevertheless, it was planned that ten production series variants were to be produced at Dornier's works in the Oberpfaffenhofen area, the main one of which, the Do 335A-1, was to be a single-seat bomber or *Zerstörer* fitted with DB 603E-1 engines and with capacity for 500 kg of bombs to be carried internally.

A 'B' series was also planned which would see the aircraft fitted with more powerful 2,000 hp DB 603LA engines and an enlarged 18.4 m-span wing to improve performance at altitude, with standard armament of one MK 103 and two MG 151s. This variant was a *Hohenzerstörer* (high-altitude destroyer), but the aircraft never saw the light of day. It was the opinion of some senior Luftwaffe officers after the war that 'even in the planning stage and in the series preparation, the High Command squandered the whole thing in talk of fast bombers, nightfighters and reconnaissance aircraft'.[4]

SPEED AND ALTITUDE – THE NEW WEAPONS

Furthermore, difficulties at Daimler-Benz meant that there were delays with the new series DB 603 engine.

If such aircraft had ever taken to the sky in numbers, there is little doubt that they would have given the bombers of the USAAF – including the B-29 – and RAF Bomber Command a battering. The ultimate proposed combined firepower of up to three MK 103 cannon (one engined-mounted and two wing-mounted) plus two 20 mm MG 151s in the cowling would have delivered a significant punch. Furthermore, weapons specialists at Tarnewitz were exploring the feasibility of fitting the Do 335 with the new Rheinmetall 55 mm MK 112 automatic aircraft cannon, which was essentially a scaled-up version of the proven MK 108.

Fortunately for the Allies, the Do 335 became a casualty of the turmoil which pervaded the Third Reich in the final two years of the war.

Towards the end of October 1944, Oberst Gordon Gollob, who had been overseeing development work on the Me 163, Hauptmann Rudolf Opitz, the acting *Gruppenkommandeur* of I./JG 400, and Hauptmann Anton Thaler, commander of E.Kdo 16, visited the HASAG plant in Leipzig to inspect work on a new 50 mm weapon known as the SG 500 '*Jägerfaust*' (Fighter Fist) and to watch a demonstration.

This vertically firing volley weapon comprised a variable number of rifled firing tubes which were to be fitted into the wing of an aircraft. Upon the triggering of a photoelectric cell (in the development of which HASAG had been engaged), shells would be fired upwards and into the underside of a bomber as the carrying fighter passed below. The tubes would then be jettisoned downwards. Because the 50 mm calibre muzzle velocity of the SG 500 was limited to 400 m per second, range to the target was reduced to 50 m to improve operational efficiency.

Gollob and Opitz felt the weapon had potential, and subsequently a contract for production was issued. For installation in the Me 163, the weapon would be adapted to fire 2 cm calibre rounds.

Tests were conducted in mid-November 1944, with the photoelectric cell installed close to a radio aerial near the ammunition bay of an Me 163. The SG 500 was first fired against a scrap wing, with no damage being sustained by the aircraft. Then, on 13 November, Leutnant August Hachtel of E.Kdo 16 took off in a *Komet* with half-full fuel tanks and the aircraft's standard MK 108 cannon removed. That test, and subsequent flights, went well, proving the weapon's effectiveness.

Thaler suggested to HASAG that only two or three shells should be fired at the same time so that two or three bombers could be engaged as an Me 163 passed below, rather than just one aircraft. HASAG concurred. Thaler also suggested that the shells should be capable of being fired by the Me 163 when flying at different speeds. The required switch necessary was already available, and once installed in the aircraft, it allowed the weapon to be fired at any time during three different speed ranges – either when the Me 163 attacked from astern; at one speed range when in a head-on attack, so that it became irrelevant whether the pilot was flying at 700–800 km/h or 600–700 km/h with thrust, or at 500–600 km/h with the engine shut down; or in making a frontal attack. Whatever the case, the switch would prevent the weapon being fired until the aircraft was being flown within the relevant speed range.

It was not until 10 April 1945 that the SG 500 was used in combat. During the early evening, in clear weather, 230 aircraft of RAF Bomber Command attacked the railway yards at Engelsdorf and Mockau in the outer districts of Leipzig – home to the HASAG works. At least one Me 163B of 2./JG 400 was scrambled from Brandis to intercept, the aircraft being flown by Leutnant Friedrich Kelb. He was observed to climb sharply above the trees at the end of the runway and then head towards the lead bombers, which were thought to be flying at an altitude of around 8,000 m. Such was Kelb's speed and course towards the RAF formation that one observer on the ground viewing events through a long-range Flak telescope feared he would ram one of the bombers.

In fact, Kelb fired his SG 500 at a Lancaster III flown by Sqn Ldr Campbell Haliburton Mussells of the Royal Canadian Air Force's No. 405 (Vancouver) Sqn as it completed its first pass over the target and was about to commence another. The projectiles from the special weapon shot away the Lancaster's rear gun turret and starboard rudder, shattered the port rudder and damaged both elevators so badly that they were rendered useless. The rear gunner, Flt Lt Melborn Mellstrom, was in his turret at the time of Kelb's attack and was killed. Damage was also caused to the H2S set and mid-upper turret, the gunner being seriously wounded.

The stricken Lancaster fell 4,000 ft, with Mussells having to use all of his strength to lash back the flying column with a length of rope to keep the nose of the aircraft up. Remarkably, Mussells remained with the aircraft and was able to return to England.

Despite his fuel being spent, Kelb evaded the Mustang escort and land back at Brandis. It was the first and only time that the SG 500 was known to have been used in combat. With that, effectively, Me 163 successes against Allied bombers had experienced their swansong.

26

Fire in the Sky

As far as Reichsmarschall Hermann Göring was concerned, the war against the *Viermots* was a long way from over, and yet he had pulled himself away from public view as much as he could. His fighter force had failed him and had failed to protect Germany's citizens, particularly those in the country's major cities.

In Bremen, for example, as a result of the bombing, for more than a year there had been an acute shortage of consumer goods, and the local authorities had been unable to honour clothing vouchers for the thousands who had been bombed out of their homes. Air raid shelters had proven inadequate and evacuation schemes had failed because of bureaucratic muddling. Amidst the rubble, the water supply for the city's 440,000 residents was unreliable as a result of damage going back to late 1943. One man complained to a local newspaper that he could not even buy a sack of lime with which to patch up his bomb-damaged ceilings. The rail yards were in ruins and transport to and from certain outlying districts no longer functioned. To rub salt in the wound, residents travelling within the city suffered the ignobility of being asked to prove that they were essential workers.[1]

In a desperate initiative, on 22 January 1945 Göring appointed General der Flieger Josef Kammhuber to the post of *Sonderbeauftragter des Reichsmarschalls für die Abwehr viermotoriger Kampfverbände* (The Reichsmarschall's Special Commissioner for Defence against Four-Engined Bombers). Ostensibly, Kammhuber was tasked with 'investigating all possibilities of defence against four-engined bombers'.

This meant forming a committee of 'experts' drawn from the Luftwaffe's Operations Staff and the Director of Air Armament, as well as specialist officers and those involved in research, along with representatives from industry, business and science. Kammhuber was responsible for recording and analysing technical and tactical data related to the enemy's employment of bombers; for keeping records of enemy strength; for conducting research into means of defence and for making recommendations as to means and tactics for attacking *Viermotors* by day and night; for overseeing experimentation; for proposing new developments; for ensuring standardisation of equipment and evaluating the success or failure of Luftwaffe operations.

One could ask why this had not been done earlier. Notwithstanding, Kammhuber was assigned a staff of six officers, a civil servant, one medium and one light car, an NCO driver, a bicycle and a twin-engined Do 217 heavy fighter or bomber as a transport.[2] Just how much he was able to achieve by this stage of the war, however, is not known.

But there was one hope to which Göring *could* cling.

The arrival of the Me 262 jet interceptor in the skies over northwest Europe in the summer of 1944 was representative of the dichotomy facing the German military at that stage of the war. The designers and engineers at Messerschmitt had created a pioneering aircraft, incorporating the most advanced design and aerodynamic refinements, and powered by the new, ground-breaking jet engine. It was an elegant aircraft, with a shark-bodied fuselage, all-round vision canopy, swept-back wings, smoothly faired engine nacelles and a tall tail, all resting on a tricycle undercarriage.

Professor Willy Messerschmitt's creation was truly a design that would change everything, and quite possibly return the strategic edge to Germany in the war in the air. But the key word here is 'possibly', because in a trend that dogged German aviation from mid-1943 onwards, while the design and engineering was there, the manufacturing capability to equip Luftwaffe units *quickly* and in *mass* simply was not.

Nevertheless, the relatively low-key arrival of the Me 262 gave a much-needed sense of hope to the Luftwaffe, to Hitler, to Göring and to the German people. When the first few examples of the sleek interceptor reached the Luftwaffe in mid-1944, they were quickly assigned to E.Kdo 262, a dedicated test unit set up the previous December.

Despite Hitler's well-known and, to a great extent, understandable desire to deploy the Me 262 as a fighter-bomber, it is important to stress that the aircraft was seen in concept as an *interceptor* and not simply as a fighter. Yet with a rate of climb of 1,200 m per minute and a maximum speed of 845 km/h at 9,000 m produced from its two Junkers Jumo 004 turbines, it was an aircraft capable of out-pacing the Mustang. While, with drop tanks, the P-51 was able to escort the USAAF's bombers to Berlin and other deep-penetration targets, its maximum speed of 438 mph (705 km/h) at 25,000 ft (7,630 m) meant that, in certain conditions, the Me 262 had the advantage.

In April 1943, the Knight's Cross-holder and 72-victory ace Hauptmann Wolfgang Späte had flown the second prototype, and subsequently reported to Galland that:

The climbing speed of the Me 262 surpasses that of the Bf 109G by 5 to 6 m/sec. The superior horizontal and climbing speeds will enable the aircraft to operate successfully against numerically superior enemy fighters. The extremely heavy armament (six [sic] 30 mm guns) permits attacks on bombers at high approach speeds with destructive results, despite the short time the aircraft is in the firing position.

After an initial introduction with operational evaluation units, albeit with mixed results, the first *Geschwader* to be equipped exclusively with the Me 262, JG 7, was established at Brandenburg-Briest to the west of Berlin under veteran of the 1939 RAF raids against Wilhelmshaven, Oberst Johannes Steinhoff. Here, it was in an ideal position to intercept American bombers on their way to targets in the northern and central Reich or against the capital. Steinhoff had to set up the unit from scratch with scant resources. In his memoirs, he recalled how the *Geschwader* received partly assembled Me 262s delivered by rail from southern Germany which were then fully assembled by teams of Luftwaffe and Messerschmitt mechanics:

By the end of November we were in the air, training in flights of three and in small formations. One weakness was the Jumo 004 turbines. Their blades could not withstand the temperatures sometimes reached, and this, together with faults in the induction system, often caused them to burn up. The life of these engines was therefore only 20 hours, and the accident rate was high.

Turbine blades and accidents aside, the Me 262 offered extraordinary speed combined with a formidable armament of four nose-mounted MK 108 cannon – just what was needed to evade the USAAF's fighters and get to the bombers. However, those Luftwaffe pilots slated to fly the jet had cause for some trepidation as a result of having to learn and then master an entirely new form of propulsion capable of unprecedented speed, and yet turn the aircraft into an efficient tactical asset.

Despite lacking numbers of aircraft, III. *Gruppe* of JG 7 commenced sporadic operations in December, but victories were few and far between. Amongst the limited number of pilots to enjoy success with the Me 262 was Oberleutnant Georg-Peter Eder, who had seen early action in the jet with *Kommando Nowotny*. A recipient of the Oak Leaves to the Knight's Cross on 25 November 1944, he would claim as many as 21 kills in the Me 262 between 6 October 1944 and 22 January 1945. The majority of these successes, many of which remained unconfirmed, were against four-engined bombers.

Steinhoff was replaced as *Kommodore* on 15 January by another wearer of the Oak Leaves, Major Theodor Weissenberger, who had been credited with his 200th victory on 25 July 1944 while serving in Normandy flying Bf 109s with JG 5. Although Weissenberger worked hard to bring III./JG 7 to a full state of readiness, it seems the Me 262 was still too precious a resource to lose in the battle against the Allied bombers. This meant that the Luftwaffe's Operations Staff had to give 'permission' to the *Gruppe* to engage enemy reconnaissance aircraft and fighters. The unit had just 17 jets at this point, with another ten promised to 'arrive soon'.

On 3 February 1945, despite the fact that III./JG 7 was still not completely ready for operations, the unit embarked upon what was its first major mission in any 'strength'. One of a range of targets for the USAAF was the marshalling yards at Berlin-Tempelhof, which was assigned to the B-24s of the 2nd AD. Some 116 Liberators reached the target, where the small force of Me 262s made its mark.

Leutnant Rudolf Rademacher claimed two 'B-17s' shot down, but it is more likely these were B-24s. Oberleutnant Joachim Weber of 9./JG 7 and Oberleutnant Günther Wegmann and Leutnant Karl 'Quax' Schnörrer of 11./JG 7 claimed one *Viermot* each. The USAAF lost 23 B-17s, two B-24s and seven P-51s during the raid that day, the only claim against a jet being made by a Mustang pilot who damaged an Me 262 south of Gardelegen.

Six days later, the Eighth Air Force returned to northern and central Germany, this time striking at oil, transport and airfield targets including Magdeburg, Lützkendorf and Paderborn. In the Berlin area, a few Me 262s from III./JG 7 attacked B-17s, with Rademacher claiming two shot down and Eder and Wegmann accredited with one each. Yet such were the debilitating odds against the Luftwaffe by this stage that in reviewing the overall German fighter response to the American raid, against which only 67 single-engined fighters were deployed, the Chief of the Operations Staff lamented that 'the employment of such a small number of aircraft is purposeless and must be regarded as a mistake'.

On 10 February OKL ordered that Fw 190A-8-equipped IV./JG 54 at Neumünster be redesignated as the new II./JG 7 equipped with the Me 262. Two days after that, meeting a deadline set by Göring, III./JG 7 finally declared itself fully operational with 50 aircraft.

On the 14th, the USAAF sent another large raid comprised of nearly 1,300 B-17s and B-24s escorted by 881 fighters to 17 assorted targets including Dresden, Prague, Brüx, Pilsen, Chemnitz and Magdeburg. Some bombers were forced to return early and were intercepted by several Me 262s from I. *Gruppe* and 11./JG 7. Rademacher and Unteroffizieren Anton Schöppler and Günther Engler all accounted for a bomber each.

Oberfeldwebel Hermann Buchner was a former ground-attack pilot who had flown on the Eastern Front, where he had destroyed no fewer than 46 tanks and been awarded the Knight's Cross in July 1944. He joined 9./JG 7 in early December, making the relatively rare transition to flying jet fighters, and later recalled:

> The Me 262 reached us too late, though it was years ahead of its time from the point of view of its technology. Of course, there were shortcomings, but with more time and sufficient operational experience, these could have been eliminated. The main problem was that the crews had to work out new methods of attack and had to learn how to manage at such high speed.
>
> In an attack we reached the target ridiculously fast, and firing time was reduced. I accounted for most of my claims by basically approaching from the rear. Of course, you had to fly through the escort. This was somewhat more difficult with the Fw 190, but was no problem with the Me 262. With a sufficient number of Me 262s deployed, the escort fighters had no chance of preventing us from making an attack.
>
> An attack began at a distance of 500 m. One had to overcome one's basic instincts and get through the defensive fire of the bomber. It was very important to make the target the tail gunner's turret, just where you made out the muzzle flash and smoke of the machine guns. If the tail gunner had been taken out, success was much more certain. And when the R4M rocket was introduced, the rate of success was even better.[3]

Just as the Me 262 was the world's first operational jet interceptor, the 55 mm R4M *Orkan* air-to-air rocket heralded the dawn of batteries of such missiles in air-to-air warfare. Manufactured by the Deutsches Waffen und Munitions Fabrik, it was a much lighter (and faster) armament than the cumbersome 21 cm mortars used by the piston-engined units. Despite its light weight, the R4M, when employed effectively, had as much, if not greater, destructive effect than the W.Gr.21 cm mortar.

Launched from a purpose-built, wooden, underwing rack, the R4M was a solid fuel-propelled, multi-fin stabilised missile. The warhead, contained in an exceptionally thin one-millimetre sheet steel case, held the Hexogen high-explosive charge. The fuse was designed to discriminate between thin skin and main aircraft structure and to penetrate 60–100 cm into a target aircraft before detonation to give maximum blast effect. Twelve R4Ms could be loaded onto one rack, and the Me 262 could carry a single rack under each wing. They would be used by JG 7 for the first time in March 1945.

Before then, however, the jet pilots were still experimenting with tactics. In the brief period that JG 7 had been operational, combat tactics and formations had been fluid, with pilots tending to adopt the traditional Luftwaffe *Schwarm* and *Rotte*, with attacks using cannon directed from any opportunistic angles. This is borne out by the events of 3 March when, following a three-day lull since the USAAF raid of 28 February, JG 7 was back in action, sending up 29 Me 262s against a raid of more than 1,000 heavy bombers with nearly 700 escort fighters targeting oil, armaments and transport targets across northern and central Germany.

The jets attacked the B-17s of the 3rd AD in line astern from 6,000–7,000 m between Braunschweig and Magdeburg. Hauptmann Heinz Gutmann, a former bomber pilot and a Knight's Cross-holder flying with 10./JG 7, Leutnant Schnörrer of 11./JG 7 and Oberfeldwebeln Helmut Lennartz and Hermann Buchner of 9./JG 7 each claimed a Flying Fortress destroyed. Buchner recalled:

We broke through the fighter escorts but then found ourselves under massive defensive fire from the bombers' turret gunners. When we were about 1,000 m from the bombers, Gutmann's cockpit flashed with fire and his fighter sheared away from our formation and dived vertically. I think he might have been killed outright, as he did not attempt to bail out.

Gutmann's Me 262 hit the ground a few kilometres south of Braunschweig. In its post-mission report, the USAAF recorded:

Analysis of Me 262 tactics on 3 March reveals that the jets preferred to attack from either 6 or 12 o'clock. In most cases, attacks from other directions turned out to be feints. No preference was shown regarding the level of approach, but high approaches were generally not very high and low ones not very low. The number making a particular pass varied from one to four, but when more than one attacked, an echelon (almost in trail) formation was used. Breakaways varied considerably, though they always combined a change in altitude with a change in direction. Bomb groups were bounced while strung out in bombing formation, and the jets completely ignored German Flak while attacking.

The Me 262 pilots did not seem to be particular as to which group of the bomber column they attacked, and they were not averse to climbing back for a second pass after diving away from the first one. In some instances, the jets seemed to glide with power off when attacking, probably to obtain a longer firing burst by lessening the rate of closure.

Six *Viermots* had fallen to the guns of JG 7 and three escort fighters also became victims. Although the USAAF claimed six Me 262s shot down, such losses are not recorded on the German side.

However, although blessed with speed, the Me 262 did suffer to some degree from a lack of manoeuvrability, and so maintaining formations in elements larger than *Schwärme* proved more difficult.

A widely recognised period of vulnerability for the Me 262 was when it prepared to take off or approached for landing. At such junctures, greater lengths of time and distance were required than for conventional fighter aircraft. The jet also needed a longer period of time to start its engines. Frequently, this would have to be done in the open, and thus there was a danger from attack by Allied fighters.

A total of 348 B-17s of the Eighth Air Force's 1st AD struck at two oil refineries in Hamburg on the 24th, and as they did so, 10. and 11./JG 7 attempted to intercept them in the airspace between the city and Lüneburg. Despite the P-51 escort, Leutnant Rademacher put in a claim for a Flying Fortress. The following day Rademacher struck again, raising his personal tally to 90 victories when he brought down a B-24 in the Halle-Leipzig area – one of two lost from the 314 Liberators of the 2nd AD sent to bomb the Halle marshalling yards.

There was no doubt that in its debut against the B-17s and B-24s, the Me 262 had given the USAAF's bomber commanders and crews a shock, but the Luftwaffe desperately needed more of them. February had seen just 42 delivered to JG 7. This was out of a total of 212 new jets squeezed from the factories, with another 12 repaired.

On the last day of March, III./JG 7 mounted 22 fruitless sorties directed at heavy bombers operating between Braunschweig and Brandenburg. By this time Allied fighters almost ruled the skies over Germany and, therefore, OKL proposed that all Luftwaffe fighters should only attack lone bombers straggling behind a formation.

On 24 December 1944, an imaginative proposal landed on the desk of the aircraft designer Professor Willy Messerschmitt from the '*Autobedarf Lagerlechfeld*', the cover name given to Lechfeld airfield, where Me 262 test flights were being conducted. The unidentified writer, clearly of some technical and scientific mind, had been inspired by fanciful rumours of a new secret weapon apparently known colloquially as 'exploding mist'.

His idea was for one or more Me 262s to make a frontal approach on an enemy bomber formation and about 500 m above it, towing winged

'*Anhänger*' (trailers). One such trailer would house a pressure-sealed container carrying 700 kg of a light gas fuel. Using a pyrotechnic propellant, the fuel could be atomised in five seconds through nozzles in the wings of the trailer. According to the writer, with a ratio of one kilogramme of fuel to 15 kg of air, an area of explosive air/fuel mixture spanning a cross-section of 20 m^2 and a length of one kilometre could be created in the air at a height of 8,000 m.

Once the outflow from the trailer ceased after five seconds, the trailer ignited automatically. If a suitable degree of atomisation of fuel (such as dissolved acetylene) could be achieved after three seconds, then 'a powerful pressure wave would emit a front of flame'. The writer further stated that, 'This should destroy a large number of the bombers, or the *Pulk* would have to break up, making it easier for individual fighters to approach'.

The report calculated that the explosive effect of this reaction would extend for about 200 m. The Me 262 would not be placed at undue risk because the releasing of the trailers would be well ahead of the target and, combined with the jet's superior speed, meant it would be able to break away and escape quickly. But questions remained as to exactly how much pressure could be expected in the 'pressure wave', what would be the most favourable fuel, and how much pressure was needed to destroy a bomber. The answers to these questions would come from consultation with thermodynamicists and combustion and ballistics specialists. The writer stated that:

> The starting point is the assumption, based on the observation of the effects of air mines, that 1,500 kg of explosives would damage a bomber at a distance of 100 m.

It is not known if the proposal was considered further by Messerschmitt.

In the late afternoon of 1 March 1945, 22-year-old Leutnant Lothar Sieber, a Luftwaffe aviator assigned to the Bachem company as a test pilot, made his way precariously along a narrow, 45-degree gangway that had been fitted several metres above the ground to a skeletal metal launch tower. The purpose-built framework rose from the cold, hard, high surface of a clearing on the Heuberg, deep in southwestern Germany near the town of Stetten am kalten Markt, its apex several metres taller than the surrounding clumps of firs.

Despite the daunting task that lay ahead of him, it seems Sieber felt he was a lucky man. A qualified, multi-engined Luftwaffe pilot, he had seen service with the covert operations *Geschwader* KG 200, and while with the unit, he was one of the few airmen, like Flieger-Haupting. Hans-Werner Lerche, to have flown a captured B-17 Flying Fortress. Indeed, such were his flying abilities that he was considered something of a daredevil, Sieber supposedly having once looped an ungainly Ju 52/3m transport aircraft. His daredevil streak also led him to volunteer for parachuting out of a He 111 over an airfield in the western Ukraine to establish whether it was usable.

But Sieber's path to KG 200 had not been a glorious one. In November 1942, his natural ebullience had fatefully led him astray when he ill-advisedly made a false report for guard duty, for which he was found out. He was court martialled, demoted from Leutnant and served six weeks in a military prison in Russia. Sieber viewed his eventual assignment to the Bachem company as an opportunity not only to redeem himself (although by this time, he had already done that) and his rank, but also to take part in the dawn of vertical take-off (VTO) rocket flight.[4]

Awaiting him at the end of the gangway was a comparatively small aircraft with short wings, set to streak vertically up the tower. Built expediently and cheaply of wood, this was a prototype of the Bachem Ba 349 *Natter*, a single-seat, VTO interceptor powered by a 1,700 kg Walter 10-9-509A rocket motor with its highly volatile fuel mix.

In a specification issued on 9 August 1944, the designer of the *Natter*, Erich Bachem, and his company, the Bachem-Werk of Waldsee, proposed an aircraft 5.67 m in length, with a wingspan of just 2.80 m and total loaded weight (with pilot, equipment, propellant and munitions) of 1,230 kg. The aircraft would be able to reach a maximum altitude of 12,000 m, with an ascent velocity of 650 km/h when taking off vertically. Acceleration at take-off would be 1.6 g, decreasing to 0.7 g during ascent. Normal cruise velocity was rated at 800 km/h, with a flight range of around two minutes and a range of operations of 16 km at an altitude of 12,000 m.

The main tactical purpose of the *Natter* was to intercept bombers in daylight. The diminutive machines would be based near key industrial plants and deployed once an enemy bomber formation was as close as possible to their launch site. In clear conditions, the interceptor was to pursue the bombers in a climbing curve and then shoot at least one down when within range. After making its attack and expending its fuel, a *Natter* would then descend earthward in a gliding dive. In the process, the pilot would jettison the nose section by means of explosive bolts and bail out using a parachute to land. Another parachute would then automatically deploy on the fuselage section and ensure the *Natter* would land safely for recovery and re-use. According to Bachem, he intended:

> Annihilation of enemy aircraft, especially bombers, by delivering a gunner within the immediate vicinity of the enemy [aircraft] and discharging rocket projectiles at it with the smallest possible amount of manoeuvring and propellant.
>
> No self-destruction of the pilot; on the contrary, he should have armoured protection. Smallest possible production cost, maximum use of wooden parts, reduction of iron. No burden on standard aircraft industry. Exploitation of large, partly underutilised timber resources. Repeated use of the most critical airframe and propulsion unit parts by parachute recovery. Little flying requirement for the pilot due to the omission of a steered take-off, as well as omission of a normal landing. Little ground input. Little transport cost. Easy transferability. Good camouflage potential.

All good theory. Operationally, if conditions allowed it, a pilot could attempt a second attack by descending towards other enemy aircraft flying further ahead, but at a lower altitude. Alternatively, more experienced pilots, if used, could climb into a loop and come in again from behind the same formation, although firm tactics still had to be agreed with whoever would fly the machine.

Various armament configurations were proposed for the *Natter*, including two MK 108 cannon or a nose-mounted 'honeycomb' battery of 32 30 mm shells known as a *Grosse Rohrbatterie*. This was intended to fire a simultaneous and highly destructive battery of shells which would saturate a bomber and destroy it. Other options included a nose-mounted 'honeycomb' of 48 R4M rockets that would be fired in three salvos of 16. The passage of the first salvo down the hexagonal tubes would cause the next salvo to be fired, and so on. All the rounds could be fired in 0.3 seconds. According to a Rheinmetall-Borsig report:

> To use the superior speed of jet fighters to best advantage, to break the enemy fighter screen and to launch surprise attacks on bombers from any desired position, development changed to the arrangement of a *Schrotschussbewaffnung* [shotgun effect armament], or multi-barrel armament. The main idea of this armament was to give the fighter pilot, whose superior speed was his greatest combat asset, the possibility of using his firepower like a blow at the shortest possible distance that he could reach tactically, and which, in any case for an attack, he would have to reach.

However:

> Its disadvantage is that its action is limited to short range only, as at greater distances, owing to the limited quantity of ammunition, neither the required area of the dispersion diagram nor sufficient concentration of shots can be obtained. Another disadvantage, which must not be underrated, is the effect on the morale of the fighter pilot, in so far as he is forced, for a certain time, to stay in the defensive zone of the bomber without being able to defend himself by firing bursts from his own weapons.

Another weapon was the SG 119. This offered a 'spray fire', 'fan fire' or '*Schrotschuss*' effect, resembling a wide 'blast' or arc of fire, rather than a single stream or 'chain fire'. The SG 119 was a cylindrical battery of 49 barrels each containing one 30 mm cannon round, held together by a metal brace and fired electrically. The shells left the barrels sequentially. The theory was that the pilot of the fighter needed to keep the target in his sights for less than one second, with all barrels being discharged within 0.3 seconds.

According to Dr. Kokott, a ballistics expert at Rheinmetall-Borsig:

> Even if we assume the *Natter* is relatively insensitive to projectiles, an attack from behind is, in our opinion, out of the question. The speed of the *Natter*, which constitutes a very high percentage of its fighting value, cannot be made full use of with this method of attack. When attacking from behind, from a central position, every fighter is within the defensive range of the bomber for the longest time. From the tactical point of view, the *Natter* should remain within the defensive range of the bomber for as short a time as possible if full advantage is to be taken of the fighting value of its high speed.

Kokott also recognised that a direct attack from the front was also out of the question due to the great closing speeds involved, which would call for pilots of outstanding ability – a luxury that Germany did not have at that stage of the war. Kokott argued:

> ... that only one method of attack remains, viz. the attack from a pursuit curve, the attack being launched at a certain angle to the direction of flight of the bomber. In such a case, it is not open to question that the *Natter* can get within 300 m of its adversary. The steeper the angle from which the attack is launched, the safer will be the *Natter* and the shorter

time it will be in its adversary's fire. It is of no consequence whether the attack is launched from above, below or from the side.

The *Natter* runs no great risk because the bomber's downwards defence is not so strong, and the bomber has now to fire with deflection allowance.

Kokott and his team of ballistics experts concluded that such a scenario demanded a weapon for the *Natter* with the highest rate of fan fire in which the simultaneous firing of a large number of rounds eliminated all margin for error. Fan fire allowed an interceptor to develop its total firepower at the moment it reached the shortest range between itself and the bomber, and the SG 119 would deliver this capability. According to Kokott:

> The method of firing could not be simpler. The pilot would be instructed to fly against the enemy formation in such a manner that at a range of 1,000 m he sees it at an angle of between 30–50 degrees. As soon as he has reached a range of 300 m – this range he can discern, as the span of the enemy is seen between two marks in his sight – he fires. All he needs to do is to strive for a fine point of aim. The necessary deflection allowance, which is about two degrees, has been set beforehand.[5]

Regardless of Kokott's scientific approach and logic, when a prototype SG 119 was tested at Unterlüss, despite relatively successful results and the inclusion of a strong buffer spring, recoil was found to be excessive and the weapon was not adopted.

Bachem also noted that:

> Apart from this method of attack, numerous other variations are still possible, as well as variations in the kind of armament. In addition, of course, even the possibility of ramming exists.

However potentially effective such weapons would be was far from the mind of Leutnant Lothar Sieber as, dressed in a one-piece flying suit, he stepped off the gangway at Heuberg, grasped the handhold on the interceptor's nose and swung his right leg awkwardly into the tiny cockpit of the Bachem *Natter* M23 prototype.

Once Sieber had settled into the hard wooden seat, a technician closed the heavy Plexiglas canopy over him and then jumped clear of the starting tower. Sieber spoke into the interphone that he was ready, and a few moments later started up the Schmidding solid-fuel, take-off booster rockets. Then the main Walter unit blasted into life and roared up to full power. The *Natter* was released and it sped upwards and away from the tower, climbing into the grey stratus-filled sky, streaming twin trails of exhaust from the boosters. At about 100 m, it veered over at about 30 degrees and the canopy hatch fell away. The *Natter* continued to climb, reaching an altitude of around 1,500 m, at which point it disappeared into cloud.

Witnessing the launch was Willy Fiedler, Bachem's technical director, who recounted:

> As planned, the manned rocket rises completely straight up into the air. We stare at its path. Is the pilot conscious, has he survived the starting forces? My hands automatically move to the right as if they handle a joystick that can influence the machine in the air. The trajectory of the projectile begins now to lean backward. The *Natter* rolls a half turn and speeds upward steeply. This manoeuvre I have agreed with Sieber two minutes earlier, so all must be well; the launch has been successful.
>
> But what is this? A dark spot is flying from the speeding machine. Immediately thereafter the *Natter* is enveloped by clouds. 'The *Natter* is gone', one of us says. We all stare into the milky clouds. One can still hear the noise of the rocket motor. Thirty seconds, 40, 50, then the sound becomes weaker. After 55 seconds I see at a distance of about ten kilometres a black body smash itself straight into the ground. It is the *Natter*.[6]

The aircraft had been airborne for 15 seconds when its rocket motor stopped. Thirty-two seconds later, it rolled over to the right and plummeted in a nose-dive back towards the earth. The M23 smashed vertically into a field near the town of Nusplingen, several kilometres from the launch site, blowing open a five-metre-deep crater. Aside from the intact cockpit canopy, only a few fragments remained from the impact. Of Sieber, there was nothing left except the remains of two limbs and a piece of skull. According to the subsequent Bachem report, 'During the entire flight the pilot made no move to save himself.'

A post-war US intelligence report, which was based on a conversation with Fiedler, asserts that 'pilot error' may have been caused by noxious gases from the fuel in the Walter rocket motor penetrating the cockpit and asphyxiating Sieber, but it was further noted that the sudden loss of the canopy with its integrated headrest may have broken the pilot's neck.

The scientific and technical endeavour behind *Projekt Natter* faded to become a fascinating footnote in aeronautical history, but there is no doubting the expertise, dedication and courage displayed by those who took part in it.

27

From 'Elbe' to the End

In many respects, in early 1945, the routine of the Me 262 interceptor pilots resembled those of the pilots of RAF Fighter Command defending southern England from German attack almost five years earlier during the summer of 1940. They were a 'few', hurriedly trained before being assigned to a small number of *Staffeln* comprised of limited numbers. They would spend much of their time waiting in primitive conditions for an *Alarmstart* order to intercept formations of enemy bombers sent to attack their cities, airfields and factories, and these would invariably be accompanied by squadrons of escort fighters. The jet pilots were always outnumbered and out-gunned, but at least they were operating over home territory, even if their combat flying time was limited as a result of their aircrafts' thirsty Jumo engines.

And on 18 March they used their new weapon – the R4M air-to-air rocket – for the first time, to devastating effect. That day, nearly 1,200 bombers attacked railway and armaments factories in the Berlin area. They were escorted by 426 fighters. 9./JG 7 put up six aircraft, each fitted with two underwing batteries of 12 R4Ms. The jets intercepted the *Viermots* over Rathenow, and a total of 144 rockets were fired into the USAAF formation from distances of between 400–600 m. Pilots reported astonishing amounts of debris and aluminium fragments – pieces of wing, engines and cockpits – flying through the air from aircraft hit by the missiles.

Oberfähnrich Walter Windisch, who had joined the Luftwaffe in 1943 and who had two victories to his credit by the time he was transferred to JG 7 from JG 52, was one of the first pilots of the *Geschwader* to experience the effect of the R4M in operational conditions:

> Flying the Me 262 was like a kind of 'life insurance'. I was on that first sortie on 18 March during which the R4M rockets were used, and I experienced something beyond my conception. The destructive effect against the targets was immense. It almost gave me a feeling of

being invincible. However, the launching grids [racks] for the rockets were not of optimum design – they were still too rough and ready, and compared with conventionally powered aircraft, when you went into a turn with the Me 262, flying became a lot more difficult because the trimming was not too good.

Leutnant Erich Müller claimed two bombers in the same mission, while Oberfähnrich Pfeiffer shot down another. On the down side, Oberleutnant Günther Wegmann was hit by the return fire from a B-17 he attacked over the Glöwen area. Despite having been severely wounded in the right leg, the 14-victory ace attempted to land his badly damaged jet back at Parchim. However, when his right engine began to burn, Wegmann decided to bail out near Wittenberge. His right leg was eventually amputated. Also lost in this mission as a result of defensive fire from the bombers was Oberleutnant Karl-Heinz Seeler, who had joined JG 7 from 5./JG 302, with whom he had scored seven victories – all four-engined bombers, including four at night.

I. and III./JG 7 had deployed 37 aircraft against the raid, of which 13 engaged. Two pilots claimed 'probables', and there were six *Herausschüsse*. The *Geschwader* suffered the loss of three pilots, with another badly wounded, while five jets had to be written off due to severe battle damage, with a further two requiring repair. Nevertheless, the action fought on 18 March was the first real indication of what impact a small, determined force of jet interceptors could have upon the enemy – even allowing for poor operating conditions. As USAAF Intelligence later recorded:

> The jets launched their attacks from out of contrails and aggressively pressed home against the last two groups, in one instance to within 50 yards. Several concentrated attacks were made by two or four jets – others attacked singly. Jets made skilful use of superior speed, and though escort fighters engaged, only one jet was claimed damaged.
>
> Some 12–15 Me 262s made strong attacks on 3rd Division from west of Salzwedel to Berlin; attacks, though not continuous, were skilful and aggressive, contrail being used to good effect; six bombers were lost to this attack. Initial attack, about 20 minutes before target, was on the low squadron of the second group in the column, which squadron at the time was strung out and in poor formation. Four Me 262s in a formation similar to that used by P-51s came out of clouds and contrails from 5 o'clock low, closing from 75 yards to point-blank range; three bombers were badly damaged in this attack. Second attack, by three

Me 262s, came in from 6:30 to 7 o'clock, low to level, resulting in the entire tail section of one B-17 being shot off.

The Allied air forces came again on 21 March, piling on the pressure. This time nearly 1,300 heavy bombers from the Eighth Air Force targeted 12 airfields across northwest Germany in an attempt to inflict damage on the jet aircraft infrastructure, while 107 B-17s of the 3rd AD went to Plauen to bomb an armoured vehicle factory. With them came 750 P-51s. Simultaneously, to the south, Liberators from the Fifteenth Air Force struck at the jet airfield at Neuburg.

As if this were not enough, to add to the Luftwaffe's woes, RAF Bomber Command operated in daylight, despatching 497 aircraft to bomb targets in the town of Rheine and its marshalling yards, a viaduct at Münster and an oil refinery in Bremen. B-17s of the 1st AD supported the RAF by striking Rheine airfield.

The *Geschwaderstab* and III./JG 7 were ordered to intercept and engage the Flying Fortresses of the 3rd AD at 0915 hrs over the Leipzig, Dresden and Chemnitz areas. Streaking out of misty skies northwest of Dresden in wedge formations of *Staffel* strength at between 6,000–7,500 m, the jets used the combined advantages of speed and surprise to evade the escort and head for the bombers, approaching from above and behind. At least six bombers were claimed shot down. Leutnant Fritz Müller fired a short burst at one B-17 from his 30 mm cannon from a range of 300 m, closing to 150 m, and watched as the left wing broke away and the bomber plunged into a spin towards the earth. The aircraft exploded before it reached the ground.

A *Kette* from 9./JG 7 led by the *Staffelkapitän*, Leutnant Joachim Weber, made its approach towards the bombers from behind and slightly to the left. However, by the time Weber allowed his pilots to open fire, a steady stream of return fire was already being aimed at the jets. The following moments were testimony to the lethal combination of the Me 262's firepower and speed – in more ways than one. Leutnant Alfred Ambs fired a short burst at a Flying Fortress, which exploded, the effect of the blast also blowing apart two other bombers in its wake. But, with no time to take evasive action, Weber flew straight into the blast and perished. 'I had never seen such an explosion', Ambs recalled. 'Terrified, I pulled up and to the left'.

The USAAF reported seven B-17s lost following the mission, as well as nine P-51s and a P-47 from the Ninth Air Force. JG 7 listed just two Me 262s and their pilots lost and two more jets damaged.

Three days later, on 24 March, it was Ambs' turn to experience a close shave when he flew one of 15 Me 262s of III./JG 7, several carrying

R4M rockets, engaging 150 B-17s of the Fifteenth Air Force on their deepest penetration raid yet from their bases in Italy to the Daimler-Benz tank engine factory in Berlin – a round trip of 2,400 km. Ambs had just attacked a B-17 and observed one wing break away from the fuselage when his own Me 262 was hit by defensive fire from the bomber. With shell splinters embedded in his face, he bailed out and came down in a wood near Wittenberg.

On the 25th, 243 B-24s of the Eighth Air Force's 2nd AD, escorted by 223 fighters, were despatched to bomb the oil depots at Ehmen, Hitzacker and Büchen. At 1010 hrs, the first jets of 9. and 11./JG 7 made contact with the enemy over Hamburg. The USAAF post-mission intelligence narrative recorded:

> Lead group of [Büchen] force reported two passes made by four jets as the bombers uncovered for the run. Jets bored in from 6 to 7 o'clock through the whole formation to within 100 yards or less. Lead and high squadrons of the second group were intercepted by five Me 262s between IP and the target, attacks being made singly and in pairs from 6 o'clock level.
>
> The hardest attack apparently hit the low left squadron of the group which had become attached to a different wing on early penetration, thus resulting in the squadron being alone and six minutes late at the target. Two jets attacked before the target and 15 Me 262s attacked for about ten minutes after bombing. Attacks were chiefly from 6 o'clock, mostly level with some high and some low. Pilots closed aggressively to within 50 yards range; attacks were mostly singly and in pairs, though in one instance jets came in five abreast. The P-51s escorting this force were able to break up attacks attempted by two formations of seven jets in line astern both before and after the target, and a P-47 group supporting the same force unsuccessfully engaged six to seven Me 262s seen attacking in line abreast.

Leutnant Fritz Müller shot a Liberator down near Lüneburg, but his victory was gained at a price, for he was hit by return fire in his port engine, forcing him to land at Stendal, where he crashed into a Ju 88 parked in a hangar. Feldwebel Fritz Taube, a former transport pilot, found himself alone shortly after take-off, having lost contact with the rest of his comrades from 10./JG 7, but he managed to bring down a Liberator at 1030 hrs, shooting off its port-side wing. Minutes later, however, Taube was set upon by Mustangs from above. His jet took hits to the fuel tank and exploded in mid-air.

1. *Jagddivision* later reported having deployed 25 Me 262s of JG 7 against the bombers, with seven claims against enemy aircraft and two probables. Four pilots were lost and a further five posted missing.

Meanwhile, the war against the bombers was about to reach desperate new heights. Following a request from Göring in early March 1945 for volunteers to take part in an operation 'from which there is little possibility of returning', a small group of pilots arrived in great secrecy at Stendal on the 24th to begin training as part of the so-called *Schulungslehrgang 'Elbe'*, known also as *Sonderkommando 'Elbe'*. This was the brainchild of *Wilde Sau* specialist Oberst Hajo Herrmann, and in a way it was a radical variation of Galland's *Grosse Schlag* concept.

Herrmann's plan was to assemble a group of pilots who would be prepared to fly their fighters in a massed attack against a large Allied bomber formation, using conventional armament but also with the intent of ramming. The chances of survival would be slim, but Herrmann was encouraged by the initial call for volunteers. Pilots from at least six *Gruppen* and even Me 163-equipped JG 400 volunteered, and soon Herrmann purportedly had 2,000 names, and agreement from Göring that 1,500 fighters – mainly Bf 109G/Ks – would be made available for the operation, which was to be codenamed '*Wehrwolf*'.

Herrmann's volunteers were to be trained for their mission by Major Otto Köhnke, the former *Kommandeur* of II./KG 54 who had been awarded the Knight's Cross for his actions on the Russian Front in 1942. Köhnke was known to be outspoken and critical of the Luftwaffe leadership, but he was blessed with exemplary leadership qualities.

He arranged for the volunteers, many of whom had come from fighter training units (mainly pupils, but also some instructors), to be briefed by Oberfeldwebel Willi Maximowitz, a pilot who had flown with *Sturmstaffel* 1 and IV.(*Sturm*)/JG 3, and who had shot down 15 bombers. Maximowitz spoke about how to ram an enemy bomber and how to best bail out of a fighter. Major Fritz Auffhammer, the *Kommodore* of JG 301, was also present to discuss issues of a tactical nature.

Further training, which lasted for about ten days, included the showing of morale-boosting films and lectures by political officers on the dangers of Jewish culture and Bolshevism. Indeed, 90 per cent of the training course consisted of political indoctrination, with the rest devoted to tactics and operations. Two professors of National Socialist ideology were on hand to deliver talks that highlighted the weaknesses of the Allied forces and the problems which purportedly affected the Allied command, while extolling the glory of the fighter pilots who had already sacrificed their lives in the defence of the Reich.[1]

The *Schulungslehrgang 'Elbe'* was to use Bf 109s adapted for the mission by the removal of their FuG 16Z transmitters and much armour protection, including that around the fuel tanks. In addition, armament was reduced to a single, fuselage-mounted MG 131 machine gun with less than 60 rounds of ammunition.

Once weather conditions were favourable enough for a ramming operation, the '*Rammkommando*' element would be provided with high escort and was to make for its respective waiting area in the normal manner and to operate under a Divisional VHF commentary. Upon receipt of the codeword '*Antreten frei*', the ram-fighters were to head for the enemy formation at a height 1,500 m above the bombers. Their approach was to consist of a long, shallow dive, if possible out of the sun and in line astern. Fire was to be opened at extreme range and continued until the final steep ramming dive towards the fuselage of the bomber, targeting immediately forward of its tail unit. If possible, the Luftwaffe pilot was then to attempt to bail out.[2] Combat with enemy fighters was to be avoided at all costs, and pilots were to climb away if attacked.

The last day of March 1945 would see another major effort by the Allies. While the Eighth Air Force struck oil refineries at Zeitz and Bad Berka, as well as other targets in central Germany, RAF Bomber Command aimed for the Blohm and Voss shipyards in Hamburg. A force of 469 Lancasters, Halifaxes and Mosquitos arrived over a cloud-covered target area, but still bombed, inflicting considerable damage to the southern districts of the port city.

Against this raid, 2. *Jagddivision* deployed some 20 jets from I. and III./JG 7. On this occasion, fortune was to favour the defenders as, in addition to 30 mm cannon shells, repeated salvos of R4M missiles streaked into the British formation. For the crews of the Lancasters, the German skies became a scene of smoke-blackened carnage as bombers exploded and shattered wings and engines spun away from fuselages. Oberfeldwebel Hermann Buchner recalled what happened after the rockets had been fired:

> I made a right turn and lined up for another attack. This was made using the nose cannon. My Lancaster lay directly in my sights and I only had to get a bit closer. Now, I opened fire, the hits were good, but

the pilot of the Lancaster must have been an old hand. He turned his Lancaster steeply over on its right wing, making a tight turn around the main axis. With my speed, I was unable to see if my shots had had any effect, or to see how he flew on. I had to think about returning home. The other pilots were also having the same problem. We had a shortage of fuel.

This first attack resulted in 13 bombers being shot down, and during the afternoon, in a second attack, five more *Viermots* and two escort fighters were claimed. The achievement of 31 March may have offered a welcome boost to the outnumbered jet pilots, but the great superiority of the Allied air forces was undeniable. The question was just how long the battle could be maintained flying an aircraft which was difficult to master, challenging to maintain and crewed by weary and mostly undertrained pilots who suffered from shortages of fuel and parts which depended on a badly disrupted transport system to reach them. The following weeks would require every measure of resolve the handful of more experienced jet pilots possessed.

On 1 April 1945, Adolf Hitler relocated his headquarters from the Chancellery building in Berlin to a deep bunker complex just behind it. It was a move redolent of defeat. In Moscow the same day, Josef Stalin enquired of his commanders, 'Well, now, who is going to take Berlin, we or the Allies?'

Three days later, B-17s and B-24s from all but one of the Eighth Air Force's bomb groups set out to attack Kaltenkirchen and 11./JG 7's base at Parchim, as well as several other airfields. U-boat yards at Finkenwarder and shipyards at Kiel were also targeted. The bombers were protected by a force of some 800 escort fighters. The B-24s of the 2nd AD led the formation, crossing the German coast west of Heide at 0900 hrs.

However, Kaltenkirchen was found to be covered in cloud, and so mid-way between Hamburg and Lübeck the formation split, with the lead combat wing making for Parchim, while the elements of the rest of the formation either turned for home or made course for the airfield at Perleberg. It was here, between 0915–0920 hrs, that 25 Me 262s of 9. and 10./JG 7, which had taken off from Brandenburg-Briest, Burg and Lärz in elements of four, some armed with R4Ms, made contact with the incoming bombers between 0915 and 0920 hrs.

The jets managed to drive their way through the P-47 escort and take down several *Viermots* using cannon and rockets, launching their R4Ms from 600 m. Immediately, several Liberators took hits, with debris flying through the air as they veered away from their formation. The USAAF noted that:

> ... some 25–30 jets in three waves were sighted heading west by fighters escorting the Perleberg force immediately after the turn onto the bomb run. Escort prevented all but the first wave of eight from hitting the bombers in formation. After the first co-ordinated attack, Me 262s darted through the formation in individual passes, and at the target some ten jets closed in from all directions. A running engagement ensued from 0940 to 0955 hrs, and two B-24s were shot down for claims of 2–0–13 against the jets.

Although six Liberators did not return from this mission, by the end of the day JG 7 reported that five of its pilots had been killed or were missing, three wounded and 23 jets battle damaged or in need of repair. By this time, the *Geschwader* was finding it difficult to cope.

Finally, at 0930 hrs on 7 April 1945, the 120 pilots of the '*Raubvögel*' (Birds of Prey) *Gruppe* of *Schulungslehrgang 'Elbe'* were placed at 30 minutes readiness at Stendal, Gardelegen, Delitzsch and Morlitz. Preparations for the mission varied between the airfields. At Stendal, days prior to the operation, the pilots had divided themselves into *Schwärme*, while at Gardelegen, pilots lined up after breakfast and counted themselves off into pairs. Furthermore, many were only assigned their respective aircraft immediately before take-off, which may explain while several pilots from Gardelegen aborted shortly thereafter with technical problems.

Fw 190s and Ta 152s of JG 301 were to provide escort. With patriotic slogans broadcast into their headsets by a female voice rather than a more useful navigational commentary, the fighters took off. Their targets were the 1,261 B-17s and B-24s escorted by 830 fighters out to bomb airfields, ordnance depots, industrial sites and marshalling yards across northern and central Germany.

Immediately after the raid, the Eighth Air Force reported:

> It appears that this was a desperation attempt on the part of the enemy, and although enemy aircraft fought aggressively and made determined efforts to get through to the bombers, our losses were comparatively light. Signs of desperation are evidenced by the fact that Fw 190 pilots

deliberately rammed the bombers, bailing out before their planes went into the bomber formations and making fanatical attacks through a murderous hail of fire. Tactics were thrown to the wind and attacks were made from all positions, mainly in ones and twos. From today's reaction, it would appear that although the enemy is fighting a losing battle, the German Air Force is preparing to fight to a finish in a fanatical and suicidal manner.

Seventeen bombers were lost during the raid, including at least five B-17s from the 3rd AD which appeared to have been rammed intentionally. In reality, and allowing for losses caused by Flak, aircraft hit by falling bombs and kills by Me 262 units also operating that day, the destruction of about 12 B-17s was attributable to *Schulungslehrgang 'Elbe'*. Research indicates that some 40 ram pilots were killed. This equates to a loss rate of 33 per cent, although the Luftwaffe lost many more aircraft during the mission. In any event, *Schulungslehrgang 'Elbe'* attempted no further operations.

On 10 April, no fewer than 1,232 B-17s and B-24s of the Eighth Air Force were active directly over JG 7's zone of operations, bringing nearly 900 fighters with them, as if the Allied planners were deliberately provoking the jets to come up and fight against such overwhelming odds. The targets were airfields, transport hubs and a military infrastructure centre.

The respective *Staffeln* of JG 7 had been placed at readiness during the morning, and the German reporting system began plotting the incursion sometime after midday. As part of JG 7's response, a force of around 30 Me 262s was airborne out of Oranienburg, Rechlin-Lärz and Brandenburg-Briest under pouring rain and with visibility down to 2,000 m. As the cloud hung at 150–200 m, take-off was staggered to avoid accidents and collisions. These jets were directed to take on the bombers of the 1st AD, which the German fighter controllers thought – wrongly – were heading for Berlin. They hit the B-17s as they reached their actual targets of Oranienburg and Rechlin. From the American perspective, it was more of the same:

> The lead and second groups were first hit by a total of about 12 Me 262s, which attacked singly and in pairs, pressing their attacks closely and in some cases flying right through the formation. Enemy aircraft were very aggressive and daring, attacking from the tail, level and above, closing to within very short distances. From these attacks

the 1st AD lost five B-17s to enemy aircraft and claim 7 1 8 Me 262s. Fighter escort was reported to have done an excellent job of breaking up any formations before they could get through to the bombers.

Despite the escort screen, Oberleutnant Walter Schuck, leading seven Me 262s of 3./JG 7, achieved the impressive distinction of shooting down four B-17s within eight minutes over Oranienburg for his 203rd to 206th victories. Schuck and his group of jets were at 8,000 m and were directed by the fighter controller towards the bombers, which were reported approaching from the northwest. To avoid the P-51 escort, Schuck brought his formation into attack on a zig-zag course at 10,000 m. With the sight of bombs raining down on Oranienburg below, Schuck fired his four MK 108s at a B-17 from 300 m. A wing immediately disintegrated as the German ace flew towards another *Viermot*. His second target took hits in its elevator and the crew jumped from their spiralling aircraft. Soon afterwards, two more bombers had exploded under his guns.

At that moment, Schuck's aircraft was fired at by a P-51 and hit in the left turbojet. His instruments told him he was at 8,200 m and that power was failing. Mindful of his dwindling fuel supply, Schuck broke away and made course for Jüterbog airfield, although he was uncertain whether the runway there would be intact. With his engine trailing smoke and chased by a pair of Mustangs, he decided to bail out at 300 m between Brandenburg-Briest and Jüterbog. He came down safely and was discovered by the local baker out on his rounds. The latter took the Knight's Cross-holder on the back of his bicycle to the refuge of his nearby mill and offered him a cup of coffee. It was the best Schuck could hope for and at least it warmed his stomach.

Inexorably, the war ground on. Soviet forces reached the centre of Vienna on 11 April, while the same day, US troops arrived at the Elbe, just south of Wittenberge and only 137 km from the centre of Berlin. OKL signalled *Luftwaffenkommando West*:

> Available jet and rocket aircraft being neutralised by strong Allied fighter forces, thus impeding landing of our own forces after operations. Alternative landing facilities therefore of decisive importance.

There is no doubt the Me 262 introduced an impressive new dimension into the air war over Europe, and one that did shock the Allies. But their numbers were just not enough, and for all their revolutionary design, sophistication and engineering, the jet interceptors were simply beaten by a force of greater strength.

Throughout April 1945, in the West, conventional fighter operations were generally limited to supporting German ground forces, with the *Jagdgruppen* conducting strafing and bombing missions against enemy troop concentrations, vehicle columns and bridges, sometimes in formations of some 20 or so aircraft, but on an increasingly less frequent basis.

By mid-April the Soviet Army was only some 16 kilometres from the northeastern outskirts of the capital, and the city shook with the impact of continuous Russian shelling. The experiences of Unteroffizier Oskar Bösch, the veteran of *Sturmstaffel* 1 who by this time flew with 14./JG 3, were typical:

> The defence of the Reich had become the defence of Berlin. But that turned into flying against the Soviet Army. On 20 April, my friend Willi Maximowitz disappeared along with four other aircraft over Frankfurt/Oder. His loss to us seemed particularly cruel; we were close to the end. He always carried a machine gun with him because he didn't want to fall into Soviet hands unprepared. Even today, nobody knows what happened to Willi Maximowitz.
>
> On 24 April 1945 it was my turn. That day, I had just landed at Prenzlau after escorting two Me 109G-8s on a photo-reconnaissance [mission] when I saw a formation of Russian Il-2s flying towards our airfield. Without orders, I took off with my comrades to catch them. In minutes we were attacked by the Soviet escort. This turned out to be tough. I had time to reach the clouds through the Yak fighters. I had the feeling that I was playing with my own life. Everywhere there were Soviet fighters.
>
> Taking advantage of a moment of relief, I decided to attack one flight of Il-2s, but could not stay unnoticed for long enough and had to move rapidly from cloud-to-cloud. As I noticed that my flight was taking me further to the east, my control ordered me back to Prenzlau. As I flew west, I was attacked head-on by one of four Yak-9 fighters. I opened fire at him. Seconds later I collided with my attacker. How I managed to parachute from the wreckage, I'll never know.
>
> I landed in the Russian frontline surrounded by hundreds of Red Army soldiers. With their weapons pointed at me and their looks of hatred, I realised that these were my final moments. Luckily, a political commissar intervened to question me. I was limping badly, but got no sympathy from my captors who were content to push me along

towards their trenches. On the way, I saw a large piece of metal which I recognised as part of the undercarriage from my aircraft and other debris from the Russian fighter.

The following three days were dreadful. I escaped on 27 April from the Garz/Oder camp and made my way to Bodensee, some 1,000 km away. This I managed, hungry and with an injured knee. I found that this backed up our motto of 'What can't kill us, can only toughen us'!

As Unteroffizier Bösch was making his way south, all over Germany the fractured units of the Luftwaffe's fighter *Gruppen* consumed the last of their fuel to reach what were considered 'safe' airfields, where they sabotaged their aircraft and waited for the end.

General der Flieger Karl Koller was the Luftwaffe's last Chief of General Staff – the seventh since 1935. He had also served as head of the Luftwaffe Operations Staff. While in Allied captivity in the aftermath of the war, he reflected on some of the reasons for the perceived failure of the Luftwaffe's fighter arm against the Allied daylight bomber offensive:

> In accordance with orders issued by Hitler, as well as Göring, there was too much clinging to the idea of fighting four-engined bombers, even after the appearance of strong enemy fighter escort formations. The enemy fighter became of no consequence – the bombers had to be destroyed.
>
> Right at the moment when enemy escort protection was initiated, it would not have been difficult for the German fighters – at the time at their very best – to thoroughly maul the so-far inexperienced enemy fighters and to create a more favourable environment for the future of this type of combat. As it was, they were not allowed to attack enemy fighters. Thus, the latter were able to fly defensive protection, and so gained experience, and their self-confidence increased. They learned to hold their own, recognised opportunities resulting from the employment of German fighters and devised offensive protection.
>
> At first, in accordance with orders, the German fighters paid no attention to them at all. Later, our fighters tried to bypass them, a manoeuvre which became more and more difficult on account of the extension in the depth of the escort protection. The offensive conduct of the escort led to more 'dogfights'. This hit the German fighters, who were no longer accustomed to dogfighting and who consisted

increasingly of young replacements lacking experience since they had only been allowed to attack bombers. This led to a feeling of inferiority – a certain '*Jägerschreck*' – a fear of fighters, along with mounting losses and a marked decline in achievement. We should have diverted greater forces against the enemy fighters from the beginning so as to clear the path to the bombers for other forces.[3]

At the time of the surrender, Koller was at OKL headquarters, and the Allies were able to seize his diaries covering the German military collapse. In a subsequent publication of the diaries, the Allied air intelligence agencies commented 'that never was there a more fitting choice of headquarters for a German staff than the lunatic asylum at Wasserburg-Gabersee'.[4]

Appendices

Appendix 1

Single-engined fighter aces with 20 or more *Viermot* victories

Meaningful analysis of this list in order to establish which pilots, on average, achieved the shortest time-to-kills ratios, and thus who were the most effective, is virtually impossible. Variable criteria such as the level of Allied bombing activity in any given area or theatre at any given time, date of death of the pilot in action, weather and operating factors such as the weight of enemy escort all come into play.

	Total victories	Known four-engined victories	Period in which four-engined victories scored
Major Georg-Peter Eder	78	36	12/42–2/45
Major Anton Hackl	192	34	7/43–12/44?
Oberleutnant Konrad Bauer	57	32	4/44–8/44
Oberstleutnant Walter Dahl	126	30	9/43–1/45?
Major Rolf-Günther Hermichen	64	26	7/43–3/44
Oberstleutnant Egon Mayer	102	26	11/42–1/44 (KIA 3/44)
Leutnant Anton-Rudolf Piffer	35	26	5/43–5/44 (KIA 6/44)
Major Werner Schroer	114	26	12/42–5/44
Major Hermann Staiger	63	26	7/43–12/44
Leutnant Alwin Doppler	29	25	2/43–12/44 (KIA 1/45)
Hauptmann Hugo Frey	32	25	1/43–3/44 (KIA 3/44)
Oberstleutnant Kurt Bühligen	112	24	7/43–7/44
Hauptmann Hans Ehlers	55	24	12/42–12/44 (KIA 12/44)
Oberfeldwebel Walter Loos	38	22	3/44–8/44

Major Friedrich-Karl Müller	140	23	1/43–5/44 (KIFA 5/44)
Hauptmann Hans Weik	36	22	9/43–7/44
Hauptmann Heinrich Wurzer	26	23	11/43–7/44 (2 night)
Oberleutnant Werner Gerth	27	22	2/44–11/44 (KIA 11/44)
Oberstleutnant Heinz Bär	221	21	2/43–3/45
Hauptmann Fritz Karch	47	21	6/43–3/44
Leutnant Willi Unger	24	21	4/44–10/44
Oberleutnant Wilhelm Kientsch	53	20	4/43–12/43 (KIA 1/44)
Hauptmann Hans-Heinrich Koenig	28	20	10/43–5/44 (KIA 5/44)
Oberfeldwebel Wille Reschke	27	20	7/44–1/45
Hauptmann Josef Wurmheller	102	20+	2/43–4/44 (KIA 6/44)

Number of pilots with 19 confirmed four-engined victories	4
Number of pilots with 18 confirmed four-engined victories	4
Number of pilots with 17 confirmed four-engined victories	5
Number of pilots with 16 confirmed four-engined victories	3
Number of pilots with 15 confirmed four-enginde victories	7
Number of pilots with 14 confirmed four-engined victories	7
Number of pilots with 13 confirmed four-engined victories	8
Number of pilots with 12 confirmed four-engined victories	12
Number of pilots with 11 confirmed four-engined victories	9
Number of pilots with 10 confirmed four-engined victories	24

Appendix 2

Zerstörer aces with ten or more *Viermot* victories

	Total victories	Known four-engined victories	Period in which four-engined victories scored
Leutnant Rudolf Dassow	22	12	10/43–6/44 (KIA 8/44)
Hauptmann Peter Jenne	17	12	12/43–12/44 (KIA 3/45)
Hauptmann Herbert Schob	17	10	10/43–3/44

Sources and Selected Bibliography

I have listed details of the archival and documentary sources used in the preparation of this book in the end notes to each chapter. In the case of files from the Bundesarchiv-Militärarchiv at Freiburg im Breisgau, more details can be found at https://invenio.bundesarchiv.de/invenio/login.xhtml (as at January 2025). Information on files used from the British National Archives at Kew can be located at https://discovery.nationalarchives.gov.uk (January 2025).

What follows is a list of the key published books consulted.

Wider air power history

Budiansky, Stephen, *Air Power*, Penguin, London, 2003
Maiolo, Joe, *Cry Havoc – The Arms Race and the Second World War, 1931–1941*, John Murray, London, 2010
Overy, Richard, *The Bombing War – Europe 1939–1945*, Allen Lane, London, 2013

Defence of the Reich

Caldwell, Donald and Muller, Richard, *The Luftwaffe over Germany*, Greenhill Books, London, 2007
Caldwell, Donald, *Day Fighters in Defence of the Reich – A War Diary*, Frontline Books, Barnsley, 2011
Corum, James S. and Muller, Richard, *The Luftwaffe's Way of War – German Air Force Doctrine 1911–1945*, The Nautical and Aviation Publishing Company of America, Baltimore, 1998

Luftwaffe units

Boiten, Theo, *Nachtjagd War Diaries – An Operational History of the German Night Fighter Force in the West: Volume One – September 1939–March 1944*, Red Kite, Walton-on-Thames, 2008

Caldwell, Donald, *JG 26 – Top Guns of the Luftwaffe: The Epic Saga of Germany's Greatest Fighter Wing*, Orion Books, New York, 1991

– *The JG 26 War Diary: Volume One 1939–1942*, Grub Street, London, 1996

– *The JG 26 War Diary: Volume Two 1943–1945*, Grub Street, London, 1998

Carlsen, Sven and Meyer, Michael, *Die Flugzeugführer-Ausbildung der Deutschen Luftwaffe 1935–1945 Band II: Fliegerwaffenschulen und Ergänzungsgruppen*, VDM Heinz Nickel Verlag, Zweibrücken, 2000

Lorant, Jean-Yves and Goyat, Richard, *Jagdgeschwader 300 'Wilde Sau' Volume One – June 1943–September 1944*, Eagle Editions, Hamilton, 2005

– *Jagdgeschwader 300 'Wilde Sau' Volume Two – September 1944–May 1945*, Eagle Editions, Hamilton, 2006

Meyer, Michael and Stipdonk, Paul, *German Fighters in the West from Poland to the Defence of the Reich*, Japo Publishing, Hradec Králové, 2022

Mombeek, Eric, *Defending the Reich: The History of Jagdgeschwader 1 "Oesau"*, JAC Publications, Norwich, 1992

– *Defenders of the Reich – Jagdgeschwader 1: Volume One 1939–1942*, Classic Publications, Hersham, 2001

– *Defenders of the Reich – Jagdgeschwader 1: Volume Three 1944–1945*, Classic Publications, Hersham, 2003

Mombeek, Eric, *Storming the Bombers – A Chronicle of JG 4: Volume 1 – 1942–1944*, La Porte d'Hoves, Linkebeek, 2003

– *Storming the Bombers – A Chronicle of JG 4: Volume 2 – 1944–1945*, La Porte d'Hoves, Linkebeek, 2011

Mombeek, Eric, with Forsyth, Robert and Creek, Eddie J., *Sturmstaffel 1 – Reich Defence: The War Diary*, Classic Publications, Crowborough, 1999

Prien, Jochen, *IV./Jagdgeschwader 3 – Chronik einer Jagdgruppe 1943–1945*, Eutin, undated

Prien, Jochen and Rodeike, Peter, *Jagdgeschwader 1 und 11 – Teil 1 1939–1943*, Eutin, undated

– *Jagdgeschwader 1 und 11 – Teil 3 1944–1945*, Eutin, undated

Prien, Jochen and Stemmer, Gerhard, *Messerschmitt Bf 109 im Einsatz bei der II./Jadgeschwader 3*, Struve-Druck, Eutin, undated

– *Messerschmitt Bf 109 im Einsatz bei der III./Jagdgeschwader 3*, Struve-Druck, Eutin, undated

Prien, Jochen, Rodeike, Peter and Stemmer, Gerhard, *Stab und I./Jagdgeschwader 27*, Eutin, undated

SOURCES AND SELECTED BIBLIOGRAPHY

– *Messerschmitt Bf 109 im Einsatz bei der III. und IV./Jagdgeschwader 27*, Eutin, undated
Prien, Jochen, *Geschichte des Jagdgeschwaders 77, Teil 3 1942–1943*, Struve-Druck, Eutin, undated
Stapfer, Hans-Heiri, *Strangers in a Strange Land*, Squadron/Signal Publications, Carrollton, 1988
Weal, John, *Osprey Aviation Elite Units 1 – Jagdgeschwader 2 'Richthofen'*, Osprey Publishing, Oxford, 2000
– *Osprey Aircraft of the Aces 25 – Messerschmitt Bf 110 Zerstörer Aces of World War 2*, Osprey Publishing, Oxford, 1999

German biographies, command, production, campaign histories, etc.

Bergstrom, Christer, Antipov, Vlad and Sundin, Claes, *Graf and Grislawski – A Pair of Aces*, Eagle Editions, Hamilton, 2003
Budraß, Lutz, *Flugzeugindustrie und Luftrüstung in Deutschland 1918–1945*, Droste Verlag, Düsseldorf, 1998
Galland, Adolf, *The First and the Last*, Methuen, London 1955
Gooden, Brett, *Natter – Manned Missile of the Third Reich: Historic Step to Human Spaceflight*, Brett Gooden/Rundle Mall, 2019
Gundelach, Karl, *Die deutsche Luftwaffe im Mittelmeer 1940–1945 Band 2*, Peter D. Lang, Frankfurt-am-Main, 1981
Hannig, Norbert (ed. John Weal), *Luftwaffe Fighter Ace – From the Eastern Front to the Defence of the Homeland*, Grub Street, London, 2004
Irving, David, *The Rise and Fall of the Luftwaffe – The Life of Erhard Milch*, Weidenfeld and Nicolson, London, 1973
– *Göring – A Biography*, Macmillan, London, 1989
– *Hitler's War*, Focal Point, London, 2002
Lerche, Hans-Werner, *Luftwaffe Test Pilot – Flying captured Allied Aircraft of World War 2*, Jane's, London, 1980
Overy, Richard, *The Air War 1939–1945*, Stein and Day, New York, 1981
– *War and Economy in the Third Reich*, Oxford University Press, Oxford, 2002
Rall, Günther, (Braatz, Kurt, ed.) *My Logbook – Reminiscences 1938–2006*, NeunundzwanzigSechs Verlag, Moosburg, 2006
Schmoll, Peter, *Nest of Eagles – Messerschmitt Production and Flight-Testing at Regensburg 1936–1945*, Classic Publications, Hersham, 2009
Suchenwirth, Richard, *USAF Historical Studies No. 174: Command and Leadership in the German Air Force*, USAF Historical Studies, USAF Historical Division, Aerospace Studies Institute, Arno Press, New York, 1969

Toliver, Raymond F. and Constable, Trevor J. *Fighter General – The Life of Adolf Galland*, AmPress, Nevada, 1990
Tooze, Adam, *The Wages of Destruction – The Making and Breaking of the Nazi Economy*, Allen Lane, London, 2006
Uziel, Daniel, *Arming the Luftwaffe – The German Aviation Industry in World War II*, McFarland & Company, Inc., Jefferson, 2012
Vajda, Ferenc A. and Dancey, Peter, *German Aircraft Industry and Production 1933–1945*, Airlife, Shrewsbury, 1998.

USAAF

Bowman, Martin W., *Castles in the Air*, Red Kite, Walton-on-Thames, 2001
– *Clash of Eagles – USAAF 8th Air Force Bombers versus the Luftwaffe in World War II*, Pen & Sword Aviation, Barnsley, 2006
Craven, W. F. and Cate, J. L., *The Army Air Forces in World War II Vol. I: Plans and Early Operations (January 1939 to August 1942)*, University of Chicago Press, Chicago, 1948
– *Vol. II: Torch to Pointblank (August 1942 to December 1943)*, University of Chicago Press, Chicago, 1951
– *Vol. III Europe: Argument to VE Day (January 1944 to May 1945)*, University of Chicago Press, Chicago, 1951
Davis, Richard G., *Carl A. Spaatz and the Air War in Europe*, Center for Air Force History, Washington, D.C., 1993
Daugherty, William J., *The US Eighth Air Force in World War II – Ira Eaker, Hap Arnold, and Building American Air Power, 1942–1943*, University of North Texas Press, Denton, 2024
Ehlers Jr., Robert S., *The Mediterranean Air War – Airpower and Allied Victory in World War II*, University Press of Kansas, Lawrence, 2015
Ethell, Jeffrey and Price, Alfred, *Target Berlin – Mission 250: 6 March 1944*, Jane's Publishing, London, 1981
Freeman, Roger A., *Mighty Eighth*, Macdonald, London, 1970
– *Mighty Eighth War Diary*, Janes, London, 1981
– *Mighty Eighth War Manual*, Janes, London, 1984
Gobrecht, Lt Col, Harry D., *Might in Flight – Daily Diary of the Eighth Air Force's Hell's Angels – 303rd Bombardment Group (H)*, 303rd Bombardment Group (H) Association, San Clemente, 1993
Hammel, Eric, *Air War Europa – America's Air War against Germany in Europe and North Africa: Chronology 1942–1945*, Pacifica Press, Pacifica, 1994
– *The Road to Big Week – The Struggle for Daylight Air Supremacy over Western Europe July 1942–February 1944*, Pacifica Military History, Pacifica, 2009
Hawkins, Ian, *Münster: The Way it Was*, Robinson Typographics, Anaheim, 1964

SOURCES AND SELECTED BIBLIOGRAPHY

Jablonski, Edward, *Flying Fortress – The Illustrated Biography of the B-17s and the Men Who Flew Them*, Echo Point Books & Media, Brattleboro, 2014

McFarland, Stephen L. and Phillips Newton, Wesley, *To Command the Sky – The Battle for Air Superiority over Germany, 1942–1944*, Smithsonian Institution Press, Washington, D.C., 1991

Miller, Donald L. *Eighth Air Force – The American Bomber Crews in Britain*, Aurum Press, London, 2006

Rein, Christopher M., *The North African Campaign – US Army Air Forces from El Alamein to Salerno*, University Press of Kansas, Lawrence, 2012

Rust, Kenn C., *Fifteenth Air Force Story*, Historical Aviation Album, Temple City, 1976

Simons, Graham M., *Consolidated B-24 Liberator*, Pen & Sword Aviation, Barnsley, 2012

Thomas, Lowell and Jablonski, Edward, *Bomber Commander – The Life of James H. Doolittle*, Sidgwick & Jackson, London, 1977

Truxal, Luke W., *Uniting against the Reich – the American Air War in Europe*, University Press of Kentucky, Lexington, 2023

RAF Bomber Command

Hastings, Max, *Bomber Command*, Michael Joseph, London, 1979

Holmes, Robin, *The Battle of Heligoland Bight 1939 – The Royal Air Force and the Luftwaffe's Baptism of Fire*, Grub Street, London, 2009

Middlebrook, Martin and Everitt Chris, *The Bomber Command War Diaries – An Operational Reference Book: 1919–1945*, Penguin Books, London, 1990

Simpson, Andrew, *Ops – Victory At All Costs: Operations over Hitler's Reich with the crews of Bomber Command 1939–1945*, Tattered Flag Press, Pulborough, 2012

Terraine, John, *The Right of the Line: The Royal Air Force in the European War 1939–1945*, Hodder and Stoughton, London, 1985

Verrier, Anthony, *The Bomber Offensive*, B. T. Batsford, London, 1968

Webster, Sir Charles and Frankland, Noble, *The Strategic Air Offensive against Germany 1939–1945 Volume I: Preparation*, HMSO, London, 1961

– *Volume II: Endeavour*, HMSO, London, 1961

– *Volume III: Victory*, HMSO, London, 1961

Notes

CHAPTER 1: 'SHOULDER TO SHOULDER'

1. The National Archives (TNA)/AIR27/125, No. 9 Sqn ORB.
2. John Foreman and Christopher Shores, 'The Battle of Heligoland', *Flypast*, April 1984.
3. Grp Capt. P. I. Harris DFC (RAF Ret), 'Wilhelmshaven Disaster', *Flypast*, June 1983.
4. Harris, 'Wilhelmshaven Disaster'.
5. Overy, *The Bombing War*, p. 241.
6. Overy, *The Air War*, p. 35.
7. Simpson, *Ops: Victory At All Costs: Operations over Hitler's Reich with the crews of Bomber Command 1939–1945*, p. 24.
8. Hastings, *Bomber Command*, p. 18; Middlebrook and Everitt, *Bomber Command War Diaries*, p. 26.
9. Report by Air Commodore Norman Bottomley, 28/12/39, cited in Holmes, *The Battle of Heligoland Bight 1939*, p. 42.
10. Webster and Frankland, *SAOAG* Vol. I, p. 191.
11. TNA/AIR2/8541, *Reconnaissance over Wilhelmshaven on 18/12/39*, HQ, No. 3 Group, 22 December 1939.
12. Holmes, p. 37.
13. Nijboer, *Flak in World War II*, p. 84.
14. See ADI(K) Report No. 406-45/1944, *GAF Signals Intelligence in the War*, 30 October 1945.
15. Mombeek, *Defenders of the Reich, Vol. One*, p. 6.
16. Bekker, *The Luftwaffe War Diaries*, p. 71.
17. Caldwell, *JG 26 Top Guns*, p. 13.
18. TNA/AIR2/8541.
19. Mombeek, p. 8.
20. Holmes, p. 80.
21. Hastings, p. 31.
22. Prien, *Jagdgeschwaders 77, Teil* 1, p. 133.
23. Wolfgang Falck, *The 'Marienkäfer' (Lady-Bug) Squadron*, at https://kalikellett.com/rk-war-heliogoland-and-wilhelmshaven.

24 Terraine, *The Right of the Line*, p. 107.
25 Hastings, p. 27.
26 TNA/AIR2/8541.
27 Caldwell and Muller, *The Luftwaffe over Germany*, p. 41.
28 Sources vary, some stating German claims amounted to 34 bombers.
29 TNA/AIR27/125, AIR27/388 No. 37 Sqn Operations Record Book and AIR 27/1000.
30 Baldwin in Holmes, p. 97.
31 TNA/AIR2/8541, *Points arising from Bomber Command reports on attacks on German fleet in Heligoland Bight*, FO2 to DHO, 3/1/40.
32 TNA/AIR2/8541, Ludlow-Hewitt to Under Secretary of State, 29/12/39 (enclosure)
33 https://kalikellett.com/rk-war-heliogoland-and-wilhelmshaven. The reason for Kellet's ire over Ludlow-Hewitt is not clear, but according to Dr Malcolm Smith, Ludlow-Hewitt was replaced as C-in-C of RAF Bomber Command because of his apparent failure to prepare adequately for war and the poor state of flying training which had made it necessary to form Operational Training Units, thus withdrawing squadrons from frontline service. (Smith, *Sir Edgar Ludlow-Hewitt and the Expansion of Bomber Command, 1939–40*, RUSI Journal, Vol. 126, 1981, Issue 1).

CHAPTER 2: 'AN EXPENSIVE MODE OF WARFARE'

1 Holmes, *The Battle of Heligoland Bight 1939*, p. 98.
2 TNA/AIR2/8541, Bottomley, BC/S.21688/2/Air, 28/12/39.
3 Webster and Frankland, *SAOAG* Vol. I, p. 197.
4 Caldwell and Muller, *The Luftwaffe over Germany*, p. 17.
5 ADI(K) Report No.406-45/1944, *GAF Signals Intelligence in the War – V: Advance Warning, Route Tracking and Forecasting of Offensives*, 30/10/45.
6 Corum and Muller, *The Luftwaffe's Way of War*, p. 122.
7 Corum and Muller, p. 153.
8 Grabmann, Gen. Maj. a.D., Walter, *German Air Defence 1933-1945, Volume I, 1933–21 March 1941*, USAF Historical Studies No. 164, 1956, p. 238.
9 Grabmann, p. 236.
10 Grabmann, p. 240.
11 Grabmann, p. 240.
12 Cited in Terraine, *The Right of the Line*, p. 87.
13 Terraine, p. 112.
14 Webster and Frankland, *SAOAG* Vol. I, p. 201.
15 Overy, *The Bombing War*, p. 242.
16 Middlebrook and Everitt, *The Bomber Command War Diaries*, p. 21.
17 Webster and Frankland, *SAOAG* Vol. I, p. 212.
18 Verrier, *The Bomber Offensive*, p. 111.

19 'Boeings for Britain?', *The Aeroplane*, 27/9/40.
20 Jablonski, *Flying Fortress – The Illustrated Biography of the B-17s and the Men Who Flew Them*, p. 28.
21 USAF Hist.Study No. 102, *Origins of the Eighth Air Force – Plans, Organization, Doctrines*, pp. 91–92.
22 Paul Bingley, *Taking the Fortress to War* at aspectsofhistory.com (accessed 3/9/24).
23 TNO/AIR 27/731 No. 90 Sqn ORB.
24 Information from Eric Mombeek, 22/9/24.
25 TNO/AIR 27/731.
26 Jablonski, p. 31 and USAF Hist.Study No. 102, p. 109.
27 USAF Hist.Study No. 102, p. 92.
28 Jablonski, p. 28.
29 Bingley, aspectsofhistory.com (accessed 3/9/24).
30 Craven and Cate, *AAF in WWII, Vol. 1*, p. 601.
31 Simons, *Consolidated B-24 Liberator*, p. 29 et passim.
32 USAF Hist.Study No. 102, p. 101.
33 Webster and Frankland, *SAOAG* Vol. I, p. 243.
34 Irving, *Hitler's War*, p. 352.
35 Grunberger, Richard, *A Social History of the Third Reich*, Penguin Books, Harmondsworth, 1971, p. 53.
36 Irving, p. 345.

CHAPTER 3: 'ONE SWALLOW DOESN'T MAKE A SUMMER'

1 Freeman, *The Mighty Eighth*, p. 5.
2 Miller, *Eighth Air Force – The American Bomber Crews in Britain*, p. 49.
3 Miller, p. 46
4 Truxal, *Uniting against the Reich – the American Air War in Europe*, p. 20.
5 Craven and Cate, *AAF in WWII, Vol. 1*, p. 613.
6 Daugherty, *The US Eighth Air Force in World War II – Ira Eaker, Hap Arnold, and Building American Air Power, 1942–1943*, p. 33.
7 USAF Hist.Study No. 102, pp. 20–25.
8 Truxal, p. 22.
9 Miller, p. 59.
10 Craven and Cate, p. 567.
11 Craven and Cate, p. 569.
12 Freeman, p. 7 and Craven and Cate, pp. 642–44.
13 Davis, *Carl A. Spaatz and the Air War in Europe*, p. 85.
14 Davis, p. 87.
15 Craven and Cate, p. 663.
16 Galland in ADI(K) Report No. 373/1945, *The Birth, Life and Death of the German Day Fighter Arm*, 15/8/45, para 245.

NOTES

17 IWM: ASPHIR, *Fighter Operations of the German Air Force*, p. 113, 6.,(1), (c).
18 IWM: ASPHIR, *Fighter Operations of the German Air Force*, Appendix XXIX, *Attacks on Heavy Bombers, Interrogation of Generalleutnant Galland*, 15/10/45.
19 TNA/AIR2/7493 *Tactical Notes on the Operations of the Fortresses (B-17F) of the USAAF in the European Theatre of War up to September 15th, 1942.*

CHAPTER 4: WEST AND SOUTH

1 For the Bf 109 see, Ebert, Kaiser and Peters, *Willy Messerschmitt: Pioneer of Aviation Design*, p. 127; Prien and Rodeike, *Messerschmitt Bf 109 F, G, and K Series – An Illustrated Study*, pp. 10–30; Fernández-Sommerau, *Messerschmitt Bf 109 Recognition Manual – A Guide to Variants, Weapons and Equipment*, pp. 45–53; and Ritger, *The Messerschmitt Bf 109 – Part 2: 'F' to 'K' Variants*, pp. 20–21.
2 Grinsell, Bob, 'Emil, Franz and Gustav – Flying the Messerschmitt 109', *Wings*, 1972.
3 IWM: ASPHIR, *Fighter Operations of the German Air Force*, p. 121, 2 (f).
4 TNA/AIR40/365, *Mission No. 17: Lille locomotive, carriage and wagon works and Abbeville/Drucat aerodrome, 8 November 1942.*
5 Toliver and Constable, p. 321.
6 Weal, *Jagdgeschwader 2*, p. 93.
7 BAMA/RL10/291, *Erfahrungen im Luftkampf gegen Boeing Fortress II und Consolidated Liberator*, Galland (*Anlage zu* I./JG 54 Nr.9/43).
8 Freeman, *Mighty Eighth War Diary*, pp. 27-28.
9 Bowman, *Castles in the Air*, p. 33.
10 TNA/AIR40/371, HQ Eighth AF, *Composite Intelligence Narrative No. 9 of Ops undertaken 23 November 1942*, 26/11/42.
11 ASPHIR, App. XXIX, *Attacks on Heavy Bombers*, 15/10/45.
12 BAMA/RL10/29 and see also ASPHIR, App. XLII, *Experiences in Combat Against Boeing Fortress II and Consolidated Liberator*, undated.
13 ADI(K) Report No. 373/1945.
14 ADI(K) Report No. 373/1945.
15 Gundelach, *Band 1*, p. 377
16 Playfair et al., *The Mediterranean and Middle East*, Vol. III, p. 207.
17 Playfair et al., Vol. III, p. 206.
18 Prien, Rodeike and Stemmer, *III. und IV./Jagdgeschwader 27*, p. 161 and p. 344.
19 Playfair et al., Vol. III, p. 93.
20 Rein, p. 49.
21 Ehlers, p. 217.
22 Playfair et al., Vol. III, p. 283 and Rein, p. 50.
23 Ehlers, p. 225.
24 Rein, p. 51.

25 TNA/AIR20/8534, CSDIC (Air), CMF, Report No. 597, *German Fighter Tactics against RAF Bomber Formations in Africa*, 23/10/45.
26 Weal, *Bf 110 Zerstörer Aces*, p. 71 and Shores et al., *Mediterranean Air War, Volume Two*, p. 674.
27 TNA/AIR2/7493, *Defence Against the Fortress*, HQ Eighth AF, 28/8/43.

Chapter 5: The Slender Sinews of Defence

1 For Luftwaffe daylight fighter pilot training, see:
   - USSBS, *The Impact of the Allied Air Effort on the GAF Program for Training Day Fighter Pilots*, HRD, Maxwell AFB.
   - TNA/AIR22/78, *The Training of a Fighter Pilot in the GAF* in Air Ministry Weekly Intelligence Summaries 187–212, April–September 1943.
   - Ketley and Rolfe, *Luftwaffe Fledglings 1935–1945*, various pages.
   - Ketley, *Fledgling Eagles*, various pages.
   - Ries, *Deutsche Flugzeugführerschulen und ihre Maschinen 1919–1945*, various pages.
   - Carlsen and Meyer, *Die Flugzeugführer-Ausbildung der Deutschen Luftwaffe 1935–1955, Band II*, various pages.
2 Gen.Maj. a.D. Walter Grabmann, *German Air Defense 1933–1945, Volume II, 21/3/41–31/12/1942*, USAFHRC Numbered Study 159, Maxwell AFB, 1954, p. 547.
3 TNA/AIR20/7711: *GAF Policy during Second World War – Comments by General der Flieger Karl Koller on a review by Oberst Bernd von Brauchitsch*, AHB.6 Translation VII/154, April 1956.
4 TNA/AIR40/2109 *Notes on the G.A.F. day fighter defence system in Western Europe: Air Defence of Great Britain, intelligence memorandum No. 2*, February 1944.
5 Caldwell and Muller, *Luftwaffe over Germany*, p. 54.
6 A.P/W.I.U. (2nd TAF), 70/1945, *Luftflottenkommando Reich*, Missunde, 28/5/45.
7 TNA/AIR40/2475, ADI(K) Report No. 16/1944, *Jafü Holland/Ruhrgebiet*, 12/1/44.
8 ADI(K) Report No. 525/1944, *Fighter Defence of Germany – Control of Fighters by the 'Y' Procedure*, 23/9/44 and ADI(K) Report No. 527B/1944, *Equipment of a Y-Site*, 25/9/44
9 Smith and Creek, *Focke-Wulf Fw 190 Volume One*, p. 181.
10 BAMA RL 8/85, Nr.52/42, *Befehl für die Kampfführung der Tag- und Nachtjagd im Bereich Jagdfliegerführer Süddeutschland*, 28/12/42.
11 Middlebrook and Everitt, p. 319.
12 TNA/AIR40/2475.
13 TNA/AIR20/7700, *A Survey of Anglo-American Air Operations against the Reich and Western Europe in 1942*, 8th Abt., 6/10/44.

NOTES

CHAPTER 6: IMBALANCE OF POWER

1. Masefield, 'Flying Fortress', *The Aeroplane*, 29/1/43.
2. TNA/AIR20/7711.
3. Adam Tooze, *The Wages of Destruction – The Making and Breaking of the Nazi Economy*, p. 409 and p. 578.
4. TNA/AIR20/7711.
5. Caldwell and Muller, *Luftwaffe over Germany*, p. 52.
6. Richard Suchenwirth, *Command and Leadership in the German Air Force*, p. 272.
7. Richard Overy, *War and Economy in the Third Reich*, p. 346.
8. Tooze, p. 405.
9. Lutz Budrass, *Flugzeugindustrie und Luftrüstung in Deutschland 1918–1945*, p. 686.
10. Richard Overy, p. 350.
11. Budrass, p. 832.
12. Caldwell and Muller, *Luftwaffe over Germany*, p. 55, and Vajda and Dancey, *German Aircraft Industry and Production 1933–1945*, p. 67.
13. Budrass, p. 822.
14. Vajda and Dancey, pp. 132–133.
15. Tooze, p. 402.
16. Joe Maiolo, *Cry Havoc – The Arms Race and the Second World War, 1931–1941*, p. 364.
17. Stephen Budiansky, *Air Power – From Kitty Hawk to Gulf War II: A History of the People, Ideas and Machines that Transformed War in the Century of Flight*, p. 253.
18. Budiansky, p. 254.
19. Maiolo, p. 372.

CHAPTER 7: 'ONCE THEY HAVE MADE CONTACT WITH THE BOMBERS, THE REST IS EASY'

1. ADI(K) Report No. 373/1945.
2. Boiten, *Nachtjagd War Diaries Volume One*, p. 151.
3. TNA/AIR40/382, *Analysis of E/A encounters – Operation No. 33, Emden, 4 February 1943*.
4. Boiten, p. 154.
5. Boiten, p. 162.
6. Stein, *Gefechtsbericht vom 18. März 1943*, via Dietmar Hermann.
7. ADI(K) Report No. 373/1945.
8. TNA/AIR20/7709, AHB.6 Translation No. VII/140, *Extracts from Conferences on Problems of Aircraft Production*, August 1954.
9. TNA/AIR2/7493, *HQ Eighth AF, Office of the Assistant Chief of Staff A-2, Defense against the Fortress*, 28/8/43.
10. TNA/AIR2/7493.

11 Hans-Ekkehard Bob, *Entwurf Gefechtsbericht, 17.4.1943*, via Bob.
12 Hans-Ekkehard Bob, *Fallschirm-Absprung Nr.2/43, 17/4/43*, via Bob.
13 Webster and Frankland, *SAOAG Volume II: Endeavour*, p. 24, and Holland, *Big Week*, p. 102.
14 Johannes Steinhoff, *The German Fighter Battle against the American Bombers*, p. 4.
15 TNA/AIR2/7493.
16 TNA/AIR2/7493.
17 Roba and Pegg, *Jagdwaffe – The Mediterranean 1943–1945*, p. 295.
18 Johannes Steinhoff, *The German Fighter Battle against the American Bombers*, p. 4.
19 Jochen Prien, *"Pik-As" – Geschichte des Jagdgeschwaders 53, Teil 2*, p. 860 and p. 927, and *Geschichte des Jagdgeschwaders 77, Teil 3 1942–1943*, p.1065–69. See also Johannes Steinhoff, *The Straits of Messina*, p. 51.
20 *Jagdfliegerführer Berlin-Mitteldeutschland*, Ia Br.B.Nr.168/43, *Bekämpfung feindlicher Kampfverbände, 28.6.1943*.
21 TNA/AIR40/1345: Air Prisoners of War Interrogation Reports: Ninth Air Force, HQ Air P/W Interrogation Detachment, 1/6/45, *Hermann Goering*.
22 ADI(K) Report No. 373/1945.
23 TNA/AIR20/7709, AHB.6 Translation No. VII/137, *Fighter Staff Conferences, 1944*.
24 Headquarters, Eighth Air Force, Operational Analysis Section, *An Evaluation of Defensive Measures Taken to Protect Heavy Bombers from Loss and Damage*, November 1944, p. 36.

CHAPTER 8: DEFENCE IN DEPTH

1 ASPHIR, *Tactical Employment: Fighter Operations of the German Air Force, Appendix XXXIII, Interrogation of Generalleutnant Galland, Oberstleutnant Bär and Oberstleutnant Dahl: The Evolution of the Defense of the Reich, 20–23 September 1945*.
2 Budrass, p. 868.
3 Speer, *Inside the Third Reich*, p. 290.
4 Dieter-Theodor Bohlmann, *Sokrates – Die Geschichte der Reichsluftverteidigung, ihrer Anlagen und Liegenschaften in und um Stade 1935–2005*, p. 159 et passim.
5 TNA/AIR40/2109.
6 TNA/AIR40/427, *HQ VIII Bomber Command Narrative of Ops, 28 July 1943, Mission No. 78*.
7 Interview, author with Horst Geyer, Ahrensburg, 18/3/93.
8 TNA/AIR40/427.
9 TNA/AIR40/427.
10 BAMA/RL8/91, *Kriegsgeschichte des I.Jagdkorps*, p. 190.
11 TNA/AIR40/427.
12 Headquarters, Eighth AF, *An Evaluation of Defensive Measures Taken to Protect Heavy Bombers from Loss and Damage, November 1944*.

NOTES

13 TNA/AIR2/7493, *HQ Eighth AF, Office of the Assistant Chief of Staff A-2, Defense against the Fortress*, 28/8/43.

CHAPTER 9: SCHWEINFURT

1 BAMA/RL10/639, *III.Gruppe/JG 3, Auszüge aus dem Kriegstagebuch.- Nachkriegsaufzeichnung von Major a.D. Langer.*
2 BAMA/RL10/565,*III./Zerstörergeschwader 26,Anlagen zu den Kriegstagebüchern Nr. 7 und 8*, 8/1943– 4/44.
3 ASPHIR, GAF Fighter Ops., Appendix XVI, Kowalewski, Nolle and Eschenauer, *A History of the GAF Twin-Engine Fighter Arm (Zerstörerwaffe)*, 8/10/45.
4 BAMA/RL10/639.
5 Prien and Stemmer, *Messerschmitt Bf 109 im Einsatz bei der III./Jagdgeschwader 3*, p. 268.
6 ADI(K) Report No. 373/1945.
7 ADI(K) Report No. 373/1945.
8 Webster and Frankland, *SAOAG Volume II: Endeavour*, p. 31.
9 Miller, *Eighth Air Force – The American Bomber Crews in Britain*, p. 193.
10 Middlebrook, *The Schweinfurt-Regensburg Mission*, pp. 29–30.
11 Mombeek, *Defenders of the Reich: Jagdgeschwader 1, Vol. Two, 1943*, p. 180.
12 BAMA/RL10/639 and Prien and Stemmer, p. 457.
13 Boiten, *Nachtjagd War Diaries Volume One*, p. 235–239.
14 BAMA/RL8/92 and Boiten, *Nachtjagd War Diaries, Volume One*, p. 238.
15 BAMA/RL10/639.
16 Mombeek, p. 180.
17 See Ken Harbour and Peter Harris, *The 351st Bomb Group in W.W.II*, p. 13 and also MACR at www.351st.org/351stMissions/Mission029/Mission29.html.
18 TNA/AIR20/7709, *Extract from Conference under the Chairmanship of Field Marshal Milch on 25 August 1943*.
19 Prien and Stemmer, p. 271.
20 BAMA/RL10/639.
21 Truxal, *Uniting Against the Reich*, pp.77–79.
22 Daugherty, *The US Eighth Air Force in World War II*, p. 222.

CHAPTER 10: BITTER HARVEST

1 ADI(K) Report No. 373/1945.
2 ASPHIR, *Appendix XXXIII, Interrogation of Generalleutnant Galland, Oberstleutnant Bär and Oberstleutnant Dahl: The Evolution of the Defense of the Reich, 20–23 September 1945*.
3 IWM/GDC, *General der Jagdflieger, Tactical Regulations for SE and TE Fighter Formations in Air Defense* [Translation], 3/9/43.

4 TNA/WO 208/4135, CSDIC(UK) SR Report: SRA 5733, 19/1/45.
 5 Michael Meyer and Paul Stipdonk, *German Fighters in the West*, p. 383.
 6 BAMA/RL10/639.
 7 BAMA/RL10/583, *Jagdgeschwader 3 "Udet", Bd. 7: III. Gruppe (Stab, 7.-9. Staffel), 1941–1944. Einsatz Sowjetunion-Süd und Reich.*
 8 Caldwell, *Day Fighters in Defence of the Reich*, p. 108.
 9 Hajo Herrmann, *Eagles Wings – The Autobiography of a Luftwaffe Pilot*, p. 199.
10 Meredith, *Phoenix – A Complete History of the Luftwaffe 1918–1945, Volume 2 – The Genesis of Air Power 1935–1937*, p.471 and see ADI(K) Report No.16/1944, *Jafü Holland/Ruhrgebiet*, 12/1/44.
11 BAMA/RL8/92, *Niederschrift über Divisionskommandeur-Besprechung am 4.11.43*.
12 BAMA/RL8/91, *Generalkommando I. Jagdkorps, Band 1*
13 General der Jagdflieger, Br.B.Nr.1759/43, *Rammen feindlicher 4-motoriger Kampfflugzeuge mit besonders gepanzerten Jagdflugzeugen*, 22 September 1943.
14 ADI(K) Report No.322/1944, *Jafü 5 – Bernay*, 30/6/44.
15 BAMA/RL10/565, *Zerstörergeschwader 26, Anlagen zu den Kriegstagebüchern Nr. 7 und 8, Aug. 1943–Apr. 1944: Gefechtsbericht, 27. Sept 1943*.
16 BAMA/RL8/91.
17 BAMA/RL8/91, *Besprechung am 27.9.1943 in Stade*.
18 BAMA/RL8/91, *Kommandeurbesprechung am 29.9.1943 in Zeist*.
19 Hoeckner, *Stab*, II./JG 1, *Abschussmeldung, Gefechtsstand*, 18 December 1943.
20 See www.frankfurt1933-1945.de/chronologie/ereignis/210/erste-massive-luftangriffe-amerikanischer-und-britischer-verbaende-auf-frankfurt and Middlebrook and Everitt, p. 436.
21 Overy, *Goering – The 'Iron Man'*, p. 201
22 Irving, *Göring*, p. 406, and Hammel, *The Road to Big Week*, p. 279.
23 Irving, *Göring*, p. 405.
24 Hammel, p. 280.
25 Irving, *Göring*, p. 406.
26 BAMA/RL10/639.
27 Budrass, p. 868.

CHAPTER 11: 'DEFENSIVE VICTORIES'

1 Letter Horst Geyer to author, 26/6/90.
2 BAMA/RL8/93
3 TNA/AIR 40/460 *Operation 111: Bremen, Deutsche Schiff U-boat yards; Weser, aircraft factory and city proper and Vegesack, Bremer Vulcan U-boat yards*, 8 October 1943.
4 BAMA/RL10/565, *III./Zerstörergeschwader 26 'Horst Wessel', Gefechtsbericht, 8.10.43*.
5 Mombeek, *Defenders of the Reich, Volume Two*, p. 186.

NOTES

6 USAF Historical Study Nos. 158–160, Gen.Lt. a.D. Josef Schmid, *The Deployment of the German Luftwaffe against the Allies in the West 1943–1945.*
7 BAMA/RL10/565, *Gefechtsbericht für 9.10.43.*
8 USAF Historical Study Nos. 158–160.
9 BAMA/RL8/92, *I.Jagdkorps: Niederschrift, 27.10.43.*
10 BAMA/RL10/565, *Gefechtsbericht für 10.10.43.*
11 BAMA/RL8/93.
12 TNA/AIR40/463, *Telegram ComBomCon Eight, 114th Operation – Mission No. 1 – 3rd Bomb Division, 11 October 1943.*
13 Hawkins, *Münster: The Way it Was*, p. 113.
14 BAMA/RL8/283, *7. Jagddivision, Auszug aus dem Kriegstagbuch vom 10.10.–15.44.43.*
15 TNA/AIR40/463.
16 BAMA/RL8/170, *Gen.Kdo. II.Jagdkorps, Korpstagesbefehl Nr.2, 15.10.1943.*
17 TNA/WO208/4341, *Interrogation of Field Marshal Milch, 3rd June 1945.*
18 Galland, *The First and The Last*, p. 257.
19 ADI(K) Report No. 373/1945.
20 TNA/WO208/4341.
21 BAMA/RL10/433, *Detlef Lüth, Abschussmeldung, 10.1.1944*
22 Joel Punches, *B-17F Flight Log (5 Sept 1943–21 Feb 1944), 8th Air Force, 385th Bomb Wing, Great Ashfield, England*, private publication, undated.
23 BAMA/RL10/565 *Gefechtsbericht für 14.10.43.*
24 BAMA/RL18/583, Zimmer, *Gefechtsbericht*, 26.10.43.
25 BAMA/RL10/639.
26 Bergström, *Graf and Grislawski – A Pair of Aces*, p. 196.
27 BAMA/RL8/92, *Niederschrift über Divisionskommandeur-Besprechung am 4.11.43.*
28 Craven and Cate, Volume II, p. 711.
29 McFarland and Newton, *To Command the Sky*, p. 129.
30 BAMA/RL8/91.
31 BAMA/RL8/92, *Gen.Kdo. I. Jagdkorps, Korpstagesbefehl Nr. 2, 25.10.1943.*
32 BAMA/RL8/92, *Niederschrift über Divisionskommandeur-Besprechung am 4.11.43.*
33 BAMA/RL18/583 and Prien and Stemmer, *III./Jagdgeschwader 3*, p. 501.

CHAPTER 12: 'WITHOUT REGARD TO LOSSES'

1 Caldwell, *Day Fighters in Defence of the Reich*, p. 144.
2 Rust, *Fifteenth Air Force Story*, pp. 5–7
3 BAMA/RL8/283, *7. Jagddivsion, Auszug aus dem Kriegstagbuch vom 10.10.–15.11.43.*
4 BAMA/RL8/92, *I. Jagdkorps, Besprechung beim Bef.Mitte am 6.11.43 in Berlin-Dahlem* and *7.11.43 in Berlin Reichssportfeld.*

5 TNA/WO208/4344 *Information on various GAF war methods and experiences obtained from former Chief of Air Command West (Luftwaffen Kommando West) Major Gen Schmid*, 11/8/45.
6 BAMA/RL10/639.
7 BAMA/RL8/92, *Besprechung am 8.11.43, De Breul.*
8 TNA/DEFE3/5, CX/MSS/T9/53 (Ultra decrypt, 21/11/43).
9 Brütting, *Das Buch der deutschen Fluggeschichte, Band 3*, p. 447; Bungay, Stephen, *The Most Dangerous Enemy*, p. 207; and www.specialcamp11.co.uk/Generalleutnant%20Joachim-Friedrich%20Huth%20(Luftwaffe).htm.
10 BAMA/RL8/92, *Besprechung in Stade am 16.11.1943.*
11 Martin Gilbert, *Second World War*, p. 478.
12 BAMA/RL8/92, *Kommandeurbesprechung am 20.11.43, Driebergen.*
13 General der Jagdflieger, Brb.Nr.2145/43, *Rammen feindlicher 4-motorige Kampfflugzeuge, 13.11.43.*
14 Petersen, KdE Brb.Nr.1187/43, *Luftverteidigung in Höhen über 10000 m bei Tage, 9.11.43.*
15 TNA/AIR2/7493.

CHAPTER 13: BATTLE GROUPS AND OPERA HOUSES

1 See BAMA/RL2 II/320.
2 TNA/AIR40/489, *Operation 138: Bremen and Paris, 26 Nov. 1943.*
3 BAMA/RL8/92; Caldwell, *Day Fighters*, pp. 151-52; Freeman, *Mighty Eighth War Diary*, p. 142
4 BAMA/RL10/565, III./ZG 26, *Nachtrag zum Gefechtsbericht vom 26.11.1943.*
5 BAMA/RL10/565, Schmid to ZG 26, 30/11/43.
6 Erprobungskommando 25, *Arbeitsberichte* Br.B.Nr.123/43 (Nr.13), 30/10/43 and Nr.142/43 (Nr.14), 16/11/43.
7 TNA/AIR40/491, BC.140, Bremen, 29/11/43.
8 TNA/AIR2/7493, *Tactical Bulletin No. 28, Current GAF Tactics against Heavy Bomber Formations Operating in Daylight, Air Ministry*, 15 January 1944.
9 BAMA/RL10/433, Schmitz *Abschussmeldung*, 14/12/43.
10 Caldwell, *Day Fighters*, p. 158.
11 Gundelach, Karl, *Die deutsche Luftwaffe im Mittelmeer 1940–1945 Band 2*, pp. 745 and 759.
12 BAMA/RL8/80, *Jagdfliegerführer Süd, Tagesbefehl Nr.10, 28.12.1943.*
13 BAMA/RL8/92, entry for 6/12/43.
14 BAMA/RL10/565.
15 ASPHIR, GAF Fighter Ops., Appendix XVI, Kowalewski, Nolle and Eschenauer, *A History of the GAF Twin-Engine Fighter Arm (Zerstörerwaffe)*, 8/10/45.
16 TNA/AIR40/503, *PNT Telegram No. 13268, Synopsis Report 11 Dec. 43 Operation 151.*

NOTES

17 Horst Geyer, interview with author, Ahrensburg, 18/3/93.
18 Horst Geyer, 18/3/93.
19 TNA/AIR2/7493.
20 *Erprobungskommando 25, Br.B.Nr.163/43, Arbeitsbericht Nr.15, 30 Nov 43.*
21 TNA/AIR40/2109, *III./ZG 26 Gefechtsbericht für 11.12.1943.*
22 *Luftwaffe Jagd Gefechtsstände, the Luftlage and types of Jagdverfahren* at www.gyges.dk/Lage%20production%202.htm and *German Day Fighter Command & Control* at www.gyges.dk/german_day_fighter_control.htm.
23 Headquarters, Eighth AF, *An Evaluation of Defensive Measures Taken to Protect Heavy Bombers from Loss and Damage, November 1944.*
24 BAMA/RL8/93, *I.Jagdkorps, Niederschrift über die Divisionskommandeurbesprechung am 29.12.1943.*
25 Schmid, *The Employment of the German Luftwaffe against the Allies in the West, 1943–1945.*
26 TNA/AIR20/7711: *GAF Policy during Second World War – Comments by General der Flieger Karl Koller on A Review by Oberst Bernd von Brauchitsch,* AHB.6 Translation VII/154, April 1956.
27 Craven and Cate, Volume II, pp. 636 and 639.
28 Headquarters, Eighth Air Force Operational Analysis Section, *An Evaluation of Defensive Measures Taken to Protect Heavy Bombers from Loss and Damage, November 1944.*
29 Vajda and Dancey, p. 80.
30 Budrass, p. 868.

CHAPTER 14: POINTBLANK AND THE BATTLE FOR AIR SUPERIORITY

1 Craven and Cate, *The Army Air Forces in World War II, Vol.III*, p. 8.
2 McFarland and Phillips Newton, p. 158.
3 Thomas and Jablonski, *Bomber Commander – The Life of James H. Doolittle*, p. 267.
4 Schmid, *The Employment of the German Luftwaffe against the Allies in the West, 1943–1945.*
5 Caldwell and Muller, *Luftwaffe over Germany*, p. 146.
6 www.gyges.dk/Gefechtsstand%20bunker%20luftflotte%20reich.htm.
7 Richard Franz, letter to author, 6/8/91.
8 Schmid.
9 TNA/AIR42/3, *Combined Operational Planning Committee, Periodic Report on Enemy Daylight Fighter Defences and Interception Tactics, 30 December 1943–22 January 1944, 3 February 1944.*
10 TNA/AIR42/3.
11 BAMA/RL/10/433, *II./Jagdgeschwader 1, Kirchmayr, Abschussmeldung, 11 January 1944.*
12 Prien and Rodeike, *Jagdgeschwader 1 und 11, Teil 2 1944*, p. 678.
13 Boiten, *Nachtjagd War Diaries, Volume One*, p. 335.

14 TNA/AIR42/3.
15 Caldwell, *JG 26 War Diary, Volume Two*, p. 198.
16 TNA/AIR2/7493, *DB Ops 21184, Attacks with trailed bombs, 16 January 1944*.
17 TNA/AIR40/529 *8th Bomber Command, Preliminary Summary of Operations, 11 January 1944*.
18 TNA/AIR40/529.
19 Schmid.
20 Schmid.
21 BAMA/RL8/93, *Gen. Kdo. I. Jagdkorps, Korpstagesbefehl Nr. 11, 28.1.1944*.
22 Hammel, *The Road to Big Week*, p. 329.
23 BAMA/RL10/433, *Meyer, Abschussmeldung, 24.1.1944*.
24 Prien, Rodeike and Stemmer, *Messerschmitt Bf 109 im Einsatz bei der III. und IV./Jagdgeschwader 27*, p. 373.
25 Schmid.
26 Schmid.
27 Schmid.
28 Davis, *Carl A. Spaatz and the Air War in Europe*, p. 306.
29 BAMA/RL10/583, *Wielebinski, Luftkampfzeugenbericht*.
30 BAMA/RL10/583, *Clemens, Abschussmeldung*.
31 BAMA/RL10/639.
32 Joel Punches, *B-17F Flight Log (5 Sept 1943–21 Feb 1944), 8th Air Force, 385th Bomb Wing, Great Ashfield, England*, private publication, undated.
33 Caldwell, *JG 26 Top Guns of the Luftwaffe*, pp. 304 and 376; *JG 26 War Diary Volume Two*, pp. 205–206.
34 BAMA/RL8/93, *Niederschrift über die Divisionskommandeur-Besprechung am 25.1.1944*.
35 Schmid.
36 Richard Franz, letter to author, 6/8/91.
37 Schmid.
38 BAMA/RL8/93, *Niederschrift des Kommandieren Generals, General Schmid, vom 9.2.–12.2.1944* and Schmid.
39 Schmid.
40 Bowman, *Clash of Eagles – USAAF 8th Air Force Bombers versus the Luftwaffe in World War II*, p. 107.

CHAPTER 15: BIG GUN – 'BIG WEEK'

1 IWM, H.E.C. No. 13661/Unterlüss Report No. 296, *Technical Report Upon the First Operational Experiences with 50 mm Automatic Weapons in Aircraft (Me 410): Discussions of the Results*, Dipl.-Ing. Kurt Buehler, 8/4/47; Rheinmetall-Borsig A.G., Unterlüss, *The 50 mm B.K., its Ammunition and Installation in Me 410 and Ju 88*, UNT.9.T., 15.9.1945; Unterlüss Report UNT.107.T., Dipl.-Ing. Johannes Linke, *Halbstarres Schiessen mit und ohne Stabilisierung: Aircraft Gun*

NOTES

Installations – Development of Larger Calibre Gun Installations for Air-to-Air Combat, translation 12/5/48; TNA/AIR40/2162: *The 50mm BK 5,* AI2(g) Report No. 1780, 28/5/45.
2. See *Erprobungskommando 25, Br.B.Nr.44/43, Arbeitsbericht Nr 5, 20 Juli 1943.*
3. ADI(K) Report No. 373/1945.
4. ADI(K) Report No. 373/1945.
5. Fritz Buchholz, letter to author, 23/7/90.
6. TNA/WO208/4344 *Information on various GAF war methods and experiences obtained from former Chief of Air Command West (Luftwaffen Kommando West) Maj Gen Schmid, 11 August 1945.*
7. Davis, *Spaatz,* p. 380.
8. Hammel, *The Road to Big Week,* p. 338.
9. Peter Schmoll, *Nest of Eagles – Messerschmitt Production and Flight-Testing at Regensburg 1936–1945,* pp. 133–134.
10. BAMA/RL8/94, *Niederschrift über die Besprechung am 23.2.1944 in Stade.*
11. TNA/AIR20/7709 *Extracts from Conferences on Problems of Aircraft Production,* August 1954; and AHB.6 Translation No. VII/137, *Fighter Staff Conferences, 1944.*
12. BAMA/RL10/565, *III./ZG 26 Gefechtsbericht vom 24.2.1944.*
13. Schmid.

CHAPTER 16: NOTES

1. Weal, John, *Jagdgeschwader 2 'Richthofen',* p. 106, but see, for example, https://falkeeins.blogspot.com/2019/03/latest-volume-in-jg-2-history-from-erik.html, *The death of Egon Mayer, 2 March 1944,* 14/3/2019.
2. BAMA/RL8/170, *Generalkommando II.Jagdkorps, Korpstagesbefehl, 10.3.44*
3. USSBS, *The Impact of the Allied Air Effort on the German Air Force Program for Training Day Fighter Pilots 1939–1945,* HRA, Maxwell AFB, undated and ADI(K) Report No. 373/1945.
4. Budrass, p. 868.
5. ASPHIR, *Fighter Operations of the GAF, Appendix XXXIII.*
6. Richard Franz, letter to author, 10/7/91.
7. Ethell and Price, *Target Berlin – Mission 250: 6 March 1944,* pp. 78–79; and see www.91stbombgroup.com.
8. BAMA/RL8/94, *Gen.Kdo. I.Jagdkorps, Korpstagesbefehl Nr.16, 10.3.1944.*
9. Prien, *IV./Jagdgeschwader 3: Chronik einer Jagdgruppe 1943–1945,* p. 355.
10. BAMA/RL10/584, Müller *Abschussmeldung,* 8/3/44.
11. IWM/GDC/Focke-Wulf, Bremen, Br.Nr.03041, *Vernichtung feindlicher Bomberverbände mittels künstlich erzeugter Böen,* Multhopp & Wendland, 8 März 1944.
12. BAMA/RL10/565, *Kogler, Meldung, 15 März 1944.*
13. Schmid, and Freeman, *Mighty Eighth War Diary,* pp. 200–201.

14 BAMA/RL8/94, *Der General spricht* (16/3/44).
15 BAMA/RL10/583 and Prien and Stemmer, *II./Jagdgeschwader 3*, p. 459.
16 BAMA/RL 10/636; Schmid; also Prien and Stemmer, *Messerschmitt Bf 109 im Einsatz bei der III./Jagdgeschwader 3*, pp. 293–294.
17 Rust, p. 17 and Prien, Rodeike and Stemmer, *III. und IV/Jagdgeschwader 27*, pp. 401 and 468.
18 Author interview with Franz Stigler, Mesa, Az., 5/10/90.
19 Prien, Rodeike and Stemmer, p. 468.
20 *Luftfahrtwissenschaft und -Technik – Wer ist Wo? I.Ausgabe: Forschung und Lehre*, DVL, Februar 1939.
21 IWM/GDC/Schmieschek, *Institut für Bildwesen der Deutschen Versuchsanstalt für Luftfahrt*, UM 1204, 20 März 1944.
22 Budrass, p. 868; Daniel Uziel, *Arming the Luftwaffe – The German Aviation Industry in World War II*, p. 31; Graham M. Simons, *Consolidated B-24 Liberator*, pp. 64–65.
23 Schmid.
24 Schmid.

CHAPTER 17: BLOODY APRIL

1 Luftflotte Reich, Ia., Br.No.1921/44, quoted in Schmid, *The Employment of the German Luftwaffe against the Allies in the West, 1943–1945*.
2 ADI(K) Report No.373/1945.
3 BAMA/RL10/433.
4 Author interview with Franz Stigler, Mesa, Az., 5/10/90.
5 Richard Franz, letter to author, 10/7/91.
6 BAMA/RL10/433, *Kurt Niedereichholz Abschussmeldung and Leo Schuhmacher Luftzeugkampfbericht*, 9.4.1944.
7 1Lt Raymond E. Smith, 78th FG, Combat Report, 11/4/44
8 BAMA/RL10/565, *Kogler, III./Zerstörergeschwader Horst Wessel Nr.26, Gefechtsbericht vom 11.4.1944*.
9 TNA/AIR40/598, *Eighth Air Force Narrative of Operations, 11 April 1944*.
10 Schmid.
11 TNA/AIR40/600, *Operation 301: Augsburg, Lechfeld and Oberpfaffenhofen fighter centres and Schweinfurt ball bearing plants*, 13 April 1944.
12 BAMA/RL10/433, *Georg Eder and Hubert Swoboda Abschussmeldung*, 13.4.1944.
13 BAMA/RL10/583, *Jürgen Hoerschelmann and Walther Dahl, Gefechtsberichte*, 19.4.1944.
14 Galland in *Jägerblatt* Vol. XL (2), 1991, p. 17 (via Caldwell).
15 Mombeek, with Forsyth and Creek, *Sturmstaffel 1 – Reich Defence: The War Diary*, pp. 89–90.

NOTES

16. Günther Rall (Ed. Kurt Braatz), *My Logbook – Reminiscenses 1938-2006*, pp .201.
17. Willi Unger, correspondence with author, 22/6/90.
18. Richard Franz, letter to author, 10/7/91.
19. *Die Wehrmachtberichte 1939–1945, Band 3*, p. 84.
20. BAMA/RL10/583, Combat reports Wielebinski, Spittler, Seel and Pankalla; and Prien and Stemmer, *III./Jagdgeschwader 3*, pp. 301, 460 and 503.
21. Oskar Bösch, *Fortress Hunter – or The Memories of a Focke-Wulf 190 Pilot*, private, undated m/s, via Boesch.
22. TNA/AIR20/7709, *AHB.6 Translation No.VII/137, Fighter Staff Conferences 1944*.
23. TNA/AIR40/613, *Berlin Raid: Bombers took the dangerous straight road*, German Telegraph Service (DNB Home), 30.4.44.
24. Schmid.
25. Bösch, *Fortress Hunter*.
26. BAMA/RL10/433, *Rüdiger Kirchmayr Abschussmeldung and Arnold Jansen, Luftzeugkampfbericht, 29.4.1944*.
27. TNA/AIR40/613, *Operation 327: Berlin, Magdeburg and Brandenburg, 29 April 1944*.
28. Schmid.
29. Freeman, *Mighty Eighth War Diary*, p. 232.
30. TNA/AIR40/613, *Berlin Raid: Bombers took the dangerous straight road*, German Telegraph Service (DNB Home), 30.4.44.

CHAPTER 18: THE LAST CHANCE

1. Adolf Galland, *The First and the Last*, pp. 266–267.
2. TNA/AIR20/7709, *AHB.6 Translation No. VII/137, Fighter Staff Conferences, 1944*.
3. TNA/AIR20/7703, *AHB.6 Translation No. VII/68, Notes on discussions with Reichsmarschall Goering, held on May 15 and 16, 1944 on the subject of fighters and fighter personnel* and USSBS, *The Impact of the Allied Air Effort on the German Air Force Program for Training Day Fighter Pilots 1939–1945*, undated, HRD, Maxwell AFB.
4. USSBS.
5. USSBS.
6. Norbert Hannig (ed. John Weal), *Luftwaffe Fighter Ace – From the Eastern Front to the Defence of the Homeland*, pp. 115–117.
7. ADI(K) Report No.334/1944, *Some Notes on the Output and Training of GAF Fighter Pilots, 6th July 1944*.
8. USSBS.
9. Hannig, pp. 115–117.

10 ADI(K) Report No. 334/1944.
11 USSBS.
12 Hannig, pp. 115–117.
13 Bösch, *Fortress Hunter*.
14 BAMA/RL10/584, *Moritz Abschussmeldungen, 8.5.1944*.
15 TNA/AIR22/417, *8th and 15th U.S.A.F. Weekly Intelligence Summaries: Nos. 26–51, 1944, May–Oct.*
16 TNA/AIR40/2016, *Combined Operational Planning Committee: Sixth Periodic Report on Enemy Daylight Fighter Defences and Interception Tactics 1–31 May, 1944.*
17 Eric Mombeek, *Defenders of the Reich: Jagdgeschwader 1 Volume Three – 1944–1945*, p. 235.
18 Mombeek, p. 235.
19 Webster and Frankland, *SAOAG Vol. III: Victory*, p. 35.
20 BAMA/RL10/584, *Nolting Abschussmeldungen, 12.5.1944*.
21 https://falkeeins.blogspot.com/2012/04/last-flight-of-lt-paul-kaschuba-and .html : *The last flight of Lt. Paul Kaschuba and 'Black 13' - the story behind the photo (Me 410 II./ZG 26 Flak 43) Zerstörer defending the Reich, Reichsverteidigung,* 17/4/2012.
22 https://falkeeins.blogspot.com.
23 TNA/AIR20/7703, *AHB.6 Translation No. VII/68, Notes on discussions with Reichsmarschall Goering, held on May 15 and 16 1944 on the subject of fighters and fighter personnel.*
24 Erprobungskommando 25, Arbeitsbericht Nr. 19, 128/44, 1/2–31/3/44.
25 Erprobungskommando 25, Arbeitsbericht Nr. 22, 335/44, 1–31/7/44.
26 Willi Unger, letter to author, 22/6/90.

CHAPTER 19: SAVAGE SKIES

1 Hans-Heiri Stapfer, *Strangers in a Strange Land*, pp. 42–43; Hans-Werner Lerche, *Luftwaffe Test Pilot – Flying captured Allied Aircraft of World War 2*, p. 31 *et passim*; see also www.airmen.dk and www.flensted.eu.com.
2 TNA/AIR20/7703, *AHB.6 Translation No. VII/68, Notes on discussions with Reichsmarschall Goering, held on May 15 and 16, 1944, on the subject of fighters and fighter personnel.*
3 Prien, Rodeike and Stemmer, *Stab und I./Jagdgeschwader 27*, p. 406.
4 TNA/AIR40/2016, *Combined Operational Planning Committee: sixth periodic report on enemy daylight fighter defences and interception tactics 1–31 May, 1944.*
5 Ernst Börngen, private account, via Hans-Ekkehard Bob to author, June 1989.
6 TNA/DEFE3/178, CX/MSS/T211/73, 26/6/44.
7 BAMA/RL8/80, *Jagdfliegerführer Süd, Tagesbefehl Nr. 5/44, 10.6.1944*; www.gyges.dk/Gefechtsstand%20bunker%20Jafu%20Sudfranch.htm and http://www.ww2.dk/ground/ln/ln51.html.

NOTES

8 BAMA/RL10/639, Information from KTB and RL10/583, *Karl-Heinz Langer, Abschussmeldung* and *Gefechtsbericht, 29.5.1944.*
9 Willi Unger, letter to author, 7/7/90.
10 Crew Interrogation Form at 95thbg.com.
11 Gray, John M. *Old Dog's Last Flight,* National Museum of the United States Air Force Friends Journal, Vol. 16 No. 1, Spring 1993; also MACR 5343, 29/5/44 and information from Roger A. Freeman, 18/9/93.
12 Schmid.
13 Headquarters, Eighth AF, *An Evaluation of Defensive Measures Taken to Protect Heavy Bombers from Loss and Damage, November 1944,* p. 64.
14 Erik Mombeeck, *Storming the Bombers – A Chronicle of JG 4: Volume 1 – 1942–1944,* p. 153.

CHAPTER 20: IMMINENT DANGER WEST

1 *Preparations for the Repulsion of the Invasion in the area of the Home Air Defence,* unpublished report, author collection.
2 Horst Geyer, interview with author, Ahrensburg, 18/3/93.
3 Michael Meyer and Paul Stipdonk, *German Fighters in the West,* p. 401.
4 TNA/AIR20/7700, *AHB.6 Translation No. VII/19, Some Aspects of the German fighter effort during the initial stages of the invasion of North-West Europe,* 18/11/44.
5 BAMA/RL10/639, Information from KTB, June 1944.
6 TNA/WO208/4134, CSDIC Report SRA.5460.
7 Hans-Ekkehard Bob, letter to author, 20/7/90.
8 Herbert Kaiser, interview with author, Felde, May 1992.
9 Galland, *The First and The Last,* p. 290.
10 TNA/WO208/4134, CSDIC Report SRA.5419.
11 Caldwell, *The JG 26 War Diary Volume Two,* p. 286.
12 AFSHRC microfilm K1026V.

CHAPTER 21: ALL-OUT DEFENCE

1 TNA/AIR20/7709, *AHB.6 Translation No. VII/137, Fighter Staff Conferences 1944, 30.6.44.*
2 Chef des Lw.Führungsstabes, Ia Nr.4532/44, *Tagesverlauf* 6/7/44 (via Irving).
3 Robert (Bob) Grinsell, *The Last Sortie,* no pub. or date; and *Focke-Wulf Fw 190,* p. 47.
4 Willi Unger, *Abschussmeldung,* 7/7/44 (via Unger).
5 Prien, *IV./Jagdgeschwader 3,* p. 175.
6 BAMA/RL10/788, *Besondere Bemerkungen zum Einsatz, Verband Jagdgeschwader Udet.*
7 Ultra decrypt: CX/MSS/T247/100 – KL 2383, 17/7/44 (via Wadman).

8 ASPHIR, German Fighter Force, Appendix XXX, Dahl, Oberstleutnant, *Conduct of a Mission in the Defense of the Reich*, 20/9/45.
9 Appendix XXXI, Dahl, Oberstleutnant, *Conduct of a Company Front Attack*, 20/9/45.
10 Oskar Bösch, interview with author, Mesa, 6/10/90.
11 Willi Unger, letter to author, 22/6/90.
12 IWM: CIOS Item No. 2, File No. XXX1-63, Alexander E. Kramer, *Development of Weapons by Rheinmetall-Borsig*, HMSO, n/d; Rheinmetall-Borsig A.G., Unterlüss, *SG 116 (Zellendusche) 3 cm Sondergerät für Flugzeugbau*, UNT.177, Dr. Grasse, 17/4/46; *H.E.C.No. 169, The Automatic Triggering of Aircraft Guns by the Target. Electrostatic and Photoelectric Devices for Making Tanks or Bombers Trigger Vertically Firing Guns Mounted in Fighter Aircraft*, P. Hackemann, no date; 16/119, *Beschreibung der Ausrüstung einer Fw 190 für den Angriff mit gesteuerten Schuß nach oben (Gerät 116) Erstes Erprobungsergebnis 1.4.44 Parchim*, Schwetzke, LFA Hermann Göring, Braunschweig, 2/7/44.
13 Horst Geyer, interview with author, Ahrensburg, 18/3/93.

CHAPTER 22: MASS AGAINST MASS

1 TNA/AIR40/714, *Operation 554: airfields, Western Germany, Holland and Belgium, 15 Aug. 1944*, RAF Signal Intelligence Service Report.
2 Harry D. Gobrecht, Lt Col, USAF (Ret), *Might in Flight – Daily Diary of the Eighth Air Force's Hell's Angels – 303rd Bombardment Group (H)*, p. 509.
3 303rd BG Narrative Report of Mission and Mission Summary, 15 August 1944 (via Ferris).
4 Letter Arno Abendroth to Jeff Ethell, 21/2/76, in author possession.
5 HQ Eighth AF, Intops Summary No. 107, 15/8/44 (via Ferris).
6 Lorant and Goyat, *Jagdgeschwader 300 "Wilde Sau"*, Volume One, p. 382
7 TNA/AIR40/117, *Schießschule der Luftwaffe, Br.6, E-6 4378, 4 September 44, Report on activity of Training Commands for EZ 40/42 with II./JG 300 13.8-29.9.44* (translation).
8 BIOS Report No. 67, *German Airborne Gun and RP Sights*.

CHAPTER 23: DARKENING SKIES

1 BAMA/RL8/186, *Bericht über Verlegung von Deelen nach Dortmund bzw. Duisburg, Ia, 3.Jagddivision, Br.B.Nr.270/44, 13.10.1944* and *Why did 3 JD relocate from Deelen to Duisburg?* at www.gyges.dk.
2 BAMA/RL8/177, I.*Jagdkorps* to 3.*Jagddivsion*, Nr.3581/44, 17/9/44.
3 AFSHRC, *Persönliches Kriegstagbuch des Generals der Flieger Kreipe*.
4 BAMA/RL8/177, *3.Jagddivision, Kommandeur, Befehl für Tageseinsatz*, 19/9/44.
5 OKL, *Operations Staff Training Sect. Nr. 1410/44, Air Defense of the Reich Volume 2 – The Fighter Arm, September 1944*.

NOTES

6 BAMA/RL8/186, IT, *3.Jagddivision, Flugzeugbestand am 20.9.44 and 30.9.44.*
7 Erik Mombeeck, *Storming the Bombers – A Chronicle of JG 4 – Volume 2: 1944–1945*, p. 15.
8 Erik Mombeeck, *Storming*, p. 21.
9 Franks, Bailey and Guest, *Above the Lines*, p. 155.
10 Lorant and Goyat, *Jagdgeschwader 300 'Wilde Sau' Volume Two September 1944–May 1945*, p. 30.
11 Gobrecht, *Might in Flight*, pp. 544–552.
12 TNA/AIR22/417, *8th and 15th USAAF Weekly Intelligence Summaries: Nos. 26–51, May–October 1944.*
13 *Jagdgruppe 10, Arbeitsberichte Nr. 23 (1–31/8/44) and 24 (1–30/9/44).*
14 HQ Eighth AF, *An Evaluation of Defensive Measures Taken to Protect Heavy Bombers from Loss and Damage, November 1944*, p. 49.
15 Craven and Cate, Volume II, p. 664.
16 Erprobungsstelle der Luftwaffe Tarnewitz, B.Nr. E6 5232/44, *Automatische Schussauslösung SG 116*, 29.11.44 and Manfred Griehl, *Arbeiten an selbstauslösenden Waffensystem, FS der Jagdgruppe 10, E-Stelle Tarnewitz*, Griehl, undated.

CHAPTER 24: BLOW AFTER BLOW

1 TNA/AIR20/7700 *The Problems of German Air Defence in 1944*, 8.Abt., 5/11/44.
2 Lorant and Goyat, *Jagdgeschwader 300 'Wilde Sau', Volume Two, September 1944–May 1945*, p. 67.
3 TNA/AIR2/9879, Gerhard Stamp in *Survey of War Situation*, 10/11/44.
4 Erprobungskommando 25, *Arbeitsbericht Nr.23, August 1944*, 1/9/44.
5 IWM, GDC, H.E.C. No.13606/ Unterlüss Report No.181, *Harfe, Jägerfaust, Bombersäge: Recoilless and Multi-Barrel Weapons*, Dr. Grasse, Work Centre Unterlüss, 2/9/46; Erprobungsstelle der Luftwaffe Tarnewitz, *Schwerpunkterprobungsberichte*, July 1943–February 1945, B.Nr.; and E6 5/45, *Optimale Bewaffnung und Treffwahrscheinlichkeit bei Senkrechtschuss mit automatischer Schusslösung*, Raabe, 30/12/44.
6 BAMA/RL7/11, *Einsatzräume der Jagddivisionen und Jagdführer im Reichsgebiet*, November 1944 and *Strategic Concentration of AAA and Flying Units in the West September 1944–May 1945*, compiled by Schmid, August–November 1956.
7 TNA/AIR40/2162, *The X4 - German Air-Launched A.A. Rocket*, AI2(g) Report No. 1773, Section E.4.D., 31/1/45; *The X.4 (8-344) German Air-Launched AA Rocket Aircraft Control Equipment*, AI2(g) Report No. 1781, 23/6/1945; and Gordon Slater, *Birth of the Air-to-Air Missile: the Kramer/Ruhrstahl X4*, Axis Wings, Volume 2, 2024.
8 Webster and Frankland, *SAOAG, Volume III: Victory*, p. 164.
9 Peloquin, Laurie, *Area Bombing by Day: Bomber Command and the Daylight Offensive, 1944–1945*, Canadian Military History 15, 3 (2006).

10 *German Fighter Tactics against RAF Day Bombers and Reply from Fighter Command* AMWIS 287, 3 March 1945 and Prien, Rodeike and Stemmer, *III. und IV./Jagdgeschwader 27*, p. 430.

CHAPTER 25: SPEED AND ALTITUDE — THE NEW WEAPONS

1 Overy, *The Air War 1939–1945*, p. 145; and Budiansky, p. 337.
2 EHAG file note 21/11/44.
3 *Das Oberkommando der Luftwaffe, Kriegstagbuch (1 February–7 April 1945)* 31/3/45. p. 3, NARS Microfilm T-321, Roll 10.
4 ASPHIR, Appendix XVI, *Kowalewski, Nolle and Eschenauer, A History of the GAF Twin-Engined Fighter Arm, 8 October 1945*.

CHAPTER 26: FIRE IN THE SKY

1 TNA/AIR22/82, AMWIS 287-304, *Bremen, 1945 – Destroyed in Heavy Bomber Attacks.*
2 TNA/AIR40/1346.
3 Hermann Buchner, various correspondence with author, 1992.
4 Gooden, Brett, *Natter – Manned Missile of the Third Reich: Historic Step to Human Spaceflight*, p.184 et passim.
5 IWM, Kokott, Dr, *Projekt "Natter": Serienschuss oder Schrotschuss*, Rheinmetall-Borsig, Unterlüss, 5/10/44.
6 Staalman, Rit, and Wagner, Monica, *The Life and Work of Willy Achim Fiedler, Designer, test pilot, aeronautical and missile engineer 1908–1998*, (via G.J.(Rit) Staalman).

CHAPTER 27: FROM 'ELBE' TO THE END

1 Fritz Marktscheffel, *Was war das 'Kommando Elbe'? Das letzte Aufgebot der deutschen Luftwaffe, Jägerblatt*, 1985.
2 ADI(K) 294/1945, *New German Ramming Units*, 26/4/45.
3 ASPHIR, *German Fighter Operations, Appendix III, Written Interrogation of General der Flieger Koller.*
4 ADI(K) 348/1945, *The Collapse Viewed from Within: the Memoirs of General Koller, the German Chief of Air Staff*, 12/7/45.

Index

Figures in **bold** refer to illustrations, tables and captions.

Achmer **12–13**, 139, 165, 177, 203, 222, 394
aerial combat 39, 67, 80, 106, 162, 179, 194, 206, 246, 251, 263, 275, 378, 405
aeronautical technology 44, 105, 196
air operations 46, 54, 88, 96
aircraft:
  Avro Lancaster 52, 171, 174, 344–345, 373, 394–396, 414, 433–434
  Boeing B-17 Flying Fortress 12–13, 15–16, 48–49, 52–53, 56–57, 60–64, 70–76, 78, 80–81, 92–93, 97–99, 102, 106–116, 118–121, 123–129, 131, 134–135, 138–141, 144–145, 147–152, 155–156, 159–162, 169–171, 173, 177–185, 187–190, 192, 195, 200–201, 206–207, 209–218, 224, 227, 231, 233–238, 240–242, 246–248, 254–255, 260, 262, 264, 266–269, 271, 273–275, 279–281, 283–292, 295–305, 311, 315–317, 319–322, 325, 328–334, 340, 351, 356–359, 360, 362–365, 370–371, 377–381, 384–385, 391, 393, 400, 405–406, 408–411, 413, 418, 420–421, 423, 429–431, 434–437
  Consolidated B-24 Liberator 15–16, 53–54, 56, 72–73, 75, 77–81, 93, 98–99, 101–102, 106–110, 112, 124, 132, 177–179, 181, 187, 192, 195, 209, 213, 215, 217, 219–221, 231, 236–238, 240, 242, 254–255, 259, 264–265, 268–269, 271, 275, 277, 279–289, 292, 298–304, 311–313, 324–326, 328–329, 331, 340, 346, 351–352, 356, 358–360, 362, 365, 368, 377, 381, 408, 418, 421, 430–431, 434–436
  De Havilland Mosquito 150, 174, 257, 344, 373, 394, 433

  Focke-Wulf Fw 190: 16–17, 62–63, 68–69, 72–73, 79, 86, 92, 94, 100, 109–113, 115, 118, 120–121, 123, 125–127, 134–135, 139–141, 147–148, 150–151, 160, 167, 169–170, 173, 176–177, 180, 182, 187, 189, 199–200, 204, 210–213, 216, 218–220, 225, 230–231, 233–236, 245, 258–259, 262, 264, 266–271, 277, 281, 283–284, 286–288, 294, 300, 305, 309–310, 312–314, 318, 323, 328–329, 332–335, 338, 340–341, 344, 346–347, 351–352, 354, 356, 358, 360–365, 368–370, 374, 377–381, 384–385, 387–388, 390, 393, 402, 410, 419, 435
  Fw 190As 13, 15–16, 69, 92, 94, 139, 202, 212, 233, 281–285, 289, 293–295, 299–300, 307, 311, 318, 335, 341, 346, 351–352, 357, 362–363, 367, 370–371, 378, 401, 418
  Heinkel He 111: 122, 219, 322, 393, 423
  He 177: 121, 209, 381, 384
  Junkers Ju 52/3m 74, 142, 342, 346, 423
  Ju 88: 86, 100, 114, 121–122, 157, 160, 180–181, 189, 235, 250, 270, 335, 388, 393, 398, 431
  Lockheed P-38 Lightning 16, **19**, 61, 106, 195, 211, 231, 237, 246, 254, 279, 281, 286, 356–357, 397
  Messerschmitt Bf 109s 13, 15, 29–30, 34–37, 51, 54–55, 63, 67–70, 72, 76–77, 81, 85–86, 92–94, 96, 100, 108–109, 112–114, 116–121, 128–129, 131, 133–135, 139, 141–142, 144–145, 147, 149–150, 152, 161–162, 170, 176, 180, 182–184, 187–190, 195–196, 198–201, 209, 211, 213–216, 225, 230–231, 234, 237, 240, 245, 254–256, 259, 264, 266, 268–269, 273–277, 280–281,

469

289–291, 293–298, 302, 304,
309–311, 313–314, 324, 328–330,
338, 342–343, 345–346, 348, 351,
355, 358, 362–363, 365, 367–370,
377, 381, 385–386, 388, 394–396,
398–399, 409–410, 417–418,
432–433
Messerschmitt Bf 110 *Zerstörer*   12–13,
36–37, 39, 46, 79–80, 96, 100,
109–110, 119, 121, 141, 143–144,
151, 157, 160, 169–171, 178, 180–
182, 186, 189–190, 193, 200, 204,
210–211, 217, 234, 251, 259, 266,
268–269, 272–273, 286–287, 356
Messerschmitt Me 109s   38, 79, 111, 113,
189, 210, 212–213, 219, 235, 241,
258, 286–287, 294, 387–388, 438
Me 110s   38, 111, 212, 218, 235
Me 163s   17, 348, 369, 403, 407–411,
413–414, 432
Me 210s   100, 121, 141, 169, 189
Me 262s   17, 196, 416–422, 428–432,
434–437
Me 410s   13, 121, 141, 160–161, 169,
178, 181, 184, 206, 249–253, 255,
260, 266, 287, 311, 316–318, 334,
350, 356
North American P-51 Mustangs   16, **19**,
145, 216–217, 246, 264, 266–268,
274–275, 281–283, 296–297,
305, 314, 316, 328, 330–331, 334,
343, 356–357, 364, 370, 378, 385,
388, 400–401, 411, 416, 418, 421,
429–431, 437
reconnaissance   150, 165, 356, 412, 418
Republic P-47 Thunderbolts   16,
19, 125–126, 135–136, 138, 141,
145, 150, 153, 170, 172–173, 178,
181–182, 187, 189, 210–211, 216,
237, 242, 246, 248, 262, 268, 279,
282, 286, 288, 307, 343, 397, 400,
430–431, 434
Supermarine Spitfires   54–55, 61, 63, 67,
69, 71, 77, 93, 106, 113, 125, 149,
153, 295, 324, 345, 370, 387, 389,
399, 411
Vickers Wellingtons   12, 27–32, 34–40,
43, 46–50, 76, 125
aircraft production   100, 253, 258, 279, 281,
284, 306, 350, 356

airframes   51, 57, 67, 100, 102, 253, 271,
289, 292, 424
Alarmstart (equivalent to RAF
scramble)   10, **20**, 118–119, 131,
138, 144, 179, 259, 272, 283–285,
288–289, 300, 302, 354, 395, 428
Allied forces   70, 77, 100, 105, 125, 127,
133, 153, 164, 168, 182, 244, 306,
323, 336, 340–341, 344–345, 347,
350, 373, 382, 384, 397, 400, 413,
432–434, 437, 440
Ansbach   **18**, 143, 328, 342
Antwerp   126, 147, 187, 382, 397–399
armour plating   40, 294–295, 300, 312, 320
Arnold, Maj Gen Henry H. 'Hap'   59–60,
101, 103, 107, 155–156, 192, 229,
253
Axis forces   67, 77–79, 81, 215

Balkans, the   116, 195, 237, 324, 382
Bär, Oberstleutnant Heinz   **14**, 247–248,
266, 268, 284, 300, 314, 398, 442
Belgium   **14, 18**, 69, 126, 137, 148, 151,
157, 163, 186, 231, 235, 240, 242,
260, 279, 313–314, 336, 382, 392,
398
Berlin   **18**, 31, 41, 69, 89, 106, 113–114,
122, 130–131, 151, 163–165, 198,
201–202, 204, 223, 239, 243–244,
250, 255, 258, 264–265, 268–270,
272, 276, 278, 282, 295, 298–300,
302–303, 305–307, 311–312, 325,
327–328, 340, 366, 401, 406, 416–
418, 428–429, 431, 434, 436–438
Berlin-Dahlem   87, 137, 197
Berlin-Wannsee   231, 239, 384, 392
Bob, Hauptmann Hans-Ekkehard   10, **15**,
116–118, 120, 344
bomb loads   29, 48, 50, 54, 62, 227, 304,
405
bombardiers   **16**, 61, 73, 118, 221, 331, 364,
379, 410–411
bombing   **15**, 27–30, 41, 46, 48–49, 51–53,
56, 60–62, 78, 102, 107–108, 110,
113–114, 121, 124, 145, 154, 161,
171, 196, 210, 232, 236, 244, 246,
248, 253, 259, 265, 275, 287, 306,
315, 319, 331, 335–336, 347, 350,
356, 394–395, 405, 408, 415, 431,
438, 441

INDEX

air-to-air 115, 121, 126, 140, 213, 219, 235
formations 9, 64, 420
policy 41, 46, 61, 171, 315
raids 9, **16**, 71, 93, 146, 166, 249, 264, 270
  daylight raids 47, 49, 53, 135, 154, 245, 327, 348, 353, 394
  night raids 48, 52, 78, 135
Bösch, Unteroffizier Oskar 10, **13**, **16**, 203, 267, 297–301, 312–313, 333, 357, 438–439
Braunschweig 46, 193, 232, 234, 236, 243, 246–248, 254, 259, 270–272, 278, 281–282, 284–285, 299–301, 311–312, 325, 420–421
Bremen 68, 93–94, 109–113, 115, 117–119, 121, 123, 126–127, 139, 177, 185, 199, 209–212, 222, 232, 244, 246–247, 270, 286, 392, 415, 430
Brest 51–54, 94
Britain **12**, 29, 44, 46, 48–49, 52, 56, 58–61, 67, 100–102, 154, 163, 243
British Air Ministry 25, 29, 40, 57, 136, 186
Browning machine gun 28, 36, 50, 57, 72, 80, 190, 410
Buchner, Oberfeldwebel Hermann 10, 419–420, 433
Bühligen, Oberstleutnant Kurt 192, 372, **441**
bullet holes 30, 38, 40, 120, 305
Bülow-Bothkamp, Major/Oberst Harry von 33, 95–96, 196

California 49, 53, 59, 101
cannons:
  cannon shells 70, 80, 118, 183, 332–333, 379, 433
  Mauser MG 151: 13, 69–70, 144, 198, 213–214, 234, 294, 355, 390
  Mauser MG 151/20 (F-4): 68–69, 75, 142, 177, 180, 202, 280, 291, 296, 302, 331, 412
  Mauser MG FF 36, 202, 365
Carinhall 113, 255, 257, 265, 353
Channel Front, the 116, 148, 150, 262, 278
Christl, Hauptmann Georg 79–80, 366, 380
Churchill, Winston 60, 107–108

cockpits 54, 57, 68, 79, 91, 117, **138**, 140, 148, 150, 152, 161, 167, 183, 190, 202–203, 214, 233–234, 237, 241, 267, 274, 283, 285, 294, 297, 300–302, 308, 316, 318, 320, 324, 332–333, 340–341, 360, 364, 378, 405, 420, 426–428
Sitzbereitschaft (cockpit readiness) **22**, 110, 116, 138, 197, 233, 240, 244, 252, 266, 272, 284, 288, 354
Cologne **18**, 60, 105–106, 144–145, 173, 213, 363, 365, 381
Combined Bomber Offensive (CBO) **20**, 107, 124, 131, 146, 156, 195, 315
communication 31–32, 43, 60–61, 77, 90, 143, 158, 169–170, 224, 244, 257, 279, 336
communications 10, 45, 58, 84, 222, 257, 279, 315
convoys 58, 78–80, 92, 335
'cornered wolf' 103, 192, 208, 278

Dahl, Oberstleutnant Walther **13**, **15**, 142, 144, 149, 155, 161–162, 175, 192, 194, 201, 218, 240, 289–291, 296, 311, 327–328, 342, 351, 353–356, 362–365, 391, **441**
Darmstadt 119, 149, 289, 363, 392
Deelen **18**, 89–90, 142, 147, 164, 169, 185, 198, 201, 223, 244, 372–373
Denmark 92, 137, 185, 222–223, 320, 336, 367
deployment 44, 56, 59, 70, 115, 121, 123, 133, 139, 142–144, 157, 199–200, 237, 252, 299, 335, 350, 376, 393–394, 400
Diehl, Leutnant Hermann 31–34, 44
Döberitz **18**, 67, 89, 137, 170, 246, 272, 392
Döring, Generalleutnant Kurt-Bertram von 89, 137, 164, 171–172, 193, 197
Deutsche Versuchsanstalt für Luftfahrt (DVL) (German Research Institute for Aviation) **20**, 276, 340
Duisburg 106, 372–374, 392

Eaker, Brig Gen Ira **12**, 59–63, 97, 103, 106–108, 112, 124, 135, 192, 208, 229
East Prussia 108, 137, 180, 319, 348

Eastern Front 70, 74, 92, 105–106, 116–117, 122, 124, 142, 145, 150, 171, 190–191, 204, 294, 307, 310, 334, 349, 351, 399, 419
Eder, Leutnant Georg-Peter 74, 282, 285, 288–289, 300, 417–418, **441**
Egypt 76–77, 81, 324
Eindhoven 188, 373–375, 398–399
elevators 40, 111, 280, 414, 437
Emden **16**, 33, 108, 169–170, 200, 217–219, 221
England 10, **16**, 35, 52–55, 57, 59–60, 94–95, 105–110, 114, 116, 127, 137, 145, 147, 151, 155, 187, 217, 231, 235, 238, 247, 252, 257, 279, 282, 305, 319–320, 324, 384, 405, 414, 428
English Channel 54–55, 71, 94, 151, 242, 331
Ergänzungsjagdgruppe (Erg.JGr. – Operational Training Group) **20**, 85–86, 135
Erprobungsstelle (test centre) **20**, 122–123, 139, 367, 384, 391
Erprobungskommando (E.Kdo) (test command) **20**, 113, 121, 212, 316
  25: **12**, **13**, **16**, **17**, 113, 121–123, 139, 143, 160, 165, 177–178, **191**, 206, 211–212, 219–220, 232, 235, 250, 316, 318, 339, 341, 359–360, 365–366, 380, 390
Europe 9, **12**, **14**, 27–28, 42, 52, 58–62, 65, 76, 82–83, 86, 92, 96, 107, 124, 146–147, 150, 162, 192, 195, 215, 230, 232, 238, 246, 253, 264, 266, 271, 324, 336, 400, 406, 416, 437
expansion 99, 107–108, 124, 134, 335

fighter escorts 10, **13**, **19**, 30, 55, 63, 76–77, 93, 96, 99, 106, 121, 124, 126–127, 136, 144, 147, 149, 173, 184, 186, 188, 192, 198–199, 213, 217–218, 236, 242–243, 246, 256, 259, 269, 274, 285, 290, 294, 300–301, 311, 325, 334, 351, 364, 368, 370, 376, 384, 386, 389, 394, 420, 437, 439
fighter groups 59–60, 126, 174, 195, 237, 253, 257, 264, 284, 325
  4th Fighter Group (FG) 135, 141, 187, 266
fighter production 101, 134, 146, 195, 258–259, 306, 348

Flak 30–34, 36, 39, 42, 45, 47, 56, 62, 87–88, 90, 111–112, 115, 119, 121, 144, 148, 159, 178, 192–193, 195, 199, 201, 206, 212, 222–223, 225, 239, 244, 257, 312, 333, 343, 359, 373, 376, 391, 399, 409, 414, 420, 436
  43: 121, 206, 316–317
Fliegerkorps:
  XII. **14**, 88, 137, 162–163
FluKo (Flugwachkommando) (air observation unit and/or filter centre) **20**, 138, 196–197, 223, 372
Ford, Henry 99, 101–102, 278
France **13**, **18**, 44, 46–47, 53–55, 61, 67, 69, 71, 85–86, 88, 92, 94–95, 101, 116–117, 126, 133–135, 137, 139, 157, 167–168, 171–172, 216, 229, 238, 240, 242, 247, 260, 262, 279, 298, 306–307, 313, 324–325, 329, 336–339, 341–342, 346, 348, 350, 362, 382–383, 398
Franz, Oberleutnant Richard 231, 244, 267, 282, 295
Franzisket, Hauptmann Ludwig 133, 325, 328
Frey, Hauptmann Hugo 192, 268, **441**
Frisian Islands, the 31–32, 34, 36, 50, 120
fuel tanks **15**, 37–38, 68, 74, 111, 292, 341, 360, 379, 413, 431, 433
  auxiliary 136, 187, 213, 243
  self-sealing 38, 40–42, 50, 53, 68
fuselage **16–17**, 28, 37–38, 40, 57, 68–69, 73, 75, 97, 114, 116, 119–120, 149, 181, 188, 202–203, 214, 220, 233–235, 267, 269, 280, 284–285, 288, 292, 294, 301, 316, 320–321, 341, 351–352, 357, 360, 363–365, 368, 378–379, 384, 390, **391**, 405, 410, 416, 424, 431, 433

Galland, Oberst Adolf 10, **13**, **15**, 54–56, 62, 74, 93, 99, 108, 112, 122–123, 128, 131, 133, 135–136, 141, 143, 145–146, 151–153, 157–161, 165–167, 174–175, 184, 186–187, 192, 198, 201–204, 206, 219, 224, 242, 250–251, 255–256, 261, 263, 273, 292–293, 298, 303, 305–308, 311, 314–315, 317–318, 322–323, 326–328, 340–342, 345, 348, 350, 359–361, 382–384, 386, 400, 416, 432

INDEX

Gardelegen 267, 269–270, 282, 302, 312, 418, 435
Gefechtsstand (battle headquarters) **20**, 136–137, 170, 193, 197
Gefechtsverband (battle group) **20**, 211–212, 265–266, 268–269, 271, 273, 281–282, 285–286, 288–289, 296, 301, 311–312, 325, 327, 329, 335, 351, 353–354, 363–364, 368–369, 374–377, 385
General der Jagdflieger (General of Fighter Forces) **20**, 54, 122, 152, 155, 166–167, 174, 204, 250, 304, 323, 400
Gerhard Fieseler Werke 93, 138–139, 362
Gerth, Oberleutnant Werner 293, 303, 352, 357, 365, 385, 442
Geschwader (air unit equivalent to a wing) **20**, 39, 45, 62, 67, 87, 92, 94, 135, 144, 151, 153, 165, 172, 180, 191, 224, 237, 247, 249, 257, 262, 265, 284, 286, 288, 293, 300, 307, 310, 323–325, 339, 344, 347, 354, 372, 391, 398–399, 401, 417, 423, 428–429, 435
Geschwaderstab (wing staff) **20**, 292, 325, 327, 369, 430
Geyer, Hauptmann Horst **13**, 122–123, 139, 143, 165, 177–178, 212, 219–221, 317–318, 339–340, 359–360, 366
Göring, Reichsmarschall Hermann **12**, 55, 98–99, 101–102, 113–114, 116, 122, 126, 128, 130–131, 135–136, 153–154, 162–165, 172–175, 178, 181, 184, 186–187, 191–194, 196–197, 199, 201–203, 205, 225–226, 236, 239, 247, 249–252, 255–257, 279, 317, 322–324, 336, 340–341, 350, 353, 360, 372, 383–384, 389–391, 397–398, 400, 415–416, 418, 432, 439
Grabmann, Generalmajor Walter **14**, 45–46, 137, 147, 149, 171, 185, 187, 197–199, 201, 205, 230, 244, 255, 372–375, 377, 392
Graf, Major Hermann 150, 191–192
groundcrews 28, 67, 142, 169, 229, 303, 342, 382, 396
Gruppe:
  III. 74, 81, 134, 147, 161, 218, 362, 370, 417

Gruppenkommandeur (officer commanding a Gruppe) **20**, 33, 55, 81, 116, 140, 142, 148, 182, 194, 204, 216, 234, 243, 257, 265, 290, 292, 294, 313–314, 323, 325–326, 329, 354, 357, 359, 376, 384, 400, 413
gunners:
  tail gunner 28, 36, 61, 73, 109, 207, 236, 267, 319, 352, 355, 357, 364, 378–379, 396, 409–410, 419 top turret gunner 61, 153, 409–411
  waist gunner 61, 71–72, 267, 357, 364, 379

Hackl, Major Anton 192, 326–327, 359, 372, 441
Hamburg **14**, 33, 106, 134–136, 179, 222, 299, 312, 392, 421, 431, 433–434
Handorf 143, 145, 149, 155
Handrick, Oberst Gotthard 137, 196, 322, 392
Harris, Air Vice-Marshal Arthur 59, 62, 106, 315, 394
Heligoland 28–29, 31–32, 34, 36, 38, 47–48, 134, 141, 222
Heligoland Bight 29, 32–33, 39, 41, 222, 392
Herausschüss 21, 145, 161–162, 170, 185, 188, 190, 194, 231, 234, 240–241, 248, 259–260, 266, 268, 270, 274, 280, 282, 291, 295–296–297, 301, 304, 313, 316, 328–329, 331, 351, 357, 359, 369–370, 396, 429
Hermichen, Major Rolf-Günther 192, 265, **441**
Herrmann, Oberst Hans-Joachim 'Hajo' 134, 164, 200, 202, 432
Hitler, Adolf 57, 83, 86, 98, 100, 105, 108, 153, 168, 174, 186, 249, 251, 324, 372, 374, 383, 397, 416, 434, 439
Höhenjagdgruppe **21**, 257, 265, 294, 328, 376
Hungary 137, 347, 368, 392, 401

Ibel, Oberst Max-Josef **14**, 95, 165, 167, 197–199, 205, 221–223, 246, 255, 257, 392
incendiaries 38, 70, 106, 189, 284, 292, 302–303, 350, 390
Industrieschwarm **21**, 94, 118, 177
infrastructure 60, 88, 197, 226, 308, 382–383, 430, 436
  defence 45, 168, 242, 392

intelligence   63, 100, 163–164, 183, 207, 232, 235, 313, 406, 427, 429, 431, 440
  officer   146, 193, 200, 206–208, 403, 406, 408, 410
interception   31, 44, 54, 68, 70, 83, 86, 91–92, 96, 132, 148, 223, 234, 280, 336
intercom   118, 170, 267, 332
interrogators   62, 79, 131, 145, 386
Italy   128, 133, 198, 215, 231, 237–238, 275, 324–325, 338, 358, 409, 431

Jafü Deutsche Bucht   89, 110, 117, 141, 160, 170, 222–223
Jafü Holland-Ruhrgebiet   **14**, 89–90, 92, 96, 137, 142, 147, 149, 161, 197
Jafü Süddeutschland   95, 196–197
Jagdabschnittsführer   **21**, 185, 223, 392
Jagddivision (fighter division):
  1. *Jagddivision*   **18**, 88, 92, 109, 137, 151, 164, 177, 179, 182, 197, 211, 214, 217, 223, 232, 238, 242, 246, 257, 271, 273, 284–285, 287, 299, 325, 392, 432
  2. *Jagddivision*   **14**, **18**, 89, 92, 126, 136–137, 139, 164, 169–171, 177, 179, 182, 185, 197–198, 200, 204, 210–211, 214, 217, 221–222, 232, 238, 242, 246, 257, 265, 271–273, 284, 299, 392, 433
  3. *Jagddivision*   **14**, **18**, 89, 137, 164, 177, 180, 182, 185, 187, 193, 197–198, 200, 205, 211, 214, 217, 232, 238, 242, 244, 246, 255, 257, 265, 271, 273, 275, 280, 284–285, 299, 372–374, 377, 392, 395, 398
  4. *Jagddivision*   **18**, 89, 137, 164, 170–171, 235, 307
Jagdfliegerführer (*Jafü*) (regional fighter controller):
  2:   94, 204, 222
  5:   168–169, 213, 325
  Höherer Jagdfliegerführer West   94, 165, 167
  Jafü Deutsche Bucht   89, 110, 117, 141, 160, 170, 222–223
  Jafü Holland-Ruhrgebiet   **14**, 89–90, 92, 96, 137, 147, 149, 161, 197
  Jafü Ostmark   **18**, 137, 196–197, 239, 265, 279, 322, 325
  Jafü Süddeutschland   95, 196–197

Jagdfliegerschule (JFS) (Fighter Training School)   **21**, 85
  4:   95–96, 309
Jagdgeschwader (JG) (fighter unit):
  JG 1:   **14**, 38, 92–93, 109–110, 112–113, 115–116, 120, 134, 139, 141, 146, 151–152, 169, 171, 177–178, 184–185, 188, 232, 248, 255, 259, 265–266, 268, 283–285, 300, 342–343, 399
  I./JG 1:   108, 113–115, 125–126, 139–140, 151, 169–170, 185, 187–188, **191**, 200, 231, 233, 245, 247, 266, 284, 288–289, 300
  II./JG 1:   **14**, 92–93, 109, 115, 151, 170, 173, 187, **191**, 200, 202, 233–234, 247, 266, 282, 284–285, 288–289, 300–301, 314, 344
  III./JG 1:   92, 126, 134, 147–149, 151–152, 187, **191**, 200, 204, 216, 257, 284, 314
  1./JG 1:   169, 173, 188
  2./JG 1:   114, 151, 248
  4./JG 1:   92–93, 109, 268
  5./JG 1:   140, 233, 283, 285, 289, 300–301
  6./JG 1:   93, 247, 285, 300, 346
  JG 2:   **13**, 55–56, 62–63, 67–68, 71, 92, 94–96, 133–134, 149, 151, 168, 213, 237, 261–262, 307, 372, 399
  I./JG 2:   89, **191**, 238
  II./JG 2:   67, 160, **191**, 262
  III./JG 2:   69, 71, **191**, 232, 262, 400
  JG 3:   89, 134, 152, 155, 158, 171, 177, 184, 260, 265, 269, 278, 281, 292, 295, 298, 312–313, 315, 334, 342, 357, 388, 399
  I./JG 3:   139, 187, 232, 240, 245, 266, 281, 285, 288, 358, 375
  II./JG 3:   169, 182, 199–200, 202, 216, 248, 266, 281, 288, 312, 343–344
  III./JG 3:   **13**, 142, 144–145, 149, 152, 155, 161, 175, 190, **191**, 196–197, 201, 209, 218, 240, 260, 273–275, 281, 289, 296–297, 311, 327–329, 342–343, 398–399
  IV./JG 3:   **15**, 215, 245, 266, 269–270, 281–283, 285–288, 292–293, 295, 301–304, 346, 358
  IV.(*Sturm*)/JG 3:   303, 312–313, 316, 333–334, 351, 354, 356–359,

INDEX

362–363, 365, 368, 370, 377, 380, 385, 432
7./JG 3: 145, 149, 155, 190, 240–241, 274, 290, 296–297, 328, 399
8./JG 3: 145, 190, 241, 273–274
9./JG 3: 161–162, 190, 241, 273, 343, 346, 399
10./JG 3: **16**, 301, 304, 316, 346
10.(*Sturm*)/JG 3: 351–352, 357
11./JG 3: 295, 316, 346
11.(*Sturm*)/JG 3: 294, 301, 303, 330, 352, 357
12./JG 3: **16**, 318, 399
12.(*Sturm*)/JG 3: 352, 357–358
15.(*Sturm*)/JG 3: 365, 377–378
JG 4: 369–370, 375, 385
II.(*Sturm*)/JG 4: 335, 356, 369–371, 377, 385
III./JG 4: 369–370, 375
I./JG 5: 254, 273, 275, 281, 289, 328–329
JG 7: **17**, 417, 419–421, 428–430, 432, 435–436
III./JG 7: 418, 421, 429–430, 433
9./JG 7: 418–420, 428, 430
10./JG 7: 420–421, 431, 434
11./JG 7: 418, 420–421, 431, 434
JG 11: 113, 134, 139, 151, 169, 171, 177, 192, 210, 232, 255, 265–266, 283–284, 294–295, 342–343, 369
I./JG 11: 126, 151, 204, 218, 248, 265, 283, 285, 329, 400
II.JG 11: 119, 126, 139, 151, 170, **191**, 192, 211, 257, 259, 294
III./JG 11: **191**, 217, 285, 326, 359, 374–375, 382
JG 26: **15**, 54–56, 71, 92, 94, 96, 116, 133–134, 139, 146–147, 151–152, 184, 213, 215, 232. 242, 259, 261, 341, 343, 349, 372
I./JG 26: 55, 69, 139, 141, 147, **191**, 199, 235
II./JG 26: 62–63, 139, 151, 153, 184, **191**, 347
III./JG 26: 54, 126, 134, 139, 148, 200, 211, 296
12./JG 26: 148, 184, 296
JG 27: 76, 79, 81, 95, 134, 158, 160, 198, 231, 260, 265, 275, 284, 342–343, 383, 386
I./JG 27: 76, 133, 144, 150, 196, 216, 325

II./JG 27: 81, 133, 149, **191**, 213, 215, 231–232, 324, 328, 330, 375
III./JG 27: 81, 325, 330–331, 381
IV./JG 27: 237–238, 275–276, 280, 325, 394, 396
6./JG 27: 190, 213, 215, 330
JG 50: 150, 183, **191**
JG 51: 122, 134, 247
II./JG 51: 133, 150, **191**, 196, 215
2./JG 51: 334, 351, 355, 357, 362, 365
JG 52: 70, 191, 399, 428
JG 53: 127, 129, 192, 215, 398–399
II./JG 53: 128, 196, 215, 254, 328, 330, 343
JG 54: 134, 204, 310
III./JG 54: 116, 118, 126, 139, **191**, 200, 232, 246, 266, 268, 328, 343, 381
IV./JG 54: 323, 374–375, 382, 418
JG 76:
JG 77: 125, 127–129, 168, 231, 247, 342, 344
II./JG 77: 33–34, 36, 95, 128–129, 171
JG 104: 96, 150, **191**, 309, 311
JG 300: **15–16**, 134, 351, 353, 362, 391
I./JG 300: 232, 351, 362–363, 368, 377, 388
II.(*Sturm*)/JG 300: 362–363, 367–370, 377–378
III./JG 300: 351, 362, 370, 375
JG 301: 342, 401, 432, 435
I./JG 302: 232, 234, 368
1./JG 400: 408–409, 411, 413
Jagdgruppen 10, 135, 138, 144–145, 199, 256, 265, 308, 323, 327–328, 337, 438
'*Höhenjagdgruppen*' ('High-altitude Fighter Groups') 257, 265, 376
Jagdstaffel (fighter squadron) **21**, 86, 121
Jägerschreck (fear of fighters) **21**, 146, 256, 440
Jägerstab (Fighter Staff) **21**, 259, 264, 298, 307, 311, 350, 381
Jeschonnek, Generaloberst Hans 87, 99–100, 133, 153
Jever 32–35, 37, 89, 112–113, 119–120, 171, 222–223
Kaiser, Oberfeldwebel Herbert 10, 344–345
General der Flieger Josef Kammhuber 162–163, 174, 415–416

Kampfraum (Battle Room) **21**, **138**, 222–223
Kanalgeschwader 92, 96, 117
Kaschuba, Leutnant Paul 178, 316–317
Kassel **16**, 93, 138–139, 295, 299–300, 328, 377
Kellet, Wg Cdr Richard 27–33, 38, 41–42, 49–50
Kette (formation of three aircraft) **21**, 72, 80, 236, 256, 430
Kiel 123, 125–127, 134, 180, 231, 434
Kientsch, Oberleutnant Wilhelm 213, 215, **442**
Knight's Cross 54–55, 71, 80–81, 87, 95, 116, 121, 128, 133, 143, 145, 150–151, 164, 168, 171, 184, 187, 191, 204–205, 216, 222, 247, 261–262, 268–269, 273, 278, 282, 295–296, 304, 307, 314, 317, 325–326, 328–329, 344, 351, 357, 362, 366, 372, 380, 385, 388, 400, 416–417, 419–420, 432, 437
Knoke, Oberleutnant Heinz 114, 170, 192
Koch, Leutnant Raimund 145, 241, 274, 281
Koenig, Hauptmann Hans-Heinrich 302, 328–329, **442**
Koller, Oberst Karl 87, 98–100, 174, 225, 350–351, 439–440
Kommando (command/detachment/unit) **21**, 167, 211–212, 339, 359, 366–369, 400, 417
Kommando der Erprobungsstellen (commander of test centres) **21**, 167, 206
Kriegsmarine 32, 44, 54, 94, 201

Leeuwarden 109, 147, 200, 217
Legion Condor 54, 199, 204
Lille **15**, 70, 93, 106, 116, 345–346
London 27, 60, 168, 177, 209, 373
Low Countries 47, 88–89, 92, 94, 101, 126, 133, 260
Ludlow-Hewitt, Air Chief Marshal Edgar 41–42, 46–47
Luftlage (air situation) **21**, 157, 223
Luftflotte (air fleet):
  2: 46, 88, 128, 215
  3: **18**, 46, 87, 94, 98, 167, 182, 184, 230, 232, 239, 260, 263, 279, 323, 342, 347, 392
Luftflotten (air fleets) 45, 87, 230

Luftnachrichten-Regiment (Air Signals Regiment) 51, 141, 170, 196, 329
201: 140, 147, 151, 177
Luftwaffe General Staff 87, 163, 225, 387
Luftwaffenbefehlshaber Mitte (central air commander) **21**, 87–88, 92–93, 137, 157, 194, 196–198, 200, 223, 230

machine guns:
  MG 17: 68–69, 86, 173, 180
  MG 131: **13**, 69–70, 214, 233–234, 274, 290, 294, 302, 433
Malta 76–77, 127, 384
Mannheim 85, 149, 161, 239–241, 275, 392
manoeuvrability **16**, 68, 77, 79, 160, 166, 206, 216, 318, 388, 402, 421
Masefield, Peter 52, 97–99, 102
materiel 105, 337, 339, 343
Mayer, Oberstleutnant Egon **13**, 64, 71–74, 76, 79, 81, 131, 213, 262, 307, **441**
mechanics **13**, 114, 138, 417
Mediterranean **15**, 67, 76–77, 79–81, 92, 105, 124, 127–128, 130, 133, 141–143, 215, 229, 247, 328–329, 344, 388
Metz **18**, 89, 137, 316, 323, 398
Meyer, Hauptmann Otto 237–238, 275, 280
mortars:
  21 cm **16**, 160, 181, 224, 232, 252, 318, 419
  W.Gr.21: **13**, **15**, **17**, 139, 141, 143–144, 151, 155, 159, 161, 170, 181, 198, 210–211, 218, 266, 317, 419
Müller, Major Friedrich-Karl 269–270, 282, 292, 295, 312, 334, **441**
Munich **18**, **19**, 46, 95, 163, 175, 195–196, 296, 321–322
Münster-Handorf 133, 142, 155
Nachtjagdschule (NJG):
  NJG 1: 96, 110, 119–120, 151, 171, 186, 205
  IV./NJG 1: 110, 126, 232
  NJG 3: 119–120, 171, 177, 232
  NJG 5: 171, 205, 232
navigators **16**, 28, 61, 73, 97, 183, 189, 221, 241, 319, 331, 364, 409
Nebelwerfer (mortar-carrying) 130, 139, 160

INDEX

Netherlands **14, 18,** 47, 71, 89, 92, 134, 137, 157, 163, 186, 201, 216, 223, 265–266, 268, 273, 336, 372, 374, 392, 398
Neumann, Oberstleutnant Eduard 76, 79, 81, 83, 198–199
Neumann, Unteroffizier Klaus 365–379
Norderney 50, 210, 217
Nordhelle-Ebbe 140, 151, 177
Norfolk 27, 31, 146, 209
Normandy 67, 168, 340–342, 344–347, 372, 398, 418
North Africa 56, 67, 76–77, 81–83, 86, 92, 106, 108, 124–125, 127, 129, 147, 150, 164, 171, 199, 216, 231, 269, 275, 278, 304, 307, 324, 344, 405
North Sea, the 30–31, 50, 89, 109–110, 125, 139, 147, 179–180, 200, 209, 217, 238, 319, 394
Norway 92, 222, 230, 310, 336

Oberkommando der Luftwaffe (OKL) (Supreme Command of the Luftwaffe) **21,** 155, 158, 263–264, 303–304, 334–335, 337–338, 341, 347, 375–377, 406, 418, 421, 437, 440
Oesau, Oberstleutnant Walter **14,** 171–172, 193, 201–202, 244, 247, 255, 268, 314
oil refineries 95, 195, 201, 391, 394, 421, 430, 433
Oldenburg 111, 116–117, 119, 170, 177, 201, 217, 222, 244, 268, 281, 381
Olejnik, Oberleutnant Robert 92, 134, 147–148, 152, 408
Operational Analysis Section 131, 141, 224, 381
operations:
  Barbarossa 88, 142, 163
  Overlord 146, 229, 253, 340
  Pointblank 146, 229, 232
Operations Record Book (ORB) 42, 50–51
Oschersleben **16,** 138–140, 232, 234–235, 258, 284, 286–287, 350–352

Panzerarmee Afrika 76, 78, 86
Parchim 340–341, 359–360, 384, 429, 434
Paris 87, 94, 99, 165, 184, 222, 239, 279, 343–345

pilots:
  instructor 93, 96, 171, 216, 280, 301, 329
  Jagdflieger (fighter pilots) **21,** 41, 77, 170, 175, 209
  Wimpy 28–29, 31, 35, 38
Plexiglas 57, 118, 152, 321, 326, 332, 340, 409, 426
Poland 44, 85, 122, 137, 230, 254, 382
Portal, Air Marshal Sir Charles 47–48, 59–60, 146
Prague **18,** 47, 321, 418
Pratt & Whitney 53, 102, 313
Priller, Oberstleutnant Josef 151–152, 341, 349, 372
propaganda 47, 76, 83, 168, 261
propellers **13,** 51, 68, 102, 120, 152, 162, 174, 219, 290, 319, 364, 366, 401
  propeller arc 68–69, 412
Prussia, East 108, 137, 180, 319, 348
Pulks (Luftwaffe slang for an enemy bomber formation) **21,** 110–111, 114, 119–120, 144, 170, 182, 188–190, 209, 214, 217–218, 233, 259, 261, 284–285, 288–290, 296–297, 300–301, 313, 318, 352, 356, 363, 365, 370, 407, 422

R/T 86, 91–92, 395
radar stations:
  Freya 31–33, 46, 90, 137, **138**
radio:
  Funkhorchdienst (Radio Listening Service) **20,** 138, 177, 181, 217, 223, 238–239, 363
  operator 61, 110, 170, 178, 182, 248, 316–317, 319, 334, 364, 379–380
  traffic 177, 181, 223
Rechlin 91, 122–123, 181, 206, 210, 219–220, 291–292, 320–321, 340, 400, 412, 436
reconnaissance (see also aircraft) 45, 60, 94, 143, 165, 205, 233, 240, 309, 343, 362, 406
  photo 52, 438
Regensburg 146–150, 154–155, 196, 229, 253–255, 258
Reichsluftministerium (RLM) (Reich Air Ministry) **21, 22,** 39, 68–69, 100, 122, 164, 206, 219, 225, 230, 239, 255, 258–259, 263, 317, 348, 350, 359, 366, 380, 406, 411

477

Reichsmarschall 98, 131, 153, 174–175, 178, 186, 191, 193, 197, 225, 250, 255, 307, 317, 323–324, 372, 391, 415

Reichsverteidigung (Aerial Defence of the Reich) 163, 230, 245, 251, 278–279, 288, 303, 323, 327, 330, 336–338, 375–376, 383

Rhine, the **18**, 126, 134, 200, 213, 238, 256, 265, 373, 382, 392, 396

Richthofen, Manfred Freiherr von 67, 83, 262

Rommel, Generalfeldmarschall Erwin 76–78, 81, 106

Roosevelt, President Franklin D. 49, 57, 60, 101–102, 107

Rotte (section of two aircraft) **22**, 34, 118–119, 123, 143, 241, 274, 283, 285, 289, 310, 420

Royal Air Force (RAF) 9, **12**, **20**, **23**, 28, 30–31, 34, 36, 38–39, 41–44, 46, 48–56, 60–62, 67, 76–79, 87, 92–95, 99, 105–107, 125, 131, 150, 171, 174, 177, 222, 257, 302, 315, 343–345, 383, 389, 393–398, 414, 417, 430
  Bomber Command 9, 27–32, 40–41, 43–44, 47–49, 52, 54, 57, 59, 62, 88, 106, 109, 135, 171, 198, 235, 373, 394, 413–414, 430, 433
    No. 3 Group 27, 29, 34–35, 38, 40, 43, 394
  Fighter Command 10, 61, 395, 428
  squadrons:
    No. 9 Sqn **12**, 27, 39
    No. 37 Sqn 27, 31, 36, 39
    No. 149 Sqn 27, 30, 35, 37, 39–40, 42

Ruhr, the 47, 52, 81, 106, 144–145, 163, 173, 201, 213, 373, 395, 397

Russia 74, 86–87, 92, 101, 116, 136, 161, 163, 168, 245, 247, 282, 294, 296, 310, 324, 326, 344, 423, 438–439
  Russian Front 296, 327, 432, 438

Saxony 203, 385
  Lower 121, 136, 217, 270

Schiphol 89–90, 139, 147, 199–200

Schleissheim **18**, 95–96, 137, 186, 254

Schleswig 141, 180, 283–284
  Schleswig-Holstein 33, 179, 222, 283, 392

Schmid, Oberst Josef **14**, 100, 162–165, 167, 170, 172, 174, 177–182, 184–186, 192–194, 197–198, 200–201, 204–205, 209–212, 216, 224, 227, 230, 236, 238–239, 242–246, 248, 252, 254–258, 260, 262, 265, 268, 273, 278–279, 288, 299, 303, 317, 322–323, 328, 334, 336–338, 353, 373–374, 388, 392

Schnoor, Hauptmann Emil-Rudolf 140, 185, 188, 200, 266

Schroer, Oberleutnant Werner 81–82, 133, 328, **441**

Schulze-Dickow, Hauptmann Fritz 143–144, 169–170, 178, 180–181, 259

Schumacher, Oberstleutnant Carl-August 33–37, 41, 46

Schwabedissen, Generalleutnant Walter 89, 162, 164, 183, 190, 194–197, 201, 203

Schwarm (flight of four aircraft) **22**, 75, 86, 94, 123, 143–144, 158, 161–162, **191**, 206, 212, 215, 221, 262, 274, 280, 285, 296, 300, 310–311, 358, 395–396, 420

Schwärme 39, 75, 86, 143–145, 159, 218, 300, 358, 395–396, 399, 421, 435

Schweinfurt **19**, 142, 146–147, 151–155, 157–158, 162, 187, 190, 192, 207, 229, 232, 288

self-sealing tanks 38, 40–42, 68

shipyards 62, 92, 125, 231, 286, 433–434

shrapnel 30, 118, 312–313, 341

Sicily 76–77, 127–129, 133, 141, 275, 324, 384

'*Sokrates*' (the 'S' denoted Stade) **14**, 136–137, 168–169, 171, 221–223, 246, 255, 259

sorties 51, 96, 175, 180, 185, 195, 214, 232, 261, 302, 314, 341, 343–344, 368–369, 374, 378, 382–383, 397, 421

Spaatz, Maj Gen Carl 'Tooey' **12**, 59–62, 229, 240, 315, 386

Spanish Civil War 54–55, 121, 169

Specht, Hauptmann Günther 139–140, 151, 170, 192, 218, 259, 369–370

Sperrle, General der Flieger Hugo 46, 94, 167, 184, 260

stabilisers 139, 267, 332
  horizontal 67, 75, 188

INDEX

Stade 14, 18, 89, 92, 111, 136–137, 164, 169–171, 178–179, 185, 204, 210, 221–223, 246, 255, 257–258, 392
Staffelkapitän (officer commanding a Staffel) 22, 34, 37, 72, 77, 81, 92, 110, 114, 121–122, 148, 162, 165, 169, 173, 188, 190, 194, 215, 234, 241, 247, 255, 268, 273–275, 280, 282, 285, 295–296, 301–302, 307, 324, 328, 334, 344, 351–352, 357, 362, 367, 370–371, 377, 384, 388, 399, 430
Stahlberg, Leutnant Erwin 145, 190, 274
Staiger, Hauptmann Hermann 148, 184, 296, **441**
Stalingrad 86, 105, 108, 153, 204, 278
starboard wing **13, 17**, 40, 53, 72, 112, 118, 285, 290, 296, 313
steel cable 123, 219–220, 276
Steinhoff, Leutnant Johannes 34–35, 39, 41, 65, 124, 128–130, 247, 417–418
Stigler, Leutnant Franz 10, 275, 280
Streib, Major Werner 171–172, 186, 205
Sturmjäger ('assault fighters') **22**, 166, 293
Sturmstaffel/-gruppe ('assault') **16, 22**, 167, 202–203, 231, 233, 248, 267, 281, 285, 287, 293, 295, 297–299, 301, 333–334
  1: **12, 13**, 167, 203, 231–233, 244–245, 247, 266–267, 269, 281–283, 285, 287–288, 295, 299, 301, 303, 312–313, 333, 335, 357, 385, 432, 438
Suffolk 27, 319, 331, 363
Switzerland 71, 162, 175, 383

tail gunners 28, 36, 61, 73, 109, 207, 236, 267, 319, 352, 355, 357, 364, 378–379, 396, 409–410, 419
tailplane 40, 50–51, 316
Tank, Dipl.-Ing. Kurt 68, 93–94, 112, 400, 411
Tarnewitz 123, 139, 367, 380, 384, 391, 412–413
Technisches Amt (RLM Technical Office) **22**, 249, 381
The Aeroplane 48–49, 52, 97, 99
Third Reich 9, **15–16, 21**, 41, 81–83, 87–88, 91, 93, 96, 105–106, 108, 116–118, 121, 128, 130–131, 133–134, 136–137, 142, 147, 155, 157–159, 162, 166, 169–172, 176–177, 179, 186, 201, 209, 215, 217, 222, 229–230, 232, 238, 240, 242–243, 247, 249, 255–256, 260, 262–263, 268–270, 278–279, 289, 293–294, 298, 304, 310–311, 323–324, 327, 330, 335–337, 339, 343, 346–348, 350–351, 354, 372, 374–375, 381–383, 386–389, 392, 401, 413, 433, 438
Tratt, Hauptmann Eduard 121–122, 139, 251, 255
training units 150, 159, 239, 247, 298, 309, 329, 432
transmitters 91–92, 257, 393–394, 433
Tunisia 67, 86, 125, 127, 150, 164, 196, 215, 324
turrets:
  ball 97, 132, 148, 233, 267, 333, 359, 379, 410
  rear 36–37, 78
  tail 55, 72–73

U-boats 54, 60, 108, 154, 195
  pens 71–72, 74, 215
  yards 108, 110, 179, 434
undercarriage 68, 84, 233, 294, 320, 412, 416, 439
Unger, Feldwebel Willi 10, **16**, 292, 294, 301, 309, 318, 330, 352, 358–359, **442**
Union of Soviet Socialist Republics (USSR) 44, 56–57, 105, 122, 133, 142
United States Army Air Corps (USAAC) 48–50, 52–54, 56, 59, 101
United States Army Air Forces (USAAF) 9, **16, 17, 19, 23**, 58, 61–63, 73–74, 77–79, 88, 94–98, 100, 107–110, 117–118, 121, 123–124, 131, 133–135, 139, 141, 144–145, 151, 154–156, 175, 177, 179, 181–182, 186–187, 192, 194–195, 198–199, 201, 206, 209–211, 215, 218, 221–222, 224–225, 231–233, 235–236, 238, 240, 242, 245, 248, 254, 261, 264–266, 269–272, 274, 279, 281–282, 284–285, 288–289, 301, 303–304, 308, 311, 313, 315, 317, 321, 325, 331, 339, 348, 351, 356, 364–365, 370–371, 374, 377–378, 380–382, 388–389, 395, 398, 400, 405, 411, 413, 416–418, 420–421, 428–431, 435

Eighth Air Force ('Mighty Eighth') 10, **12, 16**, 58–64, 70–71, 74–75, 96, 106, 113–114, 126, 131, 141, 144, 147, 155, 160, 162, 183, 199, 206, 209, 211, 213, 215–218, 224–225, 232, 234–235, 238, 240, 244, 248, 253, 264–265, 272–273, 275, 278, 284–285, 287–288, 290, 295, 298–299, 301–303, 305, 313, 315, 320, 325, 329, 331, 335, 351, 362, 365, 369, 377, 380–382, 386, 391, 397, 418, 421, 430–431, 433–436
   VIII Bomber Command **12**, 61, 63, 106, 125, 141, 146, 184, 192
bomb divisions (BD):
   1st BD   178–179, 189, 201, 210–211, 213–214, 217, 231, 235, 238, 254, 266, 281, 283, 288, 363–364, 370, 408, 410
   2nd BD   179, 181, 187, 213, 217, 231, 236, 238, 259, 271, 281–282, 285, 302, 311–312, 325, 377, 408
   3rd BD   179, 184, 189, 201, 207, 211, 217, 236, 238, 242, 246, 264, 271, 281, 283, 286–287, 312, 319, 329, 331–332, 370, 408
bomb groups (BG):
   91st BG   73, 117, 121, 266–267, 385, 410
   95th BG   92, 127, 331
   97th BG   60–61, 63, 97
   100th BG   146, 183, 332
   303rd BG   364–365, 377–378
   305th BG   109, 403, 408
   306th BG   70, 73, 235
   385th BG   14, 140, 189, 241, 319
bomb wings (BW):
   1st BW   70, 93, 109, 127, 145, 147
   4th BW   125, 127, 138, 140, 147
   5th BW   195, 281, 356
United States of America (USA)   50, 56–58, 60, 78–79, 98, 101, 124, 163, 261
United States Strategic Air Forces (USSTAF)   **22**, 229, 315, 331

Vegesack   110, 112, 177, 244
Vienna   **19**, 47, 137, 158, 265, 280, 289–290, 321–322, 324, 346, 437
Viermots ('four-engines/-ed')   **22**, 55–56, 62, 72, 81, 83, 93, 109, 116–117, 122, 124–126, 131, 139, 142, 148, 160, 165–166, 171, 178, 188, 192, 196, 198, 209–211, 231, 234, 236–237, 242, 246, 260, 262, 265, 269–270, 272, 276, 282–283, 285, 288–289, 292, 294, 296, 300–301, 304, 326, 330–331, 356, 364, 369, 383, 395, 415, 418, 421, 428, 434, 437, 441–442
Viermotorschreck (fear of four-engined bombers)   **22**, 117, 127

Wangerooge   31–34, 36–37, 46
Washington, D.C.   48, 57–58, 60, 62, 99, 146, 240
Wegmann, Feldwebel Günther   80, 82, 143–144, 189, 418, 429
Weik, Hauptmann Hans   292, 301, 316, 351, 357–358, 442
Weise, Generaloberst Hubert   87–88, 94, 137, 174, 194, 197–199, 230
Western Front   **14**, 41, 67, 89, 204, 349, 374, 378, 381–382, 392, 397–398
Wiesbaden-Erbenheim   **18**, 133, 150, 183–184, 191, 213, 289, 327, 364
Wilhelmshaven   **12**, 27, 29, 31–39, 41–42, 44, 46–50, 87, 108–110, 114, 117, 121, 126, 199–200, 210, 217, 229, 244, 417
wing roots   69, 73, 79, 202, 294, 396
Wittmundhafen airfield   119, 121–124, 143, 219, 222, 408
World War I   **14**, 67, 83, 89, 94–95, 122, 204, 276, 365, 378
World War II   9, **12**, 48, 65, 365, 400, 407

Zeist   **18**, 137, 163, 167, 172, 181, 185, 193, 216, 231, 239, 244
Zerstörergeschwader (ZG):
   (ZG) 26:   13, 158, 171, 177, 187, 200, 202, 205, 211–212, 217, 269, 299, 317
   I./ZG 26:   193, 217–218, 232, 248, 259, 334
   II./ZG 26:   232, 251, 287, 311, 316–317, 334, 350
   III./ZG 26 *Horst Wessel*:   79, 143–144, 169–170, 178–180, 182, 189, 207, 210–211, 217, 259, 266, 268, 272, 286–287, 366, 380
   5./ZG 26:   13, 251, 255, 260
   (ZG) 76:   143, 158, 187, 196–197
   II./ZG 76:   143, 218, 266, 273